A Litigator's Guide to DNA

A Litigator's Guide to DNA

From the Laboratory to the Courtroom

Ron C. Michaelis, PhD, FACMG
Robert G. Flanders, Jr., Esq.
Paula H. Wulff, JD

ELSEVIER
Amsterdam • Boston • Heidelberg • London • New York • Oxford
Paris • San Diego • San Francisco • Singapore • Sydney • Tokyo
Academic Press is an imprint of Elsevier

Acquisitions Editor: Jennifer Soucy

Associate Developmental Editor: Kelly Weaver

Project Manager: Christie Jozwiak

Publishing Services Manager: Sarah Hajduk

Marketing Manager: Kristin Banach

Design Direction: Joanne Blank

Cover Design: Brian Moore

Cover image © Chris Dascher/iStockphoto.

Academic Press is an imprint of Elsevier
30 Corporate Drive, Suite 400, Burlington, MA 01803, USA
525 B Street, Suite 1900, San Diego, California 92101-4495, USA
84 Theobald's Road, London WC1X 8RR, UK

This book is printed on acid-free paper. ♾

Library of Congress Cataloging-in-Publication Data
Application Submitted

British Library Cataloguing-in-Publication Data
A catalogue record for this book is available from the British Library.

ISBN: 978- 0-12-374036-6

For information on all Academic Press publications
visit our website at books.elsevier.com

Printed in the United States of America
08 09 10 9 8 7 6 5 4 3 2 1

Please direct all correspondence regarding this book to Dr. Michaelis at litigatorsguidetodna@gmail.com.

Dedication

I would like to dedicate this book to my parents, Robert and Dorothy Michaelis. I am keenly aware of, and deeply grateful for, the many ways in which they provided the foundation for this work (and all my other works as well). I would also like to dedicate the book to my children, Matt and Kathryn. They serve as a never-ending source of motivation and inspiration for me in everything I do. Finally, this book is dedicated to Ellen Boyd. Without her kindness and generosity there would have been no beginning; this book would have ended up as one of those things I should have done.

–Ron C. Michaelis

I dedicate this book to my wife, Ann I. Flanders, whose love and friendship have been and remain indispensable to all that I am and do.

–Robert G. Flanders, Jr.

I would like to acknowledge the dedication of the many state and local prosecutors who routinely carry full case loads and mentor others through the complexities of preparing a criminal case. Specifically I would like to thank Martha Bashford, Robert Biancavilla, Norm Gahn, Rockne Harmon, Ted Hunt, Robert Laurino, Hon. Mitch Morrissey, Melissa Mourges, Steve Redding, Hon. Matt Redle and Brian Zubel for their ceaseless energy and dedication to helping others understand the challenges presented in DNA cases. I would also like to thank my husband, John, and son, Matt, for their patience.

–Paula H. Wulff

Table of Contents

ACKNOWLEDGMENTS xi
INTRODUCTION. xiii

CHAPTER 1 The Structure of DNA and the Variability of the Human DNA Sequence. 1

You Are Out of Your Field, But Not Out of Your Depth 1
Markers, Alleles, Genotypes and Profiles. 2
The Two Sources of DNA in Human Cells 5
The Structure of DNA and RNA 6
Variability Is the Rule, Not the Exception 11
Polymorphisms Commonly Used for Forensic Testing 15
Using the DNA Profile to Identify an Unknown Perpetrator 24
References and Additional Readings 25

CHAPTER 2 The Molecular Biological Basis of Forensic DNA Tests. 27

Extraction and Quantification of DNA 27
Polymerase Chain Reaction (PCR)-Based Tests 32
Variable Number of Tandem Repeats (VNTR) Testing 50
Direct Sequencing. 51
References and Additional Readings 53

CHAPTER 3 Quality Control, Quality Assurance and Sources of Uncertainty in the Data. 55

Laboratory Accreditation, Personnel Certification and Proficiency Testing 55
Validation Studies. 59
The Inevitable Nemeses: Suboptimal Samples and Human Error. 61
Allele Dropout Due to Degradation, Preferential Amplification and Stochastic Effects 70
Artifacts Inherent in STR Analyses. 75
Hybridization Specificity in Dot-Blot Tests 87
References and Additional Readings 88

CHAPTER 4 Population Genetics, Probability Calculations and the Proper Interpretation of the Evidence 91

The Common Logical Fallacies 91

Databanks and Databases 99

Allele Frequencies, Genotype Probabilities and the Product Rule for Independent Events 106

The Principles of Population Genetics that Impact Forensic DNA Calculations 113

Applying the Product Rule—Compensating for Population Substructure and Possible Allele Dropout 119

The Likelihood Ratio (LR) Allows the Analyst to Compare the Strength of Competing Hypotheses 135

The Application of Bayes' Theorem to Paternity Disputes 142

Recommended Procedure for Analyzing Mixed Samples 147

References and Additional Readings 167

CHAPTER 5 Mitochondrial DNA (mtDNA) Analyses 171

The mtDNA Molecule—Abundant and Durable but Less Variable than nDNA 171

Laboratory Analysis of mtDNA Haplotypes 174

Matrilineal Inheritance and a Lack of Recombination 178

A High Mutation Rate Leads to Mitochondrial Heteroplasmy 180

Statistical Analysis of mtDNA Haplotype Data 187

References and Additional Readings 193

CHAPTER 6 Y Chromosome Analyses 197

Y Chromosome Evolution and its Consequences for Forensic Analyses 197

Laboratory Analysis of Y Chromosome Haplotypes 204

Statistical Analysis of Y Chromosome Haplotypes 207

References and Additional Readings 212

CHAPTER 7 DNA in Court 215

The Evolution of Standards for Admissibility of Experts and Evidence 215

The Ongoing Controversy Regarding Laboratory Error Rates 225

Counsels' Obligations Regarding Discovery 228

Expert Witnesses 232

The Durability of DNA Presents Problems for Statutes of Limitation 237

Rape Shield Laws May Limit the Use of DNA Evidence 238

Judges' and Jurors' Perceptions of DNA Evidence . . . 239
References and Additional Readings . . . 253

CHAPTER 8 Arguing for the Prosecution . . . 255
Obtaining DNA Samples . . . 255
DNA in the Courtroom: The Essentials of the Prosecution's Presentation . . . 279
References and Additional Readings . . . 312

CHAPTER 9 Arguing for the Defense . . . 313
The Defense's Choice of Strategy . . . 313
Elements of a Competent Defense . . . 326
When the Defendant Has Been Identified by a Databank Search . . . 362
References and Additional Readings . . . 367

CHAPTER 10 Postconviction DNA Testing . . . 369
DNA has the Power to Exonerate the Innocent . . . 369
Avenues for Relief . . . 370
There Are Many Procedural Obstacles . . . 373
New Evidence May Justify a New Theory of the Case . . . 379
Accessing the Necessary Samples . . . 380
Know the Specific Provisions of the Controlling Statute . . . 383
References and Additional Readings . . . 386

APPENDIX I: Using the Chi-Square Test to Determine if a Population Conforms to HWE Expectations . . . 389
APPENDIX II: How the RMP, Prior Odds of Guilt, and the PFP Influence the Posterior Odds of Guilt (POG) . . . 393
APPENDIX III: Paternity Index (PI) Calculations for Different Combinations of Maternal, Child and Alleged Father Genotypes . . . 397
APPENDIX IV: A Sample Consent Form to Collect an Oral Swab, Which Allows the Profile Obtained to Be Entered Into a Databank for Use in Additional Investigations . . . 399
APPENDIX V: Doing Your Own Research: Useful References, Websites and Strategies for Finding Current Information . . 401
GLOSSARY OF KEY TERMS . . . 411
INDEX . . . 423

Acknowledgments

The authors would like to thank the following people for their help: Krista Schmidt, Christopher Ayers and Kelly Devlin for their assistance with the research; Terry Melton from Mitotyping Technologies, Jack Tarleton from the Fullerton Genetics Laboratory, Lisa Schade and Lisa Calandro from Applied Biosystems Human Identification Business and Mike Leous from Roche Applied Science for providing figures; Donna Falcoa for assistance preparing the manuscript. We would also like to thank Amy D. Anderson from the University of Washington Department of Biostatistics for a very helpful presubmission review, and the anonymous reviewers whose comments greatly improved the book's content and focus.

Introduction

"Mere access to the courthouse doors does not by itself assure a proper functioning of the adversary process."

Hon. Thurgood Marshall

DNA evidence provides a critical component in many judicial proceedings. It can establish that a crime was committed, substantiate key elements of the crime or witness testimony, and link or exclude specific individuals to the crime. DNA evidence has the power to convict the guilty and exonerate the innocent in criminal litigation, and ensure a proper outcome in a civil proceeding. The presence of DNA evidence alone, however, does not assure a just and correct outcome to any proceeding. It is essential that counsel for both sides of the adversarial process understand the various types of DNA evidence involved in the case, as well as the scope of what that particular type of DNA can reveal and how best to present this evidence for the court's consideration. This volume intends to better prepare both sides of the courtroom to correctly understand, interpret and present DNA evidence.

DNA evidence is not biased toward any party to the case or to any particular outcome; rather, it merely provides a factual piece of the picture that the judge or jury must evaluate. Without an accurate understanding of what the DNA evidence can or cannot correctly reveal, all parties involved in the adversarial process fall short and justice is poorly served. An ill-prepared prosecutor with relatively little DNA understanding who attempts to dissect the defense expert's testimony will not recognize improper DNA interpretations. An inexperienced defense attorney who is unable to formulate a defense theory to counter the state's interpretation of DNA evidence will be swept along with the jury by having only one perspective on what the DNA evidence can provide. A judge who does not fully understand the ramifications of either side's expert witness testimony may hand down an erroneous or anomalous decision. In these instances, both the victim and defendant suffer – the victim's case may not be properly advocated, the defendant may be improperly convicted, or a true perpetrator may be set free.

This book is intended as a desk-top reference for prosecutors, defense counsel and the judiciary. It is offered as a guide to help officers of the court understand the scientific principles associated with DNA, as well as their legal application in the courtroom. It is not intended to replace the need to meet often with a forensic analyst or expert witness—and to do so well before trial—but it will serve to help all participants in the legal process to understand and reinforce some of the material gained from these meetings. The book provides a solid foundation in the complexities of DNA collection, discovery and admissibility issues. In addition, it contains advice on how to mount or overcome challenges to the evidence itself, and a discussion of DNA-related post-conviction issues.

The book represents the collaborative efforts of a biology professor, a former judge and a former prosecutor. Each of us has brought our unique professional perspectives to the material in the hope that these varied perspectives will assist the litigator in responsibly preparing a DNA-evidence related case, thus effectively serving the adversarial process.

CHAPTER 1

The Structure of DNA and the Variability of the Human DNA Sequence

CONTENTS

You Are Out of Your Field, But Not Out of Your Depth

Markers, Alleles, Genotypes and Profiles

The Two Sources of DNA in Human Cells

The Structure of DNA and RNA

Variability Is the Rule, Not the Exception

Polymorphisms Commonly Used for Forensic Testing

Using the DNA Profile to Identify an Unknown Perpetrator

References and Additional Readings

YOU ARE OUT OF YOUR FIELD, BUT NOT OUT OF YOUR DEPTH

There is no question that you are about to embark on a daunting task. Despite being microscopic in size, the world of cellular and molecular biology is gigantic in scope and complexity. You probably didn't emphasize (OK, let's be honest, you passionately avoided) science lab courses when you made your choices regarding what college courses to take. Now the Supreme Court has decided that judges have to know enough about deoxyribonucleic acid (DNA) testing to decide whether the accepted methods have been properly applied, courts are expecting attorneys to do battle with their expert witnesses sequestered, and jurors have been conditioned by the many popular forensic television shows to consider DNA evidence an essential element in the prosecution's case. Given the complexity of the science and the adversarial nature of the proceedings in which you will be participating, you may be more than a little anxious about the fact that you have no foundation in molecular biology.

Here's some good news. Most molecular biological processes, including all the ones you need to understand, are similar to processes you are already familiar with. Your body's cells maintain their infrastructure in the same way a city does: they tear down old structures and replace them with new ones. The new structures are built from raw materials that are taken in using transport processes dedicated to carrying in that raw material. In a city, trains, boats and trucks have established patterns of transporting the necessary raw materials into the city to be used to build new structures. In a cell, a variety of specialized transport systems bring in the needed raw materials. Building a new structure involves the same processes, whether it occurs inside a cell or on a city street. In a city, workers with specialized skills assemble large structures from smaller raw materials. In a cell, enzymes with specialized functions assemble macromolecules from their building blocks. Many of the formidable-sounding biochemicals you will encounter in the field of cellular biology can be seen as little workers that the cell uses to do things like build new structures or cart the debris away after it tears down old structures.

Another thing that should make it easier for you to digest the necessary molecular biological issues is the fact that many of the formidably named biochemicals that you will encounter in the field of molecular biology perform tasks similar to those we perform using our hands or common household tools. For example, once you know that the DNA molecule is shaped like a helical ribbon, it is easy to understand that a restriction endonuclease can act like a scissors and cut the DNA into pieces the way a scissors cuts a ribbon. When you try to envision the manner in which the DNA from a bloodstain on the ground is degraded by bacterial restriction enzymes, envision a helical ribbon being cut repeatedly by scissors into progressively smaller fragments. Or consider the enzyme DNA polymerase, which chains together a string of nucleotides to make a molecule of DNA. There are four different nucleotides in DNA, and DNA polymerase strings them together in a specific pattern to synthesize new DNA. As an analogy, imagine having a string of lights, with four different colored bulbs to choose from, and having instructions to string the colored bulbs in a specified order.

Throughout this book, we have tried to describe the molecular biological processes we discuss in simple mechanical terms. In addition, we have also tried to keep our focus on the significance of DNA to the litigator, not the scientist. Technical terms that may be unfamiliar to legal professionals are written in bold type, and a glossary is available at the end of the book for quick reference when you need to remember the meaning of a technical term.

MARKERS, ALLELES, GENOTYPES AND PROFILES

Before we discuss the specific polymorphisms that are used for forensic testing, let's introduce a few terms that you will encounter frequently (Figure 1.1[1]). Humans have 46 **chromosomes**, arranged in 23 pairs. The

[1] Color versions (where applicable) of the figures in the book are available at books.elsevier.com/companions/9780123740366.

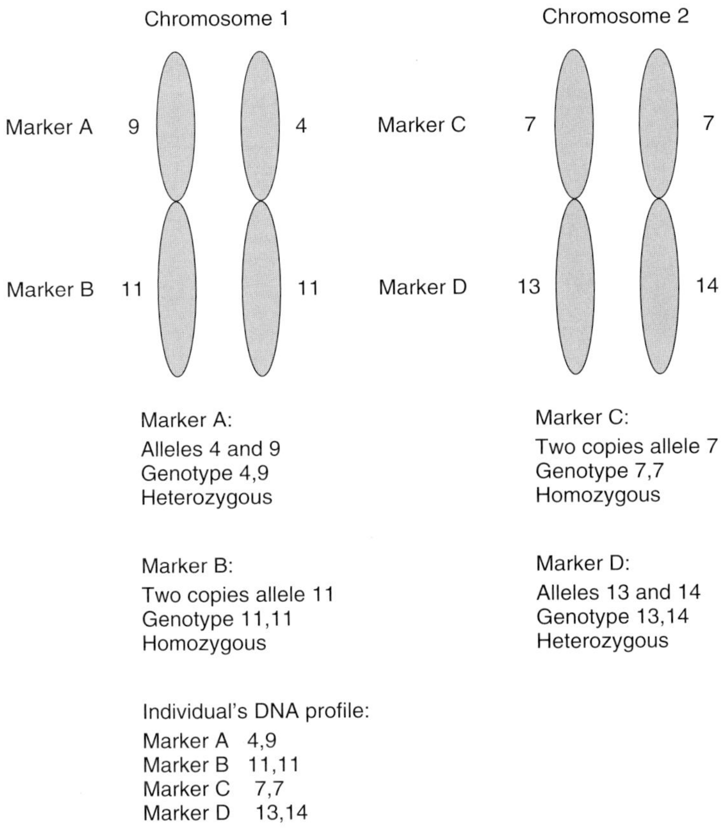

FIGURE 1.1
Diagram illustrating an individual's DNA profile at four markers. Markers A and B lie on chromosome 1, while markers C and D lie on chromosome 2. The allele numbering system is described below. For this figure, the allele numbers are arbitrary numbers intended merely to illustrate that there are several versions of each marker's sequence.

numbered chromosomes (pairs 1–22) are referred to as the **autosomes**, while the XX or XY pair (in females and males, respectively) is referred to as the **sex chromosomes**. A child inherits one set of chromosomes from his or her mother and one from his or her father, and a parent passes one of his or her two sets of chromosomes down to each of his or her children.

Because of the way in which our chromosomes are paired, we have two copies of every sequence in our DNA.[2] Each copy of a particular sequence is called an **allele**. In the vast majority of cases, an individual will only have two alleles for any marker, one on each of the two chromosomes in the relevant pair. In rare cases, however, an individual may have a small deletion or duplication of a chromosome that results in him or her having one or three alleles for a polymorphism, respectively.

As we discuss later in this chapter, the sequence of human DNA is highly variable. If you sequence the DNA of a large number of people, there are many places, or loci,[3] at which one can find slightly different sequences in

[2] Except for the sex chromosomes in males, who have one copy of the X chromosome sequence and one copy of the Y chromosome sequence.

[3] "Locus" is frequently used to refer to a stretch of sequence in the DNA molecule. There is no specific length or sequence requirement for a stretch of DNA to be a locus.

different individuals. In fact, some loci are so variable that you can find different sequences at the two alleles of a particular locus within a single individual's DNA. Any stretch of DNA sequence for which you can observe two or more different versions of the sequence in a population is considered to be **polymorphic** (from the Latin poly = many and morph = form), and is referred to as a **polymorphism**.

The two alleles an individual possesses at a locus are referred to as the individual's **genotype** for that locus. An individual for whom both alleles of a polymorphism are identical is said to have a **homozygous** genotype for that polymorphism, while someone who has two different alleles for a polymorphism is said to be **heterozygous** for that polymorphism. In the case of Y chromosome polymorphisms (discussed in Chapter 6), the individual has only one allele for each locus. The collection of alleles on the Y chromosome is referred to as the Y chromosome **haplotype**. The terms **DNA profile** and **genetic profile** are used to indicate the individual's combination of genotypes at all the polymorphisms that were tested.

Because the entire sequence of the human DNA molecule has been published, we know the location of all these different polymorphic sequences on their respective chromosomes. These polymorphisms are extremely useful for mapping the locations of genes on their respective chromosomes. Because their locations are known, they serve just like markers on a road map, indicating exactly where on the respective chromosome you are and how much distance lies between two different genes. For this reason, these polymorphisms are often referred to as **markers**.

RECAPPING THE MAIN POINTS

1. A human has 46 chromosomes, consisting of 22 pairs of autosomes, numbered 1–22, and a pair of sex chromosomes: XX in a female and XY in a male.
2. We have two copies of all the sequences on our chromosomes, except for the sequences for males' sex chromosomes. Each of the two copies of a sequence is called an allele. An individual's genotype at a locus refers to the two alleles he or she possesses at that locus.
3. Sequences for which more than one version can be found in a population are called polymorphisms, or markers. An individual's genotype is homozygous at a marker if the sequences of his or her two alleles are identical, and heterozygous if the sequence differs between the two alleles.
4. For single-copy sequences, such as a male's X or Y chromosome sequences, the individual only has one allele, and the collection of alleles on a single-copy chromosome is called a haplotype.
5. The collection of genotypes that the individual possesses is referred to as that individual's DNA profile or genetic profile.

THE TWO SOURCES OF DNA IN HUMAN CELLS

There are two types of DNA in human cells: **nuclear DNA** and **mitochondrial DNA**. Figure 1.2 illustrates the contents of a typical human cell; the **nucleus** and several **mitochondria** are labeled. Each of our cells has one nucleus, plus anywhere from a couple to a couple hundred mitochondria, depending on how much energy the cell needs to perform its specialized functions.[4] Nuclear DNA is the DNA that resides in the nucleus of all our cells; it is the DNA that is contained in our **chromosomes**. When we hear DNA discussed as the mechanism by which we inherit traits from our ancestors, or a gene mutation implicated as the cause of a patient's medical disorder, it is usually nuclear DNA that is being discussed. Mitochondrial DNA also plays an important role in our development, however, and is also useful for forensic identification purposes.

[4] One exception to this that is relevant to forensics is red blood cells, which have neither a nucleus nor mitochondria. When DNA is extracted from blood, it is extracted from the white blood cells. In addition, while this is rarely relevant to forensic investigations, a human egg, or ovum, contains over 100,000 mitochondria.

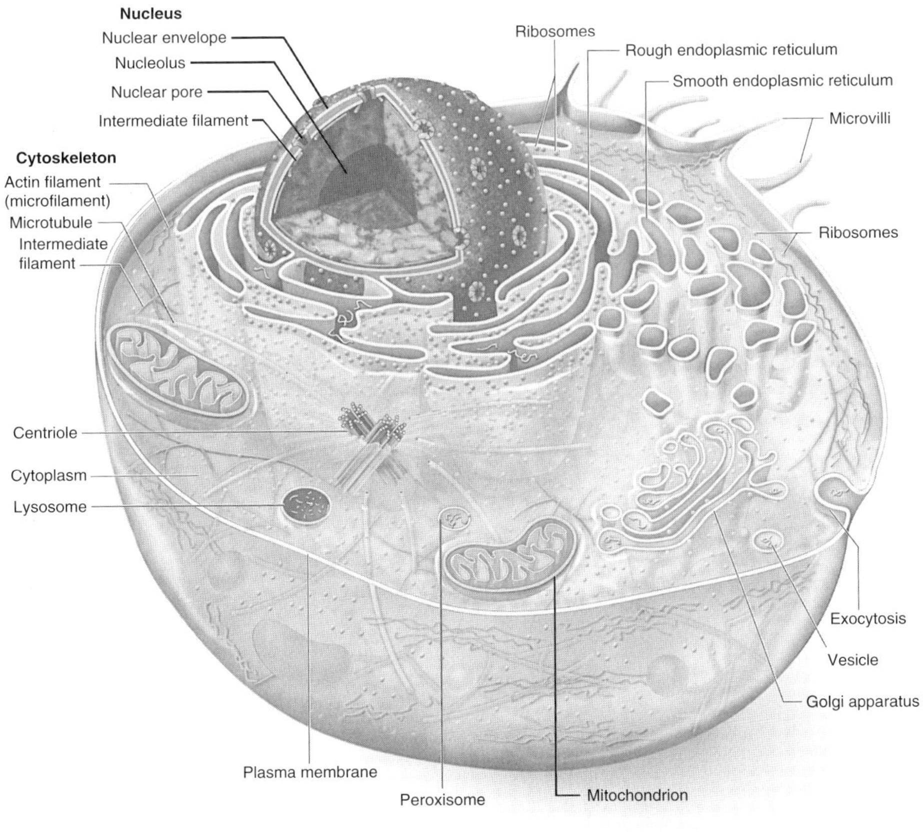

FIGURE 1.2
A typical animal cell, illustrating the nucleus and mitochondria. Reprinted from Biology, *8th ed., by Raven, Johnson, Losos, Mason and Singer. Copyright The McGraw-Hill Companies, Inc.*

The mitochondrion is not normally discussed as a source of DNA. The mitochondrion is best known for providing the cell with the energy it needs to perform all its specialized functions, in the same manner as a power plant supplies electric power to run the operations of a city. The biochemical reactions that our cells use to harvest most of the energy they derive from the foods we eat occur in the mitochondrion, and this extremely important function is usually emphasized when discussing the importance of mitochondria to human health. In addition to housing the cellular energy factory, however, the mitochondrion also has its own DNA molecule. As is true of nuclear DNA, the mitochondrial genes manufacture proteins that are essential for proper development, and mitochondrial DNA is passed from generation to generation just as nuclear DNA is, albeit with a markedly different pattern of inheritance (discussed in Chapter 5).

Although nuclear DNA is much more variable than mitochondrial DNA, and therefore much more useful for forensic identification purposes, both nuclear and mitochondrial DNA can be used for forensic testing. Chapter 5 emphasizes the differences between nuclear and mitochondrial DNA. Unless specified otherwise, the information presented in this chapter pertains to both DNA types.

RECAPPING THE MAIN POINTS

1. There are two different DNA molecules in a human cell. One resides in the nucleus and the other in the mitochondria.
2. Nuclear DNA is more variable than mitochondrial DNA, and therefore more useful for identification purposes, but mitochondrial DNA is also useful for forensic testing.

THE STRUCTURE OF DNA AND RNA

The building blocks from which DNA is built are called **nucleotides**. A nucleotide contains a nitrogen-containing **base**, a molecule of the sugar **deoxyribose** and a **phosphate group** (Figure 1.3). Each of the nucleotides in DNA contains one of four bases (**adenine**, **cytosine**, **guanine** or **thymine**), which are usually symbolized as A, C, G or T, respectively. The corresponding nucleotides are usually referred to as **adenosine, cytidine, guanidine** and **thymidine**, although their formal names (rarely if ever encountered) are **deoxyadenosine monophosphate**

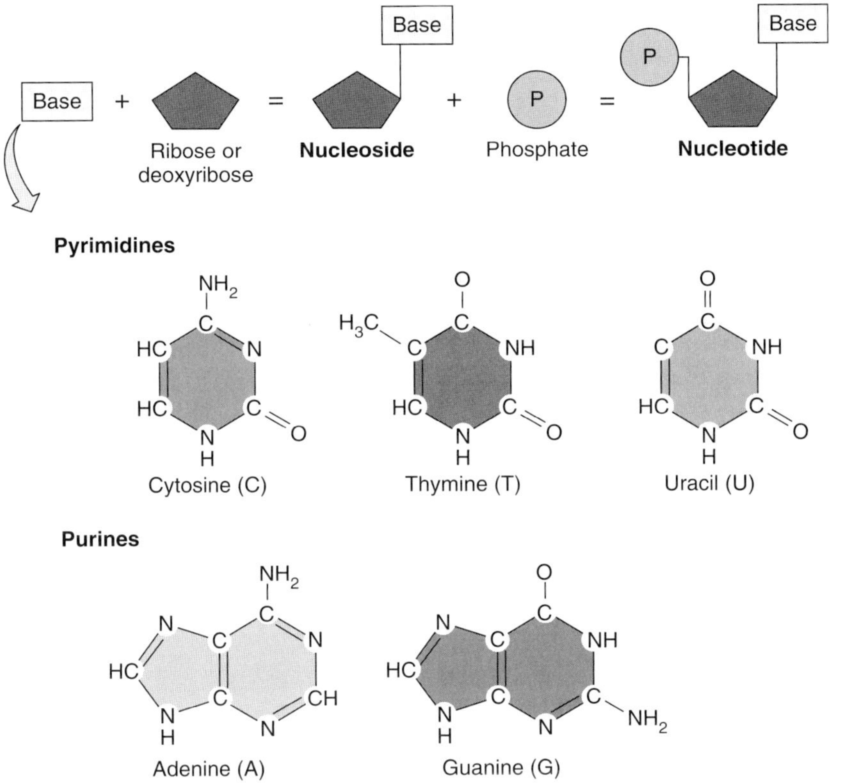

FIGURE 1.3 *The nucleotides that make up the building blocks of DNA and RNA. Reprinted from* Life: The Science of Biology, *7th ed. Purves, Sadava, Orians and Heller. Copyright Sinauer Associates, 2004. Please see the color insert for a color version of this figure.*

(dAMP), deoxycytosine monophosphate (dCMP), deoxyguanidine monophosphate (dGMP) and deoxythymidine monophosphate (dTMP). For our purposes, we can just refer to them as "A," "C," "G" and "T," and understand that the sequence of As, Cs, Gs and Ts in the DNA will differ from one person to another.

As we will discuss later in this chapter, when a gene makes its protein, the gene's DNA is first used to make the corresponding molecule of **ribonucleic acid (RNA)**, in a process called **transcription**. The sequence of nucleotides in the DNA is transcribed, one by one, into a sequence of RNA nucleotides. The nucleotides in RNA contain the sugar **ribose** instead of deoxyribose. In addition, the nucleotides in RNA contain the bases adenine, cytosine and guanine, but contain **uracil (U)** in place of DNA's thymine.[5]

Figure 1.4 illustrates the means by which the nucleotides are strung together to make the DNA molecule. The DNA molecule contains two

[5] Although this will not enter into many legal arguments, you may sometimes see the double-ringed bases adenine and guanine referred to as the **purines**, and the single-ringed cytosine, thymine and uracil referred to as the **pyrimidines**.

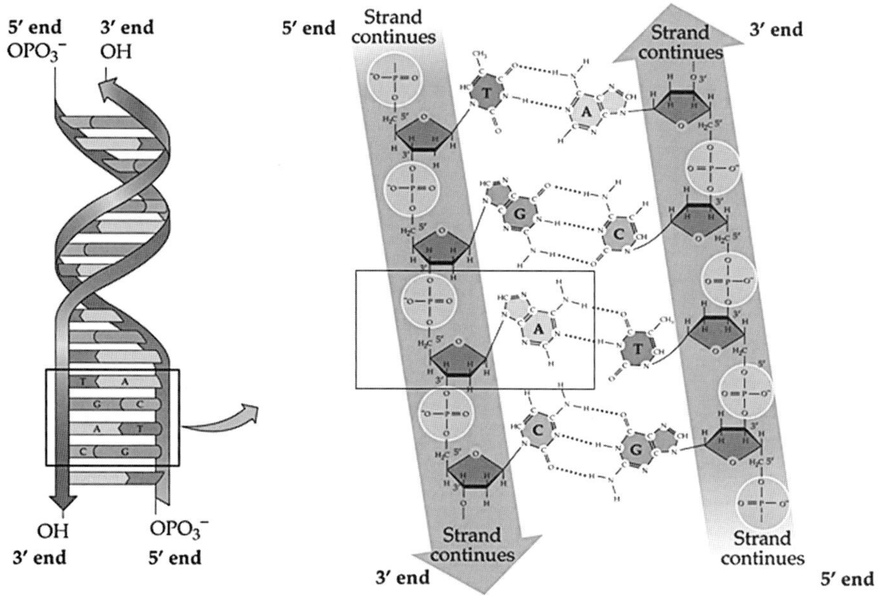

FIGURE 1.4 *The DNA double helix. A box has been drawn around a single "A" nucleotide. Reprinted from* Life: The Science of Biology, *7th ed. Purves, Sadava, Orians and Heller. Copyright Sinauer Associates, 2004. Please see the color insert for a color version of this figure.*

DNA strands, each of which is composed of a string of nucleotides. The two DNA strands are bound together in a double-stranded helix. In each of the two strands, the deoxyribose molecules and phosphate groups in the DNA nucleotides bond together to create the **sugar-phosphate backbone** of the DNA molecule, and the bases project inward from the backbone toward the center of the helix.

The easiest way to envision the double helical structure of DNA is to imagine taking a straight extension ladder and twisting it into a spiral. The handrails of the twisted ladder would illustrate the sugar-phosphate backbone of the DNA molecule. The footrungs of the ladder would depict the arrangement of the bases in the DNA molecule. Each footrung of the ladder actually depicts two bases. The two bases project toward the center of the helix from the sugar-phosphate backbone, one from each side. For the DNA molecule to maintain its proper shape, the bases must be arranged in **complementary basepairs**. As and Ts are complementary to each other, as are Cs and Gs. This means that if there is an A projecting inward from the sugar-phosphate backbone at a particular spot on one strand, there will be a T projecting inward at the corresponding point from the other strand. Similarly, where there is a C projecting inward from one strand, there will be a G projecting inward at that point from the other strand. Chemical bonding forces called **hydrogen bonds** bind the bases together and keep the helix in its double-stranded helical configuration.

The **5′ and 3′ orientation** of a DNA strand will not enter into many courtroom discussions, but it is essential that you understand this concept in order to understand the molecular biology underlying forensic testing (discussed in Chapter 2). The two strands of DNA lie in opposite orientations to each other (Figure 1.4), in an arrangement referred to as **antiparallel**. One strand of the DNA molecule is said to lie in a 5′ to 3′ orientation, and the other in a 3′ to 5′ orientation ("5′" is read as "5 prime," "3′" as "3 prime"). The terms "5′" and "3′" refer to the system by which the carbon atoms in the deoxyribose molecule are numbered. In the formal nomenclature, the carbons in the base are numbered simply as "1," "2," "3," and so on; therefore the carbons in the deoxyribose are given the "prime" character to differentiate them from the carbons in the base. In Figure 1.4, the deoxyriboses are depicted as blue pentagons. Each corner of the pentagon actually represents a carbon atom, but by convention the "Cs" that would be used to represent these carbon atoms are not usually drawn. The 5′ and 3′ carbons of the deoxyribose molecules are depicted in red in Figure 1.4. The 3′ carbon is one of the corners of the pentagon, while the 5′ carbon projects upward from the 4′ carbon, which is also one of the corners of the pentagon. Please observe from Figure 1.4 how each phosphate group (brown circle) is joined to its corresponding deoxyribose molecule at the 5′ carbon of the deoxyribose. Please note further that when a new DNA chain is synthesized, either during the natural process of DNA replication or in the laboratory, the enzyme DNA polymerase attaches each new nucleotide to the growing chain by hooking the phosphate group of the new nucleotide onto the 3′ carbon of the deoxyribose molecule in the nucleotide before it. If it helps, imagine a train of circus elephants, each one using its trunk to hold the tail of the one before it. The elephants' trunks represent the phosphate groups projecting up from the 5′ carbon of the deoxyribose (the elephants' faces), and the elephants' tails represent the 3′ carbon of the deoxyribose.

In order to understand the molecular basis for these forensic DNA tests, when you think of the DNA molecule, forget about the sugar-phosphate backbone and just focus on the sequence of bases in the DNA. You can illustrate the DNA molecule as a double strand of bases that follows the complementary basepairing rule (A-T and C-G pairings). A stretch of DNA can be illustrated simply by writing the base sequences of the two strands, as illustrated below. You will often see DNA sequence written as it is below, but without the "5′" and "3′" labels. When the 5′ and 3′ ends are not designated, it is conventional to depict the sequence in the orientation shown below.

5′-CTTAGCCATAGCCTA-3′
3′-GAATCGGTATCGGAT-5′

In addition, because the complementary basepairing rule allows you to deduce the sequence of the second strand if you see the sequence of one strand, DNA sequence is often written as a single strand of As, Cs, Gs and Ts, in the 5′ to 3′ orientation. For example, the sequence above would often be written as

CTTAGCCATAGCCTA.

Once you are accustomed to thinking about the DNA molecule in this manner, it is easy to understand the nature of the different polymorphisms that serve as the basis for forensic tests. The polymorphisms that are used for forensic DNA testing will be discussed in detail later in this chapter. Let us briefly consider an example, however, in order to illustrate this point. Consider the polymorphism that is known as a **tetranucleotide repeat**. If you know that the Latin prefix "tetra" refers to four items, then you should easily understand that a tetranucleotide repeat is merely a stretch of DNA where a specific four nucleotide motif is repeated. For example, a GAAT repeat might have the following sequence:

TGACCATAGGCT**GAATGAATGAATGAATGAAT**CTGAATCGA

Once you understand that, it is a simple matter to understand that we can differentiate between two different individuals on the basis of these tetranucleotide repeats because different people will have a different number of GAATs in the repeated sequence.

Because the sequence of bases in the DNA is usually the focus of attention, the terms "base" and "nucleotide" are often used interchangeably without causing significant confusion. In fact, the physical distance between two genes is routinely expressed as the number of **basepairs (bp)**

between the two genes,[6] despite the fact that the term "nucleotide pairs" is technically more accurate. Nuclear DNA contains 3,000,000,000 bp of DNA and approximately 21,000 genes, while the mitochondrial DNA molecule contains only 16,569 bp of DNA and 37 genes.

RECAPPING THE MAIN POINTS

1. The basic building block of DNA is the nucleotide. Each nucleotide contains a deoxyribose, a phosphate group and a base.
2. For the purpose of understanding the basis for forensic testing, the sequence of bases in the DNA is the important aspect of DNA's structure.
3. There are four different bases in DNA: adenine (A), cytosine (C), guanine (G) and thymine (T). RNA also contains the A, C and G bases but has uracil (U) in place of T.
4. There are many places in the DNA molecule where normally developed, healthy people have different specific sequences of bases.

VARIABILITY IS THE RULE, NOT THE EXCEPTION

There Is No "Normal" DNA Sequence

You have probably heard of the Human Genome Project, which has resulted in, among many other things, the publication of the entire sequence of the human DNA molecule.[7] One of the things that scientists discovered through the effort to ascertain the normal human DNA sequence is that there is no single normal human DNA sequence. On the contrary, there are many polymorphic loci in the human DNA molecule at which the sequence of bases in the DNA differs between normally developed, healthy people. In fact, there are so many polymorphisms in the human DNA sequence that it is not easy to determine which of several possible suspects is the source of a piece of biological evidence that was left at a crime scene, even if the suspects are related to each other. The only exception to this is identical twins, who have identical DNA sequences (except in the case of somatic mutations, which are discussed later in this chapter).

Some polymorphisms have no impact at all on the function of any of your proteins, but others can have measurable effects. Those that have no discernible impact on any protein functions are called **benign polymorphisms**, whereas those that do have some measurable effect on the function of their genes' proteins are called **functional polymorphisms**. For ethical

[6] The term "basepairs" is usually used because of the double helical structure of the DNA molecule and the way in which the nucleotides containing complementary bases are aligned.

[7] The term **genome** is used to refer to an individual's DNA molecule, or an individual's or species' collection of genes. The reader will frequently see the term **genomic DNA** used when discussing the DNA that is extracted from biological samples.

[8] As we will discuss in Chapter 5, the vast majority of the mitochondrial DNA is protein-coding sequence.

reasons, benign polymorphisms are used in forensic testing rather than functional polymorphisms. Some functional polymorphisms may influence one's health over the course of one's lifetime, and this information can be used to discriminate against the individual on the basis of his or her long-term health prospects. Many common diseases, such as cancer, Alzheimer disease, diabetes, asthma and cardiovascular disease, are caused by the additive, multiplicative or synergistic effects of several causative factors, including functional polymorphisms in critical genes. Many people worry that insurance companies, employers and others may use genetic information to discriminate against them on the basis of their predicted long-term health status. Because benign polymorphisms do not have any impact on one's health, however, this concern is unfounded. The information from benign polymorphisms is only useful for individual identification.

Not All Your DNA Makes Proteins—Intergenic Spaces and the Splicing Out of Introns During RNA Processing

Most people understand that our DNA contains our genes, that our genes make our proteins, and that our proteins play critical roles in our development and function. Most people would be surprised to learn, however, that only approximately 2% of our nuclear DNA constitutes protein-coding nucleotides.[8] One type of noncoding DNA is the **intergenic space** (spaces between genes) in the nuclear DNA molecule. There is considerable intergenic space in human nuclear DNA, and these intergenic spaces provide opportunities for sequence changes to occur in places where they will have no effect on the body's proteins, and therefore no effect on the person's development.

In order to understand the other major type of noncoding DNA, one must understand certain aspects of the process whereby a gene makes its protein (Figure 1.5). In a process called **transcription**, the gene first makes an RNA called the **primary transcript**, or **pre-messenger RNA (pre-mRNA)**. After the pre-mRNA is produced, large sections of the pre-mRNA, called **introns**, are cut out, and the remaining sections of the pre-mRNA, called **exons**, are spliced together to make the gene's **messenger RNA**. The mRNA is then used to direct the synthesis of the gene's protein. Because the introns are spliced out, and therefore are not included in the mRNA that is used to make the protein, changes in an intron's sequence often constitute benign polymorphisms. Although the difference in intronic

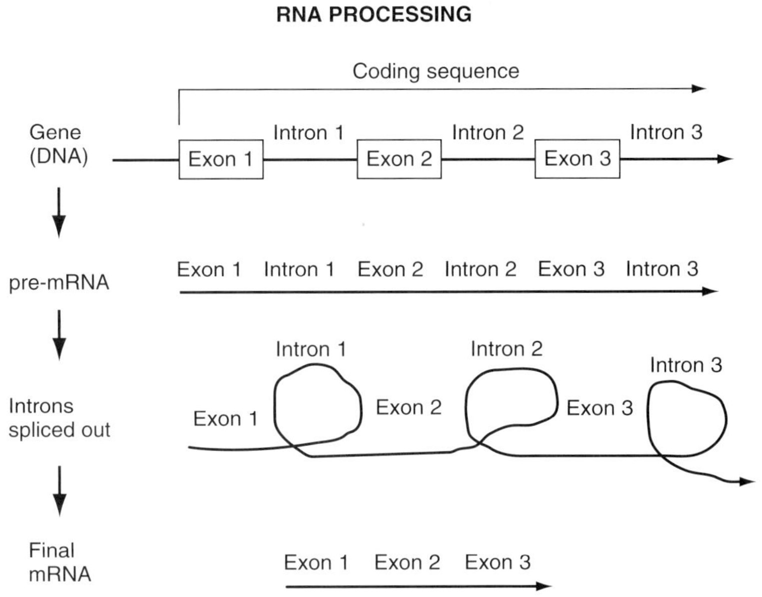

FIGURE 1.5
Introns are spliced out of the pre-mRNA to create the mRNA that is used to direct the synthesis of the gene's protein.

DNA sequence between the two individuals can be demonstrated by DNA testing, there will be no difference between these individuals with respect to the activity of their proteins, and hence no difference in the quality of the two individuals' development.

The Redundant Genetic Code Even Allows for Variability in the Protein-Coding Sequences of Genes

After the mRNA is made, it provides the instructions that enable the cellular machinery to make the gene's protein. A protein is synthesized by chaining amino acids together. This process is referred to as **translation**, because the nucleotide "language" of the mRNA is translated into the amino acid "language" of proteins. During translation, the mRNA is read three nucleotides at a time. Each three-nucleotide unit is called a **codon**, and each codon directs the cellular machinery to add a specific amino acid onto the growing chain of amino acids that will eventually become the protein.

The relationship between the three-nucleotide sequence of a codon and the amino acid that gets incorporated into the protein when that codon is read is referred to as the **genetic code**. For example, if the sequence of the mRNA codon is UGU, the amino acid cysteine is added to the growing amino acid chain. If the sequence of the codon is AAG, the amino acid

[9] Bone marrow cells produce your blood cells. Therefore, a bone marrow transplant will result in the donor's DNA being in some of the recipient's blood cells.

lysine is added to the growing chain. The genetic code is redundant; there are a number of instances in which several different codons will direct the cellular machinery to add the same amino acid to the polypeptide. This means that, if you change the DNA sequence at a single nucleotide, even though it is in the protein-coding portion of the DNA, it may not change the amino acid sequence of the gene's protein and will therefore constitute a benign polymorphism.

Rare Individuals May Have Different Genotypes in Different Tissues

Although it is very rare, it is possible for a forensic analyst to detect two different genotypes in a single individual. Blood transfusions or bone marrow transplants will enable the forensic analyst to obtain two or more different profiles from a single person's blood sample.[9] Because they came from different individuals, the two profiles can be markedly different from each other. Blood is the only tissue that will exhibit the multiple profiles, however. All other tissues, such as buccal samples (obtained by swabbing the inside of the mouth), will exhibit only one.

Another rare phenomenon that can result in two different profiles in a single individual is the **somatic mutation**. In order to understand somatic mutations, consider the manner in which an individual goes from his or her beginning as a fertilized egg to a 90-trillion-celled animal. After fertilization, the fertilized egg divides into two cells, each of which divides again into two cells, and so on. As the cells undergo repeated rounds of replication and division, different cells begin to mature and develop into different cell types. Some develop into bone cells, others into muscle cells, still others into white blood cells, and so on for all the other tissue types that are needed in the human body.

Every time a cell divides into two daughter cells, it must first replicate all its contents, including its DNA. Every time a cell replicates its DNA, there is the opportunity to introduce a mutation into the DNA sequence. If a mutation arises during one of these replication-divisions, the daughters of the cell that acquires the mutation will also have the mutation, but the other cells in the body will not. Unlike **germline mutations**, which exist in the egg or sperm that created the individual and appear in every cell the individual has, somatic mutations only appear in the tissue(s) that ultimately developed from the cell that originally acquired the mutation. If the mutation occurs early in embryonic development, the mutation may appear in several different tissues in the individual's body. If it occurs later in development, however, it will only appear in one or a few tissues. If a somatic mutation occurs in a forensic marker sequence, a forensic analyst may be able to detect different DNA profiles in different tissues from the same individual. The two profiles will be very similar, however, because the mutation will probably only affect a single marker. In addition, unlike a blood transfusion, in which two profiles can be seen in one tissue (blood), in most cases involving somatic mutations the analyst will only see one profile in any given tissue.

[10] The STR markers in the CODIS panel have between 5 and 50 repetitions of the tetranucleotide repeat in their different alleles.

RECAPPING THE MAIN POINTS

1. Forensic scientists use benign, rather than functional, polymorphisms for forensic testing.
2. Only approximately 2% of our nuclear DNA is actually used to make our proteins. The other 98% provides ample places where there can be differences in the DNA sequence between normally developed, healthy people, even if the two people are closely related (except identical twins).
3. One of the primary sources of nonprotein-coding DNA (and therefore benign polymorphisms) in the human DNA molecule is the space between genes (the intergenic space). Because these intergenic regions do not contain genes, variations in the sequence in these regions constitute benign polymorphisms.
4. The other primary source of noncoding DNA is the introns within genes. The intronic nucleotides are transcribed into the pre-mRNA, but are cut out during the process in which the pre-mRNA is transformed into the mRNA. Because they are not part of the mRNA sequence, and therefore do not influence the makeup of any proteins, most mutations in intronic nucleotides are benign polymorphisms.
5. The genetic code is redundant; some sequence variations, even in the protein-coding region of a gene, do not change the amino acid content of the gene's protein, and therefore constitute benign polymorphisms.
6. It is possible for one gene to have several different versions of its coding sequence, and for all the different versions of the coding sequence to produce proteins that perform their functions properly.

POLYMORPHISMS COMMONLY USED FOR FORENSIC TESTING

Short Tandem Repeats (STRs)

The FBI's CODIS System

STRs are currently the polymorphisms of choice for forensic DNA typing. As the name implies, in an STR, a short stretch of sequence (1–5 bp) is repeated several times, without any other nucleotides intervening between the repeats.[10] For example, a typical **dinucleotide repeat**, in which two

[11] Pentanucleotide repeats involve repetitions of a 5-bp motif, rather than the 4-bp motif found in tetranucleotide repeats.

bases (in this case, CA) are repeated a variable number of times, might have a sequence such as the following.

5′—CTAGCTACTG**CACACACACACACACA**CGTGCCGATGC—3′
3′—GATCGATGAC**GTGTGTGTGTGTGTGT**GCACGGCTACG—5′

This would be the number 8 allele for this marker, because there are eight repetitions of the dinucleotide repeat. Similarly, the number 3 allele of a **tetranucleotide repeat** (4-bp repeat; in this case, a CGGT repeat) might have the following sequence:

5′—GCTAGCTACTG**CGGTCGGTCGGT**CGTGCCGATGC—3′
3′—CGATCGATGAC**GCCAGCCAGCCA**GCACGGCTACG—5′

In 1998–1999, the FBI adopted STR testing as its standard method for forensic DNA typing and launched **CODIS (Combined DNA Index System)**. CODIS provides two searchable databanks, one containing DNA profiles from individuals who have been convicted of one of several felonies, and the other containing DNA profiles from evidence that was obtained from crime scenes. The investigator can search either databank for a match to a particular piece of evidence or individual's profile. A growing number of "cold cases," in which investigators had long ago exhausted all available leads, have been cracked when a match was obtained between evidence from the old crime and the profile of a recently convicted (and apparently serial) offender.

Tetranucleotide repeats have become the markers of choice for forensic identity testing (for reasons discussed in Chapters 2 and 3). Table 1.1 illustrates the specific repeated sequences contained in the 13 tetranucleotide markers that made up the FBI's original test battery. More recently, two more tetranucleotide markers (D2S1338 and D19S433) and two pentanucleotide markers[11] (Penta E and Penta D) have been added to the forensic testing panel. You will notice that some STRs contain the same sequence repeated a variable number of times, but others contain a combination of sequences that are repeated. In either case, there is at least one 4-bp sequence motif that is repeated a variable number of times, thereby providing the basis for the polymorphism. For each STR, different individuals, even close relatives, will have a different number of those repeated units in their DNA.

Most of the commercially available forensic DNA typing systems include the 13 CODIS loci plus an additional 2-3 STRs for individual

Table 1.1 Chromosome Band Locations and Repeated Sequence Motifs for the 13 STR Markers in the FBI's Original CODIS Database.

STR Name	Band Location	Sequence of Repeat
CSF1PO	5q33.1	$[AGAT]_n$
FGA	4q31.3	$[TTTC]_3TTTTTTCT[CTTT]_nCTCC[TTCC]_2$
TH01	11p15.5	$[AATG]_n$
TPOX	2p25.3	$[AATG]_n$
vWA	12p13.31	$TCTA[TCTG]_{3\text{-}4}[TCTA]_n$
D3S1358	3p21.31	$TCTA[TCTG]_{2\text{-}3}[TCTA]_n$
D5S818	5q23.2	$[AGAT]_n$
D7S820	7q21.11	$[GATA]_n$
D8S1179	8q24.13	$[TCTR^*]_n$
D13S317	13q31.1	$[TACT]_n$
D16S539	16q24.1	$[GATA]_n$
D18S51	18q21.33	$[AGAA]_n$
D21S11	21q21.1	$[TCTA]_n[TCTG]_n\{[TCTA]_3TA[TCTA]_3TCA[TCTA]_2TCCATA\}[TCTA]_nTATCTA$

Brackets and subscript numbers indicate the sequence that is repeated and the number of times it is repeated. Subscript "n" indicates elements that are repeated a different number of times in different people, and therefore serve as the basis for the polymorphism.
**R indicates the presence of a purine—either an A or a G—in that position.*

identification, along with a marker from the amelogenin gene for gender identification. The amelogenin gene produces a protein that is part of the enamel of one's teeth. There is a copy of the amelogenin gene on both the X and Y chromosomes. In one region of the gene, the Y chromosome's copy contains 6 bp more than the X chromosome's copy. This 6-bp difference can be used to determine the sex of the individual(s) from whom a piece of evidence was obtained, and can be particularly useful in rape cases, when evidence samples often contain a mixture of male and female material.

Marker and Allele Nomenclature

Because they each contain the same DNA sequence, and therefore the same arrangement of genes, the two members of each chromosome pair are called **homologous chromosomes, or homologs.**[12] The different alleles in an STR are named according to the number of repeats in the allele. For example, someone with a homozygous 3,3 genotype for the TH01 STR (an AATG repeat on chromosome 11) has three AATG repeats at the TH01 locus on each of his or her two chromosomes 11. Someone

[12] Again, the XY chromosome pair in males constitutes an exception to this.

with a heterozygous 4,6 genotype for the TH01 marker has four AATGs at the TH01 locus on one chromosome 11, and six AATGs at the TH01 locus on the other chromosome 11.

Some of the tetranucleotide repeats commonly used in forensic testing are imperfect. Some alleles contain a partial repeated unit in addition to the tetranucleotide repeats, and therefore their length does not differ from the lengths of the other alleles by an even multiple of four nucleotides. These imperfect alleles, or **microvariants**, are named to reflect the nature of their sequence. For example, the 6.3 allele of the TH01 tetranucleotide repeat contains three AATGs, an ATG, and then three more AATGs. The "6.3" designation indicates that this allele contains six AATGs plus an additional three nucleotides from another AATG repeat.

The sequences of two hypothetical STRs are shown below; two alleles are shown for each STR. Note that the sequences flanking the repeated region are identical in all the alleles of a particular STR. Except in very rare cases, the only difference between the sequences of two alleles of an STR is the number of repeated units. An individual who possesses the following sequences has a 6,8 genotype at the dinucleotide marker and a 3,5 genotype at the tetranucleotide marker (the sequences are shown in their double-stranded configurations).

Dinucleotide Repeat–Allele 6—contains six CA/GT repeats

5′—GCTAGCTACTG**CACACACACACA**CGTGCCGATGC—3′
3′—CGATCGATGAC**GTGTGTGTGTGT**GCACGGCTACG—5′

Dinucleotide Repeat–Allele 8—contains eight CA/GT repeats

5′—CTAGCTACTG**CACACACACACACACA**CGTGCCGATGC—3′
3′—GATCGATGAC**GTGTGTGTGTGTGTGT**GCACGGCTACG—5′

Tetranucleotide Repeat–Allele 3—contains three CGGT/GCCA repeats

5′—TCTGGATGCCG**CGGTCGGTCGGT**AGTATCTTAGC—3′
3′—AGACCTACGGA**GCCAGCCAGCCA**TCATAGAATCG—5′

Tetranucleotide Repeat–Allele 5—contains 5 CGGT/GCCA repeats

5′—GGATGCCG**CGGTCGGTCGGTCGGTCGGT**AGTATCTT—3′
3′—CCTACGGA**GCCAGCCAGCCAGCCAGCCA**TCATAGAA—5′

Each STR's sequence is unique in the human DNA molecule, because the sequence of an STR includes not only the repeated sequence, but also some of the sequence flanking either side of the repeated sequence. The sequences that flank the different STRs are all different from each other, even for two STRs for which the repeated sequence is the same. Because of the unique nature of each flanking sequence, each STR represents a stretch of sequence that only occurs once in the human DNA molecule.

In any population of individuals, there will be several different alleles for any single polymorphic marker. Some of these alleles may be found more frequently than others; the concept of allele frequency is critical to the interpretation of the DNA evidence. The best markers for forensic DNA testing are those with a large number of different alleles and a relatively even distribution of allele frequencies. When a suspect's DNA profile matches an evidence sample's DNA profile, the prosecution must provide an estimate of the probability that the profile of another person, randomly selected from the larger population, would also match the evidence's profile. The probative value of the evidence is therefore greater if that DNA profile is rare in the larger population than if it is common. For any marker, the greater the number of alleles that are observed in a population, and the more evenly the alleles are distributed among people, the rarer each genotype will be. For example, if a marker only has two alleles (call them 1 and 2), only three genotypes are possible: 11, 12 and 22. Each genotype will probably be present in a substantial percentage of the population, so finding a match between a suspect and an evidence sample does not strongly implicate the suspect as the person who left the evidence. On the other hand, a marker with 10 alleles provides 55 different possible genotypes. If the frequencies of those genotypes are approximately equal, each one will be rare, and a match between the suspect and the evidence will be highly probative. If, however, there is one genotype that is very common, and the rest are exceedingly rare, if the suspect and the evidence both exhibit the common genotype, the match is considerably less probative.

Most marker names are derived in one of two ways. If the marker lies within a known gene, its name will often reflect its location in that gene. For example, the tetranucleotide repeat TH01 is located in the first intron of the tyrosine hydroxylase (TH) gene. In many cases, however, the marker does not lie within a gene; these markers are named according to the chromosome on which they reside. For example, the marker D15S113 is named as it is because it is part of the DNA sequence (D); it is on chromosome 15 (15); its sequence only occurs once in the human genome, and it is therefore single-copy (S); and it is the 113th such marker to have been submitted to the human genome database at the **National Center for Biotechnology Information (NCBI)**, which serves as the primary repository for all human (and other organisms') DNA sequences.

In order to specify the location of a marker on its chromosome, chromosomes are divided into bands (Figure 1.6). For example, the D7S820 marker lies in band 7q21.11. The banding nomenclature comes from a technique called G-banding, which is used to search for chromosome abnormalities in children with birth defects and to map the positions of genes on their respective chromosomes. In the G-banding procedure, a cell's chromosomes are laid out on a microscope slide, treated with an enzyme that digests some of the proteins that are bound to the DNA, and stained with a dark blue-black dye called giemsa (thereby giving the procedure the name G-banding). G-banding produces a characteristic pattern of white, gray and black bands on each chromosome arm when the chromosomes are viewed under a microscope. This provides a system of standard nomenclature for specifying the location of a gene or marker in the human genome. In the case of D7S820, its band location (7q21.11) is read as "7q two-one-point-one-one," rather than as "7q twenty-one-point-eleven." The names of other bands are read in similar fashion.[13] Table 1.1 illustrates the chromosome band location, and the specific repeated sequence, for each of the 13 tetranucleotide repeat markers in the FBI's CODIS marker panel.

As you can see from Figure 1.6, each chromosome has a visible constriction called the **centromere** that divides the chromosome into what are called the **p arm** and the **q arm**. The centromere lies in the middle of some (**metacentric**) chromosomes, is offset toward one end of other (**submetacentric**) chromosomes and appears close to the end of still other (**acrocentric**) chromosomes. By convention, the shorter of the two chromosome arms is referred to as the p arm and is shown above the centromere in standard diagrams of chromosomes. The longer arm is referred to as the q arm and is depicted below the centromere. Each arm's bands are

[13] It isn't important to know why this is so for the purpose of understanding the use of DNA evidence in trials. It is only important that you avoid this gaffe when speaking. Briefly, the early chromosome banding techniques divided the chromosomes into a small number of regions, which were named 1, 2, 3, etc. As improved techniques provided better resolution, each region was subdivided into two or more subregions. For the sake of consistency, the original 1, 2, 3 nomenclature was kept, and a second number was added behind the original number to indicate the subregion. Further improvements in resolution have warranted expanding this system of nomenclature to two decimal points.

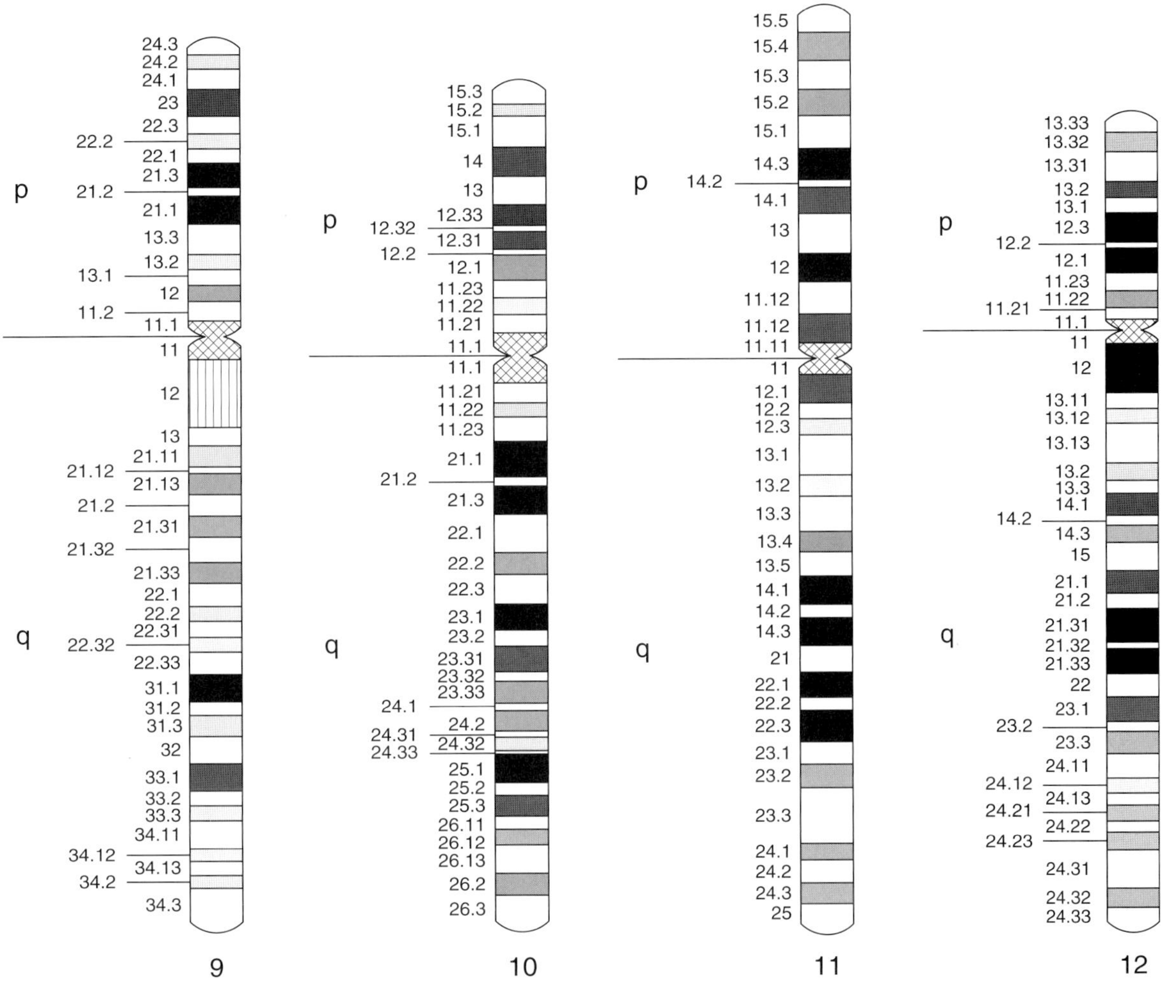

FIGURE 1.6 *G-banding patterns of chromosomes 9–12. Reprinted from Francke, U.* Cytogenet Cell Genet, *1994, 65(3), 209. Copyright S. Karger AG, Basel.*

named separately. The band nearest the centromere on each arm is numbered 11, and the numbers increase as you move toward the end of the chromosome arm.

Variable Number of Tandem Repeats (VNTRs)

The first forensic DNA tests that were developed capitalized on the existence of VNTRs in the human genome. Like STRs, VNTRs also involve the repetition of a characteristic sequence motif, but VNTRs involve the repetition of larger stretches of sequence than STRs. The repeated unit in a VNTR can be between one dozen and several hundred nucleotides in length, and can be repeated dozens, or even hundreds, of times. The VNTRs that are used for forensic work are highly polymorphic—even more so than most STRs. There are so many different alleles for each VNTR that each allele's frequency, and each genotype's frequency, is very low. It only takes a panel of 6–8 VNTR markers to provide the discriminative power of 12–15 STRs. Because of their large size, however, a VNTR analysis involves procedures that are considerably slower and more labor-intensive than those required for an STR analysis. STR protocols are not only faster and more sensitive than VNTR protocols, but they are also more easily automated, and able to produce more reliable results from suboptimal samples. For these reasons, in the period from 1998 to the early 2000s, STRs rapidly displaced VNTRs as the method of choice for forensic testing.

Coding Sequence Variations—The DQA1 and Polymarker Tests

Unlike the STRs, the polymorphisms that serve as the basis for the DQA1[14] and Polymarker™ tests involve variation in the protein-coding sequence of the gene, and not the length of a repeated sequence.[15] Recall from the earlier discussion that a gene can have several different variations in its protein-coding sequence and still have all its alleles produce proteins that function properly.

The DQA1 test determines the individual's status for several polymorphisms within a single gene. In contrast, the Polymarker™ test determines the individual's allele status at five loci: the low density lipoprotein receptor (LDLR), glycophorin A (GYPA), hemoglobin gamma globin (HBGG) and group-specific complement (GC) genes, plus the marker D7S8, which lies close to the gene that is mutated in most patients with cystic fibrosis. In any large population there are only 2–3 alleles at each of these loci, so the discriminative power of each individual test is limited. Combining the tests into one convenient assay, however, created a test that was faster and less labor-intensive than the VNTR tests, but provided a reasonable degree of discriminability. In addition, as discussed in Chapter 2, the PCR-based tests such as DQA1 and the Polymarker™ test can be used to analyze some samples that cannot be analyzed by VNTR methods because they contain minute amounts of DNA or DNA that has been degraded.

The DQA1 + Polymarker™ test was used by a number of law enforcement agencies throughout the mid-to-late 1990s, and it is not unusual to

[14] The DQA1 gene was originally named DQα, and the reader may encounter it referred to as such in earlier publications.

[15] The DQA1 gene encodes one of the proteins of the major histocompatibility complex (MHC). The MHC is a network of proteins located on the surface of all our cells. The MHC is part of the mechanism whereby your cells alert your immune system to the presence of foreign invaders such as bacterial infections. It is also a means by which doctors determine whether one person is a suitable organ or tissue donor for another person.

encounter DQA1 + Polymarker™ data in cases from that era. In addition, like the VNTRs, the DQA1 + Polymarker™ test was replaced by STR testing as the method of choice for forensic identity testing, because the STR testing protocols are faster, more sensitive, more easily automated and able to produce more reliable results from suboptimal samples like those frequently encountered in forensic work.

Single-Nucleotide Polymorphisms (SNPs)

The simplest form of a genetic variant is the **single-nucleotide polymorphism** (SNP). A SNP refers to the fact that there will be an A, for example, in one person's DNA sequence, but a C, G or T in the same place in another person's DNA sequence. There are over 1 million SNPs in the human genome, many of which constitute benign polymorphisms and can be useful for forensic testing. A SNP can be located in an intergenic space, in an intron, or even within the coding sequence of a gene. SNPs are more abundant than STRs in the human DNA molecule and can be genotyped using fast, inexpensive methods. At least two groups have developed panels of SNPs that can be used for forensic testing.[16] SNPs are limited in their variability, however, by the fact that there can only be four possible alleles for any one SNP, because one can only have either an A, C, G or T in that nucleotide position. In fact, many SNPs only exhibit two different alleles in any large population. It therefore requires approximately 100 SNPs to provide the same discriminative power as 15 STRs. In addition, SNPs are not nearly as useful for the analysis of mixed samples as the more polymorphic STRs.

One situation in which SNPs may be highly useful is in the analysis of degraded samples. Analyzing degraded DNA is often a matter of analyzing smaller fragments of the DNA than you do using the typical STR protocols. Because the SNP involves only one single nucleotide, the DNA can be analyzed in very small fragments, allowing SNP typing to yield information on some samples that cannot be analyzed using the regular STR typing protocols or even direct sequencing. Future developments in DNA array technology may increase the usefulness of SNPs for forensic testing.[17] A DNA array is capable of illustrating an individual's allele status for thousands of SNPs in one assay, allowing for excellent discriminative power with minimal processing time.

[16] Vallone et al., 2005; Kidd et al., 2006

[17] In a DNA array, thousands of different DNA sequences are micro-spotted onto a platform such as a nylon membrane or a glass slide, and a detection technique called hybridization reveals which of the target sequences matches a sequence in the individual's DNA. Needing only four micro-spots to represent all the possible alleles for one SNP, this method allows the analyst to determine the individual's allele status for thousands of SNPs in one assay, by determining which of the micro-spotted target sequences hybridize with the individual's DNA.

The allele frequencies for some SNPs vary significantly between races, and these SNPs can sometimes be used to estimate the race of the person who is the source of the evidence. The DNAprint company (Sarasota, Florida) markets a kit that determines the individual's allele status at 56 SNPs in an effort to predict the individual's race or ethnicity. Some of these SNPs are in genes whose protein products cause some of the differences that can be observed in the appearance of the different races, such as proteins that make our skin pigments. These SNPs either constitute functional polymorphisms or lie very close to functional polymorphisms in their respective genes. It is less clear for some of the other SNPs whether they contribute to the observable differences between the races, or merely occur with different frequencies in the different races by chance. As discussed in Chapter 5, SNPs are particularly useful for mitochondrial DNA analyses, where there are few STRs, no introns and little intergenic space to harbor length polymorphisms. The sequence of a hypothetical SNP is illustrated as follows.

	Allele 1-CG pair	**Allele 2-AT pair**
Single Nucleotide	—ACGTG**C**TGATCGT—	—ACGTG**A**TGATCGT—
Polymorphism	—TGCAC**G**ACTAGCA—	—TGCAC**T**ACTAGCA—

RECAPPING THE MAIN POINTS

1. Tetranucleotide repeat STRs are currently the markers of choice for forensic identity testing. The different alleles of a tetranucleotide repeat polymorphism differ from each other in the number of times a particular 4-bp sequence motif is repeated.
2. VNTR tests were the first DNA tests used for forensic purposes. VNTRs are characterized by the repetition of sequence motifs that are between a dozen and several hundred nucleotides long.
3. The DQA1 and Polymarker™ tests are based on differences in the sequence of the DNA, rather than on differences in the number of times a characteristic sequence motif is repeated.
4. SNPs represent situations in which one nucleotide has been substituted for by one of the other three nucleotides. Because many SNPs only exhibit two alleles, their discriminative power is limited, and SNPs are not frequently used for forensic testing.

USING THE DNA PROFILE TO IDENTIFY AN UNKNOWN PERPETRATOR

At this point in time, the courts have great confidence in a DNA profile's ability to identify an individual. In many jurisdictions, in order to file charges within the period specified by the statute of limitations, prosecutors will file charges against suspects who are identified solely by their DNA profiles. The first case in which such a "John Doe DNA profile warrant" led to an arrest occurred in Sacramento, California; the warrant and related arrest were both upheld by the California Superior Court in February 2001. Since then, similar warrants have been filed in Kansas, Missouri, New York, Texas, Utah and Wisconsin.[18] It is reasonable to expect that more jurisdictions will accept these warrants in the future.

[18] See Akehurst-Moore, 2006, for a review of state and federal DNA indictment and tolling statutes.

REFERENCES AND ADDITIONAL READINGS

Akehurst-Moore, Scott. (2006) *Journal of High Technology Law*, 6, 213.

Francke, U. (1994) *Cytogenetics and Cell Genetics*, 65(3), 206–218.

Kidd, K.K., Pakstis, A.J., Speed, W.C., Grigorenko, E.L., Kajuna, S.L., Karoma, N.J., Kungulilo, S., Kim, J.J., Lu, R.B., Odunsi, A., Okonofua, F., Parnas, J., Schulz, L.O., Zhukova, O.V. and Kidd, J.R. (2006) *Forensic Science International*, 164(1), 20–32.

Vallone, P.M., Decker, A.E. and Butler, J.M. (2005) *Forensic Science International*, 149(2–3), 279–286.

CHAPTER 2

The Molecular Biological Basis of Forensic DNA Tests

CONTENTS

Extraction and Quantification of DNA

Polymerase Chain Reaction (PCR)-Based Tests

Variable Number of Tandem Repeats (VNTR) Testing

Direct Sequencing

References and Additional Readings

EXTRACTION AND QUANTIFICATION OF DNA

The extraction and quantification of DNA are critical steps in the analysis procedure. Most readers are familiar with the expression "garbage in, garbage out." If the analyst wants to produce clearly interpretable results, he or she must begin with a sufficient quantity of good quality DNA.

The technical details of extraction protocols are not extremely important to the litigator. The needs of all sides converge at this stage of the process. Unlike the data manipulation part of the procedure, in which an analyst may make a decision to call a peak an artifact rather than a true allele peak, or to set the analyzer's peak detection threshold low enough that the analyzer detects peaks it usually ignores, there are few subjective decisions made by the analyst regarding the parameters of the extraction procedure. The laboratories themselves will suffer if their extraction protocols do not produce good product, and if the extraction does not produce good DNA, neither side can use the DNA evidence to bolster its arguments. With respect to the extraction of the DNA, the critical issues are whether a sufficient quantity of DNA was obtained, whether any contamination may influence the analysis, and whether the DNA in the sample has degraded. If the sample is contaminated, the analyst may not detect the contamination until he or she observes that no results were obtained for one or more markers, or that a second DNA profile is present in a single-source sample. In contrast, the analyst has several methods available for determining the quantity of DNA that was extracted and the degree of degradation the DNA has experienced before he or she analyzes it.

All the protocols used for forensic testing yield their best results when the proper amount of DNA is used in the analysis. If too much DNA is used, artifacts can appear in the data and give the impression that there are more alleles in a sample than there actually are. If too little DNA is used, alleles can drop out, and the analyst may conclude that there are fewer alleles in the sample than there actually are. Quantifying the DNA from a forensic evidence sample is often challenging because the sample includes not only human DNA, but bacterial DNA, and perhaps DNA from other species as well. Because the analyst uses human-specific reagents in order to keep the bacterial (or other species') DNA from interfering with the analysis, when one calculates how much of the sample one needs to put into the **polymerase chain reaction (PCR)**, one must be sure one is putting in the required amount of human DNA. This is so important to the outcome of the analysis that it is specified in the DAB Standards.[1] Therefore, in order to be certain one is putting the proper amount of human DNA into the analysis, one must determine the concentration of human DNA, independent of whatever bacterial or other DNA might also be in the sample.

[1] Standard 9.3.

The method that has been used most often for quantifying the human DNA in forensic samples employs what is known as a **slot-blot hybridization** procedure. For these assays, such as the Quantiblot™ method from Applied Biosystems Inc., the (negatively charged) sample DNA is immobilized (blotted) on a (positively charged) nylon membrane, and the membrane is incubated with a piece of DNA (called a probe) that has a sequence that is complementary to a set of sequences that are only found in the DNA of the higher primates. Both the membrane-immobilized DNA and the probe DNA are denatured, so they are both single-stranded and looking for complementary sequences to which they can bind. The assay uses a chemical detection method to visualize how much of the probe has bound to the sample DNA. The analyst sees a band on the membrane wherever the probe DNA has bound. The higher the concentration of the DNA sample that is immobilized on the membrane, the denser the resultant band on the membrane will be (Figure 2.1). Several control DNA samples, each having a different known concentration, are immobilized on the membrane as well, and each sample is quantified by comparing the intensity obtained from the sample with the intensities of the signals obtained from the control samples.

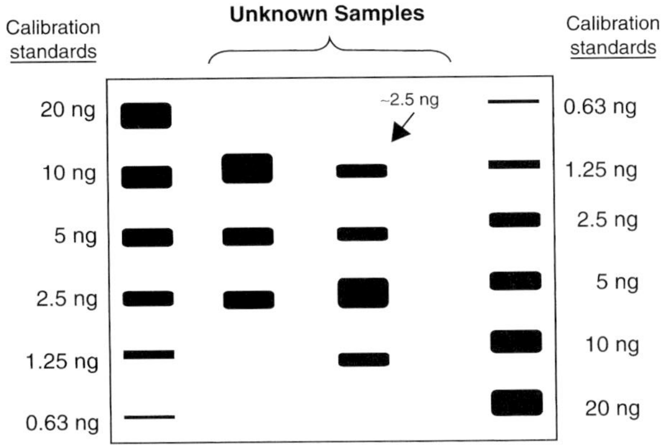

FIGURE 2.1 *Results of a slot-blot test used to quantify DNA samples. Six standard samples containing known amounts of DNA (from 0.63 ng to 20 ng) are blotted on the left side and right side of the membrane. In the center of the membrane are blotted seven samples whose concentrations are being determined. Reprinted from* Forensic DNA Typing, *2nd ed. John M. Butler, copyright 2005, with permission from Elsevier.*

Note that the probes that are used most often for the slot-blot quantification test are not completely human-specific. There are many places where the sequences of human DNA and the DNA of other higher primates are similar enough that it can be hard to design a probe that will only hybridize to one species' DNA. Therefore, in the unlikely event that a piece of evidence would contain a mixed human–gorilla or human–chimpanzee bloodstain, the investigator would not be able to specifically quantify the human DNA. In all other cases, however, the slot-blot procedure provides an accurate estimate of the concentration of human DNA in the evidence sample.

Although the slot-blot method has proven to provide reliable quantification of sample DNA, it will be replaced in the near future by real-time PCR methods such as the Quantifiler™ Human DNA Quantification Kit (Applied Biosystems Inc.). Real-time PCR methods allow the analyst to quantify several different targets simultaneously and with a finer degree of accuracy than the slot-blot procedures provide. For example, in a rape case with a mixed sample, the Quantifiler Y™ kit from Applied Biosystems enables the analyst to specifically quantify the male material in order to perform a Y chromosome STR analysis. In addition, real-time PCR methods will provide improved quantification of mitochondrial DNA. Both nuclear and mitochondrial DNA are extracted together from biological samples, and at present, the mitochondrial DNA is merely assumed to make up a certain percentage of the total DNA. Because it allows the analyst to amplify several targets simultaneously, real-time PCR methods allow the analyst to determine the quantity of both nuclear and mitochondrial DNA specifically and directly.

The easiest way to assess the degree of degradation in a DNA sample is to perform **agarose gel electrophoresis** (producing what is usually called a **yield gel**) and visually inspect the result. For gel electrophoresis, a rectangular slab of a Jello-like substance called agarose is prepared and placed in an apparatus that enables a continuous DC electric current to run through the gel. The negatively charged DNA is loaded into a set of wells at the end of the gel that lies at the negative pole of the circuit, and the electric current pushes the negatively charged DNA from the negatively charged end of the gel toward the positively charged end of the gel. The gel impedes the migration of the fragments. Shorter DNA fragments will migrate through the gel faster than longer DNA fragments, and the position of a fragment in the gel after a certain time reflects the size of the fragment. After electrophoresis, the gel is stained to reveal the DNA.

To assess the degree of degradation in the sample DNA, a **size ladder** is used. A size ladder is a collection of fragments of known sizes; it serves as a ruler against which the analyst can measure the size of the DNA of interest. A size ladder can contain fragments covering any range of sizes. For example, the size ladders that are used to measure STR allele sizes must cover a range of 50–500 bp, while those that are used to measure VNTR allele sizes must cover a range of 1,000–50,000 bp or greater. For a yield gel, a size ladder containing fragments that range from thousands to millions of bp in size is loaded into one of the lanes on the gel. The analyst compares the DNA that was extracted from the evidence and reference samples to the size ladder fragments in order to determine how extensively the DNA has been degraded. Figure 2.2 illustrates the appearance of increasingly degraded (left to right) DNA in a yield gel. A DNA sample that has not degraded will appear as a very thick band of DNA that never moves very far out of the well, indicating that all the DNA is of high molecular weight. Degradation appears as a smear in the gel lane. Slightly degraded DNA will have a faint tail of smearing extending downward a short distance from the main DNA band. Moderately degraded DNA will have a noticeable smear, extending down from the band and spreading well toward the bottom of the gel. There may be little to no

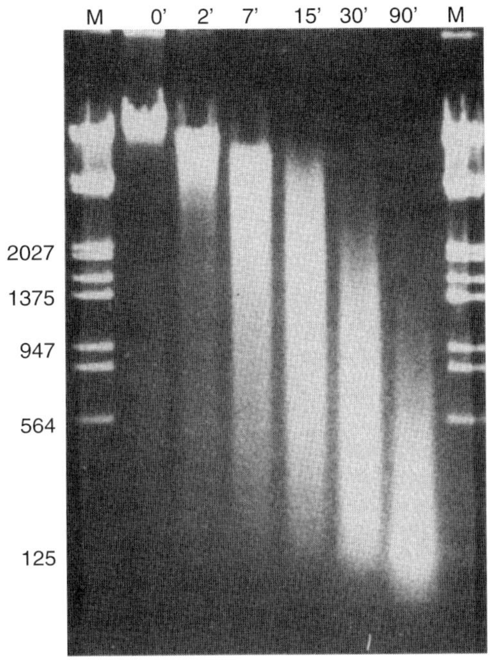

FIGURE 2.2 *Agarose gel illustrating varying degrees of DNA degradation. The numbers along the left side indicate the sizes of the fragments contained in the size ladder ("M"). The DNA was incubated with a restriction enzyme (which digests DNA) for the number of minutes indicated across the top of the figure. Note that as the incubation time increases, the degree of degradation increases, and the average size of the fragments in the DNA gets smaller. Reprinted with permission from Reynolds et al.,* Analytical Chemistry, *1991, 62, 2–15. Copyright 1991, American Chemical Society.*

high-molecular-weight DNA left in a moderately degraded sample. Significantly degraded DNA will appear as a smear, all of which appears very low on the gel, indicating that all the DNA fragments are of relatively low molecular weight. In addition, if there is sufficient bacterial DNA present, it will appear as a dense blob near the bottom of the gel.

Note that the DNA stains that are used to visualize the DNA in the gel only stain double-stranded DNA, which is what is obtained when DNA is extracted from the sample by **organic extraction**. Organic extractions are used for most samples, but a certain amount of sample loss occurs during an organic extraction. When the sample is small, a different protocol may be used, using a resin called Chelex™. This extraction protocol produces single-stranded DNA. If a **Chelex extraction** has been performed on the sample, one will not be able to determine the degree of degradation in the

DNA, because one will not be able to stain, and thereby visualize, the DNA in the agarose gel.

RECAPPING THE MAIN POINTS

1. In most labs, DNA samples are quantified using blotting and hybridization techniques.
2. Real-time PCR methods will probably soon become the methods of choice for quantifying forensic DNA samples. They are especially useful for quantifying the amount of mitochondrial versus nuclear DNA in a sample, or the amount of male material versus female material in a mixed sample.
3. A yield gel is used to determine the degree of degradation the sample DNA has experienced. Degraded DNA exhibits a smear, rather than a clear, high-molecular-weight band.

POLYMERASE CHAIN REACTION (PCR)-BASED TESTS

The PCR Acts Like a Molecular Photocopier

The PCR acts like a photocopier; it makes millions of copies of whatever portion of the DNA molecule the analyst has specified. The process is referred to as **amplification** of the target sequence, and the amplified DNA fragment is referred to as the **amplicon**.

In order to understand what PCR does for the forensic investigator, consider how small a portion of the human DNA molecule the analyst examines at any given time. The human genome consists of 3 billion basepairs (3,000,000,000 bp) of DNA. If you want to analyze an STR, you are trying to look at a 200–400 bp stretch of sequence. A 300-bp target represents a mere one ten-millionth of the human genome. If one tries to analyze the sample directly, the relative abundance of nontarget DNA will make it virtually impossible to determine the individual's allele status at an STR. If one first uses the PCR to make a million copies of the STR, however, the increased concentration of the STR sequence will make it much easier to analyze the STR's sequence apart from the rest of the DNA molecule. Just as the operator of a photocopier can specify which pages of a book the photocopier copies, the investigator designs the PCR to copy just that 200–400 bp stretch of DNA that contains the STR of interest. After the PCR is finished, the amplified sequence of interest is present in far greater concentration than any of the other sequences in the DNA molecule. The original genomic DNA is present, possibly along with some undesired products from the PCR, but if the PCR and subsequent analysis protocols are designed properly, these nontarget PCR products will not be there in sufficient quantity to confound interpretation of the results.

The PCR is optimal for amplifying the STRs and the polymorphic coding regions of the DQA1 and Polymarker™ test genes, but it is not as well suited for analyzing VNTRs. As described in Chapter 1, VNTR polymorphisms contain very large blocks of repeated sequence (a 12- to 100-bp motif, repeated up to 1,000 times); several VNTRs have alleles ranging up to 50 kilobases (50 kb = 50,000 bp) in length. Standard PCR protocols can only amplify targets up to approximately 3–5 kb in length, and while special PCR protocols that can amplify longer targets have been developed, none of them can amplify 50-kb targets reliably enough for use in criminal trials. In contrast, STRs are easily amplified by the PCR. For most of the STRs, the repeated sequence and some of the sequence that flanks both sides of the repeat are contained in a stretch of approximately 200–400 bp.

The PCR Enables Analysis of Suboptimal Samples

Although PCR-based forensic testing was not widely available until late 1990, the PCR has been used in forensic casework since 1986. The PCR has greatly expanded the power of the forensic scientist because it has enabled forensic analyses to be conducted on small, old and environmentally exposed evidence samples that could not have been analyzed by the VNTR tests or the older tests that examined blood proteins.

Two problems seen with many forensic samples is that they contain very small amounts of biological material, and/or the DNA in them has been degraded by time, chemical exposure or the elements. The PCR provides a tremendous advantage in a case involving a minute sample. For example, a bloodstained piece of clothing measuring 1 mm × 1 mm contains approximately 2 ng (1 ng = 10^{-9} grams, one billionth of a gram) of DNA. VNTR tests require a minimum of 25 ng of DNA to produce reliable results; it would be pointless to try to analyze this sample using a VNTR protocol. PCR-based protocols, however, can produce a DNA profile using 200 picograms (1 pg = 10^{-12} grams = one-trillionth of a gram) of genomic DNA as the starting material.[2] The analyst can perform ten PCR-based tests from this sample using the standard forensic PCR

[2] Budowle et al., 2003.

protocols. Special protocols have also been developed that push the limits of sensitivity even farther. Special protocols have even been developed that can produce a 5-marker DNA profile from a single cell,[3] although these protocols have not been validated for forensic work.

Because it requires much less DNA, the PCR allows many more tests to be conducted on a single evidence sample than VNTR testing does. This capability is very important, because sometimes the initial analysis raises questions that can only be answered by further testing. Current practice has been shaped by the 1996 report of the National Research Council, which established the framework for the modern-day guidelines for the processing, analysis and presentation of DNA evidence in criminal trials. In its report, the NRC clearly stated that, whenever possible, a portion of the evidence should be preserved to provide material for any further testing that is deemed necessary.

Another major advantage PCR provides for forensic analyses lies in the fact that the PCR is far more robust in the face of DNA degradation than is the VNTR procedure. This consideration is particularly important for forensic investigations that rely on the analysis of old samples or samples that have been exposed to the elements for a period of time. Time and the elements, especially soil bacteria, can degrade DNA. As the DNA degrades, it gets cut into progressively smaller fragments.

As long as the stretch of DNA to be amplified by the PCR is completely contained in one fragment, the PCR can amplify it. If the DNA is cut in the middle of a target sequence, however, that sequence cannot be amplified by the PCR. DNA that has only degraded slightly may yield good, clean DNA profiles using any of the available tests. As the DNA degrades into progressively smaller fragments, however, the tests that analyze the smallest stretches of DNA are the most likely to yield interpretable results. VNTR testing requires that the average fragment in the DNA be 20–30 kb or longer. Consequently, it is very difficult to perform VNTR tests on highly degraded samples. In contrast, most STR tests amplify fragments of 100–400 bp in length.[4] Furthermore, special protocols that amplify smaller regions (80–120 bp) around the STRs have been developed for the analysis of degraded DNA. These protocols can produce genotype profiles from samples that are too degraded to be typed by standard PCR protocols.[5]

[3] Findlay et al., 1997.

[4] Butler, 2005.

[5] For example, Chung et al., 2004; Park et al., 2007.

The PCR Mimics the Natural Process of DNA Replication

This section briefly describes the molecular means by which the PCR works. It is not strictly necessary for the litigator to understand the molecular workings of the PCR, but doing so will help the litigator understand the means by which variations in sample quality, sample handling or analytic procedures may introduce grounds for challenging the interpretation of the evidence (discussed in Chapters 3 and 9). The PCR process is illustrated in Figure 2.3. Here is an overview of what happens in a PCR, in simple mechanical terms:

The reaction mix for a typical PCR contains the following ingredients:

1. Genomic DNA from the suspect, evidence or other sources, which provides the **template DNA** sequence to be copied.
2. DNA's four nucleotides (often symbolized as dATP, dCTP, dGTP and dTTP).
3. An enzyme called **DNA polymerase** that links nucleotides together to build a new strand of DNA.
4. Two **primers**. The primers are **oligonucleotides**, or single-stranded stretches of DNA about 17–25 nucleotides long.
5. A buffered solution that maintains the pH and the concentration of ions, particularly magnesium ions, at the optimal level for the reaction to work.

The sequence of events that enable the PCR to copy a target sequence can be summarized as follows. First, recall that the DNA molecule is made of

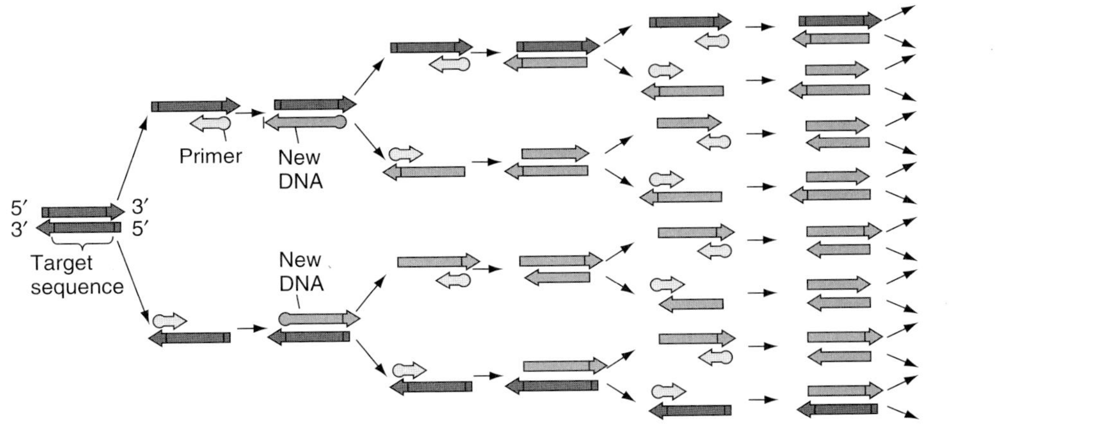

FIGURE 2.3 *The polymerase chain reaction (PCR) makes millions of copies of a desired stretch of DNA. Reprinted from* Life: The Science of Biology, *7th ed. Purves, Sadava, Orians and Heller. Copyright Sinauer Associates, 2004. Please see the color insert for a color version of this figure.*

two strands of DNA, with the bases projecting inward toward the center of the helix and hydrogen bonds between the bases holding the double helix together. To begin the PCR, the double helix is **denatured**, or opened like a zipper, where the exposed teeth of the zipper represent the bases that are projecting inward from the two sugar-phosphate backbones. Instead of a double-stranded molecule of DNA, you now have two single-stranded molecules of DNA, each of which can be used as a template against which a new DNA strand can be built. The enzyme DNA polymerase reads the sequence of bases in the template DNA strand and synthesizes a new strand of DNA that has a nucleotide sequence that is complementary to the template strand (recall the complementary basepairing rule, wherein As and Ts bond each other, as do Cs and Gs). For example, the sequence would be amplified as shown. The original double-stranded sequence is opened up, and each of the original strands (in plain font) is used as a template for the synthesis of a complementary strand (in bold font).

Example sequence	5′-CGATCAGTGACATC-3′ 3′-GCTAGTCACTGTAG-5′
Denaturing produces single strands	5′-CGATCAGTGACATC-3′ 3′-GCTAGTCACTGTAG-5′
Single strands used as templates for the synthesis of new strands (new DNA shown in bold)	5′-CGATCAGTGACATC-3′ **3′-GCTAGTCACTGTAG-5′** **5′-CGATCAGTGACATC-3′** 3′-GCTAGTCACTGTAG-5′

Recall what you learned in Chapter 1 about nucleotides being the building blocks of DNA (Figures 1.3 and 1.4). Once the DNA has been denatured, the enzyme DNA polymerase makes two new strands of DNA by stringing together the nucleotides that are complementary to the nucleotides in the template strands, in the same manner as you would follow instructions to string lightbulbs of four different colors together in a specified order. The sequence of nucleotides in the template strand specifies the sequence of nucleotides to be chained together by the DNA polymerase. The DNA polymerase reads the template DNA strand's base sequence, and selects the complementary nucleotides to be chained together to make the new DNA strand. Once you understand the PCR process in these simple mechanical terms, you can understand the following more formal and detailed description.

The denaturing of the template DNA and the chaining together of nucleotides to make new DNA strands are accomplished by subjecting the reaction mixture to repeated cycles of heating and cooling (in a machine called a **thermocycler**). Each PCR cycle contains a **denaturing stage**, an **annealing stage** and an **extension stage**. The specific temperatures and times used in a PCR vary, depending on the sequence to be amplified and the condition of the template DNA.

Typically, the reaction mix is first heated to 92–99°C, which denatures the DNA, breaking the hydrogen bonds between the A-T pairs and the C-G pairs and causing the double helix to unwind into two single strands of DNA. After the genomic DNA has been denatured, the reaction is then cooled to 55–70°C for the annealing stage of the cycle. In order for the DNA polymerase to build new DNA strands, a primer (single-stranded chain of 17–25 nucleotides) must first anneal (bind) to the template DNA. DNA's thermodynamic properties strongly favor it being in the double-stranded configuration, and when the reaction temperature is reduced, single-stranded DNA will try to return to its natural double-stranded configuration by finding a single strand of complementary sequence to which it can anneal. The thermodynamics of the process allows shorter fragments of DNA to anneal to their complementary sequences more readily than longer fragments. Therefore, a brief lowering of the temperature during the annealing stage of the PCR cycle allows the short oligonucleotide primers to anneal to the complementary sequences in the template DNA before the huge genomic DNA molecule has a chance to reanneal and return to its natural double-stranded configuration (which would prevent the PCR from working). Once the two primers have annealed to their respective complementary sequences, the DNA polymerase can extend the new DNA strands.

During the extension stage of the PCR cycle, the reaction is heated to 72°C, the temperature at which the DNA polymerase has maximal activity. The primers provide the physical starting point from which the DNA polymerase builds new DNA strands. The DNA polymerase begins at the 3′ end of each annealed primer, reads the sequence of the strand of genomic DNA to which the primer has annealed (the template strand)

and chains together the nucleotides that are complementary to those in the template DNA strand. The DNA polymerase builds the new DNA chain by hooking the phosphate group of each new nucleotide onto the 3′ carbon of the deoxyribose molecule of the nucleotide before it (discussed in Chapter 1).

A typical forensic PCR will begin with a denaturing stage, followed by 20 to 35 cycles of denaturing, annealing and extension, and then finish with a final 72°C extension stage that allows the DNA polymerase to finish extending any chains that were not fully extended during the thermal cycling.

Recall that the optimal PCR copies the stretch of DNA that the investigator specifies, and no others. The investigator specifies the stretch of DNA to be amplified by designing primers that will anneal to the template DNA right at the ends of the stretch of DNA the investigator wants to amplify. Remember that the DNA polymerase builds the new DNA strands by extending the primers from their 3′ ends. Because the new DNA strands are built out from the 3′ end of the primers only, the 5′ ends of the two primers define the ends of the amplicon (Figure 2.3). In this manner, the analyst's choice of nucleotide sequences for the PCR primers defines the specific stretch of DNA to be amplified by each PCR. By capitalizing on the complementary basepairing rule, each primer is custom designed to contain a sequence of 17–25 nucleotides that will bind to a specific complementary sequence of nucleotides on one of the two strands of the template DNA (Figure 2.3). One primer is designed to bind to one strand of the template DNA, on one side of the target sequence, and the second primer is designed to bind to the other strand of the template DNA, on the other side of the target sequence. This leaves the primers annealed to the genomic DNA at the sites chosen by the experimenter (Figure 2.3) and causes the PCR to amplify the region that lies between the two primers. The choice of primer sequences and annealing temperatures also ensures the specificity of the PCR. Analysts often use a program called BLAST to ensure that their primers will only bind to the intended targets, and not others. The BLAST program (on the NCBI website) allows the analyst to search the human DNA molecule to see if any other stretches of sequence in the DNA molecule are similar enough to the primer's binding site to allow the primer to also anneal there.

During each PCR cycle, each double-stranded DNA molecule that is present at the beginning of the cycle will provide two single-stranded templates for the synthesis of two new strands of DNA. Therefore, each PCR cycle theoretically doubles the number of double-stranded DNA molecules in the reaction mixture. At the end of 30 PCR cycles, there are theoretically one billion (10^9) molecules of the desired amplicon for each genomic DNA molecule present in the original reaction mix, although the yield is more often on the order of hundreds of thousands to ten million (10^7) molecules of amplicon per molecule of starting material.

In order to obtain maximum information from a minute sample, several pairs of primers, each one designed to amplify a different STR, are combined into a **multiplex PCR** mixture.[6] Multiplex PCR mixtures must be carefully designed. Because the annealing of short single-stranded fragments is highly favored by the thermodynamics of DNA, two primers with partially complementary sequences may anneal to each other and thereby interfere with each other's ability to amplify their intended target fragments. Multiplex PCR protocols must be validated by regular inclusion of control samples with known genotypes in the analyses. An ideal set of control samples would include all the alleles that have been reported in the human population. As discussed in Chapter 3, it is often important to demonstrate that the protocol is capable of detecting the alleles that were not detected in the evidence and suspect samples, to ensure that all the alleles that were present in the evidence and suspect samples were in fact detected.

[6] Micka et al., 1996; Dixon et al., 2005.

Some protocols also use a **nested PCR**. In a nested PCR, one PCR is performed in the manner described earlier, then a second PCR is performed, using a small amount of the first PCR's product as the template DNA. The primers used for the second PCR are designed to bind to sites inside the ends of the amplicon that the first PCR generated. Nested PCR can be a very effective means of amplifying samples that contain very small amounts of DNA. Although the first PCR cannot generate enough product from the meager starting material for subsequent analysis, it does provide enough template DNA to enable the second PCR product to be analyzed. Nested PCR protocols can produce results from as little as 33–330 femtograms (1 femtogram = 10^{-15} grams) of starting material. In addition, nested PCR can be used to selectively amplify the different alleles for multi-locus Y chromosome markers (discussed in Chapter 6). The sequences surrounding the different loci are very similar but are different at a few nucleotides. When a marker is present in multiple copies, the second PCR's primers can be designed to capitalize on the minor differences in the sequences surrounding the different copies of the marker and amplify the sequence from only one copy.

Although nested PCR can be used to amplify a minute sample, use of a nested PCR protocol increases the risk that contaminating DNA may confound the analysis. In a nested PCR, minute amounts of contaminating DNA that normally would not produce enough product to create visible peaks in the data can be amplified to the point where they do introduce visible artifacts. For this reason, nested PCRs are not used routinely in forensic work.

Direct Fragment Size Analysis—STR Testing and the D1S80 VNTR

Interpreting STR data is a matter of comparing the sizes of the PCR products that are obtained from the relevant samples. For STR analyses, the PCR is designed to amplify a DNA fragment that contains the repeated sequence, as well as a known amount of surrounding sequence. Except for a very few people who have mutations in the sequence surrounding the repeat, the sequence surrounding any given STR is constant in all people. Because the sequence around the STR is constant, the size of the PCR product will be determined by the number of repeats in the STR. The PCR primers will always bind to places in the DNA that flank the repeat. The greater the number of repeats there are in the STR, the longer the stretch of sequence between the 5′ ends of the two primers will be. For example, imagine you have designed primers for the TH01 STR (an AATG repeat on chromosome 11) that amplify a 200-bp amplicon from a person who has the number 5 allele (i.e., has 5 AATGs in the repeated sequence at that spot). Performing this PCR using DNA from someone with the number 8 allele, who has three more AATGs (a total of 12 more bp) in their repeat string than the first person, will yield a 212-bp product. Someone with a heterozygous 5,8 genotype for TH01 would show both the 200-bp and 212-bp PCR products. Someone with a homozygous 8,8 genotype, however, would only show one product, the 212-bp amplicon.

STR analyses all use some form of **gel electrophoresis** to analyze the size of the amplified PCR products in order to determine the subject's genotype for the markers tested. In gel electrophoresis, the PCR products are pushed through a gel-like medium by an electric current. The apparatus constructs an electric circuit that includes the gel, giving the gel an electrically negative end and an electrically positive end. PCR products, like all DNA, are negatively charged. The PCR products are loaded into the gel at the negative end of the gel, and because of their negative charge, migrate from the negative end of the gel to the positive end. The gel physically impedes the progress of the DNA fragments, simply by being hard to migrate through. Shorter fragments run through the gel faster than larger fragments, so the size of a PCR product, and therefore the allele it represents, can be determined by observing the speed with which the DNA fragment runs through the gel. The analyst will often add a 50- to 500-bp size ladder to each sample, which provides a ruler against which the analyst measures the sizes of the questioned alleles. The allele size ladder constitutes an **internal standard**, because it is mixed with the sample. Because they are mixed in with the sample, the internal standard's fragments run through the same gel and capillary as the questioned fragments. This eliminates the uncertainty of measurement that often arises when a questioned sample is compared to an **external standard** that was run in a different capillary or with a different batch of samples.

Most modern DNA fragment analyzers[7] use **capillary electrophoresis**, wherein the samples are run through very narrow-bore tubes, called capillaries, which are filled with a very thick liquid polymer. A capillary has a place where its coating has been removed, which serves as a detection window. The fragment analyzer shines a light into the window, and has a fluorescence detector that senses whenever something in the capillary fluoresces when exposed to the light. The samples are injected into one end of the capillary and migrate toward the other end when the electric current is applied. The fragment analyzer measures the length of time it takes for the PCR products to pass through the detection window and compares each fragment's migration speed to the migration speeds of the fragments in the internal standard. For STR analyses, one of the two PCR primers for each marker is labeled with a fluorescent molecule, or **fluor**. Several different fluors can be used to label fragments. Each one gives off a different wavelength light when it

[7] The commonly used analyzers, such as the ABI Prism 3100 Genetic Analyzer™, manufactured by Applied Biosystems Inc., can be set up either to analyze the sizes of PCR products for STR analyses, or to serve as sequencers for mitochondrial DNA testing or other sequencing tasks.

fluoresces, so each set of fragments glows with a different colored light. Even if two fragments are the same size, and therefore pass through the detection window together, if they are labeled with different fluors, the machine can detect them both. The combinations of capillaries and polymers used provide excellent resolution, and alleles that differ from each other by a single basepair can be resolved with the appropriate choice of analysis parameters.

The fragment analyzer puts out an **electropherogram** (a graph depicting the peaks detected by the analyzer) such as the one shown in Figure 2.4. There are four panels in the display; each one shows the peaks for the markers that were labeled with one of the four different fluors. The size of the allele that was amplified is indicated along the top of each of the four panels (this will be referred to as the "allele size"; the units are basepairs, or bp). In addition, the amount of PCR product generated for each allele is indicated by the strength of the fluorescent signal; the Y axis indicates peak intensity (the units are usually relative fluorescence units, or RFUs). Any single individual will have two copies, or alleles, of each STR marker. If the two alleles each have a different number of repetitions of the repeated sequence motif (i.e., the individual is heterozygous for that marker, such as vWA in Figure 2.4), the analyst will see two peaks (each of a different allele size) for that marker in that individual's sample. If both copies of the marker have the same number of repeated sequences (i.e., the individual is homozygous at that marker, such as TPOX in Figure 2.4), the analyst will only see one peak for that marker. Many forensic samples contain mixtures of material from multiple contributors, and the analyst will see more than two alleles for some or all markers in that sample. When a mixed sample is being analyzed, if there is a significant difference in the amount of material each contributor contributed to the sample, the peak intensities of the major contributor's alleles may be noticeably greater than the peak intensities of the minor contributor's alleles.

The STR analysis software will generate a report, which will include, among other things, a Table of Alleles Detected. The table lists which alleles were found for each marker in each sample that was analyzed. As discussed in Chapter 1, alleles are indicated by their number, which reflects the number of repeat motifs in that particular allele. These numbers appear below the peaks in the electropherogram. Determining

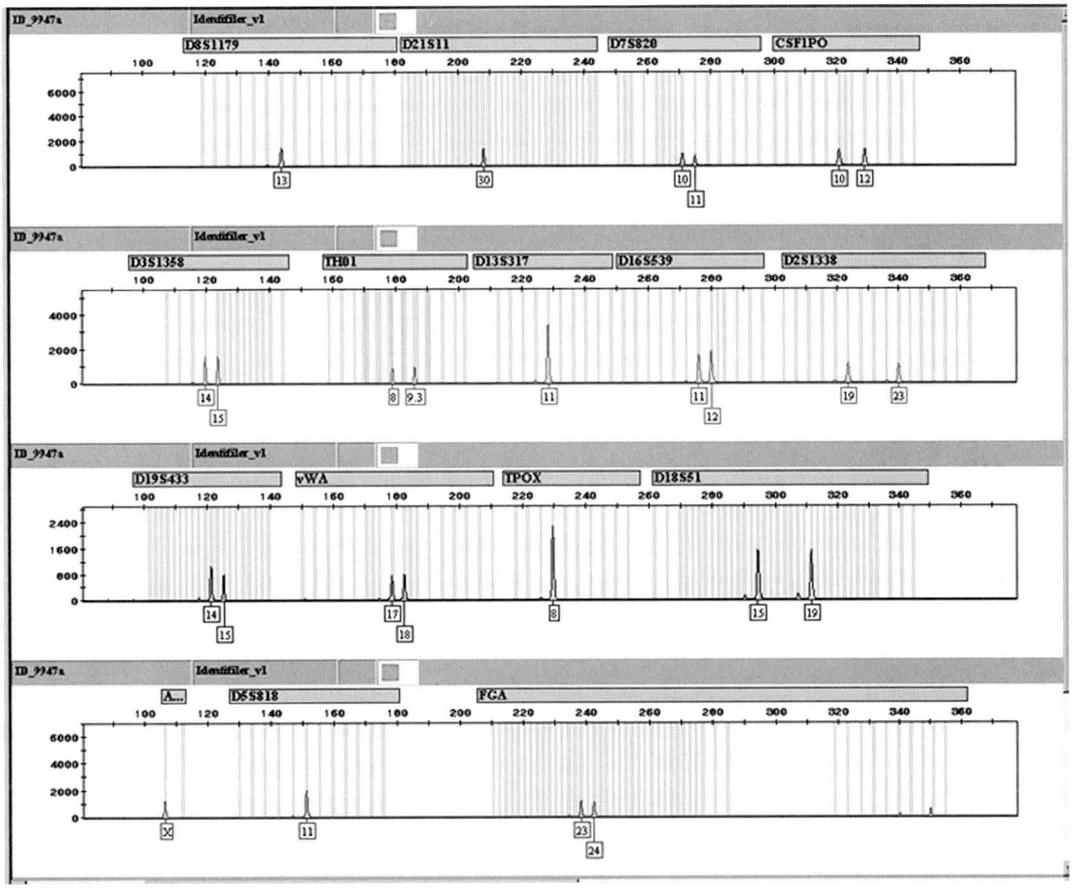

FIGURE 2.4 *A sample electropherogram illustrating the results of an STR analysis from the ABI 3100 automated sequencer/fragment analyzer. Reprinted with permission from Applied Biosystems Human Identification Group.*

whether any of the individuals whose samples were analyzed can be included on the list of people who could be the source of the evidence is merely a matter of finding which individual's sample has the same genotypes at all the markers as the evidence does. For example, in Figure 2.4, the following alleles/genotypes were detected (recall that the individual's genotype for a marker is the combination of the two alleles the individual possesses for that marker):

D8S1179—13,13	D21S11—30,30	D7S820—10,11
CSF1PO—10,12	D3S1358—14,15	TH01—8,9.3
D13S317—13,13	D16S53—11,12	D2S1338—19,23
D19S433—14,15	vWA—17,18	TPOX—8,8
D18S51—15,19	D5S818—11,11	FGA—23,24

In addition, the amelogenin marker indicated only the presence of the X allele, indicating that the sample came from a female.

Most of the alleles of any particular tetranucleotide STR will differ from each other by a multiple of 4 bp. As mentioned in Chapter 1, however, sometimes one detects a microvariant allele—one that does not differ from the others by a multiple of 4 bp, usually because the repeated sequence contains a partial copy of the repeated 4-bp motif. In Figure 2.4, the microvariant 9.3 allele was detected at the TH01 marker. On one of this individual's chromosome 11 (where the TH01 marker is located), the TH01 locus has nine full repetitions of the repeated 4-bp motif, plus another three nucleotides from a tenth repetition of the repeated 4-bp motif.

Most VNTRs have alleles that are too large to be amplified by the PCR; the D1S80 VNTR on chromosome 1, however, is an exception. The D1S80 VNTR is small enough for PCR to amplify all the known alleles (300–850 bp). The D1S80 marker is amplified, and the sizes of the alleles are determined, in the same manner as an STR. The D1S80 VNTR's usefulness is limited, however, by the fact that two alleles are very common in all ethnic and racial groups. As we will discuss in Chapter 4, the significance of a match between the evidence's profile and that of the suspect is greatly reduced if the profile contains common alleles. In addition, because of the relatively large repeated sequence motif, the D1S80 marker has a wider range of allele sizes than the STRs do. This means there is greater risk of having the largest alleles drop out when a minute or degraded sample is being analyzed (discussed in more detail in Chapter 3).

For these and other reasons, STR typing quickly replaced D1S80 as the method of choice for forensic DNA testing. D1S80 was used by a number of law enforcement agencies during the mid-to-late 1990s, however. One will still encounter D1S80 data in cases from that era.

Blotting and Hybridization Tests Using Allele-Specific Probes—The DQA1 and Polymarker™ Tests

The first PCR-based test used in forensics capitalized on the fact that there are different sequences found in the protein-coding region of the DQA1 gene[8] in different individuals (recall from Chapter 1 how this is

[8] Note that the gene was known as DQα when the test was first developed, and you will therefore see references to the DQα gene and test in earlier cases and literature.

possible). Instead of a direct analysis of the size of the PCR product, the DQA1 analysis involves a blotting and hybridization procedure similar to that described earlier for quantifying DNA. In this case, however, a set of single-stranded oligonucleotide probes is synthesized, and each one is blotted onto a specific place in a positively charged nylon membrane. The probes can be designed with any specific sequence of nucleotides the analysts wants; the ideal set of probes will contain one probe that is perfectly complementary to each of the known alleles of the gene being tested. The coding sequence from the DQA1 gene is amplified by PCR, and the product is denatured and applied to the membrane. When the nylon membrane with the single-stranded oligonucleotide probes blotted onto it is incubated with the single-stranded PCR product, the PCR product DNA will bind to whichever of the oligonuceotide probes has a sequence that is complementary to the sequence of the PCR product (i.e., complementary to the sequences of the individual's two DQA1 alleles). A color-generating reaction is then used to indicate which of the membrane-immobilized probes the PCR product bound to. The presence or absence of colored dots at the places where the different oligonucleotide probes were blotted onto the membrane indicates which of the ten different probes the PCR product annealed to, and therefore, which of the DQA1 sequences were present in the individual's DNA.

Because the probes bind to specific alleles, they are frequently referred to as **allele-specific oligonucleotides (ASO)** or **sequence-specific oligonucleotides (SSO)**. Ideally, one would like to have a set of ASO probes that would each bind specifically to one of the DQA1 alleles and not to any of the others. This would allow for unambiguous interpretation of the results. The sequences of some of the different DQA1 alleles are so similar, however, that specific probes cannot be developed for several of the alleles. Some of the different alleles' sequences are so similar that one probe will bind to more than one allele. At present, eight DQA1 alleles are recognized (referred to as alleles 1.1, 1.2, 1.3, 2, 3, 4.1, 4.2 and 4.3). These eight alleles afford 36 possible two-allele genotypes, including 8 homozygous and 28 heterozygous genotypes. A combination of ten probes, each one hybridizing to a different combination of the DQA1 alleles, is used to indicate the sample's genotype. The ten probes bind to the different DQA1 alleles as shown in Table 2.1.

Table 2.1 DQA1 Probes and the Alleles to Which They Bind

Probe Name	Binds to Alleles
All 1	1.1, 1.2, and 1.3
2	2 only
3	3 only
All 4	4.1, 4.2, and 4.3
1.1	1.1 only
1.2/1.3/4	1.2, 1.3, and 4
1.3	1.3 only
All Except 1.3	All alleles except 1.3
4.1	4.1 only
4.2/4.3	4.2 and 4.3

Because the probes are not completely allele-specific, some genotypes produce a unique pattern of positive signals, but others do not. For example, a sample from someone who is homozygous for the 3 allele (i.e., has a 3,3 genotype) will produce a unique result; positive signals (indicated by colored dots) will be seen at the 3 and All Except 1.3 probes. A sample from someone who has a heterozygous 1.2, 4.3 genotype, however, would not produce a unique result. Positive signals would be seen for the All 1, All 4, 1.2/1.3/4, All Except 1.3 and 4.2/4.3 probes (Figure 2.5). Note that the same pattern of results would be obtained from someone with the 1.2, 4.2 genotype.[9]

[9] See the discussion of the Earl Washington case in Chapter 9 for an example of how the ambiguities in DQA1 results can lead to a false conviction.

Because there are only eight different DQA1 alleles (and only six DQα alleles), the DQA1 test is limited in its ability to discriminate between individuals. However, the PCR-based DQα/DQA1 reverse dot-blot test has enabled DNA analyses to be performed on many samples that did not yield enough DNA for VNTR testing. The DQA1 test has proven very reliable. In validation trials, 180 samples, consisting of bloodstains, plucked hairs, semen stains and postcoital samples, were distributed to five different forensics laboratories for a blind trial in which the laboratory

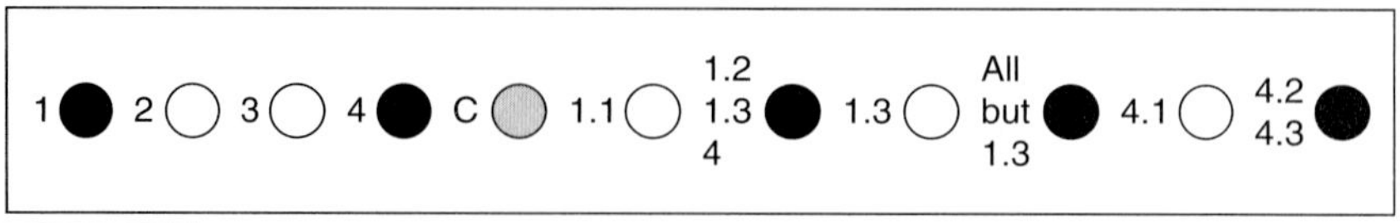

FIGURE 2.5 *Illustration depicting the DQA1 dot-blot test result for a sample with a 1.2, 4.3 genotype.*

personnel did not know the genotypes of the samples before analyzing them. The analysts were given minimal training with the kit. Results were reported for 178 of the 180 samples, and all 178 were correctly typed.[10]

The Polymarker™ test is an extension of the DQA1 test and determines the individual's allele status at five loci simultaneously. In this case, a multiplex PCR containing five sets of primers is used. The PCR mixture contains one set of primers each from the low-density lipoprotein receptor (LDLR), glycophorin A (GYPA), hemoglobin gamma globin (HBGG) and group-specific complement (GC) genes, plus one set designed to amplify the polymorphic D7S8 marker. Each of the five markers in the Polymarker™ test panel has only 2 to 3 alleles. Therefore, only 12 probes are needed to illustrate the individual's genotype for all five markers. In this case, the interpretation of the probe-target binding pattern is unambiguous; each probe binds specifically to one of its marker's alleles.

With only 2 to 3 alleles for each marker, the five Polymarker™ tests only provide a **power of discrimination** of 1/200. This means that if you ran multiple experiments in which you chose 200 pairs of people at random from a database of randomly selected unrelated individuals, on average you would only find one pair whose genotypes matched at all five markers. Combining the Polymarker™ test with the DQA1 test improves the test's power of discrimination to 1/2,000. Although this is not nearly as powerful as the VNTR tests, the Polymarker™ + DQA1 test provided several advantages over the VNTR tests that had been used until then. The most important among them is the fact that many samples that did not provide enough DNA for VNTR testing could be typed using the Polymarker™ + DQA1 kit.

The DQA1 and Polymarker™ tests are out of date. A number of law enforcement agencies used the Polymarker™ + DQA1 test throughout the mid-to-late 1990s, and Polymarker evidence has been used in cases as recently as December 2006.[11]

Real-Time PCR for Quantification of DNA

Until recently, most laboratories used a slot-blot method to quantify the DNA extracted from samples.[12] Real-time PCR is emerging as the method of choice for quantifying DNA, however. Real-time PCR is by far the most

[10] Walsh et al., 1992.

[11] *Pridgeon v. McDonough*, 2006 WL 4013728, *24 (N.D. Fla. 2006). Note that the court observed that the Polymarker tests were outdated.

[12] Walsh et al., 1992.

sensitive method available for determining a sample's DNA concentration. In addition, the virtually unlimited choice of primers for the PCR makes it extremely versatile. One can use real-time PCR to determine the relative amounts of male versus female material in a rape sample or the amount of nuclear versus mitochondrial DNA in an evidence sample.[13] Real-time PCR can also be used to quantify the level of heteroplasmy in a mitochondrial DNA sample (discussed in Chapter 5).[14]

[13] Meissner et al., 2000.

[14] Niederstratter et al., 2006.

The yield of a PCR depends on the amount of DNA that was put into the reaction and the number of PCR cycles in the protocol. In addition, if you plotted the accumulation of PCR product against the number of cycles in the PCR, you would observe a sigmoid (s-shaped) curve, as illustrated in the traces in the graph in the upper portion of Figure 2.6. The product accumulates first in an exponential manner, then in a linear manner, and finally reaches a plateau, after which there will be no significant increase in PCR product with more PCR cycles. The graph illustrates the accumulation of PCR product in six different reactions, each of which contained a different amount of template DNA (greater amounts of product are indicated by higher values on the Y, or vertical, axis). The five fainter lines

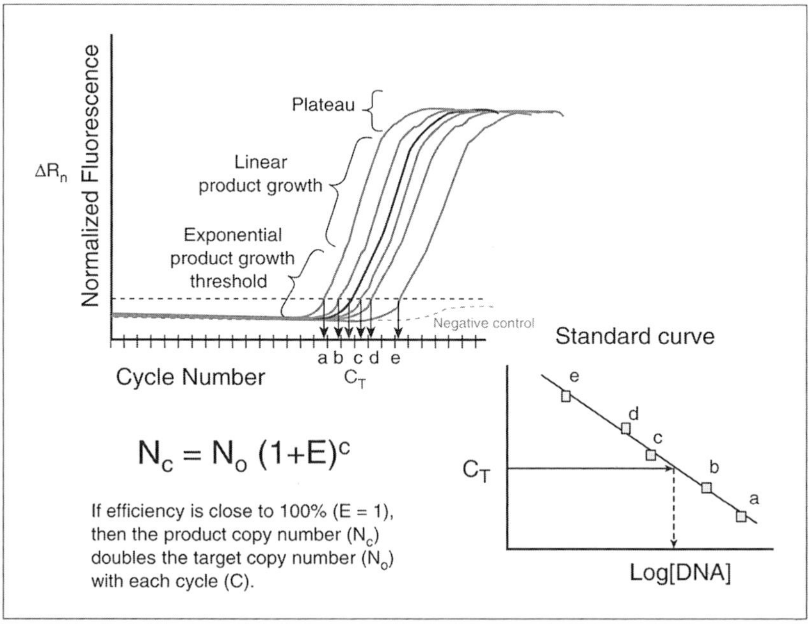

FIGURE 2.6
Upper: Accumulation of PCR product as a function of number of PCR cycles. Lower: standard curve illustrating the linear relationship between the concentration of the DNA sample and the C_T, the number of PCR cycles required to produce a specified amount of product. Reprinted from Forensic DNA Typing, *2nd ed. John M. Butler, copyright 2005, with permission from Elsevier.*

(indicated by arrows as a–e) represent the results from **standard samples**, each of which had a known concentration of DNA. The bold line, third from the left, represents the results from an evidence sample that was being quantified. Of the five standard samples, the reaction that contained the greatest amount of template DNA is represented by curve a, while the reaction containing the least amount of DNA is represented by curve e. As you can see, for any given number of PCR cycles, the curves on the left show more PCR product accumulation than the curves on the right.

The PCR protocols that are used in research settings are designed to produce maximum product for subsequent analysis. In these PCRs, the product yield is already in the final plateau stage of the accumulation curve by then, and the amount of product is not proportional to the amount of DNA that was put into the reaction. In contrast, in a real-time PCR the accumulation of the PCR product is monitored at the end of every PCR cycle. The accumulation of product in the questioned sample is compared to the accumulation of products in a set of standard samples that have had known amounts of DNA put into them. The real-time thermocycler determines the **cycle threshold (C_T)**, defined as the number of PCR cycles it takes for a sample to generate a predetermined amount of PCR product, for each standard and evidence sample (indicated by the horizontal dotted line in the graph in the upper portion of Figure 2.6). The C_T is set at a level that is designed to assess the PCR's yield at some point within the linear phase of product accumulation, when the amount of PCR product is proportional to the amount of DNA put into the PCR. The thermocycler then uses the data from the standard samples to construct a **standard curve** similar to the one seen in the lower portion of Figure 2.6. The concentration of the DNA sample is indicated on the X, or horizontal, axis (the square brackets indicate "concentration of" whatever is inside; the reason why the X, or horizontal, axis of the graph on the right is labeled in log units is not important), and the C_T is illustrated on the Y, or vertical, axis. As one would expect, as the amount of template DNA in the reaction increases (going from reaction e to reaction a), the number of PCR cycles required to produce the predetermined amount of product (the C_T) decreases. Notice from the standard curve that there is a well-defined, linear relationship between the amount of DNA put into the PCR and the C_T. When the C_T is determined for an evidence sample, it is compared to the standard curve to determine what concentration of sample would produce that C_T.

RECAPPING THE MAIN IDEAS

1. The PCR acts like a photocopier, and makes millions of copies of a portion of the DNA molecule that is specified by the experimenter. The process is referred to as amplification of the target sequence, and the PCR product is called an amplicon.
2. The PCR enables investigators to analyze samples that yield very little DNA, or DNA that has been degraded. Many samples that cannot be analyzed by VNTR tests can be analyzed using PCR-based procedures.
3. The different alleles of an STR marker or the D1S80 VNTR differ in the number of repetitions of the repeated sequence motif that are present. A greater number of repeats produces a PCR product of greater length. STRs and the D1S80 VNTR are analyzed by comparing the lengths of the PCR products from the relevant samples.
4. In the DQA1 and Polymarker™ tests, allele-specific oligonucleotide probes are used to illustrate which alleles are present in the questioned sample. Each probe binds to one specific allele, or a known combination of alleles, of its respective gene. The combination of oligonucleotide probes to which an individual's PCR product binds indicates which alleles are present in that individual's sample. A few genotypes cannot be unambiguously differentiated from each other by the DQA1 test.
5. Real-time PCR is a modification of the PCR that monitors the accumulation of the PCR product at the end of every PCR cycle and produces an estimate of the amount of DNA that was put into the PCR. Real-time PCR is becoming the method of choice for quantifying DNA samples.

VARIABLE NUMBER OF TANDEM REPEATS (VNTR) TESTING

VNTR testing is a version of a family of tests referred to as **restriction fragment length polymorphism (RFLP) tests**. Private companies began using VNTRs for forensic testing in the mid-to-late 1980s, and the FBI first used it in 1988. Its use was quickly discontinued once STR tests were developed, however, because the VNTR tests are considerably more labor-intensive than STR tests, and their results are inherently more variable and more prone to artifacts. Despite its inherent difficulties, the VNTR test represented a quantum leap forward in its day. The blood protein tests that were used before the VNTRs had significantly limited discriminative power, and VNTRs awakened the world to the power of DNA as a means of identification. At the same time, however, the poor quality of some of the VNTR data that were presented in court in the early days of VNTR testing clearly illustrated the need for quality control and quality assurance programs. At this point in time, the litigator is unlikely to encounter VNTR evidence. To the best of our knowledge, the last case in which VNTR evidence was included was tried in September 2005.[15] For this reason, we will not discuss the VNTR test in detail. Readers who require a description of the VNTR procedure are referred to the review provided by Wayne and Fourney.[16]

[15] *Murphy v. Elo*, 2005 WL 2284223, *10 (E.D. Mich. 2005).

[16] Wayne and Fourney, 1993.

DIRECT SEQUENCING

Direct sequencing allows the analyst to determine the exact nucleotide sequence of a DNA fragment. Sequencing is not generally used for the analysis of nuclear DNA. Sequencing is not as fast or as cost-effective as STR analysis, and it is far easier to interpret STR data by comparing the sizes of PCR products than to compare the sequences of all the relevant samples nucleotide by nucleotide. Direct sequencing is essential for mitochondrial DNA analyses, however, where there are very few STRs available for testing. Mitochondrial testing is usually performed by sequencing the two hypervariable regions of the mitochondrial DNA (described in detail in Chapter 5).

The technique used for sequencing DNA is called **dideoxysequencing**. Recall the structure of the sugar-phosphate backbone part of the DNA molecule. The most important aspect of this structure for the following discussion is the fact that each nucleotide is linked to the one in front of it by having the phosphate group on its 5′ carbon link to the oxygen (O) atom on the 3′ carbon of the deoxyribose of the nucleotide in front of it (Figures 1.2 and 1.3). Deoxyribose, as the name implies, is a modified version of the sugar ribose. Ribose has hydroxyl (OH) groups on both its 2′ and 3′ carbons. In contrast, deoxyribose has a hydrogen (H) atom in place of the OH on the 2′ carbon (it is missing the oxygen atom and is therefore deoxyribose). Deoxyribose still has the OH on the 3′ carbon, however. This is perfectly compatible with the molecular structure of the DNA, because only the OH on the 3′ carbon is needed to provide a place for the next nucleotide to attach.

Dideoxysequencing uses **dideoxynucleotides**—nucleotides that do not have that O (they only have an H) on either the 2′ or 3′ carbon. Without that O on the 3′ carbon, there is no place to hook the next nucleotide onto the DNA chain. Therefore, if a dideoxy nucleotide gets incorporated into a growing DNA chain, the chain stops there and cannot be extended any farther.

Dideoxysequencing involves a variation on the PCR. In a dideoxysequencing analysis, you use only one primer, so only one strand of the DNA is copied. (Remember, because of the complementary basepairing rule, if you know the sequence of one strand of DNA, you know the sequence of the other strand.) In addition, four separate reactions are run for each sample. In one reaction (the A reaction), a small portion of the A nucleotide is dideoxyATP, or ddATP. Because a small percentage of the A nucleotide in the reaction mixture is ddATP, every time an A is to be added to a newly synthesized DNA strand, a small percentage of the fragments that are being amplified will have the dideoxy A incorporated into the growing chain. Once the dideoxy A is incorporated into a growing DNA strand, that strand will not extend any farther. Therefore, the A reaction tube will contain a population of fragments that stopped at that A. The length of these fragments indicates where the A was in the sequence. Similarly, everywhere there is an A in the sequence, a small population of the DNA fragments that are being synthesized by the PCR will stop there, and thereby indicate the position of that A in the sequence. In the other three reactions (the C, G and T reactions), small portions of the C, G or

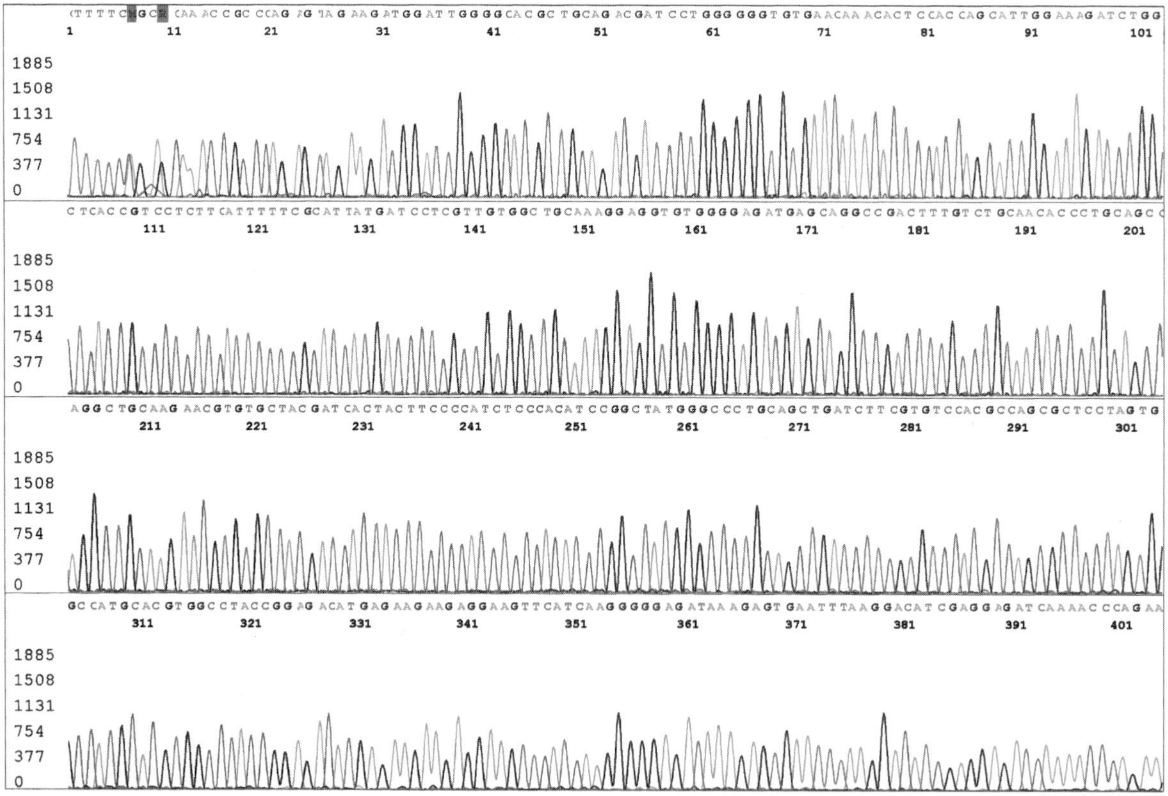

FIGURE 2.7 *Four-color output from the ABI 3100 automated sequencer/fragment analyzer from Applied Biosystems. Figure provided by Dr. Jack Tarleton, Fullerton Genetics Center, Asheville, NC. Please see the color insert for a color version of this figure.*

T nucleotides, respectively, are present in their dideoxy form. As in the A reaction, each of these tubes will contain a small portion of prematurely truncated fragments whose sizes indicate where dideoxy Cs, Gs or Ts were incorporated into the newly synthesized DNA strands.

After the sequencing reactions are run, the A, C, G and T reactions are loaded into separate lanes on the sequencer. The sequencer then determines the sizes of the fragments in the A, C, G and T reaction tubes. The sequencer's software then compiles a four-color illustration of the sequence of the fragment of interest, by ordering the fragments in increasing size order and noting which reaction tube each fragment was present in (Figure 2.7).

RECAPPING THE MAIN IDEAS

1. Direct sequencing is the "gold standard" for DNA analysis because it unambiguously indicates the sequence of bases in the locus of interest.
2. The sequencing reaction is a modification of the PCR:
   a. Four separate reactions are performed for each sample. In each reaction, a small portion of one of the nucleotides is present in the dideoxy form.
   b. When they are incorporated into a growing DNA strand, the dideoxynucleotides prevent that growing DNA strand from being extended any farther.
   c. The sizes of the fragments in the A, C, G and T reactions indicate the positions of the As, Cs, Gs and Ts, respectively, in the sequence of interest.

REFERENCES AND ADDITIONAL READINGS

Budowle, B., Sinha, S.K., Lee, H.S. and Chakraborty, R. (2003) *Forensic Science Review*, 15, 153–158.

Butler, J.M. (2005) *Forensic DNA Typing*, 2nd ed. Boston: Elsevier/Academic Press.

Chung, D.T., Drabek, J., Opel, K.L., Butler, J.M. and McCord, B.R. (2004) *Journal of Forensic Sciences*, 49(4), 733–740.

Dixon, L.A., Murray, C.M., Archer, E.J., Dobbins, A.E., Koumi, P. and Gill, P. (2005) *Forensic Science International*, 154, 62–77.

Findlay, I., Taylor, A., Quirke, P., Frazier, R. and Urquhart, A. (1997) *Nature*, 389, 555–556.

Meissner, C., Mohamed, S.A., Klueter, H., Hamann, K., von Wurmb, N. and Oehmichen, M. (2000) *Forensic Science International*, 113, 109–112.

Micka, K.A., Sprecher, C.J., Lins, A.M., Theisen Comey, C., Koons, B.W., Crouse, C., Endean, D., Pirelli, K., Lee, S.B., Duda, N., Ma, M. and Schumm, J.W. (1996) *Journal of Forensic Sciences*, 41(4), 582–590.

Niederstratter, H., Coble, M.D., Grubweiser, P., Parsons, T.J. and Parson, W. (2006) *International Journal of Legal Medicine*, 120, 18–23.

Park, M.J., Lee, H.Y., Chung, U., Kang, S-C. and Shin, K-J. (2007) *International Journal of Legal Medicine*, 121, 52–157.

Walsh, P.S., Erlich, H.A. and Higuchi, R. (1992) *PCR Methods and Applications*, 1, 241–250.

Wayne, J.S. and Fourney, R.M. (1993) Forensic DNA Typing of Highly Polymorphic VNTR Loci. In Saferstein, R. (ed.), *Forensic Science Handbook*. Englewood Cliffs, NJ: Prentice Hall.

CHAPTER 3

Quality Control, Quality Assurance and Sources of Uncertainty in the Data

LABORATORY ACCREDITATION, PERSONNEL CERTIFICATION AND PROFICIENCY TESTING

In the early days of DNA evidence, forensic DNA testing was largely unregulated. As one commentator noted, in 1989 "clinical laboratories [were required to] meet higher standards to be allowed to diagnose strep throat than forensic labs [were required to] meet to put a defendant on death row."[1] Between the technical limitations of the VNTR analyses and the lack of standards for laboratory procedures and personnel, the quality of the DNA evidence introduced in some of these early DNA cases was abominable by today's standards.

One case that was instrumental in focusing attention on the need for standardization of procedures and accreditation of laboratories and personnel was the 1987 New York State case *People v. Castro.*[2] Joseph Castro was accused of stabbing Vilma Ponce and her 3-year-old daughter to death, and an RFLP test was performed on a spot of blood from Castro's watch. The autorads produced by the testing laboratory were of very poor quality. There was a lot of nonspecific background smear in each lane, which made many of the bands that were expected to be present in the autorad hard to see. In addition, several bands were visible on the autorad that could not be explained. The quality of the autorad was so poor that four of the expert witnesses, including both prosecution and defense witnesses, took the unprecedented initiative to confer together and produce a consensus statement that asserted that the autorad was of insufficient quality to provide clearly interpretable

CONTENTS

Laboratory Accreditation, Personnel Certification and Proficiency Testing

Validation Studies

The Inevitable Nemeses: Suboptimal Samples and Human Error

Allele Dropout Due to Degradation, Preferential Amplification and Stochastic Effects

Artifacts Inherent in STR Analyses

Hybridization Specificity in Dot-Blot Tests

References and Additional Readings

[1] Lander, 1989.

[2] 545 N.Y.S.2d 985, Bronx County, N.Y. Sup. Ct. 1989.

[3] Lander, 1991; Lewontin and Hartl, 1991; Weir, 1992, 1993; Balding and Nichols, 1994.

evidence. Their statement also suggested that the admission of such evidence illustrated some of the weaknesses in the method by which the admissibility of scientific evidence was judged. The evidence was ruled inadmissible for the purpose of supporting the prosecution's claim that the blood on Joseph Castro's watch came from Vilma Ponce (an inclusion). It was ruled admissible, however, for the purpose of supporting the claim that the blood on Castro's watch was not from Joseph Castro (an exclusion).

The process of standardization was formally begun in 1988, when the FBI formed the Technical Working Group on DNA Analysis Methods (TWGDAM). TWGDAM provided a forum for forensic DNA laboratories to share data, discuss techniques and refine the methods used for forensic DNA analyses. Their work provided the basis for the National Research Council's 1992 report entitled DNA Technology in Forensic Science (hereafter referred to as the 1992 NRC report), which presented the first formal set of recommendations regarding the laboratory techniques to be used to analyze forensic evidence and the statistical procedures used to interpret the data. The 1992 report was instrumental in standardizing the laboratory aspects of the analysis, but TWGDAM had focused much less on the population genetic issues that govern the statistical interpretation of the data. The 1992 NRC report was roundly criticized by several prominent population geneticists.[3] Their criticisms focused on population genetic issues such as the need to account for population substructure in reference databases and the appropriate frequency to assign to alleles that are not found in the reference database (discussed in Chapter 4).

The debates that surrounded the 1992 NRC report generated a great deal of useful research and greatly improved forensic analysts' understanding of population substructure and the proper method for interpreting forensic DNA evidence. In 1994, Congress passed the DNA Identification Act, one consequence of which was the creation of the DNA Advisory Board (DAB) by the FBI. The DAB was established for five years, during which time it provided guidelines on a number of quality control and quality assurance issues related to forensic DNA typing. As the DAB was working, the DNA committee of the NRC reconvened with a different membership and published a second report in 1996 (hereafter referred to as the 1996 NRC report). This report focused on the statistical interpretation of the evidence and provided recommendations that reflected the findings of the recent research. As a result of the DAB's work, the FBI issued two overlapping sets of guidelines for forensic DNA analysis procedures: the 1998 *Quality Assurance Standards for Forensic DNA Testing Laboratories* and the 1999 *Quality Assurance Standards for Convicted Offender DNA Databasing Laboratories.*[4] The latter provided guidelines for the compilation of databanks containing the DNA profiles from convicted offenders as well as evidence samples from unsolved crimes. These standards define the requirements that must be met by any laboratory conducting DNA testing that wishes to participate in CODIS or to apply for federal funding to support its DNA testing.

[4] The *Standards* can be downloaded from the DAB website (http://cstl.nist.gov/div831/strbase/dabqas.htm).

Around this time, TWGDAM was renamed the Scientific Working Group on DNA Analysis Methods (SWGDAM), to reflect the increasingly comprehensive scope and research orientation of the group. At present, SWGDAM has taken over the functions of the DAB. It has adopted the recommendations from the two NRC reports as well as the DAB, and currently sets the standards for American forensic investigators regarding both DNA analysis techniques and the statistical procedures used to interpret the data. There is substantial overlap, both in terms of personnel and policies, between SWGDAM and the International Society for Forensic Genetics (ISFG), which serves as the primary source of guidelines for forensic investigations in Europe and some other parts of the world.

One important improvement that came out of this process was the development of programs to accredit laboratories and certify individual analysts. Any laboratories that wish to participate in the CODIS system must be accredited. In addition, although private laboratories are not allowed to participate in CODIS, most reputable private labs are accredited as well. Most laboratories are accredited by the Laboratory Accreditation Board of the American Association of Crime Laboratory Directors (ASCLAD-LAB). In addition, both the College of American Pathologists (CAP) and the National Forensic Science and Technology Center (NFSTC) maintain accreditation programs that are rigorous enough to satisfy the criminal justice system's requirements for quality control and quality assurance. Laboratory accreditation programs assess the laboratory's organization, the testing protocols that are used, the laboratory's quality control and quality assurance programs, and the training and qualifications of the laboratory personnel. Accredited laboratories are inspected, undergo both internal and external audits on a regular basis and participate regularly in proficiency testing programs. For the individual analysts, the American Board of Criminalistics (ABC) provides a program whereby a crime scene investigator or laboratory technician can be certified. The ABC program offers several certifications, with varying degrees of specialization in DNA analysis.

The testing laboratory is not required to be accredited in order for the DNA evidence to be admissible, nor must a criminologist or laboratory technician be certified in order for him or her to be qualified. Most courts consider a lack of accreditation a matter influencing the weight, rather than the admissibility, of the evidence and will readily admit DNA evidence from testing laboratories that are not accredited.[5] In addition, an individual criminologist or laboratory technician can be qualified by a combination of education, on-the-job training and experience in the position. If the technician followed good laboratory practices and the laboratory has validation data that illustrate that the analysis was capable of producing reliable data in the situation at hand, the evidence will most likely be considered admissible. Conversely, accreditation is no guarantee that the procedures were applied appropriately in the case at bar, nor does it shield the testing laboratory from the defense's scrutiny.

The laboratory's record of performance on past proficiency tests is considered discoverable, as are the records of all personnel who handled and processed the evidence. Under the Supreme Court's *Brady v. Maryland* ruling,[6] the defense is entitled not only to exculpatory evidence, but impeachment evidence as well. Proficiency test records are considered material to the defense, even if the prosecution does not plan to introduce them at trial, because they can be used to impeach the prosecution's DNA evidence. In some cases,[7] the prosecution has argued that compiling the records of past proficiency tests is burdensome. As the *Proctor* court observed, these arguments are without merit. The testing agency compiles test data and makes them available to the participating laboratories. Given the important role proficiency tests play in maintaining quality assurance, it would be highly unusual for a laboratory director not to keep the results of past proficiency tests accessible.

[5] *State v. Adams*, 984 P.2d 16 Ariz. 1999; *Smith v. State*, 702 N.E.2d 668 Ind. 1998; *State v. Ramsey*, 550 S.E.2d 294 S.C. 2001; *J.H.H. v. State* Ala. Ct. App., CR-02-1752, 1/30/04 Ala. Crim. App. LEXIS 22.

[6] *Brady v. Maryland*, 373 U.S. 83, 1963.

[7] Ex. *Proctor v. State*, 559 S.E.2d 318, S.C. App. 2001.

RECAPPING THE MAIN POINTS

1. The poor quality of the DNA evidence that was presented in some early trials prompted efforts to improve and standardize lab procedures, develop proficiency testing programs, accredit laboratories and certify individual personnel.
2. Most forensic testing laboratories are accredited by either the Laboratory Accreditation Board of the American Association of Crime Laboratory Directors (ASCLAD-LAB), the College of American Pathologists (CAP) or the National Forensic Science and Technology Center (NFSTC). Individual personnel are certified by the American Board of Criminalistics (ABC).
3. The current guidelines for forensic DNA testing procedures are provided by SWGDAM in the form of the 1998 *Quality Assurance Standards for Forensic DNA Testing Laboratories*, and the 1999 *Quality Assurance Standards for Convicted Offender DNA Databasing Laboratories* (http://cstl.nist.gov/div831/strbase/dabqas.htm).

VALIDATION STUDIES

The importance of validation studies cannot be overemphasized, especially in a field in which many suboptimal samples are encountered. There are two types of validation studies: those that establish the validity of the procedure in general and those that establish that the laboratory's analysis protocol can produce reliable results under circumstances similar to those that are presented by the sample being analyzed.

In most cases, the commercial company that intends to market a forensic testing kit will either perform or facilitate validation studies that demonstrate the validity of the method. These studies usually present a description of the method and the results from a series of experiments that demonstrate that the method is both sensitive and specific. Studies vary with respect to their complexity and the degree of detail reported in the results, but most will demonstrate that the study can produce the expected result from known positive controls over a range of sample DNA concentrations. Most studies will also illustrate the limits of the assay's sensitivity, and many will demonstrate conditions in which artifacts may arise. Once the product becomes commercially available, other laboratories may publish confirmatory studies, or studies that extend and clarify the original studies' findings regarding the limits of the procedure. Several laboratories may collaborate and publish work that demonstrates the reproducibility of the results from one laboratory to another.

A laboratory's internal validation studies are designed to demonstrate the limits of the procedure. When the sample in question is minute or degraded, the side opposing the evidence is highly likely to suggest that the sample was too compromised to provide highly probative evidence, or that alternative theories of the case can be supported if one considers the possibility that the test results were confounded by artifacts or allele dropout. The laboratory's validation studies provide the proponent of the evidence the most effective possible response to these suggestions. The laboratory's validation studies should clearly demonstrate the protocol's range of sensitivity. An ideal validation study includes samples representing a wide range of DNA concentrations, including several that are too extreme for the protocol to produce an interpretable result. These studies should also illustrate how robust the method is in the face of DNA degradation. They should provide yield gel data along with data from the STR analyses in order to establish the degree of DNA degradation at which alleles begin dropping out. In addition, they should illustrate which markers and alleles are most prone to dropout when a minute sample is analyzed. Although validation studies can be tedious and consume valuable time and resources, there is no more effective way to rebut suggestions that the sample in question was too minute or degraded to provide clearly interpretable results.

Validation studies should be performed regularly enough to keep up with changes in the laboratory's equipment or procedures. The laboratory's validation studies should also illustrate the sensitivity and specificity of any special protocols the analyst may choose. For example, if the analyst decides to change the number of PCR cycles or the peak detection threshold for an analysis, he or she should have validation study data demonstrating that the results will still be reliable. If an analysis is performed using parameters other than those used in the laboratory's validation studies, the defense may argue that the customary protocol was not followed, and therefore the evidence should be declared inadmissible. In this situation, solid validation study data provide the best rebuttal.

RECAPPING THE MAIN POINTS

1. There are two types of validation studies: those that establish and validate the procedure in general, and those the laboratory conducts to validate the specific set of analysis parameters it uses in its casework. The best validation studies illustrate the limits of the procedure as well as its strengths; these studies demonstrate how robust the procedure is in the face of minute sample, DNA degradation and other complicating factors. They also illustrate the validity of any special protocols the analyst may use in exceptional circumstances.

THE INEVITABLE NEMESES: SUBOPTIMAL SAMPLES AND HUMAN ERROR

Good Paperwork Habits Pay Off

Given the nature of forensic evidence, there are many cases in which an evidence sample only yields a small amount of DNA, or the DNA that is extracted from the evidence has been degraded. Many factors may promote the degradation of DNA, including heat, moisture, bacteria and fungi, ultraviolet (UV) rays and common chemicals such as bleach or acids. In addition, human error is the one source of error that can never be eliminated from any complex operation, and there will always be a chance that the evidence has been contaminated or mislabeled. Now that a general consensus has been reached that the methods used to generate forensic DNA evidence are reliable, defense attacks rarely focus on whether the procedures were appropriate; rather, they focus on whether the appropriate procedures were followed.

All the agencies that participate in the collection, handling and analysis of evidence provide their employees with forms that document each individual's role in the process. It should be emphasized regularly to criminologists and laboratory technicians that the paper reports they produce are not merely "busy work"; they serve two very important purposes. First, every individual must recognize that he or she is fallible. Every detail the individual must fill out in the report focuses his or her attention on an important aspect of the procedure; doing so reduces the chance that the individual will make an error. Second, these documents provide the means by which the prosecution can certify that the proper procedures were followed in the instant case. The criminologists and laboratory technicians who processed the samples are called upon to testify well after they have performed their duties relevant to the case at bar. Nobody expects them to remember the specifics of the analysis; they are expected to rely on their notes to recount the details of the analysis. The laboratory technician should make a regular practice of recording on the worksheet any detail about the analysis that was unusual or suboptimal. If the laboratory technician can convince the jury that he or she follows this regular practice, an absence of notes on the worksheet will serve as evidence of the absence of confounding factors. Even the records of pickup and delivery by commercial courier services are important. Without them, the opponent of the evidence may try to argue that the chain of custody of the evidence has not been properly established.[8]

[8] For example, *Snowden v. State*, 574 So.2d 960, Ala. Cr. App. 1990.

Good Housekeeping Is Necessary at All Stages of the Process

Crime scene investigators must organize their work routines to minimize the possibility of mislabeling or confusing samples. Several very good texts are available that discuss in detail the principles and practices of crime scene investigation. In this section, we will briefly discuss the aspects of crime scene investigation that are most likely to influence the quality of the evidence and provide the defense an opportunity to challenge it.

The collector of the evidence should understand that all evidence samples should be packaged in a manner that prevents them from contacting other evidence samples. DNA can transfer from a wet sample to other samples if contact is allowed. DNA-containing samples should also be kept away from heat and moisture. Plastic bags should be avoided; even a dry piece of evidence can become moist due to the condensation that can occur inside a warm plastic bag. Warmth itself will foster degradation of the DNA. Many bacteria grow well in warm environments, and the more bacteria that grow on a piece of evidence, the more extensively the DNA will be degraded by bacterial enzymes. Extreme degradation will result in an inability to produce a profile and will force the analyst to declare the results inconclusive. Ironically, more moderate degrees of degradation may present a more formidable challenge than extreme degradation. With a moderately degraded sample, the analyst may be able to obtain a partial profile, in which the data from only one or two markers is compromised. For example, if the only effect of the degradation is to cause one allele to drop out and make a heterozygous genotype look like a homozygous one, it may be difficult for the analyst to recognize that the profile he or she obtained is not completely accurate.

As DNA analysis methods get more sophisticated, they enable investigators to obtain DNA profiles from increasingly smaller samples. This has enabled investigators to solve many cases that would have gone unsolved in earlier times, but as sometimes happens, the solution has introduced new problems. One particularly dangerous problem is that of DNA transfer. As the French scientist Edmond Locard first pointed out, when two people come in contact with each other, or when someone handles an evidence object, some material (e.g., skin cells, hair) is transferred from one to the other.[9] It is also possible that someone's DNA can be transferred from them to another person, for example, by shaking hands, and then deposited onto an evidence object by the second person. Given the impressive sensitivity of the PCR-based tests, it is impossible to overstate the need for caution when handling evidence. For example, two research groups have already demonstrated the ability to obtain STR profiles from fingerprints on paper or evidence objects.[10]

DNA transfer can confound the interpretation of the evidence in several different ways. Unlike factors that always exert the same effect on the data, this may make it hard for the analyst to recognize that DNA transfer has occurred. To begin with, the amount of DNA that will be transferred by the contact will vary significantly from one person to another and will also be affected by the amount of handling.[11] If only a small amount of DNA is transferred, preferential amplification and stochastic effects (discussed later in this chapter) may result in only a few alleles being amplified, rather than the entire profile. If the transferred DNA only adds a few alleles to the data display, rather than an entire profile, the analyst may not recognize that DNA transfer has occurred.

A transfer of DNA of this nature may actually have occurred in a murder case involving a prominent physician, Dr. Dirk Greineder. Greineder was accused of killing his wife, a charge he denied. A mixture of profiles from Greineder, his wife and a third unidentified party were found on gloves and a knife that were apparently used by the murderer. Greineder denied touching these objects, and instead suggested that his DNA had been transferred to his wife's face when he and his wife had shared a towel after showering that morning. The killer struck his wife in the face, strangled her and stabbed her, allowing ample opportunity for Greineder's DNA to be transferred to the gloves and knife.

Greineder commissioned a study by forensic scientists Marc Taylor and Elizabeth Johnson from Technical Associates in Ventura, California. Taylor and Johnson's study demonstrated that just such a DNA transfer can indeed take place between individuals. They demonstrated that, if person A wipes his or her face with a towel, then person B wipes his or her face with the same towel, then person C touches person B's face with a glove, it is possible to obtain the profiles of persons A and B from the glove. In addition, if person A kisses person B on the cheek, and then person C

[9] The reader may see a reference to Locard's Exchange Principle in some publications.

[10] van Oorschot and Jones, 1997; Balogh et al., 2003.

[11] Ladd et al., 1999.

[12] Akane et al., 1994; Larkin and Harbison, 1999.

touches person B's cheek with a glove, enough DNA may be present on the glove to obtain the profiles of both person A (from saliva) and person B (from skin cells). In the face of other compelling evidence, the jury convicted Greineder. Taylor and Johnson's study, however, has clearly demonstrated that the possibility of secondary transfer must always be considered as a possible alternative explanation for an innocent defendant's DNA being found at a crime scene.

Some materials that are commonly encountered in forensic investigations can inhibit the PCR and prevent the analyst from obtaining any result from some samples. The two most frequently encountered PCR inhibitors are heme (the iron-containing compound in human blood) and one of the dyes that is used to make denim jeans.[12] Fortunately, protocols exist that can either clean the inhibitor out of the sample or adjust the PCR parameters to compensate for the contamination. In cases in which these inhibitors cannot be overcome, there will usually be no result produced, and the analyst will be forced to report that the analysis was inconclusive. There is very little chance that PCR inhibitors would act selectively on one or a few alleles and produce a profile that could be clearly identified but was inaccurate.

Crime scene investigators sometimes perform presumptive tests on evidence in order to get a preliminary assessment of what body fluids the sample contains. Investigators will always try to perform the presumptive test on a small portion of the evidence, but if the sample is minute, the entire piece of evidence may be subjected to the test. Most presumptive tests do not prevent the analyst from obtaining good quality DNA from the sample or an interpretable result from the test. If a presumptive test reagent did compromise an analysis, however, it is most likely that the analyst would not be able to obtain a profile at all. Although this is undesirable, it does not lead to false inclusions or exclusions.

The SWGDAM guidelines include several work practices designed to minimize the likelihood that a sample will be contaminated. The most dangerous sources of contamination in the DNA laboratory are amplified PCR products and the reference samples that are obtained from suspects, victims and others to be compared against the evidence samples. Amplified PCR products contain much higher concentrations of the STR sequences than evidence samples or reference samples. In addition, amplified PCR products make excellent templates for further PCR amplification. Because of this, if some aspect of the PCR setup area gets contaminated by even a small amount of product from a previous PCR (often called "carryover" contamination), it can contaminate any or all of the samples that are processed until the contamination is detected. This includes PCR products that are liberated as aerosols when the technician opens the test tube in which the PCR was performed. For this reason, forensic laboratories maintain a unidirectional workflow that prevents amplified PCR products from being carried back into the DNA extraction area or the PCR setup area. Separate rooms are used for setting up PCRs versus performing the PCR and handling the amplified PCR products. In the most demanding situations, such as mitochondrial DNA analyses (discussed in Chapter 5), laboratory technicians are not allowed to return to the PCR setup area after handling amplified PCR products earlier that day.

The laboratory should maintain separate sets of pipettes, test tubes and reagents for the different areas in which the different phases of the analysis take place.[13] All pipette tips used for extracting DNA, setting up PCRs and processing PCR-amplified samples should be of the "plugged" type. Plugged tips are packed with a material that prevents aerosolized particles from the samples from floating up into the pipette itself. Given the high concentration of DNA present in an amplified PCR product, even a small amount of aerosol material might contain enough DNA to contaminate several subsequent samples.

The other primary source of sample contamination involves the reference samples that are obtained from the suspects, victims and others to be compared against the evidence. Because these samples are usually of significantly greater volume than the evidence samples, and have not experienced whatever degradation the sample may have experienced, they represent a very large amount of DNA compared to the evidence. Any spilling or splashing of the blood when the tube is opened can place an innocent suspect's DNA from the reference sample onto the evidence sample, whereupon the innocent suspect's DNA profile will be present in the evidence (often called "cross" contamination). In order to prevent cross contamination, most laboratories maintain separate areas for the processing of evidence and reference samples.

[13] A pipette is a hand-held device used to transfer small volumes of liquids, as when a laboratory technician adds the ingredients for a chemical reaction into a test tube. The pipette is equipped with a plunger that the technician presses and releases with his or her thumb in order to draw the desired liquid into the pipette tip, and presses again to eject the liquid from the pipette tip into the test tube. The pipette is fitted with a disposable tip, which should be disposed of after a single use.

Other work practices that minimize the potential for contamination are good housekeeping practices such as changing one's gloves frequently—at the very least after each sample is processed or after any kind of spill has occurred. For samples containing minute amounts of DNA, the technician should wear a face mask and disposable sleeves, because in cases where the evidence contains minimal DNA, even a couple of skin cells falling from the technician's face or forearm can represent a significant level of contamination. In addition, the areas in which PCRs are set up and PCR products are handled should be protected from the environment. Most laboratories use laminar flow chambers, although some directors feel that an isolation hood that provides a clean work space is sufficient. Some directors provide anecdotal evidence that atmospheric contaminants may settle in the work space after a laminar flow chamber is turned off. Whichever type of chamber is used, the chambers should be equipped with sterilizing ultraviolet lights. The pipettes, pipette tips and microcentrifuge tubes used to extract the DNA should be UV-sterilized as well, as should the extraction buffer and any other reagents that will not be compromised by UV exposure. Each laboratory will have its own set of protocols for cleaning before work shifts and between samples. Most involve a combination of cleaning the work area, including the pipettors, with 10% commercial bleach and using the UV light.

In addition to these work practices, several "blank" samples will be processed along with the evidence samples in order to allow the analyst to detect contamination whenever possible. These blanks constitute **negative controls**. Negative controls are samples that are not expected to produce a result unless either the evidence or the assay reagents contained some contaminating DNA. For example, an **unstained specimen** (sometimes called the **substrate control or substrate blank**) is used to determine if a sample had been contaminated before it was collected. An unstained specimen is a sampling of the material from which the evidence has come; it is intended to ensure that the evidence object does not have any background DNA on it that might be unrelated to the crime. Testing an unstained specimen is critical for any object that might have been handled before the evidence was deposited on it, and especially for some of the heavy-wear areas in articles of clothing. For a bloodstained item of clothing, the ideal extraction blank is a piece of the garment from an unstained region that is close to the stained region. For a bloodstained countertop, it would be a swab from a nearby unstained region of the countertop. If an unstained specimen produces any detectable result, it is assumed that the object from which the evidence was obtained had some DNA on it that may be unrelated to the crime. If the bloodstain appears to be a mixed sample, its profile can be checked against the unstained specimen's profile in order to see if the profile that was seen in the unstained specimen may be contained in the evidence.

An **extraction blank** is also used to ensure that the reagents used to extract the DNA have not been compromised by contamination. An extraction blank includes everything that was used to extract the DNA from the sample, but no sample material. If the reagents used to extract the DNA are contaminated with DNA, the extraction blank will produce a profile. Similarly, a **reagent blank** is also processed in order to ensure that there is no contaminating DNA in the reagents used for the PCR and post-PCR manipulations.[14] The reagent blank contains no extracted material, but is put through all the postextraction steps of the analysis. If any of the reagents has been contaminated with DNA, the reagent blank will produce a product.

[14] Different laboratories may have different terms for these negative controls. For example, the reader may see the term "amplification blank" used instead of "reagent blank."

The procedural safeguards that are followed in forensic laboratories effectively minimize the potential for contamination of samples with extraneous DNA. In addition, these negative control samples reveal any such contamination that does occur. In some cases, the analyst can produce an accurate result in spite of the contamination. If the analyst can subtract the contaminating profile from the data, he or she can correctly determine the profile of the person who is the source of the evidence. In the most demanding situations, such as mitochondrial DNA testing (discussed in Chapter 5), analysts frequently encounter such samples. As long as the laboratory has an established procedure for separating the true profile from the contamination (especially if the laboratory's internal validation data demonstrate that this can be done reliably), the analyst may report the profile he or she obtained.

For example, if one of the evidence handlers contaminated the sample with shed skin, and the evidence handler's DNA profile shows up in the data as a minor contributor, it may be possible to subtract the handler's profile out of the data visually and report the true profile. Testing laboratories should keep a catalog of DNA profiles, not only from laboratory personnel but from everyone who had access to the crime scene, including innocent civilians and authorized personnel (these are often referred to as **elimination samples**). If a second profile is seen in a sample that is expected to have come from a single source, the analyst can check the profiles from the samples that were analyzed shortly before and during the time the sample in question was analyzed. This will enable the analyst to characterize the contamination as carryover contamination, cross contamination or sporadic contamination, which is a term used to denote contamination that is often of unknown origin and not likely to reappear in a subsequent analysis.

In addition to the negative controls, at least one **positive control** should always be included with each batch of samples. The positive control is a DNA sample for which the profile has already been determined. The best positive control sample for any particular marker contains all the known alleles for that marker. Such a control ensures that all the alleles that were present could have been detected. At minimum, the positive control should contain a relatively large allele and a relatively small allele from each marker. This helps guarantee that all the alleles that were present in the sample could be amplified. The National Institute for Standards and Technology (NIST) provides **standard reference materials (SRMs)** that serve as positive control samples for many forensic DNA tests.[15] The NIST provides SRMs for autosomal and Y chromosome STR analyses as well as mitochondrial DNA analyses.

Laboratory personnel should be aware that no detail of laboratory operation, no matter how minute, is exempt as a potential point on which a defense attorney will question the DNA evidence. For example, in a case in which a temperature-sensitive method involving hybridization of a probe to a target DNA fragment is involved (i.e., DQA1), the temperature at which the hybridization occurred is an important issue. Good laboratory procedures include regular calibration of thermometers and other temperature-dependent machines such as the thermocyclers used in PCR. In cases such as *Duarte v. Commonwealth,*[16] convicted defendants have appealed the admissibility of DNA evidence based on details as minute as a thermometer being several weeks overdue for its annual calibration. As in *Duarte*, courts have concluded that laboratory procedural errors are usually to be considered in determining the weight of the evidence, not its admissibility. The *Duarte* court observed that "[t]here is

[15] http://www.nist.gov/srd/

[16] 780 N.E.2d 99, Mass. App. 2002.

no hard and fast rule that any deviation or deficiency in laboratory procedure . . . requires the exclusion of scientific testimony." Furthermore, the court noted that the appellant had not demonstrated that the thermometer was inaccurate. In addition, the prosecution's expert witness testified that, had the hybridization temperature not been appropriate, she would have seen specific abnormalities in the data, which she did not observe.

The Many Faces of Human Error

When the subject of human error comes up, most people think of the errors made by crime scene investigators and laboratory technicians. History has also revealed another source of human error that would have been difficult to anticipate. One of the most alarming findings from the research that has analyzed the causes of wrongful convictions is the fact that unfounded or erroneous testimony by forensic scientists was a factor in a significant number of wrongful convictions.[17] As discussed in Chapter 4, people engage in many logical fallacies when presented with probabilistic evidence. Surprisingly, even forensic scientists who testify as expert witnesses sometimes commit these fallacies, or in some cases, even more deliberate, and therefore more egregious, errors.

[17] www.innocence project.org; Saks and Koehler, 2005.

One more source of human error is often overlooked but interferes far too frequently in the applied sciences. In far too many cases, the directors of government agencies such as forensic testing laboratories are subjected to pressure from politicians and government officials to produce results that are politically expedient, sometimes at the expense of quality assurance. Nowhere is this problem more applicable than in the field of forensics. Even when only a single victim is involved, violent crimes are sensational, high-profile events by their very nature, and few government officials will survive long if they are not seen as being tough on violent crime. Laboratory directors are too often pressured to produce results quickly, or to produce results that will lead to a conviction, rather than allowed to take the time required to ensure quality results. In addition, many people (especially those with no laboratory experience) consider a "top lab" one that can produce results from all samples, or worse yet, obtain a matching profile from every suspect's sample. One must accept the fact that some analyses are not going to produce properly interpretable results, and one should redefine one's concept of a "top lab" as a laboratory that always produces the correct conclusion, even if that means declaring results uninterpretable. As disappointing and politically inconvenient as it is to be unable to use a piece of evidence to secure a conviction, pressuring an analyst to produce a result from an uninterpretable sample is obviously a miscarriage of justice waiting to happen.

Resisting those political pressures requires courage and integrity; anyone who stands on principle and defies the will of his or her supervisor risks his or her immediate employment and professional reputation, without consideration of whether he or she is right or wrong. Furthermore, it is unfortunate that those who do so are often afforded insufficient protection by our legal system. It is also unfortunate that too many laboratory directors, whose professional stature should afford them some insulation against the calumnies of the unscrupulous, pass this political pressure on to their junior personnel, who feel even less empowered to resist it.

RECAPPING THE MAIN POINTS

1. The reports that crime scene investigators and laboratory analysts fill out when they collect or analyze a sample are critical documents for establishing the chain of custody and the proper handling of the evidence.
2. Crime scene investigators should take care to avoid placing evidence objects in contact with each other, or exposing the evidence to heat, moisture, UV rays and common chemicals such as bleach or acids.
3. DNA can be transferred from one person to another, or from a person to an evidence object, by contact. One person's DNA can even be transferred to another person, then from the second person onto an evidence object.
4. All forensic laboratories employ numerous work practices that minimize the potential for contamination of reagents and samples. Analysts use negative control samples to reveal any contamination that has occurred, and positive control samples to demonstrate that the assay performed as expected.
5. The potential sources for human error in forensic DNA testing are not limited to mistakes made by evidence collectors and laboratory technicians. Lawyers, judges and even expert witnesses are susceptible to the same logical fallacies that are committed by lay jurors when interpreting probabilistic evidence.

ALLELE DROPOUT DUE TO DEGRADATION, PREFERENTIAL AMPLIFICATION AND STOCHASTIC EFFECTS

When a sample yields either a minute amount of DNA or DNA that has degraded, it presents the analyst with special challenges. Ironically, the most degraded samples present the analyst with the least difficult situation. A very poor quality sample produces no result or an uninterpretable result. Although it is disappointing not to extract information from the sample, the analyst arrives easily at a confident conclusion. In contrast, a sample that is only moderately degraded can produce a DNA profile that is missing one or more alleles. This situation is obviously the more distressing of the two; it can lead to false inclusions or false exonerations.

When alleles drop out, the rule of thumb states that larger alleles are more likely to drop out than smaller alleles. As DNA degrades, it gets cut into progressively smaller fragments. Recall from Chapter 2 that in order to determine someone's allele status at a marker, the entire sequence to be analyzed must lie intact within one fragment of the deteriorating DNA. Logically, the smaller an allele is, the more likely it is to have its entire sequence contained in one of the ever-shrinking DNA fragments. If the larger of two alleles drops out of the data, the analyst may conclude that the individual providing the sample is homozygous for a small allele, when he or she is actually heterozygous for that small allele and a larger one. In addition, if the marker with the largest alleles is the only marker that is affected by the degradation, it may be difficult for the analyst to recognize that an allele has dropped out of the profile.

The small size of the repeated sequence motif in an STR helps minimize problems due to allele dropout. Because the repeated sequence in an STR is only 4 bp long, there are only minor differences between the sizes of the smallest and largest alleles. There are some samples, however, in which the DNA has degraded enough to allow the larger alleles of some STRs to drop out, but not enough to prevent the analyst from obtaining a profile. The analyst may be able to detect samples in which the DNA has degraded to the required degree by looking at the sizes of the allele peaks. In a sample that has experienced the requisite degree of degradation, if the analyst combines all the markers' data together, a general trend may emerge in which the markers with smaller alleles exhibit greater peak intensities than the markers with larger alleles.

In some samples, one or more alleles of a marker will be amplified more efficiently than the others. Degraded samples and samples that contain PCR inhibitors are especially prone to this **preferential amplification**.[18] When degradation causes the loss of some of the template DNA, or when an inhibitor reduces the efficiency of the PCR, the smallest alleles may be the only alleles that the PCR can amplify. In addition to size differences,

[18] Walsh et al., 1992.

differences in the sequences of the two alleles can cause one to amplify more efficiently than the other.

While the PCR allows the investigator to analyze impressively miniscule amounts of evidence, there are still samples for which the small amount of DNA extracted presents a special challenge to the analysis. Minute samples are often subject to **stochastic effects**, wherein there may be significantly different amounts of the two alleles amplified in the PCR. Unlike the preferential amplification discussed earlier, wherein amplification of one allele is inherently more efficient than the other because of either the lengths or sequences of the alleles, stochastic effects are due to chance. In these cases, both alleles amplify with the same efficiency, but one allele gets used as the template for more amplifications than the other, merely by chance.

To illustrate how stochastic effects can occur with minute samples, imagine that you have a bucket that contains some red balls and some white balls. The bucket of balls represents the DNA that has been extracted from the sample. The red balls represent one allele of a marker, while the white balls represent the other allele. Imagine that you want to simulate putting half your sample into the PCR by picking up half the balls in your bucket (randomly, without looking at their colors). Ideally, the sample you selected would contain an equal number of red and white balls, simulating a situation in which an equal number of copies of each allele would serve as templates in the PCR. Suppose for this example that the set of balls you pick out of the bucket contains what is very close to an even balance between red and white balls. Suppose your selected sample ended up with just one more than half the balls being red balls, and just one fewer than half the balls being white. If you began the exercise with a total of 300 red balls and 300 white balls, you would end up with approximately equal numbers of each (151 red and 149 white). If the red and white balls represent molecules of the two different alleles that you are putting into your PCR, you are simulating a situation in which there was less than a 1% difference in the number of template molecules representing each of the two alleles. However, if you began the exercise with only 10 red balls and 10 white ones, you would have 6 red and 4 white balls in the selected sample. Because there are so few molecules of template DNA to begin with, this slight deviation from an even balance between the alleles simulates a situation in which there are 50% more copies of template for the red allele than the white one. Recall that, in the PCR, the products of the previous cycle are used as templates for the next cycle. When there is an uneven amount of starting material for the two alleles, the repetitive cycling of the PCR magnifies the discrepancy. After 25–35 PCR cycles, there will be a considerable difference in the number of molecules containing one allele versus the other.

In addition to situations in which unequal numbers of template copies are put into the PCR, stochastic effects can also occur when an equal number of copies of each allele is put into the PCR. The products of each PCR cycle get used as the templates for the next PCR cycle. However, amplification efficiency is not 100%; not every available template gets used in every cycle. When only a few copies of each allele are available to serve as templates for amplification, and a small number of available templates do not get used, the result can be a significant imbalance in the amount of amplification of one allele versus the other in any given PCR cycle. If this happens in an early cycle, the effect can be magnified as the PCR progresses, and a significantly greater amount of one allele can be produced than the other. Unlike the preferential amplification discussed above, stochastic effects do not exhibit any systematic bias for smaller or larger alleles. Any of the alleles of a marker can drop out due to stochastic effects when the amount of DNA extracted from a sample is minute.

Another source of allele dropout may be encountered in rare cases. Recall that the specific stretch of DNA that gets amplified in the PCR is determined by the sequences of the primers that are put into the reaction mixture. Recall also that the primer has a sequence that is complementary to a specific stretch of DNA just to one side of the string of repeated sequence motifs. If someone has a single-nucleotide polymorphism (for example, a G substitutes for an A) in the stretch of sequence to which the primer is supposed to bind, it may leave the primer unable to bind there, because the two sequences are no longer completely complementary. If the primer cannot bind, there will be no amplification of that allele.[19]

[19] These alleles are often referred to as **null alleles**.

If the person has this single-nucleotide substitution in only one of the two alleles of the marker, the person will appear to be homozygous for that marker, because he or she exhibits only one peak, when he or she is actually heterozygous. This may complicate the analysis of the data in a paternity case if the child inherits the null allele from the father. In this

[20] Shewale et al., 2000.

case, it will appear that the child has not inherited any allele from the father for that marker. The father will appear to be homozygous, and the child will appear not to have inherited an allele that matches the one that is seen in the true father. In this case, because the child will only exhibit one allele (the one he or she inherited from his or her mother), it will appear more likely that the child's true father possesses an allele that is the same size as the allele the child inherited from his or her mother.

In the case of the amelogenin gene marker, which is used to determine the gender of the person from whom the sample is derived, the X allele can drop out because of a rare polymorphism in one of the primer binding sites. In one study, this was seen in 3 out of almost 7,000 males.[20] When a polymorphism in a primer binding site prevents amplification of an allele, designing a different primer that will bind to a locus a short distance away from the original one allows the marker to be amplified.

Allele dropout can lead to confusion if a sample is tested twice, each time using a different company's testing protocol. Usually, several different pairs of primers can be used to amplify any particular STR. As long as the primers bind to sequences flanking the repeat, the STR can be amplified. The analytical equipment used for STR analyses can accommodate PCR products ranging from 50 bp up to 500 bp, so for any one marker, often a wide range of choices of primer pairs can be used. Different companies, and even different kits from the same company, may use different primers to amplify the same STR. If an allele is dropping out because of a **single-nucleotide polymorphism (SNP)** in the primer binding site, simply using a different set of primers will allow the analyst to see the elusive allele. If a sample is tested twice with different primers, it may appear to be homozygous at that marker in one test, but heterozygous at the same marker in the other test. This is evidence of a SNP in the primer binding site used by the first testing kit. If the suspect is indeed the source of the evidence, this conclusion will be further strengthened by the observation that the profiles from the evidence and the suspect are always concordant (i.e., they always show identical genotypes), even though they produce a different result (homozygous versus heterozygous) in one test versus the other.

One other artifact can arise from a minute and degraded sample that bears mentioning; Ts can appear in the sequence where there are actually Cs.

Note from Figure 1.3 that the base cytosine can be converted into the base uracil if the amine group (NH_2) sticking up from the ring is replaced by a double-bonded oxygen (O). This deamination can occur as DNA degrades. The U nucleotide is not normally a component of DNA; it is found in place of the T nucleotide in RNA. It is similar enough to the T nucleotide, however, that it will behave as one in the sequencing reaction. When the analyst sequences the DNA, it will appear as if a T nucleotide occupies that position rather than a C. This artifact is most likely to appear in samples with minute amounts of degraded DNA in them. Archeological geneticists who analyze DNA from ancient bones will often use an enzyme to digest all the uracil residues in the DNA before sequencing, thereby avoiding the possibility that uracil-containing sequences will confound the results.

RECAPPING THE MAIN POINTS

1. In order for an allele to be amplified, the STR's entire sequence must be contained in a single DNA fragment. If, during degradation of the DNA, the DNA has been cut somewhere within the sequence to be detected, the allele will not be amplified.
2. Because of size differences, or perhaps sequence differences, some alleles amplify in the PCR with greater efficiency than other alleles of the same marker (preferential amplification).
3. Some alleles may amplify with more efficiency than other alleles merely because that copy of the target sequence was used as a template more often than the other copy was. These stochastic effects arise by chance, not as a result of differences in the alleles' lengths or sequences.
4. When only one allele of any given marker drops out of the profile, the analyst can be deceived into thinking that an individual has a homozygous genotype for that marker when he or she actually has a heterozygous genotype.
5. As DNA degrades, C nucleotides can sometimes be deaminated and become U nucleotides. If this happens, it will appear as if there is a T in the sequence where there is actually a C.

ARTIFACTS INHERENT IN STR ANALYSES

In addition to the fact that many samples will be minute or degraded, and therefore difficult to analyze, every analytical system has quirks that may even confound the interpretation of pristine samples. In addition, in some cases the analyst may manipulate the parameters of the analysis in order to maximize sensitivity or decrease artifacts. For an STR analysis, the analyst can manipulate both the parameters of the PCR and the operating parameters of the fragment analyzer. Setting these parameters at different values can result in the analyst detecting peaks that would otherwise have gone undetected, or not detecting peaks that would otherwise have been detected. If the parameters that were applied in the case at bar differ from those that were in effect during the validation studies that established the abilities of the system, the analyst must account for the difference in the analysis parameters when he or she interprets the data. If the change in parameters makes it more likely that the analyst will report an inclusion, the defense may argue that the laboratory's standard procedures were not followed, and that the modification of the procedure was prejudicial to the defendant.

The three parameters of the PCR that the analyst is most likely to manipulate are the amount of DNA that is put into the reaction, the temperature that is in effect during the annealing stages of the PCR cycles and the number of PCR cycles in the protocol. As already discussed, too little DNA may result in allele dropout. This may occur because the sample itself is minute, or because degradation has reduced the number of intact fragments that are capable of serving as templates for amplification by the PCR. Too much DNA, on the other hand, may introduce artifactual peaks that can appear to be true allele peaks, and may suggest to the analyst that more alleles are present in a sample than there actually are. Also as discussed earlier in this chapter, Standard 9.3 of the DNA Advisory Board Standards requires that the concentration of human DNA be determined in every sample. The most popular STR testing kits require between 0.5 and 2.0 ng (1 ng $= 10^{-9}$ grams) of DNA for each PCR. Each kit's protocol specifies the optimal amount of input DNA, and the laboratory should have validation study data that illustrate the range of input DNA within which their analysis is reliable. The analyst may attempt to overcome degradation by adding more DNA into the PCR or increasing the number of PCR cycles used in order to maximize amplification of faint products.

If the temperature that is in effect during the annealing stage of the PCR is too low, the PCR may produce some unwanted products that appear to be true allele peaks. Recall from Chapter 1 that nucleotides bond as complementary pairs: A nucleotides bind with Ts, and Cs bind with Gs. This complementary basepairing arrangement enables the analyst to design PCR primers that bind only to the places in the DNA where the analyst wants them to bind. At low temperatures, however, the thermodynamics of the situation favor binding, and PCR primers will bind to sites where the sequence contains only a partially complementary sequence. Anytime a PCR primer binds at a place the analyst doesn't intend it to, it may produce a product that can appear to be a true allele of that marker. In order to make sure that the primers only bind to one set of binding sites, and therefore only produce one product, the analyst programs the thermal cycler to maintain as high a temperature during the annealing stage of each PCR cycle as possible. The ideal annealing temperature is high enough so that the primers will only bind to perfectly complementary sequences, but not so high that nothing binds.

This is a particularly important consideration when dealing with multiplex PCR testing kits (assays in which the PCR contains several sets of primers, each one designed to amplify a different marker). Optimal results are obtained from the PCR when the annealing temperatures that are used are tailored to the sequences of the primers being used. Recall from Chapter 1 that there are two hydrogen bonds between an AT basepair, but three hydrogen bonds between a CG basepair. Because of the increased number of bonds, a primer with a high proportion of Cs and Gs in its sequence will bind to its target with greater affinity than an AT-rich primer will. In a multiplex PCR, where several markers are amplified using one set of temperatures, an annealing temperature that is optimal for the more AT-rich primers may allow the more CG-rich primers to bind to unintended targets and produce unwanted products. Conversely, an annealing temperature that is optimal for the more CG-rich primers may be too high for the AT-rich primers; they may not be able to bind to their intended targets efficiently and produce their intended products in the desired amount. The laboratory should have validation study data demonstrating that their chosen annealing temperature allows for specific amplification of all the intended STRs. If the annealing temperature used in the case at bar is different from the annealing temperature used for the validation studies, the analyst can expect the opposing side to challenge the evidence on the grounds that the customary protocols were not followed. The analyst should be prepared to provide evidence that the change in temperature did not prejudice the analysis against the defendant.

The number of cycles in the PCR is also a critical variable that will influence the outcome of the analysis. A PCR with too few cycles may not produce enough product to see all the alleles from a minute sample or a minor contributor to a mixed sample. Using too many cycles may allow artifacts that are usually not intense enough to be recognized by the fragment analyzer as peaks to exceed the detection threshold and appear in the data. Each manufacturer supplies recommendations regarding the number of cycles to be used with its kit. When analyzing a minute sample, however, the analyst may increase the number of PCR cycles used so as to maximize amplification. Increasing the number of PCR cycles maximizes the amplification of the intended target, but also increases the amplification of any contaminating DNA or unintended PCR products that may be present. Each laboratory should have data from validation studies that illustrate how robust the analysis is when more or fewer than the recommended number of PCR cycles are used.

One well-known case in which the use of an excessive number of PCR cycles may have contributed to a false conclusion is the 1982 rape/murder case involving Earl Washington. In this case, the initial DNA testing was done using the DQA1 test, and an error was made in the interpretation of the data. The analyst wrongly concluded that both of Washington's alleles were present in a vaginal swab sample. In 2000, the same laboratory that had performed the DQA1 test performed STR testing. During this analysis, the analyst used a greater number of PCR cycles than was recommended in both the laboratory's standard protocol and the kit manufacturer's recommendations (33 cycles versus the recommended 30), perhaps because the sample had yielded little DNA. The results of this analysis shed even less light on the circumstances surrounding the crime. The DNA of a known serial rapist was found in a sample from a blanket at the scene, but neither his, Washington's nor the victim's husband's DNA were represented in the DNA that was obtained from a vaginal swab. It was now concluded that the vaginal swab sample contained DNA from at least two unknown contributors. Subsequent STR testing (in 2004), after differential extraction of the sperm and nonsperm fractions of the vaginal swab evidence (described in Chapter 6), detected only the victim's and the serial rapist's alleles, and no others. One reason extra alleles were detected in the 2000 analysis may have been that the use of 33 PCR cycles instead of the recommended 30 allowed some artifacts that were usually not detected by the fragment analyzer to be detected and interpreted as true allele peaks.

The artifacts inherent in STR analyses do not all involve alleles dropping out; extra peaks may appear in an STR analysis as well for several reasons. Many STRs exhibit **stutter peaks**, some of which are intense enough to exceed the analyzer's peak detection threshold (Figure 3.1). A stutter peak reflects amplified PCR products that are usually one repeat shorter than the true allele's PCR product. The DNA polymerase enzyme that builds the new DNA chains in the PCR can experience slippage as it amplifies the repeat. Although most stutter peaks are one repeat smaller than the true allele peak, a stutter peak can differ from the true peak by more than that, and it can also be larger than the true allele's peak. Stutter peaks are noticeably less intense than true allele peaks and are rarely confused with true allele peaks in a single-source sample. If the sample contains material from more than one source, however, because the stutter peak is the same size as one of the other alleles that might be present in the mixture, it can be easy to confuse a stutter peak from the major contributor with a true allele peak from a minor contributor. In addition, in a minute sample, if preferential amplification or stochastic effects cause one allele to amplify with greater efficiency than another, a true allele peak may be interpreted as a stutter peak if it is one repeat smaller than

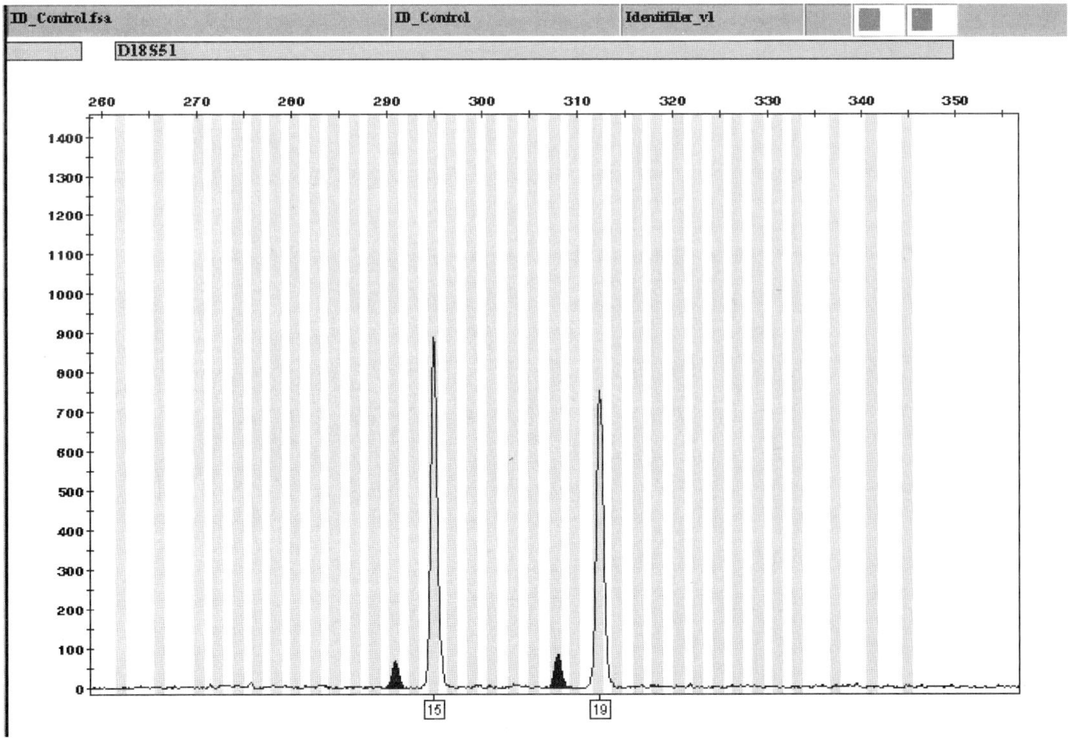

FIGURE 3.1 *Stutter peaks for the D18S51 marker. The stutter peaks are shown as low-intensity peaks with allele sizes that are 4 bp less than the true allele peaks. Figure reprinted with permission from Applied Biosystems Human Identification group.*

[21] Gill et al., 1998.

[22] Magnuson et al., 1996.

the better-amplified allele. Finally, if the fragment analyzer's peak detection threshold has been set high in order to minimize the detection of stutter peaks, the analyst may fail to detect the profile of a minor contributor to a mixed stain.

One reason tetranucleotide repeats have displaced dinucleotide repeats as the STR of choice for forensic testing is the fact that they have fewer and smaller stutter peaks. The intensities of the stutter peaks for most tetranucleotide repeats are usually 15% or less of the intensities of the true allele peaks.[21] For some dinucleotide repeats, the stutter peaks' intensities can equal 30% of the true allele peaks' intensities. Pentanucleotide repeats, in which the repeated unit is 5 bp long, may someday replace tetranucleotides as the forensic DNA markers of choice because fewer of them exhibit stutter peaks, and the stutter peaks that are exhibited are smaller than those seen with tetranucleotide repeat STRs.

Another source of extra peaks in an STR analysis arises from what is called **nontemplate-directed nucleotide addition**[22] (Figure 3.2). Simply put, the DNA polymerase used in the PCR to chain the nucleotides together to make new DNA strands has a tendency to add one more A nucleotide onto the newly synthesized DNA strand after the polymerase has gotten to the end of the template. The addition of this A nucleotide is not directed by the template because the template ended one nucleotide before. The polymerase simply has the habit of leaving many PCR products with a single A hanging from the 3′ end of the newly synthesized DNA strand (often called an N + 1 product). In most cases, this extra A does not present any problems; it usually falls off by itself within a short period of time. Depending on how recently the PCR was performed, the N+1 product may be present in greater, equal or lesser concentration than the N product. If they are present in equal concentrations, the peak may be split at the top. If they are present in unequal concentrations, a small peak will appear either close before or close after a larger peak. For example, in Figure 3.2, the N + 1 product is present in significantly greater quantity than the N product.

STR data will also occasionally include **pull-up peaks** that are an artifact of the fluorescent labeling strategy used to detect STR alleles (Figure 3.3). Recall that one of the primers used in the PCR is labeled with a fluorescent

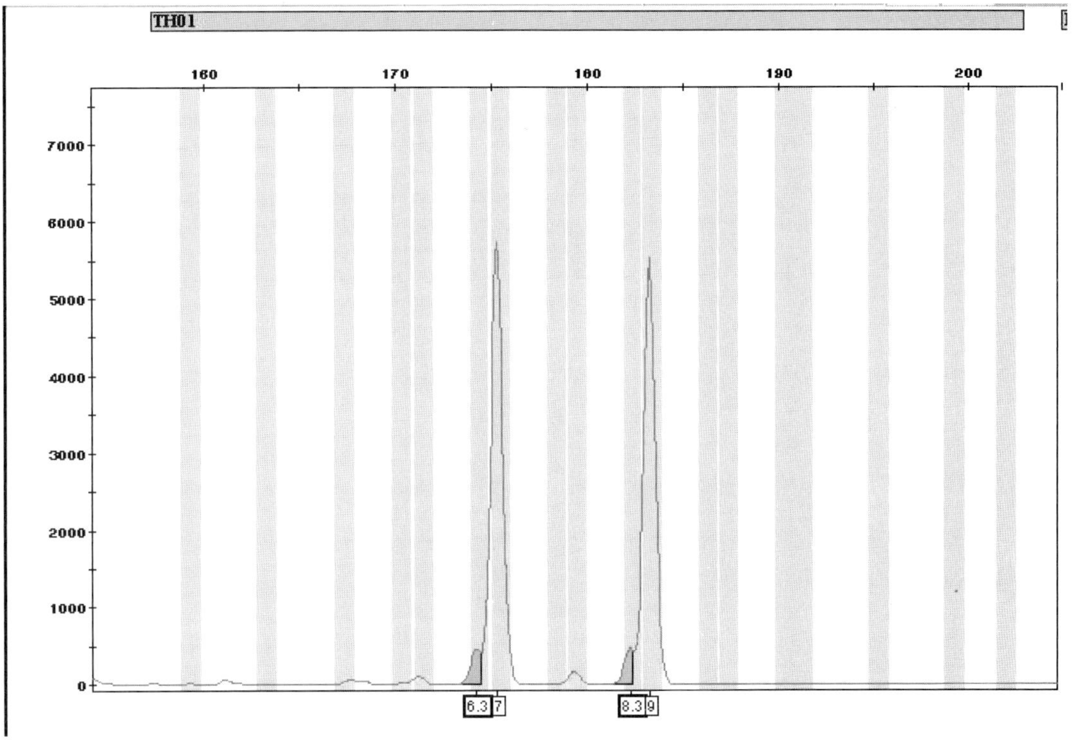

FIGURE 3.2 *Nontemplate-directed nucleotide addition. Note that a significantly greater amount of the N + 1 product is present than the N product. The N + 1 peak therefore appears as a large peak, and the N product appears as a small hump just before the N + 1 peak. Figure reprinted with permission from Applied Biosystems Human Identification group.*

molecule (also called a fluor) in order to enable the fragment analyzer to detect the PCR product. Recall also that, to maximize the efficiency with which the sample is used, four different fluors are used to label the alleles from the different markers in the test kit. Inside the fragment analyzer, a light is shone onto the PCR products, and the light is absorbed by the fluors. Each of the four different fluors then emits light at a unique wavelength. The fragment analyzer detects the alleles that are present in the sample by detecting the light that is emitted by the fluors.

In an ideal system, each fluorescent dye would emit light at a different wavelength, and there would be no overlap between the wavelengths of light emitted by the different fluors. Unfortunately, differentiating between the different fluors is not an easy task, even for a machine. The four fluors actually emit their light at very similar wavelengths. Worse than that, each fluor emits light over a band of wavelengths, and there is

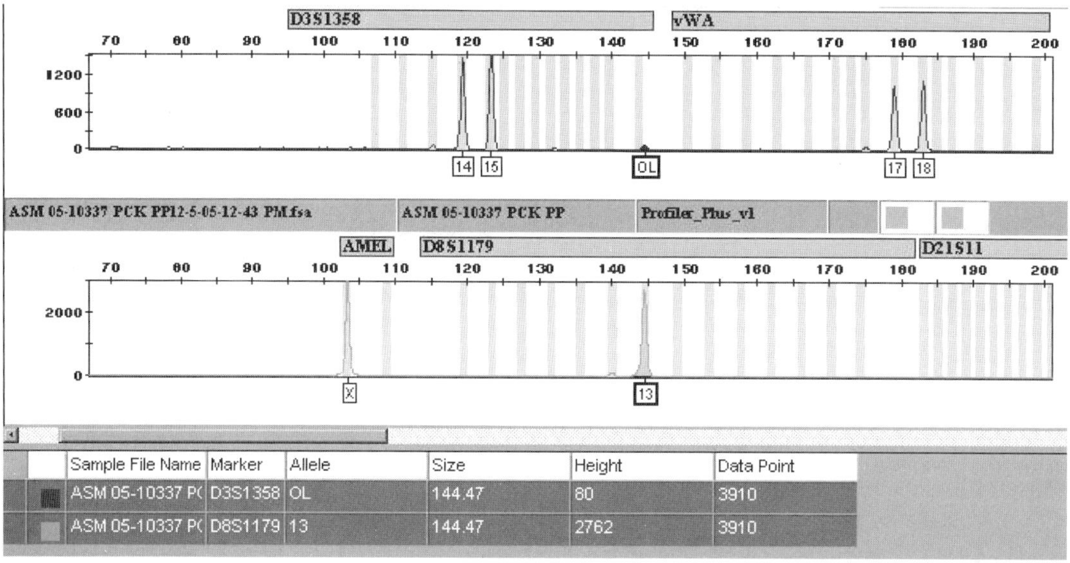

FIGURE 3.3 *A pull-up peak is seen as an off-ladder (OL) allele in the upper display. Figure reprinted with permission from Applied Biosystems Human Identification group.*

considerable **spectral overlap** between the wavelengths at which one fluor emits light and those at which the others emit it. Although each fluor emits its maximum amount of light at a different wavelength, some or all of the other fluors also emit light at that wavelength. Because of the spectral overlap between the fluors, the fragment analyzer must apply a complicated formula to measure the amount of light being emitted at one fluor's maximum emission wavelength and subtract the light that is being emitted at that wavelength by the other fluors. In order to do this, the fragment analyzer stores the emission spectra for the four fluors, as well as the expected pattern of spectral overlap between them, in a **spectral matrix**. Over time, the system can experience some slippage, and this spectral matrix occasionally needs to be recalibrated. When the spectral matrix is out of calibration, a strong signal from one fluor can be interpreted as a signal from another fluor, because the first fluor is emitting light at the second fluor's maximum emission wavelength, but the machine is not recognizing this light as representing overlap from the first fluor. Because the spectral matrix has slipped out of calibration, the fragment analyzer is interpreting the light it sees at fluor 2's maximum emission wavelength as coming from a PCR product that has been labeled with fluor 2, when no such PCR product actually exists. The light is actually coming from fluor 1's signal, and it should therefore be ignored, but the machine is not recognizing this fact. This results in the appearance of an artifactual peak among the PCR products that have been labeled with fluor 2 (i.e., the peak gets "pulled up" into fluor 2's display). This peak will appear to represent an allele that is the same length as the true allele that has been labeled with fluor 1. If this allele size is within the range of allele sizes of one of the markers that has been labeled with fluor 2, it may be mistaken for a true allele peak for that marker, and so may confuse the interpretation of the results from that test. In Figure 3.3, the pull-up peak from the number 13 allele of the D8S1179 marker is seen as an **off-ladder peak** (one that does not correspond to any of the know allele sizes) in the upper electropherogram.

Another important operating parameter the analyst programs into the fragment analyzer is the fragment analyzer's **peak detection threshold (PDT)**. The PDT is the intensity that a peak must have in order to be recognized by the machine. A certain amount of background "noise" peaks is found in any system, but the peaks associated with the amplified PCR products are usually considerably more intense, and consequently create much higher peaks in the data display, than the background noise. In most cases, the PDT is set at a level that will screen out the noise and still detect the peaks. The situation gets complicated, however, if the sample is minute or a mixture that contains a major and a minor contributor. The analyst may have to lower the peak detection threshold in order to detect the minor contributor's alleles; this increases the risk of detecting artifacts from the major contributor's material, unwanted PCR products or contaminating DNA. At present, most laboratories follow Applied Biosystems' recommendation to set the PDT at 150 **relative fluorescence units (RFU)** for routine casework, although some will use 50, 100 or 200 RFU for routine casework, and any analyst can alter the PDT for any particular sample. As with other parameters, it is best if the analyst can demonstrate that the PDT used in the analysis was shown to be reliable in validation studies.

Because it can result in entire profiles being included versus excluded in the analyst's report, the level at which the analyst sets the PDT has always been a contentious issue. It will probably become even controversial in the near future, however. The use of 150 RFU as the consensus PDT derives from a validation study that Applied Biosystems published in 1998.[23] The authors demonstrated the limits of the system's sensitivity and found that minute samples down to 0.25-ng DNA could be typed; at this level of input

[23] Wallin et al., 1998.

[24] Gilder et al., 2007.

DNA, the peak intensities were 150 RFU or greater. As Gilder and colleagues[24] have pointed out, however, this rationale runs counter to two well-established analytical chemical principles: the **limit of detection (LOD)** and the **limit of quantitation (LOQ)**. The LOD is the same as the PDT; it is the minimum intensity a peak must have in order for the fragment analyzer to recognize it as a true peak and include it in the reported data. The LOQ represents a peak intensity at which the intensity of the peak is far enough above the noise that the peak's intensity is not influenced significantly by the noise. Because the noise's contribution to these peaks' intensities is minimal, the intensity of each of these peaks reflects the amount of PCR product that generated that peak, which in turn reflects the amount of template material for that allele that was present in the PCR (assuming the parameters of the PCR were chosen appropriately). For example, the fact that the analyst can use the intensities of these peaks as a reflection of the amount of starting material enables him or her to test the hypothesis that a high-intensity allele in a mixed sample reflects the fact that two or more contributors share that allele.

In order to understand the means by which analytical chemists usually determine the LOD and LOQ for an analytical system, you must consider a couple of points about descriptive statistics: the **normal distribution** (aka the "bell curve"), the **mean** (aka the "average") and the **standard deviation (SD)**. Figure 3.4 illustrates a normal distribution with a mean of 100 and an SD of 10. The lower line of numbers on the X axis illustrates the raw

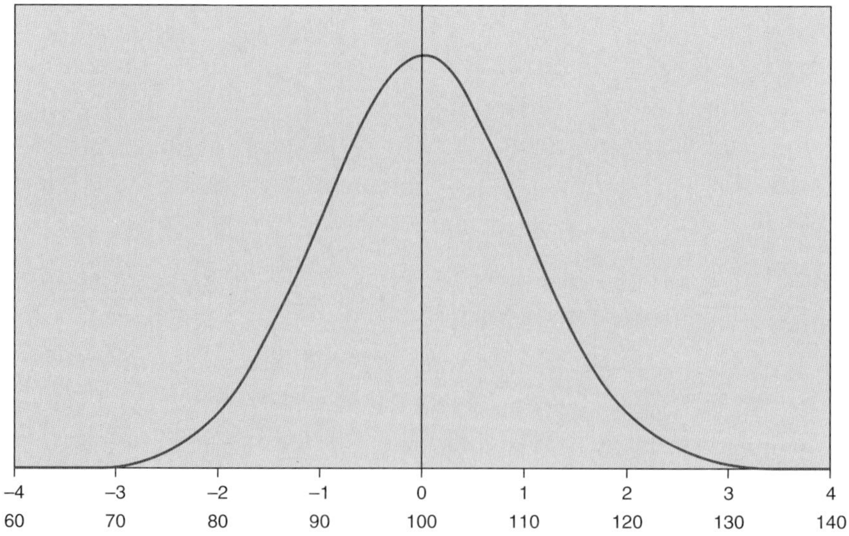

FIGURE 3.4
A standard normal distribution with mean = 100 and SD = 10. The mean is at 0 SD. The X axis illustrates the values that lie 1, 2, 3 and 4 SD away from the mean. From http://www.tushar-mehta.com.

scores of the distribution, whereas the upper line of numbers on the X axis illustrates how many SD away from the mean any value in the distribution lies. For example, a value of 70 lies 3 SD below the mean (mean − 3 SD), while a value of 120 lies 2 SD above the mean (mean + 2 SD).

Most people have a good understanding of the concept of the mean. Most people also understand the concept of the normal distribution, even if they are not comfortable talking about the statistical parameters associated with it. Few people would have trouble recognizing that, if you measured the height of a large number of people, you would find that many people's heights were close to the average height, and that the farther away from the average height you went, the fewer people you would find at that height. Most people can even envision the bell-shaped curve that would describe the data. Just like human height, if you illustrated the intensities of the peaks that constitute the fragment analyzer's background noise, you would see a normal distribution of RFUs. Most of the noise peaks' intensities would be close to the average peak's intensity, and the farther above or below the average peak intensity you looked, the fewer peaks you would find that had that intensity.

The SD is exactly what the words denote: the SD is the standard, or average, deviation from the mean. If you measured how far each value in your distribution lies away from the mean, the average of those distances would be the SD. Furthermore, it is a characteristic feature of the standard normal distribution that 68.27% of the values in the distribution fall within ± 1 SD of the mean, 95.45% of the values fall within ± 2 SD of the mean and 99.73% of the values in the distribution fall within ± 3 SD of the mean. Therefore, analytical chemists usually set their LOD at a level equal to the noise peaks' mean + 3 SD. Because 99.73% of the noise peaks fall within ± 3 SD of the mean, only 0.27% of the noise peaks' intensities fall outside (mean ± 3 SD). This means that 0.135% lie below (mean − 3 SD), while 0.135% lie above (mean + 3 SD). Because only 0.135% of the noise peaks' intensities lie above (mean + 3 SD), setting the LOD at (mean + 3 SD) enables the analyst to be 99.865% certain that, if a peak is detected, it is a true signal and not background noise. The LOQ is usually set at (mean + 10 SD) of the noise peaks' values. At this level of intensity, the noise contributes a miniscule percentage of the peak's intensity, and the peak's intensity can therefore be used to indicate the amount of PCR product present, which in turn can be used to estimate the amount of starting DNA present (if the PCR is designed appropriately).

[25] Gilder et al., 2007.

Given that the legal system often prefers to follow closely in the footsteps of the established sciences, it is curious that the LOD for forensic DNA tests has been developed in a manner that is so different from the manner in which the LOD is usually determined for analytical chemistry procedures. In fact, for most analyses 150 RFU is considerably greater than 3 SD above the mean noise peak's intensity, and in some analyses it is greater than 10 SD above the noise's mean. It is easy to see how setting the PDT that high can cause the analyst to miss true allele peaks that have low intensities. In Gilder and colleagues' study,[25] when a mixed sample containing a 10 : 1 ratio of material from the major contributor versus the minor contributor was analyzed, setting the LOD to the customary 150 RFU caused the analyst to miss 11 of the 17 alleles in the minor contributor's profile. Setting the LOD to (mean + 3 SD), however, captured the entire minor contributor's profile and still excluded all the noise. Furthermore, when run-specific LODs were established for 150 runs (50 positive controls, 50 negative controls and 50 reagent blanks), they ranged from 10.9 to 53.0 RFU—far below the 150 RFU convention. It is clear from these data that a PDT of 150 RFU is far too conservative and may cause the analyst to miss some of the true allele peaks in the evidence. The best means of determining the PDT for a sample involves using the baseline noise data from either that sample, control samples that were run along with that sample, or recent casework and validation studies, and setting the LOD to (mean + 3 SD) and the LOQ to (mean + 10 SD). The NCBI now offers a free software program entitled BatchExtract that enables the analyst to calculate the LOD and LOQ for an analysis in a manner more consistent with other analytical chemistry methods.

RECAPPING THE MAIN POINTS

1. Although all the parameters of the PCR should be examined, the three parameters that are most likely to be manipulated by the analyst are the amount of DNA that is put into the reaction, the temperature that is in effect during the annealing stages of the PCR cycles and the number of PCR cycles in the protocol.
2. Extra peaks can appear in the data as a result of stutter peaks, pull-up peaks, non-template-directed nucleotide addition, a lower-than-optimal annealing temperature or the use of too many PCR cycles.
3. The analyst programs several operating parameters into the fragment analyzer, any of which may influence the outcome of the analysis. Chief among them is the analyzer's peak detection threshold, which determines the intensity a peak must have in order to be detected by the fragment analyzer. There is a growing controversy over whether the customary settings for the PDT are appropriate.

HYBRIDIZATION SPECIFICITY IN DOT-BLOT TESTS

Recall that the DQA1 and Polymarker^{TM} tests involve hybridization of single-stranded oligonucleotide probes to the PCR products from an individual's DNA. Also recall that the probe binds to a complementary sequence in the target DNA and that the efficiency of this binding is affected by the temperature at which the hybridization takes place. The higher the temperature, the more difficult it is for binding to occur, even between perfect matches. The lower the temperature, the greater the risk that probes will bind to targets where the sequence is only partially complementary. This is a particularly important concern for the DQA1 and Polymarker assays. The sequences of the different alleles of the genes that are included in these tests differ from each other by only one or a few nucleotides. Therefore, small variations in the hybridization temperature can significantly change the results obtained from these tests.

In the DQA1 test, it is not uncommon to see faint dots at the "All 1" allele probe, even in a sample from someone who does not have any of the "1" alleles in his or her DNA. The "All 1" probe is supposed to bind only to the 1.1, 1.2 and 1.3 alleles of DQA1, but it is similar enough in sequence to some of the other alleles to exhibit **cross-hybridization** and yield a detectable dot, especially if the hybridization temperature is kept low. In order to differentiate between a true "All 1" dot and an artifactual one, the DQA1 test uses a control (C) dot, which contains a mixture of all the probes, each in a very low quantity[26] (see Figure 2.5). Because the C dot contains all the probes, all samples will show a dot at the C position. Because the probes are present in limited amounts, the C dots will be of relatively low intensity. Any dots that are less intense than the C dot are considered artifactual dots; only those dots whose intensity exceeds that of the C dot are considered to reflect true alleles. The only exception to this involves mixed samples that are known to contain very limited amounts of material from a minor contributor. In these cases, the fainter dots may be considered to represent the minor contributor's genotype for that marker.

Because the sequences of the different alleles of the DQA1 gene are so similar, some of the probes used in the DQA1 test will bind to more than one of the known alleles. Consequently, some genotypes cannot be definitively differentiated from other genotypes. For example, someone with

[26] The Polymarker^{TM} test labels their control dot with an "S."

either a heterozygous 1.2, 4.2 genotype or a heterozygous 1.2, 4.3 genotype would show hybridization to the following probes: All 1, All 4, 1.2/1.3/4, All Except 1.3, and 4.2/4.3 (see Figure 2.5).

RECAPPING THE MAIN POINTS

1. There is an optimal temperature range within which a probe binds efficiently and specifically to its one desired target sequence. Lower temperatures encourage binding to imperfect matches and can deceive the analyst into thinking that he or she has detected alleles that do not exist. Higher temperatures may prevent an allele from being detected.
2. Because of cross-hybridization between probes, it is not uncommon to see faint dots at the "All 1" allele probe, even in a sample from someone who does not have any of the "1" alleles.
3. The control spots in the DQA1 and Polymarker™ test strips help the analyst differentiate between true alleles of a minor contributor and artifacts due to cross-hybridization of probes.
4. Because the probes used in the DQA1 test are not completely specific for one target, certain combinations of alleles may leave the analyst unable to unambiguously assign a single genotype to the sample.

REFERENCES AND ADDITIONAL READINGS

Akane, A., Matsubara, K., Nakamura, H., Takahashi, S. and Kimura, K. (1994) *Journal of Forensic Sciences*, 39, 362–372.

Balding, D.J. and Nichols, R.A. (1994) *Forensic Science International*, 64, 125–140.

Balogh, M.K., Burger, J., Bender, K., Schneider, P.M. and Alt, K.W. (2003) *Forensic Science International*, 137, 188–195.

Budowle, B., Giusti, A.M., Waye, J.S., Baechtel, F.S., Fourney, R.M., Adams, D.E., Presley, L.A., Deadman, H.A. and Monson, K.L. (1991) *American Journal of Human Genetics*, 48, 841–855.

Gilder, J.R., Doom, T.E., Inman, K. and Krane, D.E. (2007) *Journal of Forensic Sciences*, 52(1), 97–101.

Gill, P., Sparkes, B. and Buckleton, J.S. (1998) *Forensic Science International*, 95, 213–224.

Haines, J.L., Korf, B.R., Morton, C.C., Seidman, C.E., Seidman, J.G. and Smith, D.R. (eds.). (2007) *Current Protocols in Human Genetics*. Hoboken, NJ: John Wiley.

Justice Department Investigation of FBI Laboratory: Executive Summary, 61 (April 16, 1997) *Crim. L. Rep.* (BNA), 2017.

Ladd, C., Adamowicz, M.S., Bourke, M.T., Scherczinger, C.A. and Lee, H.C. (1999) *Journal of Forensic Sciences*, 44(6), 1270–1272.

Lander, E. (1991) *Science*, 254, 1921–1923.

Larkin, A. and Harbison, S. (1999) *International Journal of Legal Medicine*, 112(6), 388–390.

Lewontin, R.C. and Hartl, D.L. (1991) *Science*, 254, 1745.

Magnuson, V.L., Ally, D.S., Nylund, S.J., Karanjawala, Z.E., Rayman, J.B., Knapp, J.I., Lowe, A.L., Ghosh, S. and Collins, F.S. (1996) *BioTechniques*, 21(4), 700–709.

National Research Council (1992) *DNA Technology in Forensic Science*. Washington, DC: National Academy Press.

National Research Council (1996) *The Evaluation of Forensic DNA Evidence*. Washington, DC: National Academy Press.

Shewale, J.G., Richey, S.L. and Sinha, S.K. (2000) *Forensic Science Communications*, 2(4). Available online at: http://www.fbi.gov/hq/lab/fsc/backissu/oct2000/shewale.htm.

van Oorschot, R.A.H. and Jones, M. (1997) *Nature*, 387, 767.

Wallin, J.M., Buoncristiani, M.R., Lazaruk, K.D., Fildes, N., Holt, C.L., Walsh, P.S. (1998) *Journal of Forensic Sciences*, 43(4), 854–70.

Walsh, P.S., Erlich, H.A. and Higuchi, R. (1992) *PCR Methods and Applications*, 1, 241–250.

Weir, B.S. (1992) *Proceedings of the National Academy of Sciences (USA)*, 89, 11654–11659.

Weir, B.S. (1993) *American Journal of Human Genetics*, 52, 437–440.

CHAPTER 4

Population Genetics, Probability Calculations and the Proper Interpretation of the Evidence

THE COMMON LOGICAL FALLACIES

Of all the aspects of the evidence-generating process, the application of population genetics and probability theory to determine the **random match probability (RMP)** has generated the most controversy and remains the most difficult for everyone—legal professionals and laypeople alike—to understand. The RMP corresponds to the probability that an individual who was selected at random from a population of unrelated individuals whose racial heritage matches that of the defendant will have the same DNA profile as the defendant (and the evidence).[1] If the defense proffers the hypothesis that the defendant was not involved in the crime, but his or her DNA profile matches that of the evidence by coincidence, the RMP is also the probability of that hypothesis being true.

Very few people have an instinctive understanding of population genetics and probability theory, and it is common for jurors to commit logical fallacies when they are trying to use the RMP to decide the probative value of the DNA evidence. Jurors are not the only people who are confused on this point, however. There are numerous examples of misstatements by law enforcement personnel, litigators, judges and even expert witnesses regarding the statistical interpretation of DNA evidence.[2]

Some of the common fallacies favor the prosecution, while others favor the defense. Some jurors exaggerate the significance of the DNA evidence by equating the match between the DNA profiles with the defendant being

CONTENTS

The Common Logical Fallacies

Databanks and Databases

Allele Frequencies, Genotype Probabilities and the Product Rule for Independent Events

The Principles of Population Genetics that Impact Forensic DNA Calculations

Applying the Product Rule—Compensating for Population Substructure and Possible Allele Dropout

The Likelihood Ratio (LR) Allows the Analyst to Compare the Strength of Competing Hypotheses

(continues)

The Application of Bayes' Theorem to Paternity Disputes

Recommended Procedure for Analyzing Mixed Samples

References and Additional Readings

the source of the evidence (sometimes called a "source probability error"), or worse yet with the defendant's guilt (a "guilt probability error"). There are several fallacies inherent in this reasoning. First, a reported match may not be a true match. Evidence handlers can mislabel samples, and sub-optimal samples can be very difficult to interpret properly, even for experienced analysts. In spite of the undeniable fallibility of human workers, many experts testified during the early DNA years that it is impossible to get an incorrect result on a forensic DNA test. Some commentators believe that statements such as these are misleading enough to constitute reversible error. Unfortunately, they dominated courtroom thinking for a few years, until a few human errors and the terrible quality of some of the DNA evidence that was presented in those early years made people realize that DNA evidence, though highly useful, is also fallible.

The second problem with equating a match between DNA profiles with the defendant's guilt involves the fact that even a true match may be coincidental; the crime may have been committed by someone else who happens to have the same DNA profile as the defendant. The RMP addresses this question, but in many instances even expert witnesses have misinterpreted the meaning of the RMP. The RMP tells you the probability that another person, randomly selected from the larger population, would have the same DNA profile as the defendant (and the matching evidence). Experts have testified in a number of cases, however, that the RMP represents the probability that the sample could have come from someone other than the defendant, or that an RMP of 1 in 10 million means that you would have to test 10 million more people to find a matching profile. Following this fallacious reasoning, in a few cases in which the RMP was 1 in a number greater than the population of the Earth, experts have erroneously claimed that the test definitively established the defendant as the source of the sample and that no one else on Earth could have the same DNA profile. Statements that definitively identify an individual as the source of the evidence constitute particularly egregious errors. As discussed later in this chapter, unless you have a database that contains the DNA profiles of everyone on Earth, it is impossible to state definitively that no one else possesses the DNA profile in question. Furthermore, these statements do not allow for the possibility that an error could have been made during the collection, identification and analysis of the samples. Given the well-publicized cases in which

[1] The **exclusion probability (EP)** is a related, and sometimes useful, concept. The EP represents the portion of the population that is excluded by the DNA evidence, and can be calculated simply as 1 – RMP.

[2] For example, *People v. Robinson*, 317 N.Y.S.2d 19, 1970; *United States v. Massey*, 594 F.2d 676, 681, 8th Cir., 1979. Also see Koehler, 1993, note 24, for a list of cases in which litigators, witnesses, and judges have misspoken about the interpretation of DNA evidence.

mistakes were made in the analysis or in which forensic scientists acted unethically, it should be easy to attack the credibility of statements that deny the possibility of human error or misconduct.

The third logical fallacy inherent in equating a match between DNA profiles with the defendant's guilt involves the fact that, even when the defendant is the source of the evidence, there are other explanations for the defendant's sample being at the crime scene apart from the defendant having committed the crime. The defendant's sample could have been left at the scene innocently before or after the crime was committed, or the defendant may have been present, even guilty of abetting the perpetrator, but not guilty of the crime with which he or she is charged.

One of the common logical fallacies that people commit when interpreting probabilistic evidence has been dubbed the prosecutor's fallacy.[3] When a match is found between the crime scene evidence profile and the profile of a suspect, calculating the RMP answers the question "What is the probability that the DNA profile of some other person who was randomly selected from the larger reference population would match the DNA profile from the evidence?" This question assumes that the defendant is innocent, and that the match between his or her DNA profile and that of the evidence is a coincidence. The prosecutor's fallacy involves interpreting the RMP to represent the probability that the defendant is actually innocent despite the matching DNA profiles. This question assumes that a DNA match is proof of guilt, and the usually infinitesimal RMP represents the probability that the defendant might not be guilty. This assumption is not only fallacious, but it is highly prejudicial to the defendant. The match between the DNA profiles is only one piece of evidence that establishes the perpetrator's guilt. For example, if the defendant can be proven to have been elsewhere during the time a crime was committed, he or she is innocent of the crime, and there is some other explanation for the match between his or her DNA profile and that of the evidence, even if the RMP is infinitesimal. Unfortunately, science has an aura of authority and infallibility for many laypeople, and most jurors will accept an expert witness's conclusions when the expert presents a calculated number to support his or her assertions. As the Minnesota Supreme Court has warned.[4] "Testimony expressing opinions or conclusions in terms of statistical probabilities can make the uncertain seem all but proven, and suggest, by quantification, satisfaction of the requirement that guilt be

[3] Thompson and Schumann, 1987.

[4] *State v. Carlson*, 267 N.W. 2d 170, 176, Minn. 1978.

established 'beyond a reasonable doubt.'" Mock jury research suggests that, when either the defense or prosecution makes a fallacious statement regarding the interpretation of DNA evidence, very few jurors recognize the statement as fallacious, and most jurors' decisions conform to the fallacy.[5]

[5] Goodman, 1992; Dann et al., 2006.

The prosecutor's fallacy is often referred to as the "fallacy of the transposed conditional." This means that the decisions to be made in a criminal trial involve conditional probabilities—for example, "What is the probability of A given that B is true?" The prosecutor's fallacy lies in switching the position of the hypothesis and the conditional information. When a match has been found between the crime scene evidence and the defendant, the RMP answers the question "What is the probability of finding a match between the defendant's DNA profile and that of the evidence given the assumption that the defendant is innocent?" The prosecutor's fallacy lies in transposing the hypothesis and the conditional evidence, and interpreting the RMP as if it was answering the question "What is the probability of the defendant being innocent given that a match has been found between the defendant's DNA profile and that of the evidence?"

The prosecutor's fallacy can be illustrated by applying the same fallacious logic to another problem. For example, suppose that all doctors drive a white car and that 10% of the population drive a white car. You are told that a person drives a white car, and you are asked what the probability is that this person is a doctor. Driving a white car is the trait in question. The fact that the person in question drives a white car is analogous to the defendant having the DNA profile that matches the profile from the evidence. This is the fact that you are using to establish the probability that the person is a doctor (being a doctor is analogous to being guilty). The fact that 10% of the population drives a white car is analogous to having the DNA profile in question associated with an RMP of 1 in 10 or 10%. Therefore, applying the prosecutor's fallacy that the RMP equals the probability of the defendant not being guilty, you would use the fact that 10% of the population shares the trait (drives a white car) to assume that there was a 10% chance of the person in question not being a doctor (not being a doctor is analogous to not being guilty). You would therefore conclude that there is a 90% probability that the person is a doctor.

This reasoning is fallacious because it does not take into account the prior probability of being a doctor. In order to know what the probability is that the person who drives a white car is a doctor, you need to know what percent of the population are doctors. If 1% of the population are doctors, all of whom drive white cars, and 10% of the population drive white cars, then 9% of the population drive white cars but are not doctors. The probability that a person who drives a white car is a doctor is therefore 1 in 10, or 10%. On the other hand, if 8% of the population are doctors, all of whom drive white cars, and 10% of the population drive white cars, then 2% of the population drive white cars but are not doctors. The probability that a person who drives a white car is a doctor is therefore 8 in 10, or 80%. By ignoring the base rate of doctors in the population, you arrive at an inaccurate estimate of the probability that the person who drives a white car is a doctor.

This "base rate fallacy" can be further illustrated by an example that illustrates a common fallacy committed when faced with eyewitness evidence. Suppose the population of a city is 85% white and 15% black. Suppose further that a murder has been committed and that an eyewitness has reported seeing a black man running from the scene. When you test this eyewitness's accuracy under conditions similar to those that existed on the night of the murder, he or she correctly identifies the race of a fleeing man 80% of the time but misidentifies the man's race 20% of the time. Given that the eyewitness has reported seeing a black man fleeing, what is the probability that the fleeing man was actually black?

Given the witness's 80% correct identification rate during tests, most people will claim that there is an 80% chance that the fleeing man was actually black. This, however, fails to take into account the low base rate of black men in the city. Table 4.1 illustrates the proper way in which to calculate the probability that the fleeing man was actually black. Note that there are four possible responses from the witness (and therefore the probabilities in the four cells of the table add up to 100%). The witness can see either a black man or a white man, and either correctly report what he or she saw or incorrectly report it. From these four possibilities, there are two circumstances under which the eyewitness will report seeing a black man fleeing: the witness may correctly report seeing a black man or the witness may see a white man and mistakenly report him as a black man. Most people understand that the probability of a correct witness report depends on the witness's general accuracy (the probabilities of a correct versus incorrect report are seen across the top of the table). What

Table 4.1 Probabilities of Correct and Incorrect Identification.

		The witness reported Correctly (0.80)	The witness reported Incorrectly (0.20)
The fleeing man was actually	Black (0.15)	12%	3%
	White (0.85)	68%	17%

most people do not understand, however, is that the probability of the witness having correctly reported seeing a black man also depends on the base rate of black people in the city (indicated along the left side of the table).

The probability of the witness correctly reporting seeing a black man fleeing is calculated by multiplying the probability that a citizen of the city is black (15%, or 0.15) by the probability of a correct identification (80%, or 0.80). Multiplying these probabilities together produces a 12% (or 0.12) probability that the witness correctly reported seeing a black man fleeing. By the same logic, the probability of the witness incorrectly reporting seeing a black man when he or she actually saw a white man is calculated by multiplying the probability that a citizen of the city is white (85%) by the probability of an incorrect identification (20%). This probability is 17% (or 0.17). Because of the low base rate of black people in the city, there is actually a greater chance of the report being incorrect (17%) than being correct (12%). When you consider that the witness has identified the fleeing man as black, and calculate the probability of a correct versus incorrect report, this works out to a 59% probability that the report was incorrect [$0.17/(0.17 + 0.12) = 0.59$]. Because of the low base rate of black people in the city, there is only a 41% probability that the eyewitness has correctly reported seeing a black man fleeing, not the 80% probability that most people would assume.

A relative of the prosecutor's fallacy is the fallacy that the RMP equals the probability that someone else in the larger population will match the defendant's DNA profile. As discussed later in this chapter, this is a particularly important issue when the defendant has been identified via a databank search. Few people seem to be intuitively aware that the probability of finding another matching DNA profile in a population is strongly dependent on the size of the population in which one searches. If the RMP for a DNA profile is 1 in 50,000, you would not expect to see another matching profile in a database containing 1,000 profiles. You would expect to see approximately 40 other matching profiles in a database containing 2 million profiles, however. Even though the RMP is the same in both cases, the probability that someone in the databank will also match the DNA evidence is considerably different.

Another fallacy that overstates the significance of the DNA evidence is the fallacy that the denominator (bottom number) of the RMP equals the number of people who must be tested before another matching profile will be found, or that only one matching profile will be found if that number of additional people are tested. This fallacy overstates the significance of the evidence because it overestimates the number of people who must be tested before one would expect to find another matching profile.

In order to demonstrate this fallacy, we need to take a "reverse logic" approach to our mathematical calculation. Because there are only two possible outcomes—a match or a nonmatch—in order to calculate the probability that any single individual will not match the DNA profile in question, we subtract the probability that the individual will match the profile (the RMP—let's call it 1/X for now) from 1. Therefore, the probability that any single individual will not match the DNA profile in question is $1 - (1/X)$. Because this question applies independently to every individual (whether one person's DNA profile matches the evidence has no influence on whether another unrelated person's DNA profile matches the evidence), if you test N individuals, in order to calculate the probability that nobody in the group will match the profile, you multiply the probability that a single individual will not match by itself N times, producing $[1 - (1/X)]^N$ (see below for a discussion of the product rule).

This calculation may seem complicated, but take a moment to examine how the probability of finding a match changes as the values of 1/X and N change. When the profile is rare, the RMP (1/X) is small, and $1 - (1/X)$ is less than 1 but very close to 1. When you multiply repeatedly by a number less than 1, the product decreases at every step. The closer the number is to 1, however, the smaller the decrease in the product is at each step.

[6] Thompson and Schumann, 1987.

Therefore, if $1 - (1/X)$ is close to 1 (because the profile is rare), it will take a large number of multiplications (i.e., N must be large) to get the product down to where the probability that nobody will match the profile in question is less than 0.50. If, however, the profile is relatively common, $1/X$ is relatively large, and $1 - (1/X)$ is considerably less than 1. As you multiply $1 - (1/X)$ by itself repeatedly, not only do you begin with a smaller number, but the number also gets reduced much more quickly because it is being multiplied by a much smaller number. It therefore takes a much smaller N to reach the point at which $[1 - (1/X)]^N < 0.50$.

For a numerical example, imagine a DNA profile with an RMP of 1/100, or 0.01. This fallacy would lead one to expect that an additional 100 people must be tested before another matching profile would be obtained. In contrast, however, if you use the formula $p = [1 - (1/X)]^N$ to calculate the probability that none of the individuals tested will match the profile in question, if you test 69 people ($N = 69$), the probability that none of the profiles will match the profile in question is less than 50%. Therefore, if you test 69 or more people, you have a greater probability of finding another matching profile than of not finding another matching profile. The fallacy overstates the strength of the evidence because it overestimates the number of people who must be tested before another match is likely to be seen.

Another common fallacy has been dubbed the "defense attorney's fallacy."[6] Like the prosecutor's fallacy, the defense attorney's fallacy ignores the presence of the rest of the evidence. This fallacy, however, leads the juror to undervalue the DNA evidence. The defense attorney's fallacy implies that all people who possess the matching DNA profile are equally likely to be guilty of the crime. It ignores the fact that the other evidence helps restrict the actual pool of suspects. For example, imagine a case in which the RMP of the DNA profile in question is 1 in 1,000. If the crime was committed in a city with a population of 1 million people, the defense might argue (legitimately) that one would expect to find approximately 1,000 people in that city whose DNA profile matched that of the defendant. The defense might then go on to argue (fallaciously) that, because the defendant is 1 in 1,000 people who have the DNA profile in question, there is a 999 to 1 chance that the defendant is not guilty. In committing this fallacy, the defense ignores the fact that the vast majority of the 999 other people who possess the DNA profile in question will be excluded from the suspect list because they were elsewhere when the crime was committed or because they do not fit the eyewitness's descriptions of the perpetrator. The non-DNA evidence will usually guide investigators to restrict the pool of suspects first, before any suspects are subjected to the DNA testing. There will rarely be more than one individual who was in the vicinity of the crime scene at the appropriate time, had the opportunity to commit the crime, fits the other evidence in the case and possesses the DNA profile in question.

DATABANKS AND DATABASES

The Difference Between Databanks and Databases

There are two different types of repositories for DNA profile data. Many commentators refer to both types as databases, but for the sake of clarity, we will refer to them as databanks and databases.[7] Databanks and databases are very different in their content and in the way in which they are used. Databanks are used to investigate crimes and identify suspects, whereas databases are used to provide estimates of how rare a particular DNA profile is in the larger population.

[7] Other commentators have used these two terms to distinguish between the two types of repositories, for example, Rudin and Inman (2002).

The DNA Identification Act of 1994 authorized the U.S. Attorney General to provide grant money for states to establish DNA databanks. There are three different types of databanks, each of which contains the profiles of people who were selected by a strictly defined set of criteria. All states maintain two types of databanks: one that contains the profiles from people who have been convicted of one of a list of specified crimes, and one that contains profiles from evidence samples that were obtained from previously committed crimes. In addition, some states maintain a third type of databank containing samples voluntarily contributed by relatives of missing persons. Databanks contain extensive personal information on the individuals corresponding to the profiles; they are designed to allow law enforcement officers to locate the individual if there is a match between an evidence sample and an entry in a databank.

Databanks are invaluable tools for law enforcement agencies. They allow investigators to reach across space and time to link serial crimes together, or to solve "cold cases" in which they have already exhausted all their leads. A serial criminal can no longer delay or avoid discovery by moving from state to state to commit his or her crimes. In fact, doing so only provides law enforcement officers with stronger circumstantial evidence that the person is responsible for those crimes. In addition, recidivists can often be identified as soon as they commit their first crime after being released from prison.

States differ widely with respect to their criteria for inclusion in their databanks. There is also considerable variability between states with respect to the degree to which DNA databank information is safeguarded. Some states restrict access to their databank information to law enforcement agencies, and many have made the unauthorized release of DNA databank information a criminal offense. In fact, in some states individuals whose profiles are in databanks are not even entitled to access this information for purposes unrelated to their trial.[8] Other states, however, have statutes that allow DNA databank information to be accessed by public officials for purposes other than law enforcement.[9]

It is obvious that law enforcement agencies would benefit greatly from the presence of databanks that contained profiles from as many members of the criminal element as possible. In states such as Virginia, for example, which includes samples from people convicted of certain nonviolent crimes in their databank, more than half the databank "hits" that have helped solve violent crimes for which there were no suspects have come from profiles of individuals who had previously been convicted of nonviolent crimes such as burglary. In recent years, a great push has been made to expand both the content and the use of the DNA databanks. The DNA Analysis Backlog Elimination Act of 2000 authorized the collection of DNA samples from prisoners, parolees and others on supervised release after committing one of a list of qualifying crimes. The USA Patriot Act of 2001 added terrorist acts to the list of eligible crimes, and the Justice for All Act of 2004 further expanded the list of eligible crimes to all felonies. In addition, states such as Louisiana, California, South Dakota and Virginia now allow the collection of DNA samples from people who have merely been arrested for one of a list of crimes.

It is unclear how far this trend toward expanding the databanks will go before they are reined in by concerns about civil liberties and individual privacy. Some commentators, such as former mayor of New York City (and current 2008 presidential candidate) Rudy Giuliani, have advocated taking DNA samples from all babies born in American hospitals. This is

[8] Ex. *Hull v. Pennsylvania State Police*, 768 A.2d 909, Pa. 2001.

[9] Steinhardt, 2004.

hardly a far-fetched scheme; the mechanism for doing so already exists. All babies born in America have a blood sample taken at birth. The blood is tested for biochemical metabolites that indicate the presence of a number of disorders of metabolism, such as phenylketonuria or congenital adrenal hyperplasia. A portion of that sample could easily be used for DNA testing. Having a databank of all American-born persons would obviously be of great benefit, not only in violent crime investigations but also in cases of missing persons, inheritance disputes, immigration cases and mass casualties such as airline crashes and terrorist acts. The obvious concerns over privacy and civil liberties, however, have caused many commentators to urge caution when deciding which samples to include in the databanks.[10]

One of the more interesting observations on this subject has come from the prominent population geneticist David Balding.[11] Balding has pointed out that compiling a databank containing profiles from all individuals born in a country is ethically more acceptable than allowing potentially biased agents such as law enforcement personnel and state legislators to determine whose DNA profiles are entered into the databank. In addition, as discussed in Chapter 1, an individual's allele status for the markers that are used for forensic testing does not indicate anything about the individual's long-term health status, personality or beliefs. This limits the use of the information to personal identification, which should ease people's minds regarding the potential use of that information to deny them insurance or jobs. Given the ever-increasing fear that personal information stored in databases is vulnerable to hackers, however, and the possibility that some association between a marker's genotype and health may be discovered in the future, many people are reluctant to have any personal genetic information stored in a database, regardless of the current guarantees against misuse of that information.

In contrast to the extensive personal data stored in databanks, databases usually contain only DNA profiles and the race and gender of the corresponding individuals. Databases are used to indicate how rare the DNA profile in question is in the relevant larger population.[12] The ideal database would contain the profiles from every person in the country. A database such as this will obviously never be compiled, so forensic analysts must use the data that have been collected, from a tiny portion of the population, to estimate the frequency of an allele in the larger population.

[10] Land, 2005; Maclin, 2006.

[11] Balding, 2005.

[12] The relevant larger population will vary according to the circumstances of the crime. If there is no evidence regarding the physical characteristics of the perpetrator, the relevant population may be the entire population of the city in which the crime was committed. If there were 12 members of a street gang present when the crime was committed, and nobody else, the relevant larger population is merely those 12 gang members.

Because the allele frequencies for STR markers can vary between the races, separate databases are maintained for different races such as Caucasians, African Americans, Hispanics, Asians and Native Americans. Any individual who is a member of that race may be included in that race's database; an ideal database contains thousands of profiles from people selected randomly from as many different geographic regions as possible. When a match is obtained between the DNA profile of an evidence sample and the DNA profile of a suspect, knowing the frequencies of the profile's alleles in the larger population allows one to calculate the RMP. The RMP allows one to assign the appropriate weight to the match between the evidence sample and the defendant, based on the rarity of the DNA profile in the population to which the defendant belongs.

Databases are intended to reflect the data that would be obtained from a random sampling of the population at large. Because some marker alleles can exhibit different frequencies in different racial and ethnic groups, in order to assess the weight of the evidence accurately, one must base one's RMP calculations on allele frequencies from a database that contains people whose racial and ethnic heritage is similar to the defendant's. Each of the major races contains several ethnic subgroups within it, however, and the different ethnic subgroups within one major race may have different marker allele frequencies. It would be ideal to have separate databases for as many different ethnic subgroups as possible. It would also be ideal if each racial database consisted of hundreds of thousands of samples from unrelated people who were randomly selected from all the places in which people belonging to that race live. Unfortunately, however, most databases are "convenience samples" and consist of profiles from individuals who were available to the collector through his or her normal professional activities. Few databases are compiled by a truly random sampling from many different geographic areas, and few have been rigorously scrutinized to ensure that none of the individuals in the database are related to each other.

The situation can be further complicated if the defendant is of mixed ethnic heritage. In cases in which the defendant has an unusual mixture of ethnic heritages, there may not be any data available from individuals with a similar mixed ethnic heritage. In this case, it is necessary to present several RMPs, each one calculated from a database that reflects a portion of the defendant's ethnic heritage.

The case of *Dayton v. State*[13] illustrates how using an inappropriate database can significantly skew the calculation of the RMP and result in prejudice against the defendant. Andrew Dayton was charged with sexual assault and burglary, and his initial trial ended in a hung jury. Dayton was an Athabascan Indian, a group for which Alaska had no DNA profile database at the time of the original trial. Between the initial trial and the retrial, however, the state compiled a database of profiles from Athabascan Indians, for the purpose of Dayton's retrial and other investigations, present and future. The RMPs that the prosecution presented during the retrial illustrate how different the RMPs can be when different databases are used. The RMP was 1 in 22 billion for North American Caucasians, 1 in 6 billion for African Americans, 1 in 413 million for Hispanics and 1 in 2.5 million for Athabascan Indians. There was an almost 10,000-fold difference in the RMP that was obtained by using the North American Caucasian database versus the Athabascan Indian database.

[13] 54 P.3d 817, Alaska App. 2002.

Another issue that arises when the suspect belongs to a small, isolated subgroup is the possibility that the database that does exist contains an unusually high frequency of people who are related to each other. For example, in *Dayton v. State*, Dayton attempted to obtain the names of all the individuals whose DNA profiles were contained in the Athabascan database. Dayton argued that there was a relatively high probability that he was related to several of these individuals and that this would prejudice the RMP calculation against him. The court correctly ruled, however, that if the Athabascan database did contain several of Dayton's relatives, this would cause the analyst to overestimate the frequency of Dayton's DNA profile in the Athabascan population and produce a spuriously large RMP that favored Dayton. Dayton should have argued that the danger lay in the possibility that many of the individuals in the Athabascan database were related to each other but not to him. This would produce a spuriously low estimate of the frequency of Dayton's profile in the Athabascan population and would be prejudiced against him.

Challenges to DNA Databank Statutes Are Rarely Successful

The use of DNA databanks to investigate unsolved crimes raises a particular concern about the individual's protection against suspicionless search and seizure. The databank profile is collected in association with one crime but used to investigate other, unrelated crimes. Furthermore, there are usually no grounds to suspect anyone in the databank of having committed the second crime before his or her DNA profile is matched to the second crime's evidence. Because of the lack of probable cause, some defendants have argued that the use of databank information to investigate unsolved "cold cases" constitutes unreasonable search and seizure. These arguments have usually been rejected.[14] Even when the individual has not been convicted of a crime, courts generally agree with the *King* court that "once a person's blood sample has been obtained lawfully, he can no longer assert either privacy claims or unreasonable search and seizure arguments with respect to the use of that sample."

Courts routinely uphold DNA databank statutes. In most cases, the court has either justified collection of the samples under a "special needs" analysis or has considered collecting the samples reasonable given the totality of the circumstances.[15] Collecting DNA samples from statutorily specified classes of individuals (convicted offenders, arrestees, etc.) and maintaining them in a state or CODIS databank promote important government interests. These interests include deterring and prosecuting recidivist criminal conduct and prosecuting crimes accurately to convict the guilty and exonerate the innocent.[16] The constitutionality of taking samples from convicted offenders has been repeatedly upheld at both state and federal levels, in part, because government interests in solving past and future crimes have been held to outweigh both the minimal intrusion of the collection process and convicted offenders' and arrestees' limited privacy interests.[17] In addition, the constitutionality of obtaining samples from individuals who were convicted before the statutes were enacted has been upheld.[18] In criminal investigations, DNA databases facilitate the identification of individuals "to the practical exclusion of all others."[19].

A number of defendants who were convicted before the DNA databank statutes were enacted have argued that the statutes that require them to provide DNA databank samples violate their protection against ex post facto laws and/or deny the vested interest in liberty that is associated with mandatory parole laws.[20] These arguments are usually rejected. Most courts that have heard such challenges have agreed that it would violate ex post facto laws to require someone who was convicted before the statute was enacted to provide a sample in order to be eligible for parole, because that condition did not exist at the time of the conviction, when the conditions determining the individual's eligibility for parole were decided.

[14] For example, *Jones v. Murray*, 763 F. Supp. 842, W.D. Va. 1991; *People v. King*, 663 N.Y.S.2d 610 1997; *Barkley v. State*, 551 S.E.2d 131 N.C. App. 2001.

[15] For citations exemplifying both positions, see *U.S. v. Kincade*, 379 F.3d 813, 9th Cir., 2004, pp. 830–831.

[16] *U.S. v. Kincade*, 379 F.3d 813, 820 (9th Cir.) (2004); *State v. Arvin*, 812 N.E.2d 773 (Ill. App. 2004); *Tennessee v. Robinson*, 29 S.W.3d 476 (Tenn. 2000).

[17] *Green v. Berge*, 354 F.3d 675, 677 (7th Cir. 2004); *Velasquez v. Woods*, 39 F.3d 420 (5th Cir. 2003); *Jones v. Murray*, 962 F.3d 302 (4th Cir. 1992); *State v. Sure*, 94 P.3d 345 (2004); *People v. Farvin*, 812 N.E. 2d 773 (2004); *State v. Maass*, 64 P.3d 382 (2003); *Doles v. State*, 994 P.2d 315 (Wy. 1999).

[18] *U.S. v. Hook*, 471 F.3d 766 (7th Cir. 2006).

[19] See Thomas M. Femming, Annotation, *Admissibility of DNA Identification Evidence*, 84 A.L.R. 4th 313 at § 2[b] (1991).

Requiring the parolee to provide a sample or requiring the offender who will soon be paroled to provide a sample before he or she is released is not punitive, however. It does not alter the definition of criminal behavior, and does not change the punishment attached to the crime. It is merely a procedural change and therefore does not violate any ex post facto laws. Courts have also noted that requiring convicted offenders to provide DNA samples for a databank does not constitute double jeopardy, because the individual is not prosecuted twice for the same crime.[21]

There are few situations in which the courts will not be inclined to compel a DNA sample for the state's databank. Courts may make an exception in cases involving juvenile offenders. Unless a statute exists that specifically requires juveniles convicted of certain crimes to provide DNA databank samples, the court may be reluctant to order the juvenile defendant to submit a sample for the state's DNA databank.[22] When a statute requires convicted juveniles to provide DNA databank samples, however, courts routinely uphold it.[23] The confidentiality of juvenile court records is established by statute, and most courts feel that the state legislature has the right to make exceptions by passing laws requiring convicted juveniles to provide DNA databank samples. Courts will also occasionally decline to compel a sample from parolees who were convicted decades before. For example, the federal defender's office successfully challenged the California CODIS statute on behalf of Danny Miles, who was ordered to submit a sample for the state's DNA databank while out on parole after serving a sentence for committing a bank robbery almost 30 years earlier.

The Combined DNA Index System (CODIS)

The FBI's CODIS system was established by the DNA Identification Act of 1994.[24] The CODIS system interconnects local, state and federal law enforcement agency databanks across the country (approaching 2 million profiles) and allows all participants to search all the other jurisdictions' records in order to match the profiles from their evidence and suspects to profiles associated with crimes that were committed almost anywhere in America.[25] As of March 2005, the CODIS system has produced over 21,000 identifications and assisted in over 23,000 investigations.

The standard CODIS profile contains data from the 13 STR markers listed in Table 1.1. The average random match probability for a DNA profile containing the 13 CODIS markers is 1 in 1 trillion.[26] This provides

[20] For example, *Jones v. Murray*, 763 F. Supp. 842, W.D. Va. 1991; *Kellogg v. Travis*, 728 N.Y.S.2d 645, 2001.

[21] For example, *Kellogg v. Travis*, 728 N.Y.S.2d 645, 2001.

[22] For example, *Matter of Appeal in Maricopa County Juvenile Action*, 930 P.2d 496 Arz. App. 1996.

[23] For example, *Matter of Welfare of Z. P. B.*, 474 N.W.2d 651, Minn. App., 1991; *State ex rel. Juvenile Dept. v. Orozco*, 878 P.2d 432, Ore. App. 1994.

[24] This act was part of the Violent Crime Control and Law Enforcement Act of 1994.

[25] See http://www.fbi.gov/hq/lab/codis/index1.htm. Also see Bressler, 2002, for a listing of different states' statutes and level of participation in the CODIS database.

[26] Chakraborty et al., 1999.

very strong evidence that the defendant is the source of the crime scene evidence. The quantity 1 trillion is very hard for the average person's mind to fully envision. It may help a jury appreciate the rarity of such a profile if the expert asks them to consider counting to 1 trillion at the rate of one number every second—it would take them 31,710 years.

ALLELE FREQUENCIES, GENOTYPE PROBABILITIES AND THE PRODUCT RULE FOR INDEPENDENT EVENTS

Why We Must Use Statistics to Estimate the Rarity of a DNA Profile

In an ideal situation (from the forensic analyst's perspective), forensic analysts would have access to a databank containing DNA profiles from everyone in the country. With such a databank available, identifying the source of a piece of evidence would simply be a matter of determining how many people in the country have the matching DNA profile and establishing their whereabouts at the time the crime was committed. Such a databank will never exist, however. We will never have profiles from more than a small fraction of the country's population in the available databases. Consequently, we will never be able to definitively state whether someone other than the defendant possesses the DNA profile in question. Instead, the forensic analyst must always concede that it is possible that some other person with the same DNA profile could have left the evidence in question at the crime scene, and use the data that are available to estimate how likely that alternative explanation for the match between the defendant and the evidence is.

When a match is obtained between the DNA profiles of the evidence and a defendant, in order to determine the probative value of the match, one must present a statistical interpretation of the match that reflects how rare the DNA profile in question is. Without a statistical analysis, the prosecution can state the fact that the defendant's profile matches the evidence sample's profile, but it cannot indicate how strongly this fact should be considered by those whose task it is to determine guilt or innocence. If the profile is one that can be found in a majority of the individuals in the larger population, the match between the defendant's profile and that of the evidence does not strongly associate the defendant with the crime. On the other hand, if the profile in question is extremely rare, the match suggests strongly that the defendant is the source of the evidence and is therefore associated with the crime. Numerous courts have stressed the need for a statistical interpretation of the DNA evidence.[27] The most eloquent of these decisions was handed down in the case of *United States v. Yee*.[28] In this case, the court held that "[w]ithout the probability assessment, the jury does not know what to make of the fact that the patterns match: the jury does not know whether the patterns are as common as pictures with two eyes, or as unique as the Mona Lisa." The National Research Council of the National Academy of Sciences has issued two reports in which it has developed guidelines for the statistical interpretation of DNA evidence.[29] As discussed in Chapter 7, these standards have undergone considerable evolution. The 1996 NRC report and the Scientific Working Group on DNA Analysis Methods (SWGDAM) provide the current guidelines for the procedures used to analyze forensic DNA evidence.[30]

In order to understand the need for statistical analyses, one must appreciate just how polymorphic the STR markers that are used for forensic testing are. As Table 4.2 illustrates, between 15 and 89 alleles have been found in at least one individual for each of the 13 STRs in the FBI's CODIS databank. Because each person has two alleles for each marker (recall that the two alleles together constitute the individual's genotype for

[27] For example, *Commonwealth v. Daggett*, 622 N.E.2d 272, Mass., 1993; *State v. Cauthron*, 846 P.2d 502, Wash. 1993; *State v. Hollis*, No. 2-1-04603-9, Wash. Super Ct., King County, June, 1993; *People v. Wallace*, 14 Cal. App. 4th 651, 17 Cal. Rptr. 2d 721, 1993; *State v. Carter*, 246 Neb. 953, 524 N.W. 2d, 1994.

[28] 134 F.R.D. 161, 181; N.D. Ohio 1991.

[29] NRC 1992, 1996.

[30] SWGDAM, 2000.

Table 4.2 Number of Alleles and Genotypes for the 13 CODIS Markers, Including all Reported Microvariants (from Butler, 2005, Appendix I).

		Genotypes		
Marker	**Alleles**	**Homozygous**	**Heterozygous**	**Total**
CSF1PO	20	20	190	210
FGA	80	80	3240	3320
TH01	20	20	190	210
TPOX	15	15	105	120
VWA	29	29	406	435
D3S1358	25	25	300	325
D5S818	15	15	105	120
D7S820	30	30	435	465
D8S1179	15	15	105	120
D13S317	17	17	136	153
D16S539	19	19	171	190
D18S51	51	51	1275	1326
D21S11	89	89	4005	4094

that marker), the number of possible genotypes for a marker with N alleles is N(N + 1)/2. For example, consider a marker with four alleles (N = 4): 1, 2, 3 and 4. The possible genotypes are: 1,1; 1,2; 1,3; 1,4; 2,2; 2,3; 2,4; 3,3; 3,4 and 4,4 (note that, for this purpose, a 2,1 genotype is the same as a 1,2 genotype). With four alleles, there are 10, or (4 X 5)/2, possible two-allele genotypes. To break it down one more level of detail, for a marker with N alleles, there are N homozygous genotypes (both alleles the same: 1,1; 2,2; 3,3 and 4,4) and N(N – 1)/2 heterozygous genotypes (two different alleles: 1,2; 1,3; 1,4; 2,3; 2,4 and 3,4).

To calculate the number of different DNA profiles that could exist given all the alleles that have been reported in the FBI database, you merely multiply the number of possible genotypes for the different markers together. Using the numbers in Table 4.2, there are approximately 2.6×10^{33} (2,624,716,348,000,000,000,000,000,000,000,000) different possible DNA profiles based on the 13 CODIS markers in the FBI's database. This is 4.3×10^{20} (437,452,724,700,000,000,000) times greater than the population of the Earth (approximately 6 billion, or 6,000,000,000). In other words, only a tiny fraction of the profiles that could theoretically exist on the Earth actually do exist. In addition, keep in mind that the existence or absence of a DNA profile in the world's population depends not only on the frequencies of the alleles in the profile, but also on the empirical facts of who has mated with whom. Because of the specific matings that have and have not occurred, some DNA profiles with very low theoretical frequencies will exist, while DNA profiles with higher theoretical frequencies will not exist. In order for all the possible profiles to exist, not only would there need to be many more people on Earth than there are, but people would also have to be deliberately arranged in mating pairs that allowed the proper combinations of alleles to be passed down. This obviously will never happen, so it will always remain true that the human race contains only a small fraction of the possible DNA profiles that it could contain. In addition, because we will never have the DNA profiles from everyone on Earth available, we will never know which profiles do exist and which do not, or which profiles are unique and which may be found in more than one individual. We therefore must use the data we do have available to us to estimate how rare a profile is, and how likely it is that someone other than the defendant possesses the DNA profile in question.

Frequency Estimates Are Often Accompanied by Confidence Intervals

In the following discussions, we will often use the words "frequency" and "probability" interchangeably. Although the two words can have different meanings in some contexts, in the context within which we use them they are interchangeable. In order to specify the probability that a randomly selected person from the larger population will have a particular allele for a marker, you count the number of times that allele appears in the relevant database, then divide that count by the total number of alleles in the database. This quotient represents the allele's frequency in the database. When you express the probability of an allele as a percentage, you are merely stating the number of times you would expect to see an allele with that frequency in a database containing a total of 100 alleles. For example, imagine that allele number 12 has been seen 200 times in a database that contains 2,000 genotypes. Because every person's genotype for a particular marker contains two alleles for that marker, these 2,000 genotypes represent 4,000 alleles. The number 12 allele therefore has a frequency of 200/4,000 = 1/20 = 5/100. Because you would expect to see that allele five times for every 100 alleles you counted, that allele has a probability of 5%.

Because only a tiny percentage of the nation's population is represented in the forensic databases, even the largest database can only provide an estimate of the probability associated with a particular allele, genotype or profile. In order to compensate for the fact that every estimate is subject to some degree of inaccuracy, forensic analysts often calculate a **confidence interval (CI)** when they calculate the frequency of an allele, genotype or profile.[31] The CI is a range that has the analyst's best estimate of the number in question in the center. A CI is also associated with a probability. By convention, most analysts report either a 95% or 99% CI. Although this is technically not accurate, it may be useful to consider the 95% CI as the range of numbers required for the analyst to be 95% confident that the true value of the number in question lies within the range. In actual fact, the 95% CI refers to the fact that, if the analyst measures the number in question multiple times and uses the appropriate formula to calculate the CI (discussed below) each time, 95% of the intervals that the analyst reports will include the true value of the number in question. Most readers will find the general concept behind the CI intuitive. For example, most will understand that the 99% CI will be larger

[31] Holland and Parsons, 1999.

than the 95% CI for any particular calculation, because it requires a larger range to achieve a greater degree of confidence in one's ability to estimate the true value of the number. The important point about the CI, however, is that it is used to ensure that the RMP calculation is conservative (i.e., favors the defendant). To calculate the RMP, instead of using the best estimate of the number in question, the analyst will use either the upper or lower bound of the CI, whichever endows the evidence with less weight, thereby favoring the defendant.

Three different formulas can be used for calculating the CI; the formula to be used depends on how frequently the profile in question has been seen in the reference database. For the following discussion, let the probability (p) of an allele, genotype or profile = F/N, where F equals the number of times the allele, genotype or profile was observed in the database, and N equals the total number of alleles, genotypes or profiles in the database.

From the standpoint of the criminal justice system, the analyst should avoid underestimating the frequency of the DNA profile in question because that prejudices the proceeding against the defendant by suggesting that the match between the defendant's DNA and that of the evidence is more strongly probative than it actually is. This is especially important when dealing with mtDNA and Y chromosome haplotypes, because the mitochondrial and Y chromosome DNA databases are still small enough that many of the mitochondrial and Y chromosome DNA profiles seen in forensic casework are not observed, or observed only once, in their respective reference databases. In these cases, the analyst is forced to calculate a confidence interval and produce some nonzero number for the frequency of the profile in question. After all, the fact that the defendant and the evidence have been observed to possess that particular DNA profile proves that the frequency of that profile is not actually zero, as the database suggests. When the profile in question has not been observed in a database with N entries in it, the upper bound of the CI is calculated as follows:[32]

$$1 - \alpha^{1/N}, \qquad \text{(Eq. 4.1)}$$

where $\alpha = 0.05$ for a 95% CI, or 0.01 for a 99% CI.[33] This procedure is extremely conservative, especially when the profile in question is not present in the database. For example, if a mitochondrial DNA profile was

[32] The formula that follows is valid for estimating the frequency of an allele if the population exhibits Hardy-Weinberg equilibrium, or for estimating the frequency of a profile after the data have undergone a process called logarithmic transformation. An explanation of logarithmic transformation is beyond the scope of this book.

[33] Louis, 1981.

not observed in the 604 U.S. Caucasian samples in the FBI's mitochondrial database, an analyst (using the less conservative 95% CI) would report the frequency of the profile as 0.005, or 1 in 200, which is the upper bound of the CI for the frequency estimate.

When the profile has been seen only a few times in the database, so that $Np \leq 5$, the analyst calculates the Wilson score interval.[34] For seldom-seen profiles, the 95% CI can be calculated using the following formula:

[34] Agresti and Coull, 1998.

$$\frac{p + \frac{3.84}{2N}}{1 + \frac{3.84}{N}} \pm \frac{1.96\sqrt{\frac{1}{N}\left[p(1-p) + \frac{0.96}{N^2}\right]}}{1 + \frac{3.84}{N}}, \qquad \text{(Eq. 4.2)}$$

while the 99% CI can be calculated using the following formula:

$$\frac{p + \frac{6.66}{2N}}{1 + \frac{6.66}{N}} \pm \frac{2.58\sqrt{\frac{1}{N}\left[p(1-p) + \frac{1.66}{N^2}\right]}}{1 + \frac{6.66}{N}}. \qquad \text{(Eq. 4.3)}$$

These formulas may be formidable, but keep in mind that the only variables in them are N and p, whose quantities you can easily determine. Once those values are plugged into the equation, it is merely arithmetic.

When the profile has been seen often enough that $Np > 5$, the 95% CI is calculated using the following equation:

$$p' = p \pm 1.96\sqrt{\frac{p(1-p)}{N}}, \qquad \text{(Eq. 4.4)}$$

while the 99% CI is calculated using

$$p' = p \pm 2.58\sqrt{\frac{p(1-p)}{N}}. \qquad \text{(Eq. 4.5)}$$

Note that, in the last two sets of formulas, the symbol p' (read "p'") is actually a range, not a single number. In each case, the CI is calculated by adjusting the observed p both up and down (using the "±" symbol), resulting in a range (p') that has p in the middle. Note also that the 99% CI is larger than the 95% CI, because the use of 2.58 for the 99% CI spreads the range out farther than the 1.96 of the 95% CI formula does.

The Product Rule Provides the Basis for Calculating the RMP

In order to determine the frequency of a genetic profile in the larger population, one applies a law of probability theory that many call the

product rule. Formally stated, the product rule asserts that the probability of a set of independent events happening is equal to the product of the probabilities of the individual events. More simply put, if you want to know the probability of a set of independent events happening, you take the probabilities of each of the individual events and multiply them together. The product rule is used in a situation that calls for the Boolean operator AND, as opposed to OR. For example, if you were tossing a coin and you wanted to know the probability of getting four heads in a row, you would start with the fact that the probability of getting a head on any one coin toss is 1/2. You would then multiply $1/2 \times 1/2 \times 1/2 \times 1/2$ to get 1/16, the probability of getting a head on the first toss and a head on the second toss and a head on the third toss and a head on the fourth toss. If you tossed a coin and rolled a six-sided die, the probability of getting a head on your coin would be 1/2, and the probability of getting a 3 on your die would be 1/6. The probability of getting a head and a 3, then, is $1/2 \times 1/6 = 1/12$. As long as all the events involved are independent of each other (knowing whether you got a head or a tail on the coin toss does not tell you what you are likely to roll on the die), the product rule can be applied to calculate the probability of the set of events happening. The 1996 NRC report endorsed the use of the product rule to calculate the RMP associated with a particular DNA profile, and numerous subsequent court decisions have affirmed this position.[35]

[35] For example, *Link v. State*, 25 S.W.3d 136, Mo. 2000.

In its simplest form, applying the product rule to calculate the RMP is a straightforward exercise. One first determines which database is the best match for the defendant's racial and ethnic heritage, and then consults the database to determine the frequencies of the different alleles seen in the defendant's DNA profile. The analyst next uses these allele frequencies to calculate the frequency of each of the individual markers' genotypes (using the formulas discussed later). Finally, the analyst multiplies the frequencies of all the markers' genotypes together to get the overall RMP for the profile. As we will discuss, in real forensic calculations certain correction factors must be applied to some of the markers' genotype frequencies before multiplying them. The rules for applying these correction factors are easy to understand, however, and the reader should rest assured that the application of the product rule involves a simple, straightforward multiplication.

THE PRINCIPLES OF POPULATION GENETICS THAT IMPACT FORENSIC DNA CALCULATIONS

Linkage Equilibrium and the Requirement that Marker Genotypes Be Independent

In order for the product rule to be applied, all the events under consideration must be independent of each other. For the purposes of forensic testing, this means that knowing what genotype an individual has at one marker does not allow you to predict the genotype he or she has at any other marker. For example, if everyone who had the 4,5 genotype for marker 1 also had the 6,8 genotype for marker 2, once you knew that the profile in question included a 4,5 genotype for marker 1, finding out that the profile also included the 6,8 genotype for marker 2 would not narrow down the pool of people who could be the source of the evidence any farther. This concept is critical for the interpretation of forensic DNA evidence, because the mathematical theory behind the product rule requires that there be complete independence between the different markers' genotypes in order for the product rule to produce an accurate estimate of the RMP.

When having one particular genotype for one marker makes it more likely that the individual will also have a particular genotype for a second marker, those two markers are said to exhibit **linkage disequilibrium (LD)**. In an ideal situation, the different markers used in any forensic testing panel will exhibit **linkage equilibrium (LE)**, or a complete independence between the genotypes at any one marker and the genotypes at all the other markers. Whether two markers exhibit LD or LE in any particular population depends not only on whether or not any of the genotypes of the markers are extremely common within the population, but also on the patterns of migration of and mating within that population over the course of human history. Because LD/LE is determined by factors specific to the markers and to the population in question, it is possible to find different markers in LD with each other in different populations. This means that there is no standard rule of thumb that assures the independence of marker genotypes. Markers that lie on different chromosomes can exhibit LD, so the common practice of using no more than one marker from any chromosome does not guarantee LD.[36] In addition, markers that exhibit LD in one ethnic subgroup

[36] See the section below on paternity testing for the rationale for using markers from different chromosomes in a multiplex forensic testing panel.

can exhibit LE in another, so each case's combination of markers and reference database should be tested for LD/LE.

The presence or absence of linkage equilibrium can be a crucial determinant of the weight of a match between the defendant's DNA profile and that of the evidence. Consider the case of *People v. Axell.*[37] The defense successfully argued that the prosecution's reference database exhibited linkage disequilibrium, and the prosecution was forced to recalculate the RMP in a manner that did not assume independence between markers. After the recalculation, the RMP dropped from 1 in 6 billion to 1 in 50. It is essential that the prosecution disclose its reference database to the defense, so the defense can have its expert determine whether significant linkage disequilibrium exists between any of the markers used for testing. In several cases, DNA evidence has been declared inadmissible because the testing laboratory refused to disclose the population genetic data on which its RMP calculation was based, thereby rendering the defense unable to ensure that the reference population demonstrated linkage equilibrium for the markers used for testing.[38]

Thousands of STR markers are polymorphic enough to be useful for forensic identity testing, and forensic DNA tests usually include fewer than 20 markers. Given the abundance of available markers and the obvious significance of LE, any company that markets a forensic testing kit should have data from at least the major racial databases that demonstrates that its markers are in LE with each other. Recent studies have provided empirical evidence that LE exists between the common STR markers in all the major forensic databases.[39] In addition, the calculations used to produce the RMP are all deliberately conservative; they include correction factors intended to compensate for the fact that people who belong to the same population are more likely to have similar DNA profiles than people from a different population. Because of these facts, LD should not be an issue in most cases.

[37] For example, *People v. Axell*, CR23911, Ventura Super. Ct., May 22, 1989.

[38] For example, *State v. Pennell*, IN88-12-0051, Del. Super. Ct. September 20, 1989, 1989 WL 167430; *State v. Schwartz*, 447 N.W.2d 422, Minn., 1989.

[39] Lins et al., 1998; Budowle et al., 1999, 2001.

Hardy-Weinberg Equilibrium and Population Substructure

Population genetics is, among other things, the study of genetic variation across the different geographic regions and racial and ethnic groups of the world. It is a simple fact of nature that people from different ethnic groups and different geographic regions will have different patterns of allele frequencies for these polymorphic markers. In addition, people from the same ethnic subgroup and geographic region are likely to be more closely related to each other than people from different ethnic subgroups and geographic regions, and therefore are more likely to have the same genotype for any given marker. Even distant relationships between members of the same ethnic subgroup will cause them to be more likely to share genotypes than members of different ethnic subgroups.

A population such as that which exists in modern-day America represents a mixture of people from many different ethnic groups, each of which has its own characteristic profile of allele frequencies for the forensic STR markers. In the forensic databases, people are classified into major racial groups. The American population is divided into Caucasians (or European Americans), African Americans, Asian Americans, Hispanic Americans and Native Americans. Unfortunately, the concept of race that is used to classify people is often a cultural and historical one, not a genetic one. Consequently, each race's database contains ethnic subgroups with significantly different genetic heritages. A Caucasian American database may contain individuals whose families originally came from Scandinavia, all parts of Europe, the United Kingdom and parts of Africa. An African American database contains individuals whose families originated in many different parts of Africa. The Hispanic database is the most diverse of all. It combines people whose families originated from South America, Central America, Puerto Rico, Europe, Cuba and Mexico. Forensic analysts often divide the American Hispanic population into Eastern Hispanics and Western Hispanics (including Texas and westward states). The Eastern Hispanics have considerably more African heritage than the Western Hispanics do, while the Western Hispanics have considerably more Native American heritage.[40]

[40] Irwin et al., 2007.

The existence of different ethnic subgroups, each of which has a different pattern of allele frequencies, within a larger racial population is referred to as **population substructure**. Population substructure can cause the forensic analyst to produce an inaccurate estimate of the RMP for a DNA profile, because the mathematical theory underlying the calculation of genotype frequencies (described later) assumes that the reference population is homogeneous. In fact, it assumes that people mate at random, so there will always be some population substructure. The important question is whether there is enough population substructure to cause the analyst to produce an inaccurate estimate of the RMP, and if so, how to compensate for it in calculating the RMP.

The degree of population substructure that exists within a major racial group depends on how extensively the members of the different ethnic subgroups within that major race have migrated and intermarried with members of other ethnic subgroups within their race as well as with members of other races.[41] Cultural factors strongly influence the outcome, and often significant differences are found in the amount of admixture between two ethnic groups from one geographic region to another. The analyst's choice of reference database must be tailored to the specific defendant's ethnic heritage. When the ethnic subgroups within a major race have intermingled extensively, the analyst can use the major race's database to calculate the RMP, without worrying about which ethnic subgroup the defendant belongs to. When the ethnic subgroups within a major race have not intermingled extensively, however, it is more appropriate to use data from the defendant's ethnic subgroup to calculate the RMP. Using the larger racial database for a highly substructured racial population results in spuriously low estimates of the RMP compared to using a database that contains only members of the defendant's specific ethnic subgroup.[42] This exaggerates the weight of the evidence and is therefore prejudicial to the defendant.

Two researchers by the names of Godfrey Hardy and Wilhelm Weinberg (working independently) established a mathematical method for estimating how frequently a genotype appears in a large population using allele frequency data from a small fraction of the population. For a homozygous genotype, where both alleles are alike, if the frequency of that allele $= p$, then the frequency of the homozygous genotype $= (p \times p) = p^2$. For a heterozygous genotype, if the frequencies of the two alleles $= p_1$ and p_2, the frequency of the heterozygous genotype $= 2p_1p_2$.[43] Statistical tests such as the chi-square test and Fisher's Exact test can test a population database to determine if it is in the **Hardy-Weinberg equilibrium (HWE)**.[44] An example of the application of the chi-square test is given in Appendix I.

A number of conditions must be met for HWE to be maintained in any population, including the requirement that the population engage in random mating. In human populations, however, many ethnic subgroups keep to themselves socially, even avoiding members of the same major

[41] The intermingling of different ethnic groups is referred to as **admixture**.

[42] Krane et al., 1992.

[43] The derivation of these Hardy-Weinberg predictions for genotype frequencies is illustrated in Evett and Weir, 1998, p. 84.

[44] Evett and Weir, 1998; Balding, 2005.

race. The more the ethnic groups that are contained in a major racial database stay isolated from each other, the more substructure that racial population will exhibit, and the more important it will be to use a reference database that matches the defendant's ethnic background rather than the larger racial database.

Population substructure will distort the estimates of the frequencies of homozygous and heterozygous genotypes differently. In a highly substructured racial population, the frequency of homozygous genotypes will be higher than that which is predicted by HWE theory,[45] and the frequency of heterozygotes will be correspondingly lower than HWE theory would predict. This causes the analyst who is using the larger racial population database and relying on HWE assumptions to overestimate the frequencies of the heterozygous genotypes and underestimate the frequencies of the homozygous genotypes.

[45] This excess of homozygous genotypes in a highly substructured population is referred to as the **Wahlund effect** or **Wahlund principle**.

In order to understand how population substructure causes the analyst to underestimate the frequency of a homozygous genotype for a marker, imagine a population that consists of four different ethnic subgroups (call them A, B, C and D), each of which has a different pattern of allele frequencies for that marker. Imagine that each subgroup has one allele that appears with a significantly higher frequency than in the other three subgroups (call the common alleles A, B, C and D as well). If the individuals in the population mate randomly between the four different subgroups, the children of the people from subgroup A will inherit plenty of A alleles, but because the A allele is rare in the other three subgroups, most of these children will inherit a different allele from their other parent and have a heterozygous genotype for that marker. There will be relatively few AA homozygotes. If the subgroups stay segregated for mating purposes, however, there will be a much higher frequency of AA homozygotes, because now the parents who are passing down the A allele are mating with other parents who also have a high probability of passing down the A allele. Subgroup A will have a lot of AA homozygotes, and subgroups B, C and D will have a lot of BB, CC and DD homozygotes, respectively. A highly substructured population, therefore, contains several subgroups, each of which has a higher frequency of homozygotes for certain marker alleles than HWE principles (which assume random mating) would lead one to predict. When several subgroups' data are combined into a larger population, the frequencies of these homozygous genotypes will always be smaller in the larger population than they are in their respective subgroups. This means that the genotype frequencies provided by the larger population database will always be smaller than the genotype frequencies that would be provided by a database that contained only members of the suspect's ethnic subgroup. This will cause the analyst to provide a spuriously small RMP when the larger population database is used, exaggerating the weight of the match between the defendant and the evidence.

Consider the following numerical example. Imagine that a murder has been committed in a Puerto Rican neighborhood, and you have eyewitness evidence that implicates an unspecified Puerto Rican man as a suspect. You have obtained a match between the crime scene evidence and a Puerto Rican suspect's DNA profile. In order to calculate the probability of a random match, you would use the Hispanic database to determine the population frequency of the profile in question. First consider the data from a single marker for which the evidence and the defendant are both homozygous. Imagine that the allele that is in the marker genotype in question has a frequency of 20% (0.20) in the Puerto Rican subgroup to which the suspect belongs, but is not seen very often in the other ethnic groups in the Hispanic database. Imagine also that Puerto Ricans make up only 20% of the Hispanic database population. In that case, that allele will have a frequency of 4% (0.04) in the Hispanic database. If the analyst uses a Puerto Rican database, the frequency of the homozygous genotype will be estimated as 0.04, 4% or approximately 1 in 25 ($0.20 \times 0.20 = 0.04$). If, however, he or she uses the Hispanic database, the frequency of that homozygous genotype will be calculated to be one twenty-fifth of the value that was obtained using the Puerto Rican database ($0.04 \times 0.04 = 0.0016$, 0.16% or 1 in 625). Now consider a situation in which the profile contains four such markers. The frequency of the profile will be calculated by multiplying the frequencies of the individual markers' genotypes. If all four markers had the same allele frequencies as the first one, the profile would have an RMP of 0.00000256 (1 in 390,625) when the Puerto Rican database was used, but an RMP of 0.0000000000065536 (1 in 152,587,890,600) when the Hispanic database was used. Using the Puerto Rican database as your reference for allele frequencies is not only theoretically justified in this case, but it also produces an estimate of the rarity of the genotype that is much more favorable to the defendant.

APPLYING THE PRODUCT RULE—COMPENSATING FOR POPULATION SUBSTRUCTURE AND POSSIBLE ALLELE DROPOUT

Early Recommendations Were Excessively Conservative

The conditions required for HWE are rarely met in real human populations, and HWE is the exception, rather than the rule, for human populations. One of the more controversial elements of the 1992 NRC report was the means the committee recommended to compensate for the fact that human populations do not obey the laws of theoretical mathematics.[46] As discussed earlier, population substructure in the reference database can significantly distort one's calculation of the RMP if there is enough of it. Unfortunately, the 1992 NRC committee did not have access to enough data to determine how much population substructure actually exists in the major races in America, and how strongly that population substructure actually distorts the calculation of the RMP. This problem was exacerbated by the fact that the available data were seriously flawed. The VNTR methods in use at the time often led the analyst to give a spuriously high estimate of the frequency of homozygous genotypes and caused populations to appear to deviate significantly from HWE when they actually did not.[47]

Among its recommendations for the future, the 1992 NRC stressed the need for more extensive population databases, as well as research into the effect of population substructure on calculation of the RMP. In the interim, however, it advocated the use of several correction factors that have been criticized as being considerably more conservative than necessary.[48] For example, the 1992 NRC report recommended that reference databases be tested to determine if they conformed to HWE expectations for each of the markers, and if they did not, the committee recommended that they not be used to calculate RMPs. The 1996 NRC rightly abandoned this position, however, and in doing so reminded us that statistically significant phenomena are not always significant in the practical sense. Small deviations from HWE can be statistically significant if the population is large enough. It is not uncommon to find a small but statistically significant deviation from HWE in a forensic database, but these minor deviations from HWE do not significantly distort the calculation of the RMP. Furthermore, as the size of a database increases, the

[46] Lander, 1991; Lewontin and Hartl, 1991; Weir, 1992, 1993; Balding and Nichols, 1994.

[47] Chakraborty et al., 1992.

[48] Lewontin and Hartl, 1991; Weir, 1992, 1993; Balding and Nichols, 1994; Brookfield, 1995.

likelihood of these kinds of departures from HWE increases. The 1992 NRC recommendation not only confused the difference between statistical significance and practical significance,[49] but was also prejudiced against the largest databases, which are the most reliable and useful for forensic calculations.

One of the other recommendations from the 1996 NRC that drew strong criticism was the recommendation that the analyst multiply the RMP by 10. Early studies on the subpopulation effect produced the rule of thumb that the calculated RMP was accurate within a factor of 10, and the 1996 NRC report recommended multiplying the calculated RMP by a factor of 10, to ensure a conservative calculation. Some forensic analysts have routinely applied this extra correction in order to further ensure a conservative estimate of the RMP. Given that several other measures are used to ensure a conservative calculation, and that the current STR tests are not plagued by as many technical difficulties as the VNTR tests that were in use when this policy was adopted, this is probably unnecessarily conservative.

The mathematical correction factors (described later) currently in use compensate sufficiently for population substructure when it does exist in the reference database, and they provide a very conservative estimate of the RMP when there is no population substructure distorting the calculation of the RMP.[50] The development of these correction factors has allayed the courts' worries regarding the validity of the statistical calculations used to determine the RMP of a DNA profile.[51]

Profile Probability Versus Match Probability

The research that addressed the issues raised by the 1992 NRC report suggested that the uncorrected Hardy-Weinberg formulas result in a small bias in the calculation of the RMP and that this bias usually favors the prosecution.[52] The general consensus is that the analyst must compensate for this and avoid such bias, but experts disagree regarding the best way to do so in some cases. Some experts have advocated strategies for calculating the RMP that assume that the analyst does not know whether the defendant (who is presumed innocent) and the true perpetrator are of the same ethnic heritage.[53] Others have argued convincingly, however, that in many cases it is more likely that the perpetrator and the reasonable

[49] Statistical significance is a mathematical term; it says nothing about the degree to which that phenomenon will affect life in the practical sense. For example, imagine a situation in which a population subgroup can be shown to be out of HWE by the chi-square test, but the deviation from HWE only changes the RMP from 1 in 4 billion to 1 in 3.5 billion. The deviation from HWE is statistically significant, but has no significant effect on the probative value of the evidence.

[50] Balding and Nichols, 1994; Weir, 1994; NRC, 1996; Devlin and Roeder, 1997.

[51] For example, *People v. Miller*, 670 N.E.2d, Ill., 1996; *Armstead v. State*, 673 A.2d, Md., 1996; *Commonwealth v. Fowler*, 685 N.E.2d, Mass. 1997; *People v. Soto*, 981 P.2d, Cal., 1999.

[52] Chakraborty and Kidd, 1991; Brookfield, 1992; Budowle et al., 1994a,b,c; NRC, 1996.

[53] Weir, 1993.

suspects will belong to the same population subgroup than different subgroups.[54] Many people become suspects because they match eyewitnesses' descriptions of the physical features of the perpetrator, or because they live in the area in which the crime was committed. Because police who use this kind of information to identify suspects are likely to gather a substantial number of their suspects from a single ethnic subgroup, Balding and Nichols have argued that the RMP should always be calculated using a formula (discussed later in this chapter) that assumes that the suspect and the real perpetrator belong to the same population subgroup.

[54] Balding and Nichols, 1994.

To ensure a conservative estimate of the overall RMP, the 1996 NRC recommended that the analyst adopt different strategies for homozygous versus heterozygous markers. Recall from the earlier discussion that population substructure causes the analyst who uses the standard HWE calculations to overestimate the frequency of heterozygous genotypes and provide an RMP that underestimates the weight of the evidence against the defendant. In order to be conservative, the 1996 NRC report recommended that no correction factor be applied when the genotype for the marker in question is heterozygous. The HWE term $2p_1p_2$ should be used to calculate the frequency of all heterozygous genotypes, because it overestimates the frequency of those heterozygous genotypes if the reference population has significant substructure, and it is accurate when it does not.

Because population substructure causes the HWE formulas to underestimate the frequency of homozygotes, and therefore overestimate the probative value of the DNA evidence, several efforts have been made to ensure that population substructure (real and imagined) does not cause the analyst to underestimate the RMP associated with homozygous genotypes. One of the earliest remedies involved using a straightforward "counting method" to determine genotype frequencies. As the name implies, in this method, the number of times the genotype is present in the database is counted, this count is divided by the total number of genotypes in the database, and the resultant quotient is considered the frequency of that genotype. This may seem a logical way to calculate genotype frequencies, but recall that the databases only contain a small fraction of the larger population and that a significant number of genotypes are bound to exist in the larger population but are not represented in the database. This means that if you use the straightforward counting

[55] 393 S.E.2d 436 Ga. 1990.

[56] Wright, 1951.

method, you assign a frequency of zero to the genotypes that are not in the database, thereby underestimating the frequency of all the genotypes that exist but do not happen to be in the small fraction of the population contained in the database. Because the genotypes that are not in the reference database are assigned a frequency that is less than their actual frequency, the genotypes in the database are assigned frequencies that are correspondingly greater than their actual value. The simplicity of the counting method may be appealing, but in actual fact, this method does not produce a reliable frequency estimate for the profiles present in the database or the profiles not present there.

Because the counting method overestimates the frequencies of the more common genotypes, it can be extremely conservative if the profile in question contains relatively common alleles. For example, consider the capital murder case *Caldwell v. State,*[55] which was tried before either of the NRC reports was issued. In a pretrial hearing, the judge declared the evidence of a match between the defendant's DNA and that of the evidence sample admissible; the RMP was 1 in 24,000,000. There were problems with the evidence, however. First, some technical problems had arisen with the VNTR analysis, and it was difficult to determine the size of some alleles accurately. Second, none of the state's witnesses had ascertained that the state's reference database conformed to HWE expectations. One of the defense experts investigated and found that the reference population was not in HWE. The appellate court allowed the prosecution to present the evidence but ordered them to recalculate the RMP using the counting approach. As a result, the RMP rose from 1 in 24,000,000 to 1 in 250,000—an almost 100-fold difference.

In order to ensure a conservative estimate of the RMP, the correction factor theta (θ) is used to adjust the estimate of the frequency of a homozygous genotype. The correction factor θ is derived from Wright's fixation index,[56] and compensates for the amount of population substructure that exists in the reference database. Instead of using p^2 to estimate the frequency of a homozygous genotype, the 1996 NRC report recommended that the analyst use the formula

$$p' = p^2 + p(1 - p)\theta. \qquad \text{(Eq. 4.6)}$$

Because p, $1 - p$ and θ are all positive numbers, $p(1 - p)\theta$ will always be greater than zero, and therefore $p^2 + p(1 - p)\theta$ will always be greater than p^2.

The true value of θ will vary from one subgroup to another and even from marker to marker. Most researchers estimate the true value of θ to be between 0.002 and 0.009, depending on the marker and the population subgroup one specifies. Therefore, using a value of 0.01 for θ intentionally overcompensates for the population substructure observed in most American cities and produces a conservative estimate of the genotype's frequency. In cases where the defendant is from a socially isolated group such as a Native American tribe, or the crime was committed in a geographically isolated region, the value of 0.03 can be used for θ and still ensure a conservative calculation.[57]

[57] Weir, 1994; Budowle, 1995; Roeder et al., 1995; Weir and Hill, 2002; Buckleton et al., 2004; Balding, 2005.

[58] Balding, 2005.

[59] Balding and Nichols, 1994.

Equation (4.6) does indeed provide a conservative estimate of the probability that a randomly selected individual from the reference population would have the DNA profile in question. In addition, the fact that the 1996 NRC endorsed the use of this formula has led to its acceptance in American courts. Unfortunately, however, it does not represent the most relevant assessment of the strength of the evidence. Equation (4.6) gives us the "profile probability," or the probability of seeing the DNA profile in question in the relevant reference population. As Balding[58] has reminded us, however, "[w]hat matters in practice for DNA profile evidence is not p, the overall frequency of the profile, but the probabilities of the other possible culprits having the profile *given that the suspect has it*." The more relevant probability, therefore, is the match probability, or the probability that a randomly selected person from the relevant reference population has the DNA profile in question given that the suspect has already been shown to have it.[59] For a homozygous genotype, the match probability is calculated using the formula

$$p' = \frac{[2\theta + (1-\theta)p][3\theta + (1-\theta)p]}{(1+\theta)(1+2\theta)}. \qquad \text{(Eq. 4.7)}$$

For a heterozygous genotype, the formula is

$$p' = \frac{[2\theta + (1-\theta)p_1][\theta + (1-\theta)p_2]}{(1+\theta)(1+2\theta)}. \qquad \text{(Eq. 4.8)}$$

Equations (4.7) and (4.8) look very complicated, but the only unknown terms in them are the allele frequencies (p_1 and p_2) and θ. You can find the allele frequencies in the appropriate database, and you can use 0.01 as the value of θ (or 0.03 for rare cases in which the suspect is a member of a socially isolated population subgroup). Furthermore, notice that if there is no population substructure, and $\theta = 0$, Eqs. (4.7) and (4.8) reduce to the standard HWE formulas: p^2 for the frequency of a homozygous genotype and $2p_1p_2$ for a heterozygous genotype.

The primary difference between the recommendations of the 1996 NRC versus those of Balding and Nicholls is whether to use Eq. (4.6) (with no correction for heterozygous genotypes, just using the HWE term $2p_1p_2$) versus Eqs. (4.7) and (4.8) in cases where one is uncertain whether the (presumably innocent) defendant and the true perpetrator belong to the same ethnic subgroup. When all members of the reasonable suspect pool are from the same ethnic subgroup, such as crimes committed by gangs, the NRC recommends the use of the match probability Eqs. (4.7) and (4.8). In these cases, the NRC recommends that the estimates of the frequencies of both homozygous and heterozygous genotypes be adjusted according to the appropriate formula.[60]

60 Balding and Nichols, 1994.

61 Walsh et al., 2007.

When There Is No Information Available Regarding the Race of the Perpetrator

Walsh and colleagues have recently made a point that we would like to emphasize and endorse.[61] When there is no evidence to suspect that the perpetrator of the crime belongs to one race or another, it is customary for the prosecution to report a separate RMP for each of the major racial groups. Walsh and colleagues point out, however, that it is logically more sound, and more helpful to the triers of fact, to report a single RMP that accommodates the fact that the reasonable suspect pool (e.g., the population of the entire city) contains members of different racial groups.

In order to do so, one must add the RMPs for that profile from the different races, but first one must weight each race's RMP according to the makeup of the suspect population. For example, imagine a crime for which the entire population of the city was considered the reasonable suspect pool, and the population of the city was 20% Hispanic, 30% African American and 50% Caucasian. If one symbolized the profile's RMPs in the three ethnic groups as *RMPH*, *RMPA* and *RMPC*, respectively, a single RMP for that profile and that reasonable suspect pool could be calculated as follows:

$$RMP = 0.20RMPH + 0.30RMPA + 0.50RMPC. \qquad \text{(Eq. 4.9)}$$

Because the statistical analysis must be tailored to the reasonable suspect pool in each case, we agree that calculating a single RMP that accommodates the diversity in the reasonable suspect pool is a more logical and helpful approach than calculating different RMPs for each of the different races.

When Relatives Are Suspects

When there is evidence that a close relative of the suspect could have been the source of an evidence sample, and the relative's DNA profile can be obtained, it is a simple matter of determining the relative's profile and seeing whether it matches that of the evidence. When the relative cannot be tested, however, it is possible to calculate the probability that that relative would have the same DNA profile as the suspect.[62] For unilineal relatives[63] who are not inbred, one can use a term called the kinship coefficient (symbolized by *F*) to calculate the probability of a relative having the same genotype: $F = 1/4$ for parents and offspring, 1/8 for half-siblings and uncle-nephew pairs and 1/16 for first cousins. For other relationships, *F* can be calculated using the algorithm developed by Wright.[64] For unilineal relatives who are not inbred, the probability of a relative having the same genotype as the defendant can be calculated using the following formulas:

For homozygous genotypes $p' = p^2 + 4p(1 - p)F$ (Eq. 4.10)

For heterozygous genotypes $p' = 2p_1p_2 + 2(p_1 + p_2 - 4p_1p_2)F$ (Eq. 4.11)

Full siblings are bilineal relatives; that is, they are related through both the maternal and paternal bloodlines. For full siblings, the following formulas can be used:

For homozygous genotypes $p' = (1 + 2p + p^2)/4$ (Eq. 4.12)

For heterozygous genotypes $p' = (1 + p_1 + p_2 + 2p_1p_2)/4$ (Eq. 4.13)

Once the genotype probabilities have been adjusted, they are multiplied together to calculate the overall probability that the specified relative would have the profile in question. The 13 CODIS STR markers are so highly polymorphic that even full siblings are expected to have a match probability of less than 1 in 40,000.[65]

[62] Weir and Hill, 1993.

[63] Two people who are related through only one parent's bloodline—for example, first cousins whose mothers are sisters but whose fathers are not related to each other.

[64] Wright, 1951.

[65] Chakraborty et al., 1999.

When the Suspect Is Identified Via a Databank Search

As databanks grow, investigators have ever-increasing pools of profiles they can search in order to find a match for their evidence. There has been some debate, however, regarding whether a match that has resulted from a databank search is as probative as a match that was obtained after the defendant had been identified by other means. When a match is discovered between an evidence sample and an entry in a databank, not only is the question "How rare is this profile in the larger population?" of interest, but the question "What is the probability of finding a coincidental match when searching through this many DNA profiles?" becomes an important question as well. Some commentators have claimed that the observed match between the databank profile and that of the evidence is weaker than it would be if a suspect had been identified by non-DNA evidence and then profiled, because the probability that the investigator will find a coincidental match grows as the size of the databank grows.[66] Others have disagreed, however, arguing that the fact that all the other profiles in the databank do not match that of the evidence actually strengthens the evidence against the defendant.[67]

[66] For example, NRC 1996; Stockmarr, 1999.

[67] Balding and Donnelly, 1996; Evett and Weir, 1998.

[68] For example, Balding and Donnelly, 1996; Lempert, 1997.

Both NRC reports suggested ways in which the RMP calculation could be adjusted for cases in which the defendant was identified via a databank search. The 1992 NRC report recommended that when a suspect is identified through a databank search, the suspect be tested again, using a different set of markers, and that only the data from the new test be used to calculate the RMP. This was one of the points on which the 1992 NRC report received its strongest criticism. This solution obviously discards much useful information and may be difficult to implement for minute samples. The 1996 NRC report recommended that one adjust the RMP following a databank match by multiplying the RMP of the profile in the reference population by the number of profiles in the databank. Following this reasoning, if p = the RMP of the profile in the reference population and N = the size of the database, the RMP = Np. The DNA Advisory Board has endorsed this approach, but some critics considered this a step backward for several reasons.[68] One reason is that this formula leads one to expect a match when one should not necessarily do so. For example, if the databank contained 10 million profiles (N = 10,000,000) and the profile in question had an RMP of 1 in 10 million (1/10,000,000), this formula leads one to believe that one would be guaranteed to find a match in the databank ($10,000,000 \times 1/10,000,000 = 1.0$); this is not true. Balding and Donnelly[69] provide an even more extreme illustration of the problems with this strategy. If the database contained the entire relevant population, and one identical match was found (thereby giving that profile a probability $p = 1/N$), logic would dictate that the individual with the matching profile is the source of the evidence. The "Np" formula, however, suggests that the evidence is worthless, because one is guaranteed to find a match for a profile with $p = 1/N$ if one searches N profiles [$Np = N(1/N) = 1.0$].

On the surface, obviously a conflict exists between those who argue that a match between an evidence sample and the defendant is stronger if the defendant has been identified through a databank search and those who argue that such a match is weaker than if the defendant had been identified via eyewitness or other non-DNA evidence. Interestingly, both of these conflicting arguments rest solidly on valid mathematical principles. The resolution to this conflict can be found if one invokes a full Bayesian analysis (see our later discussion of Bayes' Theorem). A Bayesian analysis combines the non-DNA evidence with the DNA evidence to produce a posterior probability of guilt. The non-DNA evidence is applied differently by the proponents of these two conflicting positions, and a full Bayesian analysis is necessary for these two different methods to produce the same result in any given situation. Without a full Bayesian analysis, including an assessment of the strength of the non-DNA evidence, the adjustment recommended by Balding and Donnelly is conservative only when the number of markers tested is large enough to produce a very small RMP in the reference population. Therefore, if one must choose between the two methods, the method recommended by the 1996 NRC and Stockmarr[70] ($RMP = Np$) is usually the more conservative. As long as the database is large, it provides a conservative estimate of the RMP in all situations. This guarantees that the RMP will always be calculated in a manner that avoids prejudice against the defendant.

Unlike the RMP calculation, there is general agreement regarding the means by which one calculates the probability of finding a matching profile in the databank. The best way to state the probability of finding a coincidental match in a databank is to calculate the probability of not finding a coincidental match and subtracting that from 1. Recall that because the only two possibilities are finding a coincidental match and

[69] Balding and Donnelly, 1996.

[70] Stockmarr, 1999.

not finding a coincidental match, the probabilities of these two events add up to 1. Let the frequency of a profile in the larger population equal RMP. Because there are only two possible outcomes—the individual matching or not matching—the probability that a randomly selected individual from the population will not match the profile in question is therefore 1 – RMP. Applying the product rule for independent events (discussed earlier), if you screen a databank with N profiles in it, to calculate the probability that none of the individuals in the databank will match the DNA profile in question, you multiply 1 – RMP by itself N times, producing $(1 - \mathrm{RMP})^N$. Finally, in order to calculate the probability that somebody from the database will match the DNA profile in question, you subtract the probability that nobody from the database will match the profile from 1, which gives you the formula $p(match) = 1 - (1 - RMP)^N$.

Logically, the more common the profile, and the larger the databank population, the larger the probability is that some individual will match the DNA profile in question by coincidence. If the profile is common, the RMP is relatively large and $1 - RMP$ is relatively small. If the databank's N is large, $(1 - RMP)^N$ means you are multiplying the small $1 - RMP$ by itself many times. As you multiply by a number less than 1, the product gets smaller; the smaller the number, the faster the product shrinks. Therefore, when the profile is relatively common and you search a large databank, $(1 - RMP)^N$ shrinks down to an infinitesimal value, and $1 - (1 - RMP)^N$ approaches 1. In plain language, the more common the profile is and the more profiles you search through, the greater your chances of finding a coincidental match. This statement should be intuitively appealing. Furthermore, this approach is mathematically conservative because it was premised on the assumption that the database being searched included randomly selected members of the population. In fact, most databanks contain the profiles of individuals who have been convicted of crimes. The high rate of recidivism among criminals leads one to expect that the prior probability of the guilty party being in the databank is greater than it would be if the databank contained an equal number of randomly selected individuals. Because this is not taken into account, the resultant calculation is conservative.

Several authorities have demonstrated the usefulness of the likelihood ratio (LR) and Bayes' Theorem for analyzing cases in which the defendant was identified through a databank search. Bayes' Theorem is very useful for guiding decisions in criminal cases because it takes into account both the DNA evidence and the non-DNA evidence, and the resulting calculation is mildly conservative.[71] Even so, few American courts embrace the use of the LR and Bayes' Theorem for any purpose other than paternity disputes or cases involving mixed samples. One insurmountable difficulty facing the use of LRs in cases in which the defendant has been identified via a databank search involves the fact that databanks are usually populated with profiles from convicted offenders, and any information that refers to the defendant's previous conviction is inadmissible. This leaves the trier of fact unable to establish the prior probability of guilt.

[71] Balding and Donnelly, 1996; Evett and Weir, 1998.

There are conflicting opinions regarding the prior probability of guilt in such a situation. One might argue that, given the rate of recidivism among violent offenders, the fact that one has a previous conviction constitutes evidence that that individual is more likely to have committed the crime in question than someone who has never been convicted of any crime. One might argue further that someone with a prior rape conviction is more likely to be guilty of a second rape than someone who had previously been convicted of auto theft. Others might insist that the presumption of innocence applies anew to every crime and suspect. These debates cannot be waged in front of a jury, however, because the evidence of the defendant's prior conviction is inadmissible.

The laws of probability that underlie the statistical interpretation of DNA evidence assume that all the profiles in a databank are independent of each other. In other words, these laws assume that none of the individuals in the databank are related to each other. If enough members of the databank population are related to each other, this will introduce some inaccuracy into any estimate of a profile's RMP that is derived from the databank, just as population substructure can distort the estimate of the RMP when the analyst uses one of the major racial databases as the reference population. When an individual is identified via a databank search, therefore, the defense may question the validity of the databank by determining the number of relatives in the databank. One way in which this is done is to use a computer program that performs all possible pairwise comparisons between the profiles in the databank, and to determine the number of matches obtained. Because even close relatives will have different profiles if enough markers are typed, these searches often use only a subset of the markers for which there are data (approximately 9).

Investigating a databank in this manner may lead to the discovery of a surprisingly large number of matching profiles. For example, the Arizona Department of Public Safety investigated their databank of 65,493 profiles and found 144 pairs of profiles that matched at nine loci.[72] This may seem like a very high number, but one must keep in mind that performing all possible pairwise comparisons involves making a huge number of comparisons, and it is therefore not so surprising to find matching profiles. This concept is sometimes referred to as the Birthday problem, or Birthday paradox.[73] In this problem, surprisingly, it requires only 23 people to produce greater than 50% probability that some pair of people in the group have the same birthday, despite the fact that there are 365 days in the year.[74]

In a group of N individuals, the number of pairwise comparisons that can be made is equal to $N(N-1)/2$ (in this situation, comparing person 1 with person 2 is the same as comparing person 2 with person 1). In the Birthday problem, 23 people allow for 253 pairwise comparisons. In a databank containing 65,493 profiles, there are 2,144,633,778 possible pairwise comparisons. Given the surprising number of comparisons involved, and the relatively small number of markers used, it is no surprise to see some matching profiles in a databank of 65,493 profiles, even if none of the people whose profiles are in the databank are related. Simulation studies using databanks consisting of unrelated people suggest that slightly over 100 matches would be expected in a databank of 65,493 profiles if none of the people in the databank were related.[75] The number of matches found in the Arizona databank exceeds the expected number, suggesting that some of the individuals in the databank are related. When one considers the number of pairwise comparisons involved, however, and the number of expected matches if the databank members were unrelated, this suggests that the number of relatives in the Arizona databank is not high enough to seriously distort estimates of the PRM.

[72] Krane, 2007.

[73] Technically speaking, it is not a paradox, but it is called that because the answer runs so counter to our intuition.

[74] A detailed explanation of the calculation is not necessary here. The reader can access a detailed explanation of the Birthday paradox at http://en.wikipedia.org/wiki/Birthday_problem.

[75] Krane, 2007.

[76] Chakraborty et al., 1999.

Determining the Probability of Uniqueness of a DNA Profile in a Suspect Population

The average RMP for a DNA profile containing the 13 CODIS markers is 1 in 1 trillion;[76] 1 trillion is approximately 167 times larger than the population of the Earth (approximately 6 billion). When the denominator of the RMP exceeds the population of the Earth, this can lead jurors to commit fallacies that may either be prosecution-friendly or defense-friendly. Some may make the prosecution-friendly assumption that a profile that rare must be unique in the human race, and therefore that the match between the profiles of the evidence and the defendant definitively identifies the defendant as the source of the evidence. Others may not be able to understand how the denominator of the RMP can exceed the population of the Earth, and may feel that any analysis that produces such an RMP is flawed.

The assumption that a profile with an RMP this small must be unique is fallacious. Recall from the discussion earlier in this chapter that the DNA profiles that exist in the human race are determined not only by the frequencies of the alleles in the profile, but also by the empirical facts of who has mated with whom. There is no guarantee that any profile, no matter what its theoretical frequency, is unique in the human race. Indeed, the fact that a theoretically rare profile exists proves that two of the rare individuals who carry these rare alleles have mated. By definition, few people carry these rare alleles, and therefore matings between these people are fewer still. Compare the probability of this profile reoccurring in a second individual versus the probability of another profile with a similarly small theoretical frequency appearing for the first time. In the latter case, because few people will be carrying this second set of rare alleles, the probability that two individuals capable of mating and creating a child with the other rare DNA profile will actually get together and mate is very small. Contrast that with the fact that we have proof that two individuals capable of producing a child with the first rare DNA profile have already mated. Given the probability that these two individuals will mate again, together with the probability that some of their relatives carry the rare alleles in question and might mate with each other, the probability of this once-seen rare profile reoccurring is greater than the probability of another, as yet unseen, profile with similar theoretical frequency appearing for the first time. Given that the reasonable suspect pool will often contain individuals from the defendant's family or population subgroup, the probability of finding a second individual with the defendant's profile in the reasonable suspect pool will always be greater than the probability of finding a profile that has never been seen before but has the same low theoretical frequency in the larger racial group as the defendant's profile.

[77] Budowle et al., 2000.

With respect to the fallacy that the denominator of the RMP cannot be greater than the population of the Earth, recall from our earlier discussion that one would have to have a database that contained the DNA profiles from everyone in the world in order for the RMP to have a lower limit of 1 in the population of the Earth. If such a database existed, the counting method could be used to produce an exact probability of a random match. Without such a database, forensic analysts do not report how frequently that profile occurs in the reference population; they estimate the probability of finding the profile in question in a randomly selected individual from the reference population. Because only a small fraction of the profiles that could exist actually do exist, the theoretical frequency can be far less than 1 in the population of the world if the profile in question contains several rare alleles.

There is a statistic for every occasion, and the question of whether the DNA profile in question is unique is no exception. Note, however, that the critical question is not whether the profile is unique in the human race, but whether the profile is unique in the reasonable suspect pool. The entire Earth's population will never be the reasonable suspect pool for any crime; the suspect pool will usually be limited by geographic location and physical characteristics. For this reason, forensic scientists usually refer to this issue in terms of "source attribution" rather than "uniqueness," in order to avoid suggesting that this individual is the only one in the world with that particular profile. When no information is available regarding the physical characteristics of the perpetrator, analysts often use the population of the city or county in which the crime occurred as the suspect pool. FBI analysts use the population of the nation as their suspect pool when they have no information about the perpetrator.

Although one can never make a definitive statement that a particular DNA profile is unique, one can calculate what the RMP must be in order to enable one to declare with a specified level of confidence that the profile is unique within the reasonable suspect pool.[77] The formula is as follows:

$$RMP \leq 1 - (1 - a)^{1/N} \qquad \text{(Eq. 4.14)}$$

where N is the number of unrelated people in the reasonable suspect pool. The $(1 - a)$ term represents your confidence level. If you want to be 95%

confident that you can claim this profile is unique in the suspect pool, you use 0.05 for the value of variable a ($1 - 0.05 = 0.95, = 95\%$). If you want the 99% confidence level, the value of variable a is 0.01. You can take it farther: you can choose any level of confidence you wish to achieve, subtract it from 1.0, and use that value as the value for variable a.

Use of this formula for source attribution presents two problems. First, Eq. (4-14) ignores population substructure and runs counter to the logic that mandates the use of the θ correction factor. Second, when the confidence level meets or exceeds 95%, some experts will say that the defendant has been proven to be the source of the evidence "to a scientific certainty." This kind of statement is a misleading oxymoron, however. A good scientist always concedes that his or her conclusion may be wrong. In fact, the field of statistics was developed to enable the scientist to specify the probability that one of his or her conclusions is wrong, and it is rare for a scientific study not to include that kind of statistical analysis. If the calculation included the 95% confidence level, there is a 5% chance that the profile is not unique in the suspect pool, but both the words "scientific" and "certainty" carry an aura of authority that will lead many jurors to feel that this definitively supports the claim that the defendant is the source of the evidence. Omitting the scientist's customary admission of uncertainty imbues the statement with an air of scientific certainty that will be very convincing for most jurors and highly prejudicial to the defendant.

In most cases in which a forensic scientist considers testifying that a DNA profile is unique, the analysis has produced an RMP that is so low that the evidence has great probative value without the prosecution having to make the point regarding uniqueness. For example, consider the FBI policy for declaring a DNA profile unique.[78] The FBI applies several conservative correction factors and uses a 99% confidence level for this calculation. If you allow N to equal 260 million (the approximate population of the United States), adopt a confidence level of 99% and apply the FBI correction factors, the RMP required to claim that the profile is unique to this degree of certainty is less than 3.9×10^{-11} (0.000000000039). This corresponds to 1 in 25,641,025,600 (over 25 billion). An RMP such as this carries significant weight in its own right. Just consider that if you counted to 25,641,025,600 at a rate of one number per second, it would take you approximately 813 years!

[78] Budowle et al., 2000.

Coping with Possible Allele Dropout When Analyzing Suboptimal Samples

As discussed in Chapter 3, when a sample is minute or degraded, some marker alleles may drop out of the profile. This always presents a problem because it makes the genotype of a marker appear homozygous when the source of the sample is actually heterozygous, or causes there to be no result for that marker when the source of the sample is homozygous. In most cases in which allele dropout occurs, it leads to false exclusions, but it can lead to false inclusions as well. A general rule of thumb is that the markers with the largest alleles are most vulnerable to dropout, but the testing laboratory should have validation studies that demonstrate which markers and alleles are most vulnerable, and how minute or degraded the sample must be for allele dropout to occur.

Cases in which this consideration is relevant will most often involve a minute or degraded crime scene sample and a marker(s) at which the defendant's reference sample is heterozygous but the crime scene sample is homozygous. If one suspects that an evidence sample is compromised enough that alleles may have dropped out of the profile, one can compensate for this possibility by adjusting the calculation of the RMP for those markers for which the evidence sample is homozygous. For markers for which the evidence is heterozygous and the defendant shares both alleles, the RMP can be calculated as described earlier. For markers for which the evidence is homozygous and the defendant is either heterozygous (possessing one copy of the evidence's allele) or homozygous (a perfect match), one must use a modified formula to calculate the RMP. If, for example, the evidence exhibits the 6 allele for the TH01 marker, but the defendant has both the 6 and 8 alleles, one can argue that the defendant's profile matches that of the evidence, but that the number 8 allele dropped out of the evidence profile because the sample was minute or degraded. In this case, you adjust the RMP for the TH01 marker to reflect the fact that you are claiming that one allele has dropped out. Following this argument, anyone who possesses the number 6 allele, either as a 6,6 homozygote or along with any other TH01 allele, would be considered to match the evidence's profile. Because an individual can only have one genotype for any marker, each of the possible 6-containing genotypes is mutually exclusive with the others. Under this reasoning, the source of the evidence could have the 6,7 genotype or the 6,8 genotype or the 6,9 genotype, and so on. This represents a logical OR situation, as opposed to the AND situation that calls for the product rule. In an OR situation, one adds the probabilities of the different events together, rather than multiplying them. Therefore, one computes the total probability of all the 6-containing genotypes by adding together the probabilities associated with each of the different genotypes that contain the number 6 allele. In this case, TH01 has 20 known alleles. There will therefore be 20 probabilities to add up, corresponding to the one homozygous and 19 heterozygous genotypes that could be obtained for a TH01 genotype that contained the number 6 allele. Each of these 20 genotypes' probabilities can be calculated as described above.

THE LIKELIHOOD RATIO (LR) ALLOWS THE ANALYST TO COMPARE THE STRENGTH OF COMPETING HYPOTHESES

The LR and Bayes' Theorem

In most cases tried in American courts, the prosecution informs the jury that the defendant's DNA profile matches that of the evidence, and then states what the probability is that a randomly selected member of the relevant reference population would also have that DNA profile. The jurors use that information to decide how probative the DNA evidence is and how to incorporate the DNA evidence into their decision regarding the defendant's guilt. In contrast, in the United Kingdom, the prosecution often uses a **likelihood ratio (LR)** approach when presenting the evidence. The LR provides a means by which the trier of fact can mathematically compare the strength of the prosecution's hypothesis against the strength of the defense's hypothesis. The LR provides a valid means of interpreting DNA evidence in all cases, including mixtures (discussed later in this chapter) and other complex cases. Unfortunately, however, the LR approach is not used routinely in American courts except for paternity cases.

Before we go any further, we should review the difference between probability and odds. Although people frequently use the terms "odds" and "probability" interchangeably, they are not the same. If we have two competing hypotheses, each with its own probability of being true, dividing one probability by the other gives us the odds in favor of or against the hypotheses. For example, imagine you have a barrel with 100 marbles. Imagine further that you have 75 white marbles and 25 black marbles in

[79] Balding, 2005; Balding and Donnelly, 1996; Evett and Weir, 1998.

the barrel. When you draw out a marble, the probability that it will be white is 75/100 = 75%. The probability that the marble will be black is 25/100 = 25%. Drawing out a white marble is three times more likely than drawing out a black marble; the odds in favor of drawing out a white marble are therefore 3 to 1. The 3:1 odds tell you that your hypothesis "the marble I draw out will be white" is three times as likely to be true as the competing hypothesis "the marble I draw out will be black." In general, the relationship between odds and probability can be given as follows:

$$Prob = Odds/(Odds + 1) \qquad \text{(Eq. 4.15a)}$$

or

$$Odds = Prob/(1 - Prob). \qquad \text{(Eq. 4.15b)}$$

The LR approach stems from **Bayes' Theorem**, which provides a mathematical model that illustrates how a purely logical mind would combine multiple pieces of information in order to determine the relative strengths of the two competing hypotheses. Several population geneticists and statisticians have demonstrated that Bayes' Theorem lends itself well to the analysis of the evidence in a DNA trial; it takes into account the rest of the evidence attending the case as well as the results of the DNA testing.[79] Recall from the discussion earlier in this chapter that many of the common logical fallacies that people commit when presented with DNA evidence stem from the fact that people ignore the rest of the evidence. Despite the fact that the DNA Advisory Board has acknowledged its validity, Bayes' Theorem is rarely used in American criminal courts, except in paternity determinations. It can, however, provide the best guidance for decision making when the analysis is complicated by factors such as multiple contributors to an evidence sample.

In Bayes' Theorem, one uses a mathematical ratio to compare how likely one hypothesis is compared to a competing hypothesis. To apply Bayes' Theorem to criminal trials, one uses what some have called the odds version of Bayes' Theorem. As the following equation illustrates, it is so named because it divides the probabilities of events assuming the prosecution's theory is true by the probability of these events assuming the defense's hypothesis is true, thereby giving the odds in favor of the prosecution's hypothesis being true. The formula for the equation is:

$$\frac{p(Hp \mid E, I)}{p(Hd \mid E, I)} = \frac{p(E \mid Hp, I)}{p(E \mid Hd, I)} \times \frac{p(Hp, I)}{p(Hd, I)}. \qquad \text{(Eq. 4.16)}$$

This is no doubt a rather intimidating formula to behold if one isn't accustomed to thinking through mathematical terms. It can be translated into easily understandable terms, however, so let's break it down. First, in words, the Bayes' Theorem formula can be onceptualized as follows:

posterior odds of defendant's guilt given the non-DNA and DNA evidence	=	LR associated with the match between the DNA profiles	×	prior odds of defendant's guilt given the non-DNA evidence

Bayes' Theorem multiplies the **prior odds of guilt**, which is derived from the non-DNA evidence in the case, by the odds of finding a match between the defendant's DNA profile and that of the evidence to get the **posterior odds of guilt**. The posterior odds of guilt tell us how much more or less likely the prosecution's hypothesis is than the defense's, and can be converted into a probability using Eq. (4.15a).

If one elects to use a Bayesian analysis to guide the decision regarding the defendant's guilt or innocence, one must decide what posterior odds of guilt will justify declaring the defendant guilty. Some commentators have referred to Blackstone's famous statement that "it is better that ten guilty persons escape, than that one innocent suffer," but several authorities, including the Supreme Court, have asserted that this principle understates the proper legal standard for conviction. Thomas Starkie's statement that "it is better that ninety-nine... offenders should escape than that one innocent man should be condemned" more closely reflects the proper standard of proof.[80] If one follows Starkie's recommendation, one would require posterior odds of guilt greater than 99 to convict the defendant.

[80] Ceci and Friedman, 2000; *Schlup v. Delo*, United States Reports, U.S. Supreme Court, 1995:513, 298–322.

Let's take a close look at the Bayes' Theorem formula. First, let's consider the characters used in the formula. The letter p indicates the probability of something, so $p(X)$ indicates the probability that X will happen or that X is true. Hp indicates the prosecution's hypothesis that the defendant is guilty, while Hd indicates the defense's hypothesis that the defendant is innocent. E denotes the DNA evidence—the match between the defendant's DNA profile and that of the evidence. I indicates the other evidence pertinent to the case (for example, eyewitness information, victim's statements). The "|" character indicates a conditional probability, that is, the probability that something will be true given the condition that is specified after the "|."

Now let's look at the three terms in the formula. The term $p(Hp|E,I)$ can be read as "the probability that the prosecution's hypothesis is true (Hp), given that the defendant's DNA profile matches the evidence's DNA profile (E) and that the other evidence implicates the defendant as well (I)." The term $p(Hd|E,I)$ gives the probability that the defense's hypothesis is true (Hd), given that the defendant's DNA profile matches the evidence's DNA profile (E) and that the other evidence implicates the defendant as well (I). The first term in the formula, therefore, tells us how much more likely the prosecution's hypothesis (the defendant is guilty) is than the defense's (the defendant is not guilty) after all the evidence has been considered.

The second term in the formula allows the trier of fact to assess the weight of the DNA evidence. The term $p(E|Hp,I)$ can be read as "the probability that the match between the profiles would be found (the evidence) given that the prosecution's hypothesis is true and considering the other evidence in the case." The term $p(E|Hd,I)$ can be read as "the probability that the match between the profiles would be found (the evidence) given that the defense's hypothesis is true and considering the other evidence in the case." This term, therefore, allows one to state how much more likely it is that the evidence came from the defendant than from some other member of the race or ethnic group to which the defendant belongs.

As we discuss later, there are some serious misgivings about whether jurors can use Bayes' Theorem properly to arrive at a valid decision regarding the defendant's guilt in the face of all the evidence. Even when the prosecutor is not using the full Bayes' Theorem, however, it is possible to use the LR represented by the second term in Eq. (4.16):

$$\frac{p(E\,|\,Hp,I)}{p(E\,|\,Hd,I)}.$$

to assess the weight of the match between the defendant's DNA profile and that of the evidence. The prosecutor can use this LR to support the claim that the defendant is the source of the evidence, and can integrate this with the non-DNA evidence to make the overall case for the defendant's guilt. Note also that this is the only portion of the evidence about which the forensic scientist is qualified to testify. The forensic analyst is only qualified to testify about what the probability of finding a match between the DNA profiles is given the assumption that the defendant is guilty versus given the assumption that the defendant is innocent. He or she is not qualified to estimate the weight of the non-DNA evidence; that is the province of the triers of fact. In order to avoid biases, the forensic analyst should conduct the analysis with no knowledge of the circumstances surrounding the case or the sample being analyzed.

In many cases, the numerator (top term) of the LR fraction is 1 because one would definitely expect the DNA profiles to match if the defendant was guilty (if Hp was true). Furthermore, the denominator (bottom term) often equals the RMP, because the defense's hypothesis is that the defendant was not associated with the crime and the match is coincidental. The LR term therefore often reduces down to 1/RMP.

Now consider the third term in the formula. The term $p(Hp|I)$ can be read as "the probability that the prosecution's hypothesis is true, given the non-DNA evidence in the case." The term $p(Hd|I)$ can be read as "the probability that the defense's hypothesis is true, given the non-DNA evidence in the case." This term, therefore, assesses the weight of the non-DNA evidence. It is this portion of the Bayesian analysis that many feel cannot be properly implemented in criminal trials.

Bayes' Theorem is not routinely used in criminal trials primarily because many experts feel that jurors are unable to assign a valid prior probability in the face of the non-DNA evidence. Unlike the DNA evidence, for which there are population databases that allow one to predict the probability of a match between the evidence and an individual, there is no database that allows a juror to accurately determine what the probability is that the defendant is guilty given that he or she matches an eyewitness's description, lives in the vicinity of the crime scene or had an argument with the victim in the past. Many feel that it is often impossible for a judge or juror to determine the prior probability of the defendant's guilt from such evidence, and that different jurors will draw drastically different conclusions if they are required to try. All these concerns are reasonable. In addition, however, some have argued that the very act of assigning a prior probability greater than zero to the prosecution's hypothesis (that the defendant is guilty) violates the basic tenet of American law that the defendant is considered innocent until proven guilty. This argument is fallacious, but unfortunately, it has been accepted in some courts, including the first appellate court that rejected the use of Bayes' Theorem.[81] In

[81] *State v. Skipper*, 637 A.2d 1101, Conn. 1994.

Skipper, Roy E. Skipper was convicted of sexual assault charges when a minor with whom he had a long relationship became pregnant. Based on Bayes' Theorem, the prosecution showed that the probability of paternity was 99.97%. Skipper appealed the conviction, claiming that the assignment of a prior probability of paternity that was greater than zero violated his right to be considered innocent until proven guilty. The appellate court agreed and remanded the case for a new trial.

The argument that the presumption of innocence translates into the prior odds of guilt being zero is fallacious. Fortunately, this has been recognized in more recent court decisions.[82] For any crime, there is a reasonable suspect pool. Furthermore, by all logical definitions of the terms, the reasonable suspect pool always includes the perpetrator. In addition, the reasonable suspect pool also includes another group of people who share one or more critical characteristics with the perpetrator (e.g., physical description, whereabouts at the time the crime was committed). Given that somebody from the reasonable suspect pool has in fact committed the crime in question, the prior odds of guilt for each individual in the reasonable suspect pool is greater than zero. In most cases, all members of the reasonable suspect pool have the same probability of being guilty, so if we let N represent the number of people in the suspect pool, the prior probability that any one of them is guilty is $1/N$. Evidence that suggests that an individual's prior odds of guilt are actually zero (e.g., the suspect being able to prove he was elsewhere at the time) precludes including the individual in the reasonable suspect pool to begin with. The presumption of innocence forces the prosecution to bear the burden of showing that one specific individual from the reasonable suspect pool (the defendant) committed the crime, but it does not dictate that a value of zero be assigned for the prior odds of guilt. If it did, the prior odds of guilt would have to be set at zero for all cases, and therefore the posterior odds of guilt would always be zero, regardless of how strong the DNA evidence against the defendant was.

Another unfortunate discrepancy between the theoretical benefits of Bayes' Theorem and the practical realities of criminal trials is the fact that people do not think in mathematical terms. As Evett and Weir[83] have aptly stated, the process of deciding a defendant's guilt or innocence is a matter of "updating uncertainty" in the face of additional evidence. This is a very appropriate way to put it; we can never be 100% certain that any of

[82] *Griffiths v State of Texas*, TX-QL 1544 No. 07-96-0140-CR, 1998.

[83] Evett and Weir, 1998.

our conclusions are correct, and we modify that uncertainty as we receive new evidence. Unfortunately, jurors do not think in terms of uncertainty. They think in categorical terms: they either believe a proposition or they don't. If the proposition is 51% likely to be true, and that is enough to get them to believe it is true, they incorporate the belief that it is true into their thinking, and forget the fact that they were not 100% certain of this conclusion as they move forward. As discussed in Chapter 7, several mock jury studies have illustrated that people do not incorporate probabilistic evidence into their decisions in the manner that Bayes' Theorem suggests they should. Other studies clearly demonstrate that many people who understand statements that are expressed as probabilities completely misunderstand statements that express the same information as a statement of odds.[84] Bruce Budowle, director of the FBI forensic laboratory, once claimed that "[w]e are all Bayesians in real day life."[85] If we were all good Bayesians in everyday life, there would be far fewer logical fallacies committed and far greater consistency in court decisions. Unfortunately, we are all presented with repeated opportunities to be Bayesians in our everyday lives, but we usually fail miserably at the task.

[84] Taroni and Aitken, 1998a,b.

[85] Budowle, 2001.

Incorporating the Possibility of Laboratory Error into the LR Calculation

This formulation of the Bayes' Theorem illustrates the importance of the controversy that still rages over how to incorporate the possibility that a laboratory made an error in the interpretation of the DNA evidence. As discussed in Chapter 7, there are several reasons why no one can provide a valid estimate of the probability of a laboratory error in any given case. This is unfortunate, because the probability of laboratory error strongly influences the probative value of the DNA evidence. When there is a match between an innocent defendant's DNA profile and that of the evidence, two explanations are possible (assuming that no close relatives are suspects and that the authorities have not tampered with the evidence): either the laboratory has made a "false-positive" type of error in declaring that the defendant's DNA profile was observed in the crime scene evidence, or the defendant's DNA profile coincidentally matches that of the person who is the true source of the evidence (a random match has occurred). The two possibilities are mutually exclusive. A coincidental match occurs when the defendant's profile matches that of the evidence, but the defendant was not involved in the crime. The probability of this is

[86] Thompson et al., 2003.

given by the RMP. A false-positive error will occur when the defendant's profile does not actually match that of the evidence, but an error in the handling, labeling or analysis of the sample causes the analyst to claim that it does. The probability of a false positive (PFP) is calculated by multiplying the probability that the profiles do not match (1 – RMP) by the probability of an error in the handling or labeling of the sample. When there are two mutually exclusive sources of error, either of which alone will cause the wrong conclusion to be drawn (a logical OR situation), to calculate the total probability of error, one adds the two probabilities together. Therefore, the total probability of false incrimination (PFI) due to either a coincidental match or a false-positive laboratory error can be calculated as follows:

$$PFI = RMP + [PFP \times (1 - RMP)]. \qquad \text{(Eq. 4.17)}$$

Following this logic, the LR that assesses the weight of the DNA evidence should be expressed not as $1/RMP$, but as $1/PFI$, or $1/\{RMP + [PFP \times (1 - RMP)]\}$. The RMP is usually very small; therefore, $1 - RMP$ is usually very close to 1. Thus, $[PFP \times (1 - RMP)]$ is usually very close to the value of PFP. The denominator of the LR, therefore, reduces down to $RMP + PFP$, and the LR to $1/(RMP + PFP)$. In many cases involving STR data, the RMP is infinitesimal—far smaller than the estimate even a laboratory director would admit for the laboratory's PFP. Therefore, $(RMP + PFP)$ essentially equals PFP, and the LR approximates $1/PFP$. Using a Bayesian analysis, Thompson and colleagues[86] have demonstrated that the PFP will have an especially important effect on the final odds of guilt in situations in which the RMP is very small. Furthermore, they have demonstrated that, if the prior odds of guilt are low, the posterior odds of guilt can be surprisingly low, even with a very small RMP for the DNA profile match. Appendix II provides a few numerical examples from their work that illustrate how the prior odds, RMP and PFP influence the posterior odds of guilt.

THE APPLICATION OF BAYES' THEOREM TO PATERNITY DISPUTES

The Concept of Linkage, Not to Be Confused with LD/LE

Earlier in this chapter we discussed the requirement for LE between the different markers that are included in a multiplex forensic testing panel. For relatedness testing, the mathematical theory that underlies the statistical calculations requires that there be no **linkage** between any of the markers included in the testing panel. Let's take a moment to draw the distinction between LD/LE and linkage. The LD and LE concepts are population concepts. Ideally, knowing the genotype an individual has for one marker gives the analyst no clue as to what genotype that individual might have for a second marker. When there is LD between two markers in a reference population, however, if the analyst knows that the individual has a certain genotype for the first marker, he or she then knows that there is an increased probability the individual will have one or more particular genotypes for the second marker. Linkage, on the other hand, refers to the process whereby a parent passes down his or her marker alleles to his or her children (the transmission of parental alleles to children is discussed in Chapter 1). Recall that each parent has two alleles for each STR marker and that he or she will pass one of the two alleles from each marker down to his or her child. In order to determine paternity, we observe which marker alleles the child has inherited from his or her mother and father. In most cases, the mother is available for testing, so the father's contribution can be determined by subtracting the mother's contribution from the child's DNA profile. When we find an alleged father whose DNA profile matches the paternal contribution to the child's DNA profile, we calculate the probability of that same set of marker alleles coming from another man who was selected at random from the alleged father's ethnic subgroup (a coincidental match). In order to use the product rule to produce an accurate estimate of the probability of a coincidental match, the different markers' alleles must be inherited independently from each other. The fact that the child has inherited a particular allele from one marker should not allow one to predict what allele the child has inherited for any of the other markers.

The reader is directed to the texts listed in Appendix V for a detailed explanation of meiosis and recombination, which underlie the concept of linkage between two markers. Fortunately, one can use a simple rule of thumb to predict the degree of linkage between two markers: the closer two markers lie, the more likely they are to be linked. Markers that lie on different chromosomes are always inherited independently from each other. For this reason, the commercially available forensic testing kits usually include no more than one marker from any one chromosome, so that linkage will not confound the interpretation of the data in cases in which the test is performed to establish the relatedness of two individuals. Markers that lie far apart on a single chromosome are also inherited independently from each other, and it is therefore acceptable to include them together if desired. For example, the AMPFlSTR Identifiler kit™ from Applied Biosystems contains one marker from the tip of the short arm of chromosome 2 and another marker from the tip of the long arm of chromosome 2. These two markers lie far enough apart on chromosome 2 to be inherited independently from each other, and can therefore be used together in a paternity testing panel.

As already mentioned, there are thousands of markers that are polymorphic enough to be useful for forensic identity testing, and forensic DNA tests usually include fewer than 20 markers. Given that, it is rare to find a forensic testing battery for which there is linkage between any two of the markers.

Using the LR and Bayes' Theorem to Calculate the Probability of Paternity

Unlike criminal cases, the LR and Bayes' Theorem are used regularly in paternity cases. As discussed earlier in this chapter, the general formula that is applied here is as follows:

$$\frac{p(Hp \mid E,I)}{p(Hd \mid E,I)} = \frac{p(E \mid Hp,I)}{p(E \mid Hd,I)} \times \frac{p(Hp,I)}{p(Hd,I)}. \qquad \text{(Eq. 4.18)}$$

In these cases, *Hp* represents the prosecutor's hypothesis that the alleged father is the true father of the child, while *Hd* represents the defense's hypothesis that the alleged father is not the true father of the child. The symbol *E* represents the DNA evidence, namely, that the child possesses one allele at each marker that could have come from the alleged father. The symbol *I* represents the other evidence in the case, including details of the relationship between the mother and the alleged father or information regarding the number of men who had sex with the mother during the relevant fertile period.

As discussed earlier in this chapter, the second term in this equation,

$$\frac{p(E|Hp,I)}{p(E|Hd,I)}$$

represents the LR associated with the DNA evidence. The LR illustrates how much more likely it would be to have observed the common alleles in the profiles of the child and the alleged father if the alleged father was the true father of the child versus if the alleged father was not the true father of the child. For paternity disputes, this LR is referred to as the **paternity index (PI)**. The **posterior odds of paternity (POP)** equal the PI multiplied by the prior odds of paternity, which are derived from the non-DNA evidence (symbolized in the conditional probabilities by *I*). One should note that the forensic testing laboratory is only in a position to provide an assessment of the PI, and not the POP. Ideally, the forensic analyst should know nothing at all about the non-DNA evidence and therefore should be in no position to give an estimate of the prior odds of paternity. The following discussion applies to most paternity cases. The reader is referred to Evett and Weir,[87] however, for instructions on how to adjust the calculations for cases of incest, cases in which the true father and the alleged father are related, and when the alleged father is not available for typing, but a close relative of his is. Fung and colleagues[88] also provide the means by which one can adjust the calculation of the power of exclusion in cases in which the true father is a relative of the alleged father.

[87] Evett and Weir (1998).

[88] Fung et al., 2002.

[89] Hageman et al., 2002, Appendix 7.

The PI will differ from one marker to the next, depending on whether the mother, child and alleged father are homozygous versus heterozygous at that marker. The PI is calculated for each marker, and then the different markers' data are multiplied together to constitute the overall PI. Hageman and colleagues[89] have provided a table that illustrates the different PIs for each possible combination of maternal, child and alleged father genotypes, including situations in which the mother is unavailable for typing. Their table is duplicated in Appendix III.

Once again, the primary weakness of this approach lies in the difficulty one encounters trying to specify the prior odds of paternity. In many cases, the parties will give conflicting testimony regarding the mother's sexual conduct during the relevant fertile period. If the mother testifies that she had sex with five men during the relevant fertile period, then the prior probability that any single alleged father is the true father, represented by $p(Hp|I)$, is 1/5. Consequently, the prior probability that the alleged father is not the father, represented by $p(Hd|I)$, is 4/5. Because the defense's hypothesis is four times as likely as the prosecution's hypothesis, the prior odds of paternity are 1/4, or 4:1 against the prosecution's hypothesis. If there is a dispute over the mother's sexual behavior during the relevant fertile period, however, the courts are often unable to arrive at a confident estimate of the prior odds of paternity. Many courts have chosen to assign the value of 1 for the prior odds of paternity. This corresponds to the court attaching as much credibility to the mother's statement as the alleged father's, and estimating that the prior probability of the defendant being the father (*Hp*) or not being the father (*Hd*) are both 50%, or 0.50. In spite of the fact that several commentators have pointed out that this policy has no scientific basis,[90] it is written into a number of states' statutes. Because of the inherent difficulty in specifying the prior odds of paternity in many cases, some have suggested that the court be provided with a table that illustrates what the posterior probability of paternity is for a range of prior probabilities.[91]

Each state sets its own criteria regarding what the posterior odds of paternity must be for the alleged father to be declared the true father of the child. Most states have adopted standards based on the Uniform Parentage Act (UPA) of 2002.[92] The UPA sets the standard for declaring a man the father of a child if tests indicate a 99% or higher posterior probability of paternity and a PI of at least 100.

Allowing for the Possibility of Mutation

One of the reasons tetranucleotide repeats are favored over dinucleotide repeats as markers for forensic testing is their lower mutation rate; the mutation rates of the commonly used STRs range from 1–4 mutations per 1,000 generations.[93] Mutation usually involves the gain or loss (usually gain) of one repeated sequence unit, but greater changes in STR length have been observed. The most common mechanism for STR mutations involves errors in DNA replication due to malfunction of the enzyme DNA polymerase, which chains the nucleotides together to make the new DNA strands (discussed in Chapter 2). The presence of the repeated sequence causes the DNA polymerase to slip, most often resulting in the addition of a single repeat unit to the repeated sequence. Different markers exhibit different mutation rates, and within a single marker, longer alleles are more likely to mutate than shorter ones.[94] In addition, some studies suggest that the mutation rate is higher when the allele is passed down from the father than when it is passed down from the mother.[95]

Exclusion is a qualitative judgment; it does not require knowledge of the population genetics or calculation of probability. In criminal cases, a mismatch at only one marker is usually considered enough to exclude the suspect. This is in part because of the stringent standard of proof in

[90] Kaye, 1990; Balding and Nichols, 1994; Evett and Weir, 1998.

[91] Evett and Weir, 1998.

[92] 42 U.S.C.S. §666(a)(5).

[93] Chakraborty et al., 1997; Butler, 2005.

[94] Kayser et al., 2000.

[95] Brinkmann et al., 1998.

criminal cases, and in part because the evidence sample is being judged as coming from the defendant, so the possibility of mutation does not enter into the calculation.[96] In paternity cases, however, when the profile of the alleged father is being compared to that of his alleged child, it is always possible that a mutation could have taken place at one (or more) of the marker loci during the genesis of the sperm that created the child. STRs have a mutation rate of approximately 1–4 per 1,000 generations.[97] This means that, if you obtain 10-STR DNA profiles from a parent and child, there is an approximately 2% probability of observing a mismatch at one of the STR loci, because the locus has gained or lost one or more copies of the repeated sequence motif as it was transmitted from parent to child.[98] In most of the reported cases in which a mutation has been detected, the parent's and child's alleles have differed at only one marker. One case has been reported, however, in which there were mismatches between a father and his son at two Y chromosome STRs.[99] For this reason, many jurisdictions require a mismatch at more than one marker before a putative father is excluded.

When one postulates that a mutation has occurred in transmission from the true father to the child, the LR for paternity calculations must be adjusted to account for this possibility. Selection of the proper correction factor is complicated. The correction factor will differ in situations in which the mutation must have come through one parent versus situations in which it could have come through either parent. The correction factor also varies depending on whether the mother, true father and alleged father are members of the same family or population subgroup. Dawid and colleagues have provided guidelines for adjusting the LR in the face of mutations, and Ayers has extended Dawid's work by illustrating how Dawid's equations can be adapted in cases in which the true parents and the alleged father belong to the same ethnic group.[100]

RECOMMENDED PROCEDURE FOR ANALYZING MIXED SAMPLES

Mixed Samples Are Especially Challenging

When a sample contains material from more than one contributor, the opportunity for confusion increases dramatically. The contributors may share one or more alleles,[101] making it hard to determine the number of

[96] Except for the possibility of somatic mutations if the evidence and reference samples are from different tissues, as discussed in Chapter 1.

[97] Balding, 2005; Butler, 2005.

[98] If a VNTR test was performed, the probability is significantly higher. VNTRs have mutation rates of 50–110 per 1,000 generations (Jeffreys et al., 1988).

[99] Kayser and Sajantila, 2001.

[100] Dawid et al., 2001; Ayers, 2002.

[101] In this situation, it is often said that one allele "masks" the other.

contributors to the sample. In addition, recall from the discussion in Chapter 3 that it may be impossible to differentiate between an STR stutter peak from the major contributor and a true allele peak from the minor contributor. Furthermore, if the mixed sample contains very little material from the minor contributor, the differential amplification and stochastic effects that plague the analysis of minute samples (discussed in Chapter 3) may make it difficult to assess the minor contribution accurately. The possibility of allele dropout is particularly difficult to incorporate into the analysis of a mixed sample. Because the alleles from the major contributor are still visible, the analyst must also consider the possibility that the minor contributor's alleles are still present but are being masked by the major contributor's alleles.

If the major contribution is from the defendant and the minor contribution is from the victim, the minor component can often be ignored, and the major component analyzed as a single-source sample. If the minor component belongs to the defendant, however, it is more likely that artifacts will interfere with the interpretation of the data. For most STR analyses, if the minor contributor has contributed 10% of the total sample, his or her profile can usually be obtained. A valid profile, or at least a partial profile, may even be obtained if the minor contributor has contributed only 5% of the total sample. In any case, the laboratory should have validation data that illustrate that the results they are reporting are within their protocol's range of sensitivity. These data are easy to generate; the analyst merely mixes two different samples whose profiles are known in several different relative proportions. As discussed in Chapter 3, the validation study should include samples representing a wide range of relative proportions of the major versus minor contributor, so that real case samples will fall within the range that was covered by the samples from the validation study.

In some cases in the past, the testing laboratory has reported that the sample was a mixture, and provided no statistical interpretation to accompany the statement. This severely limits the use of the evidence at trial, and some commentators have appropriately called this approach "unhelpful, irresponsible, and cowardly."[102] Many courts concur and will not admit any DNA evidence without an accompanying statistical interpretation, regardless of how complicated (and difficult for the average juror to understand) that interpretation may be.[103] The International Society of

[102] Rudin and Inman, 2002.

[103] For example, *People v. Coy*, 620 N.W.2d 888, Mich. App. 2000.

Forensic Genetics (ISFG) serves as the primary body for peer review of policies and practices for forensic scientists performing DNA analyses. The ISFG has published a set of recommendations for analyzing mixed DNA samples.[104] These recommendations are based largely on guidelines developed by the Forensic Science Service of the United Kingdom.[105] The following discussion is based on their recommendations, which we endorse.

Identifying the Sample As a Mixture and Determining the Number of Contributors

As in any DNA analysis, one begins by identifying the true allele peaks. This means not only determining which peaks are true allele peaks versus artifacts, but also determining the size (i.e., the number of tetranucleotides in the repeated sequence) of each allele. As discussed in Chapter 3, a size ladder is run along with the samples, and the true alleles should measure within 0.5 bp of the corresponding alleles in the size ladder. If the alleles in the samples do not measure exactly the same size as the corresponding alleles in the size ladder control, the difference between the sample's allele peak and the standard's corresponding allele peak should be identical for all peaks. In other words, if the allele sizes in the sample do not exactly match the allele sizes in the size ladder, all the peaks in the sample should measure 0.5 bp longer than the corresponding peaks from the size ladder, or all the peaks in the sample should measure 0.5 bp shorter than the corresponding peaks from the size ladder.

Once the analyst has identified all the true allele peaks, he or she must then identify the sample as a mixture and determine the number of contributors to the mixture. A mixed sample can be identified by the number of alleles seen at one or more markers, or by an imbalance in the allele peak heights or areas within one or more markers.

Barring rare chromosome duplications, each individual only has two alleles for any marker. A mixed sample is therefore indicated by the presence of more than two peaks for one or more STR markers.[106] A mixed sample may not always contain more than two alleles for every marker, however. If the two contributors to a two-source sample are both homozygous for the same allele at a particular marker, only one allele peak will be visible in the data. If the two homozygotes possess different alleles, or if the sample contains material from two heterozygotes who share both

[104] Gill et al., 2006.

[105] Clayton et al., 1998.

[106] A mixture will also be indicated if there are more than two autorad bands in a VNTR, or a pattern of positive signals in a DQA1 or Polymarker™ test that indicates the presence of more than two different alleles for one or more of the genes included in the test.

their alleles, two peaks will be visible at that marker. Because nobody has more than two alleles (barring rare chromosome duplications), you can always determine the minimum number of people who have contributed to a mixed stain. Because individuals may be homozygous or share alleles, however, you can never definitively prove the maximum number of people who could have contributed to the stain.

All scientists are trained to seek the most parsimonious, most probable and least complicated interpretation of their observations. It is also important, however, that the scientist consider all observations, including apparent "oddball" observations, and not discard any one marker's data because they suggest a different conclusion than the other marker's data do. For example, when determining the number of contributors to a mixture, the analyst should use the marker that shows the greatest number of alleles, even if none of the other markers exhibit that many alleles. As one study has demonstrated,[107] 17 to 18% of three-person mixtures (in which there are a total of six alleles at each marker) exhibit more than four alleles at only one marker. In a situation like this, because that one marker's data are inconsistent with all the other markers' data, the analyst may attribute the "extra" allele at that marker to an artifact and claim that the mixture contains DNA from only two people. If the analyst discards the "oddball" marker, these three-person mixtures will be mischaracterized as two-person mixtures. Once the analyst has identified the marker with the largest number of true allele peaks, in the interest of parsimony he or she should then assume that the sample contains the smallest number of contributors who could account for that collection of alleles.

In addition to the number of alleles seen at each marker, the relative intensities of the allele peaks may indicate that a sample is a mixture. The intensities of the STR peaks reflect (approximately) the amount of starting DNA in the PCR.[108] In addition, the peak intensities are approximately additive, so that a peak that represents two copies of an allele (as would be seen in a homozygous individual) is expected to exhibit approximately twice the intensity of a peak that represents one copy of that allele (as would be seen in a heterozygous individual). For example, if a sample exhibits two peaks at a marker, but the height or area of one peak is three times that of the other, it is unlikely that the sample is from a single source. In a situation such as this, it is more likely that the sample represents a mixture of a heterozygous contributor and a homozygous one,

[107] Paoletti et al., 2005.

[108] Gill et al., 1998; 2006.

with the homozygote having two copies of one of the alleles the heterozygote has. This combination of genotypes (let's call them 1,1 and 1,2) results in there being three copies of one allele (in this example, allele 1) and one copy of the other allele (in this case, allele 2). Allele 1's peak intensity, therefore, would be expected to be approximately three times that of allele 2.

Options for Statistical Analysis: The Probability of Inclusion/ Exclusion Approach Versus the LR Approach

Once the sample has been identified as a mixture and the number of contributors has been determined, three general scenarios may follow. In the easiest cases, one of the profiles in the mixture will match a contributor whose DNA would be expected to be present in the sample. In a case like this, the expected profile can be visually subtracted from the data display, and the other source's profile can be confidently reported. This approach can be applied frequently in rape cases. If a vaginal sample contains the victim's profile as well as that of one other person, and the victim claims not to have had sex with anyone else recently, the profile of the perpetrator can be deduced by subtracting the victim's profile from the mixture. If the profiles of the different contributors can be separated out confidently, the analyst can report a random match probability just as he or she would for a single-source sample. If the different profiles cannot be separated out, however, the analyst can either calculate the combined probability of inclusion or exclusion, or present an LR analysis to compare the probabilities of the different competing hypotheses that are proposed to explain the alleles observed in the sample.

One way to interpret the information from a mixed sample is by calculating either the **probability of inclusion (POI)** or the **probability of exclusion (POE)**.[109] The POI and POE estimate the percentage of the population that can be included or excluded, respectively, as contributors to the mixed sample. The POI is calculated simply by adding up the frequencies of all the genotypes that could possibly be contained in the mixture. The POE is also calculated simply; the analyst merely subtracts the POI from 1. For example, if the sample contains the 4, 7, 8 and 12 alleles of a marker, then the possible genotypes in the mixture include: 4,4; 7,7; 8,8; 12,12; 4,7; 4,8; 4,12; 7,8; 7,12 and 8,12. Because this is logically an OR situation, the analyst can calculate the percentage of the

[109] Devlin, 1992.

population that is included (POI) in the list of possible contributors to the mixture by adding the frequencies associated with these genotypes. In addition, by subtracting the POI from 1, the analyst can calculate the percentage of the population that is excluded from the list of possible contributors to the mixture (POE).

These calculations afford an advantage in many forensic investigations. They don't require the analyst to know how many contributors there were to the sample, or what the genotype of any individual contributor is. The POI and POE can be calculated for any sample, and in most cases can provide a (sometimes excessively) conservative estimate of the RMP. Their power is limited, however, because they do not make use of all the available genetic information. In addition, they ignore the possibility that the analyst may be able to visually differentiate between the major and minor contributions by observing the relative intensities of the two profiles' peaks. For example, if there is a clear major and minor contributor to a sample, the major contributor's allele peaks will exhibit significantly greater intensity than the minor contributor's allele peaks. In such a case, ignoring the relative intensities of the peaks allows an individual who possesses a genotype consisting of one of the intense alleles and one of the weak alleles to be wrongly included in the list of potential contributors to the sample. The POI/POE approach is best used when the analyst is confident that all the alleles that are present are visible, or when all the suspect's alleles are present in the sample and the analyst reports the findings as "The suspect is not excluded as a contributor to the sample . . ."

The likelihood ratio (LR) enables one to assess the weight of mixed-sample evidence when other methods do not.[110] Even when the combination of alleles observed in the sample lends itself to multiple alternative hypotheses, the LR can illustrate how much more or less likely the prosecution's argument is than the defense's. When the mixture does not contain an obvious major and minor contributor, there may be several plausible hypotheses regarding the genotypes that are present in the mixture. For the sake of simplicity, in the following examples we will ignore population substructure and the possibility that relatives of the defendant may be suspects.

Consider a simple example first.[111] Imagine a rape case in which the victim's genotype for a hypothetical STR marker is 7,7, the sole suspect's

[110] Evett et al., 1998.

[111] The following examples are based on examples given in Evett and Weir, 1998, Chapter 7. For the sake of simplicity, we will ignore the possibility of population substructure, relatives being suspects and technical difficulties producing artifacts or partial profiles.

genotype is 3,9 and the 3, 7 and 9 alleles are observed in a vaginal swab sample. The prosecution's hypothesis is that the evidence contains the genotype of the victim and the defendant. Given that one would fully expect to see the 3,7,9 genotype in a sample that contained material from the victim and the defendant, the probability of the vaginal swab having a 3,7,9 genotype given the prosecution's hypothesis is 1.0, and the numerator of the LR, therefore, is 1. Now imagine that the defense is arguing that the vaginal sample contains material from the victim and some other, unknown man. In this case, because one would fully expect to see the 7 allele in the mixture if the victim contributed to the sample, the probability of seeing the 7 allele under the defense's hypothesis is 1.0. The probability associated with the defense's hypothesis, therefore, is the probability that another man, randomly selected from the relevant reference population, will have the 3,9 genotype, which equals $2p_3p_9$, in which p_3 indicates the probability of allele 3 and p_9 indicates the probability of allele 9. The LR, therefore is expressed as $1/2p_3p_9$. For example, if the 3 allele had a frequency of 2% (0.02) and the 9 allele had a frequency of 1% (0.01), the LR would equal 1/2(0.02)(0.01) = 1/0.0004 = 2,500. It is therefore 2,500 times more likely that the sample contains a mixture of material from the victim and the defendant versus a mixture of material from the victim and an unidentified man.

Now consider a slightly more complicated case. Imagine that the victim's genotype at the hypothetical marker is 6,8, the defendant's genotype is also 6,8 and the vaginal sample contains the 6 and 8 alleles. Once again, the numerator of the LR is 1, because one would expect to see the 6 and 8 alleles in the sample if the prosecution's hypothesis (that the evidence came from the defendant) is correct. The defense argues, however, that there are three possible alternative explanations for the evidence: the perpetrator could be an unidentified man who has either the 6,6, 6,8 or 8,8 genotype. In this case, because only one of these three hypotheses needs to be true to undermine the prosecution's theory of the case (logically an OR situation, not an AND situation), the denominator of the LR can be calculated by adding the probabilities of the alternative hypotheses. If p_6 and p_8 represent the frequencies of the number 6 and 8 alleles, respectively, the probability of a 6,6 genotype is p_6^2, the probability of a 6,8 genotype is $2p_6p_8$ and the probability of an 8,8 genotype is p_8^2. The LR can therefore be expressed as $1/(p_6^2 + 2p_6p_8 + p_8^2)$. Note that the analyst may be able to exclude one of the defense's hypotheses using the heterozygote balance test and the mixture proportion test (discussed later in this chapter). For example, if the victim has the 6,8 genotype and the perpetrator has the 6,6 genotype, the peak associated with the number 6 allele should be approximately three times as intense as the peak associated with the number 8 allele. If the number 8 allele's peak is approximately three times the intensity of the number 6 allele's peak, it is highly unlikely that the sample contains a mixture of the victim's genotype and a 6,6 genotype, and much more likely that it contains the victim's genotype and an 8,8 genotype.

The LR can also be applied to situations in which one of the contributors to a mixed sample cannot be identified. For example, imagine a double rape case in which the sperm-rich fraction of a vaginal sample has been found to contain the 6, 8, 9 and 12 alleles of an STR. Imagine too that it is impossible to identify a major and minor contributor to the evidence; all the peaks appear in the data with approximately equal intensity. The victim identifies one of her assailants; his genotype is 6,8. The prosecution claims that the evidence was contributed by the defendant and an unidentified man with the 9,12 genotype. Because this is an AND situation, one can apply the product rule to calculate the probability of these two events having happened. One would certainly expect to see the 6 and 8 alleles if the defendant contributed to the sample, so the probability associated with that portion of the hypothesis is 1. The probability of a second man having the 9,12 genotype is $2p_9p_{12}$, where p_9 is the frequency of the number 9 allele and p_{12} represents the frequency of the number 12 allele. The numerator of the LR, then, becomes $1 \times 2p_9p_{12}$.

In this case, the defense introduces several competing hypotheses, each of which claims that the evidence has come from two unknown men. If one assumes that the defendant was not associated with the crime, then any two genotypes that together contain the 6, 8, 9 and 12 alleles might be contained in the mixture. The rapists could conceivably have any of the following combinations of genotypes: 6,8 and 9,12; 6,9 and 8,12; 6,12 and 8,9; 8,9 and 6,12; 8,12 and 6,9; and 9,12 and 6,8.[112] Each of these two-genotype combinations represents a separate hypothesis for the defense. Because each of these individual hypotheses represents an AND situation, one multiplies the probability of the first genotype by the probability of the second genotype to get the probability of each genotype combination. Because the prosecution's case will be undermined if any one of these alternative hypotheses is

[112] Notice that in this situation, having rapist 1's genotype be 8,9 and rapist 2's genotype be 6,12 is not the same as having rapist 1's genotype be 6,12 and rapist 2's genotype be 8,9.

true (an OR situation), one adds the probabilities of the individual hypotheses to calculate the denominator of the LR. The denominator of the LR, therefore, is $(2p_6p_8 \times 2p_9p_{12}) + (2p_6p_9 \times 2p_8p_{12}) + (2p_6p_{12} \times 2p_8p_9) + (2p_8p_9 \times 2p_6p_{12}) + (2p_8p_{12} \times 2p_6p_9) + (2p_9p_{12} \times 2p_6p_8)$. Although this looks like a very complicated calculation, observe that each of these six individual products within the parentheses equals $4p_6p_8p_9p_{12}$, and the denominator of the LR, therefore, equals $24p_6p_8p_9p_{12}$. The LR, then, is expressed as $2p_9p_{12} / 24p_6p_8p_9p_{12}$, which equals $1/12\, p_6p_8$.

Let us use one final example to illustrate that the LR can provide a means to estimate the relative strengths of competing hypotheses even when the alternative theories presented by the defense are not exhaustive. Imagine a double rape case in which the victim has identified both assailants. The genotype observed in the sperm-rich fraction of a vaginal sample contains the 6, 8, 9 and 12 alleles; defendant 1 has the 6,8 genotype and defendant 2 has the 9,12 genotype. Imagine further that each defendant is being tried separately and that each is represented by a different attorney. In addition to the prosecutor's hypothesis that the evidence was deposited by defendant 1 and defendant 2, there are three alternative explanations for the evidence: the evidence could have been deposited by defendant 1 and an unknown man, by defendant 2 and an unknown man or by two unknown men. Defendant 1's attorney will obviously introduce the second and third alternative hypotheses, but not the first. Similarly, defendant 2's attorney will suggest the first and third alternative hypotheses, but not the second. In this case, the LR can be used to compare the hypotheses in a pairwise manner. Following the reasoning given in the above examples, the following probabilities are associated with the four alternative hypotheses (including the prosecutor's hypothesis):

evidence deposited by defendant 1 and defendant 2 (prosecutor's hypothesis) = 1
evidence deposited by defendant 1 and an unknown man = $2p_9p_{12}$
evidence deposited by defendant 2 and an unknown man = $2p_6p_8$
evidence deposited by two unknown men = $24p_6p_8p_9p_{12}$ (because this could involve any one of six pairs of genotypes, in which each pair of genotypes contains the 6, 8, 9 and 12 alleles).

The LR can be used not only to compare the prosecution's hypothesis against any or all of the alternative hypotheses, but also to compare one of the defense's hypotheses against another.

[113] Clayton et al., 1998.

[114] Gill et al., 2005.

The LR is applicable in all situations, regardless of how many alternative hypotheses exist that can explain the combination of alleles seen in the evidence. Even in the most complex situations, there is always a finite number of plausible alternative hypotheses, and the probability of each alternative hypothesis can be calculated. No matter how complicated the situation, the LR allows the triers of fact to compare the strengths of whatever competing hypotheses are being argued.

Differentiating Between Plausible and Implausible Genotype Combinations: Heterozygote Balance and Mixture Proportion

If one chooses to use the LR approach to compare the relative strengths of the prosecution's hypothesis versus the defense's hypothesis, in order to use the available information most efficiently, one must differentiate between the plausible and implausible genotype combinations. Instead of accepting all possible genotype combinations as plausible, as the POI and POE calculations do, the analyst must consider each possible genotype combination separately and apply two tests, the heterozygote balance test and the mixture proportion test, to determine whether that genotype combination is plausible. Both of these tests involve assessing peak intensities, using either peak height or the area under the peak as the measure of the peak intensity. The peak area is technically the better measure to use, because it takes into account the shape of the peak, but peak height also provides a reliable reflection of peak intensity.[113]

The heterozygote balance test refers to the fact that, when an individual is heterozygous for a marker, the two alleles of that marker display roughly the same intensity. More specifically, it has been determined empirically that, in a heterozygous individual, when the individual's DNA is not degraded and is present in excess of 500 pg (1 pg = 1 trillionth of a gram, or 0.000000000001 gram), the ratio of allele peak intensities (less intense allele/more intense allele) is between 0.6 and 1.0.[114] Note that a ratio of 1.0 indicates that the peak intensities are equal to each other. Therefore, for each of the possible genotype combinations that might be in the mixture, the analyst looks at the two alleles that make up each of the genotypes, and determines whether the ratio of peak intensities is between 0.6 and 1.0. For example, if the sample contains the number 6, 8, 9 and 12 alleles, one of the possible genotype combinations that is considered is 6,9 and 8,12. The analyst would look at the peak intensities for the number

6 and 9 alleles, and determine if the ratio of the lesser intensity versus the greater intensity lay between 0.6 and 1.0. The analyst would then look at the peak intensities for the number 8 and 12 alleles, and determine if the ratio of the lesser intensity versus the greater intensity lay between 0.6 and 1.0. If both ratios were between 0.6 and 1.0, the analyst would conclude that it was plausible that the 6,9 and 8,12 genotype combination might be present in the mixture. If one or both of the ratios was less than 0.6, the analyst would conclude that the evidence did not support the hypothesis that the 6,9 and 8,12 genotype combination might be present in the mixture. The heterozygote balance test is not an absolute determinant of the plausibility of a genotype being in the mixture, but it is a very useful guide for interpreting mixed samples. In all cases, the analyst first applies the heterozygote balance and mixture proportion tests to compile the list of plausible genotype combinations that might be present in the mixture, and only then looks at the reference samples from the defendant and the victim to interpret the data.

Figure 4.1 illustrates three different possible results when a mixed sample is analyzed using STR testing. The middle panel of the figure illustrates the result obtained from the mixed sample, and the top and bottom panels illustrate the same markers' data from reference samples from the two individuals who contributed to the mixture. The mixture contains twice as much DNA from the individual whose profile is shown in the top panel as it does from the individual whose profile is shown in the bottom panel. For the middle-sized marker, with allele sizes in the 160- to 190-bp range (the top axis of the figure shows the allele sizes), the interpretation of the data is straightforward. Both individuals are heterozygous, and they do not share any alleles, so four alleles are seen in the mixture. If we number them from left to right, we get the following four peak heights (in RFU): Allele 1 = 480, Allele 2 = 245, Allele 3 = 250, and Allele 4 = 430.

Imagine that these data are from the sperm-rich fraction of a sample from a rape case in which there are two suspects, with genotypes 1,4 and 2,3, respectively. The prosecution's hypothesis is that the two suspects provided the evidence. Because one would expect to see the 1, 2, 3 and 4 alleles in the sample if the prosecution's hypothesis is true, the probability of the prosecution's hypothesis (and the numerator of the LR) is 1.0. The defense, on the other hand, argues that the evidence was provided by two unknown men. The defense wants to maximize the probability of its

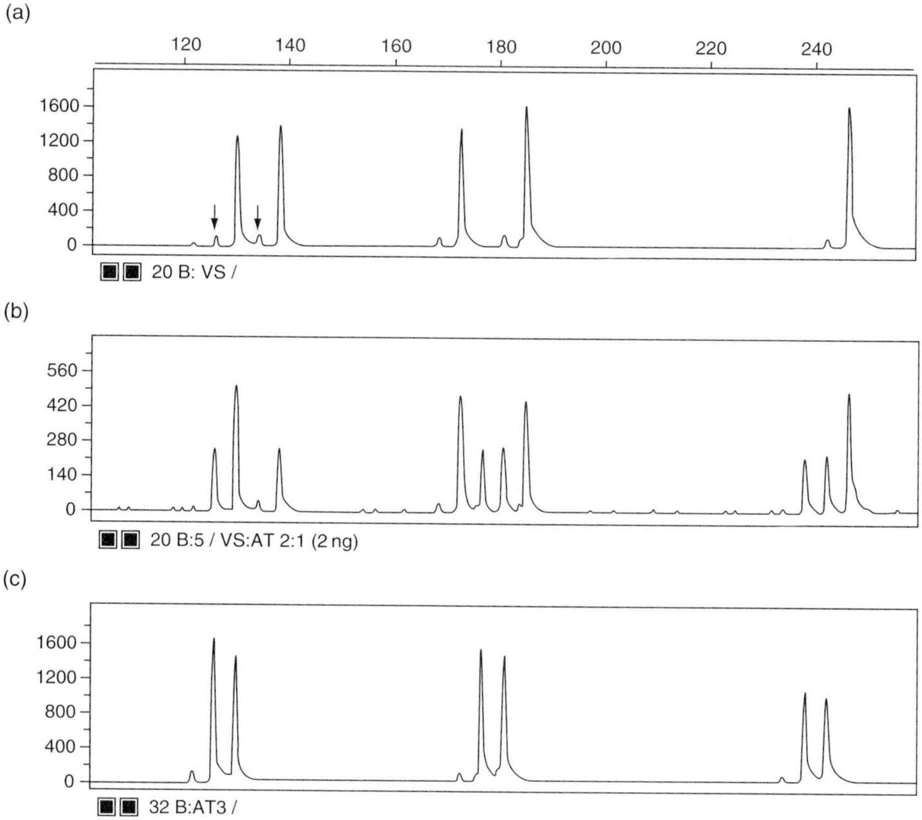

FIGURE 4.1 *Electropherograms illustrating peaks from a mixed sample (middle panel) and the two individual contributors to the mixed sample (top and bottom panels). Reprinted from Rudin and Inman, 2002, with permission from CRC Press.*

collection of competing hypotheses, and therefore maximize the denominator of the LR, which will minimize the LR itself. The best situation for the defense, then, is to argue that all possible two-genotype combinations that collectively include the 1, 2, 3 and 4 alleles could be present in the mixture. This includes the following hypotheses:

Rapist 1 had a 1,2 genotype and Rapist 2 had a 3,4 genotype.
Rapist 1 had a 1,3 genotype and Rapist 2 had a 2,4 genotype.
Rapist 1 had a 1,4 genotype and Rapist 2 had a 2,3 genotype.
Rapist 1 had a 2,3 genotype and Rapist 2 had a 1,4 genotype.
Rapist 1 had a 2,4 genotype and Rapist 2 had a 1,3 genotype.
Rapist 1 had a 3,4 genotype and Rapist 2 had a 1,2 genotype.

The heterozygote balance test is used to test the plausibility of each of the defense's individual alternative hypotheses. For example, the hypothesis that Rapist 1 had a 1,4 genotype and Rapist 2 had a 2,3 genotype is supported by the heterozygote balance test. The ratio of peak heights (smaller/larger) for alleles 1 and 4 is 430/480 = 0.90, while the ratio of peak heights for alleles 2 and 3 is 245/250 = 0.98. In contrast, the hypothesis that Rapist 1 had a 3,4 genotype and Rapist 2 had a 1,2 genotype is not supported by the heterozygote balance test. The ratio of peak heights for alleles 3 and 4 is 250/430 = 0.58, while the ratio of peak heights for alleles 1 and 2 is 245/480 = 0.51.

Note that the 0.6 ratio guideline for the heterozygote balance test applies for samples that are not degraded. Recall from Chapter 3 that degradation will impair the amplification of larger alleles more than smaller alleles. For degraded samples, if the two alleles of the marker are of significantly different sizes, the larger allele may be more affected than the smaller one, and therefore the ratio of peak heights in a single-source, heterozygous sample may be less than 0.6.

The second test that is applied to determine the plausibility of the proffered hypotheses is the mixture proportion test. In order to estimate the mixture proportion, it is best to use the amelogenin marker peaks[115] or the peaks from a marker that exhibits four alleles. For the middle-sized marker in Figure 4.1 (with allele sizes in the 160- to 190-bp range), in order to determine what mixture proportion is suggested by the hypothesis that Rapist 1 had a 1,4 genotype and Rapist 2 had a 2,3 genotype, one uses the formula (minor contributor's peaks in the numerator)

$$\frac{\text{Peak 2} + \text{Peak 3}}{\text{Peak 1} + \text{Peak 2} + \text{Peak 3} + \text{Peak 4}}$$

In the present example, these values are

$$\frac{245 + 250}{480 + 245 + 250 + 430} = 0.35$$

This suggests that the ratio of the major contribution to the minor contribution is 0.65/0.35 = 1.86:1, which is approximately equal to the actual ratio of 2:1.

Whatever the proportion of the major versus minor contributions, that proportion should be reflected in each of the markers that were tested. Therefore, if the analyst has correctly identified the two contributors' genotypes at each marker, the mixture proportion that is suggested should

115 Recall that the amelogenin gene has a copy on both the X and Y chromosomes.

[116] Clayton et al., 2005.

be similar at all markers. Some allele combinations will not allow the analyst to definitively determine the major versus minor contributor's alleles for that marker. After applying the heterozygote balance test, the analyst will be left with two or more plausible hypotheses regarding the possible genotype combinations that are reflected in the data. Each of these hypotheses will have a mixture proportion associated with it. Once all the plausible hypotheses about genotype combinations have been listed for all the markers tested, the analyst compares the mixture proportions that have been suggested at each marker. Empirical research has demonstrated that the variability in mixture proportion between different markers may be as high as ±0.35.[116] Therefore, in order for a potential genotype combination to be considered plausible, the mixture proportion associated with that genotype combination should be within ±0.35 of the average mixture proportion for all markers tested.

When there are fewer than four alleles in the mixed sample's data, it is not as easy for the analyst to differentiate between the two contributors' profiles, even though there is a major and minor contributor. For example, in Figure 4.1, the marker with the smallest alleles and the marker with the largest alleles both show three peaks in the mixed sample. In both cases, one peak is considerably higher than the other two, but there is a different explanation for why this is so for each of the two markers. For the marker with the largest alleles (in the 235- to 250-bp range), the most intense peak belongs to the major contributor, who is homozygous for that allele, whereas the two less intense peaks belong to the minor contributor, who is heterozygous. In contrast, for the marker with the smallest alleles (in the 120- to 140-bp range), the most intense peak corresponds to an allele that both the major and minor contributors share, while each of the two less intense peaks belongs to a different contributor. Clearly, if the analyst grouped the more intense alleles and the less intense alleles together, he or she would arrive at the wrong interpretation for the marker with the 120- to 140-bp alleles.

In some cases, more than one genotype combination will be considered plausible for the markers that exhibit three allele peaks. For example, for the marker in Figure 4.1 with the largest alleles (in the 235- to 250-bp range), if we number the alleles from left to right, allele 1 has a peak height = 210 RFU, allele 2 has a peak height = 215 RFU, and allele 3 has a peak height of 480 RFU. There are at least two plausible hypotheses regarding the two genotypes present for this marker. Hypothesis 1 postulates that the minor contributor has the 1,2 genotype, while the major contributor has the 3,3 genotype. The heterozygote balance ratio for the minor contributor's contribution is 210/215 = 0.98. In addition, the mixture proportion is (210 + 215)/905 = 0.47. Similarly, Hypothesis 2 postulates that the minor contributor has the 1,3 genotype, while the major contributor has the 2,3 genotype. If the analyst divides allele 3's 480 RFU between the two contributors, both heterozygote balance ratios will lie within the 0.6–1.0 guideline, and the mixture proportion will be similar to the 0.47 associated with Hypothesis 1. In this case, both genotype combinations represent plausible hypotheses because the heterozygote balance ratios associated with them are all within the 0.6–1.0 range, and the mixture proportions are close enough to the 0.35 mixture proportion that was determined for the marker exhibiting four alleles to be within the normal range of variability for this parameter.

In order to avoid bias against the defendant, it is critical that the analyst applies the heterozygote balance and mixture proportion tests before he or she knows the genotypes of the reference samples. Once all the plausible genotype combinations for all the markers tested have been listed, the analyst can then look at the reference sample genotypes to determine whether the reference sample data are compatible with any of the prosecution's or defense's hypotheses. If the reference sample data do not support one of the hypotheses, the analyst will assign a probability of zero to that hypothesis. For example, imagine the data in the middle panel of Figure 4.1 were from the sperm-rich fraction of a sample from a rape case, and the data seen in the top and bottom panels are from the two defendants in the case. Once the analyst has decided that both Hypotheses 1 and 2 from above are plausible, the reference sample genotypes allow him to clearly state that the data support the prosecution's hypothesis that these two defendants contributed to the sample. If the defendant whose profile is seen in the top panel had the 1,3 genotype instead of the 3,3 genotype, the analyst would be forced to conclude that the prosecution's hypothesis was not supported, because the data in the middle panel are not compatible with the two contributors sharing allele 1. The analyst would have already rejected the hypothesis that the evidence sample reflects a mixture of a 1,3 genotype plus a 1,2 genotype, because there is no mixture proportion that could produce the peak intensities seen in the mixed sample's data.

Accounting for Stutter Peaks and Possible Allele Dropout

The presence of stutter peaks and the possibility of allele dropout are particularly problematic when the sample is a mixture with a major and minor contributor. In a mixed sample, a stutter peak from the major contributor can have the same intensity as a true allele peak from a minor contributor. A single peak can represent a single allele, multiple shared alleles, a stutter peak or a combination of a true allele peak and a stutter peak. Depending on the number, intensities and positions of the alleles, there may be multiple plausible hypotheses regarding the genotypes present in the mixture. As is true for many issues involving the possibility of artifacts, the testing laboratory should have validation study data that demonstrate the probability that stutter peaks will be present, or that an allele may drop out, under the circumstances presented by the case at bar. Clayton and colleagues[117] have provided a thorough discussion of the issues the analyst faces when interpreting mixtures in which a major and a minor contribution can be identified. One of the examples they present is given below.

Consider the situation depicted in Figure 4.2. For this discussion, assume that allele sizes differ from each other by 4 bp. The analyst must first decide on the number of contributors to the sample. Peaks 3 and 4 obviously represent true allele peaks, but the analyst must decide if peaks 1 and 2 represent true allele peaks or stutter peaks. The intensity of a stutter peak is usually 15% or less of the intensity of the true allele peak.[118] In addition, most stutter peaks are one repeat smaller than the true allele peak. Given these guidelines, peak 1 will be considered a true allele peak. It is too intense to be a stutter peak from peak 2 and too small to be a stutter peak from peak 3. The analyst will therefore assume there were two contributors to the sample.[119] The analyst will be unable to determine whether peak 2 is a stutter peak from peak 3 or a true allele peak from the minor contributor, however, and there will therefore be two possible interpretations of these data that pass the heterozygote balance test:

Peak 2 is a stutter peak from peak 3. The minor contributor's genotype is either 1,1; 1,3 or 1,4. The major contributor's genotype is 3,4.

Peak 2 is a true allele peak. The minor contributor's genotype is 1,2. The major contributor's genotype is 3,4.

[117] Clayton et al., 1998.

[118] Gill et al., 1997; Walsh et al., 1997.

[119] In the interest of parsimony, the analyst will proceed assuming there were only two contributors to the sample, but will remain aware that this assumption may have to be revisited if the peak intensity data do not fit the assumption.

Imagine these data came from a vaginal swab sample from a rape case and the victim's genotype was 3,4. The prosecution's hypothesis would be that the defendant was the minor contributor to the sample. If the defendant had the 1,2 genotype, the prosecution's hypothesis would consider peak 2 to be a true allele peak. If the defendant had the 1,1; 1,3 or 1,4 genotype, the prosecution's hypothesis would consider peak 2 a stutter peak from peak 3.

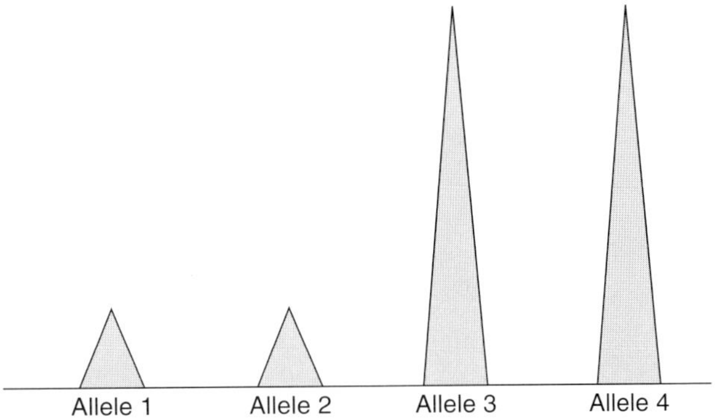

FIGURE 4.2 *Diagram illustrating a situation in which the analyst must decide whether one of the peaks in a mixed sample (allele 2) represents a true allele peak, a stutter peak or a combination of the two.*

The numerator of the LR must reflect the fact that the prosecutor's hypothesis depends not only on the fact that the defendant's alleles are present in the data, but that the prosecutor is assuming that peak 2 is or is not a stutter peak. For example, if the defendant has the 1,3 genotype,[120] the prosecution hypothesis depends on peak 2 being a stutter peak and the defendant's alleles being in the data. Because this is logically an AND situation, the numerator of the LR is calculated by multiplying the probability of a stutter peak by the probability that one would see the 1,3,4 genotype in the mixed sample if the defendant had contributed to the sample. Because the latter probability is 1.0, the numerator of the LR equals the probability that peak 2 is a stutter peak.

[120] This scenario corresponds to a Type 2d mixture in Gill et al., 1998.

The defense, on the other hand, will argue that there are several alternative possibilities, all of which involve the claim that the sample came from the victim and an unknown man. In this case, the unknown man can have the following genotypes:

If peak 2 is a stutter peak: 1,1; 1,2; 1,3 or 1,4 (Note that, if the analyst includes the 1,2 genotype as a possibility, peak 2 is considered to include both a stutter peak from peak 3 and a true allele peak from the unknown man. In many cases, this is a plausible hypothesis.)

If peak 2 is not a stutter peak: 1,2.

The defense can successfully undermine the prosecution's hypothesis if either of the above possibilities is true (logically an OR situation). Therefore, the denominator of the LR has two components: the one that considers peak 2 a stutter peak and the one that considers peak 2 a true allele peak. In order to calculate the probability of the component that assumes peak 2 is a stutter peak, remember that this hypothesis is postulating that an unknown man's alleles are present in the mixture and that stutter has occurred. Furthermore, this hypothesis postulates that the unknown man could have either of several possible genotypes: 1,1; 1,2; 1,3 or 1,4. Because any one of these genotypes will undermine the prosecution's hypothesis, these four genotypes represent an OR situation. To calculate the probability of a randomly selected person having any one of these genotypes, one adds the probabilities of the individual genotypes together. Ignoring population substructure and relatives for the sake of simplicity, the combined probability of the 1,1; 1,2; 1,3 or 1,4 genotypes is $p_1^2 + 2p_1p_2 + 2p_1p_3 + 2p_1p_4$. Because this component of the defense's hypothesis postulates that one of these genotypes is present AND there has been stutter, the combined probability of the four possible genotypes is multiplied by the probability of stutter to calculate the probability of this component of the defense's hypothesis: $[p_1^2 + 2p_1p_2 + 2p_1p_3 + 2p_1p_4]P(S)$, where p_i is the probability of allele i, and P is the probability of stutter.

Under the hypothesis that peak 2 is not a stutter peak, the only possible genotype for the perpetrator is 1,2. Therefore, to calculate the probability of the component of the defense's hypothesis that claims that the 1,2 genotype is present and that no stutter has occurred, the analyst multiplies the probability of the 1,2 genotype by the probability that there was no stutter: $[2p_1p_2]P(\overline{S})$, where $P(\overline{S})$ is the probability of no stutter having occurred [which $= 1 - P(S)$].

Because either of the two components of the defense's hypothesis undermines the prosecution's hypothesis (logically an OR situation), the probabilities associated with the two components are added together to get the final denominator of the LR. The LR is therefore calculated as:

$$LR = \frac{P(S)}{[p_1^2 + 2p_1p_2 + 2p_1p_3 + 2p_1p_4]P(S) + [2p_1p_2]P(\overline{S})}, \qquad \text{(Eq. 4.19)}$$

Determining the probability of stutter is a straightforward exercise, but it is done using empirical data. The laboratory should have data from past casework and validation studies that illustrate the intensity of the stutter peaks for each marker it uses. For a questioned peak, the analyst can determine the ratio of intensities of the putative stutter peak versus what would be the corresponding true allele peak, and then consult the laboratory's previously collected data to determine the percentage of previously observed stutter peaks that exceed the intensity ratio exhibited by the peaks in question. The probability of the questioned peak being a stutter peak equals the percent of stutter peaks that have been observed in the past for which the ratio of stutter peak intensity to true peak intensity is greater than or equal to the ratio observed for the peak in question. Moreover, because there are only two possibilities—that stutter has occurred or has not occurred—the probability of no stutter is calculated simply by subtracting the probability of stutter from 1.0.

Stutter peak intensities vary between markers and between PCR protocols, so each laboratory should collect its own data to illustrate the probability of a questioned peak being a stutter peak. Gill and colleagues[121] have published empirical data that illustrate the variability in stutter peaks between six markers used by the UK Forensic Science Service. Although it is best for each testing laboratory to collect its own data, these data can serve as a guideline for other laboratories, even for those using other markers. These data are particularly useful because they include data from D21S11, a marker that is known to exhibit more intense stutter peaks than most of the other markers used in forensic testing kits, and TH01, a marker known to exhibit less intense stutter peaks than most of the other commonly used markers. If the testing laboratory does not have its own data, the data from the D21S11 marker published by Gill and colleagues will provide a reasonably accurate estimate of the highest expected probability of stutter, and the TH01 data will provide a reasonably accurate estimate of the lowest expected probability of stutter.

The possibility of allele dropout is particularly problematic for mixed samples in which the minor contribution is very small. If the profile of the major contributor is the profile of interest, the analyst can ignore the minor contribution and analyze the sample as a single-source sample. If the profile of the minor contributor is probative, however, the analyst must try his or her best to determine it accurately and interpret the data probabilistically. This is not always possible; if the intensities of the allele peaks from the minor contributor are all close to the background noise intensity, it may be unwise to try to interpret the data probabilistically.[122]

[121] Gill et al., 1998, Table 1.

[122] Gill et al., 2006.

[123] Buckleton and Triggs, 2006.

In many cases, the analyst will be forced to acknowledge that there is more than one possible interpretation of the data. The situation may be complicated even further if replicate analyses are performed and there is a discrepancy between the results of the different analyses. In most cases, it will favor the defense to argue that any of the other alleles of that marker might have dropped out, because this maximizes the number of genotypes that might be present in the mixture, thereby maximizing the denominator of the LR. Because larger alleles are more likely to drop out than smaller alleles, however, the prosecution will often try to argue that only the genotypes that include the visible allele and a larger allele should be included among the genotypes that may be present in the mixture. Each testing laboratory should have its own validation data that empirically demonstrate what the probability of dropout is for each marker, and in fact for each individual allele, given the intensity of the remaining visible allele peak.

Historically, many analysts have adopted the "*F*" strategy and the "2p rule" to interpret a sample in which they believed dropout had occurred. The analyst would consider the genotype to be *aF*, in which "*a*" designates the visible allele and "*F*" designates the assumption that any of the other alleles of that marker may have failed to amplify. The probability of this genotype was assigned a value of $2p_a$, in which p_a represents the probability of the visible allele.

The 2p rule was originally believed to be a conservative approach to any situation because it overestimates the probability of the genotype in question. It was reasoned that the probability that an individual will have a genotype that includes one or more copies of allele *a* is calculated by adding the probabilities of the individual being a homozygote or a heterozygote. Ignoring population substructure, we find that the probability of the individual being a homozygote with the *aa* genotype is $p_a{}^2$. In addition, because the sum of the probabilities for all alleles is 1.0, the probability of having any of the other, not-*a* alleles is $1 - p_a$. Given this, the probability of the individual having a heterozygous *aF* genotype is $2p_a(1 - p_a)$. Because the individual could be a homozygote or a heterozygote, the final probability of the *aF* genotype is $p_a^2 + 2p_a(1 - p_a)$, which simplifies to $p_a(2 - p_a)$. Because p_a is always greater than zero, $2 - p_a$ is always less than 2. Consequently, $2p_a$ is always greater than $p_a(2 - p_a)$.

Buckleton and Triggs have demonstrated that the $2p_a$ rule is not always the most conservative estimate of the probability of the *aF* genotype.[123]

They have further demonstrated that the optimal formula for calculating the *LR* differs depending on whether the suspect is homozygous or heterozygous at the locus in question. Continuing to ignore population substructure for the sake of simplicity,[124] if the evidence sample has the *a* allele in it and the defendant has the *aa* genotype, the *LR* can be calculated as:

$$LR = \frac{1}{p_a[p_a + 2Pr(D)(1 - p_a)]}, \quad \text{(Eq. 4.21)}$$

where *Pr*(*D*) represents the probability that dropout has occurred. Buckleton and Triggs have shown that the 2p rule is excessively conservative when *Pr*(*D*) is very low, and actually results in a slightly higher LR when *Pr*(*D*) is close to 1.0.

When the evidence contains the *a* allele and the defendant has the heterozygous *ab* genotype, the 2p rule will seriously overestimate the LR when *Pr*(*D*) is very low, at the expense of the defendant. When the defendant is heterozygous, the formula preferred by Buckleton and Triggs is:[125]

$$LR = \frac{1}{p_a[p_a + 2\,Pr(D)(1 - p_a)]}. \quad \text{(Eq. 4.22)}$$

This formula is conservative, sometimes excessively so, for most allele frequencies and levels of population substructure.

Calculating the *LR* for a mixed sample in which one or more alleles is suspected to have dropped out can be very complex. Different formulas may be conservative for different allele frequencies and levels of population substructure. Expert systems are being developed that facilitate these analyses. Until these systems are accepted for courtroom use, however, the principles outlined by Gill and colleagues and Buckleton and Triggs provide the best available strategies for interpreting these difficult samples.

124 Buckleton and Triggs also provide the formulas that include the correction for population substructure.

125 For the sake of simplicity, we again use the formula that does not include the correction for population substructure. Buckleton and Triggs provide both.

REFERENCES AND ADDITIONAL READINGS

Agresti, A. and Coull, B.A. (1998) *American Statistician*, 52(2), 119–126.

Ayers, K.L. (2002) *Forensic Science International*, 129, 142–144.

Balding, D.J. and Nichols, R.A. (1994) *Forensic Science International*, 64, 125–140.

Balding, D. (2005) *Weight-of-Evidence for Forensic DNA Profiles*. Chichester: John Wiley.

Balding, D.J. and Donnelly, P. (1996) *Journal of Forensic Sciences*, 41(4), 603–607.

Blake, E., Mihalovich, J., Higuchi, R., Walsh, P.S. and Erlich, H. (1992) *Journal of Forensic Sciences*, 37(3), 700–726.

Bressler, D.D. (2002) *Jurimetrics Journal*, 43, 51.

Brookfield, J. (1992) *Heredity*, 69, 97–100.

Brookfield, J. (1995) *Genetica*, 96, 13–19.

Buckleton, J.S., Triggs, C.M. and Walsh, S.J. (2004) *Forensic DNA Evidence Interpretation*. Boca Raton, FL: CRC Press.

Buckleton, J. and Triggs, C. (2006) *Forensic Science International*, 159, 206–209.

Budowle, B., Monson, K.L., Giusti, A.M. and Brown, B.L. (1994a) *Journal of Forensic Science*, 39, 319–352.

Budowle, B., Monson, K.L., Giusti, A.M. and Brown, B.L. (1994b) *Journal of Forensic Science*, 39, 988–1008.

Budowle, B., Monson, K.L. and Giusti, A.M. (1994c) *American Journal of Human Genetics*, 55, 533–539.

Budowle, B. (1995) *Genetica*, 96, 21–25.

Budowle, B., Moretti, T.L., Baumstark, A.L., Defenbaugh, D.A. and Keys, K.M. (1999) *Journal of Forensic Sciences*, 44(6), 1277–1286.

Budowle, B., Chakraborty, R., Carmody, G. and Monson, K.L. (2000) *Forensic Science Communications*, 2(3), http://www.fbi.gov/hq/lab/fsc/backissu/july2000/source.htm

Budowle, B. (2001). Statistics and Mixture Interpretation Workshop. In *Twelfth International Symposium on Human Identification*. Biloxi, MS. Cited in Buckleton et al., 2005, p. 34.

Budowle, B., Shea, B., Niezgoda, S. and Chakraborty, R. (2001) *Journal of Forensic Sciences*, 46(3), 453–489.

Butler, J.M. (2005) *Forensic DNA Typing,* 2nd ed. Boston: Elsevier/Academic Press, 2005.

Ceci, S.J. and Friedman, R.D. (2000) *Cornell Law Review*, 86(1), 33–108.

Chakraborty, R. and Kidd, K.K. (1991) *Science*, 254, 1735–1739.

Chakraborty, R., de Andrade, M., Daiger, S. and Budowle, B. (1992) *Annals of Human Genetics*, 56, 45–57.

Chakraborty, R., Kimmel, M., Stivers, D.N., Davison, L.J. and Deka, R. (1997) *Proceedings of the National Academy of Sciences USA*, 94, 1041–1046.

Chakraborty, R., Stivers, D.N., Su B., Zkong, Y. and Budowle, B. (1999) *Electrophoresis*, 20, 1682–1696.

Clayton, T. and Buckleton, J. (2005). In Buckleton, J., Triggs, C. and Walsh, S.J. (eds.). *Forensic DNA Evidence Interpretation,* pp. 217–274. London: CRC Press.

Dann, B., Michael, H., Valerie, P. and Kaye, D.H. (2006) Can Jury Trial Innovations Improve Juror Understanding of DNA Evidence. *NIJ Journal* No. 255.

Dawid, A.P., Mortera, J. and Pascali, V.L. (2001) *Forensic Science International*, 124, 55–61.

Devlin, B. (1992) *Statistical Methods in Medical Research*, 2, 241–262.

Devlin, B. and Roeder, K. (1997) DNA Profiling: Statistics and Population Genetics. In Faigman D.L. (ed.), *Modern Scientific Evidence: The Law and Science of Expert Testimony.* Egan, MN: West Group.

Evett, I.W. and Weir, B.S. (1998) *Interpreting DNA Evidence: Statistical Genetics for Forensic Scientists*. Sunderland, MA: Sinauer Associates.

Evett, I.W., Gill, B.S. and Lambert, J.A. (1998) *Journal of Forensic Sciences*, 43(1), 62–69.

Fung, W.K., Chung, Y-K. and Wong, D-M. (2002) *International Journal of Legal Medicine*, 116, 64–67.

Gill, P., Sparkes, R. and Kimpton, C.P. (1997) *Forensic Science International*, 89, 185–197.

Gill, P., Sparkes, B. and Buckleton, J.S. (1998) *Forensic Science International*, 95, 213–224.

Gill, P., Curran, J. and Elliot, K. (2005) *Nucleic Acids Research*, 33, 632–643.

Gill, P., Brenner, C.H., Buckleton, J.S., Carracedo, A., Krawczak, M., Mayr, W.R., Morling, N., Prinz, M., Schneider, P.M. and Weir, B.S. (2006) *Forensic Science International*, 160, 90–101.

Goodman, J. (1992) *American Journal of Trial Advocacy*, 16, 361–389.

Hageman, C., Prevett, D. and Murray, W. (2002) *DNA Handbook*. Ontario, Canada: Butterworths.

Holland, M.M. and Parsons, T.J. (1999) *Forensic Science Reviews*, 11, 21–50.

Irwin, J., Saunier, J.L., Strouss, K.M., Sturk, K.A., Diegoli, T.M., Just, R.S., Coble, M.D., Parson, W. and Parsons, T.J. (2007) *Forensic Science International: Genetics*, 1, 154-157.

Kaye, D.H. (1990) *Family Law Quarterly*, 24, 279–304.

Kayser, M. and Sajantila, A. (2001) *Forensic Science International*, 118, 116–121.

Koehler, J. (1993) *Jurimetrics*, 34(1), 21–18.

Krane, D.E., Allen, R.W., Sawyer, S.A., Petrov, D.A. and Hartl, D.L. (1992) *Proceedings of the National Academy of Sciences (USA)*, 89, 10583–10587.

Krane, D.E. *Presentation at the 6th Annual Forensic Bioinformatics Conference*, Dayton, Ohio, August 18, 2007.

Land, G.E., Esq. (2005) *Michigan State Journal of Medicine and Law*. 9, 95.

Lander, E. (1991) *Science*, 254, 1921–1923.

Lempert, R. (1997) *Jurimetrics Journal*, 37, 439–468.

Lewontin, R.C. and Hartl, D.L. (1991) *Science*, 254, 1745.

Lins, A.M., Micka, K.A., Sprecher, C.J., Taylor, J.A., Bacher, J.W., Rabbach, D.R., Bever, R.A., Creacy, S.D. and Schumm, J.W. (1998) *Journal of Forensic Sciences*, 43(6), 1168–1180.

Louis, T.A. (1981) *The American Statistician*, 35, 154.

Maclin, T. (2006) *Journal of Legal Medicine and Ethics*, 34, 165.

National Research Council (NRC). (1996) *The Evaluation of Forensic DNA Evidence*. Washington, DC: National Academy Press.

Rudin, N. and Inman, K. (2002) *An Introduction to Forensic DNA Analysis*. Boca Raton, FL: CRC Press.

Scientific Working Group on DNA Analysis Methods (SWGDAM). (2000) Short tandem repeat interpretation guidelines. *Forensic Science Communications*, 2(3): http://www.fbi.gov/hq/lab/fsc/backissu/july2000/strig.htm.

Steinhardt, B. (2004) Privacy and Forensic DNA Data Banks. In Lazer, D. (ed.), *DNA and the Criminal Justice System*. Cambridge, MA: MIT Press.

Stockmarr, A. (1999) *Biometrics*, 55, 671–677.

Taroni, F. and Aitken, C.G.G. (1998a) *Science and Justice*, 38, 165–177.

Taroni, F. and Aitken, C.G.G. (1998b) *Science and Justice*, 38, 179–188.

Thompson, W.C. and Schumann, E.L. (1987) *Law and Human Behavior*, 11(3), 167–187.

Thompson, W.C., Taroni, F. and Aitken, C.G.G. (2003) *Journal of Forensic Sciences*, 48, 1–8.

Walsh, P.S., Fildes, N.J. and Reynolds, R. (1997) *Nucleic Acids Research*, 24, 2807–2812.

Walsh, B., Redd, A.J. and Hammer, M.F. (2007) *Forensic Science International*, April 19 (epub ahead of print).

Weir, B.S. (1992) *Proceedings of the National Academy of Sciences (USA)*, 89, 11654–11659.

Weir, B.S. and Hill, W.G. (2002) *Annual Review of Genetics*, 36, 721–750.

Weir, B.S. (1993) *American Journal of Human Genetics*, 52, 437–440.

Weir, B.S. and Hill, W.G. (1993) *Journal of Forensic Science*, 33, 219–226.

Weir, B.S. (1994) *Nature*, 369(6479), 351.

Wright, S. (1951) *Annals of Eugenics*, 15, 159–171.

Mitochondrial DNA (mtDNA) Analyses

CONTENTS

The mtDNA Molecule—Abundant and Durable but Less Variable than nDNA

Laboratory Analysis of mtDNA Haplotypes

Matrilineal Inheritance and a Lack of Recombination

A High Mutation Rate Leads to Mitochondrial Heteroplasmy

Statistical Analysis of mtDNA Haplotype Data

References and Additional Readings

THE mtDNA MOLECULE—ABUNDANT AND DURABLE BUT LESS VARIABLE THAN nDNA

The mtDNA molecule is a double-stranded, circular chain containing 16,569 bp of DNA. One strand has more A and G nucleotides in it than the other one does. Due to slight differences in their chemical structure, the A and G bases are slightly heavier than their C and T counterparts. The A/G-rich strand is therefore referred to as the **heavy strand**, while the C/T-rich strand is referred to as the **light strand**. By convention, the light strand sequence is the one used in the standard nomenclature for mtDNA sequences and SNP characterizations. Forensic analysts usually sequence both strands, however, as a means of double-checking their results.

The mtDNA sequence was first published by a research group at Cambridge University,[1] and the Cambridge Reference Sequence (CRS) was the standard against which other mtDNA sequences were compared for almost two decades. Interestingly, however, the authors could not obtain the complete sequence of the mtDNA from their human subject, and therefore filled in some gaps in the sequence with sequences from bovine (cow) mtDNA and the mtDNA from a cancer cell line called HeLa that is commonly used as a research tool. Later researchers filled in the gaps with authentic human mtDNA sequences, and the CRS was revised.[2] In spite of the fact that only 11 nucleotides needed revising, the revision presented a problem, because the C nucleotide at position 3106 in the original CRS is missing from the revised CRS (rCRS). In order to avoid having to change the numbering of all nucleotides after 3106, the rCRS includes an "N" in position 3107 as a placeholder. The rCRS is currently used as the reference sequence for naming other mtDNA sequences.[3]

The mtDNA molecule is much more efficiently organized than the nDNA molecule. Unlike the nDNA, in which the majority of nucleotides are not involved in producing proteins, 93% of the mtDNA is protein-coding sequence. The fact that so much of the mtDNA is protein-coding sequence means that there are fewer places at which a sequence variation can be tolerated, and therefore mtDNA is considerably less polymorphic than nDNA. The mtDNA does have one region, however, called the **control region**, or **D-loop**, in which no genes reside (nucleotides 16,024–16,569 and 1–576[4]). The control region contains sequences that help control the replication of the mtDNA and the expression of the genes in the mtDNA. These sequences are critical regulators of the mitochondrion's function, and therefore the function of all your cells. Very few alterations in their sequence will be tolerated, and therefore the control sequences themselves are not very polymorphic. The control sequences only occupy a portion of the D-loop region, however. Two portions of the human mitochondrial D-loop region, called the **hypervariable region I** (**HVI** = nucleotides 16,024–16,365) and **hypervariable region II** (**HVII** = nucleotides 73–340), serve no regulatory or protein-coding function, and are therefore free to vary between individuals without causing any disruptions in the individual's development. Not only can single nucleotides differ between individuals, but there are two stretches of continuous C nucleotides (poly-C repeats) in the D-loop region, the length of which often varies between individuals. HVI includes a poly-C repeat from positions 303–315, inclusive, while HVII includes a poly-C repeat from positions 16,184–16,193, inclusive.[5]

An mtDNA sequence is identified by its deviations from the rCRS. Deviations usually take the form of single-nucleotide substitutions (aka "point mutations") or variations in the length of one or both poly-C stretches. Point mutations are simply named by the position of the substitution and the nucleotide that has taken the place of the common nucleotide. For example, a sequence that is identical to the rCRS except for having a G at position 280, where the rCRS has a C, is designated as 280G. For length variations in the poly-C stretches, the extra Cs are considered to have been added onto the end of the poly-C stretch. The variant is named by using decimal notation to indicate the number of nucleotides that were added

[1] Anderson et al., 1981. The paper's first author provided the mtDNA for sequencing; the sequence is therefore also referred to as the Anderson sequence.

[2] Andrews et al., 1999.

[3] The rCRS can be found at http://www.mitomap.org or in the GenBank entry with accession number AC000021.

[4] Recall that 16,569 is the last nucleotide in the mtDNA sequence and that the mtDNA molecule is circular. Therefore, this is a single stretch of mtDNA sequence running from nucleotide 16,024-576, but because it spans the number 1 position, the sequence is designated in two pieces.

[5] In many people, the poly-C stretch between 302–315 has a T at position 310 and the poly-C stretch between 16,183–16,194 has a T at position 16,189.

after what is the final C in the poly-C repeat in the rCRS (either nucleotide 315 or 16,193). For example, if an mtDNA sequence had two more Cs than the rCRS does in the poly-C stretch that lies between nucleotides 303–315, it would be designated as 315.2C. A similar nomenclature is used to designate insertions elsewhere in the mtDNA. For example, if a T was inserted after nucleotide number 97 in the rCRS, the mtDNA type would be designated as 97.1T. Finally, deletions are identified by the nucleotides that are missing; an mtDNA that was missing nucleotide 421 would be designated as 421d.

One advantage that mtDNA affords over nDNA is abundance. Recall from Chapter 1 that there may be hundreds of mitochondria per cell, depending on the cell's energy requirements. Recall also that a single mitochondrion may contain as many as 15 copies of the mtDNA molecule.[6] Consequently, a typical cell contains between several dozen and several thousand copies of the mtDNA molecule, as opposed to only two copies of the nDNA molecule. Because of the relatively high number of mtDNA molecules per cell, minute samples that yield too little nDNA may yield enough mtDNA for analysis. This is particularly useful in cases in which a small number of hairs have transferred between the victim and the perpetrator, or when the perpetrator has picked up a few pet hairs from the scene of the crime on his or her clothing. It is even possible to obtain an mtDNA sequence from fingerprints on paper.[7] Because of the abundance of mtDNA in a typical cell, mtDNA reference samples pose a particularly high risk of contaminating other samples that are processed at the same time. Many laboratories take extra precautions to keep mitochondrial reference samples separated from their corresponding evidence samples. Laboratories either maintain separate areas for processing reference versus evidence samples or make a practice of processing the evidence samples before the corresponding reference samples.

The other advantage of mtDNA over nDNA is that of durability. The mitochondrion has a double membrane, which provides a little extra protection. In addition, the circular mtDNA molecule is less accessible to the restriction enzymes that degrade DNA by chopping off nucleotides from the ends. Because of these features, mtDNA is considerably more resistant to degradation due to time, environmental bacteria, fire, chemicals and other DNA-degrading agents than nDNA is. For this reason,

[6] Satoh and Kuroiwa, 1991.

[7] Balogh et al., 2003.

mtDNA testing has proven a highly useful tool for anthropological investigations, identification of military casualties and cases involving persons who have been missing for long periods of time.

Just as the alleles that an individual has at an STR marker is called his or her genotype, an individual's mtDNA sequence is referred to as his or her **mitotype**. The mtDNA databases are growing just as the nDNA databases are, and a system similar to the FBI's CODIS system for STR profiles has been developed to enable investigators to search mitotype databases for matching profiles.[8] The FBI's database contains two sets of data: one containing mtDNA profiles from different ethnic groups in the United States (sometimes referred to as the "forensic database"), and another containing mtDNA profiles from countries around the world. The forensic database contains the sequence of HVI nucleotides 16,024–16,365 and HVII nucleotides 73–340 from approximately 5,000 individuals representing 14 different ethnic subgroups sampled from a small handful of different geographic regions.

LABORATORY ANALYSIS OF mtDNA HAPLOTYPES

mtDNA testing has been used for years to identify military casualties, conduct anthropological research and identify long-missing persons. The methods involved have been extensively validated, and the National Institute of Standards and Technology (NIST) provides standard reference materials (SRMs)[9] to help ensure quality control. Taking notice of this authentication, the majority of courts that have heard challenges to mtDNA evidence have ruled the evidence admissible.[10]

Sequencing of large numbers of human mtDNAs has revealed the presence of very few STRs in the mtDNA molecule. There are, however, a number of loci scattered throughout the mtDNA molecule at which single-nucleotide polymorphisms (SNPs) can be observed, and the poly-C stretches in HVI and HVII may vary in length as well.[11] The sequence of the HVI and/or HVII regions of the mtDNA D-loop region is usually determined using the dideoxysequencing method (described in Chapter 2 and illustrated in Figure 2.7). In addition, a slot-blot method similar to that used for the DQA1 and Polymarker™ tests (described in Chapter 2) can be used to illustrate an individual's allele status at a number of polymorphic loci in the mtDNA (Figure 5.1).

[8] Monson et al., 2002.

[9] A listing of available SRMs for all DNA analyses can be found on the NIST SRM website—http://www.nist.gov/srd/

[10] For a listing of cases in which *Frye* and *Daubert* courts have admitted mtDNA evidence, see Kaestle et al., 2006, footnotes 145 and 146.

[11] Melton et al., 2001; Vallone et al., 2004; Coble et al., 2004; Kline et al., 2005.

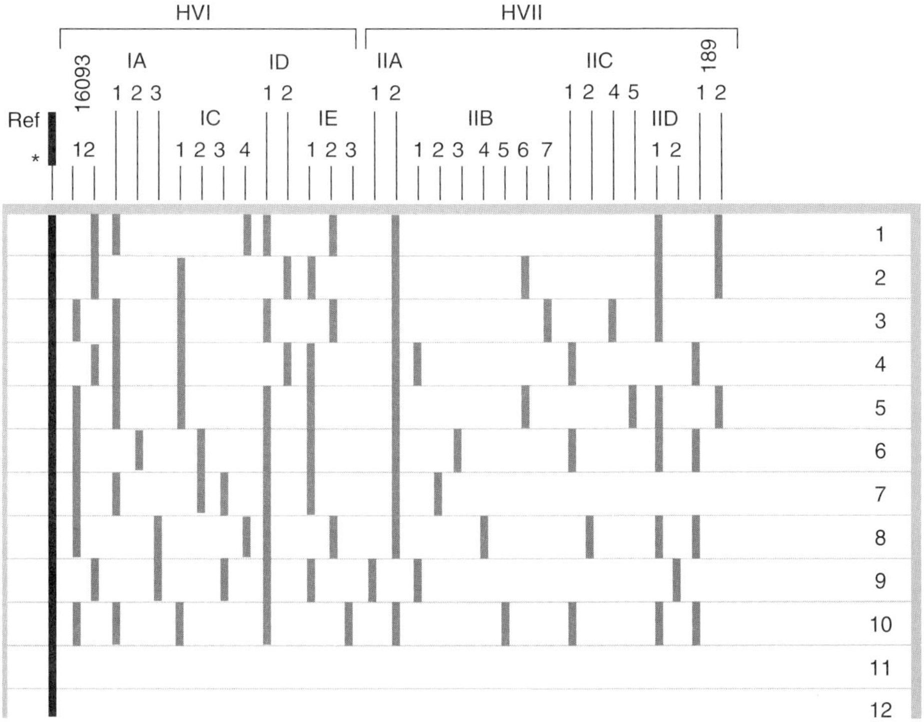

FIGURE 5.1 *Results from the LINEAR ARRAY Mitochondrial DNA HVI/HVII Region-Sequence Typing Kit. Reprinted with permission from Roche Applied Science.*

When dideoxysequencing is performed, the sequences of two samples are simply compared nucleotide by nucleotide. When the slot-blot test is performed, the analyst compares the positions of the positive signals on the two samples' test strips and observes whether they appear in the same or different positions. The LINEAR ARRAY Mitochondrial DNA HVI/HVII Region-Sequence Typing Kit™ (Roche Diagnostics) uses 31 sequence-specific oligonucleotide probes to illustrate the individual's allele status at 10 polymorphic loci in the HVI and HVII regions, each of which has between two and seven known alleles (Figure 5.1).

Combining SNP analyses with dideoxysequencing analyses has the potential to increase the discriminative power of mtDNA testing.[12] In addition, the slot-blot test has several inherent safeguards that make it acceptable for use in criminal trials. Because the slot-blot test is based on allele sequences rather than lengths, there is no risk of specific alleles dropping out due to size-related factors (discussed in Chapter 3). In most cases in which the sample has been significantly compromised, the test produces no results at all. This is desirable, as it prevents false-positive results. In addition, for mixed samples with a major and a minor contributor, the

[12] Coble et al., 2004.

relative densities of the bands on the test strip can indicate the relative amount of material contributed by the two contributors. Like all tests, however, this test has its limitations. If the two individuals have contributed equally to the sample, if the minor contributor has contributed less than 10% of the sample or if there are more than two contributors, the slot-blot test will probably not be able to sort out the individual contributions reliably.[13]

The quality control issues that were discussed in Chapter 3 also apply to mtDNA analyses. In addition, a few factors inherent in mtDNA analyses make it even more imperative that one guard against having spurious products appear in the data. Most importantly, because there are so many copies of the mtDNA per cell, extra care must be taken not to allow an mtDNA sample to contaminate other evidence. The incidence of contamination is higher with mtDNA analyses than with nDNA analyses.[14] In one study, MitoTyping Technologies reported contamination in 2.4% of PCR samples in a two-year time span.[15] A piece of evidence can be contaminated by material from within the body of the same individual, from other individuals with whom the individual had contact, from another piece of evidence collected at the same time, or by skin cells or other material shed by handlers and analysts. Because of this concern, analysts examine hairs microscopically, then wash them with detergent in an ultrasonic bath to get rid of surface contamination. Bone and tooth samples are first prepared by grinding the surface clean with a Dremel™ tool.

Another potential source of artifacts in mtDNA analyses is the fact that many mtDNA analysis protocols are designed for use in samples that are too minute for nDNA analyses, and are therefore geared for maximum sensitivity. They often use extra PCR cycles to compensate for low levels of input DNA. This makes it easier to amplify minute amounts of sample DNA, but it also makes it easier for contaminants to produce visible products. In addition, if a hair sample is being analyzed, the analyst may add extra DNA polymerase to overcome the fact that the hair pigment melanin is a PCR inhibitor.[16] This will foster amplification of all templates, even undesirable ones.

Good laboratory practices such as changing gloves, caps and sleeves frequently, the use of aerosol-resistant pipette tips and the processing of evidence samples separately from the corresponding reference samples

[13] Rudin and Inman, 2002.

[14] Isenberg, 2004.

[15] Melton and Nelson, 2001.

[16] Wilson et al., 1995.

are particularly important when mtDNA is being analyzed. In addition, in many laboratories the mtDNA samples are analyzed independently by two analysts, to further reduce the probability of error. All the appropriate negative control samples should be used in the assays, including substrate blanks and reagent blanks, to ensure that neither the evidence object nor the laboratory reagents used were contaminated by extraneous mtDNA. As with nDNA analyses, the mtDNA haplotypes of all laboratory personnel should be on file so that one can detect a situation in which the evidence was contaminated with material from one of its handlers. Note that the data from contaminated samples are not automatically discarded; if the level of contamination is low enough, the analyst will ignore it. For example, the FBI laboratory has a rule that a sample with visible contamination will be accepted if the contamination is present at one-tenth or less of the level of the target profile.[17] In these cases, it is easy for the analyst to visually subtract the contamination from the data to reveal the true mitotype. As long as the laboratory has an established procedure for recognizing contamination and subtracting a contaminating profile from the data, and validation data demonstrating the reliability of their compensatory actions (the study should include a sample with a level of contamination similar to that in the sample in question), courts should accept evidence in which the analyst has subtracted out what he or she knows to be a contaminating profile.

Another type of contamination emanates from the sample itself. Some DNA sequences have the surprising ability to make a copy of themselves and move that copy to another place in the genome; the resultant out-of-place copies of DNA are often called **pseudogenes**. Over the course of evolution, copies of portions of the mtDNA sequence have translocated into the nDNA sequence.[18] The sequences in and around these nuclear pseudogenes are different enough from their authentic mtDNA counterparts that the PCR primers and reaction parameters allow amplification of the true mtDNA targets, but not the nuclear pseudogenes. When the analyst adjusts a PCR parameter to maximize amplification, however, there is always the risk that nuclear pseudogenes may be amplified and produce visible products.

One aspect of the mtDNA analysis that will no doubt be improved upon in the near future is the fact that mtDNA is usually not quantified directly. Both the nDNA and the mtDNA are extracted from the sample together.

[17] Wilson et al., 1995; Stewart et al., 2003.

[18] Wallace et al., 1997.

[19] Meissner et al., 2000.

[20] Birky, 2001.

[21] Wiurf, 2001.

[22] Sutovsky et al., 1999; Budowle et al., 2003.

[23] Hagelberg et al., 1999; Awadalla et al., 1999; Eyre-Walker et al., 1999.

[24] Hagelberg et al., 2000; Budowle et al., 2003.

The analyst quantifies the nDNA in the sample using a procedure such as the Quantiblot™ method (described in Chapter 2) and assumes a fixed ratio of mtDNA to nDNA in order to calculate the mtDNA concentration. In the future, real-time PCR methods (described in Chapter 2) will be used to directly quantify the nDNA and the mtDNA from a sample simultaneously.[19]

MATRILINEAL INHERITANCE AND A LACK OF RECOMBINATION

There are several important differences in the ways in which nDNA and mtDNA are inherited. Recall that nDNA is inherited from both parents and that there is recombination between the maternally derived and paternally derived chromosomes. As a result, the DNA an individual passes down to his or her children contains a combination of sequences from the DNA he or she inherited from his or her parents. In contrast, all an individual's mitochondria are inherited from his or her mother.[20] In addition, mtDNA does not undergo recombination the way nuclear chromosomes do.[21] Consequently, barring a mutation, a woman passes down the same mtDNA sequence that she inherited from her mother. For this reason, one must keep in mind that mtDNA usually cannot identify a single individual. A match between the evidence and the defendant suggests that the evidence was left by either the defendant or someone related to the defendant through a line of female relatives. This relative can even be a very distant one, provided the two are related through an uninterrupted line of females.

Sperm contain ample mitochondria, but very few, if any, sperm mitochondria enter the egg at fertilization. Those few that do are destroyed, inactivated or so diluted by the relatively large number of maternally derived mitochondria that they cannot be detected by the forensic analyst.[22] Three studies have suggested the possibility of inheritance of mtDNA from the father and/or recombination between maternally derived and paternally derived mtDNA.[23] These studies have been criticized by several other researchers, and one has been retracted by its authors because of errors in the data.[24] To the best of our knowledge, only one study has described an individual who had both maternally derived and paternally derived mitochondria and withstood the peer review that followed

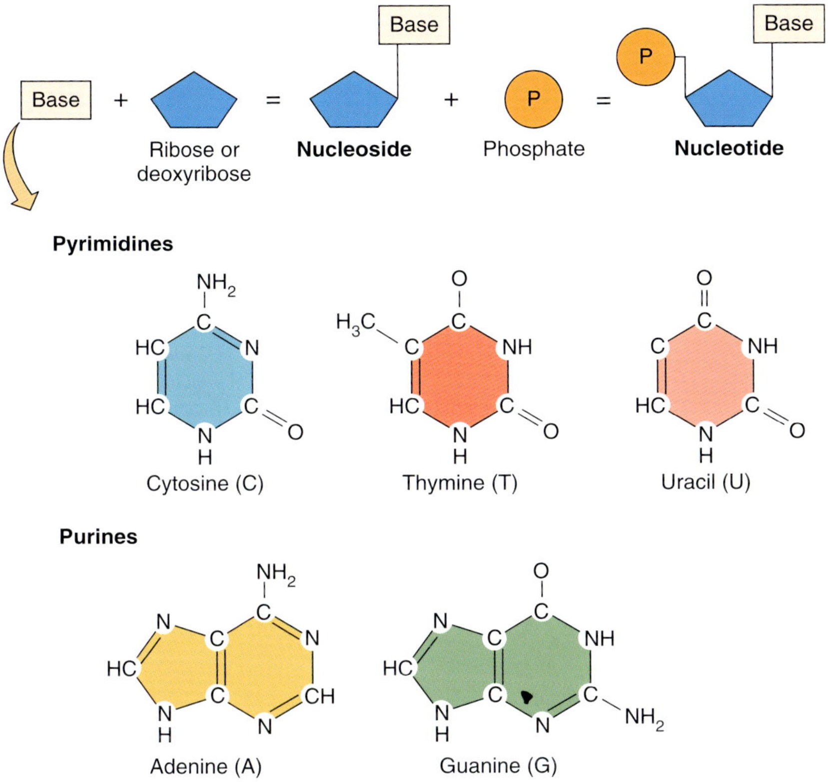

FIGURE 1.3

The nucleotides that make up the building blocks of DNA and RNA. Reprinted from Life: The Science of Biology, *7th ed. Purves, Sadava, Orians and Heller. Copyright Sinauer Associates, 2004. (see Figure 1.3 on page 7)*

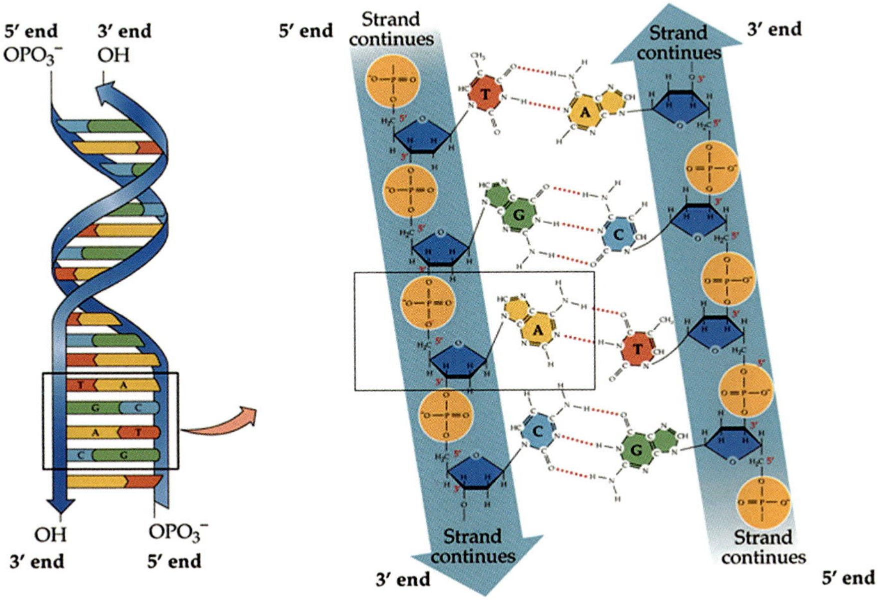

FIGURE 1.4

The DNA double helix. A box has been drawn around a single "A" nucleotide. Reprinted from Life: The Science of Biology, *7th ed. Purves, Sadava, Orians and Heller. Copyright Sinauer Associates, 2004. (see Figure 1.4 on page 8)*

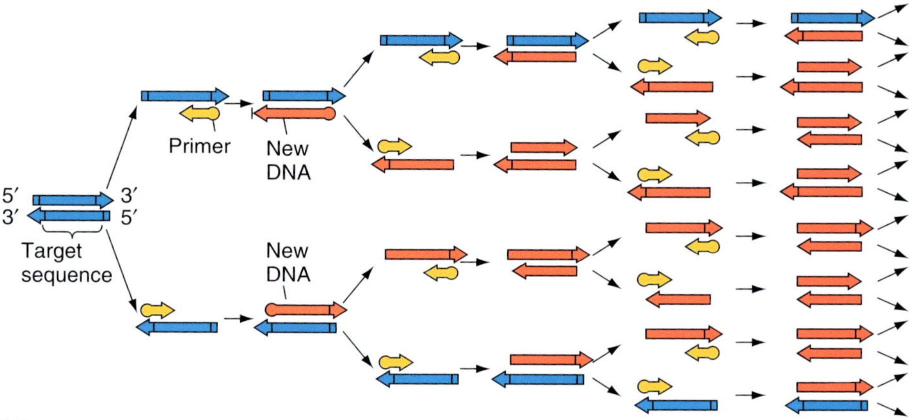

FIGURE 2.3 *The polymerase chain reaction (PCR) makes millions of copies of a desired stretch of DNA. Reprinted from* Life: The Science of Biology, *7th ed. Purves, Sadava, Orians and Heller. Copyright Sinauer Associates, 2004.* *(see Figure 2.3 on page 35)*

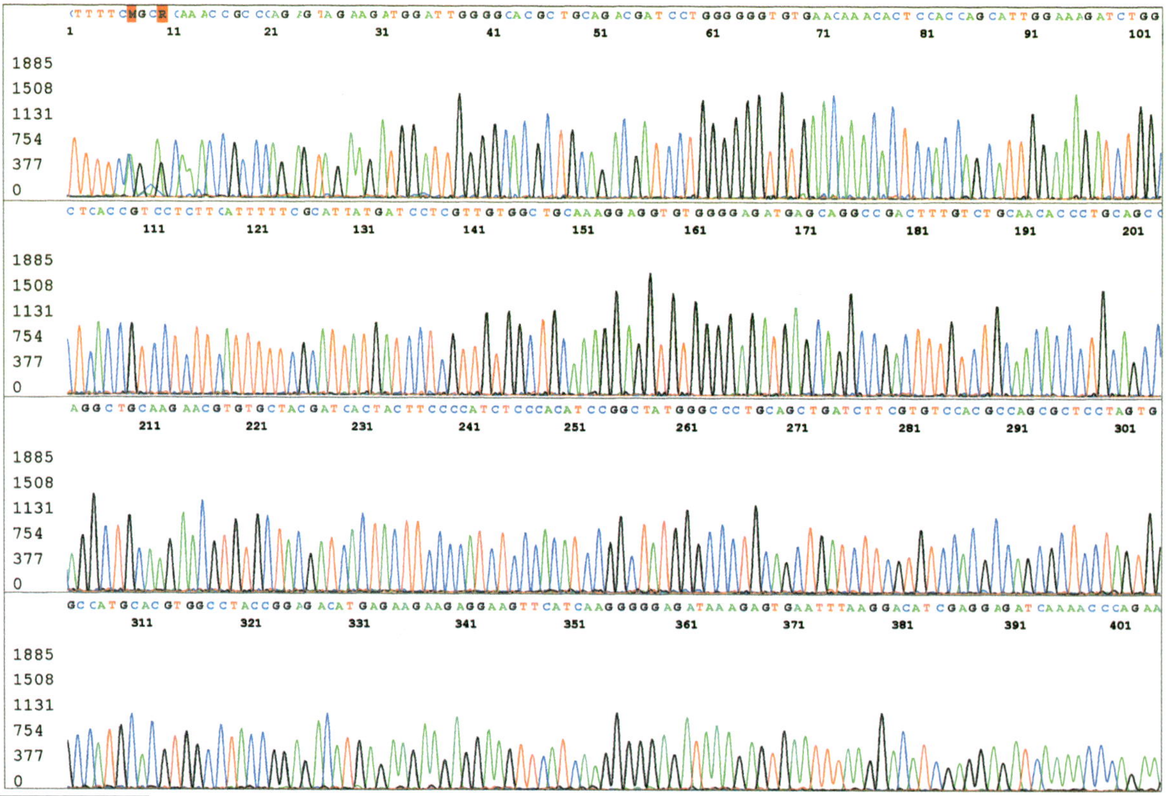

FIGURE 2.7 *Four-color output from the ABI 3100 automated sequencer/fragment analyzer from Applied Biosystems. Figure provided by Dr. Jack Tarleton, Fullerton Genetics Center, Asheville, NC.* *(see Figure 2.7 on page 52)*

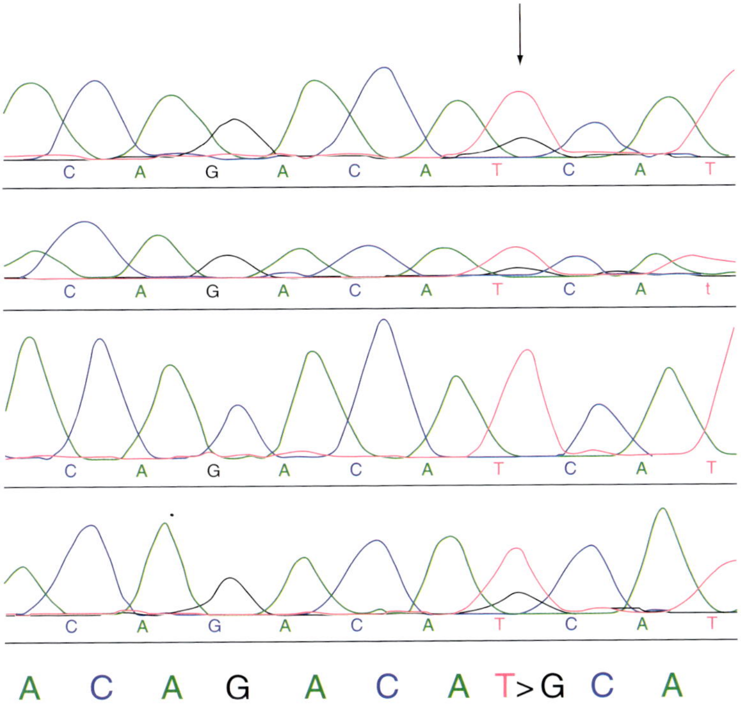

FIGURE 5.3 *Four independent sequencing assays confirm a sequence heteroplasmy at position 279 in the HVII region of the mtDNA. Figure provided by Mitotyping Technologies, State College, PA.* *(see Figure 5.3 on page 181)*

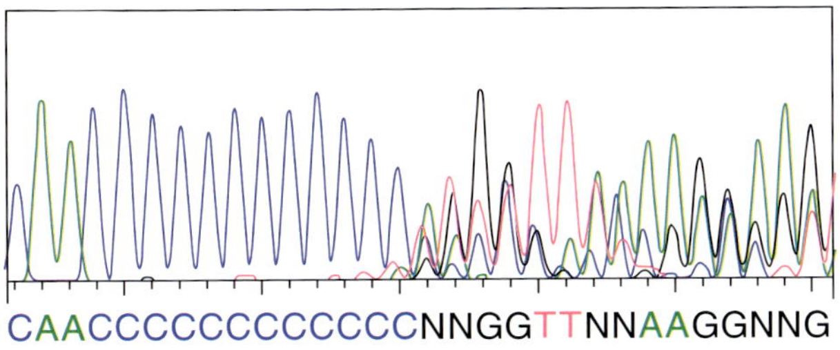

FIGURE 5.4 *Length heteroplasmy in mtDNA. Note that the sequence is clear up to the end of the poly-C string; then several sequences are laid over each other after the poly-C string. Note the number of nucleotides for which the sequencer cannot identify a major peak (symbolized with an "N"). Figure provided by Mitotyping Technologies, State College, PA.* *(see Figure 5.4 on page 183)*

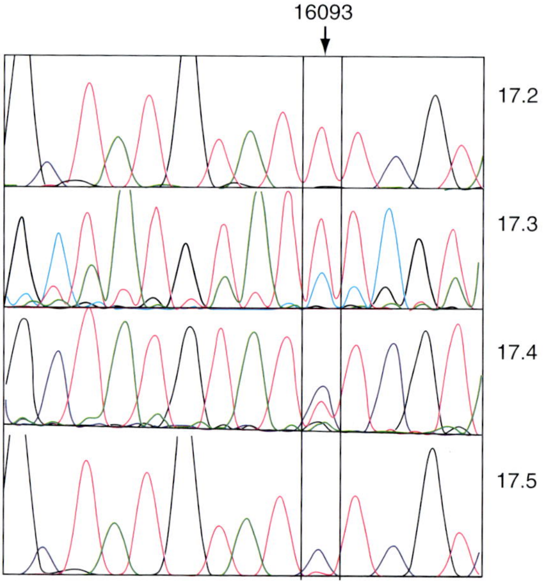

FIGURE 5.5 *Four different sections of the same hair, demonstrating different levels of heteroplasmy in the different hair sections. Reprinted from Tully et al., 2004, with permission from Elsevier.* *(see Figure 5.5 on page 185)*

publication.[25] A full 90% of the mitochondria in the patient's muscles were of paternal origin, but other tissues, such as blood and hair, contained only maternally derived mitochondria. Given that only one concrete example of paternal inheritance of mtDNA has been demonstrated, and so many thousands of examples of maternal inheritance have been proven, there is a general consensus that patrilineal inheritance, if it does occur in mitochondrial DNA, is so rare that it is highly unlikely to be encountered in a forensic investigation.[26]

[25] Schwartz and Vissing, 2002, 2004.

[26] Wiurf, 2001; Elson et al., 2001.

[27] Gill et al., 1994.

Because of the matrilineal inheritance of mtDNA, individuals who are related through an uninterrupted chain of female relatives are expected to have the same mtDNA sequence (but see the later discussion of heteroplasmy). This can be very useful when one wishes to establish an individual's membership in an extended family. The most famous investigation of this nature involved the search for Anastasia, the daughter of Tsar Nicholas II and Tsarina Alexandra of the Romanov family. Nicholas and Alexandra were executed during the Bolshevik revolution, along with their children, three servants and the family doctor who happened to be present at the time. The victims were all shot, doused with acid to render their remains unrecognizable and buried in a shallow grave. STR testing enabled investigators to separate out the parents and their children from the unrelated servants and physician, and anthropological investigations established the identities of the children whose remains were in the grave.[27] No remains were ever found from the daughter Anastasia, however, and her fate remains a mystery to this day. Over the years, several women have come forward and claimed to be Anastasia, but mtDNA testing has failed to support any of their claims. These women's claims can be tested because Prince Philip, husband of the current Queen Elizabeth II of England, is related to Tsarina Alexandra through an uninterrupted line of females (Figure 5.2). Investigators have obtained the sequence of 740 bp of DNA from the HVI and HVII regions of the mtDNA from Prince Philip, and all claimants' sequences are compared to his.

The fact that mtDNA is inherited matrilineally also makes mtDNA dragnets more efficient than nDNA dragnets. Each sample that is collected provides investigators not only with the mtDNA mitotype from that individual, but also the expected mtDNA mitotype for every relative who can be connected with that person through an uninterrupted line of

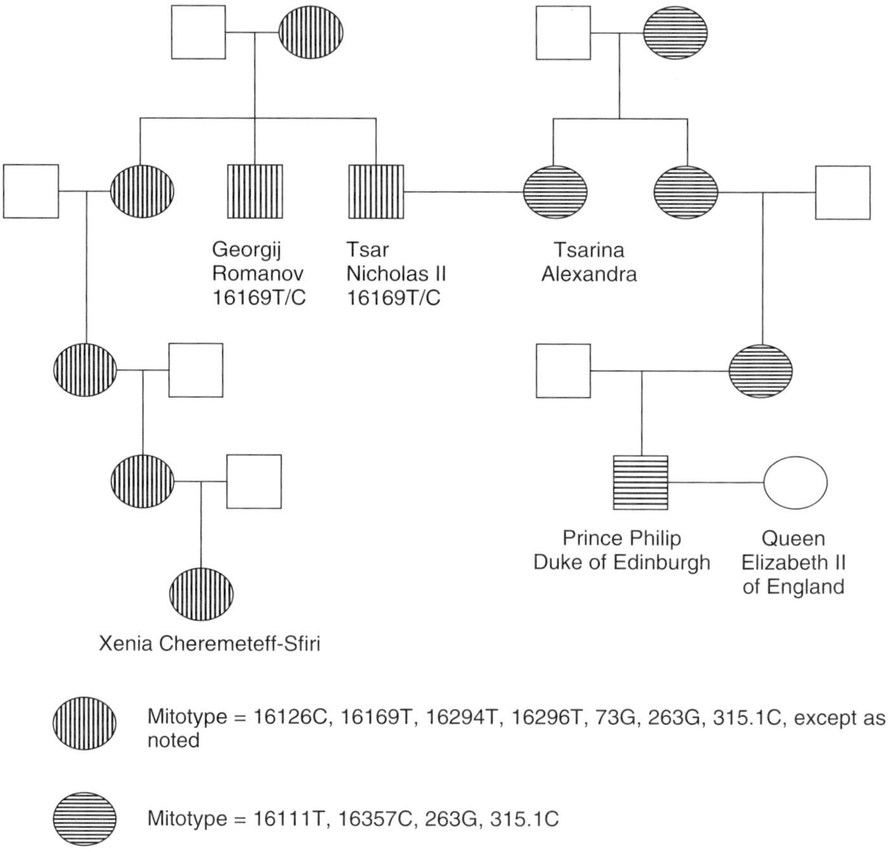

FIGURE 5.2
Pedigree of the Romanov family. Note that Prince Philip of Edinburgh is related to Tsarina Alexandra through an uninterrupted line of female relatives. Similarly, Xenia Cheremeteff-Sfiri is related to Tsar Nicholas II through an uninterrupted line of female relatives.

females. Even if the guilty party refuses to provide a sample, if one of his or her matrilineal relatives provides a sample, a match between that individual's mitotype and that of the evidence will include the perpetrator among the group of people to be investigated further.

A HIGH MUTATION RATE LEADS TO MITOCHONDRIAL HETEROPLASMY

Sequence Versus Length Heteroplasmies

mtDNA has a higher mutation rate than nDNA; in some regions of the mtDNA, the mutation rate is 6 to 17 times that of nDNA.[28] Because of the staggering number of copies of mtDNA that exists in one human body and the high mutation rate of mtDNA, all individuals are expected to exhibit some level of **heteroplasmy**, in which some copies of that

[28] Bar et al., 2000; Budowle et al., 2003.

individual's mtDNA have a different sequence than other copies of that same individual's mtDNA.[29]

The two types of heteroplasmy are sequence (or site) heteroplasmy and length heteroplasmy. In a sequence heteroplasmy, some of the individual's mtDNA molecules will have a different nucleotide in one position than others do (Figure 5.3). Some nucleotide positions appear to be "hot spots" for sequence mutations; heteroplasmy is seen more frequently at those positions than others.[30] If a sequence heteroplasmy exists, it is

[29] Bar et al., 2000; Budowle et al., 2003; Melton, 2004.

[30] Stoneking, 2000; Melton et al., 2005; Lee et al., 2007; MITOMAP, http://www.mitomap.org.

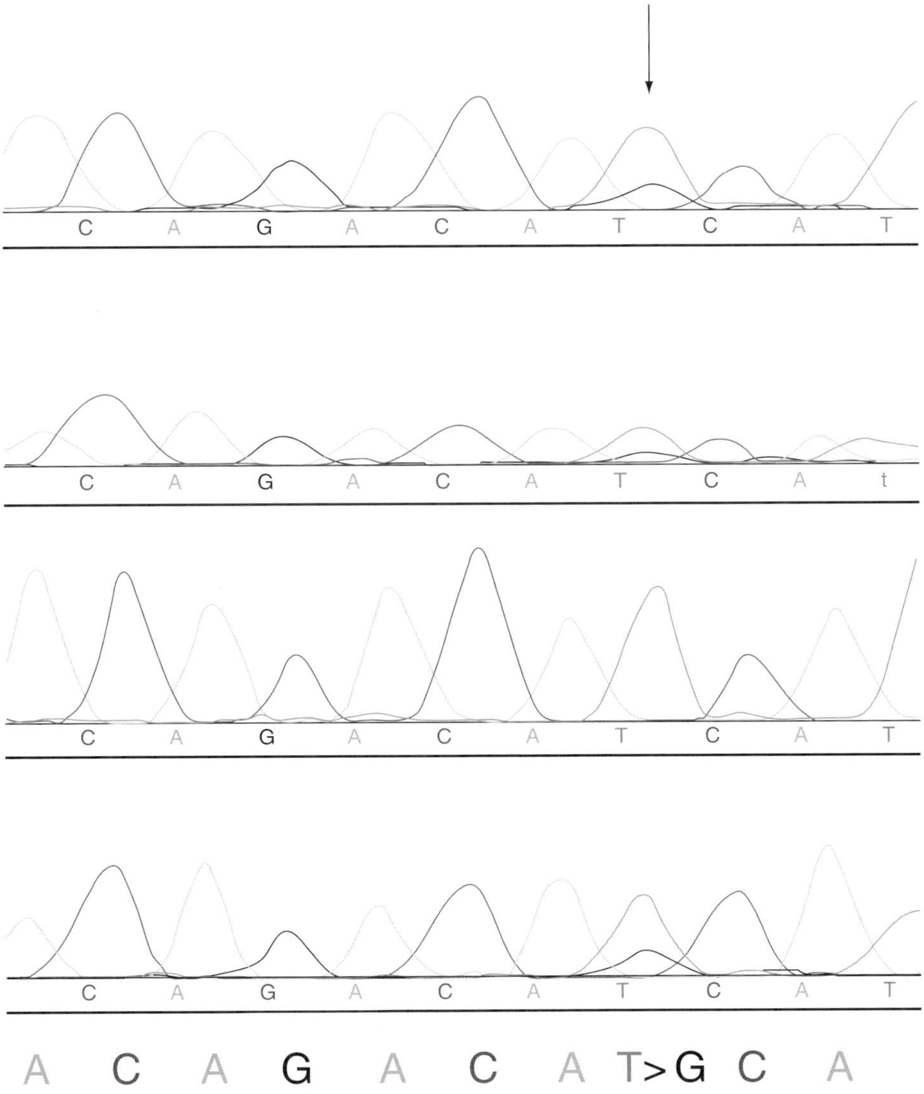

FIGURE 5.3 *Four independent sequencing assays confirm a sequence heteroplasmy at position 279 in the HVII region of the mtDNA. Figure provided by Mitotyping Technologies, State College, PA. Please see the color insert for a color version of this figure.*

usually easy to detect and characterize; if a slot-blot test is used, the analyst will see more than one signal at one of the tested loci. If the mtDNA is sequenced, the analyst who reads the DNA sequence will observe a nucleotide position at which he or she can see two peaks, corresponding to the two different nucleotides that are present in that position in different mtDNA molecules (Figure 5.3). In these cases, special letters (not the usual A, C, G and T) are used to indicate which nucleotides are recognized. For example, if both a C and a T peak are observed, the analyzer will print the letter Y in the sequence to indicate that it detected both a C and a T peak at that one nucleotide position. If one peak is of considerably greater intensity than the other, this can be indicated using the mathematical ">" (greater than) sign. For example, if the C peak predominates, but there is also a clear, smaller T peak, the position may be designated as C>T.

In some situations, the analyst can get a reasonable approximation of the relative quantities of the two sequences by comparing the heights of the associated peaks.[31] This cannot always be done, however. The different dyes used to label the A, C, G and T nucleotides incorporate into the DNA with different efficiencies, so the relative strengths of the signals will not always reflect the relative quantities of the two products. Forensic testing laboratories that perform mtDNA testing empirically determine the level at which their sequencing system can detect heteroplasmy. The NIST provides a set of SRMs that represent heteroplasmic samples that contain different proportions of the two haplotypes. When a laboratory develops a new assay for heteroplasmy, the laboratory can use these SRMs to provide the validation data that demonstrate the limits of detection. Alternatively, the analyst can mix two samples known to be homoplasmic at the locus in question in a number of different proportions and establish the system's limits of detection. The analyst may vary certain parameters of the analysis, such as the number of PCR cycles or the analyzer's peak detection threshold (defined in Chapter 3) in order to increase sensitivity and enable low levels of heteroplasmy to be detected. If different parameters are used in casework than were used in the validation study, the analyst should account for these differences when he or she interprets the data.

As mentioned earlier, the control region of the mtDNA contains two stretches in which the cytosine-containing "C" nucleotide is repeated. Some individuals exhibit a length heteroplasmy, in which their mtDNA

[31] Peak height is usually used, but the area under the peak may actually be a more reliable measure.

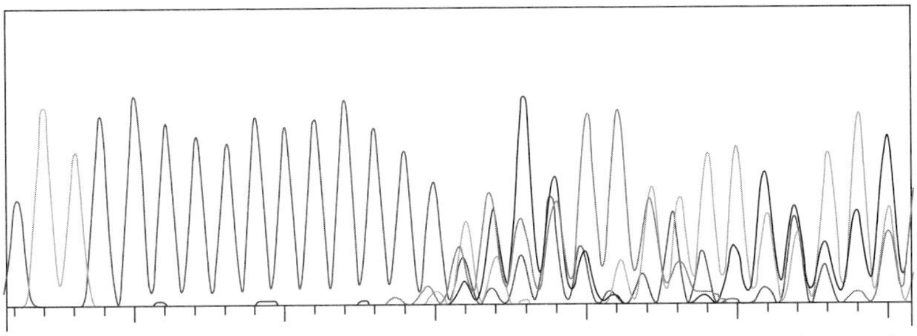

FIGURE 5.4 *Length heteroplasmy in mtDNA. Note that the sequence is clear up to the end of the poly-C string, then several sequences are laid over each other after the poly-C string. Note the number of nucleotides for which the sequencer cannot identify a major peak (symbolized with an "N"). Figure provided by Mitotyping Technologies, State College, PA. Please see the color insert for a color version of this figure.*

contains more than one subpopulation of mtDNA molecules, each of which has a different number of Cs in one of the poly-C strings. In contrast to the sequence heteroplasmies, length heteroplasmies can be difficult to characterize. The sequence will be clear up to the end of the poly-C string, but after that, the sequence analyzer is forced to read two or more sequences that are laid on top of each other (Figure 5.4). An experienced analyst can often read the sequence successfully if there are only two populations of mtDNA with different length of poly-C sequence. If there are more than two populations, however, the task gets very difficult. Because of the uncertainty inherent in trying to interpret multiple overlaid sequences, a length heteroplasmy may be noted verbally when the evidence is presented, but it is not used to calculate the RMP of the mtDNA haplotype.[32]

[32] Bar et al., 2000.

The Level of Heteroplasmy Can Vary from Tissue to Tissue

Characterizing a sequence heteroplasmy can be very difficult. The level of heteroplasmy can vary between different tissues. Consequently, a sequence heteroplasmy can manifest itself in a number of different ways. For example, an individual can be homoplasmic (all copies of the mtDNA have the same sequence) in one tissue but heteroplasmic in another. In these cases, the heteroplasmic tissue will exhibit two peaks at one nucleotide position, one of which is the same as the peak seen in the homoplasmic tissue. Alternatively, an individual can have a different allele predominate at that position in the different tissues; the major peak in one tissue will be the minor peak in the other tissue, and vice versa.

[33] Calloway et al., 2000; Alonso et al., 2002; Sekiguchi et al., 2004; Tully et al., 2004; Melton et al., 2005.

[34] Tully et al., 2004.

In a case such as this, if the minor peaks are very small, they may escape detection. The two tissues will appear to be homoplasmic, with a different nucleotide at the position in question in each of the different tissues. This obviously forces the analyst to consider the possibility that the samples came from different individuals. Conversely, this can also make it appear as if two samples that actually came from different individuals came from the same source.

Because of the potential for variability between tissues, when taking a reference sample from a suspect for an mtDNA analysis, it is always best to take a sample of the same tissue that was left at the crime scene. For example, a blood sample might have a C at nucleotide position 85, a hair sample from the same individual may show both a C and a T peak at that locus and a skin sample might show only the T peak at nucleotide position 85. If a skin sample was left by this individual at a crime scene but the analyst used a blood sample as a reference sample, the two sequences would appear to be mismatched at the 85th nucleotide. Alternatively, if a hair sample was recovered from the crime scene but the analyst used a blood sample as a reference sample, the presence of two peaks at that locus in the hair sample would force the analyst to consider the possibility that the hair had been contaminated by the DNA from a second person.

Given the number of forensic investigations that involve blood samples, it is fortunate that blood is the least heteroplasmic of the tissues that have been extensively studied. Fewer than 2% of the people whose blood samples have been analyzed were heteroplasmic at any mitochondrial loci. In contrast, hair is the most heteroplasmic of the human tissues. It is estimated that approximately 5–10% of the population exhibit heteroplasmy at one or more loci in their hair's mtDNA.[33] In addition, although this would be very rare, at least one study has demonstrated different levels of heteroplasmy in different sections of the same hair.[34] As can be seen in Figure 5.5, section 17.2 of the hair in question exhibits only a T peak at position 16093, but section 17.5 exhibits a C peak, with a very small T peak underneath it. This can easily be reported by an automated sequencer as a C peak, and the presence of two different nucleotides at that position can easily lead to confusion regarding the source of the hair. Note also, however, that the intervening sections 17.3 and 17.4 of the same hair clearly show the heteroplasmy that marks the transition between sections 17.2 and 17.5. In cases in which heteroplasmy is so marked as to produce two different,

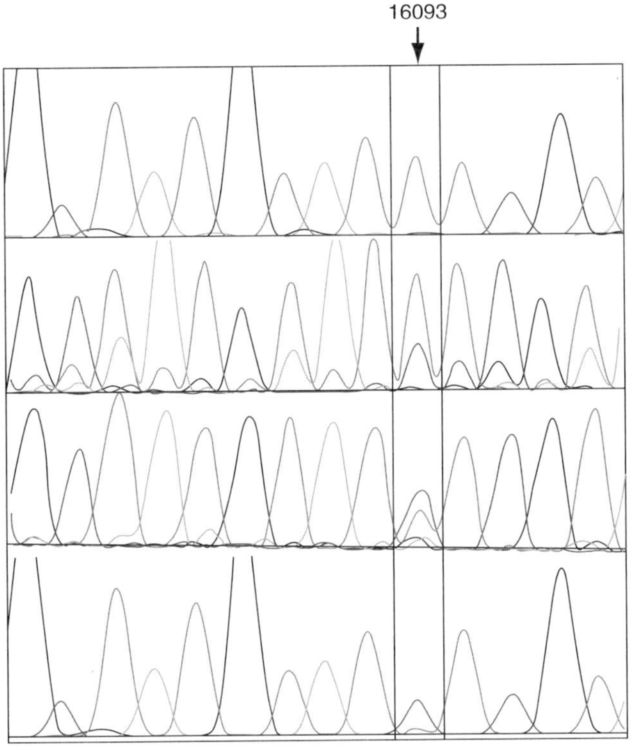

FIGURE 5.5 *Four different sections of the same hair, demonstrating different levels of heteroplasmy in the different hair sections. Reprinted from Tully et al., 2004, with permission from Elsevier. Please see the color insert for a color version of this figure.*

apparently homoplasmic, mitotypes, there will usually be tissues that clearly illustrate the heteroplasmy as well.

Despite the potential for confusion, it is usually possible to differentiate between a case of heteroplasmy and one in which the samples came from two different individuals. Heteroplasmic individuals are usually only heteroplasmic at a single-nucleotide position.[35] In contrast, when two samples do actually come from different sources, it is rare to find them differing at only one nucleotide position. If two samples differ at two or more loci, with no evidence of heteroplasmy, it is highly likely that the samples have come from two different individuals. In a single sample, if multiple signals are seen at two or more loci, the sample is highly likely to include a mixture of material from two individuals. Some courts may be cautious when faced with samples that differ at only two loci, however. Because we are presently unable to reliably estimate how much more or less likely it is that samples that differ at two loci represent heteroplasmy versus mixtures, when the samples differ at two nucleotide positions, the court may consider the results inconclusive.

[35] Tully et al., 2000; Budowle et al., 2003.

When two mtDNA profiles are identical, the analyst will report that the test failed to exclude the defendant as the source of the evidence sample. Because of the variability of mtDNA within a single individual, however, when two mtDNA samples differ by only one nucleotide, it is not automatically considered an exclusion. Some authorities feel that the probability that this represents a heteroplasmy is greater than the probability that the evidence sample came from someone who is unrelated to the suspect but whose mtDNA sequence coincidentally differs from the suspect's by only one nucleotide. Unfortunately, however, forensic analysts cannot yet unambiguously specify exactly what the two probabilities are. Because of this uncertainty, if two mtDNA profiles differ by a single nucleotide and there is evidence of heteroplasmy, the analyst will consider this a failure to exclude the suspect as a potential contributor of the evidence. If the two samples differ by a single nucleotide and there is no evidence that this may represent a case of heteroplasmy, however, the analyst must consider whether the two samples are from the same tissue and what the mutation rate is at the specific nucleotide in question. If the two samples came from a tissue with a low mutation rate, such as blood, and the specific nucleotide in question is known to have a relatively low mutation rate, the two samples have most likely come from different sources. One may not be able to state this with the degree of certainty required for criminal cases, however; in many cases, results such as these may have to be declared inconclusive.

Because heteroplasmy is rare, it is highly unlikely that two unrelated people would exhibit heteroplasmy at the same nucleotide, especially at a site that is not known as a hot spot for mutations. The existence of heteroplasmy can therefore significantly strengthen the evidence if the evidence sample and the reference sample exhibit the same heteroplasmy. For example, consider the Romanov family again. Tsar Nicholas II's mtDNA exhibited heteroplasmy (C/T) at nucleotide 16169. The body of Nicholas's brother Georgij Romanov was exhumed, and the same heteroplasmy was found in his mtDNA. This helped confirm that the remains in question were the remains of Nicholas, Alexandra and their children.[36] The conclusion was further strengthened when Xenia Cheremeteff-Sfiri, great-granddaughter of the Tsar's sister (Figure 5.2), was found to exhibit only a T at that position (all other family members tested had a C).

[36] Ivanov et al., 1996.

At one point heteroplasmy was considered a vanishingly rare event. As detection methods have improved, however, the reported frequency of heteroplasmy has increased. The fact that there is still some uncertainty regarding the frequency of heteroplasmy in mtDNA is often used as grounds to challenge the admissibility of mtDNA evidence that involves a heteroplasmic sample. This argument is aided by a study in which Grzybowski and colleagues reported heteroplasmy in 13 of 35 hair samples.[37] This level of heteroplasmy is far greater than that which has been reported by other researchers, however. If these results were accurate, they would significantly impugn the reliability of forensic hair analyses. The Grzybowski study has been convincingly criticized by several other research groups, however,[38] and the general consensus, as noted earlier, is that 5–10% of the population exhibit heteroplasmy in their hair mtDNA. In general, because mtDNA analyses have been extensively validated, most courts will admit mtDNA evidence and consider arguments regarding heteroplasmy to influence the weight, rather than the admissibility, of the evidence.

[37] Grzybowski et al., 2000.

[38] For example, Budowle et al., 2003.

STATISTICAL ANALYSIS OF mtDNA HAPLOTYPE DATA

The mtDNA Profile Must Be Treated As a Single Piece of Information

As discussed in Chapter 1, each cell's nucleus has two copies of the nDNA molecule, and the individual's allele status for an nDNA marker is referred to as the individual's genotype. Because mtDNA only has one copy, one's mtDNA profile (or mitotype) is referred to as a **haplotype**; the same term is used to describe the allele status for a single nuclear chromosome or a male's allele status for X or Y chromosome markers. Haplotypes that are very similar to each other are grouped together in **haplogroups**. A haplogroup is thought to reflect a situation in which a group of related women migrated to a location, then over time mutations arose in their mtDNA that caused the mtDNA sequences of their descendants to differ from each other by one or a few nucleotides. One can trace human migrations by observing the clustering of similar haplotypes into haplogroups in different geographic regions.

As discussed in Chapter 4, one cannot use the product rule to calculate the probability of a set of events unless the events are independent of each other. For forensic DNA purposes, this means that knowing which allele

[39] Genetic recombination is discussed in all genetics textbooks, including the one listed in Appendix V.

[40] Oota et al., 2001; Balding, 2005.

the individual has at one marker does not allow the analyst to predict which allele the individual has at any other marker. For nuclear STRs, a phenomenon known as genetic recombination[39] helps ensure the independence between marker genotypes and allows each STR to contribute independently to the effort to identify the individual. Because recombination does not occur in the mtDNA molecule, the entire mitochondrial sequence must be seen as a single piece of information, and the RMP must be obtained by directly observing the frequency of the mtDNA sequence in the appropriate database, rather than inferring the probability of profiles by multiplying the frequencies of the alleles contained therein, as is done for STRs.

Mitotypes Exhibit a High Level of Diversity Despite Concerns about Population Substructure

Because of the matrilineal inheritance of and lack of recombination in mtDNA, mtDNA mitotypes exhibit higher levels of population substructure than autosomal STR profiles do, especially in matrilocal societies in which a man usually moves to his wife's location after they are married.[40] This can lead to population substructure within the major races. Not only can different ethnic subgroups within that race have significant differences in the frequency of their mitotypes, but there can also be significant differences in mitotype frequencies between members of a single ethnic subgroup living in different geographic locations. This raises a serious concern for forensic analysts, because if the level of population substructure is high enough within a major race, the analyst needs to maintain separate databases for different ethnic subgroups and geographic regions within that race. This presents a logistical challenge, because the analyst is required to collect mitotypes from a diverse collection of geographic locations. It also decreases the effective size of the analyst's reference database and may leave the analyst with a reference database that is too small to provide a statistically valid estimate of the RMP for any particular mitotype.

Fortunately, the migration and admixture that have occurred among the ethnic subgroups within the major races in America has resulted in relatively low levels of population substructure within the major racial groups. Large-scale studies have reported that the levels of population substructure within the Caucasian, African American and Asian American populations in the United States are low enough that analysts can use the respective databases for all crimes involving defendants of that race, regardless of their geographic location.[41] These studies have also pointed out, however, that there is enough difference between the genetic heritage of southeastern Hispanics and southwestern Hispanics to require the use of separate databases for the two groups. As noted earlier, southeastern Hispanics have more African ancestry than southwestern Hispanics do, while southwestern Hispanics have more Native American ancestry than southeastern Hispanics do.[42] The analyst should use different reference databases for calculating the RMPs of mitotypes from southeastern Hispanics versus southwestern Hispanics; this is already a standard practice for some forensic analysts.

Much less information is available regarding the level of population substructure in Native Americans' mtDNA than in the mtDNA of these other races. Forensic studies using autosomal STR profiles and Y chromosome haplotypes suggest there is more population substructure within the Native Americans than within the other major races, and advocate the use of separate databases for the different Native American tribes.[43] It is therefore reasonable to believe that analysts should use separate databases for the analysis of mtDNA mitotypes in the different Native American tribes as well.

Despite the concerns about population substructure, mtDNA mitotypes are highly useful for forensic investigations, especially for the purpose of exclusion. Mitotypes are highly diverse. In all but the Native American databases, most mitotypes only occur once in their respective databases, and very few have frequencies greater than 1%. Even in the Native American tribes, however, a mitotype can eliminate the vast majority of the tribe as sources of the evidence. In the one published forensic study that reported data from Native Americans (Apache and Navajo), on average a mitotype could exclude 92.5% of the individuals in the Apache database and 95.6% of the individuals in the Navajo database.[44] Several research groups are studying other polymorphic loci and are developing marker panels that will render mtDNA testing even more useful for forensic identity testing.[45]

Although this is not the most informative analysis one can conduct, one can get a general assessment of the discriminatory power afforded by the mtDNA test by determining how frequently a pairwise comparison of two

[41] Budowle et al., 1999; Melton et al., 2001; Parsons, 2005.

[42] Parsons, 2005; Allard et al., 2006.

[43] Budowle et al., 2001; Redd et al., 2006.

[44] Budowle et al., 2002.

[45] Lutz et al., 2000; Bini et al., 2003; Coble et al., 2006.

[46] Budowle et al., 2000.

[47] Balding, 2005.

mitotypes from the database would yield a match. The FBI has developed a software program called Mitosearch that enables the analyst to compare all the sequences in the database to all the other sequences in the database.[46] This information can be used to estimate the probability that two randomly chosen individuals from that reference population would have matching mitotypes. It does not answer the most important question, however: What is the probability that a randomly chosen individual from the appropriate reference population would have a mitotype that matches that of the defendant and evidence?

Using a Confidence Interval and the Theta Correction Factor to Derive the RMP of a Mitotype

In its simplest form, the frequency of an mtDNA profile can be represented as *F/N*, where *F* is the number of times the profile appeared in the database and *N* is the total number of mitotypes in the database. This "counting method" has serious drawbacks, especially considering the size of the mtDNA databases and the level of population substructure that exists in mtDNA profiles. The mtDNA databases are too small, and sampled from too few geographic regions, to account for the relatively high level of population substructure that exists in mtDNA profiles compared to autosomal STR profiles. Consequently, many mtDNA profiles exist but have not been included in an mtDNA database. A simple counting leads the analyst to underestimate the frequencies of these mtDNA types, which is highly prejudicial to the defendant who possesses one of them.

Population geneticists have suggested several ways in which one can compensate for the small size of the available databases. David Balding[47] has suggested adding the two matching profiles (from the defendant and the evidence) into the reference population. This approach takes all the available information into account, including the observations of the defendant's and the evidence's profiles. In addition, adding the profile from the evidence as well as that from the defendant assumes that the evidence came from someone other than the defendant, which is consistent with the presumption of innocence. Following this reasoning, the frequency of the mtDNA profile is represented as

$$p = \frac{F+2}{N+2}. \qquad \text{(Eq. 5.1)}$$

John Buckleton,[48] however, has pointed out that, if one conforms properly to the principles of binary mathematics, the proper correction for the mtDNA profile frequency is

$$p = \frac{F+1}{N+2}. \qquad \text{(Eq. 5.2)}$$

Balding's formula is both more intuitive and more conservative, but Buckleton's is "mindlessly and pedantically correct."[49] In most situations, there is very little difference between the estimates produced by the two formulas.

Despite the widespread use of this modified counting approach in other countries, it is more common practice in the United States to use *F/N* to represent the frequency of the profile in question, calculate a confidence interval (defined in Chapter 4) around the frequency and report the upper bound of the confidence interval to the triers of fact.[50] If one uses a 95% or 99% confidence interval, the upper bound represents a conservative enough estimate of the RMP for use in criminal trials.[51] Three different formulas are used to calculate confidence intervals (described in Chapter 4), depending on how frequently the profile has been seen in the database and how large the database is.

All three CI formulas that were discussed in Chapter 4 consistently produce a more conservative estimate of the frequency of a DNA profile than either Balding's or Buckleton's formula does. For example, if an mtDNA profile is not seen in the FBI's African American database ($F/N = 0$, $N = 1148$), the CI method (using a 95% confidence interval, the less conservative of the two possible confidence intervals) estimates the profile's frequency at 0.26%, or 1 in 384.6. Balding's method (always the more conservative of the two alternatives), on the other hand, estimates it at 0.174%, or 1 in 574.7. If the profile is seen three times in the same database ($F/N = 0.26\%$), the CI method estimates its frequency as 0.766%, or 1 in 130.5, while Balding's method estimates it at 0.435%, or 1 in 229.9.

These methods correct the observed frequency of the mtDNA profile to account for the small size of the databases, but do not account for the relatively high degree of population substructure that is known to exist for mtDNA profiles. Because of population substructure, the frequency of the mtDNA profile must be adjusted with a θ correction factor, just as was

[48] Buckleton et al., 2004; also see Evett and Weir, 1998, p. 69.

[49] John Buckleton, personal communication, March 3, 2007.

[50] Budowle et al., 1999; Holland and Parsons, 1999.

[51] To the best of our knowledge, there are no authoritative arguments that establish whether the 95% or 99% confidence intervals should be used. Use of the 99% confidence interval is in keeping with the general goal of maximizing confidence and minimizing prejudice against the defendant, however.

described in Chapter 4 for nDNA STR profiles. Balding[52] and Buckleton[53] have provided similar suggestions regarding the appropriate way in which to compensate for population substructure in mtDNA profiles. Balding states the RMP associated with the mtDNA profile in question as

$$RMP = \theta + (1 - \theta)p, \qquad \text{(Eq. 5.3)}$$

where p is the adjusted frequency of the profile in the relevant reference database. For American courts, one can simply use the upper bound of the confidence interval for the frequency of the mtDNA profile as the value of p. This is a sound strategy, and the use of conservative estimates of θ (0.01 or 0.03, as discussed in Chapter 4) will produce RMPs that are conservative (i.e., deliberately biased in favor of the defendant).

Accounting for Heteroplasmy

Recall from the discussion above that the high mutation rate of mtDNA may result in one individual possessing slightly different mtDNA profiles in different tissues. If the crime scene evidence is from a different tissue than was used for the suspect's reference sample, one must adjust the calculation of the RMP to compensate for this fact. Most reference samples will contain mtDNA profiles from blood or buccal (mouth cavity) swab samples. If the evidence includes a tissue other than blood or buccal material, there are two observations one might make when the suspect is actually the source of the evidence: one might observe the identical profile in both tissues, or one might find that the two profiles differ by one nucleotide.[54] For example, consider the mitotype 263G, 315.1C.[55] The SWGDAM database contains 1,655 Caucasian mitotypes. Only 15 (0.89%) of these are identical matches for this mitotype, but 153 (9.3%) differ by a single nucleotide. The analyst will therefore report that there are 168 mtDNA profiles out of 1,655 (10.2%) that cannot be excluded as coming from the same source. Accounting for these other, slightly mismatching profiles obviously increases the frequency of profiles that cannot be excluded as a match and proportionally reduces the strength of the evidence against the defendant.

Calculating the actual RMP for this situation is very complicated, because among the mitotypes that differ from the evidence sample by one nucleotide, different mitotypes will differ from the evidence mitotype at different nucleotides. A different number of mitotypes will mismatch at each of the

[52] Balding, 2005.

[53] Buckleton, Triggs and Walsh, 2004.

[54] Although it is theoretically possible for two profiles from the same individual to differ by two, or even more, nucleotides, these events are improbable enough to be omitted from the calculation. Further discussion of this subject can be found in Tully et al., 2001.

[55] This example is taken from Butler, 2005, p. 278.

relevant nucleotides, and each of the nucleotides involved may have a different mutation rate. Any formula used to interpret these data must account for these facts.

Combining the RMPs from Autosomal STR Profiles and mtDNA Mitotypes

In rare cases, both nDNA and mtDNA evidence will be available. As Buckleton has stated,[56] because the inheritance of mtDNA is independent of the inheritance of nDNA, it is intuitively appealing to think that the product rule can be applied to multiply the RMP of the nDNA STR profile with the RMP of the mtDNA profile to produce an overall RMP for the DNA evidence (after adjusting both with the θ correction factor). One must keep in mind, however, that the individual's mtDNA mitotype provides some information about the ethnic group to which the individual belongs. As a result, when two individuals' mitotypes match, there may be an increased probability that they share autosomal STR alleles compared to two individuals whose mitotypes do not match. The same concern applies to combinations of autosomal and Y chromosome STR data. Walsh and colleagues have recently published a study in which they empirically determined that the Y chromosome STR match adds only a small amount of population substructure to the autosomal STR profiles.[57] Given that Y chromosome haplotypes exhibit a greater degree of population substructure than mtDNA mitotypes,[58] this conclusion probably holds for combining autosomal STR profiles and mtDNA mitotypes as well. At this point in time, however, there is no comparable demonstration regarding the degree of additional substructure that appears in autosomal STR profiles when two individuals' mitotypes match.

[56] Buckleton, Triggs and Walsh, 2004.

[57] Walsh et al., 2007.

[58] Oota et al., 2001; Schoske et al., 2004; Buckleton et al., 2004.

REFERENCES AND ADDITIONAL READINGS

Allard, M.W., Polanskey, D., Wilson, M.R., Monson, K.L. and Burowle, B. (2006) *Journal of Forensic Sciences*, 51(3), 566–573.

Alonso, A., Salas, A., Albarran, C., Arroyo, E., Castro, A., Crespillo, M., di Lonardo, A.M., Lareu, M.V., Cubria, C.L., Soto, M.L., Lorente, J.A., Semper, M.M., Palacio, A., Paredes, M., Pereira, L., Lezaun, A.P., Brito, J.P., Sala, A., Vide, M.C., Whittle, M., Yunis, J.J. and Gomez, J. (2002) *Forensic Science International*, 125, 1–7.

Anderson, S., Bankier, A.T., Barrell, B.G., de Bruijin, M.H.L., Coulson, A.R., Drouin, J., Eperon, I.C., Nierlich, D.P., Roe, B.A., Sanger, F., Schreier, P.H., Smith, A.J.H., Staden, R. and Young, I.G. (1981) *Nature*, 290, 457–463.

Andrews, R.M., Kubacka, I., Chinery, P.F., Lightowers, R.N., Turnbull, D.M. and Howell, N. (1999) *Nature Genetics*, 23, 147.

Awadalla, P., Eyre-Walker, A. and Smith, J.M. (1999) *Science*, 286(5449), 2524–5.

Balding, D. (2005) *Weight-of-Evidence for Forensic DNA Profiles*. Chichester: John Wiley.

Bar, W., Brinkmann, B., Budowle, B., Carracedo, A., Gill, P., Holland, M., Lincoln, P.J., Mayr, W., Morling, N., Olaisen, B., Schneider, P.M., Tully, G. and Wilson, M. (2000) *International Journal of Legal Medicine*, 113, 193–196.

Bini, C., Ceccardi, S., Luiselli, D., Ferri, G., Pelotti, S., Colalongo, C., Falconi, M. and Pappalardo, G. (2003) *Forensic Science International*, 135, 48–52.

Birky, C.W., Jr. (2001) *Annual Review of Genetics*, 35, 125–48.

Buckleton, J.S., Triggs, C.M. and Walsh, S.J. (2004) *Forensic DNA Evidence Interpretation*. Boca Raton, FL: CRC Press.

Budowle, B., Wilson, M.R., DiZinnio, J.A., Stauffer, C., Fasano, M.A. and Holland, M.M. (1999) *Forensic Science International*, 103,, 23–35.

Budowle, B., Wilson, M.R., DiZinnio, J.A., Stauffer, C., Fasano, M.A., Holland, M.M. and Monson, K. (1999) *Forensic Science International*, 103,(1), 23–35.

Budowle, B., Allard, M.W., Fisher, C.L., Isenberg, A.R., Monson, K.L., Stewart, J.E.B., Wilson, M.R. and Miller, K.W.P. (2002) *International Journal of Legal Medicine*, 116, 212–215.

Budowle, B., Allard, M.W., Wilson, M.R. and Chakraborty, R. (2003) *Annual Review of Genomics and Human Genetics*, 4, 119–141.

Butler, J.M. (2005) *Forensic DNA Typing,* 2nd ed. Boston: Elsevier/Academic Press, 2005.

Calloway, C.D., Reynolds, R.L., Herrin, G.L. Jr. and Anderson, W.W. (2000) *American Journal of Human Genetics*, 66(4), 1384–97.

Coble, M.D., Just, R.S., O'Callaghan, J.E., Letmanyi, I.H., Peterson, C.T., Irwin, J.A. and Parson, T.J. (2004) *International Journal of Legal Medicine*, 118(3), 137–146.

Coble, M.D., Vallone, P.M., Just, R.S., Diegoli, T.M., Smith, B.C. and Parson, T.J. (2006) *International Journal of Legal Medicine*, 120, 27–32.

Elson, J.L., Andrews, R.M., Chinnery, P.F., Lightowlers, R.N., Turnbull, D.M. and Howell, N. (2001) *American Journal of Human Genetics*, 68, 145–153.

Evett and Weir, B.S. (1998) *Interpreting DNA Evidence: Statistical Genetics for Forensic Scientists.* Sunderland, MA: Sinauer Associates.

Eyre-Walker, A., Smith, NH. and Smith, JM. (1999) *Proceedings Biological Sciences*, 266(1418), 477–83.

Gill, P., Ivanov, P.L., Kimpton, C., Piercy, R., Benson, N., Tully, G., Evett, I., Hagelberg, E. and Sullivan, K. (1994) *Nature Genetics*, 6, 130.

Grzybowski, T. (2000) *Electrophoresis*, 21, 548–553.

Hagelberg, E., Goldman, N., Lio, P., Whelan, S. and Schiefenhovel, W. (1999) *Proceedings of the Royal Society of London*, 266, 485–492.

Hagelberg, E., Goldman, N., Lio, P., Whelan, S. and Schiefenhovel, W. (2000) *Proceedings of the Royal Society of London*, 267, 1595–1596.

Holland, M.M. and Parsons, T.J. (1999) *Forensic Science Reviews*, 11, 21–50.

Isenberg, A.R. (2004) Forensic mitochondrial DNA analysis. In: Saferstein, R. (ed.). *Forensic Science Handbook. Volume II, Second Edition.* Upper Saddle River, NJ: Prentice-Hall, pp. 297–327.

Ivanov, P.L., Wadhams, M.J., Roby, R.K., Holland, M.M., Weedn, V.W. and Parsons, T.J. (1996) *Nature Genetics*, 12, 417–420.

Kaestle, F.A., Kittles, R.A., Roth, A.L. and Ungvarsky, E.J. (2006) *American Criminal Law Review*, 43, 53–88.

Kline, M.C., Vallone, P.M., Redman, J.W., Duewer, D.L., Calloway, C.D. and Butler, J.M. (2005) *Journal of Forensic Sciences*, 50(2), 377–385.

Lutz, S., Wittig, H., Weisser, H., Heizmann, J., Junge, A., Dimo-Simonin, N., Parson, W., Edelmann, J., Anslinger, K., Jung, S. and Augustin, C. (2000) *Forensic Science International*, 113, 97.

Meissner, C., Mohamed, S.A., Klueter, H., Hamann, K., vaon Wurmb, N. and Oehmichen, M. (2000) *Forensic Science International*, 113, 109–112.

Melton, T. and Nelson, K. (2001) *Croatian Medical Journal*, 42, 298–303.

Melton, T., Clifford, S., Kayser, M., Nasodze, I., Batzer, M. and Stoneking, M. (2001) *Journal of Forensic Sciences*, 46(1), 46–52.

Melton, T. (2004) *Forensic Science Reviews*, 16, 1–20.

Melton, T., Dimick, G., Higgins, B., Lindstrom, L. and Nelson, K. (2005) *Journal of Forensic Science*, 50(1), 1–8.

Monson, K.L., Miller, K.W.P., Wilson, M.R., DiZinno, J.A. and Budowle, B. (2002) *Forensic Science Communications*, 4(2), also available at http://www.fbi.gov/hq/lab/fsc/backissu/april2002/index.htm

Oota, H., Settheetham-Ishida, W., Tiwawech, D., Ishida, T. and Stoneking, M. (2001) *Nature Genetics*, 29, 20–21.

Parsons, T.J. (2005) Report for U.S. Department of Justice, Office of Justice Programs, Progress of Project 2000-IJ-CX-K010.

Redd, A.J., Chamberlain, V.F., Kearney, V.F., Stover, D., Karafet, T., Calderon, K., Walsh, B. and Hammer, M.F. (2006) *Journal of Forensic Sciences*, 51(3), 580–585.

Rudin, N. and Inman, K. (2002) *An Introduction to Forensic DNA Analysis*. Boca Raton, FL: CRC Press.

Sato, M. and Kuroiwa, T. (1991) *Experimental Cell Research*, 196, 137–140.

Schwartz, M. and Vissing, J. (2002) *New England Journal of Medicine*, 347, 576–580.

Schwartz, M. and Vissing, J. (2004) *Journal of Neurological Sciences*, 218(1–2), 99–101.

Schoske, R., Vallone, P.M., Kline, M.C., Redman, J.W. and Butler, J.M. (2004) *Forensic Science International*, 139, 107–121.

Sekiguchi, K., Sato, H. and Kasai, K. (2004) *Journal of Forensic Science*, 49(5), 1–6.

Stewart, J.E., Aagaard, P.J., Pokorak, E.G., Polanskey, D. and Budowle, B. (2003) *Journal of Forensic Sciences*, 48, 571–580.

Stoneking, M. (2000) *American Journal of Human Genetics*, 67, 1029–1032.

Sutovsky, P., Moreno, R.D., Ramalho-Santos, J., Dominko, T., Simerly, C. and Schatten, G. (1999) *Nature*, 402, 371–372.

Tully, L.A., Parsons, T.J., Steighner, R.J., Holland, M.M., Marino, M.A. and Prenger, V.L. (2000) *American Journal of Human Genetics*, 67, 432–443.

Tully, G., Bar, W., Brinkmann, B., Carracedo, A., Gill, P., Morling, N., Parsons, W. and Schneider, P. (2001) *Forensic Science International*, 124, 83–91.

Tully, G., Barritt, S.M., Bender, K., Brignon, E., Capelli, C., Dimo-Simonin, N., Eichmann, C., Ernst, C.M., Lambert, C., Lareu, M.V., Ludes, B., Mevag, B., Parson, W., Pfeiffer, H., Salas, A., Schneider, P.M. and Staalstrom, E. (2004) *Forensic Science International*, 140, 1–11.

Vallone, P.M., Just, R.C., Coble, M.D., Butler, J.M. and Parsons, T.J. (2004) *International Journal of Legal Medicine*, 118(3), 147–157.

Wallace, D.C., Stugard, C., Murdock, D., Schurr, T. and Brown, M.D. (1997) *Proceedings of the National Academy of Sciences U.S.A.*, 94, 14900–14905.

Walsh, B., Redd, A.J. and Hammer, M.F. (2007) *Forensic Science International*, April 19 (epub ahead of print).

Wilson, M.R., Polanskey, D., Butler, J., DiZinno, J.A., Replogle, J. and Budowle, B. (1995) *BioTechniques*, 18, 662–669.

Wiurf, C. (2001) *Genetics*, 159, 749–756.

CHAPTER 6

Y Chromosome Analyses

CONTENTS

Y Chromosome Evolution and its Consequences for Forensic Analyses

Laboratory Analysis of Y Chromosome Haplotypes

Statistical Analysis of Y Chromosome Haplotypes

References and Additional Readings

Y CHROMOSOME EVOLUTION AND ITS CONSEQUENCES FOR FORENSIC ANALYSES

The Y Chromosome has had a Rough Ride

The Y chromosome has gone through a striking transformation in recent evolutionary history.[1] If you go back to the point at which mammals whose young develop in pouches, such as the kangaroo and opossum, diverged from the mammals that incubate their young entirely inside the womb, you would find that the XY chromosome pair looked much like all the other chromosome pairs do now. They were both the same size, and they both contained the same genes. Over the intervening time, however, the Y has physically lost much of its material. The human Y chromosome is considerably smaller than the X. In addition, mutations have rendered many of the genes that have remained on the Y chromosome inactive.[2] Furthermore, the X and Y stopped recombining as the autosomes do. In humans, only two small regions of the X and Y chromosomes, one at each end, recombine during sperm formation. Because these regions recombine like the autosomes do, they are referred to as the **pseudoautosomal regions (PARs)** of the X and Y. The STRs that are used for forensic testing are located in the **nonrecombining portion of the Y chromosome (NRY)**, however, and not in the PARs.[3]

Because of the Y chromosome's unique evolution, Y chromosome analyses share features with both the nDNA STR analyses and the mtDNA haplotype analyses. The basic structure of a Y chromosome STR is identical to that of an autosomal STR, so the principles underlying the amplification of the STRs and the characterization of different alleles are the

[1] The details of Y chromosome evolution are beyond the scope of this book. The reader is referred to Ohno, 1967 for a detailed discussion.

same as they are for autosomal STRs. In addition, Y chromosome STRs have mutation rates similar to those seen for autosomal STRs. Unlike the other nuclear chromosomes, however, the Y markers are present in a single copy,[4] and no recombination occurs in the region of the Y chromosome in which the STR markers that are used in forensic testing lie. Y chromosome STRs are therefore inherited as a haplotype, and the statistical analysis must treat the Y chromosome STR profile as a single piece of information, just as is true for the mtDNA haplotype.

Patrilineal Inheritance and a Lack of Recombination

Between the lack of recombination in the relevant region of the Y chromosome and the low mutation rate for Y chromosome STRs, the Y STR haplotype is usually inherited unchanged from father to son. This means that when the Y chromosome profile of a suspect matches that of the evidence, the suspect and all his patrilineal relatives are included as possible sources of the sample. Furthermore, just as mtDNA can be used to connect distant relatives who are related through an uninterrupted chain of females, Y chromosome STRs can be used to connect distant relatives who are related through an uninterrupted line of males.

The most famous example of such an investigation is the recent study that concluded that Thomas Jefferson fathered at least one child (a son) with his slave Sally Hemmings[5] (Figure 6.1). Jefferson's only son by his marriage died in infancy, so there were no other direct descendants of Jefferson who could provide a Y chromosome STR profile for comparison. There are living individuals who are descended from Jefferson's paternal uncle (his father's brother) Field Jefferson through an uninterrupted line of males, however. The Y chromosome STR profiles from one of these individuals matched that from a man who claimed to be descended from Eston Hemmings, the son of Thomas Jefferson and Sally Hemmings. Given the DNA evidence and historical reports that Jefferson showed an exceptional regard for Sally Hemmings, it is most likely that Thomas Jefferson was the father of Eston Hemmings. Because of the patrilineal inheritance of the Y chromosome, however, Jefferson's brother Randolph Jefferson and his uncle Field Jefferson are also implicated as possible fathers of Eston Hemmings.[6] The Y chromosome STR analysis was able to exclude Jefferson's nephews Samuel and Peter Carr, who were also in a position to have fathered children by some of the slaves at Monticello, as Eston

[2] There is obviously at least one gene that is active on the Y chromosome that is inactive on the X–the gene that causes a child who possesses a Y chromosome to develop as a male. The development of the Y chromosome as the male-determining chromosome is beyond the scope of this book, however, and is not important for forensic purposes.

[3] The SWGDAM guidelines recommend that the following Y chromosome STR markers be used for forensic testing: DYS19, DYS385a/b, DYS389I, DYS389II, DYS390, DYS391, DYS392, DYS393, DYS438 and DYS439.

[4] The terms "homozygous" and "heterozygous" were used to describe an individual's status for autosomal STR markers. The term "hemizygous" is used instead to denote the single-copy Y chromosome haplotype.

[5] Foster et al., 1998.

[6] Randolph Jefferson is particularly implicated in this respect; he is known to have visited Monticello regularly and to have had regular interactions with the slaves there.

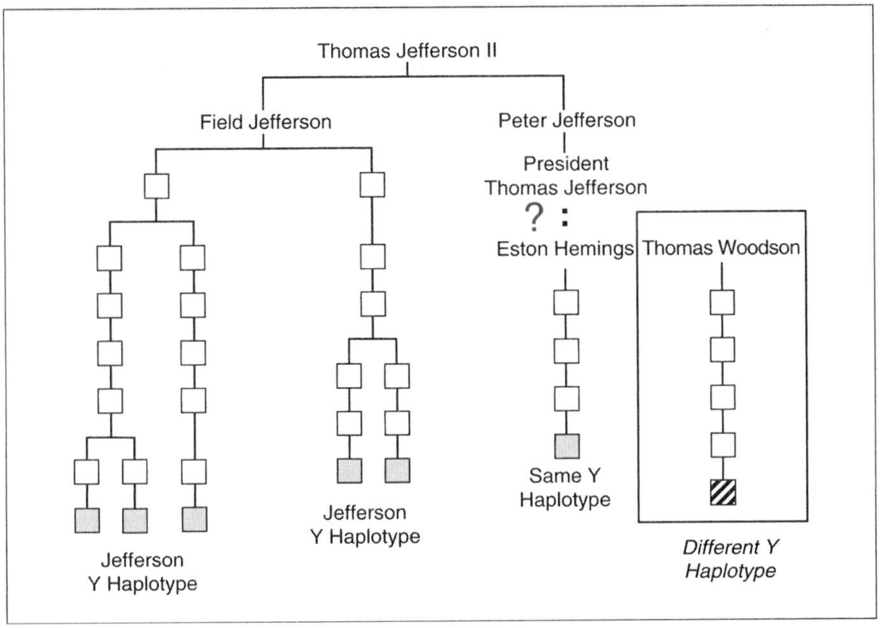

FIGURE 6.1 *Partial pedigrees (showing the relevant males only) illustrating the descendants of Field Jefferson, Eston Hemmings and Thomas Woodson. The male at the bottom of each bloodline was tested by Foster and colleagues (Foster et al., 1998). Reprinted from* Forensic DNA Typing, *John M. Butler, copyright 2005, with permission from Elsevier.*

Hemming's father. The Carr brothers were the sons of Jefferson's sister and therefore had a different Y chromosome haplotype. In addition, the Y chromosome analysis has contradicted the assertions of a group of people who claim that their ancestor Thomas Woodson was also the son of Thomas Jefferson and Sally Hemmings.

[7] A thorough discussion of Y chromosome STRs and recommendations for nomenclature are provided in Gusmao et al., 2006.

Some Y Markers Are Present in More Than One Copy

At present approximately 220 Y chromosome STRs have potential for use in forensic testing.[7] For most of the Y chromosome STRs that are used for forensic testing, there is only one copy of the sequence on the Y chromosome, and there is only one allele evident in the data. This simplifies the task of determining the number of contributors to a piece of evidence. Between the low mutation rate and the presence of only one copy of Y chromosome DNA in a cell, there are no concerns about heteroplasmy with Y chromosome DNA as there are with mtDNA. A number of intrachromosomal duplications have occurred on the Y during recent evolution, however, and a few of the commonly used markers are present on a normal Y chromosome in more than one copy. These markers are usually designated by adding lower case letters to their names. For example, there are two copies of the DYS385a/b and YCAIIa/b markers on the Y chromosome, and four copies of the DYS464a/b/c/d marker. All males are expected to show multiple alleles at these markers, unless both copies produce the same size PCR product. In this case, the individual will exhibit only one allele for this marker, similar to the result obtained when the individual is homozygous for an autosomal STR (Figure 6.2).

Litigators unfamiliar with Y chromosome STRs may find the nomenclature associated with these multilocus markers confusing. The nomenclature depends not only on the structure of the marker but also on the way the PCR amplifies it. For some of the multi-locus markers, such as DYS385, the older pairs of PCR primers amplify both copies of the marker (Figure 6.2), but new primers have been developed that amplify the two

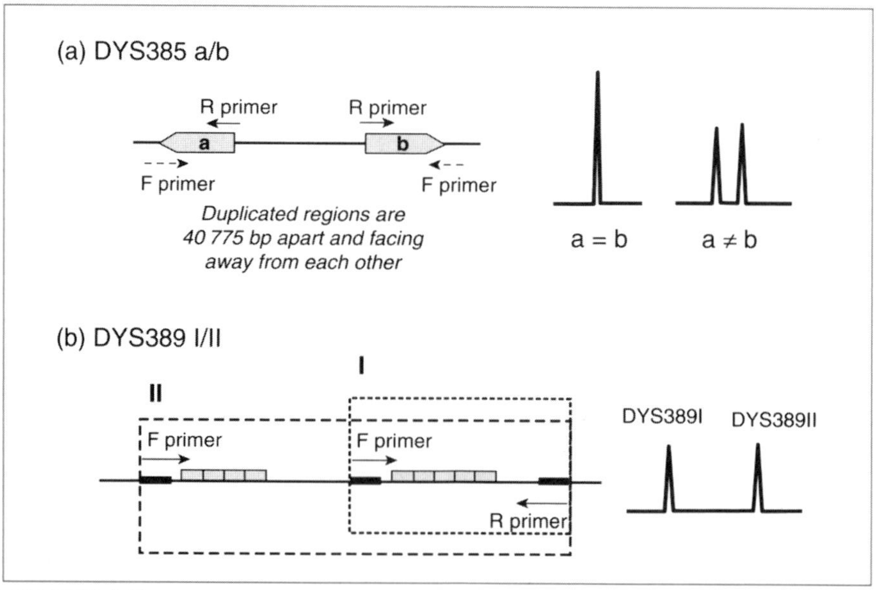

FIGURE 6.2 *DYS385a/b and DYS389I/II are multi-locus markers with different structures. The two copies of DYS385a/b are amplified separately, using completely different primers, while the DYS389I/II PCR uses a common reverse primer and different forward primers to amplify the different copies of the marker. Note how the DYS389II product includes the DYS389I sequence within it; the DYS389II PCR product will therefore always be larger than the DYS389I PCR product. Reprinted from* Forensic DNA Typing, *John M. Butler, copyright 2005, with permission from Elsevier.*

different copies separately. If the PCR protocol amplifies both copies of the marker together, the analyst will not be able to tell which allele represents which copy of the marker, and therefore will report both observed alleles' sizes together as the "DYS385" marker data. If the PCR protocol allows for the separate amplification of the different copies, the markers are designated as "DYS385a" or "DYS385b."

Another style of nomenclature is used to differentiate between the two copies of the DYS389 marker, designated as "DYS389I" and "DYS389II." This stems from the fact that the forward primer for this marker binds in two places, while the reverse primer only binds in one (see Figure 6.2). This pair of primers therefore produces two alleles, designated "DYS389I" and "DYS389II." Note from Figure 6.2 that the DYS389II amplicon includes, and will therefore always be larger than, the DYS389I marker. Figure 6.3 illustrates a result using the commercially available Y-PLEX™ 6 testing kit.

In addition to these normally multi-locus markers, some rare individuals have duplications, or even triplications, of portions of the Y chromosome that are normally present in only one copy. Because there are relatively few active genes on the Y chromosome, this rarely results in abnormal development, as it often would if it occurred on the X chromosome or one of the autosomes.[8] Y chromosome duplications are very rare,[9] although the reported frequency of these duplications is undoubtedly less than the true frequency of these duplications. Only if one of the duplicated

[8] Having an extra active copy of a gene can result in severe developmental disorders, just as missing a copy of an active gene can.

[9] Butler et al., 2005.

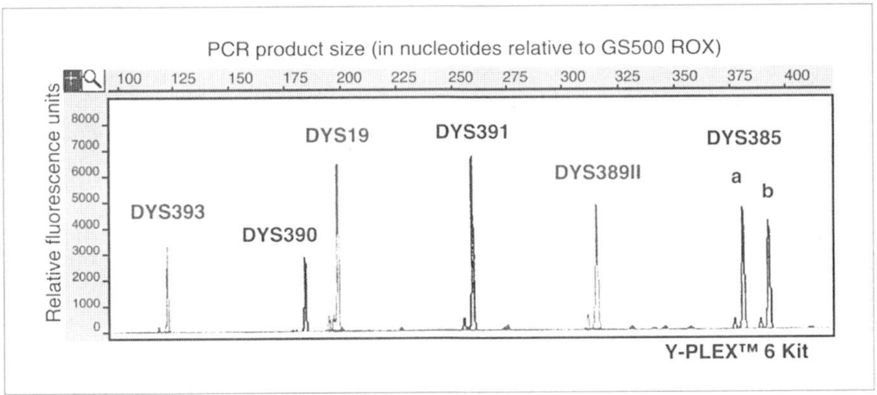

FIGURE 6.3 *The Y-PLEX™ 6 kit from Reliagene Technologies includes the DYS19, DYS389II, DYS390, DYS391, DYS393 and DYS385a/b markers. Reprinted from* Forensic DNA Typing, *John M. Butler, copyright 2005, with permission from Elsevier.*

[10] Butler et al., 2005.

[11] Butler et al., 2005.

markers undergoes a mutation either during or after the duplication will the analyst see two peaks, and therefore be certain to recognize it as a multicopy marker. If the duplication results in two identical copies of the marker, only one allele peak will be seen, and the analyst may interpret the result as a single-copy marker, especially if the height of the peak does not inform him or her that the PCR had the benefit of having more than the usual single copy of template material to amplify. The DYS19, DYS385a/b, DYS389I, DYS389II, DYS390, DYS391, DYS393, DYS435, DYS437, DYS438, DYS439 and DYS448 markers have all been reported to be duplicated in different individuals.[10] In most cases, the two copies of the marker differ by only one repetition of the repeated sequence motif. In addition, triplications of the regions containing the DYS19 and DYS385 marker have been reported in a small handful of studies.[11] Needless to say, these duplications and triplications can complicate the interpretation of the data and force the analyst to consider the possibility that a single-source sample represents a mixture of material from multiple sources.

Despite the potential for confusion, it is usually possible to differentiate between a mixed sample and one from a single source who has a duplication on his Y chromosome. As is true with mtDNA heteroplasmy, if two matching profiles contain one of these rare duplications, it greatly strengthens the probative value of the match. In most cases involving duplications, the two alleles of the multicopy marker will differ by only a single repetition of the repeated sequence motif. In contrast, when the sample represents a mixture, the alleles at the multicopy markers will often differ by more than one repetition of the repeated sequence motif. In addition, when the sample is from a single individual with a duplication, in most cases only one marker will exhibit an extra allele. If, however, an extra allele is observed at more than one marker, the markers that display the extra allele will be contiguous, because an entire block of DNA containing those contiguous markers was duplicated. In contrast, when the sample includes material from two unrelated males, multiple alleles will usually be seen at a greater number of markers, and the markers at which multiple alleles are seen will be interspersed with markers at which only a single allele is observed. Figure 6.4 illustrates the order of, and distance between, the 11 STR markers contained in the SWGDAM's recommended testing panel.

FIGURE 6.4 *Order and relative positions of the 11 STR markers contained in the SWGDAM recommended Y STR testing panel. Physical positions are represented as Megabasepairs (millions of basepairs) from the end of the p arm of the chromosome (approximate scale). Positional data derived from build 36 of the Human Genome Map Viewer at the NCBI (http://www.ncbi.nlm.nih.gov), and from Butler, 2005.*

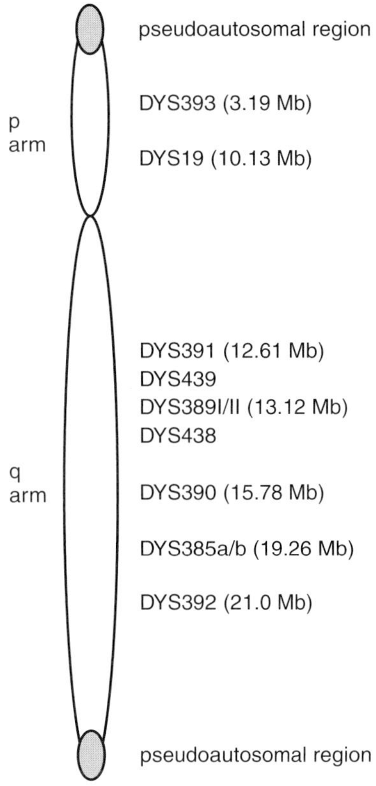

Also confounding Y chromosome analyses is the fact that for many Y chromosome sequences there are identical, or nearly identical, sequences on the X chromosome.[12] Some of these X chromosome sequences are similar enough to those on the Y chromosome to be amplified by the Y STR primers if the PCR conditions are not precisely regulated. As discussed in Chapter 2, the annealing temperature in a PCR is kept high enough so that primers only bind to perfectly complementary sequences. If the annealing temperature is less than optimal, however, a PCR primer may bind to a sequence that is only partially complementary to its intended target sequence. For this reason, any test based solely on Y chromosome markers should include a control DNA sample from a normal female. If the Y marker primers have been properly designed, they will capitalize on the differences that exist between the X and Y copies of these sequences, and will only amplify the Y copies. There should be no amplification in the female control sample; if any markers are amplified in the female control, this should be reported, and the data from those markers should not be used.

Forensic analysts capitalize on the similarity between certain X and Y chromosome sequences to determine the sex of the source(s) of some samples. As discussed in Chapter 1, several forensic testing kits use a marker from the amelogenin gene to determine whether a sample contains DNA from a male, female or a mixture of the two. The amelogenin gene has copies on both the X and Y chromosomes, and the Y chromosome copy has 6 bp in it that the X copy lacks. In this case, the primers amplify both the X and Y copies of the gene, but the 6-bp difference in the size of the PCR products makes it easy to differentiate between them. Several studies have reported that the Y allele of the amelogenin gene can be deleted in some males, especially males from India.[13]

[12] Skaletsky et al., 2003.

[13] Butler, 2005.

[14] Gill et al., 2001.

[15] A listing of available SRMs for all DNA analyses can be found on the NIST SRM website — http://ts.nist.gov/MeasurementServices/ReferenceMaterials/232.cfm

LABORATORY ANALYSIS OF Y CHROMOSOME HAPLOTYPES

Y STR Analyses Are Less Prone to Artifacts Than Autosomal STR Analyses

The laboratory techniques used to analyze Y chromosome STR profiles are identical to those used to analyze autosomal STR profiles. Consequently, all the quality control issues discussed in Chapter 3 are pertinent to Y chromosome STR analyses. The DNA commission of the International Society for Forensic Genetics (ISFG) has issued a set of recommendations for Y chromosome testing.[14] These recommendations address a number of issues, including allele nomenclature, the proper makeup of an allele size ladder, population genetic issues and methods for reporting the data. In addition, the National Institute for Standards and Technology (NIST) provides standard Y chromosome reference material (SRM2395).[15] SRM2395 contains DNA samples from five male subjects, each of which has been sequenced at over 20 STR markers, including the markers commonly included in the commercially available forensic testing kits.

Y chromosome STR analyses are slightly less prone to artifacts than their autosomal counterparts. Because only one is allele present for most Y STRs, differential amplification and stochastic effects (discussed in Chapter 3) do not cause artifacts as they do in autosomal STR analyses. In addition, because the Y chromosome STR primers bind only to Y-specific sequences, they enable the analyst to obtain a DNA profile from the male contributor to a mixed male-female sample, without introducing true allele peaks or artifacts from the female portion of the sample.

The Use of Y Chromosome Markers and Differential Extractions to Differentiate Between the Victim's and Perpetrator's Profiles in Rape Cases

In many rape cases, the vaginal swab sample contains material from both the rapist and the victim. The analyst must therefore differentiate between the two profiles. There are several means by which this can be done. In the easiest cases, the analyst can merely visually subtract the victim's profile (obtained from her reference sample) from the evidence's profile to produce the rapist's profile. Because the sample came from the victim's vagina, there is no argument that her alleles should be present in the mixture. If both the victim and the rapist are heterozygous, and they do not share any alleles, four alleles will be present for that marker, and the rapist's genotype can be unequivocally determined. If one or both of them is(are) homozygous, or they share at least one allele, the interpretation is not as easy, but if the height of the electropherogram peaks can indicate the quantity of template material in the PCR, the peaks associated with shared alleles may be noticeably higher than those associated with the alleles the victim and rapist do not share. In some cases, however, very little DNA from the rapist may be present, and his profile may be hard to see because it is overwhelmed by the victim's. When the two profiles cannot be easily differentiated, the analyst can use two strategies to more clearly discern the perpetrator's DNA profile. The analyst can use Y chromosome STRs to obtain the perpetrator's Y chromosome haplotype, or use a special extraction technique to extract the victim's DNA separately from the perpetrator's.

Using Y chromosome STRs, the analyst can get an unobstructed view of the perpetrator's Y STR haplotype without submitting the sample to differential extraction. This may be the only strategy available for minute samples that do not contain enough DNA to be divided between two assays or samples for which there is ample material from the victim but little from the perpetrator. Because the Y STR primers only bind to Y chromosome sequences, they should not produce any product from a female's DNA. This has proven particularly helpful in a number of cases in which a mixed male-female sample contained significantly more of the female's DNA than the male's. In this situation, the female's DNA provides considerably more starting material for the amplification of the autosomal STR markers than the male's DNA does. Consequently, the analyst may only see the female's genotypes when analyzing autosomal markers. The female's DNA does not compete with the male's DNA as a template for Y STR amplification, however. In a number of cases, Y STR profiles have been obtained from samples that yielded only the female's alleles for the autosomal STRs.[16] Focusing solely on the Y chromosome, which is present in only one copy, makes it easier to determine the number of assailants in a gang rape case as well. There are methods for quantifying the male-specific DNA in a mixed sample in order to ensure that the proper amount of DNA is put into the Y STR analysis. For

[16] Budowle et al., 2003.

example, Applied Biosystems has developed the Quantifiler™ Y real-time PCR method (described in Chapter 2) that specifically quantifies the male-specific DNA in a sample.

If enough sample is present, the analyst can separate the rapist's sperm from the victim's material in one of two ways. First, sperm cells have a unique appearance under the microscope, and microdissection techniques can often enable the analyst to collect the sperm cells from the mixed sample, resulting in a sample that is at least predominantly composed of material from the rapist. Because of the exquisite sensitivity of the PCR, this approach is feasible in many cases. Standard forensic DNA testing protocols can produce profiles from 60 to 100 cells' DNA. In addition, special PCR protocols have been developed that are capable of producing a 5-marker STR profile from a single cell.[17] If the analyst wishes to produce an autosomal STR profile, however, he or she should collect at least twice the minimum required number of cells. Recall that each sperm cell contains only one set of autosomal STR markers. Because this is true, unless one collects enough sperm to be certain that both sets of autosomal alleles are well represented in the template material, one risks having alleles drop out because of unequal amounts of template or stochastic effects (discussed in Chapter 3).

To extract DNA from a biological sample, one first uses chemicals and/or heat to burst the cells open (this is called lysing the cell, or lysis). This liberates the DNA from the cell, allowing the analyst to get rid of the rest of the cellular debris and extract the DNA from the liquid portion of the lysis mixture. Because of their structure, sperm cells are more resistant to lysis than the epithelial cells[18] that line the vaginal cavity. This enables the analyst to gently lyse the victim's epithelial cells first and extract the DNA from them, then go back with a more vigorous lysis procedure and lyse the sperm cells and extract the DNA from them. This technique capitalizes on the fact that the sample contains different types of cells from the victim versus the rapist (epithelial cells versus sperm cells). Unfortunately, it cannot be used to separate the two individuals' profiles from samples that contain the same types of cells from the two contributors. For example, it cannot be used to analyze fingernail scrapings, which contain skin cells from both the victim and the assailant, or on stains that contain saliva but not sperm from the assailant. The cells in saliva come from the lining of the mouth cavity, and are therefore epithelial cells.

[17] Findlay et al., 1997.

[18] Epithelial cells line cavities such as the vaginal cavity, respiratory tract, digestive system and many others.

After differential extraction, the sperm DNA fraction may contain some DNA from the victim, because some of the victim's epithelial cells may not have lysed during the first lysis. In addition, the epithelial cell-rich fraction of the sample will probably contain some of the perpetrator's DNA, because the sample will probably contain some skin cells that were rubbed off the perpetrator during the rape. In addition, the presence of saliva from the perpetrator may also contribute DNA to the epithelial cell-rich fraction. These caveats notwithstanding, the differential extraction technique frequently enables the analyst to obtain a very clear profile from the rapist's DNA, even when there is little material from the rapist to work with.

STATISTICAL ANALYSIS OF Y CHROMOSOME HAPLOTYPES

Y Chromosome STR Haplotypes Exhibit a High Level of Diversity Despite Concerns about Population Substructure

There are several Y chromosome STR databases. The markers DYS19, DYS385a, DYS385b, DYS389I, DYS389II, DYS390, DYS391, DYS392 and DYS393 make up the consensus "minimal haplotype" found in most of these databases, but the SWGDAM recommendations and at least one commercial testing kit also include DYS438 and DYS439. The two largest collaborative databases contain more than 24,000 samples from more than 224 populations around the world. In addition, several commercial companies maintain Y chromosome databases as well.[19]

In anthropological studies, Y chromosome STR profiles exhibit more population substructure than autosomal STR profiles do.[20] In addition to the biological factors involved (patrilineal inheritance and a lack of recombination), several tribal or cultural practices give rise to Y chromosome population substructure. One is the widespread practice of patrilocality, in which women move to their husband's residence after marriage. In addition, cultures in which some males are allowed to mate with more women than their contemporaries often create high local concentrations of certain Y haplotypes.

This level of population substructure raises a serious concern for forensic analysts. If the level of population substructure is high enough, a reference

[19] These websites are listed in Chapter 10.

[20] Oota et al., 2001; Schoske et al., 2004; Buckleton et al., 2004.

[21] Kayser et al., 2003; Budowle et al., 2005; Redd et al., 2006.

[22] Kayser et al., 2003; Redd et al., 2006.

[23] Redd et al., 2006.

database will only serve its purpose for cases in which the defendant was not only a member of that particular ethnic subgroup but also from that geographic region. Forensic analysts would need to collect Y STR profiles not only from as many ethnic subgroups as possible, but also from as many geographic regions as possible within each ethnic subgroup. This would result in analysts frequently being forced to work with reference databases too small to provide statistically valid estimates of the RMP for the Y chromosome haplotype in question.

Fortunately, the degree of migration and admixture that has occurred within the major races in America has greatly reduced the amount of geographical substructure within each of the major races. In the three large-scale studies of Y chromosome STR haplotypes in American populations, the genetic variance that was seen between ethnic subgroups within the major races accounted for only approximately 1 to 1.5% of the total genetic variance observed.[21] In all three studies, no significant geographic substructure was observed within the African American population. In two of the studies, significant within-race substructure was observed in both the European Americans/Caucasians and Hispanic Americans.[22] In both studies, however, the substructure was due to the fact that subjects from one geographic region had a distribution of haplotypes that was significantly different from some or all of the others. A certain number of statistically significant differences between ethnic subgroups is to be expected merely by chance in studies of these proportions, and the results from these three large-scale studies all suggest that forensic analysts do not need to compile separate databases for the different ethnic subgroups within the European American/Caucasian, African American, Hispanic American or Asian American databases.

The study by Redd and colleagues[23] is the only one to have included several Native Americans tribes. In contrast to the other races, their results indicate that there is enough substructure within the Native American population to merit maintaining separate databases for the different Native American tribes. The variation between tribes within the Native American population accounted for 9.5% of the total genetic variance. This is not only statistically significant, but also of practical significance. These findings strongly suggest that forensic analysts should continue the current practice of maintaining separate databases for the different Native American tribes.

Because it must be treated as a haplotype, the Y STR profile has less discriminative power than a profile with the same number of autosomal STRs would have. Y chromosome STR haplotypes are still variable enough to be very useful for forensic investigations, however. Studies such as the three we have discussed consistently illustrate the high degree of diversity that exists in Y chromosome STR haplotypes. Y chromosome STR haplotypes are variable enough that the 9-marker minimal haplotype analysis can exclude 98.8 to 99.8% of innocent individuals in the Caucasian American, African American and Hispanic populations.[24] There are very few common haplotypes; the vast majority of haplotypes occur only once in their respective database. In addition, the Y chromosome is indispensable in certain cases, such as rape cases with mixed evidence samples or efforts to track relatives through extended families.

[24] Melton et al., 2001; Schoske et al., 2004.

[25] Roewer et al., 2000; Krawczak, 2001.

[26] Roewer et al., 2000; Budowle et al., 2003.

Calculating the RMP for a Y Chromosome STR Haplotype

European commentators advocate the use of a Bayesian approach for interpreting Y chromosome STR data.[25] American courts, however, use a method similar to that described earlier for mtDNA analyses. The analyst begins by observing how frequently the haplotype is seen in the relevant database (which is defined by both ethnic group and geographic location). The analyst then calculates a 95% or 99% confidence interval (described in Chapter 4) around that number, and reports the upper boundary of the confidence interval as the best estimate of the haplotype's frequency. The analyst then must compensate for the level of population substructure that exists with the θ correction term, using the formula

$$RMP = \theta + (1 - \theta)p$$

where p is the adjusted frequency of the profile in the relevant reference database (the upper bound of the confidence interval).

There is general agreement that this procedure produces a highly conservative estimate of the RMP.[26] In general, the more times you observe the profile of interest in your database, the more confident you can be that the profile's true frequency is represented by the database. If the profile has been observed a number of times, the conservative estimate of the profile's frequency will be closer to the observed frequency than it will be if the profile has only been seen once or not at all. Because most Y STR profiles obtained from forensic cases are either not observed in the available databases, or observed only once, the confidence interval approach to estimating the profile's frequency usually provides a very conservative estimate of the profile's RMP.

The mutation rate for Y chromosome STRs is approximately 1.5–4 per 1,000 generations,[27] similar to the mutation rate seen in autosomal STRs.[28] In addition, as is true for the autosomal STRs, most Y STR mutations involve the addition of one more copy of the repeated sequence motif.[29] Because of the low mutation rate and the presence of only one copy of the Y chromosome DNA in any single cell, one does not encounter the heteroplasmy issues encountered when analyzing mtDNA. However, one still must account for the possibility of mutation when using Y STR evidence to prove paternity. Given this mutation rate, the probability of finding a mismatch between the 9-marker Y haplotypes of a father and son due to there having been a mutation during the making of the relevant sperm is approximately 2.5%. For this reason, just as is true of the autosomal STR profiles, a mismatch at a single marker is not sufficient to exclude the alleged father from the list of possible fathers of the child. Courts usually will consider a mismatch at two or more markers grounds for excluding the alleged father as the true father of the child. This is likely to be the correct judgment in the vast majority of cases, but there have been a few reports of verified father-son pairs in which the Y STR haplotypes differed at two loci.[30]

Combining the RMPs from Autosomal and Y Chromosome Profiles

In some cases, data will be available from both autosomal and Y chromosome STRs. Because autosomal and Y chromosome inheritance are independent from each other, it is logical to assume that one should be able to multiply the RMP for the autosomal markers by the frequency of the Y chromosome profile (after adjusting both with the θ correction factor) to produce a conservative estimate of the overall RMP for the DNA evidence. Because of the high level of population substructure inherent in Y chromosome STR profiles, however, some commentators have suggested that it may be necessary to use a more conservative calculation than usual to derive the RMP for the autosomal portion of the profile.[31] As a result of the difference between the frequencies of Y STR haplotypes from different ethnic subgroups, when two men's Y haplotypes match, it is highly likely

[27] Heyer et al., 1997; Kayser et al., 2000; Gusmao et al., 2006; Redd et al., 2006.

[28] Butler, 2005.

[29] Kayser et al., 2000.

[30] Kayser et al., 2000; Dupuy et al., 2004.

[31] Buckleton et al., 2004.

that they belong not only to the same major race, but also to the same ethnic subgroup within that race. Consequently, two men whose Y haplotypes match are more likely to have the same DNA profile than two men whose Y haplotypes do not match. Therefore, the values of 0.01 and 0.03 that are customarily used for the θ correction factor when calculating the RMP for an autosomal profile may not adequately compensate for the extra population substructure that is present in the autosomal profiles when two men have matching Y chromosome haplotypes.

Using 16 ethnic subgroups from within the United States, Walsh and colleagues have recently conducted an empirical study in which they determined the degree to which a Y haplotype match increases the level of population substructure in autosomal markers.[32] They concluded that a Y haplotype match only slightly increases the level of population substructure in the autosomal profiles. They demonstrated that the 0.01 value customarily used for the θ correction factor is conservative enough to account for the level of population substructure in many populations, and that using the value 0.02 in place of 0.01 adequately compensates for the extra population substructure in the vast majority of situations. Furthermore, when the suspect belongs to an isolated ethnic subgroup for whom one would customarily use the value 0.03 for the θ correction factor when calculating the RMP for the autosomal profile, using 0.04 in place of 0.03 adequately compensates for the increase in population substructure that is present in the autosomal profiles because of the Y haplotype match.

[32] Walsh et al., 2007.

Walsh and colleagues recommend that, in order to compute a conservative estimate of the RMP for a combined Y and autosomal marker profile, one calculate the RMP for the autosomal profile as described in Chapter 4 (and the 1996 NRC recommendation 4.2), using the formula

$$\frac{[2\theta+(1-\theta)p][3\theta+(1-\theta)p]}{(1+\theta)(1+2\theta)}$$

to represent the RMP for a homozygous marker, and the formula

$$\frac{2[\theta+(1-\theta)p_1][\theta+(1-\theta p_2]}{(1+\theta)(1+2\theta)}$$

to represent the RMP for a heterozygous marker (with either 0.02 or 0.04 as the value of θ). Once the individual markers' RMPs have been

[33] Walsh et al., 2007.

[34] Walsh et al., 2007.

calculated, they can be multiplied together to produce the RMP for the autosomal portion of the combined profile.

In order to calculate the probability of the Y haplotype match, Walsh and colleagues recommend Balding's modification of the counting method, using the expression

$$p = \frac{F+2}{N+2}$$

to represent the Y haplotype's frequency, in which $F =$ the number of times the haplotype appears in the database and $N =$ the total number of haplotypes in the database. As we demonstrated in Chapter 4, however, this method is not as conservative as the **confidence interval (CI)** method, in which one uses the straightforward F/N to represent the probability (p) of the Y haplotype in the database, and uses one of the formulas presented in Chapter 4 to calculate the CI for the estimate of p.

Once the appropriately corrected RMPs have been calculated for the autosomal profile and the Y haplotype, they can be multiplied together to produce the overall RMP for the combined profile. When there is no evidence that indicates the race of the perpetrator, it is customary to report the RMPs derived for the major racial groups separately. As discussed in Chapter 4, however, Walsh and colleagues[33] have suggested, and we agree, that it is more accurate and helpful to the triers of fact to calculate a single RMP that accommodates the fact that the reasonable suspect pool contains members of more than one race.[34]

REFERENCES AND ADDITIONAL READINGS

Buckleton, J.S., Triggs, C.M. and Walsh, S.J. (2004) *Forensic DNA Evidence Interpretation.* Boca Raton, FL: CRC Press.

Budowle, B., Sinha, S.K., Lee, H.S. and Chakraborty, R. (2003) *Forensic Science Review*, 15, 153–158.

Budowle, B., Adamowicz, A., Aranda, X.G., Barna, C., Chakraborty, R., Cheswick, D., Dafoe, B., Eisenberg, A., Frappier, R., Gross, A.M., Ladd, C., Lee, H-S., Milne, S.C., Meyers, C., Prinz, M., Richard, M.L., Saldanha, G., Tierney, A.A., Viculis, L. and Krenke, B.E. (2005) *Forenscic Science International*, 150, 1–15.

Butler, J.M. (2005) *Forensic DNA Typing* (2nd ed). Boston: Elsevier Academic Press. 2005.

Butler, J.M., Decker, A.E., Kline, M.C. and Vallone, P.M. (2005) *Journal of Forensic Sciences*, 50(4), 853–859.

Dupuy, B.M., Stenersen, M., Egeland, T. and Olaisen, B. (2004) *Human Mutation*, 23, 117–124.

Findlay, I., Taylor, A., Quirke, P., Frazier, R. and Urquhart, A. (1997) *Nature*, 389, 555–556.

Foster, E.A., Jobling, M.A., Taylor, P.G., Donnelly, P., deKniff, P., Mieremet, R., Zerjal, T. and Tyler-Smith, C. (1998) *Nature*, 396, 27.

Gusmao, L., Butler, J.M., Carracedo, A., Gill, P., Kayser, M., Mayr, W.R., Morling, N., Prinz, M., Roewer, L., Tyler-Smith, C. and Schneider, P.M. (2006) *International Journal of Legal Medicine*, 120, 191–200.

Heyer, E., Puymirat, J., Dieltjes, P., Bakker, E. and deKniff, P. (1997) *Human Molecular Genetics*, 6, 799–803.

Kayser, M., Roewer, L., Hedman, M., Henke, L., Henke, J., Brauer, S., Kruger, C., Krawczak, M., Nagy, M., Dobosz, T., Szibor, R., de Kniff, P., Stoneking, M. and Sajantila, A. (2000) *American Journal of Human Genetics*, 66, 1580–1588.

Kayser, M., Brauer, S., Schadlich, H., Prinz, M., Batzer, M.A., Zimmerman, P.A., Boatin, B.A. and Stoneking, M. (2003) *Genome Research*, 13, 624–634.

Krawczak, M. (2001) *Forensic Science International*, 118, 114–115.

Melton, T., Clifford, S., Kayser, M., Nasidze, I., Batzer, M. and Stoneking, M. (2001) *Journal of Forensic Sciences*, 46, 46–52.

Ohno, S. (1967) *Sex Chromosomes and the Sex Linked Genes*. Berlin: Springer.

Oota, H., Settheetham-Ishida, W., Tiwawech, D., Ishida, T. and Stoneking, M. (2001) *Nature Genetics*, 29, 20–21.

Redd, A.J., Chamberlain, V.F., Kearney, V.F., Stover, D., Karafet, T., Calderon, K., Walsh, B. and Hammer, M.F. (2006) *Journal of Forensic Sciences*, 51(3), 580–585.

Roewer, L., Kayser, M., de Kniff, P., Anslinger, K., Betz, A., Caglia, A., Corach, D., Furedi, S., Henke, L., Hidding, M., Kargel, H.J., Lessig, R., Nagy, M., Pascali, V.L., Parson, W., Rolf, B., Schmitt, C., Szibor, R., Teifel-Greding, J. and Krawczak, M. (2000) *Forensic Science International*, 114, 31–43.

Schoske, R., Vallone, P.M., Kline, M.C., Redman, J.W. and Butler, J.M. (2004) *Forensic Science International*, 139, 107–121.

Skaletsky, H., Kuroda-Kawaguchi, T., Minx, P.J., Cordum, H.S., Hillier, L., Brown, L.G., Repping, S., Pyntikova, T., Ali, J., Bieri, T., Chinwalla, A., Delehaunty, A., Delehaunty, K., Du, H., Fewell, G., Fulton, L., Fulton, R., Graves, T., Hou, S.F., Latrielle, P., Leonard, S., Mardis, E., Maupin, R., McPherson, J., Miner, T., Nash, W., Nguyen, C., Ozersky, P., Pepin, K., Rock, S., Rohlfing, T., Scott, K., Schultz, B., Strong, C., Tin-Wollam, A., Yang, S.P., Waterston, R.H., Wilson, R.K., Rozen, S. and Page, D.C. (2003) *Nature*, 423, 825–837.

Walsh, B., Redd, A.J. and Hammer, M.F. (2007) *Forensic Science International*, April 19 (epub ahead of print).

CHAPTER 7

DNA in Court

CONTENTS

The Evolution of Standards for Admissibility of Experts and Evidence

The Ongoing Controversy Regarding Laboratory Error Rates

Counsels' Obligations Regarding Discovery

Expert Witnesses

The Durability of DNA Presents Problems for Statutes of Limitation

Rape Shield Laws May Limit the Use of DNA Evidence

Judges' and Jurors' Perceptions of DNA Evidence

References and Additional Readings

THE EVOLUTION OF STANDARDS FOR ADMISSIBILITY OF EXPERTS AND EVIDENCE

In the early days of DNA testing, some of the evidence that was introduced into trials was of highly questionable quality. As the field of DNA testing has evolved, however, DNA testing has been subjected to considerably more intense scrutiny than any of the other forensic sciences have. At this point in time, the methods by which DNA profiles are ascertained and the statistical procedures with which the data are interpreted have withstood rigorous scientific studies and public debate in the scientific literature. Even those early critics and defense attorneys who have written extensive criticisms of forensic science evidence concede that DNA testing has been rigorously validated.[1]

The field of applied science has achieved a level of complexity and specialization that goes well beyond the ken of the average juror. Our courts have long recognized that someone with specialized training, experience and credentials may be needed to explain certain evidence if it is to be interpreted properly. Early Supreme Court decisions focused not only on the qualifications of the expert witnesses, but also on the relevance and helpfulness of the expert's testimony. In decisions such as *The Schooner Catharine v. Dickinson*, *Connecticut Mut. Life Ins. Co. v. Lathrop*, *Transportation Line v. Hope* and *Spring Company v. Edgar*,[2] the Supreme Court emphasized the need for expert witnesses in certain kinds of cases and acknowledged that this need was not restricted to the presentation of medical and scientific evidence, but could involve industrial or commercial issues that required specialized training or experience to understand. Other decisions, such as *Gillespie v. Collier*, *Beale v. Spate* and

Inland & Seaboard Coasting Co. v. Tolson,[3] while emphasizing the helpfulness of expert witnesses in trials involving scientific and technical evidence, also suggested that experts were not needed in cases in which the relevant facts could be decided upon by common knowledge and experience.

The use of expert witnesses, however, has not escaped criticism. Judge Learned Hand published the most influential of the early critiques on this subject.[4] Hand's disapproval focused on two points. First, because an expert witness is typically hired by one side of the case, the expert loses objectivity, and conducts the investigation with the mindset of an advocate rather than an objective scientist. Second, Hand believed that allowing experts to be contradicted by other experts served to confuse, rather than to enlighten, the jury. Hand stressed that average jurors would quickly become lost in the exchange of technical arguments and would be inclined to believe the more personally charismatic of the experts, rather than to make their decisions on the basis of the scientific and technical issues.

The federal courts made the first effort to develop standards for admissibility of scientific experts and evidence in *Frye v. United States*.[5] For decades, the *Frye* "general acceptance" standard provided the framework on which all the states built their standards. The *Frye* court established that expert evidence was admissible if it was "sufficiently established to have gained general acceptance in the particular field in which it belongs." The *Frye* court also acknowledged that it may be difficult to determine "when a scientific principle or discovery crosses the line between experimental and demonstrable stages." Most importantly, it gave judges the authority to decide whether the proposed expert evidence satisfied the applicable legal standards for admissibility. Finally, in an effort to ensure that the significance of the evidence was communicated clearly to the judge and jury, the court also authorized the use of expert witnesses when "the subject matter so far partakes of science, art, or trade as to require a previous habit or experience or study into it, in order to acquire knowledge of it."

A number of jurisdictions apply a hybrid *Frye-Kelly* standard.[6] In a *Frye-Kelly* state, the proponent of the evidence must show:

- The underlying theory is generally accepted as reliable in the relevant scientific community.
- The method or technique used to apply the theory is generally accepted in the scientific community.

[1] Saks and Koehler, 2005; Tobin and Thompson, 2006.

[2] 58 U.S. 170 (1854), 111 U.S. 612 (1884), 95 U.S. 297 (1877) and 99 U.S. 645 (1878), respectively.

[3] 224 F. 298 8th Cir. (1915), 74 F. 869 2d Cir. (1896) and 139 U.S. 551 (1891), respectively.

[4] Hand, 1901.

[5] 293 F. 1013 D.C. Cir. (1923).

[6] *People v. Kelly*, 549 P.2d (Cal. 1976).

It is important for prosecutors in *Frye-Kelly* jurisdictions to remember that the theory, principle or method used by the expert does not have to be unanimously endorsed by the scientific community, but rather must be generally accepted as reliable in the relevant scientific community.

The *Frye* decision created a system for evaluating proposed expert evidence that was more uniform than the common law standard that had evolved up to that point. In addition to giving judges the role of deciding whether or not proposed expert evidence was admissible, the *Frye* "general acceptance" standard also gave judges an easy way to base their opinions on the opinions of the experts in the relevant scientific or technical field. In most cases, the presence of a body of literature published in peer-reviewed journals constitutes strong support for the argument that the technique or principle involved has gained general acceptance. The peer review process practiced by scientific journals ensures that no paper gets published unless it has been accepted by at least two independent reviewers with expertise in the relevant scientific field. Therefore, even the report of a new technique or principle that is published for the first time has had at least two independent expert reviews before publication. In addition, the scientific community polices itself. The reviewers return the manuscript to the journal editor with detailed, frank comments. After that, once the paper is published, if other scientists in the field conclude there is a flaw in a published article, and refute the original authors' assertions or fail to corroborate their findings, their misgivings will be published. Finally, scientific journals strive for brevity, especially regarding the technical details of a procedure. It is common to find extensive descriptions of methods in the early articles that introduce a technique. As time passes and the technique becomes better known, however, scientific journals prefer the author to briefly describe, or even merely to mention, the technique, and refer the reader to previously published works for the details. In addition, once a technique becomes commonly accepted, certain abbreviations associated with the procedure, such as PCR—for polymerase chain reaction—are often used without explanation. One way of gauging the common acceptance of a procedure is to obtain recent articles in which there are few details given about the procedure or in which abbreviations are used without explanation.

Although many considered *Frye* a big improvement over the previous situation, the *Frye* decision had its critics. Some commentators argued

[7] 753 F.2d 1224, 3d Cir. (1985).

that it caused potentially useful evidence to be excluded when valid but novel methods are used to generate the evidence. Others argued that the standard was too vague, or too general in its focus. Some of these criticisms were summarized in *United States v. Downing.*[7] In this decision, the Third Circuit court stated that "the vague terms included in the standard have allowed courts to manipulate the parameters of the relevant 'scientific community' and the level of agreement needed for 'general acceptance.'" In addition, the court stated that "the selectivity among courts in determining whether evidence derives from 'novel' principles; the inadequacy of expert testimony on many scientific issues; an uncritical acceptance of prior judicial, rather than scientific, opinion as a basis for finding 'general acceptance'; and the narrow scope of review by which some appellate courts review trial court rulings" all contributed to some jurisdictions seeking an alternative to the Frye guidelines.

In an effort to create a uniform standard for the admissibility of evidence, the Supreme Court promulgated the Federal Rules of Evidence (FRE) in 1975. The FRE greatly expanded the judge's role as gatekeeper in cases involving scientific and technical evidence. Rule 104(a) gives the trial judge the power to determine the admissibility of the evidence and evaluate the qualifications and appropriateness of expert witnesses relative to their proposed testimony. Rule 402 allows judges to admit all relevant evidence and exclude all irrelevant evidence, and Rule 401 defines relevant evidence as "evidence having any tendency to make the existence of any fact that is of consequence to the determination of the action more probable or less probable than it would be without the evidence." Finally, Rule 702 allows judges to decide when the testimony of an expert witness is necessary to "assist the trier of fact to understand the evidence or to determine a fact in issue."

Rule 403 goes even farther than the others in expanding the judges' gatekeeping function; it allows judges the discretion to exclude even relevant evidence "if its probative value is substantially outweighed by the danger of unfair prejudice, confusion of the issues, or misleading the jury, or by considerations of undue delay, waste of time, or needless presentation of cumulative evidence." Rule 403 has no language in it that compels the judge to admit any evidence, for any reason. Legal scholars recognized immediately that it would be impossible to meld the conservative standard set forth in *Frye* with the liberal standard set forth in the FRE, and many saw this as setting the stage for abandonment of the *Frye* standard. Considerable debate ensued over which was the better standard. Some felt that it was appropriate to adopt the FRE standard and give judges unlimited discretion regarding the admissibility of evidence, but many resisted this line of thought. Some commentators felt that the simpler *Frye* test gave clearer guidelines regarding the admissibility of evidence than the FRE did, and some felt it best for judges to continue to base their opinions on the opinions of the experts in the relevant field, as reflected in the scientific and technical literature. The FRE standards were applied throughout the federal judicial system, but because of the mixed responses to the FRE, different states went to different lengths in articulating their standards for admissibility of evidence. In addition, it was not until almost 20 years after the FRE standards were promulgated that the Supreme Court rendered an opinion that weighed in on the question of whether states should keep their *Frye*-based standards or adopt those of the FRE.

In the 1993 case of *Daubert v. Merrill Dow Pharmaceuticals, Inc.*,[8] the Supreme Court clearly ruled that the Federal Rules of Evidence superseded the *Frye* test. Furthermore, the *Daubert* court provided its own test for the admissibility of DNA evidence. The *Daubert* or "relevance test" does not require a showing of general acceptance within the scientific community (although the court may take this into general advisement). Instead, the proponent of the evidence must show

- The validity of the underlying scientific theory
- The reliability of the scientific test used to obtain the evidence
- The usefulness of this scientific evidence to the jury

The prosecutor can show the reliability of the scientific test through a number of means, none of which are mandatory or exclusive.[9] These include:

- That the underlying principles involved are scientifically valid
- That this is capable of being tested
- That the method used was subjected to peer review
- The known or potential error rate
- The existence or maintenance of standards in conducting the technique
- Whether the method used is generally accepted
- Where there is a nonjudicial use or experience with the method

[8] 509 U.S. 579 (1993).

[9] *Kumho Tire Co. Ltd. v. Carmichael*, 56 U.S. 137, 119 S. Ct. 1167, 143 L. Ed. 2d 238 (1999).

The FRE and the *Daubert* ruling greatly expanded the judge's role as evidentiary gatekeeper and required judges to undertake a much more sophisticated and informed analysis of the scientific evidence than *Frye* did. Instead of merely taking notice of the relevant literature, judges must be prepared to evaluate the merits of the technology as it is applied to the criminal justice system and to the case at bar. To properly assess the admissibility of evidence under *Daubert* standards, judges must understand the scientific method and the use of controls in laboratory analyses, and be able to determine whether a test procedure has undergone the kind of tests necessary to validate the procedure for use in forensic casework. In addition, they must be able to understand the arguments about whether the appropriate statistical analyses have been used to interpret the data. Particularly in cases involving arguably novel scientific theories or methods, the increased complexity of the task virtually has necessitated the use of pretrial hearings: there experts can be examined, the range of issues can be clarified, and counsel can file motions *in limine* (under FRE 104a) seeking to preclude the admissibility of some or all of the evidence. In addition, judges have found it increasingly necessary to invoke their authority (under FRE Rule 706) to appoint their own experts to assist them in understanding the complexity of the scientific evidence and interpreting other expert witnesses' testimony.[10]

[10] For example, *United States v. Green*, 544 F. 2d 138, 3rd Cir. (1976); *Reilly v. United States*, 863 F.2d 149, 1st Cir. (1988); *Burton v. Sheheen*, 793 F. Supp. 1329, D.S.C. (1992).

It is critically important to have the DNA evidence undergo a rigorous *a priori* validation, such as that outlined in the *Daubert* decision. The jury often gives greater weight to forensic evidence than to other types of evidence in a criminal trial. The consequences of a criminal trial can be dire for all parties involved. Based on the DNA evidence, an individual may be convicted and sentenced to a lengthy prison term or even death. Alternatively, if the jury lacks confidence in the forensic evidence, it may acquit a guilty defendant. Therefore the proponent of the evidence must ensure that it has been properly collected, preserved and processed so that the jury members can both apply the proper weight in considering it and be confident that in doing so, they have reached the correct verdict in the case.

It is particularly important to police the procedures involved in generating forensic DNA evidence because the outcome of the trial usually does not illustrate any problems that might have existed in the process of collection and analysis. If a physician prescribes the wrong medicine, the patient will not get well. If an architect uses a flawed model to build a skyscraper, the building will fall down. If a defendant is wrongly convicted or acquitted based on flawed DNA evidence, however, there will often be no consequences that unambiguously illustrate that the defendant was wrongly convicted or the true perpetrator was allowed to go free.

The *Daubert* ruling preserved judges' essentially unlimited discretion regarding the admissibility of evidence. The *Daubert* court emphasized that the guidelines it promulgated were to be applied flexibly, that the four guidelines need not be applied with the same weight, and that it was not even essential that all four be applied together in any case. Because the states are not bound to follow Supreme Court rulings on evidentiary methods, however, a number of states continue to apply a Frye-based standard. All except the strictest *Frye* standards allow each trial judge considerable leeway to decide whether to allow expert testimony, with or without a pretrial hearing. Because the opinions are often as individual as the judges, the prudent litigator (whether it be the prosecutor or defense counsel) should research the previous cases in the jurisdiction where the trial will occur, particularly cases over which the trial judge assigned to the case has presided, and carefully examine any in which the judge ruled against the admission of DNA evidence.

Four years after *Daubert*, the Supreme Court reaffirmed the judges' broad discretion in the case of *General Electric Co. v. Joiner.*[11] There, the plaintiff was an electrician who worked on transformers containing a chemical that had been associated with the development of cancer. The electrician developed small-cell lung cancer and sued his employer. Despite being a smoker with a family history of cancer, he claimed that his exposure to the chemicals in the transformers caused his cancer. The District Court that originally heard the case granted summary judgment for the defendant, Joiner's employer. The court concluded that none of the evidence Joiner's experts had introduced to support their claim that exposure to the chemicals in question had contributed to Joiner's cancer was admissible. The Court of Appeals for the Eleventh Circuit reversed the decision, however, finding that the trial judge had abused his discretion by excluding the evidence. The United States Supreme Court ultimately reversed the Court of Appeals and reaffirmed the trial judge's broad discretion regarding the admissibility of expert evidence. The Court held that "in applying an overly 'stringent' review to that ruling (the Court of

[11] 522 U.S. 136 (1997).

[12] 526 U.S. 137 (1999).

[13] National Research Council, 1992.

[14] For example, Lewontin and Hartl, 1991.

Appeals) failed to give the trial court the deference that is the hallmark of abuse of discretion reviews," and that "it was within the District Court's discretion to conclude that the studies upon which the experts relied were not sufficient."

The language in the *Frye* and *Daubert* decisions refers consistently to "scientific" information and expertise. Some questioned whether these standards also could be applied to technical information and the testimony of witnesses who were not scientists, but had extensive professional experience in a technical field (for example, in a DUI case, the arresting officer who has had 20 years of experience arresting individuals under the influence of alcohol). To many others, though, the language of the *Frye* and *Daubert* rulings, and of the FRE as well, had always made it clear that there were many different ways (education, on-the-job training, long experience) in which an individual could acquire the heightened level of knowledge that could help judges and jurors better comprehend the significance of the evidence in question. The Supreme Court affirmed this view in its 1999 *Kumho Tire Co. v. Carmichael Inc.*[12] decision. In this case, the survivors of a traffic accident sued the manufacturer and distributor of the tires that were on the vehicle at the time of the accident. The plaintiff's case included the testimony of a mechanical engineer who was an expert (by dint of considerable work experience) on the subject of tire failure. In its decision, the Court held that the judge's gatekeeping function also extended to technical evidence and its sponsoring experts. It also reaffirmed that the four recommendations set forth in *Daubert* were to be applied flexibly, at the discretion of the trial judge, and that it was not necessary to apply all of them simultaneously in any single case.

Shortly before the *Daubert* decision, the National Research Council (NRC) prepared a report for the National Academy of Sciences.[13] The 1992 NRC report confirmed the potential for DNA evidence to serve the criminal justice system, and outlined a set of procedural guidelines for the production of DNA evidence and its use in court. Along with affirming its confidence in the potential of DNA analysis to serve the criminal justice system, the 1992 NRC also outlined a set of issues that future research needed to address. Several portions of the report were well received, but several prominent academic scientists voiced their adamant disagreement with a number of the policies that the NRC advocated regarding the statistical interpretation of the data.[14] The fact that several prominent population geneticists rejected the 1992 NRC committee's recommendations regarding the statistical analysis of DNA evidence made it virtually impossible to admit DNA evidence under *Frye*'s criterion of general acceptance in the field.[15] Because of *Daubert*'s greater flexibility, however, *Daubert* courts were more receptive to DNA evidence during this period than were *Frye* courts.[16]

The debates that surrounded the 1992 NRC report prompted research that has greatly improved the state of the science of DNA testing. Law enforcement agencies have increased the sizes of their reference databases, the statistical methods have been validated and several empirical studies have provided data that have helped settle the major debates. The statistical debates were settled in 1994,[17] after which the committee reconvened with a different membership, and in 1996 produced the second NRC report, which clearly stated that "The state of the profiling technology and the methods for estimating frequencies and related statistics have progressed to the point where the admissibility of properly collected and analyzed DNA data should not be in doubt." Since then, the development of STR analyses has given us an identification system that is even more reliable than the technologies available in 1996. At this point, the methods are accepted as scientifically sound, and assessing whether these established methods were applied in the appropriate manner in the case at bar constitutes a major part of the judge's role as gatekeeper of the evidence. The 2000 amendment to Rule 702 of the FRE clarifies the issue of who bears the burden to prove that the appropriate procedures have been applied; it requires that the side introducing DNA evidence demonstrate that "the witness has applied the principles and methods reliably to the facts of the case."

The 1992 and 1996 NRC reports clearly advocated the use of DNA evidence in criminal trials. In addition, appellate courts generally agree that "the Federal Rules of Evidence governing expert testimony display a preference for admissibility" and "apply a particularly stringent standard of review to the trial judge's exclusion of expert testimony."[18] These strong statements have led many courts to take judicial notice of the reliability of DNA testing.[19] In fact, the legal system's present confidence in DNA evidence is so strong that several states have enacted statutes that allow DNA evidence to be admitted without a pretrial hearing on a routine basis. Some commentators have suggested that this violates the spirit of *Daubert*. They worry that when courts take judicial notice of the validity of DNA evidence, they

[15] For example, *Commonwealth v. Curnin*, 565 N.E.2d 400, Mass. (1991); *Commonwealth v. Lanigan*, 596 N.E.2d 311, Mass. (1992); *People v. Barney*, 10 Cal. Rptr. 2d 731, Ct. App. (1992); *State v. Houser*, 490 N.W.2d 168, Neb. (1992).

[16] *United States v. Jakobetz*, 955 F.2d 786, 2d Cir. (1992); *United States v. Bonds*, 12 F.3d 540, 6th Cir. (1993); *United States v. Chischilly*, 30 F.3d 1144, 9th Cir. (1994); *United States v. Davis*, 40 F.3d 1069, 10th Cir. (1994).

[17] Lander and Budowle, 1994.

[18] *Joiner v. General Electric*, 78 F.3d 524, 11th Cir. (1996).

[19] *People v. Adams*, 195 Mich. App. 267, N.W.2d 192 (1992); *State v. Montalbo*, 73 Haw. 130, P.2d 1274 (1992); *United States v. Perry*, Crim. No. 92-474, D.D.C. Jan 11, 1994; *State v. Fleming*, 698 A.2d 503, Me. (1997).

do not ascertain that the methods have been appropriately applied in the instant case, and therefore risk admitting evidence that will not be helpful. This takes the oversight function out of the hands of the judge and places it with the jurors, who are less educated, less experienced with DNA evidence and less aware of what the important issues affecting DNA evidence are in their evaluation of the weight of the evidence. Consequently, both the advocate and the opponent of the evidence should carefully have their expert witness walk the jury through as to why the evidence does or does not, depending on the litigator's role, meet the required standards.

DNA testing procedures used by university laboratories or government agencies for basic research or applied purposes can satisfy the relevant criteria for admissibility, even if they have not been used before in criminal proceedings, providing these procedures have been accepted by the relevant scientific community. Many of the quality control issues and issues bearing on the qualifications of expert witnesses are the same whether one is performing nuclear or mitochondrial DNA testing on plant, animal or human tissue. For example, the extensive use of mitochondrial DNA testing in mass disasters, identification of wartime casualties and anthropological investigations allows it to satisfy most courts' criteria for reliability and general acceptance, whether they are based on *Frye* or *Daubert.*[20] Other types of DNA testing, such as analyses of animal hair or plant DNA, are also sufficiently established in the relevant scientific sectors to satisfy the courts' criteria for admissibility.[20] For example, plant biologists frequently use the technique called randomly amplified polymorphic DNA (RAPD) analysis to differentiate between different plant lineages. In the case of *Bogan v. State,*[21] Mark Alan Bogan was convicted of murder. At trial he argued that he had not been near the remote desert site where the victim's body was found in years. Investigators were able to use the RAPD technique to match the DNA from some palo verde tree seed pods located in the bed of Bogan's truck to specific plants that were located where the body had been found. They were also able to demonstrate that the DNA from the seed pods in Bogan's truck did not match the DNA found in seed pods from palo verde trees that grew near his home and workplace. Bogan appealed the conviction, on the grounds that the RAPD technique did not satisfy the *Frye* general acceptance criterion. The Arizona appellate court disagreed, citing RAPD's widespread use in botany research, and affirmed his conviction.

[20] For a list of court cases involving DNA evidence from dog and cat hair, see the curriculum vitae of Dr. Joy Halverson, DVM, MPVM, QuestGen Forensics, http://www.questgen.boz/cv.htm; also see Sensabaugh and Kaye, 1998.

[21] 905 P.2d 515, Ariz. App. (1995).

THE ONGOING CONTROVERSY REGARDING LABORATORY ERROR RATES

It is interesting to note one discrepancy between the *Daubert* standard and actual practice that may never be resolved. One prong of the *Daubert* test involves assessing the known or potential error rate of the technique applied in the DNA testing. As several commentators have observed, the language of the *Daubert* ruling, as well as that of Rule 702 of the FRE, considers the laboratory error rate to be a factor influencing the admissibility of the evidence.[22] Courts, however, have usually followed the 1992 NRC report and considered it to influence the weight, rather than the admissibility, of the evidence. As discussed in Chapter 4 and Appendix II, the probability that an error may have occurred in the analysis can potentially influence the probative value of the evidence, especially when the other evidence against the defendant is weak. Furthermore, when the RMP is infinitesimal, the overall probability of a false inclusion is approximately equal to the probability of laboratory error (PLE).

[22] Imwinkelreid, 1991; Scheck, Koehler, 1997.

Laboratory error is an especially aggravating issue for the proponent of the evidence, because the PLE is never equal to zero, even when the laboratory has a perfect record of performance on proficiency tests. It would require a laboratory to submit to hundreds of proficiency tests to produce a statistically reliable estimate of its probability of error. Because the number of proficiency tests most laboratories have taken is considerably smaller than that, one must compensate for the possible error in the estimate by calculating a confidence interval (CI, discussed in Chapter 4) around the observed frequency of errors and reporting the upper bound of the CI as the estimate of the probability of error. CIs are intended to produce conservative estimates of the actual number in question. If a laboratory has a perfect record on 100 proficiency tests, the upper bound of the estimate of the laboratory's probability of error (with a 95% confidence interval) is 3%. The PLE effectively puts an upper limit on the weight any DNA evidence can have, even a profile with an infinitesimal RMP.

There is widespread agreement that proficiency testing programs help ensure the quality of a laboratory's work, but less agreement on whether the proficiency testing programs in effect today provide reliable estimates of the PLE. It is universally agreed that the best type of proficiency test is a blind proficiency test. A blind test is one in which the analysts do not know the sample is a test sample, as opposed to an open test, in which the analysts know that they are being tested. Maintaining a program of regular blind proficiency tests obviously entails considerable expense and logistical challenges; among other difficulties, the samples must be packaged for each laboratory as if they came from an agency that regularly sends samples to that laboratory for analysis. The Federal DNA Identification Act of 1994 charged the director of the National Institute of Justice (NIJ) with determining the feasibility of conducting a program of blind proficiency tests. The results of the NIJ's feasibility study suggested that two blind proficiency tests could be administered to 150 forensic DNA testing laboratories per year at an annual cost of $450,000 to $3,020,000. An NIJ scientific advisory board concluded, however, that the small number of errors that would be detected by such a testing program did not justify the program's cost. Furthermore, the advisory board concluded that alternative methods existed to maintain the quality of forensic DNA analyses.

At the present time, accredited forensic DNA testing labs participate in open proficiency testing programs. The tests are conducted under simulated crime scene conditions, and the laboratory must certify that the samples were analyzed using the lab's standard operating procedures. Opinions are predictably divided as to whether these tests provide an accurate reflection of the PLE in actual casework; most prosecutors and laboratory directors claim they do, while most defense attorneys claim they do not.

Another reason a laboratory's record of performance on past proficiency tests may not reflect its present level of proficiency is the fact that one of the primary goals of a proficiency testing program is to provide laboratories with insights into ways they can improve their performance. Thus, any laboratories that made errors on proficiency tests should have remedied the reasons for the errors as soon as they learned of them. Similarly, courts have rejected suggestions to use the average rate of failure for all laboratories on proficiency tests as a universal estimate of the laboratory error rate. The NRC report has stated that this policy not only penalizes the best-performing laboratories, but also overestimates the weight of evidence generated by the poorer-performing laboratories. Attorneys routinely file motions requesting the laboratory's and analyst's records of performance on past proficiency tests, seeking to use this evidence to impeach the statements of the opposing counsel's expert regarding the weight of the evidence. Some courts have denied such motions, not only for the reasons we have discussed, but also because there is often remaining sample that can be tested to support its effort to impeach the witness. One can envision situations, however, in which proficiency test results would be admissible, even under the most stringent standards of review. For example, suppose there was a dispute between rival experts regarding whether a band represents a true allele or an artifact. One way to address this question is to survey recent work performed on the same fragment analyzer in order to ascertain if a similar band appears in data from other cases. This question could be answered by surveying either recent casework or proficiency tests. It might be preferable to survey proficiency tests, however, as a means of protecting the privacy of the individuals involved in the laboratory's other cases.

FRE Rule 403 allows evidence to be "excluded if its probative value is substantially outweighed by the danger of unfair prejudice." Some have argued that the infinitesimal RMPs are highly prejudicial to the defendant because jurors are likely to be so impressed by the tiny RMP that they will not understand that the probability that the defendant is being falsely implicated depends far more on the PFP than the RMP.[23] Several studies' findings have supported this claim. For example, Koehler and colleagues reported that mock jurors considered DNA evidence much more probative when they were presented with a PFP of 0.02 and an RMP of 0.000000001 (1 in 1 billion) than when they were presented with a PFP of 0.02 and given no information regarding the RMP.[24] Similarly, Schklar and Diamond reported that mock jurors assigned considerably greater weight to DNA evidence if they were given a PFP of 0.02 and an RMP of 0.000000001 or a PFP of 0.000000001 and an RMP of 0.02 than if they were told that the combined probability of error due to either coincidental match or laboratory error equaled 0.02.[25] Although these findings suggest that the jurors were inordinately impressed with the very small RMP, it is interesting to note that, in the latter study, most jurors remembered the larger probability more accurately than the smaller one.

Both the *Daubert* court and FRE Rule 702 considered laboratory error to be an issue that influenced the admissibility of the evidence. Most courts, however, consider the issue of laboratory error to influence the weight of the evidence, not its admissibility.[26] Despite the aforementioned misgivings regarding how well past proficiency tests reflect present performance,

[23] Lewontin and Hartl, 1991; Koehler et al., 1995. Some refer to this as the vividness hypothesis.

[24] Koehler et al., 1995.

[25] Schklar and Diamond, 1999.

[26] For example, *State v. Faulkner*, 103 S.W.3d 346, Mo. App. (2003); *United States v. Ewell*, 252 F. Supp. 2d, 104, D.N.J. (2003).

most courts agree that the laboratory's record on past proficiency tests is admissible and can be helpful to the triers of fact.[27] Thus, at present, some courts expect, or even insist, that the jury hear both the RMP and the laboratory's record of performance in recent proficiency tests.[28] This is also the position that the National Commission on the Future of DNA Evidence[29] has advocated. Although prosecutors usually have championed this point, in some cases the defense has also argued that the laboratory should provide an estimate of its false-negative error rate in cases where the laboratory reports an exclusion.

COUNSELS' OBLIGATIONS REGARDING DISCOVERY

Pursuant to Rule 16 F.R.Cr.P, or its state equivalent and the constitutional mandates of *Brady v. Maryland*, prosecutors are required to provide the defendant with copies of any exculpatory evidence in a timely manner, so that the defense has sufficient time to prepare and present its case. Exculpatory evidence is defined as any material evidence that tends to negate the defendant's guilt as to the charges. *Brady* identifies that "the suppression by the prosecution of evidence favorable to an accused upon request violates due process where the evidence is material either to guilt or punishment."[30] "Material evidence" has been held to mean substantive evidence relating to a defendant's guilt or innocence or in mitigation of what otherwise would be guilty conduct (see Chapters 8 and 9), as well as evidence that could be useful for impeachment purposes.[31] Nonmaterial evidence may be the subject of a pretrial hearing, and the judge has a wide measure of discretion in determining its disposition.[32]

Courts have traditionally looked upon *Brady* as a "rule of fairness and minimum prosecutorial obligation."[33] It is also a reciprocal process; upon filing a reciprocal discovery request, the prosecution may request material from the defense. For example, in a case in which the defense retests the evidence, the prosecutor should seek to discover the lab report itself, the names of the experts the defense intends to call, and the name of the laboratory and analyst who will do the testing. The prosecutor's responsibility in providing discovery material (and the defense's responsibility when the defense introduces the evidence) is ongoing from the commencement of the case and extends beyond the conviction. If exculpatory evidence comes to the state's attention after conviction, the

[27] For example, *Armstead v. State*, 673 A.2d 221, Md. (1996); *Williams v. State*, 679 A.2d 1106, Md. (1996).

[28] *United States v. Porter*, No. F06277-89, 1994 WL 742297, D.C. Super. Ct. Nov. 17, 1994; *Williams v. State*, 679 A.2d 1106, Md. (1996); but see *United States v. Lowe*, 954 F. Supp. 401, D. Mass. (1996); *United States v. Trala*, 162 F. Supp. 2d. 336, D. Del. (2001).

[29] National Commission on the Future of DNA Evidence, 2000.

[30] *Brady v. Maryland*, 373 U.S. 83 (1962).

[31] *Williams v. Dutton*, 400 F.2d 797 (5th Cir. 1968).

[32] *United States v. Pollack*, 534 F.2d 964, 973 (1976).

[33] *United States v. Beasley*, 576 F.2d 626, 630 (5th Cir. 1978).

prosecutor has a responsibility to provide this evidence to the defense. As stated in Chapter 8, the prosecutor is professionally and ethically responsible for complying with all discovery requests; thus, all requests should be directed to the prosecutor instead of separate requests made of the lab, law enforcement and other parties.

Prosecutors should remember that disclosure of this material is required by individual state statutes and rules, regardless of whether the defense has generated a specific request for the evidence. Thus, in trials involving DNA evidence, the prosecution is required to provide the defense with the results of all the tests that the government's agents have conducted on the evidence samples, including those for which the results were inconclusive. In addition, the prosecution should request that the analyst provide them with bench notes or other records relating to the condition of the sample and chain of custody, as well as records of the analytic procedure that the government followed in processing the DNA evidence.

Litigators should consult the applicable statutes and rules for their jurisdiction to be sure they understand the requirements that apply. The National District Attorney's Association provides prosecutors with guidelines and sample policies regarding disclosure of evidence in various situations.[34] At all stages of the proceedings, prosecutors introducing DNA evidence are urged to observe the highest ethical standards. In addition to ensuring the integrity of the criminal justice system and furthering the course of justice, these guidelines help prosecutors ensure that convictions are not reversed on appeal.[35]

Some district attorneys or individual prosecutors follow a policy of "open discovery," in which defense counsel may view all the state's evidence against the defendant and receive copies of documents, photographs and other material. Other district attorneys and prosecutors follow a policy of minimal discovery, and provide the defense only the material evidence to which it is entitled. When the defense receives only the material evidence to which it is entitled, the defense can file a motion requesting nonmaterial evidence, asserting a Sixth Amendment right to see all the evidence compiled against the defendant.[36]

In all cases, there should be a complete record of the materials provided to the defense (and prosecution, if applicable), and the dates on which they were provided. Some prosecutors make copies of the discovery given to

[34] http://www.ndaa.org

[35] Kreeger and Weiss, 2003; Roth, 2003.

[36] Friedman, 2003; Land, 2005.

defense counsel for the court file jacket. Whether the prosecutor follows an open or a minimum discovery policy, good faith shown during the early stages of the proceeding often translates into fewer challenges during the later stages and fewer avenues for postconviction appeals.

There is no better example of how important complete disclosure is to both sides than the scandal that erupted in 2003 and resulted in the suspension of operations in the Houston Police Department's forensic testing laboratory. Harris County judges had routinely denied not only defense requests for discovery of laboratory analysts' notes, but also their requests for expert assistance in reviewing DNA evidence. Had the judges granted these requests, some of the deficiencies in the Houston laboratory's operations may have come to light earlier on. The vast majority of forensic DNA labs and analysts observe admirable ethical standards as they discharge their duties. Any incidents to the contrary, however, not only provide vivid examples for defense attorneys and lay jurors of how scientific evidence can be corrupted, but may also cost the relevant locality and state the use of an important testing facility, thereby hampering legitimate efforts to prosecute perpetrators.

Prosecutors should be aware that if untested sample remains after the initial evidence typing, the defense may conduct its own independent testing. There is universal agreement that "[t]he best protection that an innocent suspect has against an error that could lead to a false conviction is the opportunity for an independent retest."[37] If the defense wishes to test the remaining evidence, counsel should formally make this request on the record, and the prosecutor, in turn and on the record, should request (1) the name of the lab the defense intends to use, (2) the type of testing to be conducted, (3) the return of any unused sample to the state by a date certain, (4) that the state be provided with a copy of any and all reports and bench notes generated pursuant to the retesting and (5) that the defense waive any chain of custody challenges. If possible, the sample should be retested at a lab with comparable accreditation status to the original testing lab.

The insistence on preserving the unused sample for independent testing is consistent with the treatment of other biological evidence during the pre-DNA era. For example, in the case of *People v. Hitch,*[38] the California Supreme Court ruled that the prosecution was obliged to preserve extra ampoules of breath sample if it planned to introduce breathalyzer evidence

[37] NRC, 1996; see also the National Commission on the Future of DNA Evidence, 2000.

[38] 12 Cal. 3d 641, 117 Cal. Rptr. 9, 527 P.2d 361 (1974).

at trial. Interestingly, in *California v. Trombetta*,[39] the United States Supreme Court disagreed. Because it considered the breathalyzer test to be extremely reliable, the Court opined that there was little chance that the results of an independent test would have been exculpatory. Some state courts, however, have rejected *Trombetta* in favor of *Hitch*. In doing so, they rely on their state constitutions and conclude that, if the prosecution destroys evidence that would have provided the defense an opportunity for an independent test that could have been exculpatory, any testimony regarding the results of the prosecution's tests is inadmissible.

The fact that many forensic samples contain a minute amount of material means that, in some cases, the samples will be completely consumed during the original testing. In some states, such as Colorado and Massachusetts, the prosecution is required to inform the defense prior to typing when the lab anticipates testing will consume the entire sample. It is best to notify the defense in writing and on the record, as failure to notify the defense in these states will result in a failure to have the DNA evidence admitted. In all cases, even absent a relevant statute, if the prosecution's testing has consumed the entire sample, the prosecution has the ethical obligation to inform the defense of this fact. Having the testing laboratory include a clear statement in its report indicating that all of the sample material was consumed during typing will satisfy the prosecution's obligation in this respect.

In those jurisdictions where the prosecution is required to inform the defense ahead of time that testing will consume the entire sample, defense counsel may request that a representative of the defense be allowed to observe the state's analysts as they perform the testing. The ability to do this is governed by the individual labs, and this request will have to be communicated to the respective lab. Given laboratory security concerns and the fact that a typical DNA analysis can take weeks or even months, however, the request may be intrusive and logistically difficult to honor. In most cases, even if the sample will be consumed by the original test, courts have deferred to the laboratory and ruled that the defense could not have an expert observe the testing.[40] In a few cases, however, the court has allowed one side to have an expert present to witness the other side's analysis.[41]

Different courts have ruled differently on the subject of whether disclosure includes all the technical details of the analysis, such as the sequences of

[39] 467 U.S. 479 (1984).

[40] For example, *Monagas v. People*, 615 N.Y.S.2d 633 (1994).

[41] For example, *Prince v. Superior Court*, 10 Cal. Rptr. 2d 855 (1992); *McKinney v. Venters*, 934 S.W.2d 241, Ky. (1996).

the primers used in the PCR tests or the population genetic data underlying the statistical analysis of the evidence. In a number of cases,[42] the courts have upheld the defendant's right to access all the details of the analysis and the supporting population genetic data. In cases such as *State v. Dykes*,[43] however, the courts have ruled that these details were not essential to the defense, and therefore not discoverable.

It is easier to understand why a court might be more sympathetic to a request for population genetic data than one for PCR primer sequences. The issues related to PCR primer sequences are those of sensitivity and specificity. If the laboratory possesses the validation study data that it should have, it will have data showing what minimum amount of input DNA is required to obtain a reliable profile (sensitivity), and how likely one is to see artifactual peaks in the data that are due to the presence of unwanted PCR products (specificity). The data from the laboratory's validation studies can provide a "bottom-line" assurance that the primer sequences, as well as the other details of the analysis protocol, pass muster for all cases. In contrast, the statistical procedures used to interpret the DNA data must be tailored to the specific case at bar. Thus, it is always prudent for the defense to scrutinize the database from which the prosecution derives its profile frequencies and the correction factors (if any) used in the RMP calculations, to be sure they are appropriate given that specific defendant's ethnic heritage.

Discovery should not only be complete, but it should be timely. Both federal and most state rules of criminal procedure specify that discovery material be provided to the requesting party within a reasonable timeframe. In some cases courts will not make exceptions for discovery material which only becomes available to the prosecution shortly before trial. Failure to provide discovery material on a timely basis may provide sufficient grounds for reversal of the conviction,[44] even if the appellate court concludes that the evidence against the defendant was strong enough to convict him anyway.[45]

EXPERT WITNESSES

Supreme Court decisions, legislation in many jurisdictions, and the NRC committees that molded current policy regarding forensic DNA testing all support a defendant's right to expert trial assistance with regard to DNA

[42] For example, *State v. Pennell*, IN88-12-0051, Del. Super. Ct. (Sept. 20, 1989); *State v. Schwartz*, 447 N.W.2d 422, Minn. (1989); *United States v. Yee*, 129 F.R.D. 629, N.D. Ohio (1990); *People v. Davis*, 601 N.Y.S.2d 174 (1993).

[43] 847 P.2d 1214, Kan. (1993).

[44] For example, *Padgett v. State*, 668 So. 2d, Ala. Cr. App. (1995).

[45] 503 S.E.2d 906 Ga. App. (1998).

evidence. In the case of indigent defendants, this right includes the state paying for this assistance. Some commentators have stated that, despite this assistance, the prosecution often has an overwhelming advantage over the indigent defendant when it comes to the availability and cost of expert witnesses.[46] Although prosecutors are limited by their individual office policy regarding the amount of resources that can be spent typing evidence samples without prior approval, state prosecutors have access to state, county, regional and metropolitan DNA laboratories. In addition, the FBI's DNA testing laboratory serves federal prosecutors, and in limited qualifying cases, these services may be available, free of charge, to state law enforcement agencies as well. In contrast, the indigent defendant is often limited to the services of expert witnesses willing to work within the allowed fee structure available through the court. Given the high costs associated with expert witnesses, this may in effect limit the quality of services available to the indigent defendant.

The Criminal Justice Act (CJA) of 1964[47] requires the federal government to provide expert assistance for indigent defendants in federal trials when the assistance is "necessary for adequate representation." The CJA recognizes the many different ways in which an expert can help a defense attorney prepare for a DNA case; in addition to court testimony, it allows for pretrial and trial consultation, as well as assistance in preparing the cross-examination of the prosecution's witnesses. The Supreme Court first recognized a constitutional right to expert assistance in *Ake v. Oklahoma.*[48] The Court based the *Ake* decision on the defendant's right to due process. Later courts have rendered similar decisions, but have cited the right to equal protection of law or the right to counsel as grounds.[49] Like the CJA, several courts have acknowledged that there are many phases of the process at which an expert can provide valuable assistance.[50] Finally, the 1992 NRC also recommended that courts appoint an expert for the defense in every case involving DNA evidence, even when the admissibility of the evidence is not in question.

The *Ake* decision left several important issues unresolved. *Ake* was a psychiatric case, and there has been some disagreement about whether *Ake* also applies to experts other than psychiatrists. A few courts have interpreted *Ake* as applying only to the appointment of psychiatrists.[51] Most courts, however, have applied *Ake* to experts of all kinds.[52] The *Ake* court seemed to allow the possibility of a range of experts. For example,

[46] Hanson et al., 1993, a study of indigent defense programs by the National Center for State Courts.

[47] CJA; 18 U.S.C., 3006A(e), 1988.

[48] 470 U.S. 68 (1985); for a complete discussion of *Ake's* impact, see Gianelli, 2004.

[49] For example, *Ex parte Moody*, 684 So. 2d 114, Ala. (1996); *State v. Van Scoyoc*, 511 N.W.2d 628, Iowa (1993); *People v. Gaglione*, 32 Cal. Rptr. 2d 169, Ct. App. (1994).

[50] For example, *Taylor v. State*, 939 S.W.2d 148, Tex. Crim. App. (1996).

[51] *People v. Leonard*, 569 N.W.2d 663, Mich. Ct. App. (1977); *Ex parte Grayson*, 479 So. 2d 76, 82 Ala. (1985); *Plunkett v. State*, 719 P.2d 834, Okla. Crim. App. (1986); *Stewart v. Commonwealth*, 427 S.E.2d 394, Va. (1993); *State v. Huchting*, 927 S.W.2d 411, Mo. Ct. App. (1996); *Weeks v. Angelone*, 176 F.3d 249, 4th Cir. (1999).

although the *Ake* Court declined to rule on the trial court's refusal to grant the defendant's requests for fingerprint and ballistics experts because the defense had not sufficiently demonstrated its need for these experts, it never suggested that fingerprint and ballistic experts fell outside the scope of its decision. Furthermore, in a previous paternity action that the Court characterized as "quasi-criminal," the Court had ruled that the indigent defendant had the right to a blood grouping test.[53]

The prosecution frequently has access to expert assistance, but this access does not, in and of itself, provide sufficient grounds for courts to appoint one for the defense. This was especially true in the early days of DNA evidence; the courts did not appreciate how much subjective judgment informed many forensic DNA analyses. In the early days of DNA evidence, the courts thought that DNA analysis was objective, precise and infallible. Because they viewed the process as completely objective, some courts considered the prosecution's DNA witnesses as neutral experts and believed that the defense did not need an expert witness, because there were no issues to dispute.[54]

Defense requests for expert assistance are now routine, but defense counsel should not assume they will be granted. Counsel should be prepared to accompany the request with an explanation as to why each particular expert is needed. For example, if the trial evidence includes several types of forensic evidence, counsel should be prepared to explain to the court why one witness's expertise does not automatically qualify them to address the unique issues inherent in another scientific discipline.

Article VII of the FRE addresses a number of issues pertinent to opinion testimony; most admissibility attacks will be premised on those provisions. In addition, there are several procedural or constitutional grounds by which courts have barred witnesses from testifying. For example, witnesses who would otherwise be judged competent have been barred as a sanction for violating discovery rules.[55] In addition, witnesses will be barred from testifying if the court determines that one side has violated a sequestration order.[56] When an expert witness's experience is found not to be optimal, most courts will try their best to admit the witness and at least a portion of his or her planned testimony, especially if that witness is the only one the defense has to offer.[57] In addition, many courts will consider the witness's experience a matter that influences the weight, rather than

[52] *Thornton v. State*, 339 S.E.2d 240, Ga. (1986); *State v. Coker*, 412 N.W.2d 589, Iowa (1987); *State v. Carmouche*, 527 So. 2d 307, La. (1988); *Prater v. State*, 820 S.W.2d 429, Ark. (1991); *People v. Dickerson*, 606 N.E.2d 762, Ill. App. Ct. (1992); *Polk v. State*, 612 So. 2d 381, Miss. (1992); *Sommers v. Commonwealth*, 843 S.W.2d 879, Ky. (1992); *Terry v. Rees*, 985 F.2d 283, 6th Cir. (1993); *State v. Ballard*, 428 S.E.2d 178, N.C. (1993); *People v. Tyson*, 618 N.Y.S.2d 796 App. Div. (1994); *Cade v. State*, 658 So. 2d 550, Fla. Dist. Ct. App. (1995); *Ex parte Dubose*, 662 So. 2d 1189, Ala. (1995).

[53] *Little v. Streater*, 452 U.S. 1 (1981).

[54] *Harrison v. State*, 644 N.E.2d 1243, Ind. (1995).

[55] For example, *Smith v. Estelle*, 602 F.2d 694, 5th Cir. (1979); *State v. Bizzle*, 608 S.W.2d 111, Mo. App. (1980); *State v. Gaskin*, 618 S.W.2d 620, Mo. (1981); *Hightower v. State*, 629 S.W.2d 920, Tex. Crim. App. (1982).

the admissibility, of his or her testimony, and leave it to the jury to decide how the witness's experience influences the jurors' perceptions of the significance of the DNA evidence.

Both sides must try to get the jury to accept their expert as an unbiased scientist or other professional rendering an objective opinion. In most cases, conveying the proper image of the expert witness presents less of a challenge to the prosecution than to the defense. Because the prosecution's expert is usually employed by a law enforcement agency or the laboratory that did the testing, the prosecutor can usually emphasize that the expert's participation is part of his or her job, and not something the individual is doing purely to enhance his or her reputation or for personal monetary gain. Under these circumstances, the witness's experience becomes a big asset. A witness who works for the testing laboratory often will have testified in a number of cases in the past, and the fact that he or she has been qualified in the past by other courts can be used to advantage. From the defense's standpoint, it is an unfortunate irony that an expert witness who has a lot of experience in court can often find his or her experience a liability—or at least, the prosecution may try to use it as such. It is extremely damaging to an expert's credibility if the other side can paint him or her as a "professional testifier," a "hired gun" or a "jukebox" who will sing whatever song is requested by the people who drop their money into the machine.

Given the fact that the most important role of the expert witness in court is that of teacher, it is important to convey to the jury that the witness is extremely knowledgeable in a specialized field. In addition, it is helpful if the expert's demeanor enables him or her to cultivate a rapport with the jurors. Jurors respect humble experts who boil the substance down to simple terms, and they may resent a pompous expert who talks himself or herself up too much, or uses technical jargon that one would not expect the average juror to understand. In his book *Trial Techniques,* Thomas A. Mauet suggests that the attorney ask leading questions of the expert witness during the early part of the witness's testimony, when the witness's credentials are being described for the jury. This allows the witness to simply answer questions "Yes," without making what might seem to be pompous statements about himself or herself. Mauet considers the use of leading questions appropriate, because the witness's credentials are preliminary matters not in dispute. Some trial judges may consider it less

[56] *United States v. Willis,* 525 F.2d 657, 5th Cir. (1976); *McCorkle v. State,* 607 S.W.2d 655, Ark. (1980).

[57] For example, *Love v. State,* 963 S.W.2d 236, Mo. App. (1997).

appropriate, and disallow leading questions during even the early part of the direct examination, but it may be good strategy to try a few to see what that particular trial judge is going to allow. Although no lawyer wants to antagonize the trial judge by persistently infringing upon the rules, it rarely hurts to "test the waters" a bit at first, to determine what the limits are in that particular court room. Ideally, this will have been determined in a preliminary hearing or outside the jury's presence.

FRE Rule 615 gives the trial judge the authority to sequester an expert witness until it is his or her turn to testify. Having the opposing side's witness sequestered works to each side's advantage, but reciprocal sequestering requests may provide more advantage for the prosecution than the defense, because the prosecution witnesses will often testify before the defense witnesses. If either counsel contemplates asking the judge to sequester a witness, counsel should ask the judge to put the witnesses "under the rule," meaning to prohibit them from discussing their testimony with other witnesses or from accessing transcripts of prior testimony. Any violations of this order may result in the judge barring the witness's testimony.[58] This is particularly important when there are multiple witnesses for the other side; the less communication there is between the other side's witnesses, the more chance there is for inconsistencies in their testimony. Even when the witnesses draw the same conclusion, they may make inconsistent statements about the analytical procedure, the statistical methods or the interpretation of the data. Any opportunity to point out inconsistencies in the testimonies of the other side's witnesses can be used to advantage. For this reason, trial lawyers should carefully coordinate the testimonies of their witnesses as part of their preparation for the case. Developing "buzz words" and key phrases for all witnesses to use will help minimize inconsistencies and maximize the effectiveness of the witnesses' testimonies.

In cases where one expert questions the other side's expert's credentials or controversial opinions, or believes that there is some other serious flaw with the other side's witnesses or evidence, counsel may consider asking the court to appoint its own expert, as authorized under FRE Rule 706. If there is a flaw in the other side's case, this is a good way to obtain a second expert whose testimony will bolster counsel's case at no expense. In addition, although this is not required, Rule 706 authorizes the judge to inform the jury that the expert is court-appointed. If the expert's

[58] *United States v. Willis*, 525 F.2d 657, 5th Cir. (1976); *McCorkle v. State*, 607 S.W.2d 655, Ark. (1980).

testimony will support counsel's case, counsel may consider asking the judge to do this; this will convey an aura of credibility on that expert that may go far with the average juror.

THE DURABILITY OF DNA PRESENTS PROBLEMS FOR STATUTES OF LIMITATION

Statutes of limitation constitute "the primary guarantee against bringing overly stale criminal charges."[59] Witness recollections and other evidence tend to deteriorate over time. Statutes of limitation are designed not only to ensure the quality of the prosecution's evidence, but also to prevent defendants from having to rely on old, unreliable evidence to defend themselves. Because of its remarkable durability, DNA evidence does not fit comfortably within the traditional time frames. DNA can provide reliable evidence long after many other forms of evidence are no longer available. Recognizing DNA's remarkable durability, some jurisdictions have extended their statutes of limitations as they apply to DNA evidence. This can present an additional burden for some defendants, forcing them to defend themselves with old, outdated evidence against the highly credible DNA evidence. If a match between the defendant's DNA profile and that of the evidence proves the defendant's guilt, then this would be reasonable. It would not matter if the defendant's alibi witness had died in the intervening period, because no jury would believe the alibi witness in the face of contradictory DNA evidence. As discussed in Chapter 9, however, there are several reasons why the DNA profile from someone who was not involved in a crime might match the profile of an evidence sample. Guilt can only be established by reviewing all the evidence pertinent to the case.

[59] *United States v. Ewell*, 383 U.S. 116, (1996); see also *United States v. Marion*, 404 U.S. 307 (1971).

In order to preserve the opportunity to prosecute the perpetrator of certain unsolved crimes, prosecutors may file charges against the suspect, identifying him or her merely by his or her DNA profile in what is referred to as a "John Doe" warrant. In the first case in which a John Doe warrant was used in the United States, Paul Eugene Robinson was convicted of five counts of sexual assault after eluding police for six years. These "John Doe" warrants have met little resistance when used because DNA is capable of providing a sufficiently unique and permanent form of identification to allow prosecutors to reliably identify the suspect when he or she is later located. Given the number of crimes that go unsolved for long periods of time, this will no doubt be an increasingly more common practice in the future.

[60] 205 W. Va. 326, 518 S.E.2d 83, W. Va., June 25, 1999 (No. 25790).

[61] 615 So. 2d 234, Fla. App. (1993).

RAPE SHIELD LAWS MAY LIMIT THE USE OF DNA EVIDENCE

Rape shield laws, which are designed to prevent a defendant from attacking the accuser on the grounds of her sexual conduct with others, occasionally limit the use of DNA evidence. For example, in *Guthrie v. State*,[60] a West Virginia court convicted Charles Guthrie of sexually assaulting his wife. His wife told the hospital personnel who examined her that, prior to the assault, she had not had sexual relations with anyone for several months. Guthrie attempted to impeach his wife's statement; DNA analysis of a vaginal sample from his wife revealed the presence of DNA from two different individuals, neither of whom was Guthrie. The trial court and appellate court both acknowledged that the rape shield statute makes exceptions for cases in which the victim makes her prior sexual conduct with others an issue at trial by testifying regarding such conduct. In this case, however, because Mrs. Guthrie did not testify in court regarding her prior sexual conduct, Guthrie could not introduce the DNA evidence as a means of attacking her credibility. Furthermore, the courts both acknowledged that the statute allows exceptions when the evidence of the victim's sexual conduct with others is directly related to the crime with which the defendant is charged. In this case, however, both courts ruled that the DNA evidence did not satisfy this criterion.

In cases in which a rape shield law precludes the defendant from presenting a full defense for himself, the court may decide that the rape shield law must be lifted in favor of the defendant's constitutional rights. For example, consider the case of *Teemer v. State*.[61] In this case, a woman had been forced at gunpoint to drive her car to a secluded area. Her assailant had then ordered her to climb into the backseat with him and remove her clothes. The victim claimed that the man forced her to insert his penis into her anus, whereupon he ejaculated moments later. The physician who examined the victim shortly thereafter at the local rape treatment center found no evidence of trauma to the victim's anus, and no evidence of semen in her anus either. The examiner did find semen in the victim's vagina and cervix, however, but the DNA profile from the semen did not match Teemer's. The victim claimed that she had had sex with her boyfriend shortly before the attack and that the semen in her vagina was his. Prior to the trial, the prosecution successfully argued that the DNA evidence was inadmissible. The prosecution argued that, because the victim had claimed that her attacker had ejaculated in her anus, the semen in her vagina was not probative regarding the identification of her attacker, but was only probative regarding her prior sexual conduct with another. Consequently, Florida's rape shield law precluded admission of the evidence. The physician at the rape treatment center testified that it was not uncommon for rape victims to report that they had been anally penetrated when no such event had occurred. Because of this phenomenon, the Florida appellate court decided that the victim must have been vaginally raped, and therefore that the semen in her vagina was probative of the identity of her assailant. The appellate court remanded the case back to the trial court for a new trial.

JUDGES' AND JURORS' PERCEPTIONS OF DNA EVIDENCE

Most Jurors Have Confidence in DNA Evidence

As the legal system and lay public become more experienced with DNA evidence, they grow more confident in the ability of DNA evidence to serve the interests of justice. Although DNA evidence may only be one part of the prosecution's case, it is being recognized as one of the most reliable types of evidence available for the state. In the early days of introducing DNA evidence, many courts assigned much greater weight to the victim's identification of his or her assailant than to the DNA evidence. When a defendant was convicted on the strength of eyewitness evidence, it was not uncommon for the trial court to deny a motion for a new trial when the defendant had DNA testing performed post-trial, or when recently developed DNA tests afforded the opportunity to obtain DNA evidence that was previously unavailable at the time of the trial.[62] Many courts considered the other evidence against the defendant, such as the victim's or other eyewitnesses' identification, strong enough that introducing the DNA evidence was unlikely to result in a different verdict.

Now that various Innocence Projects that have sprung up across the country over the last 15 years have secured the release of increasing

[62] For example, *State v. Hicks,* 536 N.W.2d 487, Wis. App. (1995).

numbers of wrongly convicted defendants, it has become apparent that either false or mistaken eyewitness identifications, often by victims, have played an important role in securing these wrongful convictions.[63] In contrast, DNA evidence is emerging as a highly reliable record that can be used years after the fact to help identify the true perpetrator of the crime. There are aspects of the public perception of DNA evidence on which both sides can capitalize. On one hand, the growing confidence in the ability of DNA evidence to help secure accurate verdicts, both guilty and not guilty, makes it easier for the prosecution to secure a conviction when there is strong DNA evidence against the defendant. On the other hand, there are those rare but sensational cases in which police or expert witnesses have behaved unethically or laboratories have made mistakes. These cases leave strong impressions in the minds of the public and can often be called upon by the defense in its effort to blunt the effect of the DNA evidence. Mock jury research suggests that, while most people feel that the probability of misconduct on the part of investigators or analysts is low, a small percentage of the population does consider it high (discussed below).

Both sides should try to gauge the jurors' levels of education and perceptions of DNA evidence during voir dire. If the DNA evidence against the defendant is strong, the prosecution should select educated people who feel that science serves humanity well, those who are familiar with the nonjudicial application of DNA (for example, medical treatment or missing person identification), and those who are generally content with their lot in life. The defense, on the other hand, wants poorly educated jurors who may be unable to understand complex technical explanations, and cynical individuals who are likely to believe suggestions that the laboratory made an error or that unethical law enforcement agents may have tampered with the evidence. Mock jury research has suggested that less educated jurors are more likely to view the DNA evidence and the process by which it was generated with skepticism than are more educated jurors.[64] In jurisdictions in which lawyers are allowed to conduct juror voir dire, the litigator should develop a set of questions designed to establish the desired attitude in the minds of all the jurors. Each question asked of a prospective juror provides an opportunity to communicate with the entire jury pool. Even a juror that a lawyer believes the other side will move to exclude can be used as a vehicle to bring issues to the attention of the others. In jurisdictions in which the judge conducts the voir dire, the

[63] www.innocenceproject.org

[64] Dann et al., 2006.

litigator may be limited to making judgments about potential jurors based on the most reliable stereotypes possible, considering the answers of the prospective jurors to the judge's standard questions.

Given the popularity of television programs and movies with forensic themes, the courts accept that many jurors will have confidence in DNA evidence and do not consider that prejudicial against the defendant. For example, in *Satcher v. Commonwealth*, the defendant argued that accepting jurors who had favorable opinions regarding DNA evidence shifted the burden of proof to the defense.[65] The *Satcher* court rejected this argument, noting that it is unrealistic to expect potential jurors not to have any knowledge of, or opinion about, something that has had as much publicity as forensic DNA testing. Furthermore, the court noted, state legislatures and courts have consistently affirmed their confidence in the reliability of DNA evidence. Given that the jurors in question had developed opinions that were consistent with the evidence that was available to laypeople, as well as with the laws of the state, the court found that accepting these jurors did not prejudice the case against the defendant.

An Alarmingly High Frequency of Fallacies

As was true during the debates that followed the 1992 NRC report, the statistical interpretation of DNA evidence continues to be one of the most controversial issues attending the use of forensic DNA evidence in criminal trials. There is little debate on the subject of whether jurors correctly incorporate probabilistic evidence into their decision making; it is widely agreed that they usually do not. The debate has centered on the question of whether jurors are more likely to make prosecution-friendly versus defense-friendly interpretations. One influential article suggested that prosecution-friendly fallacies can usually be expected to dominate jurors' thinking.[66] A review of the social psychology literature suggests, however, that one can expect defense-friendly fallacies to dominate over prosecution-friendly ones.[67] Mock jury research studies confirm this prediction; when the jurors hear both the prosecutor's fallacy and the defense attorney's fallacy, the defense attorney's fallacy is considerably more influential.[68] In addition, one study suggests that only a minority of jurors readily accept an expert witness's estimate of the RMP or PLE; most jurors maintain the impression that the RMP and PLE are actually higher than the figures provided by the expert.[69]

[65] For example, *Satcher v. Commonwealth*, 421 S.E.2d 821, Va. (1992).

[66] Tribe, 1971.

[67] Saks and Kidd, 1980.

[68] Thompson and Schumann, 1987; Goodman, 1992.

[69] Schklar and Diamond, 1999.

There are few sources of insights into how real jurors have evaluated probabilistic evidence in actual trials. The private nature of jury deliberations obviously makes it impossible to survey jurors extensively to determine how frequently they engage in fallacious reasoning. Given the alarming frequency with which lawyers, judges and even expert witnesses have made misstatements on this subject, however (discussed in Chapter 4), one can only assume that there is great potential for jurors to be affected also. On occasion, a court record illustrates the difficulties that jurors have interpreting forensic evidence. For example, in *United States ex rel. DiGiacomo v. Franzen*,[70] the jury heard testimony that there was a match between the defendant's hair and hairs that were found in the victim's car. During deliberations, the jury sent the judge a note asking whether the match proved that the defendant had been in the victim's car. Unfortunately, in this case the judge failed to provide the jurors with the proper guidance. He merely told the jurors that it was their job to decide the facts; he did not explain that the match supported this conclusion, but that there were also other explanations for a hair being in someone's car. The appellate court agreed with the defense that the jury had been misled into thinking that the match definitively established the defendant's presence in the victim's car, and remanded the case for a new trial.

An unpublished study by Stuart O'Brien[71] provides another rare insight into real jurors' thinking. O'Brien studied four people who had served as jurors in a Texas capital murder case several years earlier. He posed a hypothetical case to them that involved DNA evidence and an RMP of 1 in 100. He then presented them with a set of statements regarding the 1 in 100 figure and asked them to judge which of the statements were true. Their performance was alarmingly poor. One of the four jurors committed the prosecutor's fallacy, or source probability error, by stating that the 1 in 100 RMP meant that there was a 99% chance that the defendant was the source of the evidence sample. The other three, however, turned the concept of the RMP completely around and stated that the 1 in 100 RMP indicated that there was only a 1% chance that the evidence came from the defendant. According to this reasoning, a match with an RMP of 1 in 1 billion would have less probative value than a match with an RMP of 1 in 10. The fact that all four of the jurors in this study gave a wrong interpretation of the RMP should alert everyone connected with the criminal justice system, regardless of their specific roles.

[70] 680 F.2d 515, 7th Cir. (1982).

[71] Discussed in Koehler, 2001.

It is uncertain how well research using mock juries represents what goes on in a real jury room. Most of these studies present the mock jurors with the information in a setting that is very different from a real court trial. In addition, to eliminate the effects of other evidence, the DNA evidence is often presented alone. In real trials, when other corroborating evidence is presented as well, jurors may be more confident that the defendant is the source of the evidence.[72] Another important difference between mock jury studies and real trials is the fact that, in mock jury studies, the jurors usually answer without deliberating with other jurors. It is hard to know what effect group deliberation will have on an individual's reasoning, especially when opposing fallacies collide. Deliberations can help when error rates are low; in this situation, those who have reasoned correctly can often help correct the others. When error rates are high, however, as mock jury research suggests they are in real trials, group deliberations often foster the exchange of misinformation.[73] Despite everyone's hopes that the trial situation will promote logically sound thinking, the frequency of fallacies reported in mock jury research is so high that one must assume that the frequency of fallacies among real jurors is high enough to constitute a genuine problem. Not only do mock jurors commit a variety of fallacies, but when one of the mock attorneys makes a fallacious statement regarding the data's interpretation, few jurors realize that the attorney has made a fallacious statement, and most jurors' decisions conform to the fallacy.[74]

Some commentators have been so worried about the alarmingly high frequency of fallacious reasoning in mock jury studies that they have suggested that the jury should only be told about the match between the defendant and the evidence, and that all discussions of statistical interpretation should be avoided. In the past, to avoid prejudice against a defendant, a few appellate courts had rejected statistical evidence on the grounds that the jurors were likely to overestimate its probative value.[75] At one point, the Minnesota Supreme Court was so pessimistic about the prospects for resolving the statistical debate, as well as the average juror's ability to understand arguments regarding the proper method for calculating RMPs, that they advocated categorizing matches in qualitative, nonstatistical ways, using terms such as "rare" versus "very rare" versus "extremely rare" to characterize the weight of the match.[76]

[72] Wells, 1992.

[73] Diamond and Levi, 1996.

[74] Goodman, 1992; Dann et al., 2006.

[75] *People v. Robinson*, 27 N.Y.2d 864 (1970); *People v. Macedonio*, 42 N.Y.2d 944 (1977); *State v. Carlson*, 267 N.W. 170, Minn. (1978); *People v. McMillen*, 126 Mich. App. 203 (1984); *Padgett v. State*, 668 So. 2d 78, Ala. Ct. Crim. App. (1995).

[76] *State v. Carlson*, 267 N.W.2d 170, Minn. (1978); *State v. Bloom*, 516 N.W.2d 159, Minn. (1994).

Although all courts recognize the potential for fallacies to invade the jury room, the majority of courts do not show such a heightened level of concern over jurors' inabilities to incorporate probabilistic evidence into their thinking. At the present time, not only do courts accept DNA evidence readily, but most demand that some statistical analysis accompany it.[77] It is therefore necessary for litigators and judges to be certain that they can teach the jury exactly what the probabilistic evidence means and what information they should use to decide the weight of the evidence.

Similarly, jurors must be carefully instructed regarding the level of proof that is required to secure a guilty verdict in the various proceedings in which they are deliberating, as the level of proof differs between civil and criminal proceedings. Studies have shown that different people require markedly different levels of confidence in the defendant's guilt to declare that the prosecution has proven guilt "beyond a reasonable doubt."[78] Even different judges will define "beyond reasonable doubt" differently. Some define it as a 75–85% probability of guilt,[79] while others define it as a 95+% probability of guilt.[80] It is important to get a feel for the jurors' inclinations regarding the definitions of such important terms as "reasonable doubt." When the court allows trial lawyers to conduct jury voir dire, it may be wise for them to try to determine the prospective jurors' thresholds for deciding that the prosecution has satisfied the requisite burden of proof. They should also use the opportunity to question prospective jurors on this issue as a means of trying to establish a favorable (or at least fair) standard in all the jurors' minds.

As discussed in Chapter 4, Bayes' Theorem provides a mathematical model that illustrates how one should combine DNA evidence and non-DNA evidence to assess the relative strengths of the prosecution's versus defense's hypotheses. Mock jury studies consistently suggest that jurors' decisions are less influenced by the probabilistic evidence than a Bayesian model suggests they should be.[81] These studies consistently show that jurors are more confident in the probative value of forensic evidence when a probabilistic interpretation is presented along with it, yet they do not seem to factor the probabilistic evidence into their decision making until the probability they are presented with is extreme. This insensitivity to gradations in the probabilistic evidence reflects the fact that people think in categorical terms, rather than in gradations of probability. If the

[77] *Commonwealth v. Lanigan*, 641 N.E.2d 1342, Mass. (1994); *People v. Coy*, 620 N.W.2d 888, Mich. Ct. App. (2000).

[78] Goodman, 1992; Koehler, 2001; Nance and Morris, 2005.

[79] Underwood, 1977; Nance and Morris, 2005.

[80] *United States v. Fatico*, 458 F. Supp. 388, E.D.N.Y. (1978), aff'd 603 F.2d 1053, 2d. Cir. (1979), cert. denied, 444 U.S. 1023 (1980).

[81] Thompson and Schumann, 1987; Faigman and Baglioni, 1988; Goodman, 1992; Smith et al., 1996; Schklar and Diamond, 1999; Nance and Morris, 2005.

evidence exceeds their threshold for belief, even by a small margin, they will believe the proposition, incorporate that belief into their thinking, and forget whether that belief was based on rock-solid evidence versus barely sufficient evidence.

Some research has suggested that jurors decide the verdict they want to render, then adjust their criterion for confidence in the defendant's guilt in a manner that enables them to render their desired verdict.[82] For example, in Koehler's study, jurors who were presented with both a prosecution-friendly presentation of the evidence and a defense-friendly one were less convinced that the defendant was the source of the evidence than were jurors who were presented with only the prosecution-friendly version. In spite of reporting lower probabilities that the defendant was the source of the evidence, however, the jurors who heard both presentations voted to convict the defendant as often as the jurors who had only heard the prosecution-friendly presentation did. Because there is no objective definition of reasonable doubt, it may be easier for jurors to convict defendants of crimes involving excessive brutality. In such cases, the excessively brutal nature of the crime instills in them a stronger desire to make sure that someone is punished. Thus, they reduce their threshold level of confidence required to deliver a guilty verdict. Furthermore, the fact that women are the victims of the vast majority of rapes may prompt women to apply a lower criterion for reasonable doubt in rape cases than men do.[83]

Mock jurors consider DNA evidence highly reliable, but they seem unaware of the factors that determine the reliability of the evidence. For example, in one study,[84] mock jurors fallaciously reported greater confidence in the reliability of the evidence as the RMP got smaller. The mock jurors did not appear to understand that the validity of the techniques used to analyze the evidence affected the reliability of the DNA evidence, nor did they seem to grasp that the RMP was a reflection of a completely unrelated factor—how rare a blood type was in the population.

Despite the fact that probabilistic evidence increases jurors' confidence in the probative value of the DNA test results, the actual value of the RMP seems to have little impact on their thinking unless it is extremely high or low. For example, in one study,[85] one group of mock jurors was given no probabilistic information, while other groups were told that the RMP was 0.1%, 1%, 5% or 10%. The groups that were given probabilistic

[82] Goodman, 1992; Koehler, 2001.

[83] Goodman, 1992.

[84] Goodman, 1992.

[85] Goodman, 1992.

information were more likely to convict, and had more confidence in the defendant's guilt, than the group that was given no information. There was little difference in conviction rates or confidence levels between the groups that were given the probabilistic evidence, however, until the RMP was 10%. Because mathematical calculations convey an aura of scientific certainty on the data, providing the jurors with a probabilistic statement appeared to bolster their confidence in the evidence's probative value and to make them more likely to convict the defendant. The jurors appeared not to treat the probabilistic evidence as a continuous variable, however. If they had, a 50-fold difference in the random match probability (0.1% vs. 5%) should have had some effect on their willingness to convict. The jurors instead appeared to have a threshold for considering a trait common enough to reduce the weight of the evidence; an RMP of 10% exceeded that threshold, but an RMP of 5% did not. The mock jurors from a study by Schklar and Diamond[86] were even less discriminating. Schklar and Diamond reported that there was little difference in the likelihood that mock jurors would convict a defendant if they were given an RMP of 1 in 1 billion versus 2 in 100.

Similar findings were reported by Saks and Kidd.[87] Their subjects were given a description of a man and asked to predict the probability that he was a lawyer or an engineer. They were also told that the man had been randomly selected from a population consisting of lawyers and engineers, and they were given several scenarios in which the proportion of lawyers to engineers in the population was varied. Logically, one's prediction of whether the man was a lawyer versus an engineer should be influenced by the proportion of lawyers to engineers in the population. Saks and Kidd found that the proportion of lawyers versus engineers in the population had little impact on people's decisions about the probability of the man being a lawyer until the proportions approached 0% and 100%. Their subjects seemed to ignore the importance of the base rate of lawyers versus engineers in the population. Rather, they appeared to follow a "best guess" strategy[88] and to treat the base rate information as a categorical (yes/no) variable rather than a continuous (0 to 100%) one. To reduce the complexity of the judgment, people often consider the evidence either reliable or unreliable; evidence that is probably reliable is treated as if it were perfectly reliable, and subtle differences between evidence that is highly reliable and moderately reliable are ignored.

[86] Schklar and Diamond, 1999.

[87] Saks and Kidd, 1980.

[88] Gettys, Kelly and Peterson, 1973.

Thompson has further illustrated the difficulties jurors encounter when presented with base rate information.[89] When presented with several scenarios at once, in which the frequency of the trait and the probability of a false-positive error were varied, jurors were able to rank the scenarios in order of the reliability of the evidence. When presented with only a single set of frequency/error rate information, however, jurors were unable to correctly determine the level of reliability for such evidence. Group deliberation did not change this; jurors accorded weak but probably reliable probabilistic evidence the same weight as highly reliable evidence. The latter situation is obviously more analogous to a real courtroom situation, in which the jurors are presented with a single set of data regarding the frequency of the DNA profile and the possibility of a laboratory error. The study's findings suggest, however, that jurors may be able to assess the weight of the evidence more accurately if they are shown how changes in the frequency of the trait or probability of error would affect the RMP or the reliability of the evidence. It is possible that a graph or some other visual aid that demonstrates how changes in the RMP or other probabilistic evidence would influence the probability of guilt may help jurors use that information more appropriately than they usually do.

The specific form in which the evidence is presented may strongly influence the frequency with which jurors commit the different fallacies. Koehler has provided an elegant demonstration of the way in which the specific form in which the evidence is presented influences jurors' decisions.[90] Koehler focuses on the concept of "exemplar cueing." Simply put, a juror is less likely to convict the defendant if the juror can envision examples of other people whose DNA profiles would also match the profile in question by coincidence. Koehler presented different groups of mock jurors with different, but mathematically equivalent, representations of an RMP of 1 in 1,000. For example, in one study, one group was told that "the probability that the suspect would match the blood specimen if he were not the source is 0.1%." Another was told that "the frequency with which the suspect would match the blood specimen if he were not the source is one in one thousand." A third group was told that "[o]ne-tenth of 1% of the people in Houston who are not the source would also match the blood drops." Finally, the fourth group was told that "[o]ne in one thousand people in Houston who are not the source would also

[89] Thompson, 1989.
[90] Koehler, 2001.

[91] Koehler, 2001.

match the blood drops." All four statements are accurate, mathematically equivalent ways in which one might state that the RMP was 1 in 1,000.

Despite their mathematical equivalence, however, these statements carry significantly different psychological impacts. Koehler's mock jurors were far more likely to convict when given the first presentation and far less likely to convict when given the fourth presentation. According to exemplar cueing theory, when the presentation focuses on the defendant, as in the first two presentations, the jurors are less likely to envision other people who would also match the DNA profile in question, and more likely to conclude that the defendant is the source of the evidence. When the presentation makes reference to a larger population, as do the third and fourth presentations, the jurors are more likely to envision other members of that population whose DNA profiles will also match the profile in question, and are less confident that the match means that the defendant is the source of the evidence. Consistent with the exemplar cueing theory, reporting the probabilistic evidence as a percentage (0.1%) led to more convictions than did reporting the evidence as a frequency (1 in 1,000). This may be because the phrasing "1 in 1,000" stamps the message into the juror's mind that other members of a large population (such as citizens of the city where the crime was committed) are also expected to match. Phrasing the evidence as a probability (0.1%) does not encourage the jurors to think in terms of any broader context than the case at bar.

The magnitude of the effect that the different presentations had on jurors' perceptions was impressive. In the first group, in which the presentation focused on the defendant and the RMP was stated as a probability, 63% of the jurors declared that there was at least a 99% probability that the defendant was the source of the evidence, and 8% of the jurors concluded that there was less than a 1% probability that the defendant was the source of the evidence. In contrast, in the fourth group, who received a presentation that referred to the population of Houston and reported the RMP as a frequency, only 14% of the jurors declared that there was at least a 99% probability the defendant was the source of the evidence, and a full 32% of the jurors concluded that there was less than a 1% probability that the defendant was the source of the evidence.

Another experiment by Koehler provided further support for the exemplar cueing theory.[91] In this experiment, the experimenters presented the RMP as a frequency, which they previously showed would reduce the jurors' confidence that the defendant was the source of the evidence, presumably because the phrasing encouraged the jurors to envision examples of other individuals whose DNA profile would match that of the evidence. This time, however, they attempted to reduce this effect by presenting the frequency in terms that discouraged jurors to envision examples of coincidental matches. Six different groups of mock jurors were used. Three groups were presented with an RMP of 1 in 1,000, while the other three groups were presented with an RMP of 1 in 100,000. The groups that were presented with an RMP of 1 in 1,000 heard the RMP presented as either "0.1 out of one hundred," "one out of one thousand," or "two out of two thousand." The groups that were presented with an RMP of 1 in 100,000 heard the RMP presented as either "0.1 out of ten thousand," "one out of one hundred thousand," or "two out of two hundred thousand." According to exemplar cueing theory, the fractional numerators (0.1) should lead fewer jurors to envision examples of other individuals whose DNA profiles would match that of the evidence, because these numbers will be seen as "almost zero." Whole-number numerators (1 and 2) should be more effective at evoking images of matching individuals. The results of this experiment were very impressive. Fractional numerators were significantly more likely to cause jurors to conclude that the defendant was the source of the evidence. Furthermore, this effect was so pronounced that jurors who heard an RMP of "0.1 out of one hundred" were more likely to conclude that the defendant was the source of the evidence than were jurors who had heard an RMP of "one out of one hundred thousand" or "two out of two hundred thousand." Despite the fact that the RMP "0.1 out of one hundred" was 100 times greater than the RMP "one out of one hundred thousand" or "two out of two hundred thousand," the fractional numerator appeared to prevent jurors from envisioning examples of coincidental matches, and increased their confidence in the probative value of the evidence.

Koehler's study also reported that 6–8% of the mock jurors seemed to think that smaller RMPs indicated that the DNA evidence had less, rather than greater, probative value. If this reflects the actual percentage of confused individuals in the average jury pool, the average jury may include one such juror. This could constitute the difference between a conviction and a hung jury. No study can confirm or deny whether this is a reasonable estimate of how many laypeople have the concept of RMP backwards. As we have discussed, however, in O'Brien's unpublished study[92] of four ex-jurors, three of them had the concept backwards. This suggests that jurors must be carefully instructed about the significance of the RMP.

Another important issue is jurors' perceptions of the likelihood of either laboratory errors or deliberate tampering with the evidence. The few studies that have directly assessed laypeople's perceptions of the frequency of laboratory errors[93] have reported that the average mock juror's estimate of the probability of laboratory error (PLE) is on the order of 1 in 10 to 1 in 50. In addition, in one study, mock jurors estimated the probability of contamination as 1 in 4, despite there being no evidence presented by either side that any contamination had occurred.[94] Furthermore, in one study, the uninformed estimate of the probability that investigators may have tampered with the evidence was 1 in 50.[95]

Some of the findings in Schklar and Diamond's research also suggest that laypeople have the underlying perception that the PLE in any given case is significant.[96] These mock jurors were less likely to convict the defendant when they were given an RMP of 1 in 1 billion and no estimate of the PLE than they were when given a PLE of 1 in 1 billion and no estimate of the RMP. In addition, jurors were less likely to convict the defendant if they were given an RMP of 1 in 1 billion plus a PLE of 2 in 100 than they were when given an RMP of 2 in 100 and a PLE of 1 in 1 billion. Providing a very small PLE appears to impress jurors with the probative value of the evidence more effectively than providing a very small RMP does. This suggests that the general public recognizes the possibility that laboratories make mistakes, and factors that possibility into their thinking, even when they are not given any data that specifically refer to the issue of laboratory error.

Not all laypeople assume a high PLE in every case. There is a high degree of variability in mock jurors' perceptions about the frequencies of these errors. Although the mean, or average, scores from some of these studies suggest that jurors feel the PLE in any given case is high, the sizes of these study groups were small enough that the mean for a group of subjects can be significantly influenced by a few individuals with extreme scores. In such cases, the median is a more reliable indicator of the "typical" individual's

[92] Cited in Koehler, 2001.

[93] Koehler et al., 1995; Schklar, 1996; Schklar and Diamond, 1999; Nance and Morris, 2005.

[94] Dann et al., 2006.

[95] Schklar and Diamond, 1999.

[96] Schklar and Diamond, 1999.

status than the mean is.[97] When one considers the median estimates for these groups, the results are more encouraging. For example, in the largest of these studies,[98] the mean uninformed estimate of the PLE was 0.019, or 1.9%. In contrast, the median uninformed estimate of the PLE was 0.001, which was exactly the value the expert witness gave for the PLE. This suggests that a relatively small number of jurors consider the probability of errors and/or evidence tampering to be high, but that most hold views that conform better to the available data. If prosecutors can identify and reject those prospective jurors who are most inclined to believe suggestions about laboratory errors or evidence tampering, they may minimize the degree to which jurors' misperceptions hamper the prosecution's efforts.

Efforts to Improve Jurors' Understanding

A number of commentators have suggested ways in which jurors' use of probabilistic evidence can be improved. Pointing to the overwhelming research and anecdotal evidence that most jurors do not understand how to combine the RMP and PLE properly, some commentators have suggested that the RMP and PLE should be combined for them and that the jurors should be presented with a single probability of false inclusion.[99] Both the 1992 and the 1996 NRC committees disagreed with this suggestion, however, as do other commentators.[100] These commentators suggest that jurors should be provided with both figures because the issues of coincidental match and laboratory error are separate issues reflecting different sets of underlying factors. They feel that the jurors should be allowed to ponder both possibilities, along with their associated probabilities, independently. Furthermore, jurors may find the expert's estimate of one figure to be more convincing than his or her estimate of the other figure. If the decision of guilt versus innocence is truly left up to the jury, once the court admits the evidence, it must allow the jurors to agree or disagree with the expert witnesses' estimates of both probabilities, despite the consensus that most jurors are poorly prepared to evaluate the accuracy of the estimates of either the PLE or the RMP. At the same time, it cannot be denied that jurors rarely combine the RMP and PLE properly into an estimate of the probability of a false inclusion. It may be best to present the RMP and PLE to the jurors separately, allow them to evaluate the validity of each estimate independently, then instruct the jurors as to the proper way to combine the RMP and PLE to arrive at the probability

[97] The median is the number in the middle of the dataset. Half the numbers in the dataset are greater than the median, and half the numbers in the dataset are less than the median.

[98] Nance and Morris, 2005.

[99] Koehler et al., 1995; Koehler, 1997.

[100] Schklar and Diamond, 1999.

of a false inclusion. Schklar and Diamond have demonstrated that instructions on how to combine the probabilities of laboratory error and coincidental match do help jurors remember the combined probability of false inclusion, even if they do not remember exactly how the final combined probability was determined.[101] Although most courts insist that the jury be presented with separate estimates of the RMP and PLE, once the individual estimates have been established, it may be beneficial to explain to the jurors how to combine the two probabilities to produce an aggregate probability of false inclusion.

Just as they fail to combine the RMP and PLE properly, jurors frequently commit "misaggregation errors" in which they fail to combine the non-DNA evidence and the DNA evidence in a manner that Bayes' Theorem suggests a purely logical mind should. Some commentators have suggested that jurors can be educated to be better Bayesians, but it is unclear how much jurors' abilities to combine the non-DNA evidence and the DNA evidence can be improved by brief instructional sessions. Some studies suggest that there are situations in which people's abilities to incorporate probabilistic evidence into their decisions can be improved with the help of a brief educational presentation.[102] In contrast, however, most studies in which mock jurors have been presented with a brief instructional presentation about the proper use of probabilistic evidence have suggested that such presentations have little beneficial effect.[103]

Several studies offer some hope for the future. One study has suggested that although jurors are often unable to determine for themselves exactly what probabilistic information they need, and unable to state the reason they need it, when given the appropriate information and guidance as to why they need it, they are often able to adjust their decisions appropriately.[104] Another study has suggested that extensive trial innovations may improve jurors' understanding of DNA evidence.[105] The innovations were extensive, however, and produced only a small improvement in jurors' perceptions. These authors found that providing jurors with a checklist of questions testing their knowledge of the DNA evidence helped improve their understanding. In addition, providing them with a notebook containing the question checklist, a list of witnesses, the experts' slides, a glossary of terms relevant to the DNA evidence and paper for taking notes improved their understanding. These authors have suggested that jurors be given notebooks containing the aforementioned materials, that

[101] Schklar and Diamond, 1999.

[102] Nisbett et al., 1987; Smith, 1992; Nance and Morris, 2005.

[103] Faigman and Baglioni, 1988; Goodman, 1992; Smith et al., 1996.

[104] Beyth-Marom and Fischoff, 1983.

[105] Dann et al., 2006.

witnesses avoid presenting uncontested or inconsequential technical information, that jurors be given guidance with respect to estimating the probability of laboratory errors or sample contamination, and that jurors be given guidance on how to combine the DNA evidence with the other evidence against the defendant to arrive at the appropriate conclusion.[106] As extensive and cumbersome as these innovations are, the alarmingly high incidence of fallacious reasoning on the part of jurors may justify taking significant steps such as these to improve jurors' understanding of the significance and interpretation of DNA evidence.

[106] Dann et al., 2006.

Despite widespread agreement that jurors' abilities to incorporate probabilistic evidence need to be improved, it is unlikely that the courts will institute any measures designed to remedy the situation in the near future. The legal system relies on the adversarial nature of the process, the availability of experts on both sides and judicial instructions to help jurors avoid logical fallacies. It is obvious, however, that even judges and expert witnesses are capable of misleading a jury regarding the proper interpretation of the DNA evidence. It would no doubt behoove the criminal justice system to develop a set of instructional materials designed to help jurors better understand how to incorporate the probabilistic evidence into their decisions.

REFERENCES AND ADDITIONAL READINGS

Beyth-Marom, R. and Fischoff, B. (1983) *Journal of Personality and Social Psychology*, 45, 1185–1195.

Dann, B.M., Hans, V.P. and Kaye, D.H. (2006) *NIJ Journal*, 255.

Diamond, S.S. and Levi, J.N. (1996) *Judicature*, 79, 224–232.

Faigman, D. and Baglioni, A. (1988) *Law and Human Behavior*, 12, 1–17.

Friedman, R.D. (2003) *Seton Hall Law Review*, 33, 1047.

Gettys, K., Kelly, C. and Peterson, O. (1973) *Organizational Behavior and Human Performance*, 10, 364.

Gianelli, P. (1999) Expert Qualifications and Testimony. *Conference on Science and Law*, San Diego, CA, April 15.

Goodman, J. (1992) *American Journal of Trial Advocacy*, 16, 361–389.

Hand, L. (1901) *Harvard Law Review*, 15, 40.

Hanson, Roger A. (1993) *Report to the National Center for State Courts*.

Imwinkelried, E.J. (1991) *Washington University Law Quarterly*, 69, 32.

Koehler, J.J., Chia, A. and Lindsay, S. (1995) *Jurimetrics Journal*, 35, 33–58.

Koehler, J.J. (1997) *Jurimetrics Journal*, 37, 425.

Koehler, J.J. (2001) *Southern Caifornia Law Review*, 74, 1275.

Koehler, J.J. and Macchi, L. (2004) *Psychological Science*, 15, 540–546.

Kreeger, L. and Weiss, D. (2003) *APRI Silent Witness*, 8(2).

Land, G.E. (2005) *Michigan State Journal of Medicine and Law*, 9, 95.

Lewontin, R.C. and Hartl, D.L. (1991) *Science*, 254, 1745.

Nance, D.A. and Morris, S.B. (2005) *Journal of Legal Studies*, 34, 395.

Nisbett, R.E., Fong, G.T., Lehman, D.R. and Cheng, P.W. (1987) *Science*, 238, 625.

Roth, D.R. (2003) *High Ethical Standards: The Foundation for Every Prosecutor*. In *The Prosecutor's Deskbook*, Alexandria, VA: American Prosecutors Research Institute.

Saks, M.J. and Kidd, K.K. (1980) *Law and Society Review*, 15, 123.

Saks, M.J. and Koehler, J.J. (2005) *Science*, 309, 892–895.

Scheck, B.C. (1994) *Cardozo Law Review*, 15, 1959.

Scheck, B., Neufeld, P. and Dwyer, F. (2000) *Actual Innocence*. New York: Doubleday.

Schklar, J. (1996) Juror reactions to DNA evidence: Misperception and misaggregation. Paper presented at the meeting of the American Psychology-Law Society, Hilton Head, SC, March 1996.

Schklar, J. and Diamond, S. (1999) *Law and Human Behavior*, 23, 159–165.

Sensabaugh, G. and Kaye, D.H. (1998) *Jurimetrics Journal*, 39, 1.

Smith, B. (1992) Bayesian Presentation and Juror Use of Probabilistic Evidence. Unpublished paper presented at the American Psychology-Law Society Biennial Meeting.

Smith, B.C., Penrod, S.D., Otto, A.L. and Park, R.C. (1996) *Law and Human Behavior*, 20, 49–82.

Thompson, W.C. and Schumann, E.L. (1987) *Law and Human Behavior*, 11(3), 167–187.

Thompson, W.C. (1989) *Law and Contemporary Problems*, 52(4), 9–41.

Tobin, W.A. and Thompson, W.C. (2006) *The Champion*, 30(6), 12–21.

Tribe, M. (1971) *Harvard Law Review*, 84, 1329.

Wells, G.L. (1992) *Journal of Personality and Social Psychology*, 62, 739.

CHAPTER 8

Arguing for the Prosecution

CONTENTS

Obtaining DNA Samples

DNA in the Courtroom: The Essentials of the Prosecution's Presentation

References and Additional Readings

OBTAINING DNA SAMPLES

During the course of a criminal investigation law enforcement may need to collect a biological sample from a person or persons of interest. Federal and individual state statutes have established several procedures by which a forensic sample may be lawfully obtained and the resulting evidence admitted into judicial proceedings. As the evidence obtained from forensic samples frequently provides critical information establishing that a crime was committed and the parties involved, it is essential that prosecutors understand how these samples may be lawfully obtained and used in court. Understanding the broad scope of sample collection as well as common defense challenges will enable the prosecutor to effectively present this evidence to a jury so that the guilty may be prosecuted and the innocent exonerated.

The federal and state constitutions provide certain guarantees that citizens will not be subjected to unreasonable searches and seizures.[1] Both federal and state courts have recognized that, under certain circumstances and when certain legal requirements are met, law enforcement may compel biological samples from an individual without violating these constitutional provisions.[2] These circumstances include officers obtaining a search warrant or court order through probable cause or reasonable suspicion to believe that a crime has been committed and an identified individual is involved, or, alternatively, via a warrantless search arising from an exception to obtaining a warrant. In addition, both federal and some state statutes authorize sample collection from arrestees while others enable collection from convicted felons or probationers. Abandoned property can

[1] U.S. Const. amend. IV, Iowa Const. art. I, § 8; Article 1 §7 TN Const.; Art I § II, IN Const.

[2] *Schmerber v. California*, 384 U.S. 757, 86 S. Ct. 1826, 16 L. Ed 2d 908 (1966); *Katz v. U.S.*, 389 U.S. 347, 357, 88 S. Ct. 507, 19 L. Ed 2d 576 (1967); *Winston v. Lee*, 470 U.S. 753,767, 105 S. Ct. 1611, 84 L. Ed. 2d 662 (1985).

be lawfully collected in order to process it for forensic material. Also, when officers have some information regarding a criminal perpetrator but have not yet identified a particular individual, law enforcement has conducted DNA "dragnets" to collect biological samples from a number of consenting individuals.

Compelling Samples Through Search Warrant or Court Orders

Probable Cause Standard

The Fourth Amendment of the Constitution guarantees that all persons "shall be secure in their persons, houses, papers, and effects, against unreasonable searches and seizures."[3] In the process of identifying suspects involved in criminal activity, courts have balanced the interests of the state in resolving crime against those of citizens to evaluate the potential impact of the intrusion. Although the courts have long held that a compelled intrusion into the body for blood is a "search" within the Fourth Amendment, they have also recognized that the Fourth Amendment does not proscribe all searches—simply those that are found to be unreasonable. The Supreme Court established that the touchstone for any Fourth Amendment analysis relating to an intrusion into an individual's person is always "the reasonableness of all the circumstances of the particular government invasion of a citizen's personal security."[4] Furthermore, the Court has held that reasonableness "depends on a balance between public interest and the individual's right to personal security free from arbitrary interference by law officers."[5] The Court has repeatedly found that the Fourth Amendment permits reasonable searches and has defined such searches as those conducted pursuant to a warrant issued "upon probable cause, supported by oath or affirmation, and particularly describing the place to be searched, and the person to be seized."[6] A lawfully compelled sample can be obtained either before or after charges have been brought without violating any constitutional prohibitions.[7]

The Supreme Court also emphasized that "neither a warrant nor probable cause, nor, indeed, any measure of individualized suspicion, is an indispensable component of reasonableness in every circumstance."[8] The Court has also held that "special law enforcement concerns will sometimes justify [seizures] without individualized suspicion."[9] Rather, "where the privacy interests implicated by the search are minimal, and where an

[3] U.S. Const. Amend. IV.

[4] *Terry v. Ohio*, 39 U.S. 1, 88 S. Ct. 1868, 20 L. Ed. 2d 889 (1968).

[5] *Brinoni-Ponce*, 422 U.S. 873, 878, 95 S. Ct. 2579, 2578, 45 L. Ed. 2d 607, 614 (1975).

[6] *Florida v. Jimeno*, 500 U.S. 248, 250, 111 S. Ct. 1801, 114 L. Ed. 2d 297 (1991).

[7] *In the Matter of the Grand Jury Investigation*, 692 N.E. 2d 56 (1998).

[8] *Nat'l Treasury Employees Union v. Von Raab*, 489 U.S. 656, 665, 109 S. Ct. 1384, 103 L. Ed. 2d 685 (1989).

[9] *Illinois v. Lidster*, 540 U.S. 419, 424, 124 S. Ct. 885, 157 L. Ed. 2d 843 (2004).

important governmental interest furthered by the intrusion would be placed in jeopardy by a requirement of individualized suspicion, a search may be reasonable despite the absence of such suspicion."[10]

Depending on the procedural requirements of the jurisdiction, a law enforcement officer must appear before a judge and state facts indicating either probable cause or reasonable suspicion to believe that the requested biological sample will produce evidence linking an individual to the crime or assist in the investigation. For example, in the case of *Commonwealth v. Nina M. Draheim,* the defendant, an adult woman, was charged with two separate counts of rape of two teenaged boys. The Commonwealth alleged that each of these two counts resulted in the birth of a child. The Commonwealth sought to compel buccal swabs from the defendant, both infants and both youths. The Superior (trial) Court denied the Commonwealth's request. On appeal, the Supreme Judicial Court of Massachusetts remanded the matter and examined the Commonwealth's burden as to each party from whom it sought to compel a sample. As to the defendant, the court required the Commonwealth to establish probable cause to believe that the defendant had committed a crime and that the sample sought would "probably provide evidence relevant to the question of the defendant's guilt."[11]

On occasion defendants have successfully avoided prosecution on the basis of technical errors resulting from using an incorrect procedure or standard in obtaining a forensic sample. For example, in *McBride v. State,* McBride's blood was collected while he was in custody prior to indictment as a result of a motion. The trial court admitted this evidence. On appeal, however, the court found the state's motion was defective, because the affidavit and motion failed to make a showing of the proper standard. In reversing the lower court's ruling, the appellate court stated that, because an individual's blood does not change over time, a proper search warrant could have been secured.[12] To avoid retrying a case for a technical error, prosecutors should ensure forensic samples are collected according to the appropriate jurisdictional standard.

Reasonable Suspicion Standard

The door to a reasonable suspicion standard was opened with *Terry v. Ohio* when the Supreme Court held that stopping a suspect for questioning and contemporaneously frisking him or her for weapons was a much less intrusive process than a traditional arrest. The *Terry* decision established that the Fourth Amendment reasonableness standard could be

[10] *Skinner v. Ry. Labor Executives' Ass'n*, 489 U.S. 602, 624, 109 S. Ct. 1402, 103 L. Ed. 2d 639 (1989).

[11] *Commonwealth v. Nina M. Draheim*, 849 N.E. 2d 83, citing to Jansen, petitioner, 825 N.E. 2d 186 (2005).

[12] *McBride v. State*, 840 S.W. 111, 117 Tex. App. (1992).

satisfied by something less than probable cause.[13] Other courts have followed this line of reasoning and adopted a standard requiring the state to make a showing of "reasonable grounds to suspect" that the person named or described in the [warrant] application committed a felony, rather than a showing of probable cause.[14] "Reasonable grounds to suspect" is a lower standard for the state to prove than probable cause and requires "considerably less proof of wrongdoing by a preponderance of the evidence."[15] While probable cause requires reasonable grounds to believe that an individual has committed a crime in order to be arrested,[16] "reasonable grounds to suspect" simply requires there be a reasonable basis to think a person may be involved in an illegal activity.[17]

Grand Jury Standard

In order to determine whether sufficient grounds exist to support a criminal indictment, a grand jury may issue a subpoena duces tecum directing an individual to provide a biological sample for analysis.[18] The subpoena requiring a person to appear before the grand jury and provide a sample is not a seizure pursuant to the Fourth Amendment, as each person has the legal obligation to appear and give evidence before the grand jury.[19] The purpose of a grand jury subpoena is to ascertain whether the evidence subpoenaed contributes to the probable cause analysis regarding the facts under investigation.[20] The subpoena is therefore "limited by the general reasonableness standard of the Fourth Amendment . . . not the probable cause requirement."[21] Most courts' reasonableness analysis of the "seizure" involves balancing the extent to which the procedure might threaten the safety or health of the individual, and the extent of the intrusion upon the individual's dignity interests against the community's interest in fairly and accurately determining the suspect's guilt or innocence.

Defense Challenges

Prosecutors should anticipate that defense counsel will routinely file a motion in limine to suppress evidence obtained through a search warrant or court order. If the warrant or court order was obtained using the proper means and procedures used within a particular jurisdiction, these challenges are rarely successful. Challenges have been successful, however, when the warrant or order does not reflect the appropriate standard relevant to the warrant or order within a specific jurisdiction. For example,

[13] *Terry v. Ohio*, 392 U.S. 1, 24–25, 88 S. Ct. 1868, 20 L. Ed. 2d 889 (1968).

[14] *State v. Rodriguez*, 921 P. 2d 643 (Ariz. 1996); *People v. Madison*, 638 P. 2d 18, 32 (Colo. 1981); *Wise v. Murphy*, 275 A. 2d 05, 216 (D.C. Ct. App. 1971); *Baker v. State*, 449 N.E. 2d 1985, 1090 (Ind. 1983); *In re Order Requiring Fingerprinting of a Juvenile*, 537 N.E. 2d 186, 1288–1289 (Ohio 1989); *Bousman v. Iowa*, 630 N.W. 2d 789, 797 (Iowa 2001); *State v. Evans*, 338 N.W.2d 788 (Neb. 1983); *In re Nontestimonial Identification Order*, 762 A. 2d 1239, 1245 (Vt. 2000); *State v. Welch*, 342 S.E. 2d 789, 792 (N.C. 1989).

[15] *State v. Lamb*, 720 A. 2d 1101, 1102 (1998); *U.S. v. Sokolow*, 490 U.S. 1, 7; S. Ct. 1581, 104 L. Ed. 2d 1 (1989).

[16] *State v. Harris*, 490 N.W. 2d 561, 563 (Iowa 1992).

[17] *State v. Cline*, 617 N.W. 2d 277, 282 (Iowa 2000); *In re Nontestimonial Identification Order Directed to R.H.*, 762 A. 2d 1239, 1242 (Vt. 2000).

in *People v. Nache Afrika*,[22] the defendant was charged with robbery and sodomy in one county and sexual assault in a second county. Law enforcement in the second county obtained a blood sample through a court order. Prosecutors in the first county sought to use the second county's blood sample. A reviewing court in the first county determined that the order by which the sample had been obtained did not set forth the requisite probable cause standard linking the defendant in the sexual assault charge, and suppressed the evidence. The court determined that the blood draw was a search independent of the minimal seizure undertaken to facilitate it, and therefore collecting the sample and any resulting evidence could not be separated from the improper search and seizure.

In *Bousman v. Iowa*, the defendant filed a motion to quash a prior court order directing him to submit a buccal swab to law enforcement. Bousman claimed the order violated his constitutional protections and was issued in contravention of the authorizing statute, because the law enforcement agency's reasons for obtaining the order were "inadequate." The lower court disagreed, finding the application established reasonable grounds to suspect Bousman was involved in the commission of a felony. Bousman appealed. On appeal, the court found the underlying order was deficient because it did not include information required by the statute. The court ruled, therefore, that in the absence of the applicable reasonable grounds, the order violated both the relevant Iowa statute and the Fourth Amendment.[23]

The most successful defense challenge to forensic evidence obtained through a search warrant or court order typically is one in which the underlying order is flawed. Sometimes it is due to a technical error or when the relevant standard was not applied. While it is not always possible for prosecutors to fully review the underlying court order until a motion to suppress is filed, prosecutors should review these documents as soon as possible and evaluate how this will potentially impact the case. The inability to use forensic evidence obtained from an improperly compelled sample can be fatal to the prosecution's case.

Court-Ordered Samples from Third Parties

If a prosecutor or investigator proposes to compel a forensic sample from a third-party witness, it is essential that he or she be aware of the jurisdiction's controlling case law and ensure that the proper standards

[18] Rule 17(c) of the Federal Rules of Criminal Procedure.

[19] *Skinner v. Ry. Labor Executives' Ass'n*, 489 U.S. 602, 616, 109 S. Ct. 1402, 103 L. Ed. 2d 639 (1989); *Schmerber v. California*, 384 U.S. 757, 767, 86 S. Ct. 186, 16 L. Ed. 2d 908 (1966); *U.S. v. Mara*, 410 U.S. 19, 21, 93 S. Ct. 774, 35 L. Ed. 2d 99 (1973).

[20] *U.S. v. R. Enterprises, Inc.*, 498 U.S. 292, 297, 111 S. Ct. 722, 112 L. Ed. 2d 795 (1991).

[21] See *In re Subpoena Duces Tecum*, 228 F. Supp. 3d 341, 348 (4th Cir. 2000).

[22] *People v. Nache Afrika*, 738 N.Y.S. 2d 159 (2001).

[23] *Bousman v. Iowa*, 630 N.W. 2d 789 (2001).

are met in securing the sample. Courts continue to be split on the state's ability to compel forensic samples from third parties. For example, in *Commonwealth v. Nina M. Draheim*, the court commented that, because a defendant is entitled to compel a buccal swab from a third party, the state should have the same right. The court held that compelling physical evidence from the body of a third party not charged with a crime was within the scope of the permissible procedures, as long as the state satisfied the requirements of both the Fourth Amendment and the relevant Massachusetts statute.[24] Similarly, in *U.S. v. Pakala*, the court concluded that while requiring three third-party individuals to provide fingerprints or palm prints to the state might implicate their Fourth Amendments rights, the state had established probable cause to believe this information could be found on stolen firearms. Here, the uncharged third parties were suspected of being involved in a crime.[25]

In contrast, in *Register v. State*, the state requested a reference sample from the girlfriend of a murder suspect who claimed stains and hair found in his car belonged to his girlfriend rather than the victim.[26] The state sought the sample for comparison purposes, and the girlfriend refused. The lower court ordered the sample be obtained, and the girlfriend appealed. On appeal, the court ruled that in compelling any sample from a potential witness, the state must show probable cause that a crime has been committed and that it was committed by a particular suspect. Once both grounds are established, the state must then show (1) a clear indication that material evidence relevant to the question of the suspect's guilt will be found, and (2) that the method used to secure the evidence is safe and reliable. Unfortunately, in *Register*, the state failed to show that the girlfriend was a material witness or that the requested evidence was relevant to the question of the defendant's guilt.

A similar decision was handed down in *U.S. v. Noble*. The court denied a request to compel buccal swabs and fingerprints from two purportedly innocent third-party juveniles who were not suspected of any crime, but whose credibility the state wished to bolster as witnesses. Here the court denied the state's motion on the basis that the state was not seeking "evidence of a crime" but was seeking "evidence that tends to bolster other evidence that is evidence of a crime."[27]

[24] *Commonwealth v. Nina M. Draheim*, 849 N.E. 2d 83, citing to Jansen, petitioner, 825 N.E. 2d 186 (2005).

[25] *U.S. v. Pakala*, 329 F. Supp. 2d 178 (D. Mass. 2004).

[26] *Register v. State*, 419 S.E. 2d 771, (S.C. 1992).

[27] *U.S. v. Noble*, 433 F.2d 129 (2006).

Use of Force to Obtain Samples

Occasionally, the named individual refuses to comply with a properly issued search warrant or court order. Courts have held that an individual cannot resist a lawfully issued warrant and be rewarded by the exclusion of evidence. If law enforcement believes that a suspect will be uncooperative, a judge may authorize the use of a reasonable amount of force to obtain the sample. For example, in *U.S. v. Bullock*, the FBI properly obtained a search warrant to obtain samples of Bullock's hair and blood. Bullock refused and kicked, hit and attempted to bite seven members of the "control team" sent to issue the warrant. The court ruled that because Bullock was given multiple opportunities to comply with the warrant, the use of force needed in taking the samples was caused by his refusal and was therefore reasonable.[28]

In a similar case, North Carolina Department of Corrections officers sought to obtain blood samples from 13 state prison inmates to add to the state's databank.[29] The North Carolina General Assembly had previously passed legislation to establish the databank to assist law enforcement agencies in their effort to identify, detect or exclude individuals who were suspected of being involved in violent crimes against the person, and identify missing persons and victims of mass disasters.[30] Other states have enacted similar legislation for similar reasons, including deterring and discovering crimes and recidivistic criminal activity, identifying individuals for or excluding individuals from criminal investigation or prosecution, and searching for missing persons.[31] The inmates in *Sanders v. Coman* contended that officers used force to obtain their samples in violation of the Fourth, Eighth and Fourteenth amendments.[32] The court looked to *Jones v. Murray*, holding that inmates have no protected Fourth Amendment interest in officers drawing blood for DNA sampling.[33] In reviewing the Eight Amendment claim, the *Sanders* court noted that the Amendment prohibits the use of cruel and unusual punishment, and to successfully make this claim, the inmates would have to show that the challenged force was applied for the purpose of causing harm.[34] The court ruled that "ensuring compliance with a lawful order, such as the DNA sampling procedure, is a matter of institutional security and discipline." Therefore, the actual force used does not constitute cruel and unusual punishment simply because it caused pain to the inmates involved.[35] The court responded to the inmates' Fourteenth Amendment

[28] *U.S. v. Bullock*, 71 F. 3d 171 (1995).

[29] *Sanders v. Coman*, 864 F. Supp. 496 (1994).

[30] N.C. Gen. State. § 15A-226 et. seq. (1993).

[31] *Landry & others v. Attorney General & Others*, 709 N.E. 2d 1085,1087 (1999).

[32] *Sanders v. Coman*, 854 F. Supp. 496, 498 (N.C. 1994).

[33] *Jones v. Murray*, 962 F.2d 302 (4th Cir. 1992).

[34] *Hudson v. McMillian*, 503 U.S. 1, 112 S. Ct. 995, 117 L. Ed. 2d 156 (1992).

[35] *Sanders v. Coman*, 854 F. Supp. 496, 501 (N.C. 1994).

claim through the review provided by the U.S. Supreme Court in *Albright v. Oliver*, and concluded there was no separate due process inquiry regarding contentions involving the use of force.[36] Furthermore, the court cited *Ewell v. Murray*, indicating that an inmate's refusal to comply with DNA sampling may be treated as a refusal to comply with a direct order and may be enforced through the use of administrative penalties.[37] If the defense alleges the use of excessive force to obtain the forensic sample, prosecutors can check to determine if the procedure was taped, witnessed or otherwise documented and what, if any, other measures were taken to record the collection.

Federal law provides that the failure of individuals who have been convicted of certain federal crimes to provide federal authorities with tissue, fluid or other bodily sample on which the analysis of DNA identification information can be performed is a class A misdemeanor, punishable by up to one year's imprisonment and a fine of as much as $100,000. The federal law encompasses those who are incarcerated, or on parole, probation or supervised release.[38]

Sample Collection Is Not a Critical Stage of the Prosecution

The Sixth Amendment guarantees a criminal defendant the assistance of counsel at the initiation of adversary proceedings and at any subsequent "critical stage" thereafter.[39] After an indictment or formal charge is filed by the state, a defendant is guaranteed the presence of counsel at trial and at "any stage of the prosecution, formal or informal, in court or out, where counsel's absence might derogate from the accused's right to a fair trial."[40] Defendants have challenged the state's collection of forensic samples as a Sixth Amendment violation in instances where the collection takes place without defense counsel present.[41] For example, in *State v. Mata* the defendant was arrested and charged with sexual assault, and a public defender was appointed to represent him. An investigator from the district attorney's office requested Mata's consent to take a blood sample, and he agreed. The public defender was not notified regarding the investigator's contact with Mata. Mata later successfully filed a motion to suppress the DNA evidence, alleging the blood draw violated his Sixth Amendment right to counsel, and all reports relating to his sample were suppressed. On appeal, the court reversed and determined that an individual's right to counsel attaches

[36] *Albright v. Oliver*, 510 U.S. 266, 114 S. Ct. 807, 127 L. Ed. 2d 114 (1994).

[37] *Ewell v. Murray*, 11 F. 3d 482 (4th Cir. 1993).

[38] 42 U.S.C. §14135a(a)5; 18 U.S.C. §§ 3571 & 3581. n.3; *U.S. v. Kincade*.

[39] U.S. Const. VI amend. Article I §9; *Estelle v. Smith*, 451 U.S. 454, 101 S. Ct. 1866 68 L. Ed. 2d 359 (1981); *Thompson v. State*, 93 S.W. 3d 16 (Tex. Crim. App. 2001).

[40] *U.S. v. Wade*, 388 U.S. 218, 87 S. Ct. 1926, 18 L. Ed. 2d (1967).

[41] *State v. Mata*, 30 S.W. 3d 486 (Tex. Crim. App. 2000); *U.S. v. Hubbard*, 2007 U.S. Dist. LEXIS 3377 (January 2007).

when the state initiates adversarial proceedings and that the sample collection was not a critical stage of the pretrial proceeding, in part because a second sample could be drawn with counsel present later if necessary for trial.[42]

The analysis as to when an attorney should be present is dependent on whether at a particular stage or event the attorney is necessary to "assure fairness and the effective assistance of counsel."[43] Courts have identified "critical stages" of the proceedings at which the right to have counsel present attaches, including preliminary hearings and postindictment lineups.[44] A pretrial stage is not considered critical, however, when "confrontation with counsel at trial can serve as a substitute for counsel at the pretrial confrontation."[45] Courts have found that, because an accused has an opportunity for a meaningful confrontation of the state's case at trial through the ordinary process of direct examination and cross-examination of expert witnesses, taking a forensic sample without counsel present is not a violation of the accused's Sixth Amendment rights.[46] The court in *Mata* found that the sample would have inevitably been available to the state in due course, and that by taking the sample no new evidence was uncovered that did not already exist. Furthermore, the court ruled, Mata could confront the validity of the blood sample evidence later at trial.[47]

The Court in *U.S. v. Wade* ruled that other acts of evidence gathering, such as analyzing fingerprints, blood samples, clothing or hair, are not critical stages in the proceedings. In addition, other courts have held that collecting a DNA sample is analogous to taking a handwriting exemplar, and thus is not a critical stage in the proceedings.[48] Other courts have expanded on this ruling, saying that because the collection of DNA samples is done pursuant to established standards or practices, if subsequently there is a need to collect a second sample, the circumstances used in the collection procedure can easily be reconstructed.[49]

DNA Sampling Does Not Implicate the Fifth Amendment

The Fifth Amendment to the Constitution states that no person shall "be compelled in any criminal case to be a witness against himself." The Supreme Court has held that the privilege against self-incrimination extends no further than communication that is testimonial. DNA, like

[42] *Powell v. Alabama*, 287 U.S. 45, 57, 53 S. Ct. 55, 77 L. Ed. 158 (1932); *U.S. v. Wade*, 388 U.S. 218, 236, 87 S. Ct. 1926, 18 L. Ed. 2d 1149 (1967).

[43] *U.S. v. Ash*, 43 U.S. 300, 309, 93 S. Ct. 2568, 37 L. Ed. 2d 619 (1973); *Green v. State*, 872 S.W. 2d 717, 720 (Tex. Crim. App. 1994).

[44] *Tennessee v. Blye*, 130 S.W. 3d 776 (2004), *Coleman v. Alabama*, 399 U.S. 1, 9, 90 S. Ct. 1999, 26 L. Ed. 2d 387 (1970); *U.S. v. Wade*, 388 U.S. 218, 236, 87 S. Ct. 1926, 18 L. Ed. 2d 1149 (1967).

[45] *U.S. v. Ash*, 413 U.S 300, 316, 93 S. Ct. 2568, 37 L. Ed. 29 619 (1973).

[46] *U.S. v. Hubbard*, 2007 U.S. Dist. Lexis 3377 (Kansas 2007); *Hale v. Texas*, 220 S.W. 3d 180 (2007).

[47] *State v. Mata*, 30 S.W. 3d 486, 488 (Tex. Crim. App. 2000).

[48] *U.S. v. Wade*, 388 U.S. 218, 87 S. Ct. 1926, 18 L. Ed. 2d 1149 (1967); *Rose v. State*, 711 S.W. 2d 89 (Tex. App.-Dallas, 1989).

fingerprints or a blood sample, is nontestimonial. Thus there is no violation of the Fifth Amendment privilege when DNA evidence is lawfully obtained.[50]

Exceptions to the Search Warrant Requirement

There Are Several Different Levels of Citizen Privacy Expectation

It is well established that law enforcement taking a blood sample constitutes a search and seizure under the Fourth Amendment.[51] Unless a search falls within certain well-established exceptions to the warrant requirement, the Fourth Amendment prohibits "warrantless searches of any place or thing in which a person has a reasonable expectation of privacy."[52] Several exceptions allow officers to collect samples without a warrant, including consent, search incident to a valid arrest, inventory searches, plain view and *Terry* investigative stops.[53] In addition, the courts have held that evidence collected under the inevitable discovery doctrine, if obtained without a warrant, is admissible.

In the event the state obtains evidence from a search conducted pursuant to one of the exceptions, the state bears the burden of establishing that the exception applies, generally by a preponderance of the evidence.[54] In immediate hazard situations, law enforcement must show that, because of the existence of an actual emergency, the search and seizure was necessary to prevent the imminent destruction of any evidence, protect law enforcement officers or others, or prevent the escape of a suspect.[55] Prosecutors should be cautious in arguing the "special needs" exception for DNA collection unless the needs are obvious.[56]

Subsequent to the federal DNA Analysis Backlog Elimination Act and similar state DNA collection statutes, different levels of privacy expectations have been identified for the general public, arrestees, convicted offenders and probationers. Each has different criteria for "reasonableness" in the warrantless collection of forensic samples,[57] and the levels of law enforcement's permission to detain individuals varies according to these levels of privacy expectations. For example, the members of the general public are entitled to the highest level of expectation of privacy.[58] Courts have noted the "obvious and significant distinction between DNA profiling of law-abiding citizens" and lawfully adjudicated criminals.[59] Absent a warrant, court order, an individual's consent or other lawful

[49] *U.S. v. Hubbard*, 2007 U.S. Dist. LEXIS 3377 (2007); *U.S. v. Pridgen*, 41 Fed. App. 103 (9th Cir. 2002); *Wilson v. Commonwealth*, 2006 Va. App. LEXIS 243 (2006).

[50] *Schmerber v. California*, 384 U.S. 757 (1966); *United States v. Wade*, 388 U.S. 218 (1967).

[51] *Schmerber v. California*, 384 U.S. 757, 86 S. Ct. 1826, 16 L. Ed 2d 908 (1966); *Russey v. State*, 985 S.W.2d 316 (1999).

[52] *Mincey v. Arizona*, 437 U.S. 385, 390, 98 S. Ct. 2408, 57 L. Ed. 2d 290 (1978); *Sheler v. Commonwealth*, 566 S.E. 2d 203 (2002).

[53] *Terry v. Ohio*, 392 U.S. 1, 88 S. Ct. 1868, 20 L. Ed. 2 889 (1968), *Washington v. Ladson*, 979 P.2d 833 (1999).

[54] *U.S. v. Basinski*, 226 F. 3d 829 (2000); *Schneckloth v. Bustamonte*, 412 U.S. 218, 93 S.Ct. 2041, 36 L. Ed. 2d 854 (1973).

[55] *Britton v. Beauchaine et al.*, 2003 Mich. App. LEXIS 2804 (1993).

exception, law enforcement has limited justification for detaining members of the general public who are not linked in some way to a criminal matter as a victim, witness or suspect.

An exception can be made in a situation in which only identifying information was gathered, such as fingerprints or a DNA sample, provided no interrogation or other more intrusive procedure is conducted. For example, in *Davis v. Mississippi*, the Supreme Court acknowledged the possibility that detentions conducted only for the purpose of identifying evidence may be permissible without violating constitutional protections.[60] In *Davis* a rape victim reported that a "Negro youth" broke into her home and assaulted her. Without obtaining warrants, law enforcement officers detained 24 Negro youths, questioned and fingerprinted them before releasing them without charging them with any criminal activity. Davis's fingerprints matched those found in the victim's home, and he was subsequently convicted. On appeal, the state court affirmed, stating that fingerprint evidence was sufficiently reliable that the Fourth Amendment exclusionary rule did not apply.

The Supreme Court reversed, stating that no evidence, no matter how reliable, was admissible if it was the product of an unreasonable search and seizure. However, the Court left open the possibility that arrests made solely for the purpose of fingerprinting may conform to Fourth Amendment guidelines. The Court stated that "[d]etention for fingerprinting may constitute a much less serious intrusion upon personal security than other types of police searches and detentions. Fingerprinting involves none of the probing into an individual's private life and thoughts that marks an interrogation or search."[61] In addition, because the information obtained from fingerprints does not change over time, the Court found that a limited detention for the purpose of fingerprinting need not be done unexpectedly or at an inconvenient time for the suspect, and was therefore not overly burdensome. Similarly, in *Hayes v. Florida,* a case dealing with a suspect accompanying law enforcement officers to the police station to be fingerprinted, the Supreme Court held open the possibility that a brief detention in the field for the purpose of obtaining fingerprints might have been permissible.[62]

Taken together, the Supreme Court rulings in *Davis* and *Hayes* suggest the following propositions: (1) if law enforcement has lawfully detained an

[56] *U.S. v. Martinez-Fuerte*, 428 U.S. 543, 562, 96 S. Ct. 3074, 49 L. Ed. 2d 1116 (1976); *Ferguson v. City of Charleston*, 532 U.S. 67, 79, 121 S. Ct. 1281, 139 L. Ed. 2d 205 (2000).

[57] 42 U.S.C. § 14135a ("Federal DNA Act"), *U.S. v. Sczubelek*, 402 F. 3d 813 (9th Cir. 2005); *Groceman v. U.S. Dep't of Justice*, 354 F. 23d 411 (5th Cir. 2004); *Green v. Berge*, 354 F. 3d 675 (7th Cir. 2004); *U.S. v. Kimler* 335 F. 3d 1132 (10th Cir 2003); *Velasquez v. Woods*, 329 F. 3d 420 (5th Cir. 2003); *Roe v. Marcotte*, 193 F. 3d 72 (2d Cir. 1999); *Schlicher v. Peters*, 103 F. 3d 940 (10th Cir. 1996); *Boling v. Rober*, 101 F. 3d 1336 (10th Cir. 1997); *Jones v. Murray*, 962 F. 2d 302 (4th Cir. 1992).

[58] *Green v. Berge*, 354 F. 3d 675, 679 (7th Cir. 2004).

[59] *U.S. v. Kincade*, 379 F. 3d 813, 835 (9th Cir. 2005).

[60] *Davis v. Mississippi*, 394 U.S. 721 (1969).

[61] *Davis v. Mississippi*, 394 U.S. 721 (1969).

[62] *Hayes v. Florida*, 470 U.S. 811 (1985).

individual, it may be legal to take a DNA sample at the crime scene if the collection is conducted in a reasonable manner; (2) in the absence of either probable cause or reasonable suspicion, the donor must validly consent to giving law enforcement officers a forensic sample; and (3) if there is no probable cause to arrest an individual or other applicable standard or exception, any DNA evidence collected as a result is unlawful. The Ninth Circuit applied the *Hayes* reasoning to DNA evidence, holding that "information derived from the blood sample is substantially the same as that derived from fingerprinting—an identifying marker.[63]

The federal government and several states have established another exception to the warrant requirement; they have adopted statutes authorizing the warrantless collection of forensic samples from all or certain categories of arrestees.[64] Prosecutors should be aware of the scope of the controlling statutes on this issue. Absent such statutory authority, the defense may successfully challenge a warrantless arrestee DNA collection on the grounds that the arrestee's DNA will not change over the brief time necessary to obtain a search warrant, and thus its acquisition is not time sensitive.[65] When the DNA in question is not from the defendant but on the defendant, however, a warrantless collection may be allowed. For example, while Montana has not addressed per se arrestee DNA collection, in *State v. Madplume* the appellate court reversed the lower court's suppression of the warrantless swabbing of an arrestee's hand. Madplume was arrested on several misdemeanor charges and transported to a drunk tank. While he was there, a victim came forward and stated that Madplume had sexually assaulted and digitally penetrated her. Officers awakened Madplume and swabbed his hands and fingers for DNA evidence which, upon analysis, matched the victim's DNA. The trial court concluded that the circumstances of the case did not justify the warrantless swabbing of Madplume's hands. On appeal, the state argued that the DNA evidence collected was transient, evanescent and highly destructible, and that the DNA evidence the state sought was not from Madplume himself, but evidence he could easily have destroyed by washing or licking his hands. In reversing the lower court, the court noted that the purpose of allowing warrantless searches was to prevent an arrestee from "destroying incriminating evidence in his or her possession," and therefore the evidence obtained from the sample was admitted.

[63] *Rise v. Oregon*, 59 F. 3d 1556 (9th Cir. 1995).

[64] 42 USCS 14135a; Cal. Pen. Code 296 (2001); La. R.S. 15609 (2006); Minn. State. 299C.105 (2006); M.M Stat. Ann. 29.3-3-20 (2007); Tex. Gov't Code 411.1471 (2006); Va. Code Ann. 19.2-310.2-1 (2006).

[65] *U.S. v. Purdy*, 2005 U.S. Dist. LEXIS 40433 (December 2005).

To date, all 50 states have enacted DNA collection statutes requiring some or all convicted felons to submit to warrantless sample collection of blood, saliva or other tissue for DNA profile analysis and storage in a DNA databank.[66] Convicted offenders have rarely been successful in challenging the reasonableness of warrantless collection pursuant to the state or federal DNA collection statutes. Most courts use either a balancing test evaluation or a "special needs" analysis to evaluate the challenge. Those courts that use a balancing analysis typically conduct a two-phase evaluation of reasonableness of the collection, balancing the convicted offender's privacy interests against the government's interest in the identity of convicted persons.[67] The evaluation starts with the premise that those convicted, unlike other citizens, have a diminished expectation of privacy in their identity.[68] The courts have held that "once a person is convicted of [a serious crime] his identity has become a matter of state interest and he has lost any legitimate expectation of privacy in the identifying information derived from the blood sampling."[69] Courts using this test have frequently ruled that convicted persons and probationers have a "lesser expectation of privacy than the public at large".[70] Following this analysis, courts in the federal circuits as well as many state courts have found that drawing blood from a prisoner without a warrant and using it later in a DNA databank does not constitute an unreasonable search.[71]

Other state courts have taken a different approach to the warrantless sample collection from prisoners, and applied a "special needs" test for both the collection and inclusion of the resulting DNA profile in a DNA databank.[72] "Special needs" exceptions are intended to apply to situations outside of regular law enforcement activities, such as drug testing individuals whose job performance affects public safety. Using this analysis, the court in *Vore v. U.S. DOJ* held that the state's DNA databank statute passed the "special needs" test, because the purpose of the statute was to fill the federal DNA databank, rather than to provide evidence of the commission of a crime.[73] The court also held that collecting blood samples from prisoners was a minimal intrusion on the convicted offender's privacy interests in contrast to the significant government interest in populating the DNA databank, and was therefore not unreasonable.

Challenges to the warrantless collection of forensic samples of probationers have also been unsuccessful, with most courts following the

[66] *State v. Raines*, 857 A. 2d 19, 22 (Md. 2004).

[67] *Landry & others, v. Attorney General & Others*, 709 N.E. 2d 1085 (1999).

[68] *Jones M. Murray*, 5-6 U.S. 977, 113 S. Ct. 472, 121 L. Ed. 2d 378 (1992).

[69] *Rise v. State*, 59 F. 3d 1556, 1560, (9th Cir. 1995).

[70] *Ferguson v. City of Charleston*, 532 U.S. 67, 121 S. Ct. 1281, 149 L. Ed. 2d 205 (2000). *States v. Knights*, 534 U.S. 112, 118, 122 S. Ct. 587, 591, 151 L. Ed. 2d 497 (2001).

[71] *Shaffer v. Saffle*, 148 F. 3d 1180, 1181 (10th Cir. 1998); *Rise v. Oregon*, 59 F. 3d 1556, 1560 (9th Cir. 1995); *Jones v. Murray*, 962 F. 2d 302 (4th Cir. 1992; *Padgett v. Ferrero*, 294 F. Supp. 2d 1338 (N.D. Ga 2004); *Smalley v. State*, 889 So. 2d 100 (Fla. Dist. Ct. App. 2004); *Smalley v. State*, 889 So. 2d 100 (Fla. Dist. Ct. App. 2004); *People v. Ramos*, 353 Ill. App. 3d 133, 817 N.E. 2d 1110, 288 Ill. Dec. 460 (Ill. App. Ct. 2004); *State v. Surge*, 94 P. 3d 345 (Wash. Ct. App. 2004).

general thinking that "[p]arolees and other conditional releasees are not entitled to the full panoply of rights and protections enjoyed by the general public.[74] In a "special needs" evaluation, courts balance the goals of rehabilitation and protection of society against the probationer's diminished expectation of privacy.[75]

Inevitable Discovery

When none of the exceptions are applicable to the warrantless collection, the doctrine of inevitable discovery may apply. The doctrine of "inevitable discovery" enables the admittance of evidence that otherwise might be suppressed if the state shows, by a preponderance of the evidence, that the evidence would have inevitably been discovered by a lawful means during the course of the crime's investigation.[76] The state has the burden of showing that the information would inevitably have been obtained by the investigating officers. In order to proactively address or limit issues that the defense will raise on appeal, prosecutors can show on the record how the evidence in question would have been discovered during the natural course of the investigation.[77]

For example, in 1997 James Haynes was incarcerated for nonpayment of child support, and a blood sample was collected and entered into the state's databank. In August 2000, Haynes was convicted of a residential burglary and scheduled to be released on parole in December 2001. At the time of his conviction, the state statute that mandated DNA collection from convicted offenders did not extend to residential or commercial burglaries. At the time of his conviction in 2000, law enforcement was also investigating a residential burglary in which a 94-year-old woman was raped. The state crime lab processed a ski mask and other evidence found at the crime scene and entered the profile obtained into the state's DNA database. A positive hit came back to Haynes's profile that was entered from the 1997 blood sample. Using the hit as probable cause, the state then sought to obtain a confirmatory blood sample from Haynes. At trial, Haynes argued that the 1997 blood sample was illegally obtained and entered into the state databank, because in 1997, a conviction for nonpayment of child support did not qualify one for inclusion in the databank. Furthermore, he argued that without the database hit, the state would not have identified him as a suspect in the rape. He was convicted. On appeal, the Supreme Court of Arkansas found that the state would have inevitably

[72] *Green v. Berge*, 354 F. 3d 675 (7th Cir. 2004); *Roe v. Marcotte*, 193 F. 3d 72, 77 (2d Cir. 1999); *U.S. v. Kimler*, 335 F. 3d 1132 (10th Cir. 1983); *Balding v. State*, 812 N.E. 2d 169 (Ind. Ct. App. 2004); *In re D.L.C.*, 124 S.W. 3d 354 (Tex. Ct. App. 2003); *State v. Olivas*, 856 P. 2d 1076 (Wash. 1993); *Doles v. State*, 994 P. 2d 315 (Wyo. 1999).

[73] *Vore v. U.S. DOJ*, 281 F. Supp. 2d 1129, 1133 (D. Ariz. 2003).

[74] *U.S. v. Kincade*, 379 F. 3d 813, 830; (9th Cir. 2005).

[75] *Griffin v. Wisconsin*, 483 U.S. 868, 875, 107 S. Ct. 3164, 97 L. Ed. 2d 709 (1987, *U.S. v. Knights*, 534 U.S. 112, 115, 122 S. Ct. 587, 151 L. Ed. 2d 497 (2001).

[76] *Illinois v. Lidster* 540 U.S. 419, 428, 124 S. Ct. 885, 157 L. Ed. 2d 843 (2004); *Wilson v. Maryland*, 75 A. 2d 1250 (2000); *Michigan Dep't of State Police v. Sitz*, 496 U.S. 444, 455, 110 S. Ct. 2481, 110 L. Ed. 2d 412 (1990); *Delaware v. Prouse*, 440 U.S. 648, 663, 99 S. Ct. 1391, 59 L. Ed. 2d 660 (1979).

discovered the match between the rape scene evidence and Haynes's profile for two reasons. First, in 2001 the act authorizing the collection of blood and entry of profiles obtained into the state's databank was expanded to include residential burglaries committed on or after August 1, 1997. Second, as a condition of his parole in December 2001, Haynes's blood sample would have been collected pursuant to the statute. Therefore, the court ruled it was inevitable that the state would have matched Haynes's sample to the rape evidence.

The Standard for and Extent of Consent

Another means by which law enforcement can lawfully collect a DNA sample from a nonsuspect, free individual is through consent. A person may voluntarily waive his or her Fourth Amendment rights, thus eliminating the need for officers to obtain a search warrant or court order when obtaining a forensic sample from an individual.[78] In some cases, officers may seek a voluntary sample to exclude an individual from an investigation. For example, in a sexual assault case, a voluntary sample may be obtained from a consensual partner to aid in the analysis of a mixed sample or to identify an individual as a suspect.

A freely-given, voluntary consent is adequate justification for obtaining a sample that would otherwise constitute an illegal search and seizure.[79] In obtaining the consent, law enforcement is not required to notify the suspect that he or she has a right to refuse.[80] As long as the suspect is not coerced into providing the sample, the sample is considered lawfully obtained. Law enforcement should avoid making statements that might lead a suspect to believe that he or she had a legal duty to provide officers with a sample. If the court finds that unreasonable threats, force or deceit was used on the part of law enforcement in obtaining the donor's consent, the evidence obtained from the consent will be excluded.[81] Often a defendant will claim that his or her consent was not freely given to officers. If possible, law enforcement should document the voluntary consent through a written consent form, rather than merely relying on verbal consent.

The standard used in evaluating whether the consent was voluntary is a reasonableness analysis as construed through the eyes of the law enforcement officer conducting the search. Thus, the analysis hinges on whether an objective law enforcement officer reasonably believed that the donor's consent was voluntary after looking at the totality of the circumstances.[82]

[77] *Hayes v. Arkansas*, 127 S.W. 3d 456 (2003); *State v. Notti*, 71 P. 3d 1233 (2003).

[78] *U.S. v. Matlock*, 415 164, 171; 94 S. Ct. 988; 39 L. Ed. 2d 242 (1974).

[79] *Zap v. United States*, 328 U.S. 624 (1946).

[80] *Schneckloth v. Bustamonte*, 412 U.S. 218 (1972).

[81] *Bumper v. North Carolina*, 391 U.S. 543; 88 S. Ct. 1788; 20 L. Ed. 2d 797 (1968).

[82] LaFave, 1987.

The court reviews a number of factors in evaluating whether duress or coercion was present. These include the consenting party's vulnerability, age, education, intelligence, knowledge of his or her right to refuse consent, as well as the physical environment in which the consent was sought.[83] Thus, a lawfully obtained consent negates law enforcement's need to acquire a warrant, and the controlling test is whether the consent was given voluntarily.[84] In considering the totality of the circumstances, the court will evaluate whether the state's need to conduct the search outweighs the impact the search will have on the donor's privacy.[85]

Law enforcement officials can maximize the usefulness of a DNA sample by searching the CODIS databanks for matching samples among convicted offenders or crime scene samples. This creates a situation in which the DNA sample is used to investigate many crimes other than the one for which the DNA sample was initially obtained. The courts have held that voluntary consent implies that the suspect knows what he or she is allowing law enforcement officers to do with his or her DNA sample.[86] When a consent form is used to obtain a confirmatory sample, it is a good practice to place no limitations on the use of the sample in either the present or future investigations. Jurisdictional rules may vary according to the scope of the consent form and future use of profiles. Prosecutors should communicate with law enforcement investigators to determine the language and scope of any consent form used to obtain forensic samples. A sample consent form is provided in Appendix IV.

The legality of future use of consent samples rests on the language used to obtain the consent. Privacy concerns no longer exist after the sample has been lawfully removed from the individual's body, because the subsequent forensic analysis does not involve an additional search and seizure of the donor. Like fingerprints, there is no constitutional violation of privacy when a sample that was lawfully obtained for use in one case is used in connection with another case.[87] The courts have held that this is justified on the same grounds that lawfully collected photographs, handwriting exemplars and ballistics tests obtained in the course of one investigation are available to law enforcement for subsequent and unrelated investigations without a new Fourth Amendment intrusion being involved. For example, in *Wilson v. State*, the court stated: "Once an individual's ... blood sample for DNA testing [is] in lawful police possession, that individual is no more immune from being caught by the

[83] Grande, 2002.

[84] *Zap v. U.S.*, 38 U.S. 624; 66 S. Ct. 1277; 90 L. Ed. 2d 854 (1973); *Florida v. Jimeno*, 500 U.S. 248 (1991); *Schneckloth v. Bustamonte*, 412 U.S. 28 (1973); Greenhalgh, 1995.

[85] *U.S. v. Kincade*, 379 F. 3d 813 (9th Cir. 2004).

[86] *Florida v. Jimeno*, 500 U.S. 248 (1991).

[87] *Bickley v. State*, 489 S.E. 2d 167 (1997); *People v. Baylor*, 118 Cal. Rptr. 2d 518 (2002); *Wilson v. State*, 752 A. 2d 1250 (Md. 2000); *Patterson v. State*, 744 N.E. 2d 945 (Ind. Ct. App. 2001).

DNA sample he leaves on the body of his rape victim than he is from being caught by the fingerprint he leaves on the window of the burglarized house or the steering wheel of the stolen car."[88]

Unless the case is dismissed or prosecution is declined, there is no constitutional provision or legal precedents regarding the disposition of a lawfully obtained blood sample. A criminal defendant does not have a right to the automatic return of any property seized in a criminal proceeding without a proper demand or appropriate legal action.[89] When a forensic lab derives a DNA profile from a lawfully drawn blood sample, most courts have ruled that the resulting profile becomes the property of the crime lab, thus negating the donor's property interest in it.[90]

DNA Dragnets

DNA dragnets involve the consensual collection of biological samples from a group of individuals who fall within a nexus of qualities, for example, gender, age, race and geographic region, to assist law enforcement in the investigation of a crime. Thus, dragnets involve the collection of DNA from a number of individuals who fit the general description of an as yet unidentified suspect. They have been used when law enforcement has been unsuccessful in developing investigative leads through more traditional means. Individuals who fall within the scope of the dragnet usually live or work within the crime scene's general geographic area.[91] Because the samples are collected without a warrant, probable cause or reasonable suspicion, law enforcement must ensure that each consent is voluntary and not prompted by coercion.[92]

The first use of a DNA dragnet was in a small village in England in 1986. In investigating the rape and murder of two teenage girls, law enforcement officers obtained voluntary biological samples from men between the ages of 17 and 34. Approximately 4,000 men voluntarily provided samples. Colin Pitchfork, however, attempted to have another man provide a sample under his name. After the second man was overheard telling someone that he had provided a sample for Pitchfork, an authentic sample was obtained from Pitchfork, and he was identified as the perpetrator of the crime. Subsequent to this success, approximately 300 DNA dragnets have been conducted in the U.K., and the practice has been successfully applied in both Germany and France to identify criminals and solve crimes.

[88] *Wilson v. State*, 752 A. 2d 1250 (Md. 2000).

[89] *People v. King*, 232 A.D. 2d 111 (1997).

[90] *People v. Baylor*, 118 Cal. Rptr. 2d 518 (2002); *Smith v. State*, 44 N.E. 2d 437 (Ind. 2001).

[91] Rothstein and Talbot, 2006.

[92] *Schneckloth v. Bustamonte*, 412 U.S. 218 (1973).

The Fourth Amendment does not prevent law enforcement officers from approaching citizens and requesting their cooperation in providing a DNA sample. Case law has long held that contact between officers and citizens of the community is permitted without the use of formal search warrants in order for law enforcement to request the voluntary contribution of forensic samples. Provided the consent is lawfully obtained and there is no coercion on the part of law enforcement, officers may collect these samples for typing.[93]

The first dragnet conducted in the United States is thought to have taken place in San Diego in 1990, when law enforcement tested more than 800 African American men in an attempt to identify an individual who had stabbed six people to death. Since 1990, less than 20 DNA dragnets have been conducted to assist investigators.[94] In the few cases in which dragnets have been conducted in the United States, investigators had only had a general description of a suspected perpetrator to go on and therefore had to conduct the dragnet without a particularized suspicion as to a specific suspect. If a suspect is subsequently identified through samples obtained from the DNA dragnet, the prosecutor should be prepared for defense counsel to challenge the voluntariness of the consent. The court will apply a totality of the circumstances analysis to evaluate the voluntary nature of the consent. Ideally, before a DNA dragnet is conducted, the prosecutor should review with investigators the requirements of voluntary consent and provide a written consent form that will overcome potential defense challenges. A good practice is to include language in the consent form indicating that the reader is voluntarily providing the sample and is aware of his or her right to refuse.

Abandoned Samples

During the process of investigating a crime, law enforcement may not want to alert the suspect that he or she is under suspicion by contacting them to obtain a sample by consent or warrant. The Fourth Amendment does not prohibit the seizure of property that has been voluntarily abandoned.[95] Property has been held to be voluntarily abandoned if (1) the suspect intended to abandon it and (2) the suspect's decision to abandon the property was not due to police misconduct.[96] In cases where an officer has reasonable suspicion that someone was involved in a particular crime, officers may attempt to obtain the suspect's sample without engaging the

[93] *Davis v. Mississippi*, 394 U.S. 721, 89 S. Ct. 1394, 2 L. Ed. 2d 676 (1969).

[94] Esmaili, 2007.

[95] *Abel v. United States*, 362 U.S. 217, 80 S. Ct. 683, 4 L.Ed. 2d 668 (1960); *Mouton v. State*, 101 S.W. 3d 686 (Tex. App.—Texarkana 2003).

[96] *Shelly v. State*, 101 S.W. 3d 606 (Tex. App.-Houston 2003); *Brimage v. State*, 918 S.W. 2d 466 (Tex. Crim. App. 1994).

suspect. In many instances law enforcement has successfully collected abandoned samples such as coffee cups or glasses at a restaurant, discarded cigarette butts or Kleenex tissues, or garbage left for regular curbside collection.[97] When a suspect abandons an item or object in a public place, he or she no longer has a reasonable expectation of privacy in the discarded material. Thus, when the item or object is subsequently seized by law enforcement, there is no implication of either invasion of privacy or federal constitutional right.[98]

The Supreme Court established a general analysis as to whether the state's collection of evidence constituted an unreasonable search and seizure under the Fourth Amendment in *Katz v. United States*.[99] In *Katz* the state sought to acquire evidence by attaching an electronic listening and recording device to the outside of a telephone booth. The state argued that, because the listening device involved no physical intrusion and was installed in a public place, no Fourth Amendment violation took place. The Court ruled, however, that the Amendment protects people and not places, and that an individual has a reasonable momentary expectation of privacy inside a closed phone booth. In contrast, the Court in *California v. Greenwood* ruled that the Fourth Amendment does not enjoin the state from a warrantless search of discarded garbage left in a public place. The reasoning in *Greenwood* followed that by abandoning material, an individual also abandons any expectation of privacy attached to it.[100] The *Greenwood* court also held that an individual has the option to destroy sensitive materials before discarding them if the individual chooses to do so.

Two recent cases illustrate limitations on law enforcement's involvement in collecting forensic material and the need for investigators to avoid manipulating the abandonment process. In *Commonwealth v. Cabral*, a mentally challenged victim had been raped, and Cabral was included in the individuals being investigated because he had worked for the victim's family and had had access to the victim. The victim later delivered a child. A law enforcement officer on sick leave was hired by the victim's family to investigate the suspect covertly. The officer devised a ruse whereby the suspect was contracted to do some plumbing work at the home of a third party. While outside the building, the suspect spat on the sidewalk. This spittle was recovered, and DNA testing implicated Cabral. Cabral moved to suppress the evidence collected

[97] *Commonwealth v. Ewing*, 857 N.E. 2d 1094 (2006); *California v. Greenwood*, 486 U.S. 35, 39; 108 S. Ct. 165, 100 L. Ed. 2d 30 (1988); *Abel v. United States*, 362 U.S. 217, 241; 80 S. Ct. 683; 4 L. Ed. 2d 668 (1960).

[98] *California v. Hodari D.*, 449 U.S. 621 (1991).

[99] *Katz v. United States*, 389 U.S. 347; 108 S. Ct. 1625, 100 L. Ed. 2d 30 (1988).

[100] *Greenwood v. California*, 486 U.S. 35, 88 S. Ct. 507, 19 L. Ed. 2d 576 (1967).

[101] *Commonwealth v. Cabral*, 866 N.E. 2d 429 (2007).

[102] *Coolidge v. New Hampshire*, 403 U.S. 443, 484, 91 S. Ct. 2022, 29 L. Ed. 2d 564 (1971).

[103] *North Carolina v. Reed*, 631 S.E. 2d 320 (2007).

from his saliva and asserted an expectation of privacy claim. The court ruled that Cabral had no expectation of privacy in his saliva once he abandoned it voluntarily on a public sidewalk. On appeal, Cabral argued that the sample had been obtained as a result of a ruse devised by a state actor, thereby violating his constitutional rights. The court ruled that while Cabral had a reasonable expectation of privacy in his bodily fluids, once he expectorated in a public place and did not retrieve the fluids, he voluntarily abandoned that protection and assumed the risk of the public taking possession of his bodily fluids. The court also held that Cabral's spitting in a public area had no meaningful connection to the ruse that led him to the residence for a plumbing job, even though, but for the job, he would not have been on that particular public street.[101] Furthermore, the court held that when a person abandons an item voluntarily, collecting that sample does not constitute a search or seizure within the purview of the Fourth Amendment.[102] Prosecutors should be aware of the limitations on how far the state can reach in collecting discarded property, and ensure that these bounds are not overextended. By carefully reviewing all portions of a case file before charges are filed, a prosecutor can determine if some of the evidence or collection procedures are tainted.

In *North Carolina v. Reed,*[103] officers were investigating a burglary, robbery and sexual offense crime and went to a suspect's home to request he provide a DNA sample. The suspect agreed, but upon second thought told the officers he would like to reconsider the matter for 24 hours. While talking with the officers, a young woman entered the apartment and officers asked the suspect to continue their conversation in a more private setting. They stepped outside to a small patio in the back of the residence and continued their conversation. The defendant smoked a cigarette and after putting it out, pulled the butt apart, removed the filter's wrapper paper and shredded the filter before putting the debris in his pocket, telling officers he watched *CSI: Crime Scene Investigation,* a popular television entertainment program. During the conversation, the suspect smoked another cigarette, which he flicked into a pile of trash in the corner of the backyard patio. The butt struck the trash and rolled between the suspect and an officer who then kicked the butt off the patio into a grassy common area. The suspect and one officer went inside, and the second officer collected the still burning butt. Forensic analysis indicated a match between the biological sample collected from the butt and a stain found on the victim's shirt.

The suspect moved to suppress the evidence collected from the butt on the basis of a reasonable expectation of privacy on his patio, but the trial court denied his motion. On appeal, the court reversed the lower court's ruling, stating that the butt was removed from the curtilage of the home when the officer kicked it off the patio and into the common area. The officer's action failed to overcome the individual's reasonable expectation of privacy. Furthermore, the "furtive nature of the seizure raised a suspicion that the detective was aware that defendant would not consent to his taking the butt." The court held that while this expectation might have been overcome had the suspect placed the butt in the common area, officers may not remove evidence from the curtilage and proceed as though the evidence had been left open to the public by the defendant.[104] Prosecutors should review all the circumstances under which abandoned evidence is obtained to evaluate the case prior to indictment.

Third-Party Collection

Biological samples are collected every day for a variety of purposes, including employment applications, paternity tests, medical diagnoses, missing person and military identification, and participation in sports. These samples are taken by medical personnel, military personnel and private individuals. As of 1998, the National Bioethics Advisory Commission estimated that more than 282 million samples of human biological material were stored in the United States and that more than 20 million samples were expected to be added each year.[105] These samples are stored in a variety of institutions, including academic laboratories, commercial laboratories, teaching hospitals and armed forces' repositories of pathology specimens. Questions have been raised as to whether DNA samples collected for routine purposes might later be used by law enforcement in criminal investigations, and whether this might impact individual privacy rights. Several analyses emerge when determining the admissibility of samples collected by non-law enforcement personnel and later disclosed or provided to law enforcement.

Health Care Providers

On August 21, 1996, Congress enacted the Health Insurance Portability and Accountability Act (1996, PL 104-191) (HIPAA), which dealt, in part,

[104] *North Carolina v. Reed*, 631 S.E. 2d 320 (2007).

[105] National Bioethics Advisory Commission, 1999.

with privacy standards. The Act was created to protect the integrity, confidentiality and availability of health data, and set national standards for how health information is transmitted and protected. Hospitals, defined as a heath care provider within the Act, were required to comply after April 14, 2003 with regulations that restrict and define the ability of certain entities (health plans, health care clearinghouses and health care providers) to divulge patient medical records. Consequently, new federal guidelines were created for law enforcement, which impact investigative procedures in obtaining forensic samples from these entities. Section 164.512 (f) provides the standard for disclosures by health personnel for law enforcement purposes and permits providing information pursuant to:

(A) A court order or court-ordered warrant, or subpoena or summons issued by a judicial officer;
(B) A grand jury subpoena; or
(C) An administrative request, including an administrative subpoena or summons, a civil or an authorized investigative demand, or similar process as authorized under law, provided that

1. The information sought is relevant and material to a legitimate law enforcement inquiry.
2. The request is specific and limited in scope to the extent reasonably practicable in light of the purpose for which the information is sought.
3. De-identified information could not reasonably be used.

As of April 14, 2003, law enforcement officers must present a court order, warrant, subpoena or summons before they can obtain medical samples or records from hospitals and other medical installations.

Other Third-Party Collection

If personnel outside the scope of HIPAA conduct a search and collect biological samples that are then turned over to law enforcement, the regulations of HIPAA do not apply, and a Fourth Amendment violation does not occur. For example, in *U.S. v. Jacobsen et al.*, the Supreme Court held that Fourth Amendment issues only surface when government action is involved in a search and seizure process and, moreover, that the Fourth Amendment is "wholly inapplicable 'to a search or seizure, even an unreasonable one, effected by a private individual not acting as an agent of the Government or with the participation or knowledge of any governmental official.' "[106] In *Jacobsen*, private freight carrier employees opened a package given to them in the normal course of business and found a suspicious looking plastic bag of white powder. They contacted a federal agent, who tested the powder; he in turn contacted several other federal agents for additional field tests. A warrant was then obtained to search the address identified on the package, and law enforcement arrested two occupants. The two arrestees moved to suppress the evidence as the product of an unreasonable search.

The Court found that the initial search of the package had been done by private action; thus, the initial search did not violate the Fourth Amendment. The Court then evaluated whether the additional intrusion by the federal agents constituted an unlawful search or seizure within the Fourth Amendment, or whether society was prepared to consider it a reasonable infringement on the expectation of privacy. The Court quoted *Cupp v. Murphy*, analogizing that a warrantless search and seizure limited to scraping a suspect's fingernails was justified, even though a full search may not be.[107] In addition, the Court held that the federal agents did not infringe any constitutionally protected privacy interest that had not already been frustrated as the result of conduct of the private freight carrier employees.[108]

Later cases have held that it is the defendant's burden to establish by a preponderance of the evidence that a private party has acted as a government instrument or agent.[109] Determining whether a private citizen is a government agent is a two-part analysis, evaluating (1) the government's knowledge of and acquisition in the search, and (2) the intent of the party performing the search.[110] In evaluating the intent of the private citizen performing the search, a court must evaluate whether the party conducted the search to assist law enforcement or to further his or her own interests.[111] The court must also determine whether the private citizen conducted the search at the request of the state or whether the state offered any reward.[112]

Following *Jacobsen*, some questions and concerns have been raised as to whether biological samples collected by private, non-HIPAA related personnel can be provided to law enforcement without a warrant and without encountering Fourth Amendment issues. One analysis follows the logic

[106] *U.S. v. Jacobsen et al.*, 466 U.S. 109, 114; 104 S. Ct. 1652; 80 L. Ed. 2d 85 (1983) quoting *Walter v. United States*, 447 U.S. 649, 662 (1980).

[107] *Cupp v. Murphy*, 412 U.S. 291, 296, 93 S. Ct. 2000, 36 L. Ed. 2d 900 (1973).

[108] *U.S. v. Jacobsen et al.*, 466 U. S. 109, 126; 104 S. Ct. 1652; 80 L. Ed. 2d 85 (1983).

[109] *U.S. v. Smit*, 210 F. Supp. 2d 1096; *U.S. v. Feffer*, 831 F. 2d 734, 739 (7th Cir. 1987); *U. S. v. Reed*, 15 F. 3d 928, 931 (9th Cir. 1994).

[110] *U.S. v. Parker*, 32 F. 3d 395, 398 (8th Cir. 1994).

[111] *U.S. v. Malbrough*, 922 F. 2d 458, 462 (9th Cir. 1982).

[112] *U.S. v. Feffer*, 831 F.2d 734, 739 (7th Cir. 1987); *U.S. v. David*, 943 F. Supp. 1403, 1409 (E.D. Va 1996).

that when a sample is drawn, the donor loses ownership and standing to challenge subsequent uses of the sample. Many thoughtful commentaries have been written regarding the consequences that might ensue if biological samples collected by nongovernment agencies for medical, identification or occupational purposes were made available to law enforcement and sensitive medical information was subsequently used for non-law enforcement purposes. While these same commentators fail to provide documented instances in which this use has ever occurred, it is important to be aware of this potential challenge. If the facts suggest that this issue will be raised by the defense, either directly or by innuendo to the jury, the prosecutor can ask its expert witness to explain to the jury the safeguards, procedurally and by statute, that prevent information from being communicated to agencies outside law enforcement. In addition, recall from Chapter 1 that the markers used for forensic testing provide no information regarding an individual's health status.

Obtaining Confirmatory Samples After a Databank "Hit": A Case-Specific Strategy

All 50 states have adopted mandatory DNA collection statutes authorizing the collection, storage and analysis of DNA samples. In addition, all 50 states, the U.S. Army, the FBI and Puerto Rico participate in the FBI lab's **Combined DNA Indexing System (CODIS)**. As discussed in Chapter 4, CODIS enables law enforcement to search local, state and national databanks that contain profiles from crime scene evidence or convicted offenders searching for a match to the DNA profile of interest.[113] CODIS and similar forensic databanks play an important role in focusing a criminal investigation, convicting the guilty and exonerating the innocent.

If a DNA profile "hits" on or matches a profile already within a databank, the name associated with the profile will be sent to law enforcement for further investigation. Law enforcement will then obtain a confirmatory sample to ensure that the crime scene profile matches the identified individual. The decision regarding how to obtain the confirmatory sample may differ depending on whether the identified individual is in or out of custody. How the confirmatory sample is obtained should conform to the controlling criminal procedures of the jurisdiction. The prosecutor and case investigator should communicate when the match has been identified, and develop a strategic plan for investigating the case. In the initial

[113] http://www.fbi.gov/hq/lab/codis/partstates.htm

stages of an investigation there are valid reasons for wanting or not wanting to alert an individual to the fact that he or she is a suspect in a crime. The typical means for obtaining a confirmatory sample include a search warrant, a court order, statutory DNA collection laws and consent.

DNA IN THE COURTROOM: THE ESSENTIALS OF THE PROSECUTION'S PRESENTATION

The first criminal case in which DNA typing evidence was admitted in the United States was in 1988.[114] Subsequently, DNA-related evidence has been used in thousands of cases to identify and convict the guilty and exonerate the innocent. Every criminal prosecution in which DNA evidence is a factor contains certain similarities a prosecutor must address. Prosecutors must be familiar with such terms and principles as the product rule, random match probability, theta factor and source attribution. Understanding these terms will enable a prosecutor to address the unique challenges encountered in a DNA evidence-based proceeding.

[114] *Andrews v. State*, 533 So. 2d 841 (Fla. Dist. Ct. App. 1988).

Pretrial Preparations

Discovery—The State's Duty to Disclose and Reciprocal Discovery

Every state has statutes regarding what governs discovery in a criminal proceeding, what the prosecutor must provide to the defendant and what, if anything, the defendant must provide to the state by way of reciprocal discovery. FRCP Rule 16 establishes the federal discovery rule, and many states have patterned their own rules after this statute. Prosecutors should be very familiar with their jurisdiction's discovery rule, not only as to what they are required to provide the defense, but also what they are entitled to receive from the defendant. Most states require that the prosecutor file a formal reciprocal discovery motion to compel the defense to provide this material. FRCP Rule 16(a)(1)(F) requires:

> *Upon a defendant's request, the government must permit a defendant to inspect and to copy or photograph the results reports of any physical or mental examination, or any scientific test or experiment if:*
>
> **(i)** *the item is within the government's possession, custody, or control*
>
> **(ii)** *the attorney for the government knows—or through due diligence should know—that the item exists; and*

(iii) *the item is material to preparing the defense or the government intends to use the item in its case-in-chief at trial.*

Discovery in DNA cases, as in all prosecution, is an ongoing responsibility for both sides. In DNA cases, the prosecutor has a constitutional obligation to disclose all exculpatory material of any sort to the defense.[115] Exculpatory evidence is defined as any material information within the prosecutor's possession or control that tends to negate the defendant's guilt as to the charged offense.[116] Failure to disclose material exculpatory evidence is a due process violation. Prosecutors should be aware that the duty to disclose extends to evidence possessed by other agencies when there is a collaborative relationship between the state and other agencies.[117]

Many state statutes or court rules require the prosecutor to provide the defense with the name of the state's DNA analyst, a copy of his or her report, the analyst's curriculum vitae, a copy of the consent form used to obtain the forensic sample, the DNA search warrant, names of the evidence collection officers, copies of their reports and copies of property receipts. A good practice for the prosecutor is to disclose all forensic reports, regardless of whether or not they have been requested by the defense or whether the prosecutor intends to use them at trial. Another good practice, especially for new prosecutors, is to consult with both a supervisor and the forensic lab analyst to ensure that discovery responses are consistent with the state's affirmative obligations to disclose. Some states impose a duty to notify the defense if the state's forensic analysis will consume the entire evidence sample during typing. Failure to notify the defense may result in the evidence being declared inadmissible.

The government has a second obligation established by some state statutes to preserve materially relevant evidence. Prosecutors should be familiar with the controlling statutes in their jurisdiction regarding the preservation of biological evidence. In natural disasters such as Hurricane Katrina, the destruction of evidence stored in the New Orleans District Attorney's building or the courthouse did not establish a due process violation, as it was the result of a natural disaster. Also, in reopening a cold case, the prosecutor may find that forensic evidence was not

[115] *Brady v. Maryland*, 373 U.S. 83, 83 S. Ct. 1194, 10 L. Ed. 2d 215 (1963).

[116] *California v. Trombetta*, 467 U.S. 479; 104 S. Ct. 2528; 81 L. Ed. 2d 413 (1984); *U.S. v. Agurs*, 427 U.S. 97 (1976).

[117] *U.S. v. Risha*, 445 F. 3d 298 (3d Cir. 2006).

preserved or has been destroyed. The Supreme Court has ruled that neither the destruction nor the failure to preserve evidence is a due process violation absent the defendant showing that the loss or destruction was the result of bad faith on the part of law enforcement. The defendant must show that law enforcement knew beforehand that the evidence would have exculpated the defendant.[118] Other states do not apply a bad faith analysis to find a due process violation, but instead rely on the duty to preserve materially relevant evidence.[119]

Discovery requests may include lab-specific information such as the lab's quality assurance protocol, whether or not the testing analyst ever failed a proficiency test, or the lab's history of "false-positive" results.[120] Some laboratories have created a CD-ROM containing standard information such as operating procedures and lab protocols. When confronted by such discovery requests, prosecutors should inquire whether the forensic lab has created such a CD-ROM.

Occasionally the defense files motions that are immaterial or unduly oppressive. When this happens, the prosecutor may consider objecting to these motions on the basis that they exceed the scope of the relevant discovery statute. Following the language of FRCP Rule 16(a)(1)(F), evidence that is "material to preparing the defense" is discoverable, but it may be unclear in some cases how far this obligation extends. For example, it may or may not be relevant or material in developing a defense for the prosecutor to provide information on every failed proficiency test for every analyst ever employed at the lab. Overly broad and potentially irrelevant discovery motions should be reviewed by the prosecutor, his or her supervisor and the state's analyst. If it is determined that a motion exceeds the scope of discovery, the prosecutor should inform the defense counsel in writing regarding which requests are in question and advise defense counsel that the state intends to oppose the requests as unduly burdensome or irrelevant.

Whether or not the defense intends to retest the forensic samples or hire its own expert to review the government lab's findings, if allowed under local procedures, the prosecutor should file a reciprocal discovery motion and review any materials provided by the defense with the state's analyst.

[118] *Arizona v. Youngblood*, 488 U.S. 51, 56, 109 S. Ct. 333, 102 L. Ed. 2d 281 (1988).

[119] *Ex parte Gingo*, 605 So. 2d 1237 (Ala. 1992); *Thorne v. Dep't of Pub. Safety*, 774 P. 2d 1326 (Alaska 1989); *State v. Morales*, 657 A. 2d 585 (Conn. 195); *Lolly v. State*, 611 A. 2d 956 (Del. 1992); *State v. Okumura*, 894 P. 2d 80 (Haw. 1995); *State v. Fain*, 774 P. 2d 252 (Idaho 1989); *Commonwealth v. Henderson*, 582 N.E. 2d 496 (Mass. 1991); *State v. Schmid*, 487 N. W. 2d 539 (Minn. Ct. App. 1992); *State v. Smagula*, 578 A. 2d 1215 (N.H. 1990); *State v. Riggs*, 838 P. 2d 975 (N.M. 1992); *State v. Ferguson*, 2 S.W. 3d 912 (Tenn. 1999); *State v. Delisle*, 648 A. 2d 632 (Vt. 1994); *State v. Osakalumi*, 461 S.E. 2d 504 (W.Va. 1995).

[120] *State v. Proctor*, 348 S.C. 322 (S.C. App. 2001); *State v. Dunn*, 571 S.E. 3d 650 (N.C. Ct. App. 2002); *Cole v. State*, 835 A. 2d 600 (Md. 2003).

The defense should send all its discovery motions directly to the prosecutor. The responsibility to comply with a motion for discovery is entirely the prosecutor's, and it is improper for the defense to send such motions directly to the lab, analyst, investigator or law enforcement personnel. The prosecutor must ensure that the material provided is in compliance with the state's discovery statute and is submitted on a timely basis. Because the prosecutor has a duty to disclose exculpatory evidence within the possession of all members of the prosecution team, the prosecutor should be the point of contact for any defense request for discovery.

Pretrial Conferences with Law Enforcement and Lab Analysts

One of the first things a prosecutor should do after being assigned a DNA-related case is carefully review the complete file and contact the case officer to develop a checklist assessing what has been done and what remains to be completed. A thorough inventory of the crime scene evidence will enable the prosecutor to determine the type and quality of the evidence recovered, and whether confirmatory samples are needed. Depending on the crime, a prosecutor is often faced with a large volume of collected evidence. In light of the cost and time required to process crime scene evidence, some laboratories and district attorney's offices have set limits on the amount of crime scene evidence that can be processed without prior approval. The prosecutor should work with the investigators and the analyst to determine which of the available items are most likely to yield probative results, and which lab should be used for the testing, and to ensure that the evidence chain of custody has been properly documented.

In reality, not every prosecutor has the opportunity to repeatedly meet with a lab analyst during the initial stages of a case. Efforts should be made, however, to communicate with the analyst as time, resources and logistics allow. Whether by phone or in person, the prosecutor should communicate with the analyst early and often. The lab analyst will ultimately become one of the prime expert witnesses at trial. It is essential that the analyst and prosecutor work together to present the material so that the jury can fully appreciate the strengths and limitations of the forensic evidence. The pretrial conference gives the analyst an opportunity to help focus the prosecutor's questions to logically educate the jury regarding the information the evidence provides. The conference also gives the prosecutor an opportunity to explain the courtroom layout, where the expert will sit in relation to the judge and jury, and the kinds of questions the analyst can expect from the defense. This meeting also provides an opportunity to discuss jury education materials and exhibits.

The prosecutor should discuss the potential theory of the case with the analyst and evaluate whether the evidence supports that theory, what its weaknesses are, and whether the evidence may support other theories as well. The analyst can also help the prosecutor diffuse any red herrings the defense may introduce into the arguments. Every theory should follow the facts of the case and be evidence-driven. Thus, over the course of meetings, the theory of the case may evolve as evidence is processed.

Pretrial conferences with the lab analyst also enable the prosecutor to review the analyst's credentials and ability to communicate to the jury. The prosecutor can determine whether the analyst is prone to using jargon that might make it difficult for the jury to understand the evidence. The prosecutor can discuss the analyst's qualifications, previous court testimony, whether or not the analyst is a member of professional forensic associations, how many times the witness has been qualified as an expert and whether he or she has ever testified for the defense. During the meeting, the prosecutor should ask about the analyst's education, background and professional experience. The higher the analyst's degree and the longer his or her experience, the more compelling his or her testimony will be. The DNA Advisory Board (DAB) guidelines require that an analyst have at least six months of forensic DNA lab experience prior to independent casework, however, so even analysts who are testifying for the first time will have had at least six months of lab experience, and by the time the case goes to trial, usually considerably more. The *DNA Advisory Board Quality Assurance Standards for Forensic DNA Testing Laboratories* can be downloaded from the DAB website (http://cstl.nist.gov/div831/strbase/dabqas.htm). These standards can assist the prosecutor in preparing for the direct examination as well as the cross-examination of the defense's expert witnesses.

The prosecutor should take advantage of the fact that the DAB guidelines require an analyst to complete continuing education coursework annually. The analyst should describe any courses or in/house training he or she has completed. An independent defense expert is under no obligation to continue his or her coursework. If the defense's witness does not engage in regular continuing education activities, contrasting the continuing education of the state's witness with that of the defense witness may be insightful for the jury. Similarly, the 1996 NRC report recommends that forensic analysts undergo regular proficiency tests.[121] As with continuing education, many defense witnesses are under no such obligation. As a general rule, state and FBI laboratories conduct analyst proficiency tests at least every six months to ensure professional proficiency. During the pretrial conference, the prosecutor should inquire whether the analyst has ever failed a proficiency test and if so, the basis of the failure and what has been done to correct the deficiency. In addition, the prosecutor should inquire about what corrective action has been taken in the lab since the failed test and about the outcome of any tests the analyst has subsequently taken.

[121] Both the 1992 and 1996 NRC reports can be obtained from the National Academies Press website at http://www.nap.edu.

During the pretrial conferences, the prosecutor should ask the analyst about the lab's protocols. These protocols are essential to ensure standardization in typing procedures. The analyst should describe the lab's protocols governing educational requirements for hiring analysts, evidence management, testing and reporting procedures and the lab's compliance with quality assurance standards. The prosecutor should ask about controls that may have been instituted to ensure the proper use and operation of lab testing equipment. Commercial typing kits have internal controls to demonstrate that the kits are functioning properly, and the prosecutor should be familiar with these also.

The prosecutor should also determine whether the lab is accredited by the American Society of Crime Laboratory Directors-Laboratory Accreditation Board (ASCLAD-LAB). This is a very demanding standard, and many very proficient laboratories have not yet been qualified to receive this level of accreditation. At a minimum, the lab should meet the quality assurance standards to be a participant in the FBI's CODIS databank system. To participate in CODIS, the lab must meet two distinct standards: quality assurance standards for forensic DNA testing laboratories and quality assurance standards for government laboratories where convicted offender DNA testing is regularly performed. A copy of the standards necessary to be accepted into CODIS is available from the FBI website (www.fbi/gov/hq/codis/index1.htm). Reviewing these standards also may assist the prosecutor in developing questions for direct and cross-examination.

Reviewing the Analyst's Report

The analyst's report will include his or her findings and conclusions regarding the forensic samples that were typed. Most analysts' reports include statements identifying the samples that were received by the lab, identified as source known (typically K) or unknown (typically Q), the type of testing that was done by the lab, and the results of the testing. Not every lab includes a copy of the relevant electropherograms in its report, but these may be useful for the prosecutor in reviewing the material with the analyst and may be available upon request. The electropherogram can assist the prosecutor in understanding both the qualitative and quantitative nature of the sample. Understanding the electropherogram is beneficial in interpreting what the evidence means, how the analyst resolved a mixture, and whether or not the analyst was able to isolate separate and discrete profiles. If electropherograms are not provided with the analyst's report, they should be requested, as this is an important part of discovery and something the defense is entitled to receive. Similarly, if the sample represents a mixture, and the report states that "[s]tatistical calculations are available on request," they should be requested and the defense should be given a copy as well, as part of the ongoing discovery obligation.

The report will indicate whether there was a match, exclusion or inconclusive results between the crime scene evidence and the known (suspect's) sample. If there is a match, the report will include a statement giving the probability that this DNA profile would be found in a randomly selected member of one or more reference populations. An example of such a statement is "[t]he probability of selecting an unrelated individual at random having an STR profile matching the DNA obtained from the questioned specimen is approximately 1 in 270 billion from the African American population, 1 in 170 billion from the Caucasian population, 1 in 404 billion from the Southeastern Hispanic population and 1 in 1.4 trillion from the Southwestern Hispanic population." If the profile meets the statistical threshold of rarity established by that particular lab to make a source attribution statement, the report may contain a statement such as "Based on the STR typing results and to a reasonable degree of scientific certainty, the contributor of specimen K5 (known sample number 5) is the source of the DNA obtained from specimens Q1 and Q3 (question samples from the crime scene)."

Depending on the circumstances, the report may go on to indicate that the profile will be uploaded into the FBI's **Combined DNA Indexing System (CODIS)** and maintained by the FBI Lab for future comparisons. Finally, most reports will indicate the disposition of any remaining sample, for example: "Upon completion of all the requested examinations, the submitted items will be returned to you under separate cover."

Pretrial Analyst Check List

In the weeks leading up to a trial, the prosecutor and analyst should select and review any hearing or trial exhibits that will help the jury understand the evidence. The analyst may already have a list of question "prompts" for the prosecutor. If not, the prosecutor and analyst should develop this list together. The prosecutor should familiarize the analyst with the legal foundations necessary to have the evidence admitted, as well as the purpose of the upcoming proceeding, whether it be a motion hearing or the trial itself. For example, if the analyst will be testifying in a motion *in limine,* review with the analyst how this type of testimony differs from trial testimony. Finally, if this is the first time the analyst has testified in a particular courtroom, the prosecutor should familiarize the analyst with the courtroom orientation.

The analyst may have a prepared jury education presentation explaining DNA, where it is found in the human body and how the DNA sequence can differ from person to person. The analyst should be asked to include a brief explanation of the many ways in which DNA is used outside the courtroom, how technology is able to distinguish the DNA of one person from another, and the quality controls and assurances in place in the lab during sample typing.

Anticipate Defense Pretrial Motions

As with all types of prosecution, the prosecutor should anticipate what pretrial motions will most likely be filed by the defense and what motions the state can file proactively. Because many issues are state-specific, it is essential that the prosecutor be familiar with the governing jurisdiction's statutes and court rules.

Impact of Crawford v. Washington: Who Can Testify

By the time a matter goes to trial, a prosecutor may learn that someone other than the original typing analyst will be testifying about the forensic report. Depending on the jurisdiction, this witness may or may not be allowed to testify. In 2004 the Supreme Court ruled in *Crawford v. Washington* that "testifying statements of witnesses absent from trial have been admitted only when the declarant is unavailable, and only where the defendant has had a prior opportunity to cross-examine."[122] In the aftermath of *Crawford*, courts are split as to whether a second analyst's testimony regarding work done by another analyst constitutes hearsay and is inadmissible, or whether this testimony can be admitted on another basis.

DNA typing typically involves several analysts, including at minimum the analyst who performed the testing and a second reader who reviewed the analyst's findings and formed an independent opinion of the report. Some laboratories also require a third reviewer to scrutinize the results before the report is sent out. In addition, DNA typing may involve several different laboratories, depending on the type of DNA testing being conducted. Before *Crawford*, the original typing analyst was not required to testify as to the results. The prosecutor could reliably substitute the testimony of an analyst who may have supervised, observed or reviewed the original analyst's work, or, alternatively, another analyst whose opinion was based on information reasonably relied upon by experts in the field of DNA typing.[123] Post-*Crawford*, some courts have questioned who can reasonably testify in the absence of the typing analyst, and what sources, testimonial or nontestimonial, an expert may rely upon when developing their opinion. Some courts have looked to the business record exception as a means of admitting the analyst's report in what might otherwise be construed as hearsay.[124] Other courts have determined that *Crawford* does not extend to materials relied upon by the testifying witness in formulating his or her own opinion as it is the opinion itself that constitutes the substantive evidence.[125] If the tests the expert witness relied upon in formulating his or her opinion are the type experts in the relevant field reasonably rely upon, these courts have found no *Crawford* violation.[126] Furthemore, these courts hold that the expert's opinion is not limited to just direct knowledge of the evidence typing, but can be based on materials others reasonably rely upon in formulating scientific opinions of this sort.[127] Other courts have held that one witness's reliance on another individual's DNA analysis does not constitute testimonial hearsay.[128]

[122] *Crawford v. Washington*, 541 U.S. 36, 59; 124 S. Ct. 1354; 15 L. Ed. D 177 (2004).

[123] Chapman, 2006, www.ndaa.org.

[124] *People v. Brown*, 801 N.Y. S. 2d 709 (N.Y. Sup. Ct. 2005); *State v. Forte*, 629 S.E. 2d 137 (N.C. 2006); *People v. Bones*, 739 N.E. S. 2d 545 (N.Y. App. Div. 2005).

[125] *State v. Walker*, 613 S.E. 2d 330 (N.C. Ct. App. 2005); *State v. Wisconsin*, 709 N.W. 2d 93 (2005).

[126] *State v. Bertha*, 617 S.E. 2d 687 (N.C. Ct. App. 2005).

[127] *North Carolina v. Fair*, 557 S.E. 2d 500 (N.C. 2001); *New Jersey v. Stevens*, 345 A. 2d 804, citing *United States v. Williams* (447 F. 2d 1285 (5th Cir. 1971); *Jenkins v. U.S.*, 113 U.S. App. D.C. 300, 307 F. 2d 637 (D.C. Cir. 2006).

[128] *State v. Hocutt*, 628 S.E. 2d 632 (N.C. Ct. App. 2006).

Prosecutors should be aware, however, that at least one state court has ruled that when the original forensic analyst did not testify, it was improper to admit a report through the reviewing analyst who, the court ruled, "did not have personal knowledge of the actual DNA testing process in this case."[129] When determining who will testify regarding the analyst's report, it is essential to know how a particular jurisdiction or court has ruled on *Crawford.*

If the Defense Wishes to Retest Evidence

The 1996 NRC report states that "[a] wrongfully accused person's best insurance against the possibility of being falsely incriminated is the opportunity to have the testing repeated," and this statement has been echoed in case law.[130] Because the defendant's profile was obtained using a scientific and repeatable process, if the defendant has any concerns regarding the state's typing results, he or she can have the evidence retested. Whether by court rule, statute or case law, most jurisdictions enable defense counsel to inspect physical evidence relating to a case.[131] Prosecutors should remember, however, that while the defense may attack the state's forensic report at trial, the defense is under no burden to retest the evidence. If there is evidence available and the defense has not retested it, prosecutors should refrain, especially during the heat of closing argument, from shifting the burden of proof by suggesting that the defense could have conducted their own testing but chose not to. Arguments such as these can result in a mistrial.

Some forensic laboratories divide evidence samples to ensure that, when possible, samples for retesting are available. As soon as the prosecutor learns that unused sample is available, the prosecutor should advise defense counsel that sample is available for retesting, both on the record and in writing to be kept in the court's case file. Doing this on the record is important, as the defense's failure to retest, after being advised on the record, may constitute a lack of "due diligence" that may preclude future motions for a new trial.

When the defense intends to retest forensic evidence, the prosecutor should request that the court be provided with certain information to reasonably ensure the integrity of the sample. If the defense files a motion requesting the release of forensic evidence for retesting, the prosecutor

[129] *State v. Crager*, 005 Ohio 6868 (Ohio Ct. App. 2005).

[130] National Research Council, 1996, p. 88; *State v. Fields*, 2 P. 3d 670 (Ariz. Ct. App. 1999).

[131] Iowa Code Ann. §813.2 (Rule 13(a)(b)(1); La. Code Crim. P. Art. 718 (West 1981); Wis. State Ann. § 971.23(5) (West 1985).

should, in a response motion and/or on the record, require some of all of the following conditions prior to the transfer of the sample:

- The defense should identify the lab that will perform the testing, and certify that it is an accredited lab. The prosecutor should request that the lab be at least comparable to the state lab regarding standard compliance and accreditation.
- The defense should identify the type of testing to be performed, and the expert who will review the second test's results.
- The evidence must be transferred directly from the state's lab to the defendant's lab.
- The defendant must waive the chain of custody.
- If possible, the sample should be split by the defendant's lab for future testing.
- The state should be notified in advance if the defendant's lab anticipates consuming the sample.
- Any unused sample should be preserved and returned to the state's lab by a specified date.
- The retesting lab must provide the state's lab with any report generated as a result of the retesting.

If only a small amount of sample is available for retesting and it is apparent that the sample will be consumed in retesting, the prosecutor should object to the release of the sample unless the defense analyst is identified prior to its release.

At trial, without shifting the burden when the state's analyst is testifying, the prosecutor can ask the state's expert:

- Whether any sample remained after the analyst's testing.
- What the analyst did to preserve the unused sample.
- What quality control measures the analyst followed.
- Why preserving the remaining sample is important.

After the defense has cross-examined the witness, the prosecutor should redirect the state's witness, asking whether he or she had any of the same concerns just voiced by the defense. If the answer is no, the prosecutor should then ask why there were no concerns. The analyst will likely respond by indicating that the unused samples were preserved for future retesting if needed. The prosecutor can then ask if the analyst saw or currently sees a need to retest. Ideally, the prosecutor will be well aware that the answer is no.

In some cases, the defense will request permission for its own expert to observe the testing performed on behalf of the prosecution. Many problems are inherent in a lab allowing outsiders to observe operations, including an increased risk of contamination, breach of security and chain of custody issues.[132] Each lab has its own policy regarding granting observers access when samples are being typed. The FBI has a policy of not allowing observers during testing, whereas other laboratories will allow "remote" observation. When the testing is expected to consume the sample, however, policies may be more permissive. Several jurisdictions require that defendants be allowed to have their own experts present when typing will consume the evidence sample.[133] The prosecutor should be aware of the controlling law in his or her jurisdiction, and if it is silent, the prosecutor should consult with the analyst to determine the lab's policy regarding this type of request.

Admissibility Hearings

If the defendant does not file a pretrial motion challenging the admissibility of the DNA evidence on a Fourth Amendment basis, he or she may challenge its admissibility on other grounds. Unless a specific statute applies, admissibility of scientific evidence is generally governed by standards set out in specific case law within each state. As discussed in Chapter 7, states apply either a *Frye* or *Daubert* standard or a hybrid of one of these (*Frye-Kelly* in California, for example).[134] Prosecutors should be aware of both the governing standard in their particular jurisdiction and the requirements of each standard to overcome any defense challenge. Because DNA has gained universal acceptance in the United States, challenges now tend to focus on the application of new or novel technologies to DNA typing. Prosecutors should remember that in states following the Federal Rules of Evidence, the routine rules of evidence do not apply at admissibility hearings.[135] If the defense files an admissibility challenge that addresses interpretation, accuracy or evaluation of statistical calculations, these more properly go to the weight of the evidence for the jury's consideration rather than admissibility. The prosecutor should carefully evaluate defense counsel's motion, and if the challenge is really

[132] *People v. Monagas*, 615 N.Y.S. 2d 633 (1994); *State v. Nguyen*, 833 P. 2d 937 (Kan. 1992); *State v. Fields*, 2 P.3d 670 (Ariz. Ct. App. 1999).

[133] Ohio Rev. Code Ann. § 2925.51(e) (Baldwin 1991); *People v. Garries*, 645 P. 2d 1306 (Colo. 1982).

[134] *Frye v. U.S.*, 293 F. 1013, D.C. (1923); *Daubert v. Merrill Dow Pharmaceutical Inc.*, 509 U.S. 579; 113 S. Ct. 2786; 125 L. Ed. 2d 469 (1993).

[135] FRE Rule 104(a) (rules governing admissibility).

more one of weight, the prosecutor should require that the defense show why the requested hearing is necessary.[136]

Pretrial Depositions

Some state court systems (Florida, for example) conduct extensive depositions practice prior to trial. When a deposition of a defense forensic expert witness is held, if at all possible, the state's expert should attend.

At Trial—Presenting the Case in Chief

Strategic Voir Dire

Each week approximately 12 million people watch forensic-driven entertainment television programs. Consequently, many prosecutors have experienced what has popularly become known as "the CSI effect." They report that many jurors believe that DNA evidence is collected and processed in every case, that all investigators have extensive high-tech equipment readily available to them and that forensic evidence can be collected and processed in an hour.

Prosecutors report that jurors expect to hear about forensic evidence and, in some instances, have acquitted suspects when no DNA evidence was presented during the trial. In a survey of 102 experienced state trial attorneys, 38% described post-trial jury discussions in which jurors acquitted the defendant or the trial resulted in a hung jury simply because no forensic evidence was presented by the prosecutor. In the same survey, 74% reported that jurors "expected to be presented with forensic evidence" during the trial.[137] In some cases, prosecutors have had to put on "negative evidence testimony" in which an expert witness describes why investigators do not find DNA or other forensic evidence at a crime scene.

Voir dire provides an opportunity for the prosecutor to gauge whether an individual juror is biased in favor of or against the use of scientific evidence. The prosecutor should try to determine whether the juror feels that reasonable doubts regarding the suspect's participation in the crime can only be overcome through the neutrality of science, or whether he or she has unresolved questions regarding the criminal justice process, and by extension is uncomfortable with the state's use of DNA evidence.

Not every jurisdiction conducts attorney-directed voir dire. In those states that do, the prosecutor can elicit juror expectations as well as their source

[136] *Utah v. Butterfield*, 27 P. 3d 1133 (Utah 001); *Colorado v. Shreck*, 22 P. 3d 68 (Colo. 2001).

[137] County District Attorney, 2005.

of forensic knowledge through a series of simple inquiries. Prosecutors should draw the distinction between forensic and crime drama programs and the reality of the criminal investigations. Prosecutors in those jurisdictions where the attorney does not conduct voir dire have a more difficult task, but can educate the jury through the forensic expert witness. The expert witness can explain why DNA may be present at a crime scene, but collecting and analyzing all the evidence may not further the investigators' understanding of the crime. For example, in a stabbing, finding the victim's blood on the victim's blood-soaked clothing would be expected and nonprobative. Through voir dire or the expert witness, the prosecutors can explain that some evidence has predictable results, and therefore the choice not to test some of the evidence is not an oversight on the part of the state, but a reasonable and conservative use of resources.

Through voir dire or the state's expert witness, the prosecutor can reinforce the jury's confidence in the credibility and reliability of DNA evidence by discussing the many other uses of DNA, for example, medical applications, missing person identification, military use and paternity testing. The prosecutor should consider how much the case relies on forensic evidence and tailor the voir dire accordingly. If the case is dependent on DNA, the prosecutor should spend time educating the jury as to both the strengths and limitations of this type of evidence.

The Opening Statement

Many experienced prosecutors forgo mentioning forensic evidence in their opening and focus instead on the victim and the crime that occurred. Telling the jury in opening that they will hear from expert witnesses during the course of the trial is sometimes enough to allow the jury to anticipate the testimony without previewing the details of that testimony. Other prosecutors approach opening statements as an opportunity to tell the jury what they will hear from each expert witness regarding each type of analysis that was conducted, how the forensic evidence supports the victim's statements and how it connects the suspect to the crime. Whichever approach (or hybrid) the prosecutor takes, it is best not to overstate the evidence in the opening statement. During opening, the prosecutor does not know what theory the defense will promote, how the state's expert witness will stand up under cross-examination or what concessions will be obtained during the trial. Two points are certain: the unanticipated will occur, and a 10-minute opening statement is better than a 15-minute opening statement.

The opening statement provides the prosecutor with an opportunity to capture the jury's attention regarding the crime that took place, what the victim experienced and the suspect's role in it. The prosecutor can bring what the victim saw and experienced to life for the jury. The DNA evidence then becomes a vital "silent witness," confirming the victim's statements and the defendant's responsibility for the crime. At the conclusion of the opening statement, the prosecutor should charge the jury to hold the defendant accountable for the criminal act and request that they return a guilty verdict.

Direct Examination of the State's Expert Witness

In getting ready for direct examination, the prosecutor should meet with the lab analyst several times to discuss the theory of the case, the forensic evidence, and the analyst's background and credentials, and should review exhibits. It is important that the prosecutor not rely on "canned questions" or take a "one size fits all" approach to direct questioning of an expert witness. The prosecutor should prepare specific questions with the witness beforehand and listen carefully to the analyst's responses. Canned questions often prevent the prosecutor from listening to the nuances of the expert's testimony. The focus should be on the critical grounds to be covered with the witness, and plain language should be used to present this material to the jury.

The prosecutor can prepare himself or herself for these meeting by reading Chapters 1–6 herein, as well as being familiar with the 1992 and 1996 NRC reports and other resource materials to gain an understanding of the various types and scope of DNA evidence involved in the case. The 1992 NRC report offered defense-oriented solutions and is relied upon by many defense witnesses. The 1996 NRC report offered a more balanced resolution to statistical issues and provides a wealth of answers to statistical questions prosecutors will encounter. When defense witnesses propose the use of theories that were discussed in the 1992 NRC report, prosecutors should emphasize that the 1996 NRC report concluded that several of the suggestions found in the 1992 NRC report were excessively conservative and not necessary.

Federal Rules of Evidence Rule 702 (or the state equivalent) provides the general standards governing testimony provided by an expert witness. The rule states:

> *Fed. R. Evid. 702. Testimony by Experts: If scientific, technical or other specialized knowledge will assist the trier of fact to understand the evidence or to determine a fact in issue, a witness qualified as an expert by knowledge, skill, experience, training, or education may testify thereto in the form of an opinion or otherwise if*
>
> **(1)** *the testimony is based on sufficient facts or data;*
> **(2)** *the testimony is the product of reliable principles and methods, and*
> **(3)** *the witness has applied the principles and methods reliably to the facts of the case.*

It is important for the prosecution's expert witnesses to present the evidence "warts and all" and avoid overstating the significance of the DNA evidence. The unique value of the neutrality of scientific evidence is expressed in the phrase "the evidence is what the evidence is." Acknowledging any inherent weakness in the scientific evidence during direct examination can strengthen both the jury's confidence in the prosecution and its impression that nothing has been kept from them, enabling them to properly evaluate the weight of the evidence. Both the state's case and the prosecutor will suffer more serious damage if the jury first learns of any weaknesses in the evidence during the defense attorney's cross-examination. If there are limitations to any inferences that can be drawn from the evidence, the prosecutor should discuss these with the expert before trial in order to present the probative value of the evidence despite its inherent limitations. If the prosecutor has concerns that a controversial issue is associated with a potential lab or witness, the prosecutor may consider putting this on the record outside the jury's presence to prevent jurors from being sidetracked by the issue. This is a case-by-case decision and requires careful evaluation. On the one hand, if an issue does not directly impact on the credibility of the report or analyst, or measures have been taken to correct the issue, the prosecutor may consider presenting this directly to the jury. If the issue is merely a diversion or red herring by the defense, the prosecutor should make a careful evaluation of how to proceed.

The prosecutor's direct examination of an expert witness is often divided into two parts: laying the foundation to qualify the witness as an expert and questioning the witness regarding the evidence in the case being tried. In some jurisdictions, qualifying the expert is done outside the jury's presence, while in others it is done with the jury present. On occasion, the defense may request stipulating to the expert's qualifications, either of the state's expert witness or the defense's expert. While this approach may shorten this part of the process, most prosecutors do not recommend stipulating to the analyst's qualifications, as stipulating "short-circuits" the jury's understanding the breadth of the state's witness's qualifications and experience, especially when the defense witness is primarily an academician with little hands-on experience. In those jurisdictions where the expert is qualified outside the jury's presence, the prosecutor should repeat these qualifications for the jury to enable them to appreciate the extent of the expert's background, training and experience. Key in any qualification process is conveying to the judge that this analyst is an expert in the area he or she will be testifying about.

Typical questions used to qualify the expert analyst include:

- Where he or she is currently employed, his or her job title and professional history
- Professional training both within the lab and elsewhere
- Educational history
- How many times and for how many years the analyst has performed forensic DNA analyses
- What system of proficiency testing the witness routinely undergoes to remain qualified within his or her field.
- Publications the expert has authored or co-authored
- Professional associations to which the witness belongs, especially those that require qualifications (examination, publications) for membership
- Licenses or board certifications the witness holds
- Seminars attended in his or her specialization
- Research in his or her specialization either completed or ongoing
- Teaching experience, either in-house or other organizations, associations or professional groups
- Professional awards or commendations the witness has received
- How many times and in which jurisdictions the witness has been qualified as an expert witness and whether the expert has testified for the defense as well as the prosecution

Well before the witness takes the stand to be qualified as an expert, the prosecutor should ask whether the witness has ever failed a proficiency test. Proficiency tests identify problems that need to be corrected. The prosecutor should ask the analyst what the nature of the failure was, how it was identified, how long ago it occurred, what corrective actions were taken and what steps the expert has taken since then to maintain and demonstrate his or her proficiency. Having this knowledge in advance enables the prosecutor to ask the witness in front of the jury about the failure and what corrective action had been taken since then. Failure to address this issue directly is a guarantee that the defense will ask, and as a result the prosecutor and expert may lose credibility with the jury.

On cross-examination, the defense may assert that the analyst is not qualified to provide a statistical interpretation of the DNA typing results if the analyst does not have an academic degree in statistics or population genetics. Anticipating this objection, the prosecutor should be familiar with the Rules of Evidence and case law holding that the analyst is not required to hold such a degree to provide a statistical opinion.[138] In addition, the DAB standards require only that the analyst "have course work and/or training in statistical and population genetics as it applies to forensic DNA analysis."

[138] *Baldwin v. State*, 757 So. 2d 227 (Miss. 2000).

During the second phase of the expert's testimony, the prosecutor should have the analyst explain generally to the jury each step in the lab's procedure for receiving, documenting and storing the evidence. Under most conditions (with the exception of retesting), forensic labs require that evidence be received in sealed containers. If the lab follows this practice, this eliminates the number of individuals required to maintain the chain of custody beyond the person who sealed the evidence at the crime scene (or when the evidence was collected in the case of a rape kit) and the individual who broke the seal at the lab. By showing that the seal was intact upon the analyst's receipt of the evidence sample, the analyst demonstrates the integrity of the evidence between collection and analysis.

After being qualified as an expert witness, the analyst will be able to testify to a number of issues relating generally to DNA typing as a reliable science, the typing lab's practices and protocols, as well as issues relating directly to the evidence in the particular case. On direct examination, the prosecutor should question the analyst regarding the forensic lab itself. The prosecutor should ask if the lab meets national testing standards required by ASCLD-LAB and if the lab uploads profiles into the FBI's CODIS system. Note that some reputable labs adhere to the national standards of quality assurance but have not been certified by ASCLD-LAB.

The analyst can also testify to the internal procedural checks the lab uses to verify and validate the analyst's bench work and subsequent opinions. The National Quality Assurance Standards require that labs use a "second reader" system, which involves a second analyst independently reviewing all the testing documentation and providing an independent conclusion regarding the analyst's findings. This second reader's opinion, whether it concurs or disagrees with the testing analyst's, is included in the lab's final report. Some labs also use a third level of review, in which the lab administrator reviews both the analyst's and second reader's conclusions before the report is released. The analyst testifies as an opinion witness and as such is not bound by the same rules as a fact witness. If possible, the prosecutor should have the analyst remain in the courtroom during the defense expert witness's testimony in order to assist the prosecutor during cross-examination and possible rebuttal testimony.

During direct examination, the prosecutor can establish:

- The validity and accuracy of DNA typing: what DNA is, how it is obtained and how the sequence of DNA differs from one individual to another
- The credibility of the forensic lab: its accreditation, as well as its record of performance on proficiency tests and internal and external audits
- The qualifications of the analyst
- The proper handling of the evidence in the case according to lab protocol
- The reliability of the results of the analysis
- The reliability of the statistics obtained from the analysis

Educating the Jury on Statistics

The prosecutor can use the expert witness to educate the jurors, enabling the jurors to assign the proper weight to the evidence. As discussed in Chapter 4, this is done by developing a statistical calculation of the random match probability, which expresses the probability that the DNA profile in question would be found in an individual who was selected at random from a reference population.[139] In many jurisdictions, DNA match evidence is inadmissible without accompanying interpretive evidence regarding the likelihood of a coincidental match. The analyst must calculate a statistic to provide this clarification.[140] Some courts have held that presenting a match statement without an accompanying statistical analysis constitutes reversible error.[141]

[139] National Academy of Sciences, 1996, p. 31.

[140] *People v. Coy*, 243 Mich. App. 283 (2000).

[141] *State v. Williams*, 574 N.W. 2d 293, 298-299 (Iowa 1998); *Peters v. State*, 18 P. 2d 1224 (Alaska Ct. App. 2001).

The witness will use two primary analyses in explaining this concept to the jury, and the prosecutor should discuss in advance which of the two the analyst intends to use:

1. The random match probability analysis, in which the statistic represents the probability that a randomly selected person from the reference population would have the same DNA profile. This also allows one to calculate the number of unrelated persons within the reference population who could be expected to have the same profile as that obtained from the crime scene evidence.

2. The rate of exclusion analysis, in which the analyst describes the percentage of unrelated persons in the reference population who could be excluded as a contributor of the evidence sample.

Prosecutors should take care not to draw incorrect conclusions from the analyst's report; doing so may result in a mistrial. The analyst's findings should be stated correctly, both by the analyst and by the prosecutor in closing argument. The prosecutor should review Chapter 4 as a means of avoiding fallacious statements regarding the interpretation of the evidence.

It is also important to provide a context in which the jury can understand the value of the analyst's reported statistical calculation. For example, if the probability of finding a randomly selected individual from the general population who has the same DNA as that found in the crime scene evidence is 1 in 1 quintillion, this statistic may be difficult for the individual juror to grasp. When the statistical calculation exceeds the Earth's population, one way to put the information into context is to have the analyst calculate the Earth's current population, and tell the jury how many Earths it would take to equal that statistic. Alternatively, the analyst can inform the jury that, if one counted to 1 quintillion at a rate of one number per second, it would take approximately 31,700,000,000 (31 billion, 700 million) years.

Choosing a Format for Presenting the RMP

The prosecutor should decide the specific format in which he or she will present the RMP on a case-by-case basis, taking into account whether a full profile or partial profile was obtained, and the specific value of the RMP. Prosecutors should study Koehler's[142] theory of exemplar cueing carefully (discussed in Chapter 7). According to the theory, jurors are less likely to conclude that the defendant is the source of the evidence if the evidence is presented in a manner that enables the jurors to envision examples of other people whose DNA profiles might also match that of the evidence (coincidental matches). When presenting the RMP for the DNA evidence, the prosecutor should present it as a percentage or a fraction, rather than stating the number of people from a given population that would be expected to match. For example, if the RMP is 1 in 10,000, the expert may state that the probability of finding a coincidental match is 0.01% and illustrate that as "0.01/100." The use of a fractional numerator (0.01) will be particularly effective because that number is close enough to zero that many jurors will interpret that as indicating that almost nobody would match the profile in question. In contrast, the defense may proffer the mathematically equivalent statement that, in a city of 1 million people, 100 people would be expected to match the DNA profile in question. This form of the RMP allows the jurors to envision individuals whose DNA profiles matched by coincidence; this leaves the jurors less certain that the DNA profile match is strongly probative.

If the defense presents the RMP in a manner that encourages the jurors to envision coincidental matches, the prosecutor should remind the jurors that the DNA profile match is only one aspect of the prosecution's case. The prosecutor should remind the jurors that the non-DNA evidence will exclude the innocent individual whose DNA profile matches that of the evidence by coincidence. The jurors' minds should be kept focused on the fact that the defendant is the only individual whose DNA profile matches that of the evidence, and who was in the vicinity of the crime when it was committed, matches eyewitnesses' or the victim's description of the perpetrator, or had some motive for committing the crime. Having the expert witness present the Probability of Exclusion, which tells how many people in the general population one could expect not to have a matching profile, may also be effective. This encourages the jurors to envision all the people whose profiles do not match the one in question, keeping the jury's focus on the defendant.

142 Koehler, 2001.

Anticipating Defense Challenges to DNA

Defense challenges typically follow a pattern. If one defendant is successful in a challenge, similar challenges are seen in other jurisdictions until a sufficient catalog of case law develops to discontinue the challenge's argument. Beyond the "challenge du jour," the prosecutor should also anticipate a number of standard challenges. These challenges generally target the sample, laboratory operations or the statistics. Factors that influence the quality of the DNA evidence are discussed in Chapter 3, and strategies for challenging the evidence are discussed in Chapter 9. The prosecutor should review these chapters carefully and anticipate their use by the defense.

It is particularly important for the prosecutor to understand the process whereby the samples were analyzed, as well as how and to what degree factors such as minute quantity or degradation can affect the DNA evidence. Many factors that reduce the quality of forensic samples have predictable effects on the DNA evidence. Many of the defense's attacks that are predicated on these grounds can be countered effectively if the prosecution can point out that one can predict the specific effect that error would have on the DNA evidence and that there is no evidence that the data have been compromised in that manner. This also allows the prosecution's witnesses to emphasize how the possibility of a suboptimal sample has been considered in the interpretation of the results. In addition, every challenge presents the analyst an opportunity to reemphasize that the analysis protocol includes several safeguards that enable the analyst to detect instances in which the evidence has been impacted.

Because of the esoteric nature of the DNA analysis methods, a defense attorney has many opportunities to plant vague seeds of doubt in the mind of a naïve juror. For example, some defense attorneys will try to impress a jury with the fact that the enzyme used for the PCR, Taq DNA polymerase,[143] is known to commit errors. As described in Chapter 2, the Taq polymerase builds a new DNA strand by reading an old DNA strand and chaining together the nucleotides complementary to the old DNA strand. The polymerase will occasionally incorporate the wrong nucleotide into the new DNA strand, resulting in a PCR product whose sequence differs from the individual's true sequence at one nucleotide position. While this property of Taq DNA polymerase is well recognized, this is rarely a source of error in interpreting forensic DNA data. Most Taq DNA polymerases

[143] The term "Taq" refers to the fact that the DNA polymerase was originally extracted from the bacterium *thermus aquaticus*.

have error rates of 1 in 10,000 nucleotides or lower. Even in a sequencing analysis such as those performed to analyze mitochondrial DNA, where each nucleotide is analyzed individually, this will not introduce significant error. The PCR makes so many copies of the target sequence that, unless a specific error is made repeatedly, at the same nucleotide position every time, there will be so many more PCR products with the correct sequence than with the incorrect sequence that the product with the incorrect sequence will not be visible among the correct ones. The companies that provide PCR reagents are continually improving and developing new forms of Taq DNA polymerase, and each manufacturer will specify an error rate for each form of Taq DNA polymerase it produces. If the prosecution's witness describes how many molecules of product a PCR produces, and how rare a mistake will be, it should be easy to paint the opponent's effort to impress the jury with the fact that Taq DNA polymerase is not perfect as much ado about nothing.

Some pretrial admissibility challenges are predicated on grounds that influence the weight of the evidence and not its admissibility. If the issues being challenged go to matters of the interpretation, accuracy or evaluation of the statistical calculations, these considerations more properly go to the weight the evidence should be given by the jury. The prosecutor should carefully evaluate the defendant's request for a hearing, and if the ground for the challenge is really not an admissibility issue, the prosecutor should require the defense to show why the requested hearing is necessary. For example, challenging a laboratory's use of a commercial STR kit does not properly fall under admissibility challenges.[144]

[144] *Utah v. Butterfield*, 27 P. 3d 1133 (Utah 2001); *Colorado v. Shreck*, 22 P.3d 68 (Colo. 2001).

Quality of the Sample

Three issues that frequently impact the quality of a forensic evidence sample are degradation, contamination and the presence of PCR inhibitors. Time and the elements will degrade DNA; this is especially true for samples deposited outdoors, where enzymes from soil bacteria will degrade the DNA. If there is evidence that the sample is degraded, the defense will surely make a point of it. As discussed in Chapter 3, a yield gel can illustrate the degree of degradation the sample has suffered. In addition, the testing lab should have validation study data that illustrate how robust their analysis is in the face of the degree of degradation that has occurred in the sample in question.

Sample degradation is an issue that influences the weight of the evidence, and not its admissibility.[145] The specific effect that degradation will have on a DNA profile depends on the degree of degradation in the sample. In the most difficult cases, moderately degraded DNA can cause one or a few alleles to drop out of the profile. This can make a heterozygous genotype look like a homozygous one. In these rare cases, the analyst may feel that he or she has obtained a full 13-locus profile and will report a profile that is similar to the true profile, but characterizes one or two markers' genotypes as homozygous when they are actually heterozygous. Although these cases will be rare, they represent the most dangerous of situations because they can lead to false inclusions and exclusions. The true perpetrator will be excluded, while an individual whose DNA profile differs from the perpetrator's by being homozygous at one or two markers, where the true perpetrator's is heterozygous, will be included.

[145] *State v. Grant*, No. CR6481390, 2002, LEXIS 1127 (Conn. Super. Ct., April 9, 2002); *People v. Hickey*, 687 N.E. 2d 910 (Ill. 1997); but see *Armstead v. State*, 673 A. 2d 221 (Md. 1996); *U.S. v. Chischilly*, 30 F. 3d 1144 (9th Cir. 1994).

In many cases when degradation is present, the analyst will not be able to obtain a full profile of 13 loci. When only a partial profile is obtained, the evidence is still useful to the prosecutor, but the prosecutor must be especially careful not to overstate the significance of the evidence. Degradation is often analogized by explaining to the jury that a lightbulb may dim over time, but the passage of time does not turn a white lightbulb into a blue bulb. Assuming that allele dropout has not caused any of the typed markers to appear to be homozygous when they are actually heterozygous, the markers that could be typed will reflect the profile of the individual who is the source of the evidence, and will not change into some other person's profile. A suspect whose DNA is actually in the sample will still be included on the list of potential contributors to the sample, but because the resulting profile represents data from less than a full 13-locus profile, the RMP, if one is generated, will be less exclusionary than one obtained from a full profile. In these cases, the prosecutor should remind the jury that the DNA evidence is merely one aspect of the prosecution's case. Although the partial DNA profile does not exclude as many people as a full DNA profile would have, the non-DNA evidence will complement the DNA evidence and exclude any innocent people whose profiles match that of the evidence at the subset of markers that were typed.

Contamination is also a concern with all forensic evidence samples. Because of the nature of the evidence, samples can be contaminated by material from several sources, including the victim, the perpetrator and the people who handled and processed the evidence. The prosecutor can assure the jury that the handling protocols for forensic evidence include several work practices that minimize the potential for contamination, and "[s]ignificant contamination occur[s] only with gross deviations from basic preventative protocols and [can] not be generated by simple acts of carelessness."[146] If the defense alleges that the sample has been contaminated, the defense should be required to identify the specific timeline in which the alleged contamination occurred: collection, transportation to the lab or in the lab prior to analysis. Through witness testimony, the jury should be taken through each link in the chain of custody during the time the alleged contamination occurred. Through the testimony of officers and the analyst, the safeguards that collectively minimize or negate the potential for contamination should be explained to the jury.

Even if the evidence has been contaminated, it is not rendered inadmissible. A body of case law indicates that contamination of the crime scene evidence affects the weight, rather than the admissibility, of the evidence.[147] According to several other scholarly articles, "The primary risk of contamination is wrongful exclusion, particularly if the contaminant masks the perpetrator's profile."[148] "Most undetected contamination is likely to lead to a false-negative result; a non-match might be declared when a match actually exists."[149] Because this is less egregious than a false inclusion, contamination is not considered grounds for declaring the evidence inadmissible.

As discussed in Chapter 3, several chemicals that are frequently found in forensic evidence samples can inhibit the PCR and result in either no profile or a partial profile. The most frequently encountered chemicals are heme, the iron-containing portion of hemoglobin, and one of the dyes used in denim clothing. Protocols exist to clean up the sample or compensate for the inhibitor, however. This will usually preclude analyzing the sample only if the sample is so minute that the analyst cannot put it through the clean-up procedure, where some DNA will be lost, and still have enough DNA to perform the test.

Chain of Custody

The chain of custody for DNA cases consists of three essential parties: the person who collected and sealed the evidence at the crime scene; the individual who received the evidence into the property room; and the

[146] Scherczziner et al., 1999.

[147] *U.S. v. Morrow*, 374 F. Supp. 2d 42 (D.D.C. 2005); *Wagner v. State*, 864 A. 2d 1037 (Md. Ct. Spec. App. 2005); *People v. Ko*, 757 N.Y. S. 2d 561 (N.Y. App. Div. 2003); *U.S. v. Traia*, 162 F. Supp. 2d 336 (D. Del 2001); *State v. Pappas*, 776 A. 2d 1091 (Conn. 2001); *State v. Ramsey*, 550 S. E. 2d 294 (S.C. 2001); *People v. Johnson*, 743 N. E. 2d 150 (Ill. App. Ct. 2000); *State v. Johnson*, 743 N.E. 2d 150 (Ill. App. Ct. 2000); *People v. Wright*, 72 Cal. Rptr. 2d 246 (Cal. Ct. App. 1998); *People v. Hickey*, 687 N. E. 2d 910 (Ill. 1997); *U.S. v. Hicks*, 103 F. 3d 837 (9th Cir. 1996); *U.S. v. Beasley*, 102 F. 3d 1440 (8th Cir. 1996); *U.S. v. Lowe*, 954 F. Supp. 401 (D. Mass. 1996); *Williams v. State*, 679 A. 2d 1106 (Md. 1996).

[148] Gill and Kirkham, 2004.

[149] National Research Council, 1996.

analyst who opened it in its sealed condition and later processed it. As a result, it may only be necessary to call these three parties to establish the sample's chain of custody at trial. Each lab has written protocols that describe their procedures for receiving and processing crime scene evidence. For example, the FBI's protocol can be viewed at www.fbi.gov. Once the lab receives the sample, an internal chain of custody is created and documented (who received it, who received it for processing and where any unused sample was sent). Ideally, the chain of custody has been well documented from the time the evidence was collected through its typing in the lab and return to the submitting agency. The prosecutor should inquire about any notations on the evidence log that he or she does not understand, determine that there are no gaps in the recorded dates and times, and ensure that the log dates and the analyst's report of the sample being returned to the submitting agency agree. Carefully reviewing this information with the analyst can diffuse many challenges to the chain of custody at an early stage.

The Proficiency of the Laboratory and the Analysts

If either the laboratory or the analyst has failed previous proficiency tests, the analyst should be prepared to provide supporting documentation regarding any remedial actions that have been taken. This principle also applies to individual analyses. When a run fails, the prosecutor should discuss with the analyst how the analyst compiles an editing sheet that documents what went wrong in the test—for example, an electrical problem, too much DNA in the sample overwhelming the system, failure of the negative or positive control or a sample mix-up. These details should be discussed well beforehand, and at trial; the analyst should testify on direct examination regarding the mistake and how the lab caught it and documented it. The analyst should then testify as to what remedies were instituted, such as whether the analyst retested the material, after which the process worked properly.

Proper Interpretation of the Data

As discussed in Chapter 9, the forensic analyst often must make some subjective decisions when interpreting DNA data. From time to time, an analyst will see a peak in the data that may be a true allele peak, but it may also be an artifact such as stutter, bleed-through, pull-up or a spike. Each lab should have validation study data that illustrate how likely these artifacts are under different circumstances (degradation, minute sample), as well as exactly how these artifacts appear when they are present in the data. Each laboratory has a threshold for reporting what it considers an artifact or noise. If the analyst reports seeing artifactual peaks in the data, this finding should be discussed during direct examination, and the analyst should explain to the jury how he or she determined that these peaks were artifactual and why the presence of these artifacts did not confound the interpretation of the data.

Some defense attorneys request the analyst's raw data and have it reanalyzed using a "master program" such as the Genophiler® program. These software programs reanalyze the fragment analyzer's raw data, allowing the defense expert to perform an independent analysis of the evidence.

Even when the state's forensic lab has provided raw electronic data to the defense, prosecutors have been successful in barring testimony from defense experts who have reanalyzed the data with a master program. One objection that has been raised successfully involves the fact that these programs generally employ parameters that are different from those that were in effect during the testing lab's validation studies, and therefore have not been validated for accuracy, reproducibility and reliability. The prosecutor should determine whether the software employs a sensitivity threshold that is recognized in published validation studies to be at, or near, the level of background noise and whether the software employs a scale for its Y axis that selectively truncates all strong evidentiary DNA signals. In addition, the prosecutor should determine whether or not any private or government forensic laboratory currently employs either a sensitivity threshold or a Y-axis scale identical to those employed in the manipulating software. The prosecutor should also determine whether the software used to manipulate raw electronic data has or has not been submitted to critical independent peer review through scientific publication, which is one of the recognized touchstones of good science. If the master program detects a peak that the analyst determined to be an artifact, the defense may argue that the peak is a true peak. If challenged, however, an experienced analyst who comes to court armed with the lab's validation study data can verify the accuracy of his or her determination that the peak is indeed only an artifact.

Statistical Challenges

Expert's Qualifications

The defense may challenge the use of the forensic analyst as an expert witness to provide the statistical calculation or random match probability developed in the case. The challenge usually raised states that the analyst does not have the expertise to generate a statistical conclusion. The DAB Quality Assurance Standard 5.3 provides that in order for a witness to give a statistical calculation, the analyst must have had "course work and/or training in statistics and population genetics as applied to forensic DNA analysis." Case law has upheld this requirement.[150] Thus, if the chemist, biologist or forensic analyst has completed the relevant coursework or training, he or she should be qualified to testify under the DAB standards

[150] *Baldwin v. State*, 757 So. 2d 227 (Miss. 2000).

Mixtures

Each laboratory determines the manner in which a mixture is resolved, and prosecutors should be familiar with the thresholds or protocols the analyst used to analyze the evidence. Some laboratories attempt to identify potential contributors within the mixture, whereas other laboratories categorize the sample as an irresolvable mixture and stop there. Depending on the type of crime, some laboratories may attempt to mask the known contributor (for example, the female contribution to a mixed rape sample) and provide a report describing the remaining profile. Having resolved the mixture this way, the analyst will then report a statistical calculation that illustrates the RMP for the remaining profile.

The most common legal challenge in DNA mixture cases involves the defense questioning the analyst on the statistical analysis of the data. Prosecutors should anticipate these challenges and proactively prepare for them together with the analyst. These challenges typically center on:

- Challenging the population statistics associated with the DNA match
- Challenging the analyst's use of the product rule
- Challenging the size of the database used in developing the statistical calculation
- The analyst's interpretation of the statistical calculation itself
- Challenging the validity of the statistic when the defendant's racial background is not represented in one of the major population groups.

- In cases dealing with mtDNA, the prejudicial effect versus probative value of the statistical calculation
- A statistical calculation derived from only a partial profile.

In some states, if the prosecutor intends to present evidence from a mixed sample, the court requires that the evidence be accompanied by a statistical analysis. It is essential for a prosecutor to know the controlling state's or court's requirements well before the trial date.

The defense may argue that while the analyst can draw conclusions from a single-source profile, mixtures cannot be reliably interpreted. In response, the analyst can testify that while mixtures are more complicated than a single-source sample, the majority of mixture samples can be reliably interpreted and statistically evaluated. There has been extensive peer-reviewed literature and judicial review of statistical methods used with mixtures, including *People v. Smith*, where mixed sample analysis of DNA using STRs was shown to be generally accepted in the relevant scientific community.[151]

Challenges to the Database

The defense will often challenge the size of a database. Although the NRC reports do not specify a specific number of entries a database must contain to be valid, the NRC recommendation is "at least several hundred." In many situations, however, a database of 120 to 150 samples has been determined to be sufficient.[152] The FBI uses between 200 and 300 samples in each of its databases. Most labs use databases of similar size, and comparisons between labs have resulted in consistent statistics. Because most databases are of sufficient size, routinely validated, peer reviewed and subject to statistical analysis, defense challenges to the size of the database are typically not successful.

Another challenge may arise regarding the source of the profiles in the database. As discussed in Chapter 4, the ideal database contains thousands of samples from people who were randomly selected from as many different geographic regions as possible. In reality, most validated databases are much smaller and may contain "convenience samples" that came from blood banks, paternity testing organizations, convicted offender groups and other sources from a single geographic region. The 1996 NRC report provides authority that samples taken from these groups did not differ from samples taken from the general population at large.

[151] *People v. Smith*, 131 Cal. Rptr. 2d 230 (2d App. Dist. 2003); *People v. Soto*, 21 Cal. Rptr. 412 (1999).

[152] Chakraborty, 1992.

Also as discussed in Chapter 4, it is important for the analyst to choose a database that reflects the defendant's ethnic heritage and adjust the calculation of the RMP to reflect population substructure, if it exists, within the database population. The FBI uses five primary databases consisting of African American, Caucasian, southeastern Hispanic, southwestern Hispanic and Native American profiles. The 1996 NRC report has indicated that, given the commonality of DNA in all humans, all the major racial databases provide reasonably similar estimates of the RMP of a particular profile. In addition, research prompted by the 1992 NRC report suggests that the population substructure that does exist in the major racial populations does not distort the estimate of the RMP to a significant degree. In addition, in order to ensure that the RMP represents a conservative indicator of the weight of the evidence, many analysts use the theta correction described in Chapter 4, which inures to the defendant's benefit. In most cases, the available databases provide valid estimates of the RMP for any given profile. When the defendant is a member of a socially isolated ethic group for which no database exists, however, the defense will often challenge the analyst's RMP.

Method of Computation

The 1996 NRC report recognizes the product rule, with corrections where necessary for population substructure or relatives, as an appropriate method for indicating the probative value of the DNA evidence (discussed in Chapter 4). In addition, the NRC recognizes the LR approach (see Chapter 4) as a valid means of calculation as well. If the witness advocates an alternative system, on cross-examination the prosecutor should ask whether the witness was part of the NRC's group of recognized experts who established the guidelines for calculation. The chances are very high that the National Academy of Sciences did not include the witness in that august group of scientists.

Cross-Examining the Defense Witness

The most effective type of attack on the defense's expert witness is one that precludes the witness from testifying at all. By filing a pretrial Motion to Exclude Expert Testimony, prosecutors have successfully barred defense expert witnesses from testifying when their testimony would not meet the requirements of FRE 702 (or state equivalent). Two common reasons for excluding a witness are a lack of relevant forensic experience and/or bias and personal motivation for testifying. Another reason for excluding a witness arises when the theory or process the witness proposes was developed specifically for the litigation. *Daubert v. Merrell Dow Pharmaceuticals, Inc.*, asks whether the expert has "developed their opinion expressly for purposes of testifying."[153] In *Daubert* jurisdictions, the prosecutor has the opportunity to proactively exclude a defense expert witness from testifying if the witness has prepared a scientific theory specifically for the case at bar. For example, consider the case described earlier, in which Dr. Marc Taylor, a well-known forensic DNA expert from Technical Associates, Inc., conducted an experiment that suggested that "tertiary transfer" of DNA from one person to another, then to an object, was possible.[154] Although it is accepted that transfer of DNA does occur between individuals and from individuals to objects, when the tertiary transfer theory was first articulated, the court ruled to exclude Dr. Taylor's opinion because it was developed for the express purpose of the litigation and the defendant had commissioned the tertiary transfer study.

Prosecutors can also seek to exclude an expert witness when the expert's opinion is unfounded because "the expert has unjustifiably extrapolated from an accepted premise to an unfounded conclusion."[155] In addition, FRE 403 (or state equivalent) and *Daubert* guidelines may be used if the witness's testimony will only serve to confuse or mislead the jury. If, on the other hand, the defense attempts to preclude the prosecutor from introducing DNA evidence citing FRE 403, an offer of proof will preserve the record for subsequent review, as well as leave open the possibility that events during the trial may cause the court to reverse its earlier ruling and allow the evidence to be admitted.

When the prosecutor is notified as to whom the defense will call as an expert witness, he or she can question the state's expert regarding the background, qualifications and reputation of the defense expert. Analysts frequently are aware of the professional reputation of other analysts and how they have testified in other cases. A prosecutor may also obtain valuable insight into the defense witness's testimony from other prosecutors who have cross-examined the witness. If the witness has testified previously in other matters, the prosecutor can search through LEXIS, Westlaw, the National Library of Medicine (discussed in Appendix V) or www.google.com. In addition, several national and state prosecutor

[153] *Daubert v. Merrell Dow Pharmaceuticals, Inc.*, 43 F. 3d 1311 (9th Cir. 1995).

[154] Marc Taylor, personal communication.

[155] *General Elec. Co. v. Joiner*, 522 U.S. 136, 146 (1997).

associations maintain an electronic databank of trial transcripts that are made accessible to prosecutors.

Once the defense identifies those whom it intends to use as witnesses, prosecutors should review those witnesses' CVs with the state's analyst. Sometimes the defense witness's primary experience will be in the classroom rather than in a lab, or most of his or her training or experience will be in a field other than forensics, for example, medical genetic research. The prosecutor should find out what proportion of the witness's time is spent reviewing others' work and what time, if any, the witness spends doing bench work. Any publications attributed to the witness should be reviewed, and if appropriate, peer-review comments of the works should be requested. It is also advisable to determine who rejected the work for publication, if that is the case, and, if possible, why. In a recent instance, a witness received some unfavorable peer-review comments for a draft article to be published in a scientific journal. Rather than revising the draft to reflect the peer-review comments, the witness had the article published in a nonscientific venue. Questioning the witness on these types of issues can allow the jury to put the witness's credibility in perspective.

If the defense witness's background is in an academic, medical or research setting, the prosecutor should ask the witness whether he or she has ever held a professional position in a forensic laboratory. If the answer is no, the prosecutor should inquire as to the type and volume of samples the witness is accustomed to analyzing. Many academic and medical scientists are accustomed to receiving pristine samples with ample volumes, and are unfamiliar with the extra issues that arise when the sample is minute or degraded. If the witness has little or no experience in forensics, the state's rebuttal witness can point out that the defense's witness's perspective or interpretation is one that is common among academic experts or those with general knowledge. Prosecutors and rebuttal witness should be aware, however, that while the state's expert witness may testify that he or she disagrees with the scientific conclusions reached by the defense witness, direct comments relating to the truthfulness or credibility of a witness are generally inadmissible.[156] Evaluating or weighing the credibility of a witness is uniquely the province of the jury.[157]

Prior to the trial, the prosecutor should determine whether the defense witness is primarily a consultant or whether he or she has a full-time job

[156] *Missouri v. Link*, 25 S.W. 3d 136 (2000), quoting *State v. Love*, 963 S.W. 2d 236, 245 (Mo. App. 1997).

[157] *State v. Middleton*, 998 S.W. 2d 520, 57 (Mo. banc 1999).

and consults on the side. Once the witness takes the stand, the prosecutor should ask about his or her hourly rate for consulting in the case, whether there is a different rate for testifying, approximately how many times the witness has met with the defense for pretrial conferences and how much time he or she has spent preparing for trial. The prosecutor should also inquire into what percentage of the witness's time is spent consulting (especially if this is not the primary job) and what portion of the annual salary is from consulting. The jury is often unaware that the witness has done considerably more than just testify in court.

Because defense experts profit financially from their testimony, there is always the potential that they might be biased in favor of the defendant. If the defense witness has just testified as to how much he or she is being paid to testify on behalf of the defense, it is difficult for him or her to then claim convincingly that he or she has no interest in the outcome of the trial. The prosecutor should request a copy of any contract or engagement letters representing the terms of the witness's association with the defense. The document should be reviewed to determine whether any contingencies in those documents would create a vested interest in the outcome of the case.

Some witnesses feel that using technical jargon will enhance their credibility in the eyes of the jury. If a defense witness is prone to this type of testimony, he or she should be given free rein to do so. This tends to widen the distance between the witness and the jury and causes the jury to be less receptive to the witness's opinions.

The prosecutor should take care to avoid shifting the burden to the defense by questioning the defense witness as to why the defense did not conduct independent testing of the evidence samples. It is best not to ask the defense witness whether he or she knew that some sample remained or whether the defense chose to retest it. Without burden shifting, on direct examination the prosecutor can ask the state's expert whether any sample remained at the conclusion of the analyst's testing, what the analyst did to preserve the remaining sample, what quality control measures were followed, why preserving the remaining sample is important and whether the analyst has any concerns about the typing. On redirect, if appropriate, the prosecutor can ask whether anything in the typing procedure or results suggested the analyst should retest the remaining sample. The prosecutor should avoid any temptation to intimate, either through a witness or in closing, that the failure of the defense expert to retest the crime scene evidence constitutes an admission of the accuracy of the original test.

When cross-examining a defense witness, the prosecutor should obtain concessions, or areas in which the expert agrees with the state, such as the validity of DNA typing or the general validity of statistical analysis procedures. To date, the methods by which DNA is typed and the statistical procedures with which data are interpreted have been tested in peer-reviewed scientific studies and debated in the scientific literature. Even early skeptics now concede that the process by which DNA evidence is produced has been rigorously validated.[158]

[158] Saks and Koehler, 2005.

REFERENCES AND ADDITIONAL READINGS

Chapman, S. (2006) *Silent Witness,* 10(1), www.ndaa.org

Country District Attorney, Maricopa, Arizona. (2005) *The CSI Effect and Its Real-Life Impact on Justice, A Study by the Maricopa County Attorney's Office*.

Esmaili, S. (2007) *Chicago-Kent Law Review*, 82, 495.

Gill and Kirkhan (2004) *Journal of Forensic Scences*, 49(3), 1.6.

Grande and Jeffrey, S. (2002) *Cardozo Law Reiew*, 3, 2277.

Greenhalgh, W.W. (1995) *The Fourth Amendment Handbook: A Chronological Survey of Supreme Court Decisions*. Lanham, MD: National Book Network.

Koehler, J.J. (2001) *Southern California Law Review*, 74, 1275.

LaFave and Wayne, R. (1987) *Search and Seizure: A Treatise on the Fourth Amendment,* 2nd ed., St. Paul, MN: West Publishing Co., p. 539.

McCormick, C.T. (1999) *McCormick on Evidence,* 5th ed. In John W. Strong (ed.). St. Paul, MN: West Publishing Co.

National Research Council (1996) *Report on the Committee on DNA Technology in Forensic Science: An Update, The Evalution of Forensic DNA*. Washington, DC: National Academy Press.

Rothstein, M. and Talbot, K. (2006) *Journal of Legal Medicine and Ethics*, 34, 153.

Saks, J.K. and Koehler, J.J. (2005) *Science*, 309(5736), 892–895.

Scherczinger, C. (1999) *Journal of Forensic Sciences*, 44, 1042(5), 1045.

CHAPTER 9

Arguing for the Defense

CONTENTS

The Defense's Choice of Strategy

Elements of a Competent Defense

When the Defendant Has Been Identified by a Databank Search

References and Additional Readings

THE DEFENSE'S CHOICE OF STRATEGY

Alternative Explanations for the Match: Error, Kinship, Coincidence and Presence Unrelated to the Crime

Unlike the prosecution, which should provide the jury with a single theory of the case, the defense can introduce many alternative theories of the case in an attempt to erode confidence in the prosecution's theory. The defense's trial strategy will depend on a number of considerations, including counsel's confidence in the defendant's actual innocence. In cases in which counsel is confident their client is innocent, the DNA evidence is highly likely to exclude the defendant as the perpetrator of the crime. If the prosecution does not order DNA testing on the available evidence, the defense should do so. In the rare cases where a match is found between the DNA profile of the evidence and the defendant, but counsel is still confident of the client's innocence, counsel should come up with as many answers to the question "If my client is truly innocent, what could explain these data?" as possible.

Four general explanations can be posited for a situation in which the defendant had no connection with the crime, but a match has been reported between his or her DNA profile and that of the evidence. The first is the possibility that the laboratory may have made a "false-positive" error, or false inclusion. This error can occur for a number of reasons, including mislabeling of samples or contamination of evidence samples with reference samples. As discussed in Chapter 7, the probability of laboratory error (PLE) is often considerably greater than the random match probability (RMP), and error is often the most likely potential cause of a false inclusion.

The second reason for a false identification is kinship. The DNA sequences of close relatives are more similar than the DNA sequences of unrelated people. Given that the forensic testing only looks at the DNA at a handful of loci, samples from close relatives may well produce identical results in forensic DNA tests, when the test only produces interpretable results for a small number of markers. In order to mount this kind of third-party defense, however, the defense will be required to provide evidence that a close relative is actually a suspect.[1]

The third possible reason for the false inclusion of an innocent suspect is coincidence. As rare as any individual's DNA profile is, it is still theoretically possible for another, even unrelated, person to have the same DNA profile (again, because we are looking at the DNA at only a handful of loci). The RMP gives the probability that a randomly selected person from the larger population would match the defendant's DNA profile by coincidence. A coincidental match is possible, even for the rarest profiles. As discussed in Chapter 4, it is impossible to prove that nobody else in the human race possesses the same DNA profile as the defendant.

In rare cases, the suspect's DNA may be present at the crime scene but for reasons unrelated to the crime. If the suspect lives with the victim, his or her DNA may be on objects in the home, and the unstained sample control may contain his or her profile. Alternatively, the suspect may have had an interaction with the victim that left his or her DNA at the crime scene before the crime was committed.

The Possibility of Investigator or Analyst Misconduct

Most investigators and analysts observe an admirably high ethical standard while performing their duties, and most criminal prosecutions are conducted honestly. Unfortunately, however, there have been several high-profile examples of misconduct on the part of police officers, prosecutors, analysts and expert witnesses reported in the past, and the possibility of misconduct always exists in any human endeavor as emotionally charged as the investigation of a violent crime.[2]

The defense expert can scrutinize the injection lists, project files and other files produced by the fragment analyzer in an effort to detect instances in

[1] For example, *Taylor v. Commonwealth*, WL 80189, Va. Ct. App. (1995).

[2] Gianelli, 1997; Thompson, 2006.

which the analyst has manipulated files or replaced the data of one analysis with that of another. The sample injections occur at regular intervals, and the fragment analyzer names files according to a defined convention. If there is a gap in the injection list, or a file that is labeled with a "2," but there is no corresponding "1" file present, this may be evidence that the analyst may have deleted one or more of the run files.

Although stories involving deliberate misconduct are far more salient, it is much more likely that unconscious biases might influence the analyst's report, often in a manner prejudicial to the defendant. **Observer bias** is defined as a tendency of observers to seek out some information and avoid other information. Psychological researchers and legal commentators have demonstrated observer bias in many situations and have shown that, in many cases, the people involved are unaware that their behavior is reflecting the bias.[3] There is ample opportunity for bias, especially unconscious bias, to influence the results of forensic DNA testing. Many analysts work in settings in which it is only natural for the analyst to develop a prosecution team orientation. Even more importantly, in many cases it is possible to provide more than one interpretation for the data from a particular sample. Accordingly, the analyst must make subjective decisions, and subjective decisions always reflect whatever biases the decider possesses. In order to minimize the potential for bias, the analyst should determine the DNA profile of the evidence sample before he or she determines the DNA profile of the suspect's reference sample. This precludes the possibility that knowing the reference sample's profile will bias the analyst toward finding the suspect's profile in the evidence.

[3] Risinger et al., 2002.

For example, consider Figure 9.1. The DNA profile obtained from this sample is:

D3S1358—A questionable (low intensity, not as sharp as others) peak at the 12 allele plus a definite peak at the 17 allele

vWA—Clear peaks at both the 15 and 17 alleles

FGA—A clear peak at the 25 allele plus a broad off-ladder peak at approximately the same position as a 20 allele would be

Interpretation of these data requires the analyst to make decisions about whether the 12 allele in D3S1358 and the OL allele in FGA reflect true

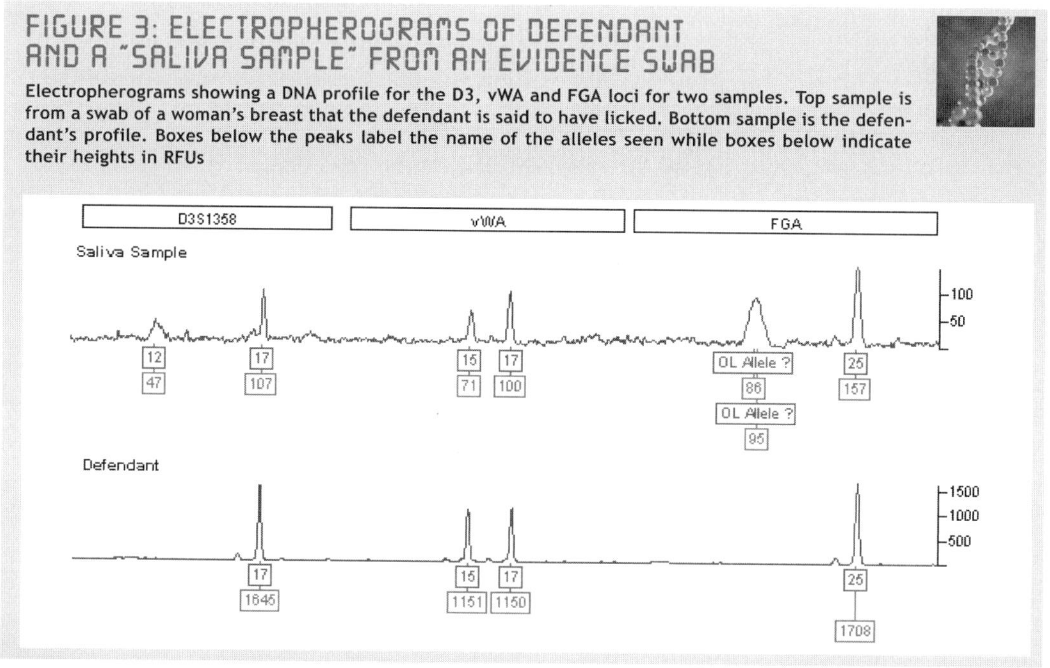

FIGURE 9.1 *Electropherogram illustrating traces from a saliva sample taken from a sexual assault victim's breast (top) and a reference sample taken from the suspect (bottom). Reprinted from Thompson et al., 2003a. Copyright the National Association of Criminal Defense Lawyers.*

allele peaks or artifacts. It is particularly important for the analyst to make these decisions before he or she knows what the profile from the suspect's reference sample is. For example, if the suspect has the 12,17 genotype at the D3S1358 marker, the analyst may conclude that minute sample or stochastic effects (discussed in Chapter 3) caused a true 12 allele to amplify poorly. Alternatively, if the suspect has the 17,17 genotype at D3S1358, the analyst may conclude that the questionable peak represents an artifact, and not a true allele peak. Similarly, if the suspect's reference sample exhibits a 25,25 genotype at the FGA marker, the analyst may declare the off-ladder peak an artifact. If, however, the suspect has the 20,25 genotype at the FGA marker, the analyst may decide that the off-ladder peak represents a combination of a true peak for the 20 allele plus some artifactual material that appeared at the same place in the electropherogram. Furthermore, if the suspect has the 15,17 genotype for the D3S1358 marker, because this was a relatively small sample, the analyst may conclude that the 15 allele could have dropped out of the data.

Given the nature of forensic work, it is unrealistic to expect most analysts not to adopt a prosecution team-oriented mindset. It is also unrealistic to expect that analysts will never receive information regarding the circumstances of a case from the investigators who have sent the samples for analysis. Because of the possibility of bias or misconduct on the part of prosecution-aligned agents, several states have created commissions charged with conducting independent reviews of forensic DNA cases. Some have even considered establishing independent testing laboratories.

Attacking the Admissibility Versus the Weight of the Evidence

In every case, the defense must decide whether to attack the admissibility of the evidence or its weight. At this point in time, attacking the admissibility of DNA evidence is difficult. Both the DNA analysis techniques and the statistical methods used to analyze forensic DNA data are routinely accepted in the courts. Prosecution witnesses are usually experienced in the field of forensic analyses and are therefore bound to be considered qualified by the court. In addition, as discussed in Chapter 7, even though the FRE and the *Daubert* decision considered the potential for laboratory error a matter influencing the admissibility of evidence, the courts now generally treat allegations of lab error as a matter influencing the weight of the evidence instead. In most cases, the defense is limited to attacking the weight of the evidence on one of the grounds we have discussed.

It is particularly important for the defense to mount any possible admissibility challenges when the DNA evidence strongly implicates the defendant; there is little to lose and everything to gain. It is also advisable to do so in a pretrial hearing, if possible, out of the presence of the jury. If counsel waits until the trial to object to the admissibility of the evidence and the judge denies the motion, it gives the jurors the impression that the judge is endorsing the DNA evidence. This will increase the jurors' confidence in the DNA evidence's probative value. Even if the challenge is successful, the jury will be aware that there was DNA evidence, and the fact that the defense wanted it dismissed may lead some to assume that the test results were damaging to the defendant. The defense is aided here by the fact that the 2000 amendment to FRE Rule 103 preserves these pretrial issues for subsequent appeal, if necessary. The amended Rule 103 obviates the need for the defense to reintroduce the objection at trial in order to preserve the matter for subsequent appeal, provided the record makes it clear that the pretrial ruling was intended to be final.

Another good reason for mounting the admissibility attack during the pretrial phase is that the judge's decisions regarding admissibility of evidence and experts may influence the defense's strategy at trial. Just as prosecutors were advised in Chapter 8, the defense should preview the weaknesses of its case with the jurors as early in the proceedings as possible, while planting the seeds of skepticism regarding the other side's evidence and witnesses. Some courts may allow the defense to preview its theory of the case during voir dire of prospective jurors; alternatively, the defense can present its theory of the case during opening arguments. If the decisions have already been made regarding the evidence to be admitted, the defense may be able to conduct a more effective voir dire of prospective jurors as well as make a more effective opening statement if it knows whether or not the DNA evidence will be presented to the jury.

When the DNA evidence against the defendant is very strong, and there is no substantive basis for an attack, the defense may consider stipulating to the fact that the DNA profiles of the defendant and the evidence match, as well as the proposed RMP. If the prosecution is going to be able to establish these facts, and the prosecution's expert witness is experienced and a good communicator, it may be less damaging to the defendant for counsel to stipulate to the facts, rather than take the chance that the prosecution's expert will captivate the jury with a charismatic and competent presentation that culminates in an infinitesimal RMP.

In some cases, DNA evidence ties the defendant to multiple crimes, but the RMP associated with each crime may differ (for example, there may be results from a different number of markers from each of the samples). In this case, the defense should try to argue that the cumulative nature of the evidence of the different crimes against the defendant is prejudicial, and that separate trials should be held for each one. The state may well argue that in the interest of judicial economy the different crimes should be tried together. If the number of charges is such that the court rules it impractical to provide a separate trial for each one, the defense should request that the charges be grouped so that the cases in which the RMP is lowest are tried together, while the cases where the RMP is less impressive are tried together. This will prevent the cases where the RMP is very low from prejudicing the cases in which the RMP is higher.

The Decision Whether or Not to Order DNA Testing

The Sixth Amendment to the Constitution guarantees a defendant the right to effective assistance of counsel. In cases in which the prosecution is not presenting DNA evidence, but evidence is available that may provide typable DNA, the defense attorney must make a strategic decision whether or not to order DNA testing. This decision depends on several factors, including the specific evidence the prosecution plans to present and the defense's level of confidence in the defendant's innocence. Where the defendant may genuinely be innocent, DNA testing will help establish that fact and may be sufficient to secure dismissal of the charges. If the prosecution's case rests on evidence other than DNA, and the defense feels it can impeach the remaining evidence successfully, DNA testing may not be necessary. If the defense feels that the non-DNA evidence against the defendant is too strong to impeach, it may order DNA testing in the hope that an exculpatory result may counteract the other evidence.

Even if pretrial DNA testing is not performed, or if the results are inconclusive, some defendants seek to have the jury informed of their willingness to submit to the testing in order to demonstrate their "consciousness of innocence." Different courts have had different opinions regarding the relevance of such "consciousness of innocence" evidence, however. For example, in the case of *Jardin v. People,*[4] a defendant who was on trial on charges of rape in the first degree and related offenses tried to introduce evidence that he had volunteered to submit to a DNA test in order to demonstrate his "consciousness of innocence" to the jury. The trial judge ruled that the statement constituted hearsay because it was "communicative and testimonial" rather than intended to establish "real or physical" evidence. The judge also ruled that the defendant had not cited any exceptions to the hearsay rule that would have rendered the statement admissible. In addition, because the results of the DNA test had been inconclusive, the court ruled that the DNA test was irrelevant, and that in turn rendered the issue of the defendant's voluntarily submitting to the test irrelevant as well. Furthermore, the court pointed out that the

[4] 584 N.Y.S.2d 732 (1992).

defendant would have been compelled to give a reference sample anyway, so voluntarily submitting to the test was not the sort of bold act that was capable of proving the state of the defendant's conscience.

In other situations, the courts have ruled that the fact that the defendant acquiesced to the testing spoke to his or her state of mind and was relevant. For example, in the case of *Santana-Lopez v. State*,[5] Miguel Angel Santana-Lopez was convicted of sexually assaulting a six-year-old girl by forcibly licking and digitally penetrating her vagina. Santana-Lopez had volunteered to submit to a DNA test, but none had been performed. At trial, Santana-Lopez tried to argue that volunteering to submit to the DNA test was evidence of his consciousness of innocence. The trial judge did not reject Santana-Lopez's argument, but instead ruled that Santana-Lopez's state of mind was not relevant. The appellate court disagreed, however, and ruled that the issue of Santana-Lopez's state of mind was relevant. It did not reverse the conviction, however. Apart from ruling that Santana-Lopez's state of mind was relevant, the appellate court left the remainder of the process in the hands of the trial court. The appellate court remanded the case to the trial court "for a finding . . . whether Santana-Lopez believed DNA could detect the sexual assaults of which he was charged." Because the assault had involved only licking and digital penetration, and there was no semen to provide a good DNA sample, the possibility exists that a DNA test may not have been informative. Thus, the central issue for the trial court to decide was how much Santana-Lopez understood about the capabilities and limitations of DNA testing. The trial court was ordered to determine whether Santana-Lopez truly believed that a DNA test could provide evidence capable of implicating the guilty or exonerating the innocent in this case, or whether he believed that a DNA analysis could not provide such evidence, and his volunteering to submit to the DNA test was merely a deceptive ploy. In addition to leaving the decision up to the trial judge, the appellate court also kept the DNA evidence in perspective. It ruled that if the trial court found that Santana-Lopez truly believed that a DNA test would provide relevant evidence, then the court should consider his willingness to submit to testing evidence of his consciousness of innocence. The trial court, however, was to consider this within the context of the body of evidence against Santana-Lopez and determine whether the decision not to admit this testimony was prejudicial to the defense or merely harmless error.

[5] 613 N.W.2d 918, Wis. (2000).

In some cases, the defense may have a perfectly sound strategy that does not require DNA testing. This is especially true when counsel plans to argue an alibi defense,[6] or when the sole evidence against the defendant is the testimony of the victim or an eyewitness.[7] In these cases, failure to have DNA testing performed does not constitute ineffective assistance of counsel. In fact, in the majority of appeals in which the defendant claimed ineffective assistance of counsel due to a failure to order pretrial DNA testing, appellate courts have ruled that the failure to order testing was consistent with the defense's sound strategy, or that the other evidence against the defendant was sufficiently compelling that adding DNA evidence would not make a difference in the verdict. Unless the convicted defendant can demonstrate that the results of the DNA testing would have resulted in an exoneration, there is little chance of any court accepting the claim that the failure to order pretrial DNA tests alone constituted ineffective assistance of counsel.

[6] *Thomas v. State*, 492 N.W.2d 410, Iowa (1992).

[7] For example, *Helton v. State*, 924 S.W.2d 239 Ark. (1996).

[8] 536 N.W.2d 487 Wis. App. (1995).

In contrast, a case in which a defense attorney's failure to order DNA testing was considered to constitute ineffective assistance of counsel is *State v. Hicks.*[8] Anthony Hicks was charged with burglary, robbery, and sexual assault. The state presented evidence from the microscopic analysis of head and pubic hairs, but no DNA testing was performed by either side during the original trial. Although the prosecution's expert admitted that microscopic analysis of hairs was not capable of providing an individual identification, she testified that the results of her analysis were "consistent" with Hicks having been the assailant. Hicks was convicted. The evidence against him included the fact that the victim identified him in a lineup; circumstantial evidence also indicated he had the opportunity and means to have committed the crime.

After his conviction, Hicks had DNA testing performed on the pubic hair samples. Several samples yielded inconclusive results, but the single set of interpretable results that was obtained excluded Hicks as the assailant. The trial court denied Hicks's motion for a new trial. The trial court concluded that his defense counsel's failure to order DNA testing was not prejudicial to Hicks. The trial court downplayed the importance of the hair analysis results to the original verdict. Because of the victim's eyewitness identification and the circumstantial evidence, the court concluded that it was unlikely that a new trial, including the DNA test results, would result in a different verdict. In addition, because only one of several hairs provided interpretable DNA results, the court concluded that there was a possibility that the other hairs could have belonged to Hicks.

In *Hicks*, the Wisconsin appellate court concluded that Hicks's defense counsel provided ineffective assistance by failing to order the DNA testing. Hicks had never told his counsel that he had committed the crime with which he was charged, and Hicks's counsel admitted that he was aware that DNA testing could have been performed on the hairs. Hicks's attorney claimed that his trial strategy was to expose the weaknesses of the evidence from the microscopic hair analysis and that he made a "strategic decision" not to pursue the DNA testing. The appellate court decided, however, that ordering DNA testing was not inconsistent with the defense's stated strategy. In addition, there had been no pretrial hearing regarding the admissibility of the hair analysis findings. The court ruled that, in the absence of this hearing, Hicks's counsel should have anticipated the possibility that the court would admit the evidence over counsel's objection (which it did). The court further opined that the fact that some other samples (semen, blood, saliva) had been tested, with inconclusive results, also did not preclude performing a DNA analysis on the pubic hairs. The appellate court pointed out that, because the hair analysis results were a prominent part of the prosecution's case, it rejected the trial court's assertion that the new DNA evidence would have no impact on the verdict. The appellate court reversed the conviction, and the case was remanded for a new trial. The Wisconsin Supreme Court later affirmed the appellate court's decision.[9]

All private defense attorneys realize that they can be sued for legal malpractice. Under some circumstances, court-appointed attorneys can be sued as well, in spite of the fact that they are government employees. Although the principle of sovereign immunity insulates many state and federal agents from malpractice suits, in some jurisdictions, court-appointed attorneys are employees of the county, and as such do not enjoy this protection. For example, consider the case of *Johnson v. Hallora.*,[10] Richard Johnson was wrongly convicted of rape in 1992 by an Illinois circuit court judge (Johnson had chosen a trial by judge rather than by jury). No DNA evidence was presented at trial; the prosecution's case relied heavily on the victim's identification of Johnson from a mugbook photograph. The conviction was affirmed on appeal.

[9] *State v. Hicks*, 549 N.W.2d 435, Wis. (1996).

[10] 742 N.E.2d 741, Ill. (2000).

While in prison, Johnson was able to have DNA tests performed on the crime scene evidence; the results excluded him as the source of the evidence. His conviction was vacated, and he was released after serving approximately 3½ years. Johnson then sued his court-appointed public defender, Michael Halloran, for legal malpractice, claiming that he had been negligent in not ordering DNA testing for the trial. Furthermore, a serological test had been performed on body fluids that had been found on the victim. The test excluded Johnson as the source of the material, but this was not introduced in court. Halloran had instead presented a motion *in limine* to prohibit the prosecution from introducing any evidence of blood, semen, or saliva testing.

Halloran requested summary judgment, arguing that, as a public defender, he was a state employee and therefore entitled to sovereign immunity. The trial court agreed and summarily dismissed the civil suit. Johnson appealed the decision, and the appellate court reversed it; Halloran then appealed to the Illinois Supreme Court. The court ruled that, as a public defender, Halloran was a county employee, not a state employee. The public defender's office had been established by the Counties Code, and was financially and logistically supported by the county. Moreover, although a statute existed extending sovereign immunity to certain county employees, public defenders were not included in the protected group.

The Defendant's Rights Regarding Testing and Expert

As discussed in Chapter 7, the Supreme Court has established the defendant's right to expert assistance through its decision in *Ake v. Oklahoma,*[11] and state courts have followed suit.[12] The Criminal Justice Act of 1964[13] (CJA) also evinces an understanding of the fact that there are many phases of the process during which an expert can render counsel valuable assistance. In addition, an indigent defendant has a constitutional right to an expert witness hired on his or her behalf at the state's expense when the subject matter for which the expert is needed will likely be a significant factor in presenting the defense, and the defense would be prejudiced if the defendant were denied this assistance.[14] Thus if the defense is predicated on several types of forensic subject areas, the defendant may be entitled to several experts at the state's expense.[15] One limitation, however, is that only one expert can be hired per specialized subject area. The defense cannot take it for granted, however, that

[11] 470 U.S. 68 (1985).

[12] *State v. Van Scoyoc,* 511 N.W.2d 628, Iowa (1993); *People v. Gaglione*, 32 Cal. Rptr. 2d 169, Ct. App. (1994); *Ex parte Moody*, 684 So. 2d 114, Ala. (1996); *Taylor v. State*, 939 S.W.2d 148, Tex. Crim. App. (1996).

[13] 18 U.S.C. 3006A(e), 1988.

[14] *Ake v. Oklahoma,* 470 U.S. 68; 105 S. Ct. 1087; 84 L. Ed. 2d 53 (1985); *Dubose v. State*, 6 62 So. 2d 1156 (Ala. Crim. App. 1993).

[15] *Hodges, v. Commonwealth*, 492 S.E. 2d 846 (Va. Ct. App. 1997).

requests for expert assistance will be granted automatically by the court. The court will assess the "probable value of the assistance sought, and the risk of error in the proceeding if such assistance is not offered."[16]

Now that DNA has come of age in the courtroom, defense attorneys are expected to be able to shoulder a significant amount of the burden themselves and be able to articulate exactly which aspect of the DNA evidence they need the expert's help to address. As discussed in Chapter 7, some appellate courts have ruled that the trial court's refusal to appoint an expert for the defense was harmless error when the appellate court considered the defense attorney's cross-examination of the prosecution's expert effective and comprehensive.[17]

An expert can help a defense attorney in many different ways. For example, one British study of defense attorneys who had litigated DNA trials reported that 94% of the defense attorneys who had consulted with an expert felt that the expert had provided them valuable assistance in evaluating the evidence or managing the trial.[18] Furthermore, as any litigator has learned, there is a substantial difference between directing one's own expert and cross-examining a witness for the opposing side.[19]

Expecting a defense attorney who does not also have an advanced degree in molecular genetics to navigate the intricacies of a DNA trial without the services of an expert is as unrealistic as expecting a DNA scientist who does not also have a law degree to defend himself on a murder charge without the services of an attorney. The prosecution has an overwhelming advantage in terms of access to forensic testing laboratories and expert witnesses, and many forensic analysts, because they testify frequently for the state, have close ties with the law enforcement agencies that send them samples and the prosecutors.[20] Given the numerous factors with which the defense has to contend, the inability to secure for the defense the services of an expert all but guarantees a suboptimal defense.

Whether or not the defendant is indigent, the defense should routinely request or seek the services of a DNA expert, or of any expert the defense feels would be helpful, for several reasons. First, it preserves the issue for appeal; if counsel does not make the motion, there is no denial of the motion on which to base an appeal.[21] In addition, failure to make an *Ake* request may constitute ineffective assistance of counsel.[22] Moreover, the defense may be able to use this issue to gain leverage for a plea bargain. For the indigent defendant, the fact that the defense is not required to pay for the

[16] *Ake v. Oklahoma*, 470 U.S. 68, 77 (1985).

[17] *People v. Bell*, 253 N.W.2d 726, Mich. Ct. App. (1977); *People v. Leonard*, 569 N.W.2d 663, Mich. Ct. App. (1977); *People v. Anderson*, 276 N.W.2d 924, Mich. Ct. App. (1979); *Plunkett v. State*, 719 P.2d 834, Okla. Crim. App. (1986); *Frias v. State*, 547 N.E.2d 809, Ind. (1989).

[18] Steventon, 1993.

[19] *United States v. Wilson*, 361 F. Supp. 510, D. Md. (1973); *State v. Dean*, 307 N.W.2d 628, Wis. (1981); NRC, 1992.

[20] Peterson et al., 1985; Moenssens, 1993; Bernstein, 1996; Wilson, 1994.

[21] *People v. Redd*, 670 N.E.2d 583, Ill. (1996).

[22] *Knott v. Mabry*, 671 F.2d 1208, 8th Cir. (1982); *United States v. Tucker*, 716 F.2d 576, 9th Cir. (1983); *Lindstadt v. Keane*, 239 F.3d 191, 2d Cir. (2001); *Pavel v. Hollins*, 261 F.3d 210, 2d Cir. (2001); *Spencer v. Donnelly*, 193 F. Supp. 2d 718, W.D.N.Y. (2002).

expert if the request is granted presents no downside to making an *Ake* request. The defense can request several experts but should remember that the court is only required to appoint one expert per individual specialization.

The most difficult situation in which to make a convincing argument that an expert's assistance is required involves a situation in which the expert is needed to help the attorney determine if there are critical technical issues involved in the development of the suspect's defense. Many courts will deny *Ake* requests if the request sounds merely exploratory.[23] The defense should argue, however, that there are times when an *Ake* request is necessarily exploratory in nature. In these cases, it is critical for defense attorneys to be able to articulate the limits of their own knowledge and illustrate why the expert's assistance is needed to assess the relevance of a particular technical issue for trial. In evaluating the indigent defendant's request for an expert, the court may request that the defense disclose its theory of defense. When this request is made, defense counsel may submit a motion ex parte and under seal and request that any court proceeding addressing the request be held *in camera* with the record remaining under seal. By doing so, the defense ensures the creation of a full record and allows for appellate review if the request is denied, without revealing its strategy to the prosecution. In addition the court may require the expert to review the evidence and render an affidavit before the court considers the need for the expert to have been sufficiently demonstrated.[24]

In order to maximize the chances for success, the defense's request for the expert witness should include the following features: (1) the name, field of expertise, qualifications and fees charged by desired expert; (2) the specific reason the expert's assistance is needed (in this case, counsel should specify the scientific or technical issues that are in question and illustrate why the resolution of these questions is beyond the ken of a competent defense attorney); (3) a demonstration that the expert's fees are reasonable; (4) a statement making it clear which element of the prosecution's argument the expert will be used to attack; (5) an argument outlining the indigent defendant's legal entitlement to an expert; and (6) a statement explaining that there are no government experts available who could adequately fulfill the role.

If the defense is denied an expert, in order to successfully appeal the ruling, the defense must demonstrate that the request for an expert was

[23] *Yohey v. Collins*, 985 F.2d 222, 5th Cir. (1993).

[24] *Harrison v. State*, 635 So. 2d 894 Miss. (1994).

timely, that the intention to use the expert was properly disclosed to the prosecution, and that denying the defendant the assistance of an expert denied defendant's right to due process. Untimely disclosure of the expert can result in the defendant being denied use of the expert as a sanction.[25] If the defense can demonstrate that the expert would have introduced exculpatory evidence, however, even decisions such as that handed down by the trial court in *Passino* can be reversed.[26]

A third perspective on the evidence is available to the bench through a developing trend among trial judges to appoint an expert witness to assist the judge in evaluating the testimony of both the state's and defense's expert witnesses. This individual interprets the experts' statements and reports and provides a neutral perspective for the bench.

[25] For example, *State v. Passino*, 640 A.2d 547 Vt. (1994).

[26] For example, *Passino*; also *People v. York*, 727 N.E.2d 674, Ill. App. (2000).

[27] Thompson et al., 2003b.

ELEMENTS OF A COMPETENT DEFENSE

The Discovery Checklist

During discovery, the prudent defense attorney will ask for all items relevant to the collection, processing and analysis of the evidence. Sample discovery requests are available in several published articles.[27] The prosecutor's duty to provide the defense with discovery is ongoing, and defense is entitled to any exculpatory evidence the prosecutor receives during the pendancy of the case. Items to be discovered include, but are not necessarily limited to:

1. All forms and worksheets that document the procedures used to collect, package, and label the sample. The request may include evidence that each person who was involved in collecting, packaging and labeling the evidence was properly trained and qualified. Criminologists must have proper certifications or experience, and even veteran police officers should have a short course in forensic evidence collection in order to ensure that they know how to collect the evidence properly.

2. All records required to document the chain of custody of the evidence. These records should be scrutinized to determine if there was any possibility for mislabeling or contamination of the evidence.

3. The laboratory's records of receiving the sample. These records should include not only the date and time the sample was received, but also notes regarding the condition of the sample, the means by which it was labeled and the location in which it was stored in the laboratory. Any documents that were sent by the agent(s) who collected the evidence should be scrutinized as well, to be certain they did not contain statements about the condition of the sample or the circumstances of the case that may have biased the analyst.

4. Complete documentation describing the portion of the evidence that was actually used for the analysis, and what procedures were in place to minimize the potential for contamination as the sample was collected.

5. A record of the standard operating procedures that were in place in the laboratory when it analyzed the evidence, covering not only the DNA extraction and analysis, but also the reporting of the data and the operation of the relevant instruments and equipment. This includes a wide range of things, including the laboratory protocols, the records of calibration and preventive maintenance of the relevant instruments, and the results of recent quality control tests on the equipment. In addition, the defense should request the names of all software programs that were used to analyze and interpret the data, and a description of any macros used by the program as well.

6. The raw data from the fragment analyzer. For the Genescan™ and Genotyper™ software packages, this includes all injection lists and log files that show which samples were injected into the analyzer, all Genescan files, including sample files and project files, and all Genotyper files, including templates and macros.

7. The analyst's complete case file, including photographs of the yield gel or other reports of the performance of the standard quality control procedures, and any notes the analyst made during the processing of the evidence.

8. The specific operational parameters that had been programmed into the instrument for that analysis. Note that this is not the same as the technical details of the analysis protocol, such as the number of PCR cycles used to amplify the DNA (these should be contained in the laboratory protocols). These are the parameters that are programmed into the fragment analyzer, such as the allele size ranges and the peak detection threshold (discussed in detail below), and any macros used to make allele calls.

9. A description of the reference database(s) used to calculate the RMP(s). In addition to a table of allele frequencies for each marker that was tested, this should include the number of entries in the database, the racial and ethnic makeup of the database's population, and the results of statistical tests indicating that the database conforms to Hardy-Weinberg equilibrium expectations, and that there is linkage equilibrium between the markers that were used for testing (discussed in Chapter 4 and below).

10. All records related to the accreditation of the laboratory and its personnel, especially the results of proficiency tests taken during the time period surrounding the analysis. These should include the laboratory's overall proficiency test results and any tests taken by the individuals involved in processing the evidence as well. In addition, the results of any internal or external audits conducted around the time of the analysis should be obtained. The DNA Advisory Board issued a guideline in 1998 that required forensic DNA laboratories to "follow procedures for corrective action whenever proficiency testing discrepancies and/or casework errors are detected," as well as to "maintain documentation for the corrective action." The defense should be certain that all necessary remedial actions have been instituted and documented.

11. All documents that certify the validity of the reference samples used in the analysis, such as control DNA samples or the molecular-size ladders used to assign sizes to the alleles that are identified.

12. Records indicating that the reagents used in the analysis were subjected to quality control tests and have not yet reached their expiration date.

13. A list of the samples that were processed immediately before and along with the sample in question. These are among the most likely sources of contamination.

14. Documents related to any internal audits that included that particular analysis.

15. Records of the laboratory's workload during the time of the analysis, and documentation of the number of employees who were working to process that workload.

16. A catalog of DNA profiles. The testing laboratory should maintain a catalog of DNA profiles from their technicians, analysts and anyone else who handles, and therefore could conceivably contaminate, the samples that pass through the laboratory. A complete list of these "elimination samples" would also include everyone who had access to the crime scene and who could have left the evidence, including innocent civilians and authorized crime scene investigators.

The prosecution is required to provide the defense with the results of all the tests that were conducted, including those for which the results were inconclusive. In addition, the prosecution should turn over any notes or other records that suggest that the sample was suboptimal or that there might have been a problem with the chain of custody or the analysis procedure. The defense should always ask for these "bench notes" specifically, however, to be certain there are no omissions in the discovery material it receives. These notes will contain the analyst's recollections regarding the quality of the evidence and the effect it may have had on the analysis. If any of the evidence introduced at trial comes from a sample that was contaminated, degraded or otherwise suboptimal, the defense will thereby have ammunition to attack the evidence. The defense should ask whether other samples were collected but not analyzed. The existence of other samples that were not analyzed is neither exculpatory nor inculpatory, but the defense should scrutinize the circumstances that led to documented contamination of any unused samples, in case they provide the defense a means of attacking the evidence the prosecution did present.

The Defense's Expert Witnesses

It is often difficult for the defense to find witnesses who not only have the right kind of experience but are also willing to commit the time and effort required to assist properly in the defense of the client. Ideally, the expert will have experience in the field of forensics, but this is not a requirement, even in strict *Daubert* courts. The courts have frequently accepted experts who had no direct experience in forensics.[28] Laboratory techniques such as STR analyses have many applications in molecular genetics, including medical diagnostic tests and gene research studies. An individual with appreciable experience with one application of the technique may be qualified to testify regarding issues of validation and quality control for that technique, regardless of its application. Similarly, the field of population genetics concerns itself with the study of the biological variability that exists in the human race. This variability is a fact of nature; as such, it often must be considered at one point or another in any analysis of human DNA. Consequently, many scientists who routinely perform DNA analyses need to use these statistical techniques to analyze their data, and to consider the principles of population genetics in their interpretations of their data. Because the formulas that should be used to calculate random match probabilities have been published, along with articles explaining how to decide which formula is appropriate for a given case, someone who has experience with other applications of population genetic principles may be able to testify regarding the validity of the statistical analyses used in the case at bar, even if that person has no direct experience with forensic analyses. For most forensic analyses, it is not strictly necessary for the expert witness to have direct experience in a forensic laboratory, although if the state's expert does, the defense counsel should anticipate that the jury will be informed of the disparity between the state's expert's experience and that of the defense expert. In cases involving minute or degraded samples, it may be necessary to use an expert who has appreciable experience analyzing suboptimal samples, such as an experienced forensic laboratory scientist. Many witnesses with experience in the medical field are accustomed to receiving samples that contain ample volume and were obtained under aseptic conditions; they may not be accustomed to dealing with the special considerations that attend minute or degraded samples.

[28] For example, *State v. Colbert,* 896 P.2d 1089, Kan. (1995); *Commonwealth v. Blasioli*, 685 A.2d 151, Pa. Super. Ct. (1996); *State v. Harvey*, 699 A.2d 596, N.J. (1997).

Experienced defense attorneys often rely on academic scientists rather than on forensic scientists from private labs. Many feel that most forensic scientists will have the same mindset as the prosecution's forensic scientists and will be less likely to question the subjective judgments and circular reasoning that are sometimes evinced in an analyst's interpretation of the DNA data.[29] An academic scientist is more likely to approach the DNA analysis from a different perspective, and is less likely to accept the analyst's conclusion that the unexpected results from a control procedure can be overlooked, or the analyst's dismissal of some questionable extra peaks as artifacts.

[29] Thompson et al., 2003b.

One important principle that applies differently to the prosecution witnesses versus the defense witnesses involves the influence that courtroom experience will have on the jurors' perceptions of the witness. The prosecution's experts will often be employees of a law enforcement agency or the forensic testing laboratory, and most jurors will not be inclined to question their motive for being in court. The more courtroom experience the prosecution's witnesses have, the more experienced and credible they will seem to the jury. Courtroom experience can be a liability for the defense's expert witness, however, especially those with only academic backgrounds. The defense must take care not to have its expert seen as a "juke box"—one who will sing whatever song is requested by the person who puts the money in. The defense team should emphasize that their experts are necessary to provide the defendant with a competent defense, and that they are being compensated for their time and expertise, not simply being rewarded for giving favorable testimony. It may also be helpful to use the defense witness to remind the judge and jury that DNA has proven to be a powerful tool for exonerating the innocent, and that expert witnesses have been instrumental in preventing wrongful convictions as well as securing the release of the wrongly convicted. Some jurors may think of DNA more as a tool to convict the guilty rather than a means to exonerate the innocent. Reminding them that it works for justice via both means may help soften some of their prejudices.

Defense counsel should be aware that in some jurisdictions all communication between the defense attorney and the client may not be considered privileged. For example, in Texas, when the defense gives notice of an expert and decides, after the named expert reviews the state's report, not to call the named expert, the prosecutor can, without violating the Texas work-product doctrine, inform the jury that another expert has reviewed the state's analyst's conclusions. The state may then argue that "if there were a witness to rebut our expert, the defense would surely have called him."[30] The Advisory Committee note accompanying the draft of Rule 503 endorsed the application of the attorney-client privilege to expert testimony, but the version of Rule 503 that was enacted leaves the recognition and development of these privileges in the hands of the courts. Despite the Texas exception, most courts consider communications between experts and counsel privileged, citing either the need to ensure effective assistance of counsel or merely fundamental fairness as the ground.[31] These courts recognize that the defense attorney may be reluctant to consult with an expert if that expert, having rendered an adverse opinion, can then be used by the prosecution against the defendant. Some courts disagree, however.[32] These courts may limit the privilege to discussions between the attorney and the client, or to the expert's review of information that came directly from the client. For example, in *State v. Cosey*,[33] the defense used all that remained of an evidence sample for its own test, thus precluding the prosecution from conducting further tests on the sample. Because the prosecution could not obtain the information it required, the court ruled that the prosecution was entitled to a copy of the report.

Courts and commentators have opined that, because allowing the prosecution to call nontestifying defense experts as witnesses may make the defense reluctant to consult experts, this may impact on the Sixth Amendment right to effective assistance of counsel.[34] In addition, courts have invoked the effective assistance of counsel principle to deny the prosecution the right to have a representative observe the defense's independent analysis of an evidence sample or to discover reports prepared by the defense expert for other cases.[35] This argument will be strongest when the defense has been allowed to hire a partisan expert, but if the court hires the expert, even if the hiring is done at the defense's request, the expert's opinion may not be considered a privileged communication. For example, in *Taylor v. State*,[36] the trial court appointed an expert, at the defense's request, to review the analysis of DNA from a semen sample from a rape case. The defendant's profile matched that of the evidence, with an RMP of 1 in 12 million. Upon hearing this report, the prosecution included the expert on its list of witnesses. Because the expert had been hired by the trial court, the appellate court rejected the defendant's claim that the expert's conclusions were privileged. The appellate court remanded

[30] *Pope v. State*, 207 S.W. 3d 352 (Tex. Crim. App. 2006).

[31] *State v. Pratt*, 398 A.2d 421, Md. (1979); *Commonwealth v. Noll*, 662 A.2d 1123, Pa. Super. Ct. (1995); *State v. Dunn*, 571 S.E.2d 650, N.C. Ct. App. (2002); also see Imwinkelried, 1990, for a survey.

[32] *State v. Carter*, 641 S.W.2d 54, Mo. (1982); *State v. Schaaf*, 819 P.2d 909, Ariz. (1991); *State v. Hamlet*, 944 P.2d 1026, Wash. (1997); *State v. Riddle*, 8 P.3d 980, Or. (2000).

[33] 652 So. 2d 993, La. (1995).

[34] *United States v. Alvarez*, 519 F.2d 1036, 3d Cir. (1975); *State v. Mingo*, 392 A.2d 590, N.J. (1978); *Hutchinson v. People*, 742 P.2d 875, Colo. (1987).

[35] *Prince v. Superior Court*, 10 Cal. Rptr. 2d 855 Ct. App. (1992); *State v. DeMarco*, 646 A.2d 431, N.J. Super. Ct. App. Div. (1994).

[36] 939 S.W.2d 148 Tex. Crim. App. (1996).

the case to determine whether the defendant had satisfied the requirement for demonstrating the need for a partisan expert.

Either side may request that the judge sequester the other side's witnesses until they are called to testify. FRE 615 and similar state procedural rules allow, with judicial approval, an exception to sequestration for an expert whose presence can be shown to be essential to the litigator's management of the case. This rule applies equally to the prosecution and defense, and both sides should arrange to have their expert present during the trial to ensure that any inaccurate or inconsistent statements are noticed. This enables both sides to be fully conversant regarding each other's representations about the evidence. This approach to case management is uniformly endorsed by the CJA, the NRC reports and others. Each side should be prepared to state specific reasons why it requires its experts to be present during the entire trial. Some courts need little convincing if there is to be considerable discussion of scientific or technical matters.[37]

Other courts, however, require the trial attorney to understand the fundamental issues and have required a showing that the presence of the expert was essential, not merely helpful.[38] For example, in *Evans v. State*, the trial judge ordered all witnesses sequestered during trial. Evans's counsel requested that the defense expert be exempted from the order to assist him in cross-examining the prosecution witnesses. Evans's counsel complicated the matter, however, by telling the court that he was undecided as to whether the defense's expert would actually testify, and that, in fact, it was unlikely that he would. The prosecution objected, claiming that allowing the defense's expert to hear the testimony of the prosecution's witnesses before deciding whether he would testify was counter to the purpose of the sequestration order. The defense responded by asking if it was permissible for the expert to sit at the defendant's table and assist with cross-examination if the expert did not testify later at trial. The judge denied counsel's request. Evans appealed, and the appellate court upheld his conviction, claiming that counsel had not made a specific enough case to demonstrate the necessity for having the expert present. The fact that an expert is merely helpful to the defense is not sufficient for the court to automatically grant an FRE 615 request; the expert's presence must be necessary to the defense's case managment, and this fact must be demonstrated by referring to a specific aspect of the effort to defend the client or a specific issue that pertains to the witness's expertise.

[37] For example, *People v. Valdez*, 223 Cal. Rptr. 149 (1986); *People v. Santana*, 600 N.E.2d 201, N.Y. (1992).

[38] For example, *Evans v. State*, 617 N.W.2d 220, Wis. (2000).

New Advances in DNA Testing Technology May Reshape the Debate on Discarded Materials

As discussed in Chapter 8, the courts consistently affirm an investigator's right to collect discarded materials from suspects in order to obtain a DNA profile. Following Supreme Court decisions such as *Katz v. United States*[39] and *California v. Greenwood*,[40] the courts have ruled that the individual retains no expectation of privacy in nontestimonial materials such as drinking cups, cigarettes and tissues that he or she voluntarily discards into the environment. Furthermore, the courts have noted that the individual has the opportunity to destroy the material before discarding it, thereby rendering the information contained in it inaccessible to others.

As new advances in DNA testing technology enable analysts to derive DNA profiles from more and more materials, situations may arise in which the logic of *Greenwood* does not apply. DNA profiles can now be obtained from fingerprints on glassware or from hairs that have been shed naturally. In order to avoid leaving behind any fingerprints or shedding any hairs into the environment, an individual would have to practice extraordinary containment and cleanup measures. There is clearly less of an intent to abandon these materials than there is for used tissues thrown in a trash can or a cigarette butt thrown on the ground.

[39] 389 U.S. 347 (1967).

[40] 486 U.S. 35 (1988).

Challenging the Quality of the Sample

One of the defense's best chances for impugning the DNA evidence lies in the possibility that the sample may be of poor quality. As discussed in Chapter 3, forensic DNA samples can be minute in quantity, degraded or contaminated by extraneous material. Any of these factors can make it difficult for the analyst to obtain a profile from the sample.

Degradation of the DNA sample will manifest itself in several ways. The simplest and most unambiguous way to determine whether degradation has occurred is to examine the yield gel that was run after extraction of the DNA. As discussed in Chapter 3, degradation of the DNA reduces the amount of amplifiable template in the DNA, even when the appropriate total amount of DNA is put into the PCR mixture. Because the amount of amplifiable DNA that is placed in the PCR is such an important parameter in the analysis, it is standard procedure to run a yield gel for every sample except those that are expected to yield very little DNA. If the DNA has been degraded, the yield gel will clearly show a smear in the corresponding lane, rather than a tight, high-molecular-weight band. In some cases, to save time or sample, a yield gel is not run. In this case, there is always the possibility that the sample has been degraded, and the defense should be primed to notice other things that may indicate this degradation, such as small peaks or an unexpected number of homozygous genotypes among markers with relatively large alleles.

A severely degraded sample will usually not produce any result. A more moderate degree of degradation, however, may result in an inability to detect the largest alleles in the population. With a moderately degraded sample, the peak heights across all markers may show a tendency to decrease as the allele sizes go up, because the largest alleles are the most difficult to amplify. If several markers' data are displayed in a single plot, you will see a downward trend in peak heights as you move from left to right along the allele size axis (the horizontal X axis). You may find that the analyst was unable to get a proper result for the marker with the largest allele range, despite being able to get satisfactory results from the markers with smaller alleles.

Allele dropout presents a challenge for the analyst, because there is no way to independently verify that the allele has dropped out. The only evidence that exists to suggest that an allele has dropped out is the fact that the profiles of the evidence and the defendant match at other markers. For the defense, the obvious explanation is that the defendant has a DNA profile that is similar to the actual contributor of the crime scene evidence sample, but the defendant should be excluded because of the lack of a match at that marker. Further testing using additional markers may strengthen one's confidence that the defendant is the source of the evidence, but there is nothing anyone can do to definitively determine whether the situation represents allele dropout or a profile mismatch.

Scrutinizing the Chain of Custody

FRE Rule 901 requires that the proponent of the evidence prove the evidence's authenticity. When it comes to scientific evidence, however, the issue is not merely the identity of the sample; the condition of the sample may impact on its proponent's ability to establish authenticity. Completely documenting the chain of custody is the only way to prove that the sample that was analyzed was the sample that was obtained from the crime scene, and that it had not been contaminated or otherwise compromised during the collection and handling process. For any evidence that comes from a biological sample, proving the chain of custody is a necessary element in the expert's testimony. If the authenticity of the sample cannot be proven through the chain of custody, the evidence or the expert's testimony may be rendered inadmissible.[41]

The chain of custody typically consists of three essential parties: the person who collected and sealed the evidence at the crime scene; the individual who received the evidence into the property room; and the analyst who opened it in its sealed condition and later processed it. At every step in the custody chain, there should be a record of the physical characteristics of the evidence sample. These characteristics may include volume, size, weight or some other characteristic that helps quantify and characterize the sample. Not only do all the links need to be established, but also the defense should scrutinize the level of safekeeping exercised at each level. If the level of safekeeping is judged to be suboptimal, however, the relatively lenient standards for admissibility set forth in FRE Rules 104(b) and 901(a) will probably cause the court to rule that this influences the weight, rather than the admissibility, of the evidence.

Scrutinizing the Testing Laboratory and Its Personnel

As discussed in Chapters 3 and 7, the poor quality of the DNA evidence used in some of the early DNA trials prompted the government to establish an accreditation program and quality assurance standards for DNA testing laboratories. Although all parties agree that a procedure for accreditation and external proficiency testing is a good way to maintain quality in forensic testing laboratories, the issue of whether a laboratory is accredited is of little practical significance to the defense in most cases. Even if the laboratory that has performed the testing is accredited, the defense must scrutinize each analysis carefully, to be certain that the laboratory made no mistakes in that particular analysis. In states that do not have statutes mandating the admission of DNA evidence without pretrial hearings, a lack of lab accreditation may provide grounds for a pretrial hearing. Absent specific evidence that some portion of the procedure actually went awry, however, most courts consider a lack of accreditation a matter influencing the weight, rather than the admissibility of the evidence and will readily admit DNA evidence from testing laboratories that are not accredited.[42]

[41] *Birge v. Alabama*, 2007 Ala. Crim. App. LEXIS 82 (May 25, 2007); *State v. Britt*, 231 S.E. 2d 644 (NC S. Ct. 1977); *State v. Chavez*, 508 P.2d 30 (N.M Ct. App. 1973); .ex. *Rogers v. Commonwealth*, 197 Va. 527, 90 S.E.2d 257 (1955); *Robinson v. Commonwealth*, 212 Va. 136, 183 S.E. 2d 179 (1971).

[42] *State v. Adams* 984 P.2d 16, Ariz. (1999); *Smith v. State*, 702 N.E.2d 668, Ind. (1998); *State v. Ramsey* 550 S.E.2d 294, S.C. (2001); *J.H.H. v. State* Ala. Ct. App., CR-02-1752, 1/30/04 Ala. Crim. App. LEXIS 22.

With respect to the actual methods used to generate the evidence, the 1996 NRC report and the National Quality Assurance Standards that came from the FBI's DNA Advisory Board (DAB) constitute the current guidelines regarding both the DNA analysis methods and the statistical analyses used to interpret the data.[43] Keep in mind, however, that even if the laboratory's procedure is not completely in line with the recommendations of the NRC and DAB, the prosecution may still be able to satisfy the court's *Frye*- or *Daubert*-based criteria for admissibility in a pretrial hearing. For example, in the case of *Henyard v. State,*[44] Richard Henyard was convicted of multiple murders and sentenced to death. On appeal, Henyard argued that the RFLP procedure that the Florida Department of Law Enforcement (FDLE) laboratory had used did not completely conform to the recommendations of the 1996 NRC, and therefore the evidence should not have been admitted. The state had argued successfully in a pretrial hearing that the laboratory's procedure, though not completely consistent with the NRC's 1996 recommendations, satisfied the *Frye* criteria of acceptance within the scientific community. In addition, it provided evidence that the FDLE analyst who had performed the analysis was subjected to regular proficiency testing and had performed satisfactorily on recent proficiency tests. Finally, the state was able to show that the FDLE laboratory's quality control and quality assurance measures were consistent with the 1996 NRC recommendations. The appellate court affirmed Henyard's conviction.

All accredited laboratories will have records of good performance in recent proficiency tests. Keep in mind, however, that some laboratories have only recently achieved accreditation and that some may have had significant deficiencies in their operation before correcting them and becoming accredited. As discussed in Chapter 7, attempts to challenge lab performance based on events that occurred before the evidence samples were processed are rarely successful. The defense should scrutinize the laboratory's record on proficiency tests from the era during which the sample was analyzed and afterward. In particular, the defense may use any errors that were made in the proficiency tests administered after the samples in question were analyzed to suggest that there were deficiencies in the laboratory's performance during the period when the samples were analyzed, and that these deficiencies were only brought to light by the subsequent proficiency tests. The defense should also carefully review the proficiency test performance of any analysts involved in generating the case DNA evidence.

[43] http://www.fbi.gov/hq/lab/codis/qualassur.htm

[44] 689 So. 2d 239, Fla. (1996).

Given the suboptimal nature of some forensic samples, there are many analyses for which the initial data will present ambiguities. Some studies have suggested that crime lab analysts may resolve these ambiguities in a manner that supports the prosecution's efforts.[45] An impressive body of research suggests that an analyst's work product can be biased when the analyst is aware of other facts concerning the case, or aware of the expectations of other investigators involved in the case.[46] Many forensic testing laboratories take samples solely from law enforcement agencies, and in some laboratories that analyze samples for both law enforcement agencies and defense attorneys, most analyses are performed at the request of law enforcement agencies. It is not unusual for investigators and analysts to communicate, and it takes a deliberate effort on their part not to communicate biasing information. Although this might not be a frequent occurrence, commentators have cited instances in which investigators have asked analysts questions such as "Would it help if I told you we know he's the guy who did it?[47]" It is critical to discover any documents the analyst received along with the sample or bench notes describing the scope and nature of the communications between the analyst and the prosecutor, submitting law enforcement agency or others. One very important matter counsel should determine is whether the reference sample from the defendant was analyzed before the evidence sample was typed. If the analyst already knew what the suspect's DNA profile was, it may be hard for even the most unbiased analyst to avoid having that knowledge influence the interpretation of the data from the evidence. In spite of the many ways a zealous defense attorney can challenge inculpatory DNA evidence, forensic testing laboratories receive discovery requests from only 10 to 15% of defense attorneys when the results of the DNA test have incriminated the defendant.[48]

[45] Thompson, 1995, 1997, 2003a.

[46] Risinger et al., 2002.

[47] Risinger et al., 2002.

[48] Thompson et al., 2003a.

In every case there will be a laboratory report describing the testing, reporting the results and providing an interpretation of the data. The report should clearly state which samples were tested, the type of tests performed, and whether each of the suspects whose samples were tested is included or excluded as a possible source of the evidence. When a match is declared, the report should include an estimate of the RMP and provide a table showing the frequencies of the different alleles for the different markers in at least one reference population. In addition, the report should clearly state if there was anything noteworthy or unusual about the appearance of the sample, the performance of control samples in the analysis, or any other event that may influence the reliability of the test results.

There is a constant push to develop DNA analysis systems that allow the analyst to perform the analysis faster and with a minimum of human involvement. For example, New York has validated a system that prioritizes allele calls and allows the analyst to focus time and energy on less clear data for use in the New York State Convicted Offender databank.[49] In addition, many government laboratories are so overloaded with cases that they have to outsource many cases to private laboratories. Standard 17.1.1 of the DNA Advisory Board's Standards for Forensic DNA and Convicted Offender DNA Databasing Laboratories requires these laboratories to compare the results obtained by the outside laboratory's analytical system with the results that would have been obtained with their system. Another system has been developed that allows for a speedier comparison between two different platforms' analyses. Just as the analyst can influence the results of an analysis by altering the operating parameters of the fragment analyzer, the analyst will be required to specify the rules that the new system uses to prioritize its allele calls or declare the results of the two different systems a match. There is always the potential for the analyst to introduce some bias into the analysis via his or her choice of parameters.

Challenging the Test Itself

The Defense's Obligations When Alleging Error

If the defense plans to call an expert witness to allege that an error was made during the DNA analysis, and there is untested sample remaining, the defense should have the sample retested to provide evidence supporting the allegation. (Note that this theory does not apply if the defense brings up the probability of laboratory error during cross-examination of the prosecution witness.) Replication is a hallmark of the scientific method, and any time scientists doubt the veracity of an experiment's results, they can simply repeat the experiment. If the defense expert alleges that the laboratory made an error in the analysis, but has not ordered an independent test of the sample to support the allegation, this may raise doubts with the jury regarding the witness's sincerity.[50] In this situation, under FRE Rule 105, the defense will be entitled to a limiting instruction to the effect that the expert's failure to perform independent tests on the sample does not demonstrate that the original test result was correct, but merely

[49] Kadash et al., 2004.

[50] *People v. Oliver*, 713 N.E. 2d 727, Ill. App. Ct. (1999); *State v. Varnado*, 753 So.2d 850, La. App. Cir. (1999); *State v. Saleh*, Wash. App. LEXIS 1461, Div.1 (2001); *State v. Faison*, 59 S.W.3d 230, Tex. (2001); *State v. Ledet*, WL856433 (2001); *Seager v. Iowa*, US LEXIS 6343 (2002).

demonstrates that the expert is not sincere in asserting that the original analysis was flawed. Ironically, although it is intended to help the defense, this instruction may inure to the benefit of the prosecution. The instruction may raise doubts regarding the defense witness's credibility that the prosecution would not have been allowed to raise on its own.

The test that is usually applied here is whether "it would be natural" for the defense experts to order a retest of the sample if they truly doubted the veracity of the results. It is easy to argue that, if a defendant had been unjustly implicated by an erroneous DNA test, it would by all means be natural for a skeptical expert witness to order retesting of the sample.[51] This approach provides an advantage for the prosecution over the previously mentioned approach. Because an admission by conduct qualifies as substantive evidence under FRE Rule 105, the defense is not entitled to a limiting instruction, as above.

If the defense does not order the sample retested, prosecutors may be tempted to emphasize during closing arguments that the defense has failed to introduce any evidence that contradicts the prosecution's DNA evidence, despite having the opportunity to independently test the sample. As discussed in Chapter 8, the prosecutor may ask the state's witness whether there was any sample remaining after the analyst typed the evidence sample. The prosecutor may ask the analyst before or after the state's witness has been cross-examined whether anything in the results would cause them to feel the need to conduct additional tests on the unused samples. Furthermore, the prosecutor can comment on the defendant's failure to present evidence or call witnesses.[52] A fine line must be understood between what comments a defendant may object to and what comments are permissible by the prosecutor. For example, the Fifth Amendment of the U.S. Constitution states that no person shall be compelled in any criminal case to be a witness against himself. It is improper for the prosecutor to comment on the accused's silence. This rule prohibits direct reference to the suspect's failure to testify and prohibits the prosecutor from suggesting to the jury that it may consider the defendant's silence as evidence of guilt.[53] The courts will sustain the defense's objection in this situation.[54]

STR Tests

The STR tests truly do provide the criminal justice system with a powerful tool for ascertaining a suspect's guilt or innocence. Many defense

[51] McCormick, 1999.

[52] *Van Woudenberg v. State,* 211 F. 3d 560 (10 Cir. 2000).

[53] *People v. Guzman,* 96 Cal. Rptr. 2d 87 (CA Ct. App. 2000).

[54] For example, *People v. Harbold*, 464 N.E.2d 734, Ill. App. Ct. (1984); *People v. Wills*, 502 N.E.2d 775, Ill. App. Ct. (1986); *Hayes v. State*, 660 So. 2d 257, Fla. (1995); *State v. Primus*, 535 S.E.2d 152, S. Ct. App. (2000).

attorneys get discouraged when facing STR evidence and feel that the best thing they can do is to negotiate a guilty plea. Keep in mind, however, that although STR testing has the potential to produce virtually unassailable evidence, that potential is not realized in every case. STR analyses are plagued by issues of suboptimal samples, equipment malfunctions and human error, just as any other type of forensic DNA test. The defense should combine high-tech scrutiny of the analytical procedure with a simple determination of "whether all the 'i's have been dotted and the 't's have been crossed." For example, if there is a gap in the injection schedule, or evidence that a sample has been analyzed more than once or had any changes made to its label, the defense should find out why.

In order to properly manage a defendant's case, a defense attorney must acquire a thorough working knowledge of the technical details of an STR analysis. Even with such knowledge, however, a complete defense review of the DNA evidence may require an independent test of the sample, or at the very least, an independent analysis of the analyst's raw data. Each analytical system has its own proprietary software that is required in order to analyze the data from that system. For most systems, the defense expert must have access to that company's software in order to reanalyze their data. For the most commonly used system, the Prism 310 Genetic Analyzer™ from Applied Biosystems, Inc.™, one can either use ABI's Genescan™ and Genotyper™ programs, or contact Forensic Bioinformatics,[55] which has developed an "expert system" program called Genophiler® that is capable of conducting a Genescan™ or Genotyper™ analysis. The Genophiler® program conducts an independent analysis of the raw data and allows the defense expert to review the analyst's decisions regarding where to set the fragment analyzer's peak detection threshold or which peaks to call true allele peaks versus artifacts.

[55] www.bioforensics.com

Requests for raw data should be made on the record through a discovery motion. Providing the raw data requires the analyst to copy the relevant files onto a portable medium. A "record-only- style" compact disc is the preferred medium because it creates an unalterable version of the data provided by the laboratory. The importance of an independent analysis of the raw data cannot be overstated. No matter how closely the defense attorney scrutinizes the testing laboratory's final report, without the raw data he or she will never be able to detect instances in which the analyst may have made a subjective judgment about the presence or absence of an allele in the sample.

56 Thompson et al., 2003b.

In addition to examining the technical details of the analysis, the defense attorney should ascertain whether all the standard control procedures have been followed pursuant to recognized protocols. Any time a control sample does not perform as expected, the defense can argue that the entire batch of data obtained along with that control should be discarded. All proper laboratory protocols contain a section in which the technician is advised to take corrective measures if a control sample has not performed as expected. These corrective measures may involve discarding the entire set of data and repeating the analysis. If the technician has not follow his or her laboratory's standard operating procedure, this provides an opportunity for the defense to attack the admissibility of the evidence because the accepted, validated procedure has not been followed in the case at bar.

In addition to examining the technological details of the assay, the defense should also examine the more mundane aspects of the quality control procedure. For example, some defense counsels report that laboratories sometimes omit standard control procedures that are considered good laboratory practices.[56] As described in Chapter 3, every STR analysis should include the following in-laboratory quality control measures:

1. A yield gel should illustrate the quality of the DNA that was obtained from the sample.
2. The analyst should have quantified the human DNA in the sample apart from bacterial or other DNA that may be present.
3. An unstained sample should have been used to ensure that there was no typable DNA on the evidence object apart from that associated with the crime.
4. An extraction blank should have been used, in order to ensure that there was no contaminating DNA in the reagents used for extracting DNA.
5. A reagent blank should have been used in order to ensure that there was no contaminating DNA in the reagents used for the PCR.
6. Size ladders should have been used in the yield gel as well as in the samples subjected to gel electrophoresis.

When performing automated analyses such as the STR analyses, the analyst must specify a number of parameters related to the function of the fragment analyzer. For example, the analyst sets the **allele size window** for each marker. This specifies a range of expected sizes for that marker's alleles. In order to be considered an allele for that marker, the allele must fall within that size range. If a sample contains an allele that is smaller or larger than the range of alleles that have been reported for that marker, it may fall outside the size range that the analyst has specified for that marker, and will not be recognized as one of that marker's alleles. One individual could have a heterozygous genotype for that marker, but only have one of his or her alleles recognized by the machine. If the evidence sample is homozygous for that allele, the individual's profile will appear to match that of the evidence, because the other allele that exists in his or her sample was not recognized.

Another machine parameter that is set by the analyst is the **peak detection threshold (PDT)** or **limit of detection (LOD)**. As discussed in Chapter 3, the PDT specifies the amount of fluorescence intensity required for a peak to be recognized by the machine. This applies to both true allele peaks and artifacts; any peak that exceeds the threshold will be reported in the data. In contrast, any peak that does not have the specified intensity will be considered by the machine to be part of the machine's ever-present background "noise." The companies that manufacture fragment analyzers provide recommendations regarding the level at which to set the PDT, but analysts are not bound by these recommendations. For example, ABI recommends a peak detection threshold of 150 RFU for the ABI Prism 310 Genetic Analyzer™ with the Profiler Plus™ set of markers, but laboratories may use a PDT anywhere between 50 and 200 RFU for their analyses.[57] The key point for the defense attorney who is reviewing a forensic laboratory's report is whether the PDT used in the case at bar is the same as the one that was in effect during the most recent proficiency tests and validation studies, and conforms to the lab's established threshold level. If it is not, the defense should review the fragment analyzer's raw data in order to determine whether any peaks were either included or omitted as a result of the analyst applying the new PDT. If this appears to prejudice the analysis against the defendant, the defense may be able to cite that as grounds for a motion *in limine*.

[57] Gilder et al., 2004.

The peak detection threshold is especially likely to influence the results of the test when a mixed sample with a minor contributor or a sample containing a minute amount of DNA is analyzed. If there is very little starting DNA to work with, the true allele peaks' intensities will be limited. Depending on how little DNA is present, the result may be anything from the loss of the alleles that are most vulnerable to dropout (discussed in Chapter 3) to the entire profile going undetected. The genotype of a minor contributor to a mixed stain or a sample with very little DNA may be impossible to analyze unless the peak detection threshold is set below the normal level. The defense should carefully check the PDT for each analysis, to ensure that the laboratory has validation study data illustrating that reliable results can be obtained with that PDT. Furthermore, if the fragment analyzer's hardware or software has recently been updated, all peak intensities may systematically increase or decrease.[58] If any such updates have occurred since the most recent validation studies and proficiency tests, the defense should first consider whether or not the change in the analyzer's performance will prejudice the results against the defendant, and if so, consider a motion *in limine*.

[58] Gilder et al., 2004.

There are several reasons why artifactual peaks that should not be there might appear in the electropherogram (discussed in detail in Chapter 3). For example, **stutter peaks** appear with most STR markers; even adjusting the parameters of the PCR cannot get rid of some of them. Stutter peaks rarely confuse the analyst when they occur in a single-source sample, especially at markers for which the subject is heterozygous. In these cases, the analyst can see two full-intensity true allele peaks with two stutter peaks of considerably less intensity. When the sample represents a mixture, however, and the stutter peak is exactly one repeat smaller than the true peak, the stutter peak from the major contributor may be interpreted as a true allele peak from the minor contributor.

Noise spikes are sharp peaks in the electropherogram that occur due to voltage fluctuations in the fragment analyzer's power supply, urea crystals in the electrophoresis polymer, air bubbles or other contamination in the sample. They are usually of low intensity, but can possess enough intensity to get over the machine's peak detection threshold. They are usually visible in all four sets of differently labeled markers. They are momentary "glitches" in the system and are not reproducible. They will almost never appear in a second test of that sample; even if the system has recurring problems that cause regular noise spikes, they will appear at random times and will therefore almost never appear in the same place in two runs of the same sample.

Pull-up peaks, also called "bleed-through" peaks, are described in detail in Chapter 3. They are due to a failure of that portion of the fragment analyzer that detects the signals of the different colored fluors. A pull-up peak occurs when the fragment analyzer detects an authentic peak for a marker that has been labeled with one fluor, registers it properly, but also acts as if it has seen a peak, representing the same allele size, for one of the markers that has been labeled with a different fluor. This will produce a spurious peak in the group of markers that have been labeled with the other fluor. If that peak is within the range of alleles of one of the markers that has been labeled with the other fluor, it can be interpreted as a true allele for that marker.

Dye blobs will also produce spurious peaks, but these are often easy to differentiate from real peaks. Dye blobs occur when some of the fluorescent label that has been applied to the markers comes off. When it is carried past the detection window by the flow of the polymer in the capillary, the machine detects it and draws the corresponding trace in the electropherogram. Dye blob "peaks" are usually considerably wider and less peaked than true peaks or even artifactual peaks from the other sources we have mentioned. In addition, they appear only in the set of markers that have been labeled with that particular fluor.

As discussed in Chapter 1, some STR markers have microvariants, or off-ladder alleles. Markers FGA, D18S51 and D21S11 have all been shown to have microvariants that enable two alleles with different sequences to be declared a match. These microvariants will only provide an explanation for a false inclusion in very rare cases. If a partial profile has been obtained, and data from these STRs are crucial to the prosecution's case, it may be prudent to challenge the results by having these STRs sequenced. In most cases, however, there will be data from several other STRs as well. The probability that an individual would match the evidence's DNA profile on 10 to 13 markers, but have a microvariant produce a false match on one additional marker, is extremely low.

DQA1 and Polymarker™ Tests

Because of the inability to produce probes that are completely single-allele-specific for the DQA1 dot-blot test, it can be impossible to unambiguously determine a sample's DNA profile if certain specific combinations of alleles are present. For example, consider the 1982 case in which Rebecca Adams was raped and stabbed. Before dying, she told police that her attacker was a single black male. In 1984, Earl Washington Jr. confessed to the rape and murder, and the Virginia Department of Forensic Sciences

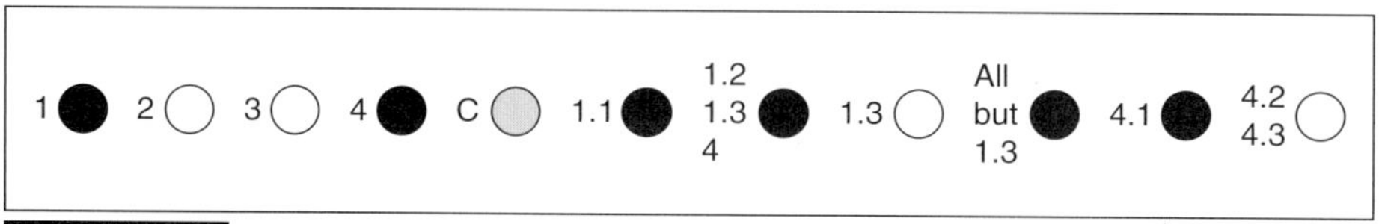

FIGURE 9.2 *Simulation of the DQA1 test results for the vaginal sample in the Earl Washington case. Notice that this pattern of results would be obtained from someone with either a 1.1, 4.1 genotype or a mixed sample with the 1.1, 1.2 and 4.1 alleles present.*

(VADFS) performed the forensic testing for the prosecution. Figure 9.2 illustrates the DQA1 test results from a vaginal swab taken from the victim. The vaginal swab was interpreted to contain the 1.1, 1.2, and 4 alleles. Washington's genotype was determined to be 1.2, 4 for the DQA1 gene. The victim and her husband were both determined to have the homozygous 4,4 genotype. Because of his confession and the analyst's conclusion that his 1.2 and 4 alleles were present in the evidence sample, Washington was sentenced to death. The presence of the 1.1 allele in the sample also suggested that there was another, unknown male contributor to the vaginal swab sample. It was unclear, however, whether this occurred as part of the rape and murder; Adams may have had consensual sex with someone shortly before the attack and correctly reported to the police that her murderer acted alone.

If you examine the dot-blot results from the vaginal swab carefully, you can see that the analyst erred when he or she reported that the vaginal swab sample had a 1.1, 1.2, 4 genotype. A sample with the 1.1, 4 genotype will give the same pattern of results in the DQA1 test as a mixed sample with a 1.1, 1.2, 4 genotype. Both samples will give a positive signal at the All 1, All 4, 1.1, 1.2/1.3/4, All but 3, and either the 4.1 or 4.2/4.3 probes, depending on which 4 allele is present.

Unfortunately, because of the lack of complete specificity in the probes, if a 4 allele is present along with either a 1.1 or 1.3 allele, it will be impossible to determine whether there is also a 1.2 allele in the sample. No probe is completely specific for the 1.2 allele. If a 4 allele is not present, the results from the All 1, 1.1, 1.2/1.3/4, and 1.3 probes can indicate the presence of the 1.2 allele. This is based on the fact that you will see a positive signal at the 1.2/1.3/4 probe, and the 1.3 and All but 1.3 probes will tell you whether or not that dot is due to a 1.3 allele. If a 1.3 allele is not present, and there is no hybridization at any of the 4, 4.1, or 4.2/4.3

probes, then the positive signal at the 1.2/1.3/4 probe is due to a 1.2 allele. Unfortunately, if the 4 allele is present, the 4 allele will give a positive signal with the 1.2/1.3/4 probe, and it will be impossible to determine whether that positive signal is due to the presence of the 4 allele alone or a combination of the 4 allele and the 1.2 allele. If the 1.3 probe shows no hybridization signal, you know there is no 1.3 allele present, but you still cannot tell whether or not there is a 1.2 allele in the sample, because there is no 1.2-specific probe that allows you to differentiate whether the positive signal at the 1.2/1.3/4 probe is due to the 4 allele alone or a combination of the 4 and 1.2 alleles.

In the Washington case, if the vaginal sample's genotype had been reported as 1.1, 4, which were the alleles the analyst did have direct evidence for, the interpretation would have been that the 4 allele represented the victim's homozygous 4,4 genotype, and the attacker would have had either a homozygous 1.1, 1.1 genotype or a heterozygous 1.1, 4 genotype. Washington would have been immediately excluded based on his 1.2, 4 genotype.

The Washington case illustrates mistakes made by several people involved in the analysis and interpretation of the data, as well as either the prosecutor or Washington's defense attorney. To begin with, an independent review by the ASCLD/LAB accreditation committee found that the analyst's conclusions were simply wrong. They stated that the analyst should not have concluded that the sample contained the 1.2 allele; he or she should have specified the several possible interpretations that could have been derived from the data, or reported the results as inconclusive. One specific aspect of the analysis that was called into question was the fact that the analyst used 33 cycles for the PCR, when the laboratory's standard protocol and the manufacturer's recommendations both stated that 30 cycles was optimal. As discussed in Chapter 3, forensic analysts will sometimes employ more than the standard number of PCR cycles when the sample contains little DNA, as it did in this case. Unfortunately, doing so always carries with it the risk that artifactual alleles that are usually not intense enough to be recognized as peaks may be intensified and recognized as true alleles. The laboratory was criticized not only for the use of a nonstandard number of PCR cycles, but also for the fact that the analyst had not recorded this variation from the standard protocol on his or her work sheets; it was discovered by the ASCLD/LAB review team. The problem was further compounded by the fact that the laboratory did not have any data from validation studies that illustrated how the test performed when 33 PCR cycles were used.

The controversy was further inflamed when the official in charge of the VA DFS blindly stood by the initial interpretation of the data and dismissed critics as "scientific naysayers" who were wrongly opposed to the use of DNA evidence in general. It was only when pressure from the public and the media accumulated that an independent review was requested. Finally, at least one of the attorneys involved committed procedural errors. The jury was never told that serology tests on the vaginal swab sample excluded Washington as a contributor to the sample. Whether this omission was due to the prosecution's lack of disclosure or the defense's oversight is not clear. It is highly likely, however, that this omission played a significant role in Washington's wrongful conviction (although the 4th circuit court rejected postconviction claims that this constituted ineffective assistance of defense counsel).

The evidence was subjected to STR testing in 2000 (by the lab that performed the initial tests), and again in 2004 (by Dr. Ed Blake of Forensic Science Associates). After the 2000 analysis, it was concluded that a stain on a blanket contained DNA from the victim and Kenneth Tinsley, a serial rapist whose physical description matched that given to the police by Adams. Tinsley, Washington and Adams's husband were all excluded from the vaginal sample, however, and it was then postulated that at least two unknown males' DNAs were present in the vaginal sample. There were several other anomalous findings from the 2000 report as well. There are several markers for which one of the victim's alleles was not present in the vaginal samples. The sample contained only a small amount of DNA, which suggested that some of the alleles may have dropped out, casting doubt on the reliability of the other markers' data.

In the 2004 analysis, a differential extraction was performed to separate the sperm and nonsperm fractions of the vaginal sample, and clean profiles were obtained from both. The nonsperm fraction contained the victim's alleles and no others. The sperm fraction contained DNA from Tinsley alone. No other DNA was detected. Washington was pardoned, but he was never exonerated.

Scrutinizing the Reference Database

In order to calculate the RMP properly, the analyst must consult a valid reference database in order to obtain the appropriate allele or genotype frequencies. Defense counsel should be familiar with the four primary litmus tests associated with the validity of a database. The first is whether the choice of reference database was appropriate for that defendant's ethnic heritage. As discussed in Chapter 4, genotype frequencies can vary between ethnic groups, and the RMP can differ markedly depending on the reference database the analyst used to calculate it. Most cases in which this is an issue involve Native American populations or other primarily self-contained communities in which there has been little or no intermatings with other groups. For some tribes there are little or no data available, and using either the Caucasian, African American or Hispanic databases can significantly underestimate the RMP of the defendant's DNA profile. This does not mean however, that the analyst is unable to create an RMP statistic associated with a defendant who is not associated with one of the four databases used by the FBI. Many jurisdictions are compiling local and regional databanks containing samples from the different ethnic communities in that region. Thus, counsel should not be tempted to consider that if a client belongs to a unique ethnic group a RMP cannot be generated reflecting the statistical probability with which the client's profile may be found within the relevant population.

For example, consider the case of *Dayton v. State.*[59] Andrew Dayton was convicted of sexual assault and burglary by an Alaska court. Dayton appealed, on the grounds that the reference database used to calculate the RMP was inappropriate for his ethnic background. Dayton was an Athabascan Indian, a group for which Alaska had no DNA profile database. Between the time of Dayton's initial trial (which ended in a hung jury) and his retrial, the state compiled a database of profiles from Athabascan Indians. During the retrial, the prosecution presented several RMPs, using the four traditional databases as well as the new Athabascan database. The RMP was 1 in 22 billion for North American whites, 1 in 6 billion for African Americans, 1 in 413 million for Hispanics, and 1 in 2.5 million for Athabascan Indians. Dayton objected, arguing that the state was required to demonstrate the reliability of the database in a preliminary hearing before it could be used at trial. In addition, he argued that none of the individuals who provided samples for the database were

[59] 54 P.3d 817 (Alaska App. 2002).

required to prove that they were Athabascan Indians. In addition, he asked for the names of the individuals who were represented in the database, claiming that some of them may have been his relatives. At the retrial, the court ruled that a hearing was not required to establish the validity of the newly created Athabascan DNA database. The appellate court revisited the case and found this to be error, stating that Dayton was entitled to litigate this issue for a determination of whether the database contained the type of data that experts in the field would reasonably rely upon.[60]

The court affirmed the trial court's decision not to provide Dayton with the names of the individuals contributing samples to the database. The court noted that if there were a disproportionate number of Dayton's relatives in the database, it would appear that Dayton's marker genotypes were present in greater frequency in the Athabascan Indian population than they actually were. The spuriously high RMP that would result from using this database would favor the defense. Subsequent research has indicated that "inclusion of some relatives in the database will not invalidate allele frequency estimates."[61]

The second litmus test is simply one of size. Statistics are sometimes referred to as representing the "laws of large numbers," because statistics are used to estimate the characteristics of a large population using a relatively small amount of data that has been taken from a sample of individuals from within that population. Most written opinions, including the NRC reports, do not specify a specific number of entries a database must have to be valid. The 1992 NRC report proposes collecting 100 samples from a number of ethnic groups to create different population databases, and one noted forensic analyst has concluded that 100 to 150 individuals per population will be sufficient.[62] Others have reached similar conclusions, indicating that "100–120 individuals per locus per population were sufficient for robust likelihood calculations."[63] Alternatively, some laboratories, both state and private, have created databases using between 225 and 300 samples, making the consensus "at least several hundred."[64] Forensic scientists have concluded that additional information from more samples typically only improves the precision of the result rather than the accuracy of the allele count.[65] All the current databases for Caucasians, African Americans and Hispanics contain many more entries than that, and for these databases, size is not an issue.

[60] *Dayton v. State*, 89 P.3d 806 (Alaska App. 2004).

[61] Butler, 2005.

[62] Chakraborty, 1992, p. 94.

[63] Evett and Gill, 1991.

[64] *Commonwealth v. Blasioli*, 685 A.2d 151 (PA Sup. Ct. 1996); *State v. Sivi*, 646 A.2d 169 (Conn. 1994); *U.S. v. Jakobetz*, 506 U.W. 834 (1992).

[65] Foreman and Evett, 2001.

When the defendant belongs to a small, socially isolated group such as a Native American or Eskimo tribe, however, the available reference database may not yet contain the generally accepted number of entries to provide a probative RMP statistic that can be admitted in court. Frequently used databases, such as the FBI databases, are periodically validated. In order to admit an RMP statistic created from a newly created database, however, the prosecutor must show that the database complies with the requirements set out in FRE 703, namely, that the database contains the type of data that experts in the field would reasonably rely on. Failing to do this may result in the RMP statistic not being admissible.

Counsel for the defense should be diligent in researching the size of the database being used to create the RMP, especially when a private laboratory is involved. For example, in *Huang v. People,* the defendant, an ethnic Chinese, was charged with several felony crimes. The state submitted crime scene evidence consisting of blood samples to Lifecodes Corporation, a private forensic lab. In calculating the RMP, Lifecodes used its database consisting of 167 blood samples of what originally had been 200 samples contributed by individuals from mainland China. At trial, the state's expert testified that 200 samples was the amount usually required for a valid statistical analysis of an ethnic group.[66] The defendant failed to challenge the use of the small database either by putting on his own witnesses or other evidence. While the court expressed concern for the number of samples comprising the Chinese statistical database as well as its scientific reliability, the court concluded that, because the defendant had offered no expert testimony to contradict the state's witness's conclusions, the sample was sufficient and reliable. The court cautioned, however, that because the database was smaller than the minimum suggested by the state's expert the court would only allow testimony as to the lowest figure of probability in the RMP. Defense counsel should review the database size used to generate the RMP with its expert in order to avoid the court accepting the RMP by default and in the absence of other testimony.

[66] *People v. Shi Fu Huang,* 546 N.Y.S.2d 920 (1989).

The third litmus test for a database is whether the data conform to Hardy-Weinberg equilibrium (HWE) expectations (refer to Chapter 4 for the discussion of HWE). The defense attorney should be cautious about using this test as grounds for objection or appeal, however. Failure to conform to HWE indicates that there is significant population

[67] Dann et al., 2006.

substructure in the reference database. In most cases, however, unless the departure from HWE is extreme, and can be seen for several of the markers used for testing, the correction factor theta can compensate for it. Raising an objection on the grounds that the database does not conform to HWE expectations may only provide the opposition with an opportunity to reinforce the message that the process of interpreting the data is conservative and actually stacks the deck in favor of the defense. The other caution the defense must observe when considering matters of HWE is that noted by the Alaska 2002 appellate court in *Dayton v. State*. Some departures from HWE will artificially inflate the RMP and work in the defense's favor. Defense attorneys should study Chapter 4 carefully, so that they can fully understand whether any apparent statistical aberrations are favorable to versus prejudicial against the defendant.

The final litmus test is that of linkage equilibrium (LE) between markers. As described in Chapter 4, in order to allow the product rule to be used to calculate the RMP, the genotype an individual possesses for one marker should not allow the analyst to predict what genotype the individual will have for another marker. The defense should have a population geneticist examine the database to be certain there is LE between the different markers.

In the opinion of most courts, the issue of the validity of the reference database relates to the weight of the evidence, not its admissibility. When the defense demonstrates a deficiency in the reference database, the courts will quite often admit the DNA evidence, rightfully allowing the jurors to decide what impact the articulated problems have on the weight to be given the evidence.

Helping the Jury Avoid Prosecution-Friendly Fallacies

In the brief time that litigants have used DNA evidence in criminal trials, the world has seen examples of both the ability of DNA evidence to secure just verdicts and the ability of counsel for both sides to confuse the jury with misinterpretations or misstatements regarding the forensic evidence. Having uneducated jurors who do not feel they understand modern science may work in the defense's favor. Mock jury research has suggested that less educated jurors are more likely to view with skepticism the DNA evidence and the process by which proponents have generated it than are more educated jurors.[67] The less apt the juror is to be able to comprehend all the details pertinent to the DNA analysis, the more easily the juror can be influenced by a charismatic defendant, defense attorney or witnesses. As noted earlier, the defense also wants cynical, distrustful jurors who are likely to believe a suggestion that unscrupulous law enforcement agents may have tampered with a sample, or that evidence handlers may have carelessly mislabeled a sample. One cannot overstate the importance of determining prospective jurors' confidence in the integrity of the process. Several studies have shown that people's prior beliefs about the probability of laboratory error or evidence tampering strongly influence their decisions, even if the evidence with which they are presented countermands their prior beliefs.[68] Any lack of confidence the jurors may have regarding the process whereby proponents have generated or presented DNA evidence may translate into a reluctance to convict someone of a crime that will carry a heavy sentence.

[68] For example, Schklar and Diamond, 1999.

It is important for both sides to determine each prospective juror's perception of how reliable DNA evidence is, but it is particularly important for the defense to explore the issue of DNA evidence with the jurors as early in the process as possible if the evidence strongly supports the prosecution's case. The renowned trial lawyer Edward Bennett Williams frequently advised defense attorneys to share their case's greatest weaknesses with the jury during voir dire and the opening statement because it helped defuse the prosecution's strongest arguments and weakened the impact the evidence would have on the jury. The specific format of the questions the advocate asks the jurors may help influence their attitudes in a direction favorable to that side's argument. Thus, the defense should ask if the juror has ever heard or read any of the publicized stories in which unethical behavior or a laboratory's error contributed to a wrongful conviction or a medical catastrophe, or whether they have heard the statistic that almost 100,000 people die in America every year because of medical mistakes. The defense should remind the jurors about the difference between opinions and facts, and ask the jurors whether they understand that different, but equally experienced, experts may have opinions that disagree with each other. The fact that forensic testing laboratories and personnel undergo regular proficiency testing will provide the prosecution with an opportunity to remind the jury that quality control measures are constantly applied in the testing laboratory. The defense can ask jurors, however, if they are aware of the fact that a laboratory or an analyst is allowed to get less than a perfect score on the proficiency tests and continue to operate. Finally, if the defense can find a way to work it into the voir dire, history has provided us with several high-profile scandals that have tarnished the forensic laboratories of several law enforcement agencies. According to the Innocence Project, misconduct on the part of law enforcement agents or prosecutors has contributed to a significant number of wrongful convictions.[69] Interestingly, the Innocence Project cites bad lawyering by defense counsel just below government misconduct as a contributor to this statistic.

[69] http://www.innocence project.org

[70] www.innocenceproject.org; Saks and Koehler, 2005.

If the defense plans to attack the prosecution's expert vigorously, it should prepare the jurors to interpret its attack appropriately as early as it can. It should also avoid giving the appearance that the attack is reflexive or overly zealous. Rather, counsel should emphasize not only that experts are fallible, but also that unfounded or erroneous testimony by forensic scientists is the second most frequent cause of wrongful convictions.[70] Also, the defense should agree with the jurors that someone committed the terrible crime that they will be hearing about during the trial, and also that justice demands that someone be punished for it. Finally, the defense should remind them, however, that many people have been wrongly convicted of serious crimes in the past, and it is the lawyer's duty, as well as theirs, to ensure this doesn't happen in this particular case.

From the defense's standpoint, one of the most alarming findings from the research on jurors' perceptions of DNA evidence is that jurors do not seem to intuitively appreciate the concept of presumption of innocence. Many jurors will consider probatively neutral evidence, such as the simple fact that an individual has been arrested and charged with a crime, as incriminatory. This is a prejudice the defense must work to overcome. The innate desire to see someone punished for the crime at hand may lead many jurors to lower their requirements of proof, even when they have been told that the defendant's guilt must be proven beyond a reasonable doubt (discussed in Chapter 7). This may be particularly important if the crime for which the defendant is being tried was excessively brutal, or involved a child or a prominent member of the community. The defense should be aware that, when no specific instructions are given regarding the probability of guilt that is necessary to satisfy the reasonable doubt criterion, not only will different people have markedly different thresholds for declaring guilt proven, but many people will have thresholds that are surprisingly low. Several studies have shown that mock jurors who were given verbal instructions to convict only if they felt that the defendant's guilt had been proven beyond a reasonable doubt voted to convict the defendant, despite reporting probabilities of guilt that ranged down to 50%.[71] If the defense is not allowed to question prospective jurors about whether they understand the concepts of presumption of innocence and beyond reasonable doubt during voir dire, counsel should emphasize these concepts during opening and closing arguments.

Defense attorneys should study Koehler's work on exemplar cueing (described in Chapter 7) carefully. Koehler's work suggests that jurors are less likely to conclude that the defendant is the source of the evidence if the probabilistic evidence is presented in a manner that enables the jurors to envision examples of people other than the defendant whose DNA profiles would also match that of the evidence. The defense expert witnesses should express the RMP in terms of frequency rather than probability, and point out that one would expect to find other matching profiles in a larger population. Reporting a frequency (1 in 1,000) leads the jurors to envision other individuals whose DNA profiles match that of the evidence more effectively than reporting a percentage (0.1%) does. In addition, using a larger numerator—for example, using 5 in 5,000 or 10 in 10,000 instead of 1 in 1,000—may further encourage jurors' perceptions that there are multiple individuals whose DNA profiles would be expected to match that of the evidence. In addition, it behooves the defense to inform the jury how many individuals within a given population would be expected to have a DNA profile that matches the DNA profile of the evidence. This encourages the jurors to envision examples of other individuals whose DNA profiles will match that of the evidence, and will render them less confident that the defendant is the source of the evidence. Of course, if the RMP is infinitesimal, for example, 1 in 1 billion, it will be difficult to encourage jurors to envision examples of other individuals whose DNA profile would match that of the evidence. Koehler[72] has reported that the linguistic form in which the evidence is presented, which strongly influences jurors' decisions when the RMP is on the order of 1 in 1,000 or 1 in 100,000, has little effect on jurors' decisions when the RMP is 1 in 1 million or 1 in 1 billion.

In cases involving infinitesimal RMPs, the defense should focus, if relevant, on the possibility of laboratory error or evidence tampering as an alternative explanation of the match between the defendant and the

[71] Goodman, 1992; Koehler, 2001.

[72] Koehler, 2001.

evidence. As discussed in Chapter 7, when the RMP is infinitesimal, the probability of a false identification is essentially equal to the probability of a laboratory error. This may be a more fruitful avenue of attack than the defense attorney may realize. Research studies indicate there is a definite upper limit to the degree to which DNA evidence has been shown to convince mock jurors. Several studies have shown that, even when presented with an RMP of 1 in 1 billion, many jurors are unwilling to assign near-100% probabilities that the defendant is the source of the evidence.[73] One possible reason for this is the common perception that there is a substantial probability of laboratory error (PLE) or evidence tampering. The best estimates of potential laboratory error rate that can be derived from proficiency test records is in the range of 1 in 75 to 1 in 1,000.[74] The few studies that have directly assessed laypeople's perceptions of the frequency of laboratory errors,[75] however, have reported that the average mock juror's estimate of the PLE is on the order of 1 in 10 or 1 in 15. In one study, mock jurors estimated the probability of contamination as 1 in 4, despite the lack of evidence from either side that any contamination had occurred.[76] In addition, in one study, the uninformed estimate of the probability that investigators may have tampered with the evidence was 1 in 50.[77] As discussed in Chapter 7, these findings may reflect the fact that a relatively small number of jurors think the PLE for any given analysis is high, while most accept the estimate of the PLE that is given by the expert witness.

Some of the findings in Schklar and Diamond's research may suggest that there is an underlying perception among laypeople that the PLE in any given case is significant.[78] Their mock jurors were more likely to convict the defendant when they were given an RMP of 1 in 1 billion and no estimate of the PLE than they were when given a PLE of 1 in 1 billion and no estimate of the RMP. In addition, jurors were more likely to convict the defendant if they were given a RMP of 1 in 1 billion plus a PLE of 2 in 100 than they were when given a RMP of 2 in 100 and a PLE of 1 in 1 billion. Providing a very small PLE appears to reassure jurors that the evidence is probative more effectively than providing a very small RMP does. This suggests that the general public recognizes the possibility that laboratories make mistakes, and that they factor that possibility into their thinking, even when they are not given any data that specifically refer to the issue of laboratory error.

[73] Koehler et al., 1995; Schklar and Diamond, 1999.

[74] Koehler et al., 1995; National Research Council Report, 1996.

[75] Schklar, 1996; Schklar and Diamond, 1999.

[76] Dann et al., 2006.

[77] Schklar and Diamond, 1999.

[78] Schklar and Diamond, 1999.

Helping the Jury Interpret Mixed Samples

When an evidence sample represents a mixture of material from multiple donors, the defense must make the jury understand that multiple possible combinations of alleles are represented. For example, suppose the evidence is a vaginal sample from a woman who has been raped by two men. The victim's genotype at the exemplary marker is 6,8, and there are two suspects in custody whose genotypes are 4,9 and 7,10. If the vaginal sample contains all six alleles, 4, 6, 7, 8, 9 and 10, the prosecution will argue that the six alleles represent three contributors, with genotypes of 6,8 (the victim), 4,9 (one suspect), and 7,10 (the other suspect). The defense should emphasize to the jury, however, that several other possible allele combinations could exist in the mixture. Just because the prosecution's interpretation of the data is plausible, it is not the only possible interpretation. In this example, one rapist could have had a 4,7 genotype and the other one a 9,10 genotype. Alternatively, one rapist could have had a 4,10 genotype, and the other could have had a 7,9 genotype. Obviously, either of these two alternative interpretations excludes the defendant as a possible source of the evidence.

If the analyst has used relative peak heights to define the major versus minor contributor, the defense should ascertain that the laboratory has validation study data demonstrating that the data produced in this manner are reliable, and that the accepted procedure was followed. If the established procedure has not been followed, the defense may be able to convince the court that the criterion has been applied in the case at bar in a manner that is prejudicial to the defendant.

Chapter 4 illustrates the appropriate statistical analyses to be used when analyzing a mixed sample. In some cases, the prosecution may have to calculate the probability of exclusion rather than the standard RMP that would be applied to a single-source sample. As counsel can imagine, with several possible genotype combinations present, the probative value of the evidence may be reduced, which will provide the defense the opportunity to present the probabilistic evidence in a manner that encourages the jury to envision other individuals who could be included in the list of possible sources by coincidence. Furthermore, if the sample has been degraded by time and the elements, it may be impossible to detect the true profile of one or more of the contributors. The different contributions may be present in different amounts, or may have suffered different degrees of degradation. If the yield gel or the profile of alleles suggests that the sample has been degraded, it will be very difficult for the analyst to correctly identify the DNA profiles of all the contributors.

Strategies for Attacking the Prosecution's Witnesses

When scrutinizing the prosecution's witnesses, the defense should ascertain that each witness's experience provides a proper foundation for their specific testimony. In addition, the defense should choose witnesses who can pass the same tests to which the prosecution witnesses will be subjected. Judges in *Daubert* jurisdictions are taking an increasingly more stringent look at witnesses' specific experiences before declaring them qualified to testify regarding forensic DNA evidence. The more the defense can limit the expertise of the witness, the more limitations there will be on the witness's ability to aid the prosecution. Given that many prosecution witnesses are employees of a law enforcement agency or a forensic testing laboratory, however, it will often be difficult to attack them on the subject of the relevance of their experience.

In most cases, the prosecution's witness will testify before the defense's does. If the defense's expert has not been sequestered during the testimony of the prosecution's expert, the defense's expert should be aware of the state's explanation of the DNA evidence to the court. It is important that the judge and jury avoid the "prosecutor's fallacy" that was described in Chapter 4, but the defense must decide whether to have its expert emphasize to the jury what the prosecutor's fallacy is and why it is to be avoided. It may be very hard to gauge whether or not to have the expert emphasize this point to the jury. Having the expert explain the prosecutor's fallacy may prevent some jurors from falling into it. In some cases, however, it is difficult not to think of something when you have been told to ignore it. Introducing the idea of the prosecutor's fallacy may prompt some jurors to think about this erroneous interpretation of the evidence when they would not have done so otherwise.

As summarized by Imwinkelried,[79] the defense attorney has the choice of four strategies when cross-examining the prosecution's expert witness. To begin with, sometimes it may be best not to cross-examine the witness at all. When the evidence is strong and no evidence of error exists in the process whereby the evidence was generated, it may be prudent to waive

[79] Imwinkelried, 2004.

cross-examination and not allow the witness to reiterate damaging points. In addition, in some cases, the defense will be planning to introduce a theory of the case that explains why the innocent defendant's DNA profile matches that of the evidence sample, and does not need to focus on attacking the DNA evidence itself. In other cases, if the prosecutor and witness have made a confusing presentation of the DNA evidence, it may be best to leave the jury on that note; cross-examining the witness opens up an opportunity for the prosecution to conduct a redirect that may clarify the confusion sown during the direct examination. Similarly, if the prosecution has failed to develop a critical point pertinent to the DNA evidence, cross-examination may remind him or her of the omission, and he or she may try to correct it during redirect examination. Most redirect examinations are limited to topics introduced by the cross-examination, but courts have been known to grant exceptions to this limitation, so in prosecution-friendly courts, it may be best not to take the risk.

If there is evidence that the sample was suboptimal or that some error occurred in the evidence-generating process, the defense attorney may choose to cross-examine solely to elicit favorable facts. Even in the face of an impressively small RMP, several favorable facts can be exploited. For example, if the laboratory or any of the specific analysts involved have a record of errors on past proficiency tests, it will be useful to bring this record out if it has not already been addressed on direct by the prosecutor. If the yield gel suggested that the DNA had been degraded, or if one of the control samples did not perform optimally, this problem should be emphasized. Any entries from equipment maintenance logs indicating that one of the instruments used in the analysis needed maintenance at that time may help plant a seed of doubt regarding the validity of the evidence. Keep in mind the earlier discussion (from Chapter 7) that the laboratory's potential false-positive error rate is usually a much better approximation of the probability of a false identification than the RMP is. If the RMP is very low, the defense attorney should elicit a reasonable estimate of the laboratory's error rate and replace the infinitesimal RMP in the jurors' minds with this much larger number. Note that these issues are more properly left to the juror's consideration of the weight, rather than the admissibility, of the evidence. Note also that this attack is a reasonably safe one. Counsel is not waging a frontal assault on the expert and therefore will provide few opportunities for the expert to use his or her answers to defense questions to reiterate key prosecution points.

If the expert witness has presented damaging testimony, the defense must cross-examine, even if the defense does not have firm grounds to impeach the expert or his or her testimony. Failure to cross-examine will give the jurors the impression that the witness's testimony was truthful and unimpeachable, and may provide the prosecution with the opportunity to point out during closing that the defense never challenged the evidence. When the defense does not actually have substantial grounds on which to impeach the expert or the evidence, this situation is quite obviously a very difficult one to manage. A frontal assault on strong DNA evidence allows the witness to reiterate damaging points. The defense must confine the cross-examination to peripheral issues, and wage what amounts to an apparent attack on the expert or the evidence. One effective strategy may be to question the validity of the facts that underlie the witness's opinion. If any important facts have come from the defendant himself, the source of these facts can be called into question. In most cases, the prudent defense attorney wants to avoid the appearance of a "fishing expedition" by not introducing too many improbable hypothetical scenarios. If the evidence has been devastating, however, and the defense has little ammunition for a substantive attack, this may be the only option available.

In any situation, the defense should carefully think through all lines of attack, even those based on notes that suggest that the sample may be suboptimal or that there may have been some irregularity in the analysis procedure. In many cases, the effects that the potential error would have on the data are known. If the defense cannot demonstrate some aspect of the data that shows the expected effect, bringing the topic up will allow the prosecution to follow up on redirect examination and emphasize that the potential error did not appear to compromise the data. Cross-examining an expert is always dangerous; it always provides a composed expert the opportunity to turn his or her answers to your questions into reaffirmations of the prosecution's arguments. When counsel does not have a solid foundation on which to attack the testimony, it may be better to elicit what favorable facts are available or attack factual premises during cross-examination, and then use closing argument to generate inferences favorable to the defense's alternative theory of the case.

The fourth potential strategy for cross-examining the witness is to mount an actual assault on the witness or the evidence. If the prosecution has not laid the proper foundation for some aspect of the expert's testimony, the defense may object to questions raised during the witness's direct examination. If the defense believes that the proper foundational requirements outlined by FRE Rule 104(a) have not been satisfied, the defense may request permission to question the witness on voir dire in order to support the objection. This amounts to interrupting the direct examination to conduct a limited cross-examination. In addition, the defense may request that the court excuse the expert briefly, in order to allow the defense to introduce other witnesses whose testimony will attack the qualifications and credibility of the prosecution's witness.

Whenever possible, the defense should arrange to argue about the admissibility of the evidence or expert out of the presence of the jury. If the objection is made at trial and overruled, the jurors may conclude that the judge endorses the witness and his or her testimony. For justification, the defense can cite FRE Rule 103(c), which provides that proceedings be conducted in a manner that prevents potentially inadmissible evidence from being presented in the presence of the jury. Courts will differ in their readiness to accept this argument, and logistical and time considerations will influence decisions as well.

During cross-examination, the prudent defense attorney will question the prosecution's expert witnesses exhaustively regarding the details of the evidence-generating process. The more descriptions and explanations the prosecution's witnesses are forced to give, the harder it is for the jurors to digest it all. Outpacing the jurors' capacity for new knowledge with multiple lengthy descriptions full of technical details may help sow a feeling among the jurors that they "just can't understand this technical stuff." This may make them less confident that they can develop their own opinions about the weight of the evidence, and more likely to accept what they are told by a credible and charismatic defense attorney or expert (sometimes referred to as jury nullification). In addition, the more details that can be brought out, the better the chance that the prosecution's witness will say something that the defense can capitalize on to sow a seed of doubt regarding the evidence. Most of the admissions the defense will extract from the prosecution's witnesses during cross-examination will be matters that influence the weight, rather than the admissibility, of the evidence. It may be possible, however, to elicit an admission that calls the admissibility of the evidence into question, and allows the defense to move that the witness's direct testimony be stricken from the record. In such a case, if the witness's direct testimony has been very damaging, the impression made in the jurors' minds may be indelible. Although a judge can offer the jury a curative instruction, if the testimony has been very impressive, the defense should argue for a mistrial, because even a judge's curative instructions may not be sufficient to remove the prejudicial impression the direct testimony has left in the jurors' minds. If the judge refuses to strike the direct testimony, the defense should urge the jury during closing arguments to ignore the testimony.

The form of the judge's instructions to the jury may also influence the jury's perceptions of the significance of the expert's testimony. In many jurisdictions, the judge's standard instructions will include statements that an expert's opinion is merely an opinion, that the jury is not bound to accept the conclusions of an expert, or that the expert's testimony should be viewed with caution. In some cases, judges have even warned jurors that statistics are inherently slippery by nature.[80] If the judge's instructions to the jury do not include some statement to this effect, request that the judge add such a statement. Even if the judge refuses, the defense has preserved an appealable issue.

[80] *McAlester v. United Air Lines*, 851 F.2d 1249, 10th Cir. (1988).

WHEN THE DEFENDANT HAS BEEN IDENTIFIED BY A DATABANK SEARCH

Identifying a suspect through a databank search is different from identifying a suspect through eyewitness evidence or victims' statements. In a case in which the suspect was identified through a databank search, there is no probable cause to believe the suspect committed the crime before the databank search identified him or her. In terms of Bayes' Theorem (discussed in Chapter 4), the prior odds of guilt are extremely small. Furthermore, it is logically intuitive that the probability of finding a coincidental match between the evidence and an individual is greater if one searches a databank of 100,000 profiles than if one investigates the DNA profile of one suspect. This means not only that one's conclusion regarding guilt versus innocence must be tempered by the small prior odds of guilt, but also by the fact that searching a large database increases the probability of finding a coincidental match. Chapter 4 provides a discussion of how the RMP calculations change when a defendant is identified through a databank search. The formula to be applied in these cases is more conservative than the one that is applied when the defendant has been identified by other evidence, such as eyewitness testimony, and will therefore produce a larger, less impressive, RMP. If the defendant has been identified through a databank search, counsel should ensure that the appropriately conservative formula has been used to calculate the RMP.

The DNA Analysis Backlog Elimination Act of 2000 requires the DNA profile to be expunged if the individual's conviction is overturned, but most statutes that authorize the collection of samples do not address the issue of expungement. Even statutes that authorize the collection of samples from individuals who have merely been arrested may not specify whether the profile is to be expunged if the arrestee is not later charged or convicted. When the defendant has been identified through a databank search, the defense should carefully scrutinize the applicable statutes, as well as the circumstances under which the defendant's profile was entered into the databank, to be sure that the defendant's profile was legitimately entered and retained in the databank.

Police will sometimes conduct "DNA dragnet" operations, in which they collect large numbers of samples as part of an investigation. For example, as part of a 1994 investigation of several sexual assault cases in which the victims had reported that their assailants were black, police in Ann Arbor, Michigan collected samples from 160 black men from the area. In another case, police in Costa Mesa, California spent four years investigating a crime, during which time they took 188 samples from randomly selected people who lived in the neighborhood where the crime was committed. Even larger "DNA dragnets" have been used in other cases, including cases in Florida (2,300 samples collected) and Louisiana (600 samples collected). In these cases, the collections are technically voluntary, and therefore the Fourth Amendment is not implicated. If the defendant's DNA sample has been obtained via a dragnet, the defense should ascertain that no coercion was involved. For example, when police in Truro, Massachusetts requested that all the male residents of the town submit DNA samples to aid in a murder investigation, some residents allege they were told that law enforcement would "pay close attention to those who refuse to provide DNA."

[81] 744 N.E.2d 437, Ind. (2000).

As discussed in Chapter 8, once the police have obtained a DNA sample lawfully, they are free to use it in other applications. Often when a DNA dragnet results in the identification of the guilty party, law enforcement agencies are under no obligation to purge the other DNA profiles collected in the dragnet and entered into the databank. In most states it is the individual's responsibility to seek expungement of their sample. Before the profile is removed, however, investigators may search it against other profiles in the local or state databanks to see if it matches profiles collected from other crime scenes. If the defendant has been identified in this manner, it may be possible to challenge the databank search.

When critical evidence has been obtained in violation of the state's databank laws, it is no surprise to see the evidence declared inadmissible. Many would feel that, because the state's laws lay out the rules for obtaining evidence, any violation of those rules would render the evidence inadmissible. Surprisingly, however, having the evidence declared inadmissible is not necessarily an automatic consequence of finding that the method by which the evidence was obtained violated state databank laws. At least one court has placed the state's need to prosecute the perpetrators of violent crimes above the state's obligation to follow its own databank laws. For example, consider the case of *Smith v. State.*[81] Damon Smith was charged with rape and forced to provide a blood sample for DNA testing. Smith argued successfully that the sex was consensual, and he was found not guilty of the rape. While the trial was ongoing, the Indianapolis-Marion County Forensic Services Agency searched their databank of unsolved crimes against Smith's profile and found that his profile matched the evidence from another, unrelated rape. Smith tried to have the evidence declared inadmissible for the second trial because the Indiana statute clearly limits the state's authority to place DNA profiles in their databank to the profiles of individuals who have been convicted of certain crimes. Because Smith had been found not guilty of the first rape, he argued that the prosecution had no right to have retained his profile in their databank. The appellate court affirmed the judgment of the trial court, and Smith appealed to the Indiana Supreme Court. The Indiana Supreme Court conceded that Smith's DNA profile should not have been in the databank, but affirmed the trial court's denial of Smith's request nonetheless. In its opinion, the court stated that "[t]he rule excluding evidence seized in direct violation of the state constitution... is entirely a creation of judicial precedent. Nothing in the state or federal constitution requires it." The court further noted that there was "no statutory direction as to the admissibility of DNA profiles included or retained in the database without statutory authorization." The court conceded that provisions of the statute clearly demonstrated that there was concern for the individual's right to privacy. The court ruled, however, that "[e]xclusion of extremely valuable evidence in crimes that often leave little other trace is a major social cost" and that "[a]n exclusionary rule would prioritize the need for compliance by the authorities with the statute over the cost of exclusion of obviously critical evidence as to a serious crime."

When a defendant has been identified through a databank search, the defense should be sure to check that the match between the evidence and the defendant was perfect. When the client has been identified through a databank search, this does not necessarily mean that his or her profile will be a perfect match for the evidence. The databank searching software does not declare a match; it merely provides the analyst with a list of profiles to be investigated further. Forensic analysts recognize that there will be many suboptimal samples for which some markers' data will be compromised. For that reason, databank searching programs do not require a perfect match in order to report that profile as one the analyst may want to investigate further. Instead, the analyst sets the level of stringency he or she wants the program to apply to the search. A high stringency search requires perfect matches for all alleles at all markers in order to flag the profile for further review. In a moderate stringency search, if either the evidence or the suspect has a homozygous genotype at any particular marker, then the other sample only has to match that allele for a match to be declared. Even if the other sample is clearly heterozygous, if its genotype contains the allele that was seen in the homozygous genotype, the program will consider the two samples matching. At low stringency, a match will be declared at a marker if there is one allele that is shared by both the evidence and the suspect. Even if both are clearly heterozygous, and their second alleles clearly do not match, the program will still consider them matching. When the defendant has been identified by a databank search, defense counsel should determine the level of stringency used to identify the profile, especially when a relative of the defendant may be a suspect as well. If the level of stringency that gets applied to the search is low enough, there is a good chance that more detailed investigation will reveal that the two profiles are not a perfect match.

All the considerations that have been discussed in Chapter 3 regarding the possibility for sample contamination pertain to samples that have been collected for databanks as well. Several false "hits" have been obtained from databanks because the sample that was in the databank was not actually from the individual of record due to a mislabeling of samples or a transfer of DNA from one sample to another.[82] If the defendant has been identified through a DNA databank search, the state will obtain a reference sample. In addition to scrutinizing all the aspects of the evidence we have discussed, it may be prudent for the defense to obtain a separate reference sample and have it tested by an independent laboratory. At the very least, the defense attorney should be aware of any samples that his or her client has provided in the past, for any reason, and determine if any of the defendant's previous samples were processed along with the evidence sample that the defendant has been shown to match.

Defense counsel should be aware that prosecutors may occasionally seek to classify the defendant's offense in a manner that compels the defendant to provide a DNA sample for the state's databank. Consider the case of *Kelley v. State*[83] in which Sheryl D. Kelley was convicted by a Washington court of possession of drugs with intent to deliver. The maximum sentence for her crime was 10 years. Because Kelley had prior convictions for similar crimes, her case fell under a statute that allowed the court to double her sentence, to a maximum of 20 years. Under Washington's criminal statutes, crimes carrying sentences of 20 years or more are classified as class A felonies. Furthermore, one statute defines a violent offense as "[a]ny felony defined under any law as a class A felony." Because of the 20-year maximum sentence now associated with Kelley's crime, the prosecution argued that Kelley was a class A felon. The prosecution further argued that being a class A felon also meant that she was classified as a violent offender, and therefore compelled to provide a DNA sample for Washington's DNA databank. The trial court ruled that the prosecution was wrong to use prior convictions for nonviolent offenses as justification for getting Kelley classified as a violent offender, and prohibited the state from entering Kelley's DNA profile in its databank. (Kelley had provided a sample under threat

[82] Thompson, 2006.

[83] 889 P.2d 940, Wash. App. (1995).

of sanctions.) The appellate court agreed, citing one of the statutes that limited the state's power to compel samples to individuals convicted of sex crimes or crimes involving injury to others.

REFERENCES AND ADDITIONAL READINGS

Bernstein, D.E. (1996) *Yale Journal of International Law*, 21, 123–171.

Borteck, D. (2004) *Cardozo Law Review*, 25, 1429.

Butler, J.M. (2005) *Forensic DNA Typing*, 2nd ed. Boston: Elsevier/Academic Press, 2005.

Dann, B.M., Hans, V.P. and Kaye, D.H. (2006) *NIJ Journal*, No. 255.

Evett, I.W. and Gill, P. (1991) *Electrophoresis*, 12, 226–230.

Foreman, L.A. and Evett, I.W. (2001) *International Journal of Legal Medicine*, 114, 147–155.

Gilder, J.R., Ford, S., Doom, T.E., Raymer, M.L. and Krane, D.E. (2004) *Journal of Forensic Sciences*, 49(1), 92–95.

Goodman, J. (1992) *American Journal of Trial Advocacy*, 16, 361–389.

Imwinkelried, E J. (1990) *Washington University Law Quarterly*, 68, 19–23.

Imwinkelried, E.J. (2004) *The Methods of Attacking Scientific Evidence*, 4th ed. Lexis Nexis.

Koehler, J.J., Chia, A. and Lindsey, S. (1995) *Jurimetrics Journal*, 35, 201.

Lander, E.S. and Budowle, B. (1994) *Nature*, 371, 735.

National Research Council. (1992) Committee on DNA Technology In Forensic Science: DNA Technology In Forensic Science Washington, DC: National Academy Press.

National Research Council (1996). Committee on DNA Technology in Forensic Science: An Update, The Evaluation of Forensic DNA Evidence. Washington, DC: National Academy Press.

Peterson, J.L., et al. (1985) *Journal of Forensic Sciences*, 30, 10–13.

Risinger, D.M., Saks, M.J., Thompson, W.C. and Rosenthal, W.C. (2002) *California Law Review*, 90, 1.

Schklar, J. (1996) Juror reactions to DNA evidence: Misperception and misaggregation. Paper presented at the meeting of the American Psychology-Law Society, Hilton Head, SC.

Schklar, J. and Diamond, S. (1999) *Law and Human Behavior*, 23, 159–165.

Steventon, B. (1993) Royal Commission on Criminal Justice, The Ability to Challenge DNA Evidence.

Thompson, W.C. (1995) *Genetica*, 96, 153.

Thompson, W.C. (1997) *Jurimetrics*, 37, 405, 1997.

Thompson, W.C., Ford, S., Doom, T., Raymer, M. and Krane, D.E. (2003a) *The Champion*, 27, 16.

Thompson, W.C., Ford, S., Doom, T., Raymer, M. and Krane, D.E. (2003b) *The Champion*, 27, 24.

Thompson, W.C. (2006) *The Champion*, 30, 10.

CHAPTER 10

Postconviction DNA Testing

CONTENTS

DNA has the Power to Exonerate the Innocent

Avenues for Relief

There Are Many Procedural Obstacles

New Evidence May Justify a New Theory of the Case

Accessing the Necessary Samples

Know the Specific Provisions of the Controlling Statute

References and Additional Readings

DNA HAS THE POWER TO EXONERATE THE INNOCENT

The defense attorney who plans to present DNA evidence as a means of undermining the prosecution's theory of the case will find many of the issues discussed in Chapters 7 and 8 useful. When the suspect is in fact innocent of the crime, efforts such as these have a high probability of producing an exclusion, which may or may not secure an acquittal for the defendant depending on the other evidence in the case. Furthermore, one of the most beneficial of all uses of DNA evidence involves the exoneration of defendants who were wrongly convicted of crimes and sent to prison. Demonstrating an exclusion is considerably simpler than demonstrating a match. In criminal trials, if the defense can demonstrate a mismatch of the genotype at even one marker, it will usually be enough to be considered an exclusion; no statistical analysis is required in these cases. If the individual is actually innocent, it is highly likely that the individual's profile and that of the evidence will be mismatched at several markers.

Before the advent of DNA testing, most efforts to exonerate the wrongfully convicted took the form of attacking the trial evidence with evidence of similar type and credibility, and few attempts were successful. Now, however, DNA evidence is considered so much more reliable than most other types of evidence, including in some cases eyewitness testimony or even the victim's statement, that it can be used to overturn convictions that were based on other sources of evidence. The advent of DNA testing in the late 1980s–early 1990s provided many wrongly convicted prisoners an effective vehicle for bringing their claims of actual innocence before the court. The first published trial court decision in which a conviction was vacated because of newly available DNA evidence was *People v. Dabbs.*[1] It did not take long, however, for it to become apparent that there were many wrongly convicted individuals behind prison bars in many jurisdictions.[2] In 1992, Barry Scheck and Peter Neufeld, law professors at the Benjamin Cardozo School of Law in New York, founded the Innocence Project.[3] This group alone has been successful at securing the release of over 200 wrongly convicted prisoners. In the wake of their success, a number of similar Innocence Projects have been established by other law schools and several states. Today the release of a wrongfully convicted prisoner after exoneration by DNA evidence has become commonplace enough that several released prisoners have been surprised to find that the news media did not consider their story worthy of much coverage.

[1] 587 N.Y.S.2d 90 (1991).

[2] Connors et al., 1996.

[3] www. innocence project.org

Postconviction test results are not always exculpatory. In addition, exculpatory test results will not necessarily free the convicted individual. If the evidence does exclude the petitioner, the court must weigh the significance of the exclusion in relation to all the other evidence. Convicted offenders often believe that if crime scene evidence does not contain their DNA they will automatically be exonerated. Not finding the petitioner's DNA does not automatically indicate the case should be overturned, however. In a rape case, for example, the perpetrator may have worn a condom, or not ejaculated. In some cases, the absence of evidence is not necessarily evidence of the defendant's absence or lack of involvement in the crime.

AVENUES FOR RELIEF

The convicted defendant has several avenues by which he or she can challenge either the conviction or the sentence imposed. Many procedural requirements complicate all applications for postconviction relief, but if the sole ground for appeal is actual innocence, the individual faces an even more difficult procedural labyrinth. All states provide some mechanism for postconviction relief for prisoners who have been convicted in state court. Federal courts provide mechanisms for relief for prisoners convicted in federal courts, and in some cases prisoners who have been convicted in state courts. In most cases, if the defendant is convicted in a state court, he or she is required to first pursue all opportunities for appeals through the state system before seeking federal relief. As discussed in this chapter, however, there are a few exceptions to this rule.

The first appeals to be pursued is the direct appeal, which focuses on matters that are in the trial record. Direct appeals can constitute trial remedies, in which motions are made to the convicting court, or appellate remedies, in which motions are made to an appellate court. Requests for trial remedies usually take the form of writs of error, whereas appellate remedies usually take the form of writs of certiorari. In a direct appeal, the prisoner can request a new trial, move to arrest judgment or move to withdraw a guilty plea (under Federal Rules of Criminal Procedure Rules 33, 34, and 32(d), respectively). The Uniform Post-Conviction Procedure Act [subsection 1(a)(4) of the 1966 version] provides for postconviction relief if there exists "evidence of material facts, not previously presented or heard, that requires vacation of the conviction or sentence in the interest of justice." Both the 1968 and 1978 versions of the American Bar Association Standards that regulate postconviction procedures endorsed this provision. Direct appeals must be filed within a specified time after conviction, and different states' statutes of limitation provide for different time periods during which direct appeals will be heard.

If all direct appeals fail, the convicted defendant can mount collateral attacks on the conviction, often referred to as postconviction review. Postconviction review is most often requested on jurisdictional or constitutional grounds, but other grounds can be claimed as well, including processing untested forensic evidence for DNA. In most jurisdictions, and under most circumstances, there is a 1-year statute of limitations for filing a postconviction relief claim. However, if the petition is brought on the basis, in part, of untested DNA evidence, the time frame to file has been expanded.

Postconviction review is the forum for requesting a new trial based on newly discovered evidence or other statutorily outlined reasons. In some cases, there may be samples that were not available at the time of trial, or the prosecution may have chosen not to test the samples that were available, relying on other evidence to convict the defendant. More commonly, new developments in DNA testing methods will enable analysts to obtain information from the evidence that could not be obtained using the methods in use at the time of trial.[4]

[4] For example, *People v. Callace*, 573 N.Y.S.2d 137, N.Y. (1991); *People v. Kellar*, 605 N.Y.S.2d 486, N.Y. (1993); *Whitsel v. State*, 525 N.W.2d 860, Iowa (1994); *Mebane v. State*, 902 P.2d 494, Kan. Ct. App. (1995).

Postconviction remedies take the form of habeas corpus, coram nobis or remedies in the nature of coram nobis.[5] Under 28 U.S.C.§2241, habeas corpus relief is available to prisoners who are in custody due to a wrongful conviction. Although the writ of habeus corpus was originally intended to correct procedural errors, it has evolved into a vehicle by which newly discovered evidence can be introduced. As discussed here, however, the Supreme Court has erected a number of procedural obstacles that complicate the process for the appellant who is introducing newly discovered evidence to support a claim of actual innocence, but has no constitutional or jurisdictional grounds for appeal.

[5] See Wilkes, 1983, for review.

In addition to habeas corpus writs, collateral attacks may include writs of error coram nobis (28 U.S.C.§1651). The writ of error coram nobis is a petition to the trial court to review its own judgment based on errors of fact. It cannot be used to get a higher court to reverse a lower court's decision, nor is it a remedy for procedural errors or errors of law. The writ of error coram nobis can be used, however, to secure a new trial by introducing new evidence, provided that evidence was not available at the time of the original trial. Coram nobis can be used by prisoners whose habeas corpus petitions have been rejected on procedural grounds. For example, consider the Nebraska case in which Mohamed El-Tabech was convicted of murdering his wife.[6] At the time of the trial, DNA testing was not available. After El-Tabech's conviction, however, DNA testing became available, and El-Tabech filed a postconviction motion to have DNA testing performed on the evidence. The motion was denied because the Nebraska Supreme Court had not yet recognized the admissibility of DNA evidence. After the Nebraska Supreme Court accepted DNA testing, El-Tabech filed another motion seeking DNA testing. The trial court denied this motion as well, claiming that the request constituted a successive petition. To El-Tabech's relief, however, the Nebraska appellate court ruled that El-Tabech's motion could be treated as a writ of coram nobis.

[6] *State v. El-Tabech*, 610 N.W.2d 737, Neb. (2000).

Coram nobis is highly limited in its scope. Moreover, the burden of proof is on the defendant to show that the evidence would have prevented a conviction, not merely provided a probability of a different decision. For this reason, it is necessary for the defendant to have exculpatory DNA evidence in hand to demonstrate grounds for a writ of error coram nobis. As with writs of habeas corpus, an inability to access the relevant samples often impedes wrongfully convicted defendants' efforts to file writs of error coram nobis.

Remedies in the nature of coram nobis apply both to individuals in custody and not in custody.[7] These appeals may involve a motion to vacate, set aside or correct the sentence (under 28 U.S.C.§2255), a motion to correct an illegal sentence or a sentence imposed in an illegal manner [FRCP Rule 35(a)], or a motion to reduce the sentence [FRCP Rule 35(b)].

THERE ARE MANY PROCEDURAL OBSTACLES

Once the defendant has been convicted, the legal system's concern for the finality of verdicts, federal-state comity and the efficiency of the judicial system often overrides its concern for the prisoner's actual innocence. Once convicted, the defendant loses the presumption of innocence, and along with that much of his or her right to due process. Furthermore, the primary purpose of our constitutionally mandated protections is not to ensure that the innocent are not convicted, but to ensure that the procedures that were followed provided the defendant a fair opportunity to mount a defense.[8] Rather than provide a judicial remedy for the actually innocent, courts have consistently emphasized that executive clemency has historically been the channel through which the wrongfully convicted pursued their claims of actual innocence.[9] Although it is obviously beneficial for wrongfully convicted prisoners to have this avenue for relief, some commentators are disturbed by the fact that the clemency process is completely subjective and unregulated. The clemency executive can base his or her decision on any factors he or she wishes, and the Supreme Court has allowed the clemency process to remain completely free from judicial oversight.[10] As Justice John Paul Stevens observed in his dissenting opinion in *Woodard*, there are no safeguards in place to prevent the clemency process from being "infected by bribery, personal or political animosity, or the deliberate fabrication of false evidence."

The judicial system tries to ensure the finality of its verdicts. All states have a limited time period during which a convicted defendant can introduce new evidence to challenge the conviction and to prevent a convicted offender from wasting the court's time with an endless series of frivolous challenges. These statutes of limitation are often severe; more than half the states allow six months or less, and few statutes extend the period

[7] Federal Rules of Criminal Procedure Rule 35.

[8] *Patterson v. New York*, 432 U.S. 197 (1977).

[9] *Herrera v. Collins*, 506 U.S. 390 (1993); *Lucas v. Johnson*, 132 F.3d 1069, 5th Cir. (1998); *Royal v. Taylor*, 188 F.3d 239, 4th Cir. (1999).

[10] *Conn. Bd. of Pardons v. Dumschat*, 452 U.S. 458 (1981); *Ohio Adult Parole Auth. v. Woodard*, 523 U.S. 272 (1998).

beyond three years. Furthermore, when a defendant petitions for access to a sample, the court may determine when the requested testing became available, and require the prisoner to make the request within the specified time period after the test became available (sometimes referred to as a laches test). For example, in *Ziegler v. State,*[11] the Florida Supreme Court denied an application for DNA testing that was made in 1994, because the testing had been available since 1991, and Florida provided only a two-year period during which new evidence could be introduced.

The rationale for having a statute of limitations for introducing newly discovered evidence is based on the assumptions that verdicts are accurate, that the quality of witness recollections and other evidence declines over time, and that a final verdict and sentencing allow the victims and their families a sense of closure that enables them to get on with the healing process. This reasoning is valid for many types of evidence, such as witness recollections. DNA is considerably more durable than these other types of evidence, however, and valid DNA evidence can often be obtained long after a state's statute of limitations has precluded the introduction of new evidence.[12] In 1999, the National Commission on the Future of DNA Evidence published a report for the National Institute of Justice entitled "Postconviction DNA Testing: Recommendations for Handling Requests."[13] In its report, the commission suggested waiving time limits on the introduction of new evidence in certain cases where new DNA evidence is available. The commission acknowledged that "[f]inality is a fundamental value that can be properly ignored only in the extraordinary case." It added, however, that "DNA analysis now provides us with the ability to do justice in the exceptional situation." With the success of the various Innocence Projects, it is becoming increasingly clear that the system whereby violent crimes are prosecuted is badly flawed and that DNA evidence has enormous potential to exonerate the falsely convicted. Unfortunately, the desire for finality has denied a number of prisoners who were convicted years before the advent of DNA testing the opportunity to use DNA testing to secure new trials because the period during which they could introduce new evidence had expired. Many states have enacted habeas corpus laws, or have case law citing the "interests of justice," that enable the state to waive the time limitation on introducing new evidence.[14]

Another principle that is often invoked as justification for restricting prisoners' rights to challenge their convictions is the desire to ensure

[11] 654 So. 2d 1162, Fla. (1995).

[12] Gianelli, 2001; Houch and Budowle, 2002.

[13] National Institute of Justice, 1999.

[14] For example, *Tuffiash v. State*, 878 S.W.2d 197, Tex. Crim. App. (1994); *Davi v. Joseph Class*, Warden, unpublished decision, Case No. 19844, Order of Remand, S.D. (1998).

federal-state comity by requiring state prisoners to exhaust their state remedies before requesting the federal government to step in. The Supreme Court has repeatedly emphasized that one of the principles underlying our system of federalism is the concept that the federal government should avoid meddling in the legitimate affairs of the states.[15] Allowing a prisoner to appeal immediately to a federal court denies the state the opportunity to correct a constitutional violation. For this reason, in many cases if a prisoner files a petition for federal habeas corpus relief before he or she has exhausted all the available state remedies, the petition will be considered procedurally flawed. The convicted defendant must first exhaust all his or her opportunities for direct appeals, then collateral attacks, in state court before filing a petition in federal court.

State prisoners have brought a large number of frivolous petitions to federal courts, hampering the judicial system's efficiency. In response, Congress has enacted several laws that have the effect of delaying the prisoner's right to petition for federal relief until all available state appeals have been exhausted. One such example is the Prison Litigation Reform Act (PLRA).[16] The PLRA was written to cover a broad range of issues pertinent to the conditions of prison life, such as overcrowding or abusive behavior on the part of prison officials. The request for access to a sample is not pertinent to conditions of prison life and should not be controlled by the PLRA.

The Anti-Terrorism and Effective Death Penalty Act (AEDPA)[17] contains a similar exhaustion provision intended to limit the number of petitions received by federal courts. The Ninth Circuit court has recently ruled that the AEDPA applies to claims of actual innocence that are based on newly acquired evidence,[18] so this act will regulate many petitions for postconviction DNA testing. In response to criticism that the exhaustion requirement unfairly delays the wrongfully convicted prisoner's effort to prove his or her innocence and gain release, DNA testing requests have been exempted from the provisions of the AEDPA. Furthermore, the Advancing Justice Through DNA Technology Act of 2003 (AJTDTA) specifically states that its provisions, one of which is a similar exhaustion requirement, do not affect "the circumstances under which a person may obtain DNA testing or post-conviction relief under any other law." The AJTDTA allows a prisoner to request a new trial or resentencing based on the availability of newly acquired DNA evidence. It does not provide the exoneration and release that is provided by a writ of habeus corpus or executive clemency,

[15] For example, *Ex parte Royall*, 117 U.S. 241 (1886); *Darr v. Burford*, 339 U.S. 200 (1950); *Younger v. Harris*, 401 U.S. 37 (1971); *Wainwright v. Sykes*, 433 U.S. 72 (1977).

[16] PLRA, 42 U.S.C. § 1997e, 2000.

[17] AEDPA, Pub. L. No. 104-132, 110 Stat. 1214, 1996.

[18] *Redd v. McGrath*, 343 F.3d 1077 (2003).

but it does provide another avenue by which a wrongfully convicted prisoner can pursue justice.

Prior to 1977, the Supreme Court was generally receptive to state prisoners' habeas petitions. For example, in *Fay v. Noia,*[19] the Court ruled that a federal court could consider a habeas petition from a state prisoner, even if the petition did not conform to the relevant state procedures, provided the prisoner had not deliberately bypassed the state's procedures in filing with the federal court. More recently, however, the Supreme Court has dramatically restricted prisoners' rights to have procedurally defaulted habeas petitions heard. The Court requires petitioners not only to exhaust all available state remedies and follow all applicable state procedures, but also to raise all applicable constitutional issues in the first petition. This has created three classes of improper habeas petitions: procedurally flawed petitions, which do not conform to state procedures; successive petitions, which raise the same principles that were raised by a previous, procedurally defaulted, petition; and abusive petitions, which are premised on grounds that were available to the petitioner at the time of a previous petition but not used.

With the decision in *Wainwright v. Sykes,*[20] the Supreme Court established that the petitioner was required to demonstrate some excusable cause for not having followed the required state procedures, and moreover, to demonstrate that a refusal to hear the petition was prejudicial to the petitioner. In addition, in 1986, the Court rendered three decisions that further defined the concepts of cause and prejudice, as well as extended the principle of actual innocence to include the possibility that the defendant could be innocent of the sentence that was imposed.[21] The courts have interpreted factors such as ineffective assistance of counsel or novelty of a legal claim as justifiable causes for not following state procedures.[22] As for prejudice, if one has exculpatory DNA evidence in hand, it should be easy to argue that precluding the defendant from introducing it is prejudicial to his or her case.

Unfortunately for those whose sole ground for challenging their conviction is actual innocence, these early Supreme Court decisions all required the petitioner to demonstrate a constitutional error in addition to actual innocence. Six years later, in *Sawyer v. Whitley,*[23] the Supreme Court reaffirmed the requirement for a constitutional error. In *Sawyer*, the Court expanded its analysis of the actual innocence exception and gave a more

[19] 372 U.S. 391, (1963).

[20] 433 U.S. 72 (1977).

[21] *Kuhlmann v. Wilson*, 477 U.S. 436 (1986); *Murray v. Carrier*, 477 U.S. 478 (1986); *Smith v. Murray*, 477 U.S. 527 (1986).

[22] For example, *Reed v. Ross*, 468 U.S. 1 (1984); *Murray v. Carrier*, 477 U.S. 478 (1986).

[23] 505 U.S. 333 (1992).

objective definition of actual innocence than it had before. It borrowed from the Eleventh Circuit Court of Appeals' ruling regarding defendants who are seeking to reverse a death sentence, which requires that the defendant demonstrate "by clear and convincing evidence that but for constitutional error, no reasonable juror would find him eligible for the death penalty." Once again, by requiring there to have been a constitutional error, the Court denied relief to those prisoners who had been wrongfully convicted in a constitutionally valid trial.

For many wrongly convicted prisoners, these procedural obstacles are so difficult to overcome that they violate the principles of fundamental fairness that constitute the foundation of our criminal justice system. Recognizing this, Justice O'Connor wrote in *Murray* that "the principles of comity and finality that inform the concepts of cause and prejudice must yield to the imperative of correcting a fundamentally unjust incarceration." The Court established one final means by which a procedurally defaulted, successive or abusive habeas petition could be heard. The Court ruled that such a petition could be heard if the refusal to do so would constitute a fundamental miscarriage of justice. Furthermore, the Court did not place the burden of demonstrating a miscarriage of justice on the petitioner. Instead, it charged the Court itself with the task of ascertaining that such a miscarriage of justice would not take place if the petition was rejected.

Despite the decision against the defendant, the Supreme Court's *Herrera* decision represented a significant turning point in the court's treatment of claims of actual innocence.[24] In *Herrera*, the Court disagreed with the defendant's contention that the incarceration of an innocent prisoner violated the Constitution's Due Process clause. Once again, the Court's emphasis was on procedural due process rather than substantive due process. Writing for the majority, however, Chief Justice William Rehnquist briefly visited the subject of substantive due process. His opinion left open the possibility that a prisoner who had been convicted of a capital crime but could provide a "truly persuasive demonstration of 'actual innocence'" would have the right to do so. Rehnquist stated that such a demonstration would "render the execution of the defendant unconstitutional, and warrant federal habeas relief if there were no state avenue open to process such a claim." He went on to state further, however, that the petitioner would be required to meet an extraordinarily high standard for the demonstration.

[24] *Herrera v. Collins*, 506 U.S. 390 (1993).

Several state and federal courts interpreted the *Herrera* decision as an acknowledgment that claims of actual innocence could be entertained in the absence of constitutional error. For example, the courts in Connecticut and Illinois ruled shortly thereafter that, while *Herrera* controlled decisions regarding federal habeas corpus petitions, state constitutional jurisprudence recognized claims of actual innocence under the principle of due process.[25] Even as they opened this new avenue of relief, the courts reemphasized Rehnquist's admonition that the standard for demonstrating innocence was extremely high.[26] It is unclear exactly what the standard is; most courts have never specifically defined this standard, either in general or as it applied to the instant case. The *Wilson* court is one exception, however. The *Wilson* court required the defendant to demonstrate that "it is more likely than not that no reasonable juror would have convicted [the prisoner]." Despite the lack of a universal definition, it is clear that the standard is very high; it is apparently not sufficient merely to introduce exculpatory DNA evidence. The courts have noted that, while the presence of DNA at a crime scene associates the individual with the crime, the absence of DNA at a crime scene does not necessarily mean that the defendant was not associated with the crime. The prisoner who is using exculpatory DNA evidence to petition for habeas relief will be required to demonstrate exactly how the exculpatory evidence fits within the framework of the other evidence against him to cast doubt upon the validity of the verdict.

The excessively high standard for proving actual innocence has contributed to the execution of a number of innocent prisoners.[27] Nonetheless, most courts have historically maintained a standard for demonstrating actual innocence that has proven too high for innocent petitioners to attain. In a jarring departure from *Herrera*, however, Judge Jed S. Rakoff of the United States District Court for the Southern District of New York ruled that new advances in DNA testing were capable of providing the "truly persuasive demonstration" of actual innocence alluded to by Chief Justice Rehnquist in *Herrera*.[28] This in itself opened up a new avenue of hope for wrongfully convicted prisoners. In addition, Rakoff extended this reasoning to declare the death penalty unconstitutional. Rakoff reasoned that, because new developments in technology might make new evidence available to the prisoner at any time, executing him "cuts off the opportunity for exoneration, denies due process, and indeed, is tantamount to

[25] For example, *Summerville v. Warden*, 641 A.2d 1356, Conn. (1994); *People v. Washington*, 665 N.E.2d 1330, Ill. (1996).

[26] *Spencer v. Murray*, 5 F.3d 758, 4th Cir. (1993); *Wilson v. Greene*, 155 F.3d 396, 4th Cir. (1998); *Jenner v. Dooley*, 590 N.W.2d 463, S.D. (1999); *Cherrix v. Braxton*, 131 F. Supp. 2d 756, E.D. Va. (2001).

[27] Bedau and Radelet, 1987.

[28] *United States v. Quinones*, 205 F. Supp. 2d 256, S.D.N.Y. (2002).

foreseeable, state-sponsored murder of innocent human beings." Rakoff's ruling has generated much discussion regarding the judicial system's treatment of actual innocence and the appropriateness of the death penalty. Most courts, however, continue to apply the very high *Herrera* standard when considering claims of actual innocence.

NEW EVIDENCE MAY JUSTIFY A NEW THEORY OF THE CASE

All would agree that, if the relevant facts do not change, counsel's arguments during postconviction proceedings should be consistent with the arguments he or she proffered during the trial. When postconviction testing produces new information, however, the new information may justify the prosecution constructing a new theory of the case that is inconsistent with a portion of the theory of the case it had developed for the original trial. For example, after Roy Criner was convicted in 1990 of sexual assault and murder in a trial that included serological testing of semen found in the victim, he requested DNA testing of the semen sample. The results were exculpatory, but the Texas Court of Criminal Appeals denied his request for a new trial. In doing so, the court accepted the prosecution's argument that the semen may have been deposited during a prior act of consensual sex with another, and that Criner could have either worn a condom or failed to ejaculate. At trial, the prosecution had claimed that the victim had not had sex with anyone else shortly before the crime and that it was Criner's semen that had been found in the victim. This theory was supported by the fact that the serological testing included Criner. Once the DNA evidence excluded him, however, the prosecution argued that this did not mean that Criner was innocent; it merely meant he was not the source of the semen in the victim's vagina. The non-DNA evidence that supported the conviction was still strong enough to support the theory that Criner raped the victim, and to preserve the conviction.

If the new DNA evidence contradicts evidence that was presented at trial, the defense's odds of securing a reversal of the conviction may be improved if it can convince the court to apply a harmless error test to the motion for a new trial, rather than the newly discovered evidence test.[29] Under the harmless error test, if the reviewing court rules that the judgment was not substantially affected by the error, the error is ignored.[30] In addition, the prosecution has the burden to prove that

[29] Federal Rules of Criminal Procedure 52 defines a harmless error as "any error, defect, irregularity or variance that does not affect substantial rights," and directs that they be disregarded.

[30] *Kotteakos v. United States*, 328 U.S. 750 (1946).

introduction of the now-impugned evidence did not affect the jury's verdict. Placing this burden on the prosecution forces the prosecution to argue within the framework of the original case and prevents the prosecution from adapting to the new information by introducing novel theories of the crime. In most cases, the forensic testing evidence that was introduced at trial will have had a strong influence on the jury's decision, and it should be relatively easy for the defense to argue that the use of the now-impugned evidence was not a harmless error. In spite of the elemental appeal of this argument, some courts have been reluctant to accept it.[31]

ACCESSING THE NECESSARY SAMPLES

Historically, one of the biggest obstacles to the effort to introduce new evidence, whether for the purpose of requesting a new trial or appealing for clemency, is the difficulty some defendants have had in accessing the relevant samples. There is clearly no constitutionally mandated right to request a new trial based on new evidence or to obtain postconviction DNA evidence to be used in writs of habeas corpus or petitions for executive clemency. In *Herrera*, the Supreme Court recognized the states' right to develop whatever method they wished, or no method if they wished, to enable a prisoner to request a new trial based on newly discovered evidence.[32] Absent a postconviction DNA testing statute, a prisoner who wants access to samples must request the samples from the prosecutor or petition the court. Some prosecutors have refused to turn over samples, claiming that even exculpatory DNA evidence would not ensure a different verdict in the face of the rest of the evidence against the defendant.

If the prosecutor refuses to turn over samples that had been preserved, the prisoner can file an action under U.S.C. § 1983, alleging that the prosecutor deprived him of his right to due process under the Fourteenth Amendment.[33] The courts differ with respect to the defendant's right of access to the sample for the purpose of further DNA testing. Several courts have upheld the defendant's right to access old samples, asserting that DNA testing is capable of providing the truly persuasive demonstration of actual innocence hypothetically alluded to by Chief Justice Rehnquist in *Herrera*.[34] In contrast, however, several circuit courts have ruled that the defendant has no constitutionally mandated right to access evidence for the purpose of DNA testing.[35] These courts' denials have been based on

[31] For discussion, see *State v. Armstrong*, Nos. 01-2789 and 02-2979, 2004 Wisc. App. LEXIS 453, Wis. Ct. App. May 27, 2004.

[32] *Herrera v. Collins*, 506 U.S. 390 (1993).

[33] U.S.C. § 1983 enables someone to bring an action against anyone who, acting as an agent of the state, deprived the individual of a federally protected right.

[34] For example, *Cherrix v. Braxton*, 131 F. Supp. 2d 756, E.D. Va. (2001).

[35] *Boyle v. Mayer*, 2002 WL 31085186, 6th Cir. Sept. (2002); *Harvey v. Horan*, 278 F.3d 370, 4th Cir. (2002), rehearing denied en banc, 285 F.3d 298, 4th Cir. (2002); *Kutzner v. Montgomery County*, 303 F.3d 339, 5th Cir. (2002).

their interpretation that the prisoners were trying to assert claims of actual innocence. Consequently, the courts have cited *Heck v. Humphrey*[36] and *Preiser v. Rodriguez*[37] to support their assertion that claims of actual innocence should be brought as petitions for habeas corpus. In both *Heck* and *Preiser*, the Court opined that the request for postconviction DNA testing was by its very nature an attack on the merits of the conviction, and therefore that it threatened the finality of the conviction.

In some cases, the samples were not available for postconviction testing, through no fault of the prosecution. As discussed in Chapter 7, the NRC, many courts, the federal Innocence Protection Act and a number of state statutes have all affirmed the importance of preserving a portion of the evidence for independent testing by the defense. Unfortunately, however, even the most cooperative law enforcement agencies do not have the space required to store all the biological samples they have ever collected indefinitely. Recognizing the practical realities, the Supreme Court has twice ruled that the *Brady* decision only extends to evidence that is known to be exculpatory, and that the state has no obligation to preserve potentially exculpatory evidence, provided the state did not act in bad faith in disposing of the evidence.[38] Even so, a number of state courts have ruled that the state has an obligation to preserve potentially exculpatory evidence, and will not consider the issue of whether the prosecution acted in good versus bad faith when a defendant challenges the disposal of a sample.[39]

A number of states are currently contemplating legislation to address the issue of evidence sample retention. Some contemplate retaining the evidence through the convicted offender's term of incarceration, while others contemplate a time certain in years from date of conviction. If the defense attorney feels there is a high probability that the defendant will want further testing on a sample some day, it may be prudent to request that the court issue an order instructing the preservation of the evidence sample.

Despite the lack of a constitutional entitlement, many commentators have emphasized that denying the defendant access to samples violates the fundamental principles of fairness that underlie our criminal justice system.[40] Even as they confirmed the lack of entitlement, some judges have asserted that principles of fairness should provide the prisoner the

[36] 512 U.S. 477 (1994).

[37] 411 U.S. 475 (1973).

[38] *California v. Trombetta*, 467 U.S. 479, 81 L. Ed. 2d 413, 104 S. Ct. 2528 (1984); *Arizona v. Youngblood*, 488 U.S. 51, 102 L. Ed. 2d 281, 109 S. Ct. 333 (1988).

[39] *State v. Fain*, 774 P.2d 252 Idaho (1989); *Thorne v. Dep't of Pub. Safety*, 774 P.2d 1326 Alaska (1989); *State v. Smagula*, 578 A.2d 1215 N.H. (1990); *People v. Nation*, 604 P.2d 1051, Cal. (1990); *Commonwealth v. Henderson*, 582 N.E.2d 496 Mass. (1991); *Lolly v. State*, 611 A.2d 956 Del. (1992); *Ex parte Gingo*, 605 So. 2d 1237 Ala. (1992); *State v. Schmid*, 487 N.W.2d 539 Minn. Ct. App. (1992); *State v. Riggs*, 838 P.2d 975 N.M. (1992); *State v. Delisle*, 648 A.2d 632 Vt. (1994); *State v. Morales*, 657 A.2d 585 Conn. (1995); *State v. Okumura*, 894 P.2d 80 Haw. (1995); *State v. Osakalumi*, 461 S.E.2d 504 W. Va. (1995); *State v. Ferguson*, 2 S.W. 3d 912 Tenn. (1999).

[40] Neufeld, 1993.

right to access the relevant samples.[41] The wrongfully convicted prisoner's effort to exonerate himself or herself obviously begins with access to the relevant samples. State and federal courts all expect a prisoner to have exculpatory evidence in hand when applying for habeas corpus relief.[42] In addition, without the ability to produce exculpatory DNA evidence, a prisoner has little chance of presenting a meaningful petition for executive clemency. Finally, without access to the sample, the defendant cannot take advantage of newly developed and potentially more sensitive typing technologies.

Some courts have melded the concerns over fundamental fairness with the right to exculpatory evidence that was established in *Brady v. Maryland*,[43] and adapted these principles to requests for postconviction DNA testing. Although the *Brady* decision concerned exculpatory evidence that the prosecution had in hand for the trial, some courts have applied *Brady* to requests for samples that could provide potentially exculpatory DNA testing after the conviction.[44] This opinion also finds support in *Arizona v. Youngblood*.[45] In *Youngblood*, the Supreme Court was asked to vacate a conviction because the state had destroyed evidence samples. While the court focused on the question of whether the state had acted in good versus bad faith in disposing of the samples, the wording of its decision implies that the petitioner would have been entitled to the samples if they had still existed. Although this argument has persuaded several courts, other courts have been less convinced.[46]

The state's Freedom of Information Act (FOIA) statutes may provide one final means by which a prisoner may access samples. The FOIA statutes often refer to tangible materials; one may be able to argue that this includes biological samples.

Once the defense makes the decision to have a sample retested, the next challenge may be finding whatever samples are still available. Counsel should also try to discover any ancillary material—reports, bench notes and other documents—that accompany the sample or may have been archived in the typing lab. Samples and other information may be located in police department property rooms or property warehouses, public or private forensic laboratories, hospitals or medical facilities (especially in rape cases), the coroner's or medical examiner's office, courthouse property rooms, the prosecutor's office or the investigators' files. If the

[41] For example, *Harvey v. Horan*, 278 F.3d 370, 4th Cir. (2002), rehearing denied en banc, 285 F.3d 298, 4th Cir. (2002), Judge Luttig invoked the basic "principles of justice," citing *Mathews v. Eldridge*, 424 U.S. 319 (1976), and *Medina v. California*, 505 U.S. 437 (1992), quoting *Speiser v. Randall*, 357 U.S. 513 (1992); see also *Jenner v. Dooley*, 590 N.W.2d 463, S.D. (1999).

[42] National Institute of Justice, 1999.

[43] 373 U.S. 83 (1963).

[44] *Dabbs v. Vergari*, 570 N.Y.S.2d 765 (1990); *State v. Thomas*, 586 A.2d 250 (1991); *Commonwealth v. Brison*, 618 A.2d 420, Pa. Super. Ct. (1992); *Jenkins v. Scully*, No. CIV-91-298E, 1992 WL 32342, W.D.N.Y., February 11, 1992; *Sewell v. State*, 592 N.E.2d 705, Ind. App. (1992); *Toney v. Gammon*, 79 F.3d 693, 8th Cir. (1996); *Jones v. Wood*, 114 F.3d 1002, 9th Cir. (1997).

[45] 488 U.S. 51 (1988).

[46] For example, *Ohio v. Wogenstahl*, No. C-970238, 1998, WL 306561, Ohio Ct. App. June 12, 1998, unpublished opinion.

defendant has been tried for a crime before, counsel may find relevant evidence at the facilities of the agencies involved in that prosecution.

KNOW THE SPECIFIC PROVISIONS OF THE CONTROLLING STATUTE

Almost all states have enacted postconviction legislation that maximizes the use of DNA testing in criminal trials, makes it easier for convicted defendants to get access to the relevant samples, pays for testing for indigent defendants, extends the statutes of limitation on the introduction of newly discovered DNA evidence and compensates the wrongfully imprisoned.[47] There are significant differences between the provisions of the different statutes, however, so the litigator should be aware of the specific requirements and exclusions attending the relevant statute.

Some common elements found within these statutes include:

- The felony petitioner must be incarcerated at the time of petition.
- The petition must be in written form.
- The petitioner must make an assertion of actual innocence under penalty of perjury.
- The forensic evidence must be in a testable condition and not previously been tested, or tested with outdated technology and new technology is currently available.
- Identity was an issue at trial.
- Evidence the petitioner wishes to have tested is material and goes to the issue of identity.

There are a number of important differences in the provisions of the different statutes, however.

Statutes differ in their criteria for deciding who may file the petition for postconviction relief. Many statutes provide testing only for petitioners who assert their actual innocence and seek complete exonerations; those who seek to reduce their sentence are denied. In addition, many require the petitioner to demonstrate that identity was an issue at trial. This has the desirable effect of excluding petitioners whose defenses were based on other claims, such as a consent defense or a defense of diminished mental capacity.[48] Unfortunately, however, it also has the undesirable effect of

[47] See Swedlow, 2002, for a review of state statutes, and Kleinert, 2006, for a review of the federal Innocence Protection Act.

[48] *Halsey v. State*, 748 A.2d 634, N.J. (2000).

[49] *North Carolina v. Alford*, 400 U.S. 25 (1970); Leo and Ofshe, 1998; Borteck, 2004; www.innocenceproject.org

tacitly precluding defendants who have pleaded guilty from petitioning. Many commentators, and the Supreme Court as well, acknowledge that a surprising number of innocent defendants plead guilty.[49] Many defendants who are innocent but pleaded guilty nonetheless may have been more inclined to plead not guilty if they felt that they had strong exculpatory DNA evidence on their side.

Most states' postconviction DNA testing statutes require that the testing produce new, noncumulative evidence. This usually requires the petitioner to demonstrate the existence of evidence that was not available to him or her at trial. This may involve evidence samples that were not tested before trial, new developments in testing technology, or testing that was not available due to ineffective assistance of counsel. All postconviction DNA testing statutes require the petitioner to demonstrate, or the court to find, that the DNA evidence is material. The different statutes differ in their standard for materiality, however. Some states, such as New York, only require that there be a probability that the verdict would have been more favorable to the defendant. Others require conclusive proof that there would have been a different verdict.

Almost all states' statutes require proof of an unbroken chain of custody. Some statutes require the petitioner to prove the chain, while others require the court to make its own determination. On this subject there appears to have been an important oversight. In jurisdictions that require the petitioner to prove the unbroken chain of custody, none of the statutes specifies the mechanism by which the petitioner can do so. The petitioner relies on the agents that produced the DNA evidence to respond to discovery requests and disclose all the necessary information. According to the National Commission on the Future of DNA Evidence, "when an inmate is truly innocent, interests converge." The Commission recommended that "participants in postconviction DNA proceedings need to consider the category of the case in which the DNA testing is sought and whether participants need to adjust the roles they customarily play in adversarial proceedings." Despite the Department of Justice's recommendation that "the prosecutor should make every effort at cooperation and coordination with defense counsel," the defense may still find that some state agents are hostile to the defense's requests. If the postconviction DNA testing statute has been codified as part of the traditional postconviction statute, the petitioner can argue that he or she has the same right to discovery as does a traditional postconviction petitioner. In addition, during postconviction proceedings, the prosecution has an ethical duty to disclose any newly available information that casts doubt on the validity of the conviction, even if the defense has not requested such information.[50] A petitioner who is still within the prescribed time period for direct appeals may be able to use his subpoena power to procure the necessary documents. If the time period for appeals has expired, however, the petitioner may lack the jurisdiction of the court to invoke his subpoena power.

[50] *Imbler v. Pachtman*, 424 U.S. 409 (1976), note 25; Model Code of Professional Responsibility EC 7-13, 1969.

[51] Swedlow, 2002.

Most states' statutes differ from the traditional postconviction practices regarding the timing of the petition. Poorly timed petitions can cost the prisoner opportunities to challenge the conviction. In the interest of federal-state comity, federal courts have historically required petitioners to exhaust their state appeals before seeking federal habeas corpus relief. In contrast, U.S.C. § 1983 and most postconviction DNA testing statutes allow the petitioner to seek *habeas* relief at any time after the conviction.[51] The defense must first know what avenues are available for pursuing relief, and must then determine whether any of these actions will have an effect on any of the statutes of limitation that control any of the other available actions. For example, if the defense focuses on requesting a new trial on the basis of newly available DNA tests, it is possible that the litigation of the petition for DNA testing might extend beyond the period during which constitutional/statutory appeals may be filed. If the request for postconviction DNA testing is denied (for example, because the evidence has been discarded), the statutes of limitation may have closed off other avenues of appeal.

This issue is further complicated because these provisions interact with the provisions of the federal Anti-Terrorism and Effective Death Penalty Act (AEDPA). The AEDPA requires petitioners to file habeus corpus petitions within one year of the date their convictions become final. However, this time limit may be tolled if any "properly filed application for State postconviction or other collateral review" is pending. One can argue that postconviction DNA testing petitions constitute applications for collateral review and should therefore statutorily toll the AEDPA's one-year time limit. The AEDPA requires the petitioner to assert a federal constitutional error within the motion, however, in order for the request for testing to toll the AEDPA time limits. Absent such an assertion, the AEDPA time limit will not be tolled, and the petitioner will lose his or her opportunity for review of his or her case in federal court. To avoid such complications, some states' testing statutes automatically stay the request for DNA testing until after the opportunity for direct appeals has been exhausted. This is obviously highly inconvenient for the defendant who is actually innocent, because it requires him or her to remain incarcerated for a longer period of time and delays the day when the DNA evidence will free him or her. It does, however, ensure that the defendant does not have to sacrifice one potential avenue of relief to pursue another.

Different states' statutes also differ with respect to their provisions for appointment of counsel and payment of testing fees for indigent defendants. Some do not address the issue, others allow the defendant to request counsel (with no guarantee that one will be provided) and still others explicitly provide for counsel. Even if the statute provides for counsel, however, if the time period for direct appeals has expired, the defendant's Sixth Amendment right to effective assistance of counsel is significantly restricted. For example, consider the case of *People v. Love.*[52] In *Love*, the petitioner sought DNA testing one year after the conclusion of his state postconviction proceedings. At a hearing to decide on the motion for testing, which Love did not attend, the state argued that the evidence had been destroyed. In addition, the state also argued that the issue of destruction of the evidence had been litigated during direct appeal. When the court asked Love's counsel whether a factual hearing should be convened to determine whether the evidence had been destroyed, Love's counsel declined, and the petition was dismissed. Love tried to argue on appeal that his counsel had rendered ineffective assistance because he had not requested the hearing. The appellate court affirmed the conviction, however. The court held that, because Love's opportunity for direct appeals had been exhausted, Love was statutorily entitled to the appointment of counsel, but was not constitutionally entitled to effective assistance of counsel (or even a reasonable level of assistance). This decision echoed one that had been handed down by the Court of Appeals of Ohio a few years earlier.[53]

[52] 727 N.E.2d 680, Ill. App. Ct. (2000).

[53] *State v. Scudder*, 722 N.E.2d 1054, Ohio Ct. App. (1998).

REFERENCES AND ADDITIONAL READINGS

Bedau, H.A. and Radelet, M.L. (1987) *Stanford Law Review*, 40, 21.

Borteck, D. (2004) *Cardozo Law Review*, 25, 1429.

Connors, E., Lundregan, T., Miller, N. and McEwen, T. (1996) Convicted by Juries, Exonerated by Science: Case Studies in the Use of DNA Evidence to Establish Innocence after Trial, National Institute of Justice, NCJ161258. Available at http://www.ncjrs.org/pdffiles/dnaevid.pdf

Gianelli, Paul. (2001) *Arizona State Law Journal*, 33, 113–117.

Houch, M.M. and Budowle, B. (2002) *Journal of Forensic Sciences*, 47, 964–966.

Kleinert, M.E. (2006) *Brandeis Law Journal*, 44, 491.

Leo, R.A. and Ofshe, R.J. (1998) *Journal of Criminal Law and Criminology*, 88, 429.

National Institute of Justice. (1999) Postconviction DNA Testing: Recommendations for Handling Requests.

http://0-www.ncjrs.org.wncln.wncln.org:80/txtfiles1/nij/1776.26.txt

Neufeld, P.J. (1993) *Journal of Criminal Law and Criminology*, 84, 189.

Swedlow, K. (2002) *California Law Review*, 38, 355.

Wilkes, D.E., Jr. (1983) *Federal and State Postconviction Remedies and Relief*. Norcross, GA: Harrison Company.

Appendix I

Using the Chi-Square Test to Determine if a Population Conforms to HWE Expectations

Recall that HWE theory allows one to take the frequencies of the different individual alleles of a marker and use them to predict what the proportion of homozygous versus heterozygous genotypes should be in a population. The chi-square test compares the proportion of homozygous and heterozygous genotypes that was observed in the population against the proportion of homozygous and heterozygous genotypes that HWE theory would predict should exist. The application of the test for a biallelic (only two alleles) marker can be easily demonstrated. Multiallelic markers call for an adaptation of the formula given below, but are easily handled by the various statistical packages that include the chi-square test. Note that in most real cases, a test such as Fisher's Exact test will be used to test a population for HWE. The chi-square test and the Exact test are founded on the same principles, however, and the chi-square is simpler and more straightforward for the novice.

Quite simply, the farther apart your observed numbers and your expected numbers lie, the more likely you are to declare that your population is not in HWE. For the chi-square test, you perform four mathematical operations:

1. For each of the three genotypes, subtract your expected number from your observed number (obs – exp).
2. Square each of the three differences $(\text{obs} - \text{exp})^2$.
3. Divide each of the three squared differences by its expected number of that genotype $\frac{(\text{obs} - \text{exp})^2}{\text{exp}}$.

4. Add those three numbers together to produce the chi-square statistic. If the value of your chi-square statistic exceeds a critical number, you can declare that your population does not conform to HWE expectations. If your observed values are close to your expected values, the differences will be small, the squared differences will be small, and the sum of the squared differences will in turn be less than the critical value for the chi-square statistic.

Consider the following numerical example involving a biallelic (only two alleles) marker. Imagine that allele 1 is the more frequent of the two, with a frequency of 70% ($p_1 = 0.70$). This means that allele 2 has a frequency of 30% ($p_2 = 0.30$). Imagine you have a population of 1,000 people.

The three possible genotypes for this marker are 11, 12, and 22. According to HWE theory, using p_1 and p_2 along with the product rule, one can predict the following probabilities for the three genotypes:

$$p(11) = p_1^2$$

$$p(12) = 2p_1p_2$$

$$p(22) = p_2^2$$

With $p_1 = 0.70$ and $p_2 = 0.30$, HWE theory predicts the following:

$$p(11) = 0.70^2 = 0.49 \times 1{,}000 \text{ people} = 490 \text{ expected } 11 \text{ genotypes}$$

$$p(12) = 2 \times 0.70 \times 0.30 = 0.42 \times 1{,}000 \text{ people}$$
$$= 420 \text{ expected } 12 \text{ genotypes}$$

$$p(22) = 0.30^2 = 0.09 \times 1{,}000 \text{ people} = 90 \text{ expected } 22 \text{ genotypes}$$

If you actually have 510 people with 11 genotypes, 440 people with 12 genotypes and 50 people with 22 genotypes, do these proportions differ from HWE expectations enough for you to declare that the population is not in equilibrium?

In order to answer this question, the chi-square statistic is computed as illustrated in Table AI.1, and the resultant number is compared to a table of critical values.[1] The critical value depends on the probability of error one accepts. It is customary to accept either a 5% or 1% probability of declaring a population out of HWE when it actually is not. The critical

[1] The table of critical chi-square values can be found in any statistics textbook or online through any of the popular search engines.

Table AI.1 Calculation of the Chi-Square Statistic

	Genotypes		
	11	**12**	**22**
observed	510	440	50
expected	490	420	90
obs – exp	20	20	–40
$(obs - exp)^2$	400	400	1600
$(obs - exp)^2/exp$	0.82	0.95	1.78
		0.82 + 0.95 + 1.78 = 3.55	

value also depends on a concept known as the degrees of freedom (df). The df is a function of the design of the experiment. For a marker with N alleles, the df can be calculated as $N(N-1)/2$. For a biallelic marker, therefore, $df = 2(1)/2 = 1$.

As you can see, the calculated value for our chi-square statistic is 3.55. The critical value for the chi-square statistic, with 1 df and a 5% probability of error, is 3.84. With 1 df and a 1% probability of error, the critical value of chi-square is 6.63. Because the value of chi-square does not exceed either of these critical values, we must conclude that our population does conform to HWE expectations. Because the value of chi-square is so close to the critical value, however, any greater deviation from expectations would produce a chi-square large enough for us to conclude that our population does not conform to HWE expectations.

Appendix II

How the RMP, Prior Odds of Guilt, and the PFP Influence the Posterior Odds of Guilt (POG)[1]

I. THE PFP AFFECTS THE POG ESPECIALLY STRONGLY WHEN THE RMP IS LOW

Consider four situations in which the DNA profile of the defendant matches that of the crime scene evidence. In each situation, the prior odds of guilt are 1/100. This corresponds to a suspect being identified by an eyewitness' somewhat vague report that the perpetrator belonged to a certain ethnic subgroup. The situations are as follows:

Situation 1: A common profile and a low probability of laboratory error. Let the RMP = 1 in 1 thousand (0.001) and let the PFP = 1 in ten thousand cases (0.0001).

Situation 2: A common profile and a high probability of laboratory error. Let the RMP = 1 in 1 thousand (0.001) and let the PFP = 1 in one hundred cases (0.01).

Situation 3: A rare profile and a low probability of laboratory error. Let the RMP = 1 in 1 billion (0.000000001) and let the PFP = 1 in ten thousand cases (0.0001).

Situation 4: A rare profile and a high probability of laboratory error. Let the RMP = 1 in 1 billion (0.000000001) and let the PFP = 1 in one hundred cases (0.01).

Bayes' Theorem states that the posterior odds of guilt can be calculated as follows:

$$\frac{p(Hp \mid E, I)}{p(Hd \mid E, I)} = \frac{p(E \mid Hp, I)}{p(E \mid Hd, I)} \times \frac{p(Hp, I)}{p(Hd, I)}$$

[1] These examples are excerpted from Thompson, W.C., Taroni, F. and Aitken, C.G.G. (2003) *Journal of Forensic Sciences*, 48, 1–8.

posterior odds of guilt = Likelihood ratio (LR) associated with DNA match × prior odds of guilt

Using the formula given in Chapter 4 for calculating the LR:

$1/\{RMP + [PFP \times (1 - RMP)]\}$, we get the following numbers to plug into the equation:

Table AII.1 The Influence of the RMP and the PFP on the POG

	RMP	PFP	LR	Prior Odds	Posterior Odds (POG)
Situation 1	0.001	0.0001	900/1	1/100	9
Situation 2	0.001	0.01	100/1	1/100	1
Situation 3	0.000000001	0.0001	10,000/1	1/100	100
Situation 4	0.000000001	0.01	100/1	1/100	1

Comparing Situations 1 and 2 illustrates the effect of the PFP when the RMP is high, and comparing Situations 3 and 4 illustrates the effect of the PFP when the RMP is low. When the profile was relatively common (Situations 1 and 2, RMP = 0.001), the 100-fold difference in the PFP made only a 9-fold difference in the POG. When the profile was rare, however (Situations 3 and 4, RMP = 0.000000001), the 100-fold difference in the PFP made a 100-fold difference in the POG.

II. THE POG CAN BE SURPRISINGLY LOW, EVEN IF THE RMP IS LOW, IF THE PRIOR ODDS ARE LOW

Consider two situations in which the DNA profile of the defendant matches that of the crime scene evidence. In both cases, the RMP is relatively low, 1 in 1 billion (0.000000001), and the PFP is 1 in 1,000 cases (0.001). The situations are as follows:

Situation 1: The defendant was arrested because the victim made a very credible statement that the defendant perpetrated the crime.

Situation 2: The defendant was identified through a search of a DNA databank.

In Situation 1, the prior odds of guilt are very high—let's call them 100:1 in favor of the defendant being guilty. In Situation 2, the prior odds of the defendant's guilt are no higher than for any other person. Let's let them be 1 in one thousand (0.001). Using the same formulas given above for calculating the LR and the POG, we get the following numbers to plug into the equation:

Table AII.2 Effect of Prior Odds of Guilt on the POG

	RMP	PFP	LR	Prior Odds	Posterior Odds (POG)
Situation 1	0.000000001	0.001	1,000/1	100/1	100,000/1
Situation 2	0.000000001	0.001	1,000/1	1/1,000	1

Comparing Situations 1 and 2, one can see that, even with an impressive RMP like 1 in 1 billion, in a situation in which the defendant has been identified through a databank search, the extremely low prior odds of guilt will result in there being as good a probability that the defendant is innocent as guilty.

Appendix III

Paternity Index (PI) Calculations for Different Combinations of Maternal, Child and Alleged Father Genotypes

Marker alleles are called P, Q, R and S, with respective frequencies = p, q, r and s. Reproduced from Hageman, C., Prevett, D. and Murray, W. (2002) *DNA Handbook*. Ontario, Canada: Butterworths.

Table AIII.1 Paternity Index for Different Child, Maternal and Alleged Paternal Genotypes

Child	Mother	Alleged Father	Paternity Index
PP	PP	PP	1/p
PP	PP	PQ	1/2p
PQ	PP	PQ	1/2p
PQ	PQ	PQ	1/(p + q)
PP	PQ	PP	1/p
PQ	PQ	PP	1/(p + q)
PP	PQ	PQ	1/2p
PQ	PP	QQ	1/q
QR	PQ	RR	1/r
PR	PP	QR	1/2r
QR	PQ	PR (or RS)	1/2r
PR	PR	QR	1/[2(p + r)]
QR	PR	QR	1/2q
RR	PR	QR	1/2r
PQ	Absent	QR	1/4q
PQ	Absent	QQ	1/2q
PQ	Absent	PQ	(p + q)/4pq
QQ	Absent	QR	1/2q
QQ	Absent	QQ	1/q

Appendix IV

A Sample Consent Form to Collect an Oral Swab, Which Allows the Profile Obtained to Be Entered Into a Databank for Use in Additional Investigations

Consent to Collect an Oral Swab

DATE:

TIME:

LOCATION:

I, ________________ by signing below, am consenting to provide an oral swab to obtain my DNA sample. I understand that I have the right to refuse and that I am under no obligation to provide such a sample. I also understand that this swab will be subjected to DNA analysis, and that the DNA profile generated will be maintained in a databank and compared to samples from this and other cases. This DNA profile will be used by the XXXXXXX Police Department and the Medical Examiner's Office for investigative purposes, and may be used against me in any criminal prosecution. No promises have been made to me in connection with signing this consent form and providing this sample.

____
Defendant's Name

____
Defendant's Address

____
Defendant's Signature

____
Witness

____
Assistant District Attorney

Appendix V

Doing Your Own Research: Useful References, Websites and Strategies for Finding Current Information

This listing is not intended to be exhaustive. There are many publications and websites that contain useful information on forensic DNA. The publications and websites listed below are selected because they represent the most complete and/or most easily understood treatments of their respective topics.

ADDITIONAL READINGS

- *Introduction to Genetic Analysis*, 9th ed. Anthony J.F. Griffiths, Susan R. Wessler, Richard C. Lewontin and Sean B. Carroll. Freeman, 2008.

  This basic genetics textbook provides useful discussions of recombination and linkage, linkage disequilibrium and equilibrium, and mtDNA, among other topics. One of the authors (Lewontin) was a prominent participant in the debate over the application of population genetic principles that raged after the 1992 NRC report was published.

- *Forensic DNA Typing*, 2nd ed. John M. Butler. Elsevier/Academic Press, 2005.

  This book provides a thorough, detailed discussion of the biology, technology and population genetic issues pertinent to STR testing. It is the only book one needs for a complete foundation reference on

STR testing, and it also provides a great deal of information on mtDNA testing.

- *An Introduction to Forensic DNA Analysis*, 2nd ed. Norah Rudin and Keith Inman. CRC Press, 2002.

  This book provides a thorough, detailed discussion of crime scene investigation and the laboratory aspects of the DNA analysis. It is well written and easy to read. It includes several very useful appendices, including listings of decisions U.S. courts have made regarding the admissibility of STR and mtDNA and different states' DNA statutes (as of 2001).

- *Interpreting DNA Evidence: Statistical Genetics for Forensic Scientists.* Ian W. Evett and Bruce .S. Weir. Sinauer Associates, 1998.

  There are three excellent books that discuss the population genetic and statistical issues relevant to forensic DNA testing. For those with no background in statistics, this one provides the best foundation and presents the esoteric material in the most readable form. It is also the only one of the three that is written by an American author; consequently, it is the most relevant for American litigators. For those interested in using a likelihood ratio to interpret DNA data, however, the following two books will also be useful:

- *Weight-of-Evidence for Forensic DNA Profiles*. David Balding. John Wiley and Sons, 1995.

- *Forensic DNA Evidence Interpretation.* John S. Buckleton, Christopher M. Triggs and Simon J. Walsh. CRC Press, 2004.

- *Encyclopedia of DNA and the United States Criminal Justice System.* Louis J. Palmer, Jr., McFarland and Company, 2004.

  This encyclopedia includes everything from technical terms to case law. Its best assets are the numerous well-chosen excerpts from trial court, appellate court and supreme court rulings. Its content is not exhaustive, but it is worth checking to see if it contains an entry for the case you are interested in. It can also serve as a glossary of technical terms that many litigators will find useful.

- *Reference Guide on DNA Evidence.* David H. Kaye and George F. Sensabaugh, Jr. In *Reference Manual on Scientific Evidence,* 2nd ed. Federal Judicial Center, 2000.

  This publication of the Federal Judicial Center provides guidelines relevant to all aspects of the trial process for both litigators and judges.

- *1992 National Research Council Report: DNA Technology in Forensic Science.* National Academy Press, 1992.

  This NRC report laid down some guidelines for the laboratory aspects of the DNA analysis that are still relevant, although some of the guidelines that are pertinent to VNTR analyses have been rendered moot since STRs have replaced VNTRs as the markers of choice for forensic DNA analyses.

- *1996 National Research Council Report: The Evaluation of Forensic DNA Evidence.* National Academy Press, 1996.

  This NRC report provides guidelines for the statistical interpretation of forensic DNA data that are still relevant today. The 1996 NRC report and the SWGDAM guidelines provide the current standards for all aspects of forensic DNA testing.

- Lothridge, K. and Jones, R.W. (2006) Principles of forensic DNA for officers of the court: An interactive, computer-based training tool for attorneys and judges. *Drake Law Review,* 54, 671.

  This interactive, computer-based program was funded by the National Institute of Justice and developed by the Office of Justice Programs and the National Forensic Science Technology Center. The program is intended to help lawyers and judges better understand the technical, scientific and legal issues they will encounter in DNA cases. The program gives a wide-ranging but superficial overview of the relevant issues. It is a good starter reference because it addresses all the relevant topics, but it does not expand extensively on any background information or the history of developments in any specific area.

- DNA Advisory Board Recommendations on Statistics (2000): Statistical and Population Genetics Issues Affecting the Evaluation of the Frequency of occurrence of DNA Profiles Calculated from Pertinent Population Database(s). Forensic Science Communications, 2(3). http://www.fbi.gov/hq/lab/fsc/current/index.htm.

The duties of the DAB have been assumed by SWGDAM, but this document outlines the DAB recommendations on which the current standards are based.

- References detailing unethical behavior by forensic scientists:

  http://www.corpus-delecti.com/forensic_fraud.html

  This is "an archive of cases where forensic and police experts have provided sworn expert testimony, documents, or reports to the court that contain deceptive or misleading information, findings, opinions, or conclusions, deliberately offered in order to secure an unfair or unlawful gain."

  Also see Turvey, B. (2003) Forensic Frauds: A Study of 42 Cases. *Journal of Behavioral Profiling,* Vol. 4, No. 1.

USEFUL WEBSITES

Professional Organizations

- National District Attorney's Association/American Prosecutor' Research Institute website (http://www.ndaa-apri.org)

  The NDAA-APRI provides prosecutors with ethical and procedural guidelines for all aspects of their practice, including assistance in developing policies for prioritizing cases and responding to discovery requests.

- National Legal Aid and Defender Association (http://www.nlada.org)

  This website provides a highly useful online forensics library, which includes summaries and reviews prepared by criminal defense attorneys and accessible only to other criminal defense attorneys. It also includes a place for defense attorneys to contribute pieces that will benefit others.

- National Association of Criminal Defense Lawyers (http://www.nacdl.org)

  This site is more commercial than the NLADA website, but NACDL members can avail themselves of a number of useful resources. Its publications service offers a wide range of materials, including manuals describing the procedural recommendations and standard operating procedures that are provided to a number of prosecution-aligned organizations, including the FBI's forensic testing laboratory.

- American Bar Association's Criminal Justice Section: http://www.abanet.org/crimjust/home.html

  This website links to the ABA's publications, including *Criminal Justice Magazine*, as well as a section that details the Criminal Justice section's standards on DNA evidence.

- Association of Federal Defense Attorneys

  http://www.afda.org

  This website is dedicated exclusively to criminal defense attorneys who litigate cases in federal court. Among other features, it includes a searchable database of federal circuit court opinions, a variety of instructional materials, a message board and a chat room.

- National Institute of Justice—National Commission on the Future of DNA Evidence

  http://www.ojp.usdoj.gov/nij/topics/forensics/dna/commission/welcome.html

  The Commission was established in 1998 in response to a report of several dozen cases in which DNA evidence had exonerated wrongly convicted individuals. The Commission's mission is to improve the usefulness of DNA evidence in criminal trials. Their published reports include recommendations for crime scene investigators, as well as recommendations for litigators and judges regarding postconviction DNA testing.

- FBI forensic laboratory website: http://www.fbi.gov/hq/lab/labhome.htm

This website provides links to the FBI's journal *Forensic Science Communications*, the CODIS system and manuals describing the FBI's methods for nDNA and mtDNA testing.

- American Society of Crime Laboratory Directors-Laboratory Accreditation Board (ASCLD-LAB) http://www.ascld-lab.org/

  This is the body that accredits most forensic DNA testing laboratories.

- American Board of Criminalistics (ABC)—http://criminalistics.com/ABC/A.php

  The ABC certifies individual crime scene investigators and laboratory technicians, with several different classifications within the field of DNA testing.

- American Academy of Forensic Sciences (AAFS)—http://www.aafs.org

  The AAFS is the preeminent professional organization for forensic scientists.

Autosomal STR, Y STR and mtDNA Databases

- National Institute of Standards and Technology website (http://www.cstl.nist.gov/biotech/strbase)

  This website provides a wealth of information on STRs (autosomal and Y chromosome), SNPs and mtDNA haplotypes. Their offerings include instructional material, an exhaustive list of literature references, sequence information (including PCR primer sequences), mutation rates for individual STRs and allele frequencies that have been observed in American populations and around the world.

- Y STR Haplotype Reference Database (http://www.yhrd.org or www.ystr.org)

  This website contains information from a number of laboratories around the world. In addition to providing haplotype frequencies from a number of population databases, it also allows one to compare the frequencies of Y chromosome STR haplotypes between any two populations.

- Applied Biosystems, Inc.'s Y STR database:

  http://www.appliedbiosystems.com/yfilerdatabase

- Promega Corporation's Y STR database:

  www.promega.com/techserv/tools/pplexy/

- MITOMAP website: http://www.mitomap.org/

  This website contains the human mtDNA sequence, a complete listing of articles pertinent to mtDNA and a listing of mitochondrial mutations and polymorphisms.

- Human mtDNA sequence:

  http://www.ncbi.nlm.nih.gov (search the nucleotide database, accession number AC_000021.2)

  mtDNA database that is useful for calculating frequencies of specific polymorphisms—http://www.genpat.uu.se/mtDB/

Good Laboratory Practices

- The DNA Advisory Board Quality Assurance Standards can be found at

  http://www.cstl.nist.gov/biotech/strbase/dabqas.htm and at

  http://www.fbi.gov/hq/lab/codis/qualassur.htm and at

  http://www.fbi.gov/hq/lab/fsc/backissu/july2000/codis2a.htm

- National Institute of Standards and Technology website http://www.cstl.nist.gov/biotech/strbase

  The NIST provides Standard Reference Materials (SRMs) for a wide variety of forensic tests.

- International Society of Forensic Genetics website http://www.isfg.org

  The ISFG website provides the ISFG guidelines for forensic DNA testing, as well as information about *Forensic Science International: Genetics*, the first journal dedicated to forensic genetics.

RESEARCHING THE CURRENT LITERATURE ON FORENSIC TESTING

The National Library of Medicine's PUBMED Search Engine

PUBMED is one of the major sections of the National Center for Biotechnology Information (NCBI; http://ncbi.nlm.nih.gov). From the NCBI website, click on PUBMED at the top left, then use the PREVIEW feature of PUBMED to search the literature. In the PREVIEW screen, you will be provided with a drop-down window that lists numerous options for search strategies. You can search by author, publication date (year), major topic (forensics, DNA, mitochondrial DNA and Y chromosome are all major topics), or for words in the title and abstract. You can combine your search terms using Boolean functions such as AND, OR or NOT. You can build searches that gather all references on a broad topic or only those references for which a single phenomenon was the focus. The PREVIEW feature allows you to see how many articles your search will turn up, so you know when to stop refining it.

The Title/Abstract option often allows you to refine the search very efficiently. Plugging a search term into the Title/Abstract option identifies all articles that have that term in either their title or abstract. For example, imagine that you are dealing with DNA evidence that is unambiguous except for an anomalous result for one marker. If you want to see if this odd result has ever been reported before, plugging that marker's name into the Title/Abstract search will identify all articles that have reported unusual genotypes for that marker.

Once you have identified an article that focuses on your desired topic, you can click on the Related Articles feature at the right of the article's listing to bring up other articles that occupy the same niche in the PUBMED classification scheme. This enables you to identify all the articles that have been published after the article in question, allowing you to access the most recent information on that topic.

FBI Publications

Many of the publications that have come from the FBI, including those from the FBI's DNA Advisory Board (DAB) and the Scientific Working Group on DNA Analysis Methods (SWGDAM), can be found in the journal *Forensic Science Communications* at http://www.fbi.gov/hq/lab/fsc/current/index.htm.

National Institute of Standards and Technology website (http://www.cstl.nist.gov/biotech/strbase)

The NIST website includes an exhaustive list of literature references on all aspects of forensic DNA testing.

Glossary of Key Terms

5′ and 3′ orientation Refers to the numbering of the carbons in the sugar molecule of the nucleotide. The two DNA strands lie in the opposite 5′ to 3′ orientations.

acrocentric A chromosome in which the centromere is close to one end of the chromosome.

adenine One of the bases in DNA and RNA nucleotides.

adenosine One of the nucleotides in DNA and RNA nucleotides.

admixture The intermating of one population with another population that has a different ethnic heritage.

agarose gel electrophoresis A process that separates DNA fragments according to their size, by using an electric current to push them through a gel-like substance called agarose.

allele A version of the sequence of a gene or a marker. Any polymorphism represents a sequence for which there is more than one known allele for that sequence.

allele size ladder A set of DNA fragments with known sizes, used as a ruler against which to measure the sizes of the fragments in the samples.

allele size window The range within which the analyst expects the allele sizes for a particular marker to fall.

allele-specific oligonucleotides (ASO)

amplicon One of the amplified products of the PCR.

amplification The process whereby the PCR makes millions of copies of the desired stretch of DNA.

annealing stage The stage of a PCR cycle in which the mixture is cooled slightly to allow the primers to bind to their complementary sequences.

antiparallel Refers to the fact that the two strands of the DNA molecule lie in opposite orientation to each other.

autosomes The numbered chromosomes.

band shifting Because of inconsistencies in the gel or the electrical field that is applied for electrophoresis, the fragments in one lane of an electrophoresis gel will sometimes run at a different speed than the fragments in the other lanes of that same gel.

base The portion of the nucleotide that determines which specific protein the gene makes. In DNA, A, C, G and T; in RNA, A, C, G and U.

basepairs (bp) Refers to the complementary basepairing within the DNA molecule; used as a measure of the distance between two markers, or between any two genomic elements.

Bayes' Theorem A mathematical model that illustrates how a purely logical mind would combine multiple pieces of information in order to determine the relative strengths of the two competing hypotheses.

benign polymorphisms Places in the DNA molecule at which one can find different specific sequences in different people. These sequence variants have no effect on an individual's development or function, however, so differences in sequence are not accompanied by differences in personality, health status or other characteristics.

blotting and hybridization A procedure in which test probes and PCR products are incubated together; the binding or lack of binding of the PCR product to the individual probes indicates which alleles were present in the DNA sample.

capillary electrophoresis A process whereby DNA fragments are pushed through very narrow tubes called capillaries by electric current. The DNA fragments are separated according to their size.

centromere The constriction that separates the p arm from the q arm on a chromosome.

Chelex extraction Sometimes used for minute samples, an extraction procedure that uses a special resin and produces single-stranded DNA that cannot be quantified using the standard yield gel.

chromosomes In the nucleus of each cell, our DNA molecule is organized into 46 chromosomes. Each chromosome acts as an independent unit for the purposes of passing down our genetic information to our children.

CODIS (Combined DNA Indexing System) A system of interconnected databases and search-and-compare software that enables local, state and federal law enforcement agents to search each others' DNA databanks to help them investigate crimes, for example, by searching for matches to crime scene evidence among convicted felons.

codon The ribosome reads the mRNA in 3-nucleotide "words." Those three-nucleotide units are called codons, because they are the means by which the mRNA code is translated into the amino acid sequence of the polypeptide.

complementary basepairs As bind with Gs; Cs bind with either Ts or Us.

confidence interval (CI) The range of values that the analyst feels, with the specified level of confidence, includes the true value of the parameter in question.

control region or D-loop region A region of the mtDNA molecule in which no genes reside (nucleotides 16,024–16,569 and 1–576). The control region contains sequences that help control the replication of the mtDNA and the expression of the genes in the mtDNA.

control samples Samples for which the expected result is already known. If control samples do not perform as expected, the data from the analysis are suspect.

cross-hybridization Hybridization of a probe with a sequence that is similar, but not identical, to the one with which it is supposed to hybridize.

cycle threshold (C_T) In a real-time PCR protocol, the number of PCR cycles required for a sample to generate a predetermined amount of product.

cytidine One of the nucleotides in DNA and RNA nucleotides.

cytosine One of the bases in DNA and RNA nucleotides.

denatured Forced to adopt an unnatural 3D shape, as when the DNA double helix is unwound into two single strands.

denaturing stage The stage of a PCR cycle in which the mixture is heated to unwind the double helix into single strands.

deoxyadenosine monophosphate (dAMP) The formal name for the A-containing nucleotide.

deoxycytosine monophosphate (dCMP) The formal name for the C-containing nucleotide.

deoxyguanidine monophosphate (dGMP) The formal name for the G-containing nucleotide.

deoxyribose The sugar portion of a DNA nucleotide.

deoxythymidine monophosphate (dTMP) The formal name for the T-containing nucleotide.

dideoxynucleotides Nucleotides that lack an oxygen atom at the 3′ carbon; a DNA strand that is being synthesized cannot be extended further once a dideoxynucleotide has been incorporated into it.

dideoxysequencing A process for determining the nucleotide sequence in a stretch of DNA.

dinucleotide repeat A polymorphic stretch of DNA sequence characterized by the repetition of a 2-bp sequence motif.

DNA polymerase An enzyme that links nucleotides together to build a new strand of DNA.

DNA profile, aka genetic profile The individual's genotype status at all the markers that were tested.

dye blob A broad signal that arises when some of the fluorescently labeled molecule that is used to allow the fragment analyzer to detect the PCR products does not get cleaned out of the sample during purification.

electropherogram The figure put out by the fragment analyzer, displaying peaks that represent the size of the PCR products that were produced in the different samples.

elimination samples DNA profiles from laboratory personnel, crime scene investigators and anyone else who may have been in a position to contaminate evidence with their own DNA.

exclusion probability (EP) The portion of the population that is excluded by the DNA evidence, calculated as 1 – PRM.

exons The portions of the gene's coding sequence that are used to make the gene's protein.

extension stage The stage of a PCR cycle in which the temperature is held at 72°C, the temperature at which the DNA polymerase works best.

external standard A collection of DNA fragments of known sizes that is used as a ruler against which to measure the sizes of the alleles in the questioned sample. Unlike the internal standard, which is mixed in with the sample itself, the external standard is assays in a separate gel lane or capillary, or even with a separate batch of samples.

extraction blank A negative control that includes everything that was used to extract the DNA from the sample, but no sample material. An extraction blank is used to detect contaminating DNA in the reagents employed to extract DNA from samples.

fluor A fluorescent molecule that allows a fragment analyzer to detect the PCR products that were produced in the samples being analyzed.

functional polymorphisms Places in the DNA molecule at which one can find different specific sequences in different people. These sequence variants cause minor changes in the activity of the gene's protein and contribute to interindividual differences in personality, long-term health status, response to stress and other characteristics.

gel electrophoresis A process whereby DNA is pushed through a gel-like substance by an electric current. The gel separates fragments of DNA according to their size.

genetic code The translation between the nucleotide language of mRNA and the amino acid language of a protein. A table that illustrates the genetic code shows which amino acid will be incorporated into the polypeptide when the ribosome reads each of the 64 possible three-nucleotide codons.

genetic profile, aka DNA profile The individual's genotype status at all the markers that were tested.

genome An individual's DNA molecule, or an individual's or species' collection of genes. The reader will frequently see the term **genomic DNA** used when discussing the DNA that is extracted from biological samples.

genotype The alleles an individual possesses for any particular polymorphism.

germline mutations DNA mutations that exist in the sperm or the egg that create the individual. These mutations will appear in all the cells in that individual's body.

guanidine One of the nucleotides in DNA and RNA nucleotides.

guanine One of the bases in DNA and RNA nucleotides.

haplogroup A cluster of mtDNA or Y chromosome profiles that are similar to each other, often thought to reflect a relatively recent common ancestry.

haplotype A single-copy DNA profile, such as that which is inherent in mtDNA or Y chromosome STRs.

Hardy-Weinberg equilibrium (HWE) Mathematical rules that allow one to predict the frequency of homozygous and heterozygous genotypes in a population.

heavy strand The A/T-rich strand of the double-stranded mtDNA molecule.

heteroplasmy A situation in which some copies of an individual's mtDNA have a different sequence than other copies of that same individual's mtDNA.

heterozygous A situation in which the two alleles that the individual possesses for a polymorphic marker are not identical.

homologous chromosomes, or homologs The two members of a chromosome pair.

homozygous A situation in which the two alleles that the individual possesses for a polymorphic marker are identical.

hydrogen bonds Bonds that form between the bases that project inward into the DNA helix from each side and hold the DNA in its double-helical configuration.

hypervariable region I A highly polymorphic region of the mtDNA molecule (nucleotides 16,024–16,365).

hypervariable region II A highly polymorphic region of the mtDNA molecule (nucleotides 73–340).

intergenic space The nucleotides that are contained in the spaces between genes.

internal standard A set of DNA fragments of known size that is added to a sample in order to provide a ruler against which the analyst can measure the sizes of the PCR products that were generated from the sample by the PCR. The internal standard is mixed in with the sample itself and therefore experiences the same assay conditions as the sample does.

introns The portions of the pre-mRNA that get spliced out as the pre-mRNA is processed into mRNA.

light strand The C/G-rich strand of the double-stranded mtDNA molecule.

likelihood ratio (LR) In a Bayesian analysis, the LR is a mathematical expression that compares the probability of finding the DNA profile in question given the prosecution's hypothesis that the defendant is guilty versus the probability of finding the DNA profile in question given the defense's hypothesis that the defendant is innocent.

limit of detection (LOD) The intensity a peak must have in order for the fragment analyzer to recognize it as a true peak and include it in the reported data.

limit of quantitation (LOQ) The intensity above which the intensity of a peak is considered to reflect the amount of PCR product that was generated for that allele, and not be influenced significantly by the system's background noise. A peak whose intensity is greater than the LOQ is thought to reflect the amount of template material that was present for that allele in the PCR, and can be used for quantitative analyses, such as must be considered when multiple contributors to a sample share one or more alleles.

linkage The tendency of alleles that lie close together on a single chromosome to be passed down together from parent to child.

linkage disequilibrium (LD) The tendency of genotypes of different markers to occur together more frequently than one would predict would happen by chance alone.

linkage equilibrium (LE) Complete independence between the genotypes of different markers, so that knowing the individual's genotype for one marker does not allow the analyst to predict that individual's genotype at any of the other markers.

markers Polymorphic sequences, the locations of which on their respective chromosomes are known.

mean The arithmetic average of a set of numbers.

messenger RNA The RNA that is produced after the introns are spliced out of the pre-mRNA. The mRNA is read by the ribosome and provides it instructions for stringing the appropriate amino acids together to make the gene's polypeptide.

metacentric A chromosome in which the centromere is in the middle of the chromosome.

microvariants Alleles that contain a partial repeated unit in addition to the tetranucleotide repeats. The length of a microvariant allele does not differ from the lengths of the other alleles by an even multiple of four nucleotides.

mitochondrial DNA The DNA in the organelle known as the mitochondrion, better known for its role in providing the cell the energy it needs.

mitochondrion Better known for its role in supplying the cell with the energy it needs, the mitochondrion also contains its own DNA molecule.

mitotype An mtDNA profile.

mtDNA D-loop region, aka control region A region of the mtDNA molecule in which no genes reside (nucleotides 16,024–16,569 and 1–576). The control region contains sequences that help control the replication of the mtDNA and the expression of the genes in the mtDNA.

multiplex PCR A PCR that uses more than one set of primer, thereby producing more than one product.

National Center for Biotechnology Information (NCBI) The nation's foremost repository for biotechnology information (http://www.ncbi.nlm.nih.gov).

negative controls Control samples that are not expected to produce any result; used to detect contamination of reagents or equipment.

nested PCR A two-phase PCR in which a PCR is performed, after which the product of that PCR is used as a template for a second PCR.

noise spike A usually sharp signal peak that comes from a disturbance in the machine's electric supply, air in the capillary or some other artifact.

nonrecombining portion of the Y chromosome The majority of the Y chromosome, minus the PARs at both ends, in which no recombination occurs with the X chromosome.

nontemplate-directed nucleotide addition The tendency of the DNA polymerase to add one more A nucleotide onto the newly synthesized DNA strand after the polymerase has gotten to the end of the template.

normal distribution When one measures the distribution of a trait (e.g., height, weight) across a large population, many biological phenomena exhibit a bell-shaped curve, in which values are distributed symmetrically around the mean, or average.

nuclear DNA The DNA in the nucleus of all our cells; the DNA that is contained in our chromosomes.

nucleotide The basic building block of DNA and RNA; composed of a nitrogen-containing base, a phosphate group and a sugar—either deoxyribose (DNA) or ribose (RNA).

nucleus A specialized compartment that resides within each of our cells and contains the chromosomes.

null alleles Alleles that exist, but do not appear after the PCR has been performed, because a polymorphism in the stretch of DNA to which one of the primers is supposed to bind prevents the primer form binding, and therefore prevents the allele from being amplified.

observer bias As it applies to forensic DNA analyses, the tendency of a forensic analyst's judgment to be biased in favor of the prosecution, because most forensic testing laboratories receive samples solely or primarily from law enforcement agencies.

off-ladder allele or off-ladder peak An allele (or peak) whose size does not exactly match that of any known allele, usually because there has been an insertion or deletion of 1 to 3 nucleotides in this person's sequence.

oligonucleotides Short (10–40 nucleotides) single-stranded stretches of nucleotides.

organic extraction The standard method for extracting DNA from samples.

p arm The shorter of the two arms of a chromosome; usually depicted above the centromere in diagrams.

paternity index (PI) In a paternity case, the LR that illustrates how much more likely it would be to have observed the common alleles in the profiles of the child and the alleged father if the alleged father was the true father of the child versus if the alleged father was not the true father of the child.

peak detection threshold (PDT) The intensity that a peak must have in order for the fragment analyzer to recognize it as a peak.

phosphate group The phosphate group alternates with the sugar molecule to make up the sugar-phosphate backbone that gives the DNA molecule its double-helical shape.

polymerase chain reaction (PCR) A chemical reaction in which millions of copies of a desired stretch of DNA are made.

polymorphisms Places in the DNA molecule at which one can find different specific sequences in different people. Adjective form = **polymorphic**.

population substructure The existence of different ethnic subgroups, each of which has a different pattern of allele frequencies, within a larger racial population.

positive control A sample that is expected to produce a specific result if the analysis ran properly.

posterior odds of guilt In a Bayesian analysis, the posterior odds of guilt is the final number that indicates the relative strength of the prosecution's hypothesis versus the defense's hypothesis. Posterior Odds = Prior Odds × Likelihood Ratio

posterior odds of paternity (POP) The final calculation in a Bayesian analysis of the DNA and non-DNA evidence in a paternity case. The POP equals the PI multiplied by the prior odds of paternity.

power of discrimination A measure of how often you would find a match if you compared randomly selected profiles two-by-two.

preferential amplification A situation in which one allele of a marker is amplified by the PCR with greater efficiency than the other allele.

pre-messenger RNA, aka primary transcript The first RNA produced by the gene; it is processed into mRNA.

primary transcript, aka pre-messenger RNA The first RNA produced by the gene; it is processed into mRNA.

primers Short (17–22 nucleotides) single-stranded stretches of nucleotides that are used to specify which stretch of DNA sequence is to be amplified in the PCR.

prior odds of guilt In a Bayesian analysis, the prior odds of guilt are derived from the non-DNA evidence in the case.

probability of exclusion (POE) The percentage of the population that can be excluded as contributors to the mixed sample. The POE is calculated by subtracting the probability of inclusion (POI) from 1.

probability of inclusion (POI) The percentage of the population that can be included as contributors to a mixed sample. The POI is calculated simply by adding up the frequencies of all the genotypes that could possibly be contained in the mixture.

product rule A law of probability that asserts that the probability of a set of independent events happening is equal to the product of the probabilities of the individual events. This allows the analyst to calculate the PRM for a DNA profile by multiplying the probabilities of the individual genotypes in the profile.

pseudoautosomal regions The tips of the p and q arms of the sex chromosomes, so named because these regions recombine like the autosomes do.

pseudogenes Partial duplications of genes, the duplicated copy of which has translocated to a different portion of the DNA molecule, or between the mtDNA and nDNA molecules.

pull-up peak An artifact that arises when the spectral matrix has slipped out of calibration. The fragment analyzer interprets a signal as coming from a PCR product that has been labeled with one fluor, when it is actually coming from a PCR product that has been labeled with a different fluor.

purines The A or G bases or nucleotides.

pyrimidines The C, T or U bases or nucleotides.

q arm The longer of the two arms of a chromosome; usually depicted below the centromere in diagrams.

random match probability (RMP) The probability that the defendant's DNA profile matches that of the evidence purely by coincidence.

reagent blank A negative control that contains no extracted material, but is put through all the postextraction steps of the analysis. A reagent blank is used to detect contaminating DNA in the reagents used to amplify the DNA markers.

restriction fragment length polymorphism (RFLP) tests Forensic DNA tests that involved cutting the DNA with a restriction enzyme, separating the resultant fragments by electrophoresis, transferring the fragments to a nylon membrane and hybridizing the membrane with a probe.

ribonucleic acid (RNA) There are three types of RNA: messenger RNA, tramsfer RNA and ribosomal RNA. All of them are integral to the process whereby the cell uses the instructions in the mRNA to synthesize the polypeptide that will be processed into the gene's protein.

sequence-specific oligonucleotides (SSO) A single-stranded piece of DNA that is designed to bind only to one allele of a polymorphism.

sex chromosomes The X and Y chromosomes, so named because they determine one's sex.

short tandem repeat (STR) A polymorphic stretch of DNA sequence characterized by the repetition of a 2- to 5-bp sequence motif.

Single-nucleotide polymorphism A situation in which some people can be found to have an A, C, G ot T in one position, while other people have a different nucleotide in that same position.

size ladder A set of DNA fragments with known sizes, used as a ruler against which to measure the sizes of the fragments in the samples.

slot-blot hybridization A procedure that capitalizes on the fact that two single-stranded DNAs with complementary sequences will anneal into a stable, double-stranded DNA. One DNA is immobilized on a nylon membrane, and the other is applied to the membrane as a liquid solution.

somatic mutations DNA mutations that are not present in the egg and sperm that make the individual, but arise after fertilization, when the cells are replicating and increasing their numbers. These mutations only appear in a subset of the body's cells, as opposed to appearing in every cell of the body, as they would if they came down in either the egg or sperm that created the individual.

spectral matrix The fragment analyzer keeps a catalog of the emission spectra for the four fluors, as well as the expected pattern of spectral overlap between them. This spectral matrix is then used to decode the raw data into peaks.

spectral overlap The different flours used to label PCR products emit light over overlapping wavelength bands.

standard curve The data obtained from a set of samples whose values with respect to an important parameter (e.g., DNA concentration) are known. The standard curve serves as the ruler by which one measures the value of the same parameter in test samples.

standard deviation When a trait (e.g., height, weight) is measured in a large number of people, the standard deviation provides a measure of how widely dispersed the distribution of values is.

standard reference materials Positive control samples for forensic DNA tests.

standard samples Samples for which the expected result is already known. If standard samples do not perform as expected, the data from the analysis are suspect.

stochastic effects A difference in the degree to which the two alleles of a marker have been amplified. These effects occur purely by chance; one allele gets used as a template more often than the other.

stutter peaks A stutter peak reflects amplified PCR products that are usually one repeat shorter than the true allele's PCR product. Stutter peaks are thought to be caused by slippage of the DNA polymerase as it amplifies the repeat.

submetacentric A chromosome in which the centromere is somewhat offset toward one end of the chromosome.

substrate control or substrate blank (aka **unstained specimen**) A piece of the evidence sample that appears not to have any body fluids on it; used to detect any background DNA that might have been on the evidence object before the crime was committed.

sugar-phosphate backbone When sugar molecules and phosphate groups alternate in a chain of nucleotides, they form a helical backbone from which the bases project toward the inside of the helix.

template DNA A sequence to be copied.

tetranucleotide repeat A polymorphic stretch of DNA sequence characterized by the repetition of a 4-bp sequence motif.

thermocycler The machine in which the polymerase chain reaction is performed.

thymidine One of the nucleotides in DNA nucleotides.

thymine One of the bases in DNA nucleotides.

transcription The process whereby the cell uses a DNA template to make an RNA molecule.

translation The process whereby the ribosome reads the mRNA and joins together the appropriate sequence of amino acids.

unstained specimen (aka **substrate control or substrate blank**) A piece of the evidence sample that appears not to have any body fluids on it; used to detect any background DNA that might have been on the evidence object before the crime was committed.

uracil One of the bases in RNA nucleotides.

variable number of tandem repeats (VNTR) A polymorphic stretch of DNA sequence characterized by the repetition of one or more large sequence motifs, sometimes hundreds of bp long, repeated up to 1,000 times.

Wahlund effect or Wahlund principle An excess of homozygous genotypes in a highly substructured population.

yield gel An agarose gel that enables the analyst to determine the amount of DNA extracted from a sample.

Index

Accreditation, forensic labs, 57–58, 284
Acrocentric, definition, 20, 409
Adenosine
  definition, 6, 409
  structure, 7
Admissibility
  defense challenge, 317–319
  evolution of standards, 215–224
  hearings, 290–291
Admixture, definition, 409
Advancing Technology Through DNA Technology Act of 2003 (AJTDTA), 375
AEDPA, *see* Anti-Terrorism and Effective Death Penalty Act
Agarose gel electrophoresis, definition, 30, 409
AJTDTA, *see* Advancing Technology Through DNA Technology Act of 2003
Ake v. Oklahoma, 233, 323, 325
Albright v. Oliver, 262
Allele
  definition, 4, 409
  nomenclature, 17–21
Allele dropout
  mixed samples, 162, 165–167
  overview, 70–75
  suboptimal sample analysis, 134–135
Allele size window
  defense challenge, 342–343
  definition, 409
Allele-specific oligonucleotides (ASO), definition, 45, 409
Amplicon, definition, 32, 409
Amplification
  definition, 409
  PCR, 32
Annealing stage
  definition, 409
  PCR, 37
Anti-Terrorism and Effective Death Penalty Act (AEDPA), 375, 385
Antiparallel, definition, 9, 409
Arizona v. Youngblood, 382
ASO, *see* Allele-specific oligonucleotides
Autosomes, definition, 3, 409

Band shifting, definition, 409
Base, definition, 6, 410
Basepairs (bp), definition, 10–11, 410
Base rate fallacy, 95
Bayes' Theorem
  applications
    paternity cases, 142–146
    practical aspects, 140–141
  definition, 410
  formula, 136–139
  mock jury research, 244
Beale v. Spate, 215
Benign polymorphisms, definition, 11–12, 410
Blotting and hybridization, definition, 410
Bogan v. State, 224
Bousman v. Iowa, 259
bp, *see* Basepairs
Brady v. Maryland, 58, 228, 381–382

Caldwell v. State, 122
California v. Greenwood, 273, 334
California v. Trombetta, 231
Capillary electrophoresis
  definition, 410
  DNA fragments, 41
Centromere, definition, 20, 410
Chain of custody, DNA evidence, 303–304, 335–336
Chelex extraction
  definition, 410
  DNA, 31
Chi-square test, Hardy-Weinberg equilibrium, 116, 389–391
Chromosomes
  definition, 2, 410
  nuclear DNA, 5
CI, *see* Confidence interval
CODIS, *see* Combined DNA Indexing System
Codon, definition, 13, 410
Combined DNA Indexing System (CODIS)
  confirmatory sample collection after databank hit, 278–279
  databanks, 16
  definition, 15–16, 410
  features, 105–106
  statistical analysis of markers, 107–108
  uploads for later comparison, 286
Commonwealth v. Cabral, 273–274
Commonwealth v. Nina M. Draheim, 257, 260
Complementary basepairs, definition, 8, 410
Confidence interval (CI)
  calculation, 110–111
  definition, 410
  random match probability for mitotype, 190–191
  statistical analysis, 109–110
Connecticut Mut. Life Ins. Co. v. Lathrop, 215
Consent
  sample form, 399
  standards and extent, 269–271
Contamination, *see* Polymerase chain reaction
Control region, definition, 411
Control samples
  definition, 411
  real-time polymerase chain reaction, 49
Crawford v. Washington, 286–288
Criminal Justice Act of 1964, 233, 323
Cross-hybridization, definition, 87, 411
C_T, *see* Cycle threshold
Cupp v. Murphy, 277
Cycle threshold (C_T), definition, 49, 411
Cytidine, definition, 6, 411

Cytosine
  deamination, 74–75
  definition, 411
  structure, 7

D1S80 marker, 44
DAB, *see* DNA Advisory Board
dAMP, *see* Deoxyadenosine monophosphate
Databank
  challenges to statutes, 103–105
  features, 99–101
  suspect identification, 126–130
Database
  defense challenges at trial, 307–308
  features, 101–103
  reference database scrutiny by defense, 349–352
Daubert v. Merrill Dow Pharmaceuticals, Inc., 219–223
Davis v. Mississippi, 265
Dayton v. State, 103, 349
dCMP, *see* Deoxycytosine monophosphate
Defense
  challenges to DNA collection, 258–259
  databank search suspects, 362–367
  defendant rights regarding testing and expert, 323–326
  discarded material testing, 334
  discovery checklist, 326–329
  expert witness
    finding, 330–333
    prosecution witness examination, 358–362
  jury education
    mixed sample interpretation, 357–358
    prosecution-friendly fallacy avoidance, 352–356
  motion anticipation by prosecution
    chain of custody, 303–304, 335–336
    data interpretation, 304–305
    overview, 300–301
    pretrial, 286
    proficiency of laboratory/analyst, 304, 336–339
    sample quality, 301–303, 334–335
    statistical challenges, 306–312
  retesting of evidence, 288–290, 319–323
  strategies
    admissibility, 317–319
    alternative explanations for match, 313–314
    investigator or analyst misconduct, 314–317
  test challenges
    defense obligations, 339–340
    DQA1 and Polymarker™ tests, 345–348
    reference database scrutiny, 349–352
    short tandem repeat tests, 340–345
Defense attorney's fallacy, 98–99, 241
Denatured
  definition, 411
  DNA in PCR, 36
Denaturing stage
  definition, 411
  PCR, 37
Deoxyadenosine monophosphate (dAMP), definition, 6, 411
Deoxycytosine monophosphate (dCMP), definition, 7, 411
Deoxyguanidine monophosphate (dGMP), definition, 7, 411
Deoxythymidine monophosphate (dTMP), definition, 7, 411
Depositions, 291
dGMP, *see* Deoxyguanidine monophosphate
Dideoxynucleotides, definition, 51, 411
Dideoxysequencing
  definition, 411
  mitochondrial DNA, 175
  principles, 51–53
Dinucleotide repeat, definition, 15–16, 411
Discovery
  counsel's obligations, 228–232
  defense checklist, 326–329
  inevitable discovery, 268–269
  prosecutor responsibilities, 279–282
D-loop, mitochondrial DNA, 172, 414
DNA
  amplification, *see* Polymerase chain reaction
  evidence handling, 62–64
  extraction and quantification, 27–32
  sequencing, 51–53
  structure, 6–11
DNA Advisory Board (DAB), 56–57
DNA Backlog Elimination Act, 264, 363
DNA dragnets, 271–272, 363
DNA Identification Act of 1994, 99, 105, 226
DNA polymerase
  definition, 411
  PCR, 35
  Taq polymerase fidelity, 300–301
DNA profile
  definition, 4, 411
  probability of uniqueness in suspect population, 130–133
  unknown perpetrator identification, 24–25
DNA sample acquisition
  compelling through search warrant or court order
    defense challenges, 258–259
    exceptions
      abandoned samples, 272–275
      citizen privacy expectation, 264–268
      consent standard and extent, 269–271
      DNA dragnets, 271–272
      health care providers, 275–276
      inevitable discovery, 268–269
      third-party collection, 275–278
    grand jury standard, 258
    probable cause standard, 256–257
    reasonable suspicion standard, 257–258
    third party court-ordered samples, 259–260
    use of force, 261–262
  confirmatory sample collection after databank hit, 278–279

consent sample form, 399
constitutional protections, 255–256
Fifth Amendment implications, 263–264
Sixth Amendment critical stage status, 262
DQA1 test, 22–23, 44–47, 78, 87, 345–348
dTMP, *see* Deoxythymidine monophosphate
Duarte v. Commonwealth, 68–69
Dye blob
defense challenge, 345
definition, 412

Electropherogram
definition, 42, 412
example, 43
Elimination samples, definition, 68, 412
EP, *see* Exclusion probability
Ewell v. Murray, 262
Exclusion probability (EP), definition, 412
Exons, definition, 12, 412
Expert witness
defense, 330–333
examination by prosecution, 358–362
direct examination, 293–297
cross-examination, 308–312
guidelines, 232–237
qualification challenge by defense, 306
Extension stage, PCR, 37
External standard, definition, 41, 412
Extraction, DNA, 27–32
Extraction blank, definition, 67, 412

Fallacy of the transposed conditional, 94
Fay v. Noia, 376
Federal Rules of Evidence (FRE), 218–220, 222, 227, 234–235
Fisher's exact test, Hardy-Weinberg equilibrium, 116
5′ and 3′ orientation, definition, 9, 409
Fluor
definition, 41, 412
spectral overlap, 82
FRE, *see* Federal Rules of Evidence
Frye v. United States, 216–217, 222–224, 337
Frye-Kelly standard, 216–217
Functional polymorphisms, definition, 11, 412

Gel electrophoresis
amplicon analysis, 41
definition, 412
General Electric Co. v. Joiner, 221
Genetic code, definition, 13, 412
Genetic profile, definition, 4, 412
Genome, definition, 412
Genotype, definition, 4, 413
Germline mutations, definition, 14, 413
Gillespie v. Collier, 215
Guanidine, definition, 6, 413
Guanine
definition, 413
structure, 7
Guthrie v. State, 238

Haplogroup
definition, 413
mitotype, 187
Haplotype
definition, 4, 413
mitotype, 187
Hardy-Weinberg equilibrium (HWE)
chi-square test, 116, 389–391
database testing, 351–352
definition, 413
determination, 116
population substructure, 114–118
Hayes v. Florida, 265–266
Health Insurance Portability and Accountability Act (HIPAA), 274–275
Heavy strand
definition, 413
mitochondrial DNA, 171
Heck v. Humphrey, 381
Heme, PCR inhibition, 64
Henyard v. State, 337
Herrera v. Collins, 377–380
Heteroplasmy
definition, 413
mitochondrial DNA
probability calculations, 192–193
versus sequence length, 180–183
tissue variations, 183–187
Heterozygote balance, analysis, 156–161
Heterozygous, definition, 4, 413
HIPAA, *see* Health Insurance Portability and Accountability Act
Homologous chromosomes, definition, 17, 413
Homozygous, definition, 4, 413
Huang v. People, 351
Human error, sources, 69–70
HWE, *see* Hardy-Weinberg equilibrium
Hydrogen bonds, definition, 9, 413
Hypervariable region I
definition, 413
mitochondrial DNA, 172
Hypervariable region II
definition, 413
mitochondrial DNA, 172

Inevitable discovery, 268–269
Inland Seaboard Coasting Co. v. Tolson, 216
Innocence Project, 239–240
Intergenic space, definition, 12, 413
Internal standard, definition, 41, 413
Introns, definition, 12, 413

Jardin v. People, 319
Jefferson, Thomas, Y chromosome analysis, 198–199
Johnson v. Hallora, 322–323
Jones v. Murray, 261
Jurors
defense education
mixed sample interpretation, 357–358
prosecution-friendly fallacy avoidance, 352–356
DNA evidence perceptions, 239–241
education, 251–253
mock jury research of fallacies, 241–251
prosecutor education on statistics, 297–298

Katz v. United States, 273, 334
Kelley v. State, 366
Kumho Tire Co. v. Carmichael Inc., 222

Laboratory error
incorporation in likelihood ratio calculation, 141–142
proficiency testing, 225–227
rates, 225–228
LD, *see* Linkage disequilibrium
LE, *see* Linkage equilibrium

Light strand
  definition, 413
  mitochondrial DNA, 171
Likelihood ratio (LR)
  allele dropout in mixed samples, 167
  applications
    overview, 135–141
    paternity cases, 142–146
  definition, 413
  laboratory error incorporation in calculation, 141–142
  mixed sample analysis, 152–156
  stutter peaks in mixed samples, 164
  validity in court, 308
Limit of detection (LOD)
  defense challenge, 343
  definition, 84, 414
  forensic DNA tests, 86
Limit of quantitation (LOQ), definition, 84, 414
Linkage disequilibrium (LD), definition, 113, 414
Linkage equilibrium (LE)
  database testing, 352
  definition, 113, 414
  forensic DNA calculation impact, 113–114
Linkage, definition, 142–143, 414
LOD, *see* Limit of detection
LOQ, *see* Limit of quantitation
LR, *see* Likelihood ratio

Markers
  definition, 4, 414
  nomenclature, 17–21
McBride v. State, 257
mDNA, *see* Mitochondrial DNA
Mean, definition, 84–85, 414
Messenger RNA (mRNA), definition, 12, 414
Metacentric, definition, 20, 414
Microvariants, definition, 18, 414
Mitochondrial DNA (mDNA)
  advantages over nuclear DNA analysis, 173–174
  D-loop region, 172, 414
  databases, 174
  definition, 5, 414
  features, 171–173
  haplotype analysis
    laboratory practices, 174–178
    statistical analysis, 187–193
  heteroplasmy
    probability calculations, 192–193
    versus sequence length, 180–183
    tissue variations, 183–187
  matrilineal inheritance, 178–180
  overview, 5–6
  strands, 171
Mitotype
  combining with other data, 193
  definition, 174, 414
  statistical analysis of data, 187–193
Mixed sample
  allele dropout, 162, 165–167
  challenges, 147–149
  defense challenges at trial, 306–307
  heterozygote balance and mixture proportion, 156–161
  identification, 149–151
  juror education, 357–358
  number of contributors determination, 149–151
  statistical analysis, 151–156
  stutter peaks, 162–165
mRNA, *see* Messenger RNA
Multiplex PCR
  definition, 39, 415
  optimization, 77
Mutation, possibility in paternity cases, 146–147

National Center for Biotechnology Information (NCBI)
  definition, 415
  marker submission, 20
NCBI, *see* National Center for Biotechnology Information
Negative controls, definition, 66, 415
Nested PCR
  applications, 39–40
  definition, 39, 415
Noise spike
  defense challenge, 344
  definition, 415
Nonrecombining portion of the Y chromosome, definition, 197, 415
Nontemplate-directed nucleotide addition, definition, 80, 415
Normal distribution, definition, 84, 415
North Carolina v. Reed, 274
Nuclear DNA, definition, 5, 415
Nucleotide, definition, 6, 415
Nucleus, definition, 415
Null alleles, definition, 415

Observer bias, definition, 315, 415
Off-ladder allele, definition, 83, 415
Ohio Adult Parole Auth. v. Woodward, 373
Oligonucleotides, definition, 35, 416
Opening statement, prosecution, 292–293
Organic extraction
  definition, 416
  DNA, 31

p arm, definition, 20, 416
Paternity index (PI)
  calculations, 145, 397
  definition, 416
PCR, *see* Polymerase chain reaction
PDT, *see* Peak detection threshold
Peak detection threshold (PDT)
  defense challenge, 343
  definition, 83, 416
  forensic DNA tests, 86
People v. Castro, 55–56
People v. Dabbs, 370
People v. Hitch, 230
People v. Love, 386
People v. Nache Afrika, 259
PFI, *see* Probability of false incrimination
PFP, *see* Probability of false positive
Phosphate group, definition, 416
PI, *see* Paternity index
PLE, *see* Probability of laboratory error
POE, *see* Probability of exclusion
POG, *see* Posterior odds of guilt
POI, *see* Probability of inclusion
Polymarker™ test, 22–23, 44–47, 87, 345–348
Polymerase chain reaction (PCR)
  allele dropout, 70–75
  contamination prevention, 64–66, 176–177
  controls, 66–68
  cycle number, 77–78
  definition, 416
  DNA quantity requirements, 28, 76
  inhibitors, 64
  mitochondrial DNA, 176
  principles, 32–33, 35–40
  real-time PCR, 47–49
  sensitivity, 33–34
  Y chromosome analysis, 203

Polymorphisms
benign versus functional, 11–12
definition, 4, 416
POP, *see* Posterior odds of paternity
Population substructure
definition, 115, 416
DNA forensic calculation impact, 117
match probability with no information on race, 124–125
mitotype diversity, 188–190
Y chromosome haplotype diversity, 207–209
Positive control, definition, 68, 416
Postconviction DNA testing
avenues for relief, 370–373
controlling statute provisions, 383–386
exoneration of innocent, 369–370
new evidence and new case theory, 379–380
procedural obstacles, 373–379
sample access, 380–383
Posterior odds of guilt (POG)
definition, 416
influences
prior odds of guilt, 394–395
probability of false positive, 393–394
random match probability, 393–395
Posterior odds of paternity (POP)
calculation, 145
definition, 137, 416
Power of discrimination
definition, 416
Polymarker™ test, 47
Pre-messenger RNA, definition, 12, 416
Preferential amplification, definition, 71, 416
Preiser v. Rodriguez, 381
Primary transcript, definition, 12, 416
Primers
definition, 416
PCR, 35
Prior odds of guilt
definition, 137, 417
posterior odds of guilt influences, 394–395
Prison Litigation Reform Act (PRLA), 375
PRLA, *see* Prison Litigation Reform Act
Probability
correct identification of witnesses, 95–96
DNA profile uniqueness in suspect population, 130–133
logical fallacies, 91–98
paternity calculations, 144–146
profile probability versus match probability, 120–124
Probability of exclusion (POE)
definition, 417
mixed sample analysis, 151–152
Probability of false incrimination (PFI), calculation, 142
Probability of false positive (PFP)
calculation, 142
posterior odds of guilt influences, 393–394
Probability of inclusion (POI)
definition, 417
mixed sample analysis, 151–152
Probability of laboratory error (PLE)
calculation, 225
juror education, 251–252
mock jury research, 250–251
Product rule
definition, 417
statistical analysis, 111–112
validity in court, 308
Prosecution
DNA sample acquisition, *see* DNA sample acquisition
pretrial preparations
admissibility hearings, 290–291
analyst checklist, 286
analyst report review, 285–286
conferences with law enforcement and lab analysts, 282–284
defense motion anticipation, 286
defense retest, 288–290
depositions, 291
discovery, 279–282
eligible analyst testimony, 286–288
trial
defense motion anticipation
chain of custody, 303–304
data interpretation, 304–305
overview, 300–301
proficiency of laboratory/analyst, 304
sample quality, 301–303
statistical challenges, 306–312
expert witness direct examination by prosecution, 293–297
jury education on statistics, 297–298
opening statement, 292–293
random match probability presentation, 299
strategy voir dire, 291–292
Prosecutor's fallacy, 93–94, 241, 352–356
Pseudoautosomal regions, definition, 197, 417
Pseudogenes
definition, 417
mitochondrial DNA, 177
PUBMED, 407–408
Pull-up peak
defense challenge, 344–345
definition, 80–81, 417
Purines, definition, 417
Pyrimidines, definition, 417

q arm, definition, 20, 417
Quantiblot™, 28
Quantifiler™, 29

Race, *see* Population substructure
Random match probability (RMP)
allele dropout, 134–135
calculation, 111–112, 123
definition, 91, 417
guidelines, 119–121
juror education, 251–252, 298
logical fallacies, 91–98
mitotype, 190–192
mock jury research, 245–250
population substructure effects, 118
posterior odds of guilt influences, 393–395
probability of uniqueness in suspect population, 130–133
profile probability versus match probability, 120–124
prosecution presentation, 299

Random match probability (RMP) *(Continued)*
suspect identification with databank search, 126–130
Y chromosome haplotype calculations, 209–210
combination with autosomal profiles, 210–212
Randomly amplified polymorphic DNA (RAPD), admissibility, 224
RAPD, *see* Randomly amplified polymorphic DNA
Rape shield law, DNA evidence limitations, 238–239
Reagent blank, definition, 67, 417
Real-time polymerase chain reaction, 47–49
Recordkeeping, importance, 61–62
Register v. State, 260
Relative fluorescent unit (RFU), definition, 83
Relatives, as suspects, 125
Restriction fragment length polymorphism (RFLP) tests
definition, 417
overview, 50
RFLP tests, *see* Restriction fragment length polymorphism tests
RFU, *see* Relative fluorescent unit
Ribonucleic acid (RNA)
definition, 417
processing, 13
structure, 6–11
transcription, 7, 12
RMP, *see* Random match probability
RNA, *see* Ribonucleic acid

Sample acquisition, *see* DNA sample acquisition
Sanders v. Coman, 261
Santana-Lopez v. State, 320
Satcher v. Commonwealth, 241
Sawyer v. Whitley, 376
Schooner Catharine v. Dickinson, 215
Scientific Working Group on DNA Analysis Methods (SWGDAM), 57, 64, 107
SD, *see* Standard deviation
Sequence-specific oligonucleotides (SSO), definition, 45, 418
Sex chromosomes, definition, 3, 418
Short tandem repeat (STR)
artifacts inherent in analysis, 75–86
defense challenge of tests, 340–345
definition, 418
direct fragment size analysis, 40–44
Single-nucleotide polymorphism (SNP)
allele dropout, 74
allele frequency, 24
definition, 23, 418
degraded sample analysis, 23
heterozygosity, 73–74
mitochondrial DNA, 174–175
Size ladder, DNA degradation analysis, 30
Slot-blot hybridization
definition, 418
DNA quantification, 28–29
Smith v. State, 364
SNP, *see* Single-nucleotide polymorphism
Somatic mutations, definition, 14, 418
Spectral matrix, definition, 82, 418
Spectral overlap
definition, 418
fluors, 82
Spring Company v. Edgar, 215
SRMs, *see* Standard reference materials
SSO, *see* Sequence-specific oligonucleotides
Standard curve
definition, 418
real-time PCR, 49
Standard deviation (SD)
definition, 84, 418
principle, 85
Standard reference materials (SRMs), definition, 68, 418
Standard samples, definition, 418
State v. Cosey, 332
State v. Dykes, 232
State v. El-Tabech, 372
State v. Hicks, 321–322
State v. Madplume, 266
State v. Mata, 262–263
State v. Passino, 326
Statutes of limitation, DNA evidence, 237–238
Stochastic effect
causes, 72–73
definition, 418
STR, *see* Short tandem repeat
Stutter peaks
characteristics, 78–80
defense challenge, 344
definition, 78, 419
mixed samples, 162–165
Submetacentric, definition, 20, 419
Substrate control, definition, 66, 419
Sugar-phosphate backbone, definition, 8, 419
SWGDAM, *see* Scientific Working Group on DNA Analysis Methods

Taq polymerase, fidelity, 300–301
Taylor v. State, 332
Technical Working Group on DNA Analysis Methods (TWGDAM), 56–57
Teemer v. State, 238
Template DNA
definition, 419
PCR, 35
Terry v. Ohio, 257, 264
Tetranucleotide
definition, 419
forensic identity testing, 16
repeats, 10, 15–16
Thermocycler
cycle threshold, 49
definition, 419
PCR, 37
Theta correction factor, random match probability for mitotype, 190–192
Thymidine, definition, 6, 419
Thymine
definition, 419
structure, 7
Transcription, definition, 7, 419
Translation, definition, 13, 419
Transportation Line v. Hope, 215
TWGDAM, *see* Technical Working Group on DNA Analysis Methods
2p rule, 166

Uniform Parentage Act of 2002, 146
United States ex rel. DiGicomo v. Franzen, 242
United States v. Bullock, 261
United States v. Downing, 218
United States v. Jacobsen et al., 276–277
United States v. Noble, 260
United States v. Pakula, 260
United States v. Wade, 263

United States v. Yee, 107
Unstained specimen, definition, 66, 419
Uracil
  definition, 419
  structure, 7

Validation studies, 59–60
Variable number of tandem repeats (VNTR)
  D1S80, 40–44
  definition, 419
  properties, 21–22
  testing, *see* Restriction fragment length polymorphism tests
VNTR, *see* Variable number of tandem repeats
Vore v. U.S. DOJ, 267

Wahlund effect, definition, 419
Wainwright v. Sykes, 376
Wilson v. State, 270

Y chromosome
  evolution, 197–198
  haplotype analysis
    artifact advantages, 204
    rape cases, 204–207
    statistical analysis
      haplotype diversity, 207–209
      random match probability calculation and combination with autosomal profiles, 210–212
  markers
    copy number, 199–202
    nomenclature, 199–201
  mixed sample analysis, 202
  patrilineal inheritance, 198–199
  polymerase chain reaction, 203
Yield gel, definition, 30, 419

Ziegler v. State, 374